Law and the Christian Tradition in Italy

Firmly rooted on Roman and canon law, Italian legal culture has had an impressive influence on the civil law tradition from the Middle Ages to present day, and it is rightly regarded as "the cradle of the European legal culture." Along with Justinian's compilation, the US Constitution, and the French Civil Code, the Decretum of Master Gratian or the so-called Glossa ordinaria of Accursius are one of the few legal sources that have influenced the entire world for centuries.

This volume explores a millennium-long story of law and religion in Italy through a series of twenty-six biographical chapters written by distinguished legal scholars and historians from Italy and around the world. The chapters range from the first Italian civilians and canonists, Irnerius and Gratian in the early twelfth century, to the leading architect of the Second Vatican Council, Pope Paul VI. Between these two bookends, this volume offers notable case studies of familiar civilians like Bartolo, Baldo, and Gentili and familiar canonists like Hostiensis, Panormitanus, and Gasparri but also a number of other jurists in the broadest sense who deserve much more attention especially outside of Italy. This diversity of international and methodological perspectives gives the volume its unique character.

The book will be essential reading for academics working in the areas of Legal History, Law and Religion, and Constitutional Law and will appeal to scholars, lawyers, and students interested in the interplay between religion and law in the era of globalization.

Orazio Condorelli is Professor of Ecclesiastical and Canon Law in the University of Catania, Italy.

Rafael Domingo is the Spruill Family Professor of Law and Religion at Emory University in Atlanta, USA, and Alvaro d'Ors Professor of Law at the University of Navarra, Spain.

Law and Religion

The practice of religion by individuals and groups, the rise of religious diversity, and the fear of religious extremism, raise profound questions for the interaction between law and religion in society. The regulatory systems involved, the religion laws of secular government (national and international) and the religious laws of faith communities, are valuable tools for our understanding of the dynamics of mutual accommodation and the analysis and resolution of issues in such areas as: religious freedom; discrimination; the autonomy of religious organisations; doctrine, worship and religious symbols; the property and finances of religion; religion, education and public institutions; and religion, marriage and children. In this series, scholars at the forefront of law and religion contribute to the debates in this area. The books in the series are analytical with a key target audience of scholars and practitioners, including lawyers, religious leaders, and others with an interest in this rapidly developing discipline.

Titles in this series include:

Christianity and Global Law
Edited by Rafael Domingo and John Witte, Jr.

Christianity and Criminal Law
Edited by Mark Hill QC, Norman Doe, R H Helmholz and John Witte Jr

Law and the Christian Tradition in Italy
The Legacy of the Great Jurists
Edited by Orazio Condorelli and Rafael Domingo

For more information about this series, please visit: www.routledge.com/Law-and-Religion/book-series/LAWRELIG

Law and the Christian Tradition in Italy

The Legacy of the Great Jurists

Edited by Orazio Condorelli and Rafael Domingo

Produced by the Center for the Study of Law and Religion, Emory University

Routledge
Taylor & Francis Group
LONDON AND NEW YORK

First published 2021
by Routledge
4 Park Square, Milton Park, Abingdon, Oxon OX14 4RN

and by Routledge
605 Third Avenue, New York, NY 10158

First issued in paperback 2022

Routledge is an imprint of the Taylor & Francis Group, an informa business

Publisher's Note
The publisher has gone to great lengths to ensure the quality of this reprint but points out that some imperfections in the original copies may be apparent.

British Library Cataloguing-in-Publication Data
A catalogue record for this book is available from the British Library

Library of Congress Cataloging-in-Publication Data
Names: Domingo, Rafael, 1963– editor. | Condorelli, Orazio, editor. | Emory University. Center for the Study of Law and Religion, sponsoring body.
Title: Law and the Christian tradition in Italy : the legacy of the great jurists / edited by Rafael Domingo and Orazio Condorelli.
Description: Abingdon, Oxon ; New York, NY : Routledge, 2020. | Series: Law and religion | "Produced by the Center for the Study of Law and Religion, Emory University" | Includes bibliographical references and index.
Identifiers: LCCN 2020006192 (print) | LCCN 2020006193 (ebook) | ISBN 9780367857103 (hardback) | ISBN 9781003014539 (ebook)
Subjects: LCSH: Christian lawyers—Italy—Biography. | Law—Italy—Christian influences—History. | Christianity and law—History. | Law—Italy—History. | Canon law—History.
Classification: LCC KKH105 .L39 2020 (print) | LCC KKH105 (ebook) | DDC 262.9092/245—dc23
LC record available at https://lccn.loc.gov/2020006192
LC ebook record available at https://lccn.loc.gov/2020006193

ISBN: 978-0-367-85710-3 (hbk)
ISBN: 978-0-367-50871-5 (pbk)
ISBN: 978-1-003-01453-9 (ebk)

DOI: 10.4324/9781003014539

Typeset in Galliard
by Apex CoVantage, LLC

Contents

Contributors

Romeo Astorri, Professor of Church and State Relations, Catholic University of the Sacred Heart, Milan, Italy.

Italo Birocchi, Professor of Legal History, Sapienza University of Rome, Italy.

Giovanni Chiodi, Professor of Legal History, University of Milano-Bicocca, Italy.

Peter D. Clarke, Professor of Medieval History, University of Southampton, United Kingdom.

Orazio Condorelli, Professor of Ecclesiastical Law and Canon Law, University of Catania, Italy.

Emanuele Conte, Professor of Legal History, Roma Tre University, Italy; and Professor of Legal History, École des hautes Études en Sciences Sociales, Paris, France.

Kathleen G. Cushing, Reader in Medieval History, Keele University, U.K.; and President of the Iuris canonici medii aevi consociatio (ICMAC).

Wim Decock, Professor of Legal History, Universities of Leuven and Liège, Belgium.

Olivier Descamps, Professor of Law and Legal History, Panthéon-Assas University (Paris II), France.

Rafael Domingo, Spruill Family Professor of Law and Religion, Emory University, Atlanta, GA, USA; and Alvaro d'Ors Professor of Law, University of Navarra, Spain.

Carlo Fantappiè, Professor of Canon Law, Roma Tre University, and Professor of History of Canon Law, Pontifical Gregorian University, Rome, Italy

R. H. Helmholz, Ruth Wyatt Rosenson Distinguished Service Professor of Law University of Chicago, IL, USA.

Julius Kirshner, Professor Emeritus of Medieval and Renaissance History, University of Chicago, IL, USA.

Atria A. Larson, Assistant Professor of Theology, Saint Louis University, MO, USA

Susanne Lepsius, Professor of Learned Law, German and European Legal History and Civil Law, Ludwig Maximilians-University of Munich, Germany.

Alberto Lupano, Professor of Legal History, University of Turin, Italy.

Marco Nicola Miletti, Professor of Legal History, University of Foggia, Italy.

Giovanni Minnucci, Professor of Legal History, University of Siena, Italy.

Andrea Padovani, Professor Emeritus of History of Medieval and Modern Law, University of Bologna; and Professor of History of Canon Law, Saint Pius X Institute of Canon Law, Venice, Italy.

Kenneth Pennington, Kelly-Quinn Professor of Ecclesiastical and Legal History, Catholic University of America, Washington, DC, USA.

Charles J. Reid, Jr, Professor of Law, University of Saint Thomas, Minneapolis, MN, USA.

Maria Gigliola di Renzo Villata, Professor of Legal History, University of Milan, Italy.

Jean-Pierre Schouppe, Professor of Canon Law, Pontifical University of the Holy Cross, Rome, Italy.

Lorenzo Sinisi, Professor of Legal History, University "Magna Graecia" of Catanzaro, Italy.

Giuseppe Speciale, Professor of Legal History, University of Catania, Italy.

Alain Wijffels, Professor of Comparative Law and Legal History, Leiden, The Netherlands; KU Leuven and UCLouvain, Belgium; and Senior Research Fellow, CNRS, Lille, France.

John Witte, Jr., Robert W. Woodruff University Professor, McDonald Distinguished Professor of Religion, and Director of the Center for the Study of Law and Religion, Emory University, Atlanta, GA, USA.

Foreword

John Witte, Jr.

"Thrice has Rome conquered the Western world," Rudolf von Jhering once wrote: "by her arms, by her church, and by her law." Another volume in this series analyzes the first of these conquests, and the shaping influence of the ancient Roman Empire on law and religion in the first millennium Western world. This volume takes up the second and third of these "conquests"—the transformative power of the Roman Church and Roman law on the Italian peninsula ("Italy" today) in the second millennium. Italy was the site of the "papal revolution," when Pope Gregory VII (r. 1073–85) and others established the Roman Catholic Church as the preeminent legal and political ruler of medieval Christendom. Italy was the site of the rebirth of Roman law when scholars rediscovered the *Digest* of Justinian in ca. 1070 and created the first law faculties in Bologna, Padua, Naples, and Siena dedicated to its intense study and new application in statutes and cases. Italy was the site of the rebirth of the Church's canon law with the publication of Gratian's *Decretum* in ca. 1140 unleashing a massive new industry of Church legislation and canonical jurisprudence, built in part on Roman law prototypes. And Italy was the birthplace of scholastic theology and philosophy, catalyzed by the rediscovery of Greek, Roman, and patristic sources and brought to sublime expression in the monumental *Summae* of Thomas Aquinas and others.

This Italian story of birth and rebirth in law and religion repeats itself in the middle of the second millennium. The Italian renaissance brought the world not only breathtaking new art, architecture, and literature, based in part on classical Roman prototypes. It also brought the Church comprehensive reforms and renewals of its doctrine, liturgy, catechesis, and governance set out in the monumental decrees of the Council of Trent (1546–63), the Church's definitive response to Protestant and other reform movements in Christendom. The Tridentine decrees also transformed the canon law, leading to the publication of the Roman edition of the books of the *Corpus Iuris Canonici* in 1582 and the (re)establishment of canon law faculties and methods in many major universities around Italy and well beyond. The Renaissance renewed Roman law and civilian learning both through application of the famous *mos gallicus* method to numerous public, private, penal, and procedural law questions and through publication, with the new printing press, of masterful new legal treatises, the best of them gathered in the massive *Tractatus universi juris* of 1584 issued under the auspices of Pope Gregory XIII. And this was the time of a brilliant neo-Thomist renaissance in theology, philosophy, and jurisprudence, led more centrally by the University of Salamanca in neighboring Spain, but also transformative of legal, political, and social scholarship in many Italian universities.

And rebirth and renewal in law and religion recur yet again at the end of the second millennium. The Catholic Church, badly shaken by the attacks of modern liberalism and sharply divided across a vast new colonial empire, responded with another renewal of Thomistic thought in the sweeping new social teachings movement inaugurated by Pope Leo XIII and culminating in the constitutions, declarations, and decrees of the Second Vatican Council (1962–65) a century later. The Church transformed its canon law with the promulgation of a new Code of Canon Law, first in 1917 and again in 1983, reviving anew deep canon law jurisprudence, now regularly taught in seminaries and law faculties. Renewal and reform of state law came with the great legal codification movements of the nineteenth and twentieth centuries, the constitutional transformation of Italy in the grim aftermath of Mussolini and two world wars, and the negotiation of a whole series of brilliant new concordats between the Holy See and Italy and various nation-states in Europe and the Middle East.

This volume tells this millennium-long story of law and religion in Italy through a series of twenty-six well-chosen and well-written biographical case studies. The chapters range from the first Italian civilians and canonists, Irnerius and Gratian in the early twelfth century, to the leading architect of the Second Vatican Council, Pope Paul VI. Between these two bookends, we get exquisite case studies of familiar civilians like Bartolo, Baldo, and Gentili and familiar canonists like Hostiensis, Panormitanus, and Gasparri but also a number of other distinguished jurists who deserve much more attention today from nonspecialists. A few famous popes and cardinals who shaped the law, Innocent IV, Cajetan, Bellarmine, and Paul VI, make an appearance on these pages. So do a few theologians and philosophers with profound legal insights and reforms, such as Aquinas and Sturzo. But most of the case studies focus on canon law and civil law jurists—judiciously selected from the 2,159 jurists who appear in the two-volume biographical dictionary of Italian jurists (*Dizionario biografico dei giuristi italiani*, 2013), and collectively represent the major schools and shifts in thought about the multiple interactions of law and Christianity over the second millennium. And almost all the case studies feature devout Catholics who dominate the religious landscape of Italy until the twentieth century when creative freethinkers begin to reconstruct and reform traditional teachings yet again.

This volume is part and product of an ongoing project on "Great Christian Jurists in World History." The project is directed by the Center for the Study of Law and Religion at Emory University, where the editors Professors Orazio Condorelli and Rafael Domingo are senior fellows. Each volume in this global Great Christian Jurists series focuses on a specific country, region, or era, and samples the life and work of a score or more of its greatest legal minds over the centuries. These legal minds include not only civil and canon lawyers and judges but also theologians, philosophers, and Church leaders who contributed decisively to legal ideas and institutions, or who helped create landmark statutes, canons, or cases. Thus, familiar Christian jurists like Gratian, Grotius, Blackstone, Kuttner, and Scalia appear in this series, but so do Augustine, Isidore, Aquinas, Calvin, Barth, and Romero. This biographical approach is not intended to deprecate institutional, doctrinal, social, or intellectual histories of law, nor will it devolve into a new form of hagiography or hero worship of dead white males. It is instead designed to offer a simple method and common heuristic to study the interaction of law and Christianity around the world over the past two millennia. In due course, we hope to produce some fifty volumes and one thousand biographical case studies all told.

Columbia University Press opened this series in 2006 by publishing a three-volume work titled *Modern Christian Teachings on Law, Politics, and Human Nature*, divided into case studies of nearly thirty modern Catholic, Protestant, and Orthodox Christian figures. Cambridge University Press has in print or in press newly commissioned studies on great Christian jurists in the first millennium, as well as in English, Spanish, French, Lowlands, and American history. Routledge will publish major new volumes on Great Christian Jurists in Nordic, Russian, Welsh, and Latin American history. Mohr Siebeck is taking up the German story; Federation Press the Australian story. The Center for the Study of Law and Religion aims to commission similar studies for other parts of the world, particularly countries in Eastern Europe and Eurasia, and discrete regions and eras in the Middle East, Africa, and the Pacific Rim.

This volume was made possible by a generous grant from the McDonald Agape Foundation which supported the work of the editors and contributors. On behalf of the editors and my colleagues in the Center for the Study of Law and Religion, we express our deep thanks to Ambassador Alonzo McDonald, Ms. Suzie McDonald, Mr. Peter McDonald, and the other members of the Foundation board for their generous support for this and many other related volumes on law and Christianity. We are also most grateful for the perennial support, counsel, and encouragement of Gonzalo Rodríguez-Fraile for Rafael Domingo's work on fundamental questions of law, religion, and spirituality viewed in rich interdisciplinary perspective.

We are deeply grateful to Dr. Gary S. Hauk, former Emory University historian and current senior editor in our Center, for sharing his superb editorial talents so generously in copyediting this manuscript. We also express our warmest thanks to our Center colleagues, Ms. Amy Wheeler and Ms. Anita Mann for their skillful administration of this and other scholarly projects.

It was a joy for me to work with Professors Condorelli and Domingo and to learn from the two dozen leading scholars from European and North American universities whom they commissioned to write fresh chapters. We are especially grateful that so many great Italian jurists and legal historians were kind enough to join this volume and present their work in English form—no easy task for those scholars grounded in Latin sources and accustomed to writing in Italian, French, or Spanish, and no easy method to accept in a day when doctrinal, social, and political historiography is more fashionable.

It is a delight to publish this volume and several others in the distinguished Law and Religion series edited by one of the world's preeminent scholars of law and religion, Professor Norman Doe. Professor Doe and his many colleagues in the Cardiff Centre for Law and Religion have been vital trans-Atlantic allies with our Emory Center for the Study of Law and Religion. We give thanks for their leadership in this expanding global field of interdisciplinary legal study, and for their partnership with us in publishing this and parallel volumes on law and Christianity.

Finally, we express our warm thanks to Alison Kirk and her colleagues at Routledge in taking on this volume and applying their usual standards of excellence in their editing, production, and marketing.

John Witte, Jr.
Director, Center for the Study of Law and Religion
Emory University

Introduction

Orazio Condorelli and Rafael Domingo

In the current sociocultural context, the historical problem of the role of Christianity in the formation of the common legal tradition of the Western world is inescapable. This volume on the relationship between law and the Christian tradition in Italian history, represented here by a gallery of great jurists, constitutes an attempt to offer a partial answer to this question.

In 1942, while the Second World War was raging, and part of Europe was dominated by totalitarian regimes, the Italian idealist philosopher Benedetto Croce wrote a short essay titled "Why We Cannot but Say We Are 'Christians'" (*Perché non possiamo non dirci cristiani*).[1] We think that the core of Croce's answer is still valid. He considered, in the light of history, that Christianity "was the greatest revolution that humanity has ever accomplished," a revolution that "operated in the center of the soul, in the moral conscience," and that the members of Western society, regardless of the adhesion of individuals to the Christian faith, "in the moral life and in thought" are "children of Christianity." Croce felt the need to state this belief in a highly tragic historical moment, in which the compression of fundamental freedoms and horrible crimes against humanity manifested themselves—even in the eyes of a secular spirit, as he was—as an open denial of the Christian commandment of love: "And to preserve and rekindle and nourish the Christian sentiment is our ever recurring need, acute and tormenting today more than ever, between sorrow and hope."

The editors of this volume share the conviction that the Western world cannot but be said to be Christian. And yet, we are not sure that this belief can generally be shared today, sometimes due to ideological rejection, sometimes simply due to ignorance or neglect of history and, for our concerns, ignorance of European legal history.

The Western world today tends to present itself as a society in which religion is (or should be) confined to the sphere of the conscience of each person, while law and politics should be built regardless of the demands of religion. In liberal democratic societies, as well as in supranational institutions inspired by the principles of democracy and human rights, such a premise nevertheless leaves open a way of communication between the sphere of religion and conscience and the dimension of law: this way passes through the dynamics of democracy and rights to freedom. But it would be difficult to deny that in the same Western world a certain sense of intolerance circulates towards other cultural and legal experiences in which the process of secularization has just begun or to which it is totally foreign. In fact, attempts to exclude religion from the public sphere clash with a growing pressure, also fueled by migrations and globalization, aimed at giving legal and political recognition to demands coming from religion and conscience. Religion today, as always, is an unstoppable driving force behind the development of societies. On the other hand, the separation between the sphere of secular law and that of religious law is called to be reassembled in a deeper unity of the human person. In practice, however, effects are not always satisfactory, and sometimes people remain existentially divided because of the impossibility of reconciling the conflict between the law of God and human laws.

The problem of how we must build our present and our future is inevitably connected with the understanding of our past. It would be unrealistic to think of being able to act independently of any religious conditioning coming from the common European legal past, or from solicitations that arise from the confrontation with different legal cultures. In the current geopolitical context, the processes of globalization coexist with forces emerging from cultural and religious pluralism. Even legal history has a role in the process of building up a common home for humanity and a global law. In facing different cultures, the Western world still considers itself the depository of some Christian values that distinguish it from other societies. One of these values consists in the healthy distinction (not intolerant separation or exclusion) among politics, law, and religion.[2] This distinction is today accompanied by the recognition of a catalog of human rights in which religious freedom emerges as the first freedom that individuals historically have claimed from the public power.

We believe that the essays collected in this volume can help explain the contributions that the values of Christianity, through the mediation of the thought of the jurists, gave to the formation of the Western legal tradition.

Our volume is part of a larger research project on Christian jurists in the history of the Western world, led by John Witte, Jr., director of the Center for the Study of Law and Religion at Emory University. The project aims to explore the ways in which Christianity has forged the conformation of law and the sense of justice from within. More precisely, how the thought of Christian jurists has interpreted, throughout history, the teachings of Christ and has contributed to the formation and consolidation of legal and social Christian values. It is clear that the interpretation of the core values of Christianity has not been uniform throughout history. The historical perspective is therefore necessary both to recognize the roots—sometimes ignored or intentionally neglected—of our present, and to understand the extent to which our present is detached from some interpretations given in the past (e.g., about the value of human life or the legitimacy of the death penalty), or has changed on the basis of revised anthropological convictions that were undisputed until a few decades ago (e.g., the concepts of marriage and family).

Our volume is placed, in spirit as well as formal structure, next to the volumes already published, in which the relationship between Christianity and law has been explored through the thought and writings of jurists belonging to the legal traditions of some Western countries. Between 2017 and 2019 the volumes dedicated to English, Spanish, French, and American jurists appeared,[3] along with a volume on the great Christian thinkers of the first millennium.[4] Our volume also shares the ideals and principles which have recently inspired a book on the interactions between Christianity and global law.[5]

This volume has a biographical structure. The historical and theoretical interest at the basis of the research is pursued through a gallery of jurists who, because of their Italian background, belong to the Catholic tradition (though not exclusively) and, in any case, were involved from the sixteenth century onwards in the dialogues (and conflicts) with other churches or denominations.

On the model of the other volumes of the series, our book also starts from a broad meaning of the category of "jurist"—a term that deserves some clarification. After the eclipse of the Roman civilization and the parenthesis of the early medieval period ("an age without jurists"[6]), it was between the eleventh and twelfth centuries (the "medieval renaissance")[7] that the jurist emerged from the masters of liberal arts as a new intellectual figure. The jurist was distinguished from other thinkers such as philosophers and theologians by his specific scientific training and his professional activity, exercised in the universities as a teacher, in the courts as a judge or lawyer, and in secular or ecclesiastical administrations.

In this volume we adopt a broad interpretation of the category of jurist. The reader might be surprised to find that some chapters concern theologians (Thomas Aquinas, Thomas Cajetan, and Robert Bellarmine), while other jurists are more commonly known for their philosophical speculation (Giambattista Vico), or were intellectuals and men committed to political action (Luigi Sturzo and Alcide De Gasperi) or a pope (Innocent IV and Paul VI). In our book, in short, we have included personalities who, beyond the specific social role of the jurist in the strict sense, in our opinion have made a significant contribution to the interpretation and development of the law in the broadest sense of the term. Without disregarding the epistemological reasons for a more restrictive approach, we think that an enlargement of the horizon and an inclusive approach allows us to fruitfully integrate the law with other perspectives of analysis (politics, economics, sociology, theology, etc.). Moreover, in making these choices the editors did not act alone, because the final choices were agreed upon by the contributors to the volume. If it is true that some personalities included in the book are not jurists in the strict sense, we think that the unity of the perspective of interpretation is guaranteed by the fact that all the authors of the individual chapters are themselves renowned jurists and law historians.

This volume is neither a dictionary nor an encyclopedia: excellent works of both types have been published recently.[8] The book is divided into twenty-six chapters that trace the biography of twenty-seven authors (one chapter deals with Azo and Accursius together). The selection was not easy, as one may guess in recalling that the *Dizionario Biografico dei Giuristi Italiani*, published in 2013, includes the biographies of 2,159 jurists from the twelfth century until 2010. We are aware that every selection involves a certain degree of discretion, and that the final choice can cause approval or discontent according to the tastes or expectations of the reader. We chose twenty-seven jurists whom—due to their intellectual commitment or the way in which they translated their Christian vision into civil action—we consider particularly representative in order to illustrate the interactions between Christianity and legal thought. It is inevitable that not all the authors included in the list appear at first sight to be figures of universal importance, but the purpose of the volume is also to reconstruct a particular intellectual milieu, embodied, so to speak, in the Italian legal tradition.

The choice of jurists was conditioned primarily by the need to maintain the length of this volume in line with the other volumes of the series. The selection was oriented in the sense of privileging the jurists of the high and late medieval period (1100–1500) and early modern period (1500–1800), respectively, twelve and seven jurists each. In the twelfth through eighteenth centuries, Europe was characterized by a profound cultural unity rooted in the Christian faith founded on the texts of the Old and New Testament and in the living tradition of the Church. This cultural unity was also expressed in the field of law: the legal culture based on the *ius commune* (civil and canon law: *utrumque ius*) remained the basis of the training of jurists in European universities until the age of codifications.[9] It cannot be denied that the religious differences originating in the Reformation of the sixteenth century reverberated in their effects on this common experience, but they did not break this unity. The nineteen jurists selected for the twelfth through eighteenth centuries were undisputed protagonists of European legal culture and its projections into the New World.

The selection of jurists of the nineteenth and twentieth centuries was thornier and more difficult. In general, and not only in the context of Italian history, the processes of secularization made the incidence of religious thought in the elaboration of law less evident and full blown. This was, generally, an effect of the processes that tended to lead religion back into the private sphere of the citizens, but the phenomenon is more directly connected with the policies of Church-State separation that tended to secularize the legal systems of the States, freeing them from the structures of the confessionalism that had stratified over the centuries. This process would lead to the consolidation and exaltation of legal positivism, which reduces law (*ius*) to the law produced by the nation-state (*lex*), excluding thus the sources of religious laws.

The seven personalities chosen for these last two centuries are partly central figures of these events and partly forerunners of the twentieth-century cultural and political renewal, which, in the Catholic Church, culminated in the ecclesiology of the Second Vatican Council. Through this renewal, the new coordinates of the relations between law and religion were outlined within the framework of the rights to freedom and of democratic dynamics.

In examining the relationship between Christianity and law through the legacy of some great Italian jurists, the volume presupposes a historical fact, namely, that Christianity and law have merged into the historical experience of the Western world, and that this fusion has given a peculiar mark to Western civilization that distinguishes it from other civilizations and from other ways of relating law, politics, and religion. This awareness does not mean to deny that in the contemporary world various combinations of factors—such as postsecularization, globalization, and the accentuation of cultural and religious pluralism—produce new social scenarios that require jurists and politicians to find shared solutions by reasoning according to cultural categories that are no longer monolithic or homogeneous. From this perspective, we cultivate the hope that this volume will stimulate an intellectual dialogue among Christians of all denominations, as well as between Christians and non-Christians in general.

Italian Christian jurists in the Middle Ages

The two jurists whose portraits open our gallery occupy a unique and incomparable position in the European legal tradition. Irnerius and Gratian can rightly be considered the founders of medieval legal science, respectively in the fields of civil law and canon law.[10] Irnerius recomposed and restored Justinian's *Corpus Iuris*, which in the early Middle Ages had been known in incomplete form, and he made these texts the basis of the new science of civil law. Gratian was the author of a canonical collection, the *Concordia discordantium canonum*, otherwise known as *Decretum magistri Gratiani*, the book on which the science of canon law was built. Both Irnerius and Gratian worked in the early decades of the twelfth century in Bologna: the city is rightly considered the mother or cradle of legal studies (*alma mater studiorum*).

Medieval legal science was born therefore as interpretation of texts of authority: on one hand the ancient laws of the emperor Justinian (the so-called *libri legales*, legal books), and on the other a private work, the *Decretum*, which collects a very wide selection of the sources of Church law (about four thousand passages). Irnerius and Gratian were not isolated geniuses but participated in a broad movement of cultural renewal, from which the formation of an autonomous legal science arose, born from the bosom of the liberal arts (*artes liberales*). Hence the jurist emerged as a new intellectual figure.

The work of Irnerius and Gratian gave a decisive impulse to the new science, both in its methods and in its contents. Irnerius could do his work because he was a master of liberal arts, and perhaps even a theologian. Andrea Padovani presents the portrait of a man that medieval jurists themselves considered the *primus illuminator* of legal science, that is, the one who lit the light of the new science. His teaching is handed down mainly through extremely concise glosses, sometimes requiring arduous interpretation, which touch with great acuteness and incisiveness the main themes which medieval legal thought is discussed: the great themes of legal theory, such as the meaning of justice and of equity, the natural freedom of the human person, the idea that individual will is the basis of contractual relations between private individuals, the fundamental questions concerning sovereignty, and the relations between citizens and political power.

Gratian, the father of the science of canon law, was a jurist with deep knowledge of theology, perhaps matured in French schools, as Atria Larson suggests. His contribution consists not only in the compilation of a canonical collection but also in an original style of thought transmitted through his *dicta*, that is, those passages of the *Decretum* in which Gratian carries out the hermeneutical work directed at rediscovering the intimate harmony of the multiple and discordant sources handed down over a millennium of Church history. The *Decretum* presents a true system of Church law. Gratian's brilliant approach manifests itself in the first twenty *distinctiones* (distinctions), in which the author proposes a hierarchically articulated picture of the sources of law. His scientific contribution on this point is invaluable: Gratian gives his readers, for the centuries to come, a vision of law as a unitary reality articulated in the distinction between natural law and human law, in which canon law, founded on divine revelation, concerns the supernatural dimension of the relation between the baptized person and God in the body of the Church.

Irnerius and Gratian were the two pillars on which the legal science of the second millennium was built. From their schools sprang generations of jurists, who, from the method they adopted, are called glossators and, specifically, decretists, inasmuch as they made Gratian's *Decretum* the basis of their science. With Azo and Accursius our gallery presents two fundamental authors of the school of glossators of Roman law. About a century after Irnerius, the scientific path of the civil-law glossators found two moments of high synthesis in the works of these great jurists, in particular in Azo's *Summa aurea* (which gathered the *Summa Codicis*, the *Summa Institutionum* and the *Summulae Digestorum*) and in Accursius's *apparatus* on the five volumes into which the Justinian's *Corpus Iuris* was divided in the medieval tradition. Accursius's glosses were received by schools as the standard gloss on the *libri legales*, and therefore were constantly reproduced on the margins of Justinian's *Corpus*, first in manuscripts and later in printed editions. The works of Azo and Accursius—as Emanuele Conte highlights—are an extraordinary testimony to how the glossators used the ancient laws of Justinian to affect the fabric of medieval society and to give a new direction to social and economic developments. An example concerns the network of relations between the urban world, rural society, and feudal lordships, with the related theme of the bonds of personal dependence, which were seen as a sort of wound brought to natural human freedom, an idea that arose from Christian teaching grafted onto Justinianic sources.

While Justinian's *Corpus Iuris* was a collection of laws inherited from the ancient Roman and Byzantine past, from the second half of the twelfth century the new legal system of the Latin Church developed on the foundation of the canonical tradition collected by Gratian in the *Decretum*. The tools of this development were the decretals of the popes and the decisions of the general councils of the Latin Church. These materials were selected and published in a series of collections by the Roman pontiffs which, along with the *Decretum*, represent the large nucleus of the series that would be known as *Corpus Iuris Canonici*: the

Decretales of Gregory IX (1234), the *Liber Sextus* of Boniface VIII (1298), and the *Clementinae* of Clement V (published by John XXII in 1317).

The school of the decretalists arose in the second half of the twelfth century and had its heyday between 1250 and 1350 approximately. Sinibaldo Fieschi, Enrico da Susa, and Giovanni d'Andrea are recognized as the triad of the most authoritative canonists of that era. Sinibaldo was a master canonist and became Pope Innocent IV; Enrico da Susa was a teacher, bishop, and cardinal (with the Latin title of Hostiensis); Giovanni d'Andrea was a layman who acquired an incomparable authority in his time as master in the *Studium* of Bologna. Sinibaldo Fieschi, whose profile is outlined by Kathleen Cushing, in his apparatus on the *Decretales* of Gregory IX defined some thematic paths which, in the wake of his original teaching, would later be examined in depth by the jurists of the following decades and centuries: the relationship between the *societas christiana* and the infidels, the modalities of the missionary action of the Church, the theme of the crusade, the relations between secular and ecclesiastical power, and the definition of the respective spheres of competence.

As Kenneth Pennington shows in the chapter on Enrico da Susa, these themes and the doctrinal approaches of the decretalists would resurface as main points of reference in the discussions that, after the discovery of America, accompanied the penetration of European institutions and culture into the New World. Giovanni d'Andrea, whose portrait is presented by Peter Clarke, explores the internal problems of the *societas christiana* and shows some methodological trends that herald legal humanism.

In this context, it seemed appropriate to insert a chapter on Thomas Aquinas, whose figure is introduced by Charles J. Reid, Jr. A volume on the great Christian jurists could not overlook this theologian and philosopher, whose thought was decisive for the development of many legal concepts. First of all, his teaching on law (*ius* and *lex*) became an essential point of reference for jurists of the medieval and modern ages. Moreover, the idea of law (*ius*) as a *res iusta* (the right thing) and the idea of the law (*lex*) as an order given by reason (*ordo rationis*) proposed again, in the clarity of an impeccable philosophical construction, a teaching that was coherent with the doctrines elaborated by the jurists in the wake of Isidor of Sevilla and Gratian. In the works of Thomas Aquinas, such conceptions of law take place along ramifications that touch virtually all areas of civil life. His teachings (for example, his contribution to the theory of just war, a theme particularly relevant in the modern age) came fully into the discourse of the jurists.

The thirteenth and fourteenth centuries in Italy and wider Europe were characterized by an intense process of normative production linked to the development and consolidation of the various political and social institutions (kingdoms, city communes, guilds of arts and crafts, etc.). A great variety of local and particular laws (called *iura propria* in the wake of a teaching of Gaius handed down in the Digest 1.1.9) was joined to the *ius commune* (civil and canon law) which was scientifically created in the universities. *Ius commune* and *iura propria* were the two poles of a legal system of which the jurists elaborated the rules of interpretation and resolution of conflicts. However, the *ius commune* remained the basis for the training of jurists, because it offered the indispensable categories and principles for interpreting the *iura propria*.[11]

Cino Sinibuldi da Pistoia, Bartolo da Sassoferrato, and Baldo degli Ubaldi testified in an exemplary way to the developments of legal science in the renewed political, social, and cultural framework of the fourteenth century. First-rate jurists, all three of them worked in the institutional context of Italian cities. They represent the continuity and the development of a teaching line that was formed in the relationship between master and pupil: Cino was Bartolo's master, and Bartolo was Baldo's master. In the peculiar political context of central and northern Italy, Cino and Bartolo experienced the profound crisis of the imperial institution. Like Dante Alighieri, they cultivated the hope of a restoration of the role of the empire as supreme guarantor of order and justice and regulator of the conflicts that lacerated the Italian city communes, but they also proved the disappointment of political ideals founded on the concord between *ecclesia* and *imperium* as the foundation of the order of Christian society. New city lords emerged from the crisis and the conflicts: medieval political thought, inspired by the tradition of the fathers of the Church, qualified them as tyrants.

Cino da Pistoia, whose portrait is offered by Giuseppe Speciale, was a jurist and a poet contemporary of Dante. Cino passed on to Italy the methods and teachings of the French jurists of Orléans (Jacques de Revigny and Pierre de Belleperche) and is considered the leader of a methodological renewal from which the school of commentators emerged. Bartolo, presented by Orazio Condorelli, was a master of the highest authority, whose work ended up identifying the characteristics of the school of commentators. In Bartolo's work, the relationships among ethics, law, and theology, between the external forum and the forum of conscience, are clearly highlighted as internal problems of legal discourse and political thought. Baldo went down in history as "the most philosophical of jurists." Julius Kirshner highlights Baldo's outstanding contribution to the identification of the legal forms inspired by the ideals of Christian economic ethics. With their *consilia* (legal consultations) the jurists, alongside the theologians, acted as authoritative moral guides for the operators of economic life.

The overview of medieval jurists closes with two bright stars of the first half of the fifteenth century, Paolo di Castro and Niccolò Tedeschi, whose profiles are outlined by Susanne Lepsius and Richard Helmholz. Respectively a layman and an ecclesiastic (bishop and cardinal), a civilian and a canonist for education and academic life, both Paolo di Castro and Tedeschi expressed a unitary conception of law, which manifested itself in the system of *utrumque ius*, that is, the system in which civil law and canon law were competing forces in governing the life of the *societas christiana*.[12] Both lived, albeit in different phases and with different roles, at the time of the Great Schism that divided Western Christianity in the decades between 1378 and the Council of Basel (1431). Both stand out for their clear and original thought, for they were able to gather the best of what medieval legal science had elaborated, and to pass it on to future generations who would recognize their excellent merits. They were not isolated thinkers in an ivory tower, but their thought was constantly elaborated in the dialectical confrontation with the practice of economic and social relations and with the grievous emergencies of the divided Church.

Italian Christian jurists in the early Modern Age (1500–1800)

The early modern age was a period of crisis. The signs can be seen in the social, political, epistemological, and anthropological perspectives inherited from the Middle Ages, but these multiple upheavals did not demolish the unity of European legal culture.[13] A fundamentally homogeneous experience continued until the social and political transformations of the second half of the eighteenth century led to the codification of national laws. From the Iberian Peninsula to Poland and Hungary, from Scandinavia to Sicily, this experience was nourished by substantially homogeneous legal studies grafted onto the trunk of medieval legal science and cultivated in the European universities.[14]

The European exploration of America beginning in 1492 disclosed new geographical and anthropological horizons that forced European culture to confront itself with situations that were not entirely new (relationships with peoples who had not known Christianity), but this phenomenon had absolutely new quantitative proportions. The moral issues emerging from the conquest and colonization of America fueled the persistent connections between theology and law that had characterized medieval legal culture. In the confrontation with the Indo-American populations, European culture identified a suitable instrument of juridical dialogue in natural law and in the principles that flow from it: natural law, elaborated by jurists and theologians, became a true "intercultural" law *ante litteram*.

The Protestant Reformation caused multiple institutional and intellectual upheavals. The various reformed churches and denominations experienced different processes of institutionalization. This plurality of churches and denominations within the same political contexts imposed the search for forms of peaceful coexistence and urged an intense reflection on the topics of tolerance and religious freedom as barriers against bloody religious conflicts.[15]

The Catholic Church, with the great enterprise of the Council of Trent (1545–63), confirmed and reformulated the truths of the Catholic faith, but was also forced to react to the crisis of ecclesiastical institutions, of the moral life, and of the discipline of the faithful and of the clergy. This new rupture of European religious unity did not, however, diminish the fundamental unity of European legal culture and did not interrupt the processes of communication among intellectuals of the various religious affiliations.

In this framework, there were also important innovations in the methodology of legal studies. The application of the humanistic method in the science of law aimed to introduce a historical and philological approach in the study of traditional sources. Legal humanism aimed to study the texts of civil and canon law as sources for the knowledge of the history of Roman and Byzantine civilization or the history of the Church; however, the historical-philological interests of the humanists could not eliminate the traditional approach based on the need to coordinate—for the demands of practice and for civil and ecclesiastical government—the *ius commune* with local or national laws. France is normally considered the cradle of the new humanistic method applied to law (*mos gallicus*), while Italy remained the homeland of the traditional legal method—a method which, under the name of Bartolo ("bartolism"), is qualified as *mos italicus.*

Andrea Alciato—as Alain Wijffels points out—consciously embodied, with excellent results, the different tendencies rooted in the humanistic method. In Alciato the tradition of *mos italicus*—also acquired in legal practice, which required the mastery of traditional methods—was combined with an extraordinary historical and philological expertise acquired in the schools of Italian humanists during his youth. His teaching in France, in Avignon, and later in Bourges, and the intellectual relations with European humanist circles are evidence of a persistent circulation of ideas that fertilized the intellectual environment of sixteenth-century Europe despite religious divisions.

Our gallery includes two theologians who, in different times between the sixteenth and seventeenth centuries, had a very important presence in the development of legal doctrines on the themes involved in the social, religious, and political events we have mentioned. Thomas de Vio (know as Cajetan), whose profile is outlined by Wim Decock, testifies to the continuity of the authority of the thought of Thomas Aquinas in the modern era. Cajetan's commentaries on the *Summa theologiae* not only favored the dissemination of the teaching of Aquinas but also constituted a tool for updating Aquinas's doctrines in relation to new historical developments. Cajetan was immersed in the theological controversies of the time (he was an examiner charged with identifying the heretical statements contained in Luther's writings). The connection between theology and law, already widely experienced in medieval centuries, in Cajetan arises in the moral-theological approach to the thorny legal questions of his time, such as those concerning the lawfulness of commercial operations. The authority of his writings, which certainly reflects the authority of the teaching of Aquinas, was very significant in European and Latin American theological and juridical literature.

Lorenzo Sinisi introduces the central figure of Robert Bellarmine, who lived and worked when the effects of the Reformation were consolidated and the Catholic Church was engaged in defending the orthodoxy of the faith and in working for deep ecclesiastical and moral reform. In his *Disputationes de controversiis Christianae Fidei adversus huius temporis haereticos*, Bellarmine systematically outlined Catholic doctrine in comparison with the ideas of the reformers and on the basis of the treasure of Catholic doctrine. One of the central themes of his ecclesiology consists in defining the position of the Roman pontiff in the constitution of the Catholic Church in connection with the intent to defend the *libertas ecclesiae* against interference by Catholic sovereigns in the government of the Church (variously named "jurisdictionalism," "regalism," "Gallicanism," etc.) and, correlatively, with the aim of defining the powers of the ecclesiastical authority in temporal matters. His doctrine of the *potestas indirecta in temporalibus* (indirect power in temporal matters) was rooted in the medieval teaching of the *potestas ecclesiae in temporalibus ratione peccati* (power of the Church in temporal matters by reason of sin), and became the cornerstone of the Catholic teaching on the relations between the Church and civil authority up to the threshold of the Second Vatican Council.

The dialectic of positions and methods is well manifested by Alberico Gentili, whose figure is presented by Giovanni Minnucci. Gentili is an extremely original author in the picture we have described. A jurist trained in the method of the *mos italicus*, later in his life he also approached the method of legal humanism. He had to flee Italy for having adhered to the religious ideas of the Reformation and had a brilliant career in England. Deservedly counted among the founders of modern international law, Gentili was a staunch supporter of the distinction of the roles of theology and law and expressed his impatience with the confusion of the two perspectives. If theology deals with the relations between humankind and God, law should concern the relations between persons: theologians, therefore, should maintain silence in the field that is not their responsibility. Gentili, who had a personal experience of the religious conflicts that ravaged the Europe of his time, identified religious freedom as a necessary solution to establish a peaceful coexistence in a society marked by different confessions and religious groupings. This *diversitas religionis* no longer concerned the relationship between Christians and infidels but connoted the Christian world from within.

The gallery continues with Giovanni Battista De Luca, who is recognized as the greatest Italian jurist of the seventeenth century. Italo Birocchi points out that De Luca's work is centered on the idea that practice is the highest moment in jurisprudence, since the principles of law are applied to the regulation of human relations in function of the common good. From the point of view of method, his work marks the crisis of the *mos italicus* and of the scholastic method inherited from the Middle Ages and is also characterized by the convinced promotion of the Italian language as an instrument of legal communication. These trends translated into a pronounced attention to the demands of legal practice and the experiences of the great courts. The legal system was still centered on the two common laws (*iura communia*), but it also had to confront the territorially defined dimension of local law (*ius patrium*) in a coordination which gave rise to the features of "today's law" (*ius hodiernum*). According to De Luca, the jurist is the depositary of the virtue of prudence, which must be exercised in relation to a positive law that at that time was mainly entrusted to the legislation of territorial princes. In his thinking, the practical dimension of prudence is tinged with a certain realistic skepticism, still nurtured by a Christian vision of the world. This realistic approach aims for "the things of this world," for the definition of reasonable solutions rather than the implementation of an abstract idea of truth or common good.

The transition from the century of the Baroque to the Enlightenment is illustrated through Giambattista Vico: his presence in the gallery of the great Italian jurists gives a well-deserved space to a thinker who occupies an undisputed place in the history of philosophical thought, but who has not received equal attention in the perspective of the history of legal thought. Marco Nicola Miletti highlights how religiosity deeply permeates Vico's vision of law and institutions. His speculation on law is contained both in specifically juridical works and in his masterpiece, *Scienza nuova* (*The New Science*). More than analyzing contingent norms, Vico turned his attention to identifying the philosophical principles that govern the historical reality of law, which he found in the convergence between nature and law (*ius*) and between truth and fact (*verum* and *factum*). Vico discovered the religious roots of law in the universal history of humankind and proposed them as the foundations for the idea of law in dialogue with the skeptical, libertine, or relativistic currents of his time. His works reveal original perspectives that resulted in acute contributions in the field of philology, anthropology, and legal history.

With Cesare Beccaria, whose profile is outlined by Maria Gigliola di Renzo Villata, we enter the heart of the Enlightenment. His universal fame is linked to a booklet, *Dei delitti e delle pene* (*On Crimes and Punishments*), which represents a manifesto of the Enlightenment tendencies towards the reform of the legal system and the modernization and humanization of criminal law. Beccaria lived in Milan, where ideas of renewal circulated with the prospect of reforming the legal system through the promulgation of a code of laws—a trend in Europe during the second half of the eighteenth century. Beccaria's adherence to Enlightenment thought matured in this milieu open to reforms, under the influence of the writings of Montesquieu, the Encyclopedists, and Rousseau. The fruit of this turning point was the work *Dei delitti e delle pene* (1764), which brought the author universal fame. The idea of reforming criminal law is here connected to a broader prospect for reform of the legal system, which included criticism of the system of sources and the methods of traditional jurisprudence and was rooted in the idea of a social pact based on human freedom. The prospects for reform and modernization of criminal law were based on several principles: the idea that criminal repression must affect acts that endanger civil coexistence; the principle of legality (a punishment can be imposed only when an action is previously defined as a crime by criminal law, since the judge is subjected to law); the presumption of innocence; punishment proportionate to the crime; and the refusal of judicial torture. The purpose of these reforms was to guarantee legal certitude and to limit judicial arbitrariness. Beccaria's work received the praise of Enlightenment authors (Voltaire, Bentham), but in reactionary circles it was judged as an expression of a spirit that aimed to pervert religion and subvert the established order. In our eyes as observers of the twenty-first century, the ideas advocated by Beccaria appear as indisputable cornerstones of a modern and secularized criminal law, inspired by an idea of justice and humanity that is fully consistent with a Christian vision of social relations.

Italian Christian jurists in the nineteenth and twentieth centuries

In the history of European society, the last two centuries have experienced changes that created a clear break with the past. Past times began to be seen as an *ancien régime* from which the new course was intended to stand out in terms of freedom and progress. The French Revolution marked the beginning of a process of irreversible changes, which took place in different times and modes in the various European countries. The processes of secularization of European society went hand in hand with institutional changes that were driven by the idea of the nation-state.

From the perspective of the history of law, such changes marked the end of the age of European *ius commune*, in which the coexistence and application of particular laws was guaranteed by the connective tissue of a culture that was common because it was founded on the methods and values that legal science had built over centuries on the texts of Justinian's law and canon law.

The codes were instruments of this desire for change. The codification of national laws was motivated by the intention of bringing order to the confused system of sources and building a new civil order on the basis of the primacy of positive law. National codifications, imposed during the nineteenth century, were built with ancient materials filtered through eighteenth-century rationalism and doctrines of natural law and reread through the values proposed by the Enlightenment and the French Revolution. If, to a certain extent, this process testifies to a continuity in the cultural tradition of European law, the new legislation was nevertheless based on the idea that law is a phenomenon produced by the sovereign will of the State and substantially coinciding with sources produced by the State or with sources that State law recognizes and accepts as productive factors of legal effects. The nineteenth-century code generally appears as a complete law with no gaps, which does not admit to being integrated by external sources (natural law, equity, custom, etc.). The law of the codes, therefore, reduces or deletes the spaces that in previous experiences were occupied by canon law or by the laws of other religious confessions. Canon law, which had contributed in a decisive way to the formation of a common legal tradition, was therefore confined as positive law to an area of irrelevance with respect to civil relations or was considered relevant only to the extent that State law permitted it.

At the same time, even legal science was forced to "nationalize" itself, due to the need to build the new legal order on the basis of the new laws. This phenomenon did not prevent jurists from maintaining an awareness of a permanent supranational dimension of legal science, because the sharing of methods and the memory of that common juridical past nurtured relations between the differentiated codified laws of the European nations.

Such historical processes took a peculiar turn in the Italian institutional situation of the nineteenth century. The conclusion of the Napoleonic experience and the restoration dictated by the Congress of Vienna gave birth to the new political structure of the "preunification" States. And yet the design of the new territorial map also marked the beginning of an irreversible process of political unification. Italian national unity was achieved in 1861 and was the fruit of ideals, revolutionary movements, and wars of independence that gave substance to the Italian Risorgimento. Vittorio Emanuele II of Savoy, king of Sardinia, became the first king of Italy.

Political unification was the premise of national legal unification.[16] The statute that Carlo Alberto had granted for the Kingdom of Sardinia in 1848 became the Statute of the Kingdom of Italy: it laid the foundations of a constitutional monarchy founded on liberal principles. The Civil Code of 1865 was the first legislative monument of united Italy.

The fact that Rome is the see of the pope—head of the Catholic Church but also, at that time, temporal monarch of the Papal States—deeply conditioned the process of Italian unification and the subsequent political vicissitudes of the Kingdom of Italy. In 1870 the Italian army conquered Rome and ended the centuries-old history of the Papal States. The supreme pontiff retired to the Vatican, declaring himself a prisoner, and Rome became the capital of the Kingdom of Italy. Although the Statute of the Kingdom declared that the Roman Catholic apostolic religion was the "only religion of the State," and that other cults were "tolerated in accordance with the laws" (Article 1), the ecclesiastical policy of the Kingdom of Italy was hostile to the Church and anticlerical. The progressive secularization of the structures of the State passed through the equalization of citizens before the law without distinction of religion, the abolition of historical privileges of the Church (ecclesiastical immunities, such as the privilege of the forum), the secularization of marriage (civil marriage was introduced in the Civil Code of 1865), the suppression of ecclesiastical institutions, and the confiscation of their assets.

Camillo Benso, count of Cavour, first president of the Council of Ministers of the Kingdom of Italy, had prefigured the design of a "free Church in a free State." This program was only partially implemented in the direction of the separation between State and Church; rather, it took place in the line of a sort of "liberal jurisdictionalism," which still granted relevant powers for the State in the life and organization of the Catholic Church.

The end of the temporal power of the popes opened the "Roman Question," which was the source of deep disagreements that for many decades would condition the relations between State and Church and the participation of Catholics in Italian political life. With the Law of Guarantees, the Italian State regulated unilaterally the prerogatives of the pope and the Holy See, and the relations of the State with Church (Law 214/1871). The solution of the Roman Question and religious pacification were achieved only during the fascist regime, with the stipulation of the Lateran Pacts and the creation of the Vatican City State (1929), which guaranteed a territorial basis for the spiritual sovereignty of the Holy See.[17]

The first two personalities who open the gallery of contemporary jurists operated in this context.[18] Contardo Ferrini—whose profile is outlined by Rafael Domingo—belongs to a generation of Italian jurists who include several eminent scholars of Roman law. During the nineteenth century the national codifications had removed the force of positive law from Roman law; in Germany this point of arrival was reached with the *Bürgerliches Gesetzbuch*, the civil code that went into effect in the German empire in 1900.[19] These developments gave Roman law back to history, and thus favored a reorientation of research interests towards the historical studies of Roman and Byzantine law. In Italy, the affirmation of the French codification model caused the success of the method of the so-called French exegetical school. But these new achievements went hand in hand with the maturation of awareness, fueled above all by German Pandectism, that Roman law offered the essential legal tools with which nineteenth-century jurists built an autonomous theoretical system of legal principles, institutions, and legal dogmas. In the outline of the secular jurists included in this volume, Ferrini is a unique figure, since in a short and intense life he gave testimony of Christian faith and values, for which he was beatified in 1947.

Pietro Gasparri—whose figure is presented by Alberto Lupano—was an eminent canonist but also a person endowed with uncommon practical skills, which he put to profit at the highest levels of the government of the Catholic Church. His work as a jurist took place at a time when canon law had lost much of its relevance in civil life due to the secularization of European society. Canon law suffered a sort of scientific marginalization due to the breakdown of the methodological unity of legal science provoked by the exclusive supremacy of national State law. In Italy, in the last two decades of the nineteenth century, this tendency gave rise to the so-called State ecclesiastical law, that is, the legal area concerning the laws of the State which govern religious matters. Francesco Scaduto and Francesco Ruffini, although following different doctrinal guidelines, are the two recognized founders of this branch of Italian legal science.[20] As a jurist, Gasparri was an heir to the classical tradition of canon law, which he illustrated with important contributions, among which a treatise on marriage stands out. He was also the true architect of the Church law codification, which concluded in 1917, when Benedict XV promulgated the first Code of Canon Law (*Codex Iuris Canonici*). As Secretary of State of the Holy See during the pontificate of Pius XI, Pietro Gasparri conducted the negotiations with the Italian State that led to the conclusion of the Lateran Pacts in 1929.

Luigi Sturzo and Alcide De Gasperi—introduced by Romeo Astorri and Olivier Descamps, respectively—lived during extremely tumultuous and changing times of Italian, European, and world history between the last three decades of the nineteenth century and the fifties of the following century. After the capture of Rome in 1870, the Holy See declared that it was not appropriate for Catholics to participate in the political life of the Italian State (*Non expedit*, 1874). This prohibition remained formally in force until 1919. In that year the Italian Popular Party, inspired by Catholic social teaching, was founded among others by Luigi Sturzo, a Sicilian Catholic priest, and Alcide De Gasperi, who later founded the Christian Democracy Party.

The March on Rome (1922) marked the beginning of the fascist regime and the starting point of a political and institutional process that transformed the structures of the liberal State into a totalitarian regime.[21] Realizing that religion is a powerful *instrumentum regni*, Benito Mussolini obtained the consent of Catholics by promoting conciliation between the Kingdom of Italy and the Catholic Church; his political action, however, provoked a tragic involution towards a model of a totalitarian State that denied the civil and religious values of freedom, equality, and solidarity. The publication of the racist laws (1938) and the subsequent adherence to the Hitlerian plan to exterminate the Jews was one of the saddest and most execrable pages of fascist politics.[22]

Luigi Sturzo represented an incessantly critical voice against the idolatry of the omnipotent State, the dangers of nationalisms, and the aberrations of totalitarianism. In his long intellectual journey, which extended from the last decade of the nineteenth century to the second postwar period, he elaborated a coherent and organic doctrine on international organization and war, on the relations between democracy and totalitarianism, on cooperation between Church and State, and on the ways of Catholic participation in political life. His thought exalted the Christian roots of the values of peace, justice, and freedom.

After the fall of fascism (1943) and the end of the Second World War, the institutional referendum marked the end of the monarchy and the birth of the Italian Republic (June 2, 1946). The Constituent Assembly had the task of tracing, on the ruins left by the war and the fascist regime, the path that the republic should take.

It was a choral effort in which all the parties that sat in the Assembly participated, and in which the Catholic forces made a fundamental contribution. Among the leading exponents of the Catholic world who took part in the Assembly, two jurists deserve mention: Giuseppe Dossetti (professor of canon law and ecclesiastical law) and Giorgio La Pira (professor of Roman law)—two men endowed, like De Gasperi, with intense religious faith. Dossetti and La Pira contributed to providing the Constitution of the Italian Republic a Christian inspiration (1948). This inspiration is found at the beginning of the Constitution, in Article 2, which is located in the section of the Fundamental Principles: "The Republic recognizes and guarantees the inviolable rights of the person, as an individual and in the social groups where human personality is expressed. The Republic expects that the fundamental duties of political, economic, and social solidarity be fulfilled." This article, in turn, "inspires so much of the principles and the very organizational structure determined by the Constitution."[23] From 1946 to 1953 De Gasperi was the head of the Italian government. In his activity, constantly nourished by his fervent Catholic faith, De Gasperi is considered to be one of the founding fathers of the European integration on the basis of the ideals of freedom, democracy, and peace.

Francesco Carnelutti and Arturo Carlo Jemolo embodied, each according to his personality, the figures of "well-rounded" jurists. The long spans of their lives allowed them to experience the profound evolution of Italian and world society between the last decades of the nineteenth century and the seventies of the twentieth century. The prestige of Carnelutti, as Giovanni Chiodi highlights, went beyond national boundaries due to the extraordinary breadth of the fields of law which he mastered with great skill. His works range from civil procedural law to criminal and procedural criminal law, from civil law to commercial and labor law, and from the methodology of law to the general theory of law. Moved by a deep religious faith, in his old age Carnelutti experienced the sense of the insufficiency of the legal dimension as a key to understanding human life: this led him to broaden his horizons as a scholar and writer, and to challenge himself in interpreting the Gospel message in writings in which law, ethics, and religion are intertwined.

Jemolo, whose profile is outlined by Carlo Fantappiè, was likewise able to combine the methodological conviction of the unity of legal science with an extraordinary ability to dominate multiple fields of law. Jemolo was a promoter of the Italian civil conscience not only with his scientific writings but also with an intense activity carried out in newspapers and magazines. The relations between law and religion and between civil society and religious society were the fields of research that he pursued with greater passion and with a rare mastery that allowed him to combine law with history and theology. Jemolo was endowed with a Catholic faith as profound as it was critically restless and pessimistic, a faith that resulted in a tormented political thought and in a preference for the model of separation between State and religion. When the republican constitution came into force, Jemolo repositioned the fulcrum of juridical analysis from the traditional question of relations between State and Church towards the centrality of the rights of freedom and of equality of citizens without distinction of religion. His intellectual convictions and his religious positions found a landing point in the idea of "secular conscience" (*coscienza laica*).

The concept of secularism (expressed in Italian with the noun *laicità* and the adjective *laico*) has taken a central position in legal thought and in the political debate in Italy in the second half of the twentieth century, up to the present day.[24] The convergence of the right of religious freedom with the principles of equality and of cooperation between the State and religious confessions led the Italian Constitutional Court to identify secularism as a supreme principle of the Italian constitutional order. According to the Court, the principle of secularism "implies not the indifference of the State before religions, but a guarantee of the State for the safeguarding of freedom of religion, in a system of confessional and cultural pluralism" (Judgment n. 203/1989). In another judicial decision, the Court specified that the principle of secularism involves "equidistance and impartiality" of the State in the face of religious confessions, and that it characterizes "in a pluralistic sense the form of our State, within which different faiths, cultures, and traditions have to coexist, in equality of freedom" (Judgment n. 508/2000). This meaning of secularism has now become a stable pillar of the living law and distinguishes the Italian experience from other ways, such as the French one, to conceive the sense of secularism.[25]

Jean-Pierre Schouppe introduced the last personality of our gallery: Giovanni Battista Montini, archbishop of Milan and later Pope Paul VI, who was canonized by Pope Francis in 2018. Paul VI followed the steps of his predecessor, John XXIII, of whom Montini was a friend and collaborator in the preparation and development of the Second Vatican Council (1962–65). The council, convened by John XXIII but suspended upon his death, was reopened by Paul VI. The ecumenical assembly started a process of renewal in the tradition that continues to this day. Paul VI not only completed the council but was also the first of a series of pontiffs who had the task of implementing the conciliar principles concerning the internal life of the Catholic Church, the dialogue with other Christian churches and denominations and with non-Christian religions, as well as relations with the political community.

The major contributions of Paul VI to the life of law consist in the promotion of the culture of human rights (encyclical *Populorum progressio*, 1967, in the wake of John XXIII's *Pacem in terris*, 1963) and in the work of revising the legislation of the Catholic Church on the basis of the principles of Vatican II. This process was completed by John Paul II with the promulgation of the *Codex Iuris Canonici* (Code of Canon Law, 1983) and the *Codex Canonum Ecclesiarum Orientalium* (Code of the Canons of the Eastern Churches, 1990). According to John Paul II the new Latin code (but the same can be said of the Eastern code) "could be understood as a great effort to translate this same doctrine, that is, the conciliar ecclesiology, into canonical language" (Apostolic Constitution *Sacrae disciplinae leges*, 1983).

The teaching of the Second Vatican Council presents the Catholic Church as people of God and emphasizes the dignity and equality of the faithful within the diversity of their functions. This teaching has also produced a significant reorientation of the doctrine of relations between Church and State and, more generally, of the role of the Church in the contemporary world (Pastoral Constitution *Gaudium et spes*, 1965). The conciliar teaching abandoned the centuries-old language of the *potestas in temporalibus* (direct or indirect), entrusted the lay faithful with the task of animating the world and giving witness of Christ, and recognized the rightful autonomy of temporal realities and the mutual independence of the political community and of the Church. But the council also claimed the right of the Church

> to preach the faith, to teach her social doctrine, to exercise her role freely among men, and also to pass moral judgment in those matters which regard public order when the fundamental rights of a person or the salvation of souls require it.
>
> (Gaudium et spes, n. 76)

The Second Vatican Council therefore outlined the path of a Christian secularism, linking the council's own teaching to the problems of the contemporary world, the function of the faithful in society, and the specific mission of Christian jurists.[26]

Conclusion

It is superfluous to reaffirm how great and profound was the contribution of Italian Christian jurists to the development of European and Western legal culture. This contribution lies at the very origins of medieval legal science (twelfth century), is expressed in the formation of a European *ius commune* in the centuries of the *societas christiana*, and in modern times continues during the centuries of divided *Christianitas* until the end of the *ancien régime*. In the twelfth through eighteenth centuries, the work of Italian jurists took place in a cultural and scientific dimension that did not know national boundaries, and in which jurists spoke a common language, despite the differentiation of the legal experiences of the different European territories. Their work continued in the nineteenth and twentieth centuries, but in a context in which the formation and consolidation of national States led to the emergence of new national laws. Christian values, according to the collective consciousness developed over the centuries, represented a leaven of legal culture and, through the convergence of civil law and canon law, contributed to the formation of a common legal tradition.

We expect that this volume will contribute to nourishing an academic conversation on the role of Christianity, and more generally of religions, in the building of a common home for humanity which, within the framework of the current processes of globalization, can be considered an inclusive place, respectful of cultural and religious diversity, and active in protecting rights and promoting peace.

We believe, in particular, that Christianity has much to say in the era of globalization because at the heart of Christianity lies a message of divine love and loving fellowship among individuals created in the image of God. Such a contribution can even be expressed in accordance with the secular standards accepted by the dynamics and proceedings of liberal democracies.[27] From this point of view, present-day Western democracies show conflicting tendencies: on one hand is the attempt to confine religion to the private sphere and to exclude it from the public dimension; on the other hand, the plurality of faiths and cultures that characterizes global society stimulates an irresistible push towards the public emergence of religious instances and the claim of individual rights based on cultural and religious foundations.

The passionate debate about the opportunity or nonopportunity to mention the Christian roots of Europe in the preamble to the (never entered into force) European Constitution has been temporarily dismissed, but this dismissal does not cancel the substance of the problem.[28] From one point of view, since the Christian roots are an unquestionable historical fact, not to mention them may appear to be an adequate choice, inasmuch as it is justified by the desire to define a more inclusive formula. From a different perspective, this choice conceals the ideological tendency to want to build the future by obliterating a fundamental part of the European legal tradition, which would be like cutting a plant, Europe, from its roots. In other words, this choice implies the secularist idea (and perhaps, after all, a nonreligious vision of life) that Christianity, and more generally religions, must be confined to the sphere of individual conscience, which, however, is anthropologically difficult to separate from the public dimension. The individual person who believes (or the one who does not believe) is always a human person who acts in society, who aspires to act in accordance with his or her beliefs, who yearns for building a society in which beliefs and religious experiences are recognized as bearers of values to be shared or at least to be respected.

The relationship between Christianity and law remains one of the fundamental questions of our day. Cultivating the memory and deepening the understanding of this crucial relationship should be regarded as a necessary task of theologians and legal scholars for helping understand our secular present and building our *postsecular* future.

Notes

1 Croce, 289, 297.
2 Lombardía, 53.
3 Hill and Helmholz; Domingo and Martínez-Torrón; Descamps and Domingo; Dreisbach and Hall. See also Schmoeckel and Witte.
4 Reynolds.
5 Domingo and Witte.
6 Bellomo, *The Common Legal Past*, 34–54.
7 See Benson and Constable; Berman, *Law and Revolution*, vol. 1.
8 Birocchi, et al.; Cappellini, et al. Many Italian Jurists are included in Domingo, *Juristas Universales*. A fundamental reference work is *Dizionario Biografico degli Italiani*. The series is not yet completed; ninety-five volumes have been published until 2019; the entries are available online: www.treccani.it/biografico/index.html#
9 Dauchy, et al.
10 For further reading see Bellomo, *The Common Legal Past*; Cortese; Brundage; Helmholz, *The Spirit of Classical Canon Law*; Stein; Ascheri; Padoa Schioppa; Hartmann and Pennington, *History of Medieval Canon Law*; Hartmann and Pennington, *History of Courts and Procedure*.
11 Bellomo, *The Common Legal Past*; Pennington, "Learned Law."
12 Condorelli, et al.
13 *L'unità giuridica dell'Europa* is the title that Piero Fiorelli, editor of the volume, gave to a collection of essays by Francesco Calasso. This unity arose from the foundations of the medieval *ius commune*: see Calasso, *Medio Evo del diritto*.
14 Wieacker; Coing, *Europäisches Privatrecht*, vol. 1; Birocchi, *Alla ricerca dell'ordine*; Caravale; Grossi, *History of European Law*, 39–137; Fantappiè, 163–230.
15 A classic and still-useful book is Ruffini. See also Witte, *Law and Protestantism*; Berman, *Law and Revolution*, vol. 2; Schmoeckel.
16 On these developments, see the books by Ghisalberti.
17 Jemolo, *Chiesa e Stato in Italia negli ultimi cento anni*, remains a magnificent overview of these developments. Further reading: Binchy; Seton-Watson; Finocchiaro; Traniello; Pollard; Pertici; Cardia.
18 For an overview, see Grossi, *Scienza giuridica italiana*, and the chapters included in Cappellini, et al. (above, note 8).
19 Coing, *Europäisches Privatrecht*, vol. 2.
20 Miele.
21 Aquarone.
22 Speciale; Gentile; and the contributions collected in *Il Diritto Ecclesiastico* 129.1–2 (2018).
23 De Siervo, "Giorgio La Pira," and La Pira, *Principi contro i totalitarismi e rifondazione costituzionale*.
24 Tedeschi; Dalla Torre.
25 Ferrari, "State and Church in Italy"; Ferrari and Ferrari, "Religion and the Secular State."
26 Cf. Benedict XVI. See also Cartabia and Simoncini. The term had already been used by John Paul II, who had repeatedly spoken of the "appropriate secular character" of the political structures (*giusta laicità*).
27 See Domingo, *God and the Secular Legal System*; Domingo and Witte, *Christianity and Global Law*.

28 Cf. *Treaty establishing a Constitution for Europe* as signed in Rome on October 29, 2004, Preamble: "Drawing inspiration from the cultural, religious and humanist inheritance of Europe, from which have developed the universal values of the inviolable and inalienable rights of the human person, freedom, democracy, equality and the rule of law."

Bibliography

Aquarone, Alberto. *L'organizzazione dello Stato totalitario.* Torino: Einaudi, 1995.

Ascheri, Mario. *The Laws of Medieval Italy (1000–1500): Foundations for a European Legal System.* Leiden/Boston: Brill, 2013. Original Italian edition: *I diritti del medioevo italiano. Secoli XI–XV.* Roma: Carocci, 2000.

Bellomo, Manlio. *Breve storia della scienza giuridica dal rinascimento medievale alla modernità in crisi.* Leonforte: Euno, 2019.

Bellomo, Manlio. *The Common Legal Past of Europe: 1000–1800.* 2nd ed. Translated by Lydia G. Cochrane. Washington, DC: Catholic University of America Press, 1995. Last version of the original Italian edition: *L'Europa del diritto comune. La memoria e la storia.* Leonforte: Euno, 2016.

Benedict XVI, Pope. *Address to the Participants in the 56th National Study Congress Organized by the Union of Italian Catholic Jurists*, December 9, 2006. Available at https://w2.vatican.va/content/benedict-xvi/en/speeches/2006/december/documents/hf_ben_xvi_spe_20061209_giuristi-cattolici.html

Benson, Robert L., Giles Constable, and Carol D. Lanham, eds. *Renaissance and Renewal in the Twelfth Century.* Cambridge, MA: Harvard University Press, 1982.

Berman, Harold J. *Law and Revolution.* Vol. 1, *The Formation of the Western Legal Tradition.* Cambridge, MA/London: Harvard University Press, 1983.

Berman, Harold J. *Law and Revolution.* Vol. 2, *The Impact of the Protestant Reformations on the Western Legal Tradition.* Cambridge, MA/London: Harvard University Press, 2003.

Binchy, Daniel. *Church and State in Fascist Italy.* Oxford: Oxford University Press, 1941.

Birocchi, Italo. *Alla ricerca dell'ordine. Fonti e cultura giuridica nell'età moderna.* Torino: Giappichelli, 2002.

Birocchi, Italo, Ennio Cortese, Antonello Mattone, and Marco N. Miletti, eds. *Dizionario Biografico dei Giuristi Italiani.* 2 vols. Bologna: il Mulino, 2013.

Brundage, James A. *Medieval Canon Law.* London/New York: Longman, 1995.

Calasso, Francesco. *L'unità giuridica dell'Europa.* Edited by Piero Fiorelli. Soveria Mannelli: Rubbettino, 1985.

Calasso, Francesco. *Medio Evo del diritto.* Milano: Giuffrè, 1954.

Cappellini, Paolo, Pietro Costa, Maurizio Fioravanti, and Bernardo Sordi, eds. *Enciclopedia Italiana di scienze, lettere ed arti. Il contributo italiano alla storia del pensiero. Ottava Appendice, Diritto.* Roma: Istituto della Enciclopedia Italiana, 2012. Available at www.treccani.it/enciclopedia/elenco-opere/Il_Contributo_italiano_alla_storia_del_Pensiero:_Diritto

Caravale, Mario. *Alle origini del diritto europeo. Ius commune, droit commun, common law nella dottrina giuridica della prima età moderna.* Bologna: Monduzzi, 2005.

Cardia, Carlo. *Risorgimento e religione.* Torino: Giappichelli, 2011.

Cartabia, Marta, and Andrea Simoncini, eds. *Pope Benedict XVI's Legal Thought: A Dialogue on the Foundation of Law.* Cambridge: Cambridge University Press, 2015.

Coing, Helmut. *Europäisches Privatrecht*. Vol. 1: *Älteres Gemeines Recht (1500–1800)*. München: C.H. Beck, 1985.

Coing, Helmut. *Europäisches Privatrecht*. Vol. 2: *19. Jahrhundert. Überblick über die Entwicklung des Privatrechts in den ehemals gemeinrechtlichen Ländern (1800 bis 1914)*. München: C.H. Beck, 1989.

Condorelli, Orazio, Franck Roumy, Mathias Schmoeckel, Yves Mausen, and David von Mayenburg, eds. *Der Einfluss der Kanonistik auf die europäische Rechtskultur*. 6 vols. Köln/Weimar/Wien: Böhlau, 2009–2020.

Cortese, Ennio. *Il diritto nella storia medievale*. 2 vols. Rome: Il Cigno, 1995.

Croce, Benedetto. "Perché non possiamo non dirci 'cristiani.'" *La Critica* 55 (1942): 289–97.

Dalla Torre, Giuseppe, ed. *Lessico della laicità*. Rome: Studium, 2007.

Dauchy, Serge, Georges Martyn, Anthony Musson, Heikki Pihlajamäki, and Alain Wijffels, eds. *The Formation and Transmission of Western Legal Culture: 150 Books that Made the Law in the Age of Printing*. Cham: Springer, 2016.

Descamps, Olivier, and Rafael Domingo, eds. *Great Christian Jurists in French History*. Cambridge/New York: Cambridge University Press, 2019.

De Siervo, Ugo. "Giorgio La Pira." In Cappellini, et al., *Il contributo italiano alla storia del Pensiero—Diritto*, 589–93.

Dizionario Biografico degli Italiani. Rome: Istituto della Enciclopedia Italiana, 1960. Available at www.treccani.it/biografico/index.html#

Domingo, Rafael. *God and the Secular Legal System*. New York/Cambridge: Cambridge University Press, 2016.

Domingo, Rafael, ed. *Juristas Universales*. 4 vols. Madrid/Barcelona: Marcial Pons, 2004.

Domingo, Rafael, and Javier Martínez Torrón, eds. *Great Christian Jurists in Spanish History*. Cambridge/New York: Cambridge University Press, 2018.

Domingo, Rafael, and John Witte, Jr., eds. *Christianity and Global Law*. London/New York: Routledge, 2020.

Dreisbach, Daniel L., and Mark David Hall, eds. *Great Christian Jurists in American History*. Cambridge/New York: Cambridge University Press, 2019.

Fantappiè, Carlo. *Storia del diritto canonico e delle istituzioni della Chiesa*. Bologna: Il Mulino, 2011.

Ferrari, Alessandro, and Silvio Ferrari. "Religion and the Secular State: The Italian Case." *The Cardozo Electronic Law Bulletin* 16/1 (2010): 431–48.

Ferrari, Silvio. "State and Church in Italy." In *State and Church in the European Union*, edited by Gerhard Robbers, 209–30. Baden-Baden: Nomos Verlagsgesellschaft, 2005.

Finocchiaro, Francesco. *Diritto ecclesiastico*. 12th ed. Edited by Andrea Bettetini and Gaetano Lo Castro. Bologna: Zanichelli, 2015.

Gentile, Saverio. *La legalità del male. L'offensiva mussoliniana contro gli ebrei nella prospettiva storico-giuridica (1938–1945)*. Torino: Giappichelli, 2013.

Ghisalberti, Carlo. *La codificazione del diritto in Italia 1865–1942*. 13th ed. Rome/Bari: Laterza, 2009.

Ghisalberti, Carlo. *Storia costituzionale d'Italia 1848–1948*. 7th ed. Rome/Bari: Laterza, 2010.

Ghisalberti, Carlo. *Unità nazionale e unificazione giuridica in Italia*. 13th ed. Rome/Bari: Laterza, 2018.

Grossi, Paolo. *A History of European Law*. Chichester: Wiley-Blackwell, 2010. Original Italian edition: *L'Europa del diritto*. Rome/Bari: Laterza, 2007.
Grossi, Paolo. *Scienza giuridica italiana. Un profilo storico 1860–1950*. Milano: Giuffrè, 2000.
Hartmann, Wilfried, and Kenneth Pennington, eds. *The History of Courts and Procedure in Medieval Canon Law*. History of Medieval Canon Law. Washington, DC: The Catholic University of America Press, 2016.
Hartmann, Wilfried, and Kenneth Pennington, eds. *The History of Medieval Canon Law in the Classical Period, 1140–123: From Gratian to the Decretals of Pope Gregory IX*. Washington, DC: The Catholic University of America Press, 2008.
Helmholz, Richard H. *The Spirit of Classical Canon Law*. Athens: University of Georgia Press, 1996.
Hill, Mark, and Richard H. Helmholz, eds. *Great Christian Jurists in English History*. Cambridge/New York: Cambridge University Press, 2017.
Jemolo, Arturo Carlo. *Chiesa e Stato in Italia negli ultimi cento anni*. Torino: Einaudi, 1971. English translation (incomplete): *Church and State in Italy 1850–1950*. Oxford: Basil Blackwell, 1960.
La Pira, Giorgio. *Principi contro i totalitarismi e rifondazione costituzionale*. Edited by Ugo De Siervo. Florence: Firenze University Press, 2019.
Lombardía, Pedro. *Lecciones de derecho canónico. Introducción. Derecho constitucional. Parte general*. Madrid: Tecnos, 1984.
Miele, Manlio, ed. *Gli insegnamenti del diritto canonico e del diritto ecclesiastico dopo l'Unità d'Italia*. Bologna: Il Mulino, 2015.
Padoa Schioppa, Antonio. *A History of Law in Europe: From the Early Middle Ages to the Twentieth Century*. Cambridge: Cambridge University Press, 2017. Original Italian edition: *Storia del diritto in Europa. Dal medioevo all'età contemporanea*. Bologna: Il Mulino, 2007.
Pennington, Kenneth. "Learned Law, Droit Savant, Gelehrtes Recht: The Tyranny of a Concept." *Rivista internazionale di diritto comune* 5 (1994): 197–209.
Pertici, Roberto. *Chiesa e Stato in Italia. Dalla Grande Guerra al nuovo Concordato (1914–1984)*. Bologna: Il Mulino, 2009.
Pollard, John. *Catholicism in Modern Italy: Religion, Society and Politics since 1861*. London/New York: Routledge, 2008.
Reynolds, Philip L., ed. *Great Christian Legal Thinkers in the First Millennium*. Cambridge/New York: Cambridge University Press, 2019.
Ruffini, Francesco. *La libertà religiosa. Storia dell'idea*. Torino: Bocca, 1901. Reprinted with introduction by Arturo Carlo Jemolo and afterword by Francesco Margiotta Broglio), Milano: Feltrinelli, 1992. English translation: *Religious Liberty*. Translated by J. Parker Heyes, with a preface by J.B. Bury. London: Williams & Norgate/New York: G.P. Putnam's Sons, 1912.
Schmoeckel, Mathias. *Das Recht der Reformation*. Tübingen: Mohr Siebeck, 2014.
Schmoeckel, Mathias, and John Witte, Jr., eds. *Great Christian Jurists in German History*. Tübingen: Mohr Siebeck, 2020.
Seton-Watson, Christopher. *Italy from Liberalism to Fascism, 1870–1925*. London: Methuen/New York: Barnes & Noble, 1967.
Speciale, Giuseppe. *Giudici e razza nell'Italia fascista*. Torino: Giappichelli, 2007.
Stein, Peter. *Roman Law in European History*. Cambridge: Cambridge University Press, 1999.

Tedeschi, Mario, ed. *Il principio di laicità nello Stato democratico*. Soveria Mannelli: Rubbettino, 1996.

Traniello, Francesco. *Religione cattolica e Stato nazionale. Dal Risorgimento al secondo dopoguerra*. Bologna: Il Mulino, 2007.

Wieacker, Franz. *A History of Private Law in Europe with Particular Reference to Germany*. Oxford: Clarendon Press, 1995. Original German edition: *Privatrechtsgeschichte der Neuzeit unter besonderer Berücksichtigung der deutschen Entwicklung*. Göttingen: Vandenhoeck und Ruprecht, 1967.

Witte, John, Jr. *Law and Protestantism: The Legal Teaching of the Lutheran Reformation*. Cambridge: Cambridge University Press, 2002.

1 Irnerius (ca. 1055 to ca. 1125)

Andrea Padovani

Biographical introduction

The details of Irnerius's biography and activity still remain disputed. Sources are twofold: documentary and literary. The first consist of fourteen instruments produced from 1112 to 1125 and edited since 1970 by Enrico Spagnesi.[1] They record a certain lawyer named, variously, Guarnerius, Varnerius, Warnerius, Vuarnerius, Wernerius, and Gernerius, acting first as the main pleader (*causidicus*) in two judicial proceedings at the court of the countess Matilda of Tuscany (1112–13), then as judge appointed by the emperor Henry V in judgments made in northern Italy. The last document, from 1125, which introduces Irnerius passing sentence in Casale Barbato, near Mantua, now seems to be false.[2] In any case, it is certain that Irnerius supported Henry V when, in 1118, the German emperor promoted Mauritius Burdinus as antipope, in Rome, against Gelasius II. There, before the assembly, a reader swiftly expounded the imperial rights to replace the pope, as asserted by some pontifical decrees: indeed, presumably, spurious documents of the late eleventh century, such as the *privilegium minus* from Leo VIII to Otto I.[3] The Council of Reims, the following year, therefore pronounced the excommunication of both Irnerius and Henry.[4]

The most ancient literary source concerning Irnerius dates back to some years after 1175. In his chronicle, Robert of Torigni, monk of Bec and later abbot of Mont St. Michel, in Normandy, writes that Lanfranc of Pavia and Garnerius, his pupil (*socius eius*), having found, near Bologna, the Roman laws—which the emperor Justinian had amended and shortened in the year 530—[5] started to teach and expound them to others. While Guarnerius (the name is modified slightly again a few lines later) persevered in this activity, Lanfranc became a teacher of liberal arts and holy scriptures as a monk (and later abbot) in Bec.[6]

Years later (1179–89) an English theologian, Ralph Niger, who taught in Paris, remembers master (*magister*) Pepo—praised as "rising dawn"—and master Warnerius, who had the merit of propagandizing the Roman laws with great honor in many countries.[7] Some time after 1230, Burchard of Biberach, in his chronicle, says that the lord (*dominus*) Wernerius "renewed, at the request of the countess Matilda, the books of law compiled by Justinian that until then had been neglected and never studied by anyone."[8] After roughly twenty years, the lawyer and teacher in Bologna Odofredus describes to his students the birth of the school of law in these terms:

> Irnerius was a lamp of the law among us, that is, he was the first to teach law in this city. For when at first a school of arts began in this city, and when the school at Rome was destroyed, the books of law were brought to the city of Ravenna and from Ravenna to this city. A certain lord Pepo began to teach law on his own authority. Nevertheless, whatever knowledge he had, he was of no importance. But because lord Irnerius taught the arts in this city, when the books of law were brought here, he began to study these law books on his own, and while studying them began to teach law. He was of great importance and was the first interpreter of our science. Because he was the first who wrote glosses in our books, we call him the lamp of the law.[9]

All of these literary sources have been widely discussed by historians from the time of Friederich Carl von Savigny. Until recently, Robert of Torigni's testimony was rejected as groundless because in 1032 (the year for which the chronicler chose to insert his note, striking out a less important event from that year) Irnerius was not yet born. To understand correctly this statement of the Norman abbot—usually well informed about cultural events—one must recall that he was compelled to concentrate in a few lines the more diffuse information received by Vacarius—an old student of Bologna—on the occasion of the council of Westminster (1175), where he had followed his lord, Roger, archbishop of York.[10] Robert's decision to insert the statement about Lanfranc and Irnerius under the year 1032 was imposed by the necessity of taking unaltered the chronological and logical sequence of the events reported in his already completed chronicle.[11] The year 1032 indicated approximately, in Robert's reestablishment of events, the departure of Lanfranc from Italy to France, where he met Irnerius. On his own, Robert added to Vacarius's information what the Italian lawyer ignored: that is, the adherence of Irnerius to Lanfranc, otherwise well known in the monastic environment of Bec or Caen. In what sense and field of application, we will see further.

Recently, scholars like Johannes Fried, Richard W. Southern, and Anders Winroth[12] have rejected Irnerius's teaching activity, observing that the documents already mentioned called him only advocate or judge, never schoolmaster. His world—they say—was law courts and high politics, not a classroom. Irnerius's role in the foundation of the University of Bologna must be, in their view, a mere invention spread by Odofredus, a really unreliable storyteller. One can reasonably object that the simple fact that the documents call him advocate, judge, or—as in the excommunication of 1119—expert in law (*legis peritus*) depends on the judicial nature of those acts. In that context, the didactic activity of the lawyer was, indeed, totally unimportant and out of place.

Moreover, although Irnerius is called "bononiensis iudex," this does not mean that he was a native of Bologna. In the Middle Ages it was usual to privilege the place where one earned fame instead of one's birthplace.[13] On the other hand, it was well known in Bologna, until the eighteenth century, that Irnerius was German. Recently discovered manuscripts confirm this point. Although late (from the second half of the thirteenth century), a note probably from Franciscus, Accursius's son, not only corroborates Irnerius's teaching in the school's early period but states that he left Bologna, wishing to go back to his home (old aged, adds another source).[14] Unfortunately, we do not know when this move happened. Probably Irnerius died a few years after 1120. Mazzanti has recently supposed that the date of his birth could be around 1055.[15]

The works of Irnerius

The edition of the *Liber Divinarum Sententiarum*—[16]a collection of patristic sentences taken mostly from Augustine and Ambrose, joined together in ninety-four chapters like a mosaic and mutually connected by means of short notes by its author—has reopened an old discussion dating from 1901 and resumed during the last century. Generally rejected, the authorship of Irnerius now seems very probable. New evidence places this work in the wake of the burning controversy on the Eucharist between Berengarius and Lanfranc, the latter of whose opinions the work substantially restates. Just such fidelity—shared by other pupils of Lanfranc, such as Ivo of Chartres and Guitmond de La Croix-St.—Leufroy again credits Robert of Torigni's assertion of Lanfranc's mentorship of Irnerius in theology if not also, indeed, in dialectics and textual critical exegesis.[17]

After historians from the end of the nineteenth century and early years of the twentieth century rejected some works previously attributed to him (*Brachylogus, Epitome exactis regibus, Questiones de iuris subtilitatibus, Summa Codicis Trecensis, De natura actionum, Summa legis Langobardorum, Summa Institutionum Vindobonensis, Formularium Tabellionum*, a short *De equitate*), Irnerius's activity as a jurist is testified to solely by his glosses on the whole *Corpus Iuris* of Justinian. Some of these glosses reveal an impressive expertise in dialectic and logic that confirms Odofredus's tale about Irnerius as formerly a master of arts. Other evidence is lacking, including anything testifying to his arrival in Bologna and his status (was he lay or cleric?), but it is certain that the Bolognese documentation regarding the period of the investiture struggle was purged and consequently destroyed. At any rate, later lawyers, from Azo to Jacques de Revigny, insist on the point alike, often remarking on the sublety of certain of Irnerius's glosses. Thus, for instance, Odofredus writes about a gloss at C. 2.21(22).9:

> Lord Irnerius, because he was a logician and a teacher in our city in the arts before he taught law, wrote a sophisticated gloss that is more obscure than the text. And this is what he wrote: 'it takes off the consequence, does not infer the opposite, because it is a part of it.'[18]

Another gloss, edited by Pescatore, says:

> Y. Whoever asserts that something 'is' can prove it by means of related concepts (*affinia*): that is, by means of genus and difference. But whoever simply denies does not put anything. The nature of things is such, that what 'is

> not' has neither genus, nor difference, nor something similar. Consequently, no argument is useful about it.[19]

To be sure, the first gloss shows Irnerius's knowledge of the theory of consequences spread throughout France by masters of logic such as Garlandus (1045/64–1084/1112) and Abelard (1079–1142); the second one calls genus and difference, in Latin, *affinia*. The only available example of such a definition, as far as we know, occurs in Abelard's *De divisionibus*.[20]

One could quote other passages like these, but what is really interesting is noting the difficulty of the Bolognese cultural environment in understanding Irnerius's thought. This was true not only of lawyers like Odofredus, who writes, "This question (of Irnerius) widens out in immensity and flies in the skies."[21] It was true as well of a teacher in arts, like Boncompagnus, who harshly criticizes Irnerius's "sophistic" gloss at C. 2.21(22).9: "Guarnerius here wonderfully dreamt. Or, rather, he undoubtedly raved."[22] Such reactions reveal the great distance between Irnerius's cultural (perhaps French) background and the Bolognese milieu.

Odofredus is certainly wrong in assuming that the "first lamp" was also the first one in writing glosses: that kind of scientific approach to authoritative books was diffused before him among philosophers, theologians, grammarians, and lawyers. At any rate, Irnerius was the first to gloss the whole *Corpus Iuris* of Justinian.

As is well known, the manuscripts report Irnerius's glosses with an impressive variety of sigla—*Warn.*, *Varn.*, *G.*, *Guua.*, *Gar.*, *Garn.*, *Guarn.*, *Gir.*, but overall *Y.*, *Yr.*, and sometimes *Yrne.*—that embarrassed legal historians. The main problem seems to be the use of "Y." and its linguistic genesis. As I have explained elsewhere—and I have no reason to modify my point of view—that siglum is a quite normal transition from *Girnerius* or *Gernerius*.[23] In order to understand the diversity of sigla, one must keep in mind that, very probably, Irnerius did not subscribe or sign his own glosses. This was an initiative of subsequent glossators who seemingly used some books in collecting the writings of the old master. The various, free individual initiatives in propounding the sigla mirrored, in some way, the uncertainty or the difficulty of adjusting a foreign name (at least in Italy) to vernacular language. This was a difficulty already faced by the notaries drawing up the documents in 1112–18, who wrote *Wernerius, Vuarnerius*, or *Warnerius*, although the same lawyer subscribed simply *Wernerius*. The same can be said about Robert of Torigni's chronicle, noted earlier, which speaks first of *Garnerius* and immediately afterward of *Guarnerius*. In the burlesque, multilingual Bolognese environment, the confusion grew more pronounced over time. That the *Y.* is—as supposed by Dolezalek—a misunderstanding of the sign § is not likely.[24] In that case, it would appear also in canonistic manuscripts, but it does not. Nor does it seem credible that learned, almost contemporary readers could incur such a gross mistake. Lastly, if *Y.* is fitting for Irnerius, so is *I.* Documents of the twelfth century attest to the mutual interchange of both letters, as the Italian pronunciation makes no distinction between them. A neat distinction about *Y* and *I* was propounded by Pietro Bembo (1470–1547), but it was accepted only in learned milieus. The usual practice went on in the old way. Pescatore was therefore right when, in his *Glossen*,[25] he first ascribed to Irnerius the glosses signed *I.* in the ms. Berlin 275; but he was wrong, in my opinion, when he later advanced the authorship of Irnerius's pupil Iacobus,[26] neglecting the fact that his siglum is regularly *Ia.*, *Ja.*, *Jac.*, *Iaco.*, or *Iacob.* The restitution of paternity of the glosses by *I.* to Irnerius helps explain the theological depth of some assertions contained in the ms. of Berlin, as I have noted elsewhere.[27] Here one can add that two glosses appended to C. 1.1.8(7)—a letter from Pope John II to Justinian, then assumed as an imperial decree—explain the words *montes* and *colles*, respectively:[28] "mountains: who are of eminent life. I."; "hills: smaller saints. I." Both notes depend on the ordinary gloss of Gilbertus Universalis (also resumed elsewhere by *I.*) to Isaiah 2.2.[29] As far as I know, no other lawyer, than the former theologian Irnerius of the *Liber Divinarum Sententiarum*, could have been attracted by those two words (apparently of little importance, in that legal context), and then propounded about them with biblical considerations and appropriate references to the ordinary gloss.

A further question concerns when Irnerius taught law. Seemingly he had no possibility of teaching while serving Henry V as an imperial judge, in northern Italy, after 1116 and immediately after the excommunication of 1119. His former role as a pleader (*causidicus*) at Matilda's court (1112–13), in places not very far from Bologna, was not very heavy. At any rate, De Vergottini supposed that Irnerius's scientific activity started long before 1111 or even 1102.[30] As a matter of fact, his formula of emphyteusis was already commonly used in Bologna after 1116, with relevant social effects, as we will see further. Such a refined formula certainly required long training and deep competence in Roman law. Over time, a secluded, personal study of law was probably accompanied by didactic tasks. Lonely or not, as that work might have been, it is certain that the impressive number of glosses attributed to Irnerius and his insertion of the *Authenticae* (a collection of the *Novellae*, the latest constitutions issued by Justinian) into the Code to update it, absorbed all the time and the intellectual energy of that genius. It is really inconceivable, therefore, as Winroth asserts, that Irnerius "only started to scratch the surface of Roman Law."[31] According to Winroth, the true promoter of Roman law in Bologna who first studied and taught it there, was Gratian II, and Bulgarus and his colleagues therefore began the study of Roman law after the publication of the *Decretum*. All of these assertions are hardly credible. More attention has to be paid to scholars who raised doubts about Irnerius's didactic activity and a question related to this one, already put by Savigny, as to whether he really was the teacher of the "four doctors": Bulgarus, Martinus, Ugo, and Iacobus. Irnerius was called "master" by Landulfus Junior,[32] Ralph Niger, and Burchard of Biberach, all sources not reciprocally connected in any way. Robert of Torigni also writes that Irnerius engaged "in reading and expounding" the Roman laws. The same is reported by Boncompagnus and, before him, Otto Morena ("the old lord doctor Irnerius was the teacher of the four doctors and of many others").[33] Furthermore, Besta refers to two glosses ("this is the case where my lord Guar[nerius] says . . ."; and

". . . said my lord G.")[34] that Horst Heinrich Jacobs recently was unable to find in the manuscript of Turin used by Besta (who really was wrong in referring to their proper position in the code).[35] Moreover, a gloss from ms. Fulda D.4, says: "That [namely, about emphyteusis] feels m. uuarnerius," where "m." looks like an abbreviation of "master."[36]

Major themes and contributions

Legal historians made clear over time that Irnerius was not the only one dealing with law between the end of the eleventh century and the first decades of the following one. In his glosses it is not rare to find some hints about contemporary (though often unnamed) doctors or interpreters. But surely he surpassed them all. There is something true in Odofredus's account in which he compares Pepo with Irnerius. The former reads and interprets Justinian's texts by means of his own skill (*auctoritate sua*); the latter lightens them in a radically new way. Irnerius starts a revolution, a real turning point in legal sciences. He accomplishes this first of all in methodology, using and spreading the techniques of Scholasticism, later extensively used by following glossators: divisions (*divisiones*), distinctions (*distinctiones*), solution of contraries (*solutio contrariorum*), *notabilia*, and so on. In his glosses we also find some examples of questions (*quaestiones*), as well as of dialectical arguments (*a minori, a maiori*, and so on). When required, he employs the four Aristotelian causes. Irnerius also brings into juridical literature the *exordia* or *materiae*, an introduction which deals with certain general aspects of the subject matter treated in the writings to which it belongs. Thus, we read in the *Exordium Institutionum* about its author: "As this book bears the name of Justinian, one deduces that he was the only author and the promulgator of such an important work." Further, regarding the subject matter, he writes:

> The matter regards the equity and justice of contracts, whether equity is not constituted yet, or constituted but scorned. It deals also with law and what is considered in the same way, like the lawful will of living men (as expressed in contracts) and dying men (e.g., last wills). This matter is therefore tripartite.

Again, regarding the scope (*intentio*) of the work: "The scope is also threefold: the emperor's aim is, indeed, simply setting the law itself or, if it is obscure, interpreting it." About the cause of the work, he writes:

> The final cause can be drawn by the opportunity (*occasio*). . . . The opportunity was this: some were ignorant or in error, so that it was necessary to make them obedient to the emperor. Others were not ignorant or in error but disobedient and therefore contumacious. So it was necessary to enact a law in order to compel them and to make the ignorant ones and those in error finally learned. The emperor did it by four means: commanding, forbidding, punishing, permitting.

To conclude, the *exordium* insists again on scope:

> The aim (of this book) is to treat about justice. Many are the kinds of justice: the first is religion, by which are bound again the souls separated by false gods from the true God. So [this book] deals primarily with religion. Further, in treating religion, it considers its ground, namely faith, and then the other parts of religion.[37]

Once again, Irnerius's use of *exordia* (*materiae*) echoes French literary models, still unknown in Italy at the time.

Innovations can be found also in the content of his works. It is really impossible to recall here all the points where Irnerius gave a proof of his theoretical competence and profound insights about Roman law. It suffices to examine only a few points of major interest. About politics, first of all, at D. 1.3.32, where the Roman jurisconsult Iulianus exalts the role and the strength of custom, Irnerius glosses:

> Here the law speaks considering his times, when the people had the power to make laws and, consequently, they were abrogated by common consent of all the people. But, as today that power has been transferred to the emperor, the disuse (of a law) no longer has any effectiveness.[38]

Shortly, Irnerius assumes that the transfer of sovereignty from the people to the emperor is definitive and irrevocable; no custom can therefore invalidate imperial decrees.

This point of view was repeatedly confirmed in other Irnerian glosses, but we can find it already in the *Liber divinarum sententiarum*: "The people create and elect their own king. But as soon as the king has been made and confirmed in the kingdom, he has power over subjects, and the people cannot throw the yoke off their neck."[39] In the same book, Irnerius celebrates the eminence and the providential role of the empire: "The Roman Empire, before Christ and also after, suffered adversities. Though once plagued, it never changed, and has been created again, reviving from that affliction. That is a reason for not giving up hope in our times."[40] Is this an echo of Henry IV's misadventures and troubles in reigning? To be sure, Irnerius later reaffirmed his loyalty to Henry's son, Henry V, in the difficult years 1118–19 (the election of the antipope Mauritius Burdinus and the consequent excommunication of Henry V and Irnerius).

Social and political ideas emerge also when the lawyer is exploring a private law contract such as emphyteusis at the *Authentica Qui res* (*post* C. 1.2.14). The formula proposed by Irnerius aims to reduce the submission of the petitioner before his counterpart, a formula that in preceding times had been permeated by feudal models.[41] The new wording, rapidly successful in Bologna, burdens the grantor with heavier bonds and responsibilities than the emphyteuta. It was a turning point of relevant importance, shaking off the old feudal order, its abuses and liberties. Moreover, the formula was the choice of a courageous man, as Odofredus says: "Lord Irnerius was the first one who dared to address his heart to this law," thus announcing a new spirit of freedom.[42]

Regarding freedom, Irnerius sketches views of strong ethical import. According to him, it is true and certain what one reads at D. 1.1.4: "under natural law all human beings are born free." Moreover, all things are common to humankind. But in both cases, "facts and civil law resist what has been introduced by natural law."[43] Odofredus explains Irnerius's position in these terms:

> Lord Irnerius, lamp of the law, wrote here (D. 1.1.4) an interlinear gloss in very elegant words: he well says that civil law neither recedes nor serves at all the natural law and the law of nations. When something is added to or detracted from the common law, then it is civil law.[44]

Therefore, slavery and property are both examples of iniquity, modifying the original dictate of natural law.

The assumption of the natural and inviolable freedom of every person also leads Irnerius to consider inadmissible a hiring of labor (*locatio operarum*) that does not include a deadline. Such a contract would substantially resemble—he maintains—a bond of slavery.[45] His Christian education, then, does not admit any cruelty towards slaves. At C. 6.1.3—which provides sentences of amputation of a foot, hard labor, or similar punishments of a slave taking refuge in hostile lands (*apud hostes*)—he glosses: "That is a punishment inflicted by judge's liberty: but nothing can be written on his face, which has been created after the likeness of heavenly beauty. Writing is admitted on his hands, as for thieves."[46] Along the same line, commenting on D. 1.6.1.7, which forbids any Roman citizen to treat his slaves ruthlessly, beyond measure and without a cause admitted by laws, Irnerius hurries to make clear: "in any case, also, if there is a cause for being cruel."[47] A position like this can be found in the *Liber divinarum sententiarum* as well: "There are lords; there are slaves as well. The names are different, nevertheless both are human beings and bear the same name: human beings."[48]

The doctrines examined to this point are inspired by deep religious sensibility and strong perception of justice and equity. Although Irnerius finds in nature the equal dignity of all humankind and the common destination of earthly goods, he does not engage—as far as we know—in a precise analysis of natural law, often recalled by Justinian's *Corpus Iuris* and widely investigated by later glossators. In the *Liber Divinarum Sententiarum* Irnerius added to a quotation from Augustine's *De doctrina christiana* a few words remarking on the immutability of natural law, valid also for brute animals. This was an unusual view among theologians but was held by Ulpian at D. 1.1.1.3.[49] As a lawyer, Irnerius once curtly wrote, "In a mistake of law (*in iuris errore*), natural and civil law are on the same level."[50] Usually understood as a depreciation of natural law, this gloss articulates instead a rule—that is, the impossibility of claiming back what has been paid, because of ignorance of the law, to fulfill a natural debt—that in some way could be drawn by the principle stating the inadmissible ignorance of natural law.[51]

In any case, Irnerius's rare and fragmentary hints at nature, equity, and justice can be tentatively arranged in order to get at least a coherent view of these terms. That nature is governed by divine providence is shown, for example, in two glosses: "*Nature.* y. Given (*prodita*) by God in general and singularly"; "*Nature.* y. Given by God's wisdom in general and singularly in the nature of every citizen."[52] (The "y." in these glosses is the initial for Inerius, whose comment follows his initial.) Such statements are quite normal for a Christian and medieval scholar. To explain the impressive but otherwise mysterious regularity of behaviors characteristic of every being in the universe, Irnerius had already recalled in the *Liber Divinarum Sententiarum* (after centuries of silence by other authors) the notion of *lex aeterna*,[53] quoting Augustine's *Contra Faustum*, 22.27: "A divine reason or will that commands the preservation of natural order and forbids its violation." Perhaps, it is just that complex compound of reason and will that Irnerius bears in mind and tries somehow to resolve when he glosses D. 1.1.1.1: "Justice: here he calls justice good and equitable. But equity differs from justice; equity, indeed, is perceived in things themseves and, when it descends from will—by intervention of form (*forma accepta*)—becomes justice."[54] Once again, according to his pithy and concise style, the old master contains in few words theoretical hints of relevant difficulty that demand a precise understanding of each word he uses.

Here one must get rid of the modern meaning of "equity." In this passage the term alludes rather to the harmony governing all things in mutual correspondence and perceived by every observer. That order cannot be the result of mere chance but derives from an eternal reason. For a faithful philosopher, equity reflects the wisdom of the divine Word, as "all things were made by him, and without him was not any thing made that was made" (John 1:3). Other jurists will later see, in the Logos/Divine Word, the roots of natural law. "Equity," in Irnerius's gloss, alludes to the rational, divine plan that, in the Son/Word, eternally conceived the whole Creation. But to make the things that actually exist—the concrete world that we see and touch—it was necessary for a will to accomplish that ideal, merely virtual order. According to Augustine's treatise on the Trinity, the will is a special attribute of the Holy Spirit that perfects and brings to an end the work of the Triune God in the universe. By means of the will of God, justice is therefore established, as is said at Inst. 1.1.pr.: "Justice is constant and perpetual will."

In short, Irnerius perceives justice as nothing other than the universal order conceived by the eternal Word and completed in its actuality by the good will (or love) that is the attribute or peculiar quality and characteristic of the Holy Spirit.[55] Thus, we are brought back to the concept of Augustine's eternal law, in which reason and will are as inextricably bound as are, in their divine nature, the Son and the Holy Spirit, distinguishable only by the "form" of their proper activity on the outside (*ad extra*).

Seemingly far from the level of human activity and interests—almost fixed in an abstract, metaphysical sky—the Irnerian view contains a perennial teaching, related to human activity. Here, justice is seen as a virtue. So he writes in the *Exordium Institutionum*:

> Notice that in the definition of justice (Inst. 1.1.pr: "Justice is the constant and perpetual will to give each his due") is given the definition of its genus,

namely virtue. When, indeed, "constant" is written, this means "well constituted," as constancy cannot be understood otherwise than in its good sense; when, then, "perpetual" is written, this means a habit: habit, indeed, is a will difficult to be moved and enduring through life. Thus, one could say that justice is the habit of a well- constituted mind giving each his due. This, only, is the right definition of justice.[56]

Here, the definition of habit is taken from Boethius's commentary on Aristotle's categories, where he distinguishes habit (as a permanent, mental constitution) from simple disposition (natural inclination easily changing over time).[57] Once again, we have further evidence of Irnerius's competence in dialectics and liberal arts.

What is more surprising, and unnoticed until recently, is the correpondence between this passage in Irnerius's writing and a passage of Abelard's *Sententiae*:

> So philosophers define justice: 'justice is a habit of the soul giving each his due for the preservation of common utility.' Justinian wrote down the same, saying 'Justice is constant and perpetual will, etc.' When saying 'his just due,' he pointed out the best (*optimum*).[58]

This is not the place to discuss the problems concerning the possible relations between these two authors. But if David Luscombe is right in stating that Abelard was the first one to insert in theological inquiry a reflection about human virtues,[59] equal merit has to be credited to Irnerius in the legal field.

As a virtue, justice puts into coherent effect a right reasoning about values. Once assumed as true that justice is the "will of giving everybody his due" (Inst. 1.1.pr.; D. 1.1.10), it is necessary to know first of all "his due" or the merit that each person consists of. Misconceiving this point, in a tragic obscuring of the reason, it was possible to write, over the gate of Buchenwald: "To each his due" ("Jedem das Seine").

Further, the identification of equity with justice raises the question of their relation to law (*ius*). Irnerius deals with this question in two glosses:

> Equity. Namely, unwritten, so that, when law seems to be contrary to justice, it is necessary to abandon the words of the law and privilege justice, since the same law wants it. But as law prescribes what justice prescribes (though obscurely), it is better to adhere firmly to the words of the law than to look for something else and so wander arbitrarily.[60]

And again:

> Though equity and law deal with the same things, yet they are different. Indeed, it is peculiar to equity simply to propound what is right. Law, then, propounds the same end through will: that is to say, by making use of some authority. But by reason of human faults, law sometimes withdraws from

equity, partly containing to a lesser extent what equity dictates, partly propounding more. Besides, equity and law are different under many other aspects; in such cases, their disagreement must be resolved only by a prince's interpretation, which has the value of law.[61]

Summing up: there is no doubt that, in Irnerius's view, justice—the manifestation of the harmonious balance conceived by God's plan in Creation—is the first and fundamental aim to be pursued by the legal system. It happens, nevertheless, that sometimes human laws order things differently. While the still-unknown authors of the *Exceptiones Legum Romanarum Petri* and of the *Questiones de iuris subtilitatibus* resolutely propound radical solutions (that laws contrary to equity must be canceled or, rather, trampled down), Irnerius shows a more cautious and substantially pragmatic attitude. With deeper insight, he finds that law, with its authority, shares the same goal as equity, namely the pursuit of justice. This must be found precisely by means of patient and accurate investigation, because words, far from making the meaning of the law clear, sometimes obscure it. If the effort to clarify justice proves useless and the contrast between law and justice looks really insoluble, then—as enacted by C. 1.14.(17).1—it is the emperor's duty to give his interpretation, which is binding for everyone. As he is "living law on the earth," justice will—hopefully, at least—prevail. Irnerius's solution balances ethical expectations and observance of the positive legal order. This is the persistent attitude or intellectual mark that characterizes Irnerius's work: the precocious but already ripe fruit of a legal culture that will flourish, for centuries, in the West.

Notes

1 See Spagnesi, *Wernerius bononiensis iudex.*
2 See Mazzanti, "Un falso irneriano?," 37–44.
3 Capitani, 184–5.
4 Holtzmann, 137: "Gwarnerius Bononiensis legis peritus."
5 The point is discussed by Padovani, "Roberto di Torigni," 82–5, 89–92.
6 Robert of Torigni, x, 25–6.
7 Kantorowicz, 242.
8 Burchardus Urspergensis, *Chronik*, 15–16.
9 Odoffredus, *In undecim primos pandectarum libros* 7rb at D. 1.1.6. Also Kantorowicz, 232.
10 Padovani, "Roberto di Torigni," 126–7.
11 Padovani, "Matilde e Irnerio," 206.
12 Fried, *Die Entstehung des Juristenstandes im 12*, 102–3; Id., "'. . . auf Bitten der Gräfin Mathilde'," 173; Southern, 279–80; Winroth, *The Making of Gratian's Decretum*, 147–8.
13 Padovani, "Alle origini dell'università di Bologna," 17.
14 Pace, 124, 131.
15 Mazzanti, "Irnerio: contributo a una biografia," 165.
16 Guarnerius, *Liber Divinarum Sententiarum.*
17 Padovani, "Matilde e Irnerio," 207–42; Id., "Il titolo *De Summa Trinitate et fide catholica*," 1076–87.
18 Odofredus, *In Primam Codicis*, 101va at C. 2.21(22).9.
19 Pescatore, *Kritische Studien*, 97–8 at C. 4.19.23.

20 Abelard, *Scritti di logica*, 179, 182–3; Abelard, *Dialectica*, 475–6, 540.
21 Odofredus, *In undecim primos pandectaruum libros* 75ra, n. 11 at D. 2.14.7.5.
22 Boncompagnus, x, 292.
23 Padovani, "Il titolo," 1090–101.
24 Dolezalek, 465, n. 1.
25 Pescatore, *Die Glossen des Irnerius.*
26 Pescatore, *Kritische*, 191–202.
27 Padovani, "Il titolo," 1101–9.
28 Pescatore, *Die Glossen*, 84.
29 Mazzanti, "Anselmo di Laon."
30 De Vergottini, 708; Fasoli, 35.
31 Winroth, "The Teaching of Law," 44.
32 Landolfo, 28.
33 Morena, 58. See Padovani, "Sull'uso del metodo," 83, n. 78.
34 Besta, II, vi; I, 83.
35 Heinrich, "Irnerius Sigle," 471, n. 62. The Irnerian gloss *nam ceteris*, for instance, has to be found not at D. 15.1.31, but at D. 15.1.38(39): Besta, *L'opera*, I, 97.
36 Dolezalek I, 198.
37 The complete text can be seen in Kantorowicz and Buckland, 233–9.
38 See Cortese, *La norma giuridica*, 126, n. 56.
39 Guarnerius, *Liber Divinarum Sententiarum*, XXIIII, 175.
40 Ibid., 173.
41 Orlandelli, 504, 518, 525, 532.
42 Bellomo, *Elogio delle regole*, 64, 71, emphasizing "Irnerius' courage": "a man of action."
43 Besta, *L'opera*, II, 8 at D. 1.5.4. About Irnerius's conception of freedom (also related to slaves) see Torelli, 60–9.
44 Odoffredus, *In undecim primos pandectarum libros*, 7ra, n. 1 at D. 1.1.4.
45 Bellomo, "Il lavoro nel pensiero," 143 and n. 6.
46 Pescatore, *Kritische*, 122.
47 Besta, II, 11.
48 Guarnerius, *Liber Divinarum Sententiarum*, LV, 265.
49 Ibid., XXII, 168.
50 Besta, II, 232 at D. 22.6.8.
51 Condorelli, *L'idea di diritto naturale alle origini della scienza giuridica medievale. Percorsi di ricerca*, in press. Thanks to my friend Orazio for sharing with me the results of his research.
52 Weigand, 18.10, 11 respectively at D. 1.1.1.3 and Inst. 1.2.pr.
53 Guarnerius, *Liber Divinarum Sententiarum*, XXII, 169.
54 Besta, II, 1.
55 Padovani, "Metaphysical Thought," 31–6, 63–5.
56 Kantorowicz and Buckland, 240.
57 Boethius, *In Categorias Aristotelis*, PL 64 241–242.
58 Abelard, *Opera Theologica*, 134–5.
59 Abelard, *Ethics*, xxv.
60 Loschiavo, 225, n. 26.
61 Pescatore, *Kritische*, 91 at C. 1.14.1.

Bibliography

Abelard, Peter. *Dialectica: First Complete Edition of the Parisian Manuscript*. Edited by L.M. De Rijk. Assen: Van Gorcum, 1956.

Abelard, Peter. *Ethics.* Edited and translated by David E. Luscombe. Oxford: Clarendon Press, 1975.

Abelard, Peter. *Opera Theologica.* Vol. 6: *Sententie Magistri Petri Abaelardi.* Edited by David Luscombe. *Liber Sententiarum Magistri Petri.* Edited by Constant J. Mews. Turnhout: Brepols, 2006.

Abelard, Peter. *Scritti di logica. "Introductiones dialecticae": editio super Porphyrium. Glossae in Categorias. Editio super Aristotelem de interpretatione. De divisionibus. Logica "Ingredientibus": super Topica glossae.* Edited by Mario Dal Pra. Florence: La Nuova Italia, 1969.

Bellomo, Manlio. *Elogio delle regole. Crisi sociali e scienza del diritto alle origini dell'Europa moderna.* Leonforte: Euno Edizioni, 2012.

Bellomo, Manlio. "Il lavoro nel pensiero dei giuristi medievali." In *Il doppio medioevo*, 141–56. Rome: Viella, 2011.

Besta, Enrico. *L'opera d'Irnerio: Contributo alla storia del diritto italiano.* Turin: Loescher, 1896. Reprinted Bologna: Arnaldo Forni, 1980.

Boncompagnus. *Rhetorica Novissima.* Edited by Augusto Gaudenzi. *Scripta Anecdota antiquissimorum glossatorum.* Vol. 2. Bologna: Petrus Virano, 1892.

Burchardus, Urspergensis. *Die Chronik des Propstes Burchard von Ursperg.* Edited by Oswald Holder-Egger and Bernhard von Simson. Hannover/Leipzig: Hahnsch, 1916.

Capitani, Ovidio. "Politica e cultura a Ravenna tra Papato e Impero dall''XI al XII secolo." In *Storia di Ravenna.* Vol. 3: *Dal Mille alla fine della signoria Polentana*, edited by Augusto Vasina, 169–98. Venice: Marsilio, 1993.

Cortese, Ennio. "Irnerio." In *Dizionario biografico degli italiani.* Vol. 62, 600–5. Rome: Istituto della Enciclopedia Italiana, 2004.

Cortese, Ennio. "Irnerio (XI sec.-1119 . . .)." In *Dizionario biografico dei giuristi italiani (XII–XX secolo)*, edited by Italo Birocchi, Ennio Cortese, Antonello Mattone, and Marco Nicola Miletti, 1109–13. Bologna: Il Mulino, 2013.

Cortese, Ennio. *La norma giuridica. Spunti teorici nel diritto comune classico.* Vol. 2. Milan: Giuffrè, 1964.

Cortese, Ennio. "*Wernerius* (Irnerio) (. . . 1112–1125 . . .)." In *Autographa: Giuristi, giudici e notai (sec. XII–XV)*, edited by Giovanna Murano. Vol. 2, 3–7. Imola: La Mandragora, 2016.

De Vergottini, Giovanni. "Lo Studio di Bologna, l'Impero, il Papato." In *Scritti di Storia del Diritto Italiano*, edited by Guido Rossi. Vol. 2, 689–792. Milan: Giuffrè, 1977.

Dolcini, Carlo. "Postilla su Pepo e Irnerio." In Giovanni De Vergottini, *Lo Studio di Bologna, l'Impero, il Papato*, edited by Carlo Dolcini, 83–100. Spoleto: CISAM, 1996.

Dolezalek, Gero. *Repertorium manuscriptorum veterum Codicis Iustiniani.* Frankfurt am Main: Vittorio Klostermann, 1985.

Fasoli, Gina. "Ancora un'ipotesi sull'inizio dell'insegnamento di Pepone e di Irnerio." *Atti e Memorie della Deputazione di Storia Patria per le Province di Romagna* 21 (1971): 19–37.

Fried, Johannes. "'. . . auf Bitten der Gräfin Mathilde.' Werner von Bologna und Irnerius. Mit einem Excurs von Gundula Grebner." In *Europa and der Wende von 11. zum 12. Jahrhundert. Beiträge zu Ehren von Werner Goez*, edited by Klaus Herbers, 171–206. Stuttgart: Steiner, 2001.

Fried, Johannes. *Die Entstehung des Juristenstandes im 12. Jahrhundert. Zur sozialen Stellung und politischen Bedeutung gelehrter Juristen in Bologna und Modena.* Köln/Wien: Bölau, 1974.

Guarnerius Iurisperitissimus. *Liber Divinarum Sententiarum.* Edited by Giuseppe Mazzanti. Spoleto: CISAM, 1999.

Heinrich, Jacobs Horst. "Irnerius Sigle." *Zeitschrift der Savigny-Stiftung für Rechtsgeschichte, Romanistische Abteilung* 134 (2017): 444–90.

Holtzmann, Walther. "Zur Geschichte des Investiturstreites, (Englische Analekten, II). Vol. 4. Eine Bannsentenz des Konzils von Reims 1119." In *Beiträge zur Reichs- und Papstgeschichte des hohen Mittelalters. Augewählte Aufsätze.* Bonn: Röhrscheid, 1957.

Kantorowicz, Hermann. "An English Theologian's View of Roman Law: Pepo, Irnerius, Ralph Niger." *Medieval and Renaissance Studies* 1 (1941–43); now in *Rechtshistorische Schriften*, edited by Helmut Coing and Gerhard Immel, 231–44. Karlsruhe: Müller, 1970.

Kantorowicz, Hermann, and William W. Buckland, eds. *Studies in the Glossators of the Roman Law: Newly Discovered Writings of the Twelfth Century.* Reprint Aalen: Scientia, 1969.

Landolfo di S. Paolo o Iuniore. *Historia Mediolanensis ab anno MXCV usque ad annum MCXXXVII*, edited by Carlo Castiglioni. Rerum Italicarum Scriptores, n.s. Vol. 3. Bologna: Zanichelli, 1934.

Lange, Hermann. *Römisches Recht im Mittelalter, Band 1: Die Glossatoren.* München: C.H. Beck, 1997.

Loschiavo, Luca. *Summa Codicis Berolinensis. Studio ed edizione di una composizione "a mosaico".* Frankfurt am Main: Vittorio Klostermann, 1996.

Mazzanti, Giuseppe. "Anselmo di Laon, Gilberto l'Universale e la 'Glossa Ordinaria' alla Bibbia." *Bullettino dell'Istituto Storico Italiano per il Medio Evo e Archivio Muratoriano* 102 (1999): 1–18.

Mazzanti, Giuseppe. "Irnerio: contributo a una biografia." *Rivista Internazionale di Diritto Comune* 11 (2000): 117–82.

Mazzanti, Giuseppe. "Un falso irneriano? Riconsiderazioni sul documento del 1125." In *Il contributo del monastero di S. Benedetto Polirone alla cultura giuridica italiana (secc. XI–XVI). Atti del convegno San Benedetto Po, 29 September, 2007*, edited by Pierpaolo Bonacini and Andrea Padovani, 37–44. San Benedetto Po: Publi Paolini, 2009.

Morena, Ottone. *Das Geschichtswerk des Otto Morena und seiner Fortsetzer über die Taten Friedrichs I. in der Lombardei*, edited by Ferdinand Güterbock. MGH SS Rer. Germ. 8. Berlin: Weidmann, 1930.

Odofredus. *Domini Odoffredi in iure absolutissimi matura, diligentissimeque repetita interpretatio in undecim primos pandectarum libros. . . .* Lugduni: Petrus Compater et Blasius Guido, 1550.

Odofredus. *Odofredi Iuris Utriusque peritissimi dicaearchi in primam Codicis partem complectentem I.II.III.IIII. et V. lib. Praelectiones (quae lecturae appellantur).* Lugduni: Petrus Compater et Blasius Guido, 1552.

Orlandelli, Gianfranco. *Scritti di paleografia e diplomatica.* Edited by Roberto Ferrara and Giovanni Feo. Bologna: Istituto per la Storia dell'Università di Bologna, 1994.

Pace, Giacomo. "Garnerius Theutonicus. Nuove fonti su Irnerio e i 'quattro dottori'." *Rivista Internazionale di Diritto Comune* 2 (1991): 123–33.

Padovani, Andrea. "Alle origini dell'università di Bologna. L'insegnamento di Irnerio." *Bulletin of Medieval Canon Law* 33 (2016): 13–25.

Padovani, Andrea. "Il titolo *De Summa Trinitate et fide catholica* (C. 1.1) nell'esegesi dei glossatori fino ad Azzone. Con tre interludî su Irnerio." In *Manoscritti, editoria e biblioteche dal medioevo all'età contemporanea: Studi offerti a Domenico Maffei per il suo ottantesimo compleanno*, edited by Mario Ascheri and Gaetano Colli. Vol. 3, 1075–123. Rome: Roma nel Rinascimento, 2006.

Padovani, Andrea. "Matilde e Irnerio. Note su un dibattito attuale." In *Matilde di Canossa e il suo tempo: Atti del XXI Congresso Internazionale di studio sull'alto medioevo in occasione del IX centenario della morte (1115–2015): San Benedetto Po, Revere, Mantova, Quattro Castella, 20–24 ottobre 2015*. Vol. 1, 199–242. Spoleto: CISAM, 2016.

Padovani, Andrea. "The Metaphysical Thought of Late Medieval Jurisprudence." In *The Jurists' Philosophy of Law from Rome to the Seventeenth Century*, edited by Andrea Padovani and Peter G. Stein, 31–78. A Treatise of Legal Philosophy and General Jurisprudence 7. Dordrecht: Springer, 2007. Available at https://books.google.com/books?id=-5SRCwAAQBAJ&dq=Andrea+Padovani,+%E2%80%9CThe+Metaphysical+Thought+of+Late+Medieval+Jurisprudence&source=gbs_navlinks_s

Padovani, Andrea. "Roberto di Torigni, Lanfranco, Irnerio e la scienza giuridica anglo-normanna nell'età di Vacario." *Rivista Internazionale di Diritto Comune* 18 (2007): 71–140.

Padovani, Andrea. "Sull'uso del metodo questionante nel *Decretum*: Un contributo." *Bulletin of Medieval Canon Law* 34 (2017): 61–87.

Pennington, Kenneth. "Odofredus and Irnerius." *Rivista internazionale di diritto comune* 28 (2017): 11–27.

Pescatore, Gustav. *Die Glossen des Irnerius*. Greifswald: Julius Abel, 1883.

Pescatore, Gustav. *Kritische Studien auf dem Gebiete der civilistischen Litterärgeschichte des Mittelaters*. Greifswald: Julius Abel, 1896.

Robert of Torigni. *The Chronicle of Robert of Torigni Abbot of the Monastery of St. Michel-in-Peril-of-the-Sea*, edited by Richard Howlett. *Rerum Britannicarum Medii Aevi Scriptores (Roll Series 82)*. Vol. 10. London: Eyre and Spottiswoode, 1889. Reprinted Millwood: Kraus, 1964.

Savigny, Friedrich Carl von. *Geschichte des Römischen Rechts im Mittelalter*. Vol. 4. Heidelberg, 1850; Reprinted Bad Homburg: Hermann Gentner, 1962.

Southern, Richard W. *Scholastic Humanism and the Unification of Europe*. Oxford: Blackwell, 1995.

Spagnesi, Enrico. "Irnerio." In *Enciclopedia Italiana*. Appendix 8, *Il contributo italiano alla storia del pensiero*, edited by Paolo Cappellini, Pietro Costa, Maurizio Fioravanti, and Bernardo Sordi, 43–6. Rome: Istituto della Enciclopedia Italiana, 2012.

Spagnesi, Enrico. "Irnerio teologo, una riscoperta necessaria." *Studi Medievali* 42 (2001): 325–79.

Spagnesi, Enrico. *Wernerius bononiensis iudex: La figura storica d'Irnerio*. Florence: Olschki, 1970.

Torelli, Pietro. *Scritti di storia del diritto italiano*. Milan: Giuffrè, 1959.

Weigand, Rudolf. *Die Naturrechtslehre der Legisten und Dekretisten von Irnerius bis Accursius und von Gratian bis Johannes Teutonicus*. Munich: Max Hueber, 1967.

Winroth, Anders. *The Making of Gratian's Decretum*. Cambridge: Cambridge University Press, 2000.

Winroth, Anders. "The Teaching of Law in the Twelfth Century." In *Law and Learning in the Middle Ages: Proceedings of the Second Carlsberg Academy Conference on Medieval History*, edited by Helle Vogt and Mia Münster-Swendsen, 41–62. Copenhagen: Diøf, 2006.

2 Gratian (Late Eleventh Century to ca. 1145)

Atria A. Larson

If men are to be judged by the legacies they leave behind, Gratian (Italian: Graziano) was a great man. If men are to be judged by their character and their accomplishments during their lifetime, we cannot assess whether Gratian was great. His biography is notoriously shrouded in mystery.[1] Scholars can be confident that he was born in Italy, likely in central Italy, probably towards the end of the eleventh century. His textbook and the numerous identifications of him as *magister* by commentators on his work prove that he taught, and scholars can presume that he spent at least much of his teaching career in Bologna, the center for the recently revived study of Roman law which, after and because of Gratian, quickly became the center for the study of canon law too. He probably died in the 1140s as a bishop, possibly in 1144 or 1145 as bishop of Chiusi. The qualifications, even on so brief a sketch, are considerable, and really the best evidence scholars have about Gratian comes from the one work he left behind, his *Concordia discordantium canonum*, later referred to simply as the *Decretum*.

The *Decretum*, which scholarship often refers to as a "canonical collection" (that is, a collection of the Church's *canones*, or rules governing Church life and administration), is in fact *sui generis*. The *Decretum* constitutes a mix between a canonical collection, a collection of patristic *sententiae*, and a topical biblical commentary. In all of this, it is much like Peter Lombard's *Sentences*, completed in the late 1150s and destined to become the textbook for advanced theology students. Unlike Peter Lombard's work or any other, however, it is largely constructed around thirty-six ecclesiastical cases, or *causae* (in the *secunda pars* of the *Decretum*), for each of which it poses and then answers questions about what is canonically lawful arising from a supposedly real-life scenario. And unlike any canonical collection before or after him, Gratian opened his work with a treatise on law (*prima pars*, distinctions 1–20) and a lengthy treatment (*prima pars*, distinctions 21–101) of the qualifications of clerics. Like Peter Lombard's *Sentences*, and expanding upon early scholastic methodology evident in writers such as Bernold of Constance, Alger of Liège, Anselm of Laon, and Peter Abelard, Gratian demonstrated an awareness of potential conflicts or points of discord among authoritative sources in the Christian tradition as well as a desire to bring them into harmony (hence the title *Concordia discordantium canonum*). Like Alger before him and Peter Lombard after him, Gratian interwove his own commentary and logical argumentation with excerpts from the tradition. These passages of Gratian's own words are referred to as his *dicta*, and passages quoted from the Church fathers, Church councils, papal decretals, and other sources are his *auctoritates*. Gratian set the *auctoritates* against each other, on opposite sides of a question, and then reasoned and made distinctions in order to come to the right, or better, answer and reconcile the seemingly contradictory canons to his conclusion.

The formal, or intermediate, sources from which Gratian copied his *auctoritates* (his library, as it were) support the idea that Gratian worked in Italy; he worked from largely Italian collections (Alger of Liège's *De misericordia et iustitia* is a notable exception).[2] The learning revealed in his *dicta* discloses that he had a strong background in the trivium (grammar, logic, and rhetoric), as any well-educated man of his time would have. His particular affinities for modes of argumentation and approaches to scripture as taught in the school of Anselm of Laon, together with his usage of Alger; his extensive theological and exegetical knowledge; and his usage of early versions of the *Glossa ordinaria* on the Bible being worked on at Laon suggest that Gratian, like others of his talented Italian peers, traveled to northwestern France to study the *sacra pagina* and then returned to Italy, invigorating the theological scene there and bolstering their teaching on various subjects with the early scholastic methods for study of scripture.[3]

Scholars disagree on when Gratian started teaching and for how long he taught. Some think he was working on his text already in the 1120s and had a long career into the early 1140s; others believe he began in the late 1130s and composed the bulk of the *Decretum* only after the Second Lateran Council of 1139.[4] The debate here is intricately tied to philological issues connected to various recensions of Gratian's text surviving in extant manuscripts.[5] Some scholars think Gratian composed a first recension and another person nearly doubled the work after Gratian became a bishop. Others see a longer process in which the *Concordia discordantium canonum* grew in stages, several of which are discernible in extant manuscripts, into the complete *Decretum* and believe that one man, Gratian, could have been responsible for the entire work in all of its pre-Vulgate redactions. Regardless, there is an early recension, which I call R1, that was preserved in the manuscript tradition and circulated in Europe. This recension, R1, demonstrates a greater usage of the methods of the trivium and the early scholastic approach to biblical and patristic *auctoritates*, whereas the later stages, resulting in a finalized R2, has more the character of a traditional canonical collection, consisting largely of additional canons with much less commentary.[6] For this reason, and because the scholarly consensus is that Gratian was responsible for at least R1, this essay will focus on texts present in that recension.

Irrespective of the foggy details of Gratian's life and career and the development of his textbook, his *Decretum* and its influence leave no doubt about either Gratian's importance in the history of Christian law or his commitment to a specifically *Christian* approach to law. Scholars have questioned whether Gratian was more of a theologian or a jurist/canonist. The question is somewhat misguided.[7]

Gratian was a man of his times, which did not have distinct academic faculties of theology and canon law, and in which every well-educated baptized person's worldview was imbued with biblical principles and exempla and whose ultimate guide for truth and justice was to be found in the holy scriptures and the God testified to in them. Gratian studied the Bible, and then, more than any of his predecessors or peers, he applied his knowledge of the scriptures to practical questions about what could be right and just in the administration of ecclesiastical offices, duties, and courts. In the end, he composed a work that inspired a highly refined canonistic jurisprudence and formed a fundamental part of the body of laws that governed the Church until the new *Codex iuris canonici* of the Roman Catholic Church went into effect in 1918. This essay will examine four influential areas of Gratian's juristic teaching that were impacted heavily by his understanding of scripture in application to issues in the Christian church: (1) the hierarchy of laws, (2) penance, (3) culpability and dispensation, and (4) procedure.

Hierarchy of laws

Gratian opened his *Decretum* with the statement, "The human race is ruled by two things, namely, natural law (*ius naturale*) and usages (*mores*)" (D.1 pr.).[8] He identified *ius naturale* with what is contained in the law and gospel, that is, all of scripture, and associated it most concisely in a double formulation of the Golden Rule, both positive (do to others what you want done to you) and negative (do not inflict on others what you do not want done to you). Drawing heavily on the *Etymologies* of the seventh-century Iberian Church father Isidore of Seville, Gratian connected natural law to the divine and what is eternally morally good (*fas*), and usages to the human and what is historically handed down and recorded. If usages are recorded, they are written laws (*leges*), but if not, they are custom (*consuetudo*). Gratian then offered a different taxonomy of law from Isidore's work: natural law, civil law, and the law of nations (*ius gentium*).

Gratian next introduced ecclesiastical or canon law. Crucially, he introduced ecclesiastical law as a species of human *lex* or *ius*; canon law was not divine law or natural law. "One kind of constitution is civil," he wrote, "another ecclesiastical. . . . An ecclesiastical constitution is known by the name of 'canon'" (D.3 pr.). Canons can be divided into papal decretals and statutes from Church councils, and, among councils, universal councils should be differentiated from provincial ones. For Gratian, all *leges*, whether civil or ecclesiastical, were meant to "command what must be done, prohibit evil from being done, permit what is licit . . . or certain illicit things, lest worse things happen" (D.3 d.p.c.3).

Gratian to this point remained descriptive, situating various laws into a categorical schema, without giving more authority to one kind over another, but he quickly began to consider a hierarchy: which law is the highest? His answer was unequivocal: "Natural law obtains the first place among all others, both by its age and its dignity. For it began from the beginning of rational creatures, and it does not change with time but remains immutable" (D.5 pr.). Since he had started his book with an association between natural law and the Bible, Gratian knew that he needed to make a clarification. After all, many prescriptions found in the Bible no longer held. The example he used was the prohibition of women entering the temple during menstruation or within a certain period of time after giving birth. The same restrictions were not in effect for women entering churches. Gratian specified that natural law is contained in the Bible but that not everything in the Bible constitutes natural law. He distinguished moral from ceremonial law; the underlying moral significance of the rituals remained, but the symbols and rituals themselves might change (D.6 d.p.c.3). Since all human laws, including canon law, are subordinate to natural law as contained in the Bible, this distinction provides an important hermeneutical key for understanding why, and with what perspective, Gratian returned so often to the scriptures for guidance on canonical problems. Gratian never read Old Testament prescriptions for Israel as eternal laws that should be transferred to his day; he never took the examples of biblical persons as models to follow literally in any situation. Gratian instead believed that every concrete historical law or person or action in scripture pointed to some other, higher, eternal reality, and Church practice in his day should fall in line with that higher reality, the natural law, from the standpoint of its own historical context.

Gratian grew more specific in his hierarchy. Custom is subordinate to natural law (D.8), as are *leges* of all kinds (civil and ecclesiastical) (D.9). If any custom or law ran counter to natural law, it should be considered null and void (D.8 d.p.c.1). Gratian set ecclesiastical law over civil law, but the *auctoritates* he cited were quite moderate, essentially giving different spheres of action to the two and making clear that secular laws cannot abrogate ecclesiastical laws nor dictate how cases are settled in ecclesiastical courts (see, e.g., D.10 c.1). Gratian did not advocate for ecclesiastical intervention in secular laws but instead indicated that secular laws that opposed decrees from the New Testament or canon law should be resisted but otherwise should be held "worthy of all reverence" (D.10 d.p.c.6). Custom fell for Gratian below written law (D.12), even though it was also clear that sometimes contrary longstanding usage superseded laws that had not been followed for a long time (D.4 d.p.c.3). Gratian then set a standard of justice for defining what is licit in all actions (D.12 pr.) and also introduced the notion of dispensation—that in some cases, in consideration of specific circumstances, the rigor of custom or *lex* should be relaxed (D.14).

Finally, Gratian turned specifically to the hierarchy within ecclesiastical law, first specifying the authoritative councils of the early Church (DD.15–16), then ascribing to the papacy the authority to convoke councils (D.17), then placing episcopal councils under the general enactments of papal councils (D.18), and lastly considering the authority of papal decretal letters and their position in relationship to conciliar law and the writings of the Church fathers (DD.19–20). Decretal law was equal to conciliar law, but when thinking about decretals and patristic writings, Gratian made an important distinction (D.20 pr.). Church fathers like Augustine and Jerome might have greater grace (*gratia*), cling more strongly to reason (*ratio*), and possess more knowledge (*scientia*) than certain popes, but expounding scripture is one thing and deciding cases another. Popes and theologians might share *scientia*, but only popes had the power (*potestas*) to decide cases. With this distinction, Gratian separated papal power from the personal merits of individual popes so that papal letters had legal authority regardless of whether the pope was more knowledgeable or virtuous.[9] Gratian did not mean to denigrate the authority and stature of the Church fathers. In fact, he integrated hundreds of excerpts from them into his work and took them as a guide for thinking through questions of canon law. Nonetheless, when it came to rendering a verdict on a case, papal decretals carried greater, and even decisive, legal weight because of the office to which they were attached.

With these first twenty distinctions of his work, the *Tractatus de legibus*, Gratian formulated a unique and influential preface for his textbook, compelling all the students of canon law after him to reflect on the various types of law and their mutual relations. His work fostered heightened reflection on natural law and its relationship to Christian scriptures and universal humanity, contributing to the vibrant natural law tradition in Western jurisprudence. Significantly for the history of the Church, this section of Gratian's work provided a theoretical basis to ground the legal authority for the much higher numbers of papal decretals coming out of the papal curia in the decades after the *Decretum*'s composition. In this subsequent period, recent papal decretals surpassed conciliar decrees numerically in canonical collections and became a more regular form for churches in Christendom to receive legal guidance from the increasingly centralized and powerful papacy.[10] Gratian's work, in spite of all of its theological content and reasoning, provided a strongly juridical basis for Petrine authority over the whole of the Church while also providing the Western legal tradition with a basic notion of the distinction of person and office in matters of justice.

Penance

In the middle of the twentieth century, no scholars would have selected "penance" as a category for discussing Gratian's importance and impact. This is largely because they viewed the *Tractatus de penitentia* that appears embedded within his *Decretum* (at C.33 q.3) as of dubious authenticity. Anders Winroth's confirmation of earlier suspicions, that Gratian's work had developed in stages, solidified *De penitentia* as belonging to Gratian—it appears in the R1 text and could have been completed in the early 1130s, if not earlier. When read as part of the design for an early stage of the *Decretum* and set beside numerous other texts in the *Decretum* that refer to penance, *De penitentia* becomes rather central to Gratian's project. After all, many matters of Church discipline were, for Gratian, also matters of sin before God, and if God was willing to forgive repentant sinners, that should effect how the ministers of God in the Church handled erring members.

Gratian's views had potentially enormous impact on ecclesiastical discipline. On the one hand, the Church had always preached repentance and forgiveness, and in debates in the early Church about how to handle those returning from heresy or a lapse in faith in the face of persecution, the orthodox Church had decided in favor of welcoming Christians back into the fold. The Church was not for the perfect, but for sick sinners. On the other hand, in the Church reforms leading into Gratian's day, the Church insisted on the moral purity of the clergy. There was a danger that such insistence could prove practically devastating for the Church. Was every cleric who fell into sin to be deposed? In fact, several heresies arose in the twelfth century taking the notion of clerical purity to an extreme and rejecting officeholders in the Church precisely because they did not meet the moral standards that they were supposed to keep.

Gratian dealt with the issue of priests who fell into sin in the first part of his *Decretum*, where he discussed qualifications for clerical office. First he argued that lapsed priests should not retain their office, but then he argued that, if they truly performed penance, they should (D.50 d.p.c.12). In a passage reminiscent of sections of *De penitentia* (cf. *De pen.* D.2 d.p.c.39, D.3 d.p.c.26), he argued his point using biblical exempla of persons who sinned but afterwards regained or gained their office:

> Miriam, Aaron's sister, after she had been struck with leprosy since she had grumbled against Moses, was cleansed by an act of penance and received her original grace of prophesying (cf. Numbers 12). After he raised up the [golden] calf, Aaron was even consecrated high priest (cf. Exodus 30, 32). After his adultery and murder, David received the spirit of prophecy and remained in his current office (cf. 2 Samuel 11–12). After the death of Naboth, a most holy man, Ahab was humbled through penance and remained in his royal seat (cf. 1 Kings 21). And, in order to pass over multiple examples of the Old Testament, Peter denied Christ and nevertheless was afterwards made the prince of the apostles (cf. Mark 14); Paul stoned Stephen and nevertheless was elected by God to the apostolate (cf. Acts 7).

Gratian stipulated that the penance must be genuine; the cleric could not simply go through the motions in order to make a show of false piety for purposes of ambition (D.50 d.p.c.24 and d.p.c.28). He observed as well that, historically, many clerics who had fallen into heresy retained their rank when returning to the orthodox communion (D.50 d.p.c.12). Later in the *Decretum*, he presented several authorities that seemed to bar from office clerics who had lapsed into heresy, but he then observed that "these authorities did not prohibit men to be received in their orders when they had denounced their heresy with true penance" (C.1 q.7 d.p.c.4). In other words, priests who had lapsed into heresy had been and could conceivably be received at their same rank back into the Church. These considerations threw Gratian into a discussion of dispensation, where the rigor of discipline is sometimes relaxed.

Gratian's understanding of penance had implications for clerics as well as for laypersons under their care. The internal discipline of the hierarchy, determining who fills the ranks of the clergy and thus who exercises pastoral care and jurisdiction over the faithful, is central to the Church as an institution. Gratian's position was moderate but not soft: the hierarchy could not be filled with offenders of canon law and God's law, yet, where true penance seemed evident, those who had fallen could regain their dignity. Gratian's, and the medieval Church's, perspective on repentance as a factor in considerations of justice, discipline, and punishment has contributed to discussions in Western jurisprudence about the purpose of punishment, the possibility of redemption, and the conditions on which law-breakers reenter society or disgraced public officials regain office.

Culpability and dispensation

In matters of discipline and judgment, requiring demonstrations of penance makes sense only if the object of the discipline and judgment is guilty to begin with. This is another area in which Gratian made important strides, namely, considerations of culpability. In Christian justice in imitation of God's justice, a punishment can be rendered only when there is fault. Gratian's thinking about culpability largely occurred in relationship to the ecclesiastical hierarchy and considerations of clerical qualifications. Within an institution such as the Church, moral culpability is not the only factor when determining whether someone should achieve or lose an office. Guilt is one thing, unsuitability another. In canon law, certain qualities constituted an "irregularity" (*irregularitas*), rendering the person having those qualities unfit for clerical office.[11] For Gratian and the canonistic tradition afterwards, in cases where guilt was lacking and certain elements of suitability (such as superior virtue or learning) outweighed elements of unsuitability, special dispensations could permit a person to be ordained and perform their office who, by the letter of law, was unsuitable for office.

Gratian sometimes considered culpability in connection to family relationships—for instance, in terms of whether children can be held guilty and punished for their parents' sins of which they had no knowledge. The entire first *causa* is premised on just such a situation. A father paid for his young son's entry into a monastery; the son was too young to know anything about this act of simony, or purchase of spiritual things. The boy grew, became a priest, and then was elected bishop, not knowing that his father once again intervened with payments to higher officials. Gratian asked, "Is a person guilty of a crime that his father commits but of which he is ignorant?" In his discussion, two general categories emerged that excuse a person from a crime, making them not culpable. One was force (*violentia* in C.1 q.1 d.p.c.106). Another was ignorance (cf. C.1 q.1 d.p.c.106; C.1 q.4 d.p.c.10; C.1 q.5 d.p.c.2).

Gratian argued from biblical examples first that ignorance does not excuse anyone or anything, and that those who are ignorant still receive punishment for the sins of others. As in sections of *De penitentia*, his interpretation of the biblical passages relied on the *Glossa ordinaria* stemming from exegetical work at the school of Laon in northwestern France. For instance, in 1 Samuel 15, King Saul was commanded to kill the Amalekites down even to their animals. Canaan was cursed for the sin of his father, Ham, in Genesis 9. Gratian argued that these passages must not be understood as teaching that it is just to punish things or people for sins of which they are ignorant. Drawing on the biblical gloss on

"Amalekites" in Numbers 14:45, as those who lick blood (*lingentes sanguinem*, in C.1 q.4 d.p.c.11 §7), Gratian interpreted the Amalekites as those who are greedy and lustful, thus rendering their animals as figuratively signifying "the irrational movements of vices."[12] The point of 1 Samuel 15 is not, then, that those who are ignorant but incapable of knowing can or should be punished for the sins of others but that Christians should slay vices. Similarly, the curse of Canaan and similar episodes only show that sometimes children are punished corporally for the sins of others, and the sins of prelates and parents sometimes have an effect on their subordinates and children as part of God's punishment for those who have sinned, not as punishment for those who were ignorant and innocent (C.1 q.4 d.p.c.11; cf. C.24 q.3 d.a.c.1). Gratian dismissed and explained away numerous other biblical narratives that might seem to argue that ignorance does not excuse anyone from the guilt of a crime and that therefore the ignorant can be punished. As when he questioned whether sons of priests could be ordained (D.56 d.p.c.1), Gratian fell back on the idea of imitation—those who imitate the sins of their fathers are held guilty of those sins and punished for them, but those who are ignorant of the sins of their fathers and do not imitate them are not held guilty (C.1 q.4 d.p.c.11 §12, d.p.c.12).

Gratian distinguished among kinds of ignorance, however, for not every ignorance was exculpatory. He divided *ignorantia facti* from *ignorantia iuris* (C.1 q.4 d.p.c.12). Sometimes it is reasonable for someone to be ignorant of a fact, which Gratian proves from 1 Corinthians 10, where it is acceptable for Christians not to ask any questions about the meat placed before them and to partake without worrying whether the meat had been sacrificed to idols. But it was not acceptable or reasonable (*non oportuit*), Gratian argued, for the Jews to be ignorant of the fact that Jesus was the long-awaited Messiah. They should have recognized in Jesus that he fulfilled everything the Old Testament prophets had foretold, and thus that ignorance does not excuse them.

Gratian then returned to fundamental categories of law to distinguish acceptable from unacceptable *ignorantia iuris*. Ignorance of natural law is "damnable in all adults." Ignorance of civil law is permissible in some, in others not. In the specific case of the boy who was ignorant of his father's payment, he could not be held culpable, for his ignorance was of the fact of what had happened, and such ignorance was excusable; even if he could have known, his ignorance was excused based on his young age when it occurred.

Gratian discussed issues that would pertain intimately to the canonistic jurisprudence of culpability elsewhere too. Once again, the discussions occurred within questions of clerical qualifications and discipline.[13] What was the Church to do with a cleric at whose hands blood was shed? Gratian differentiated accidental homicide, manslaughter (where someone was moved by wrath but did not intend to kill), and premeditated murder (where someone was moved by wrath and had an intent to kill) (D.50 d.p.c.35, d.p.c.36). In the case of manslaughter and premeditated murder, the priest was to be deposed forever. The priest (it is implied) was guilty and merited punishment. In the case of accidental homicide, the priest did not merit punishment because (it is implied) he was not guilty, and yet the fact that blood had been shed at his hands created a problem for the dignity of his office within his community; in terms of how canonistic jurisprudence developed around holy orders, it created an *irregularitas.* Gratian said, then, that such a cleric was allowed to remain in his office *ex dispensatione* (D.50 d.p.c.35).

Dispensation means that normal regulations are relaxed under certain circumstances. It does not abrogate the law but suspends its normal application with regard to a particular person.[14] Gratian frequently used the term in relationship to the administration of the ecclesiastical hierarchy and what circumstances warranted a man remaining in or gaining an office even if some irregularity stood in the way. When he discussed those circumstances, most thoroughly in C.1 q.7, he spoke of them as the reasons that things were tolerated in the Church that otherwise were not tolerated. It was on the basis of decretist commentary on this section that canonistic jurisprudence about dispensation developed. Gratian's treatment had developed the ideas in Ivo of Chartres's *Prologue*, which was widely distributed in the decades just prior to Gratian's career and which discussed dispensation as a temporary *mitigatio* of the rigor of the law.[15]

Gratian's fullest explanation of dispensation occurred where he addressed whether a heretic who renounced his heresy could be bishop. A precondition of a heretic retaining an office received previously was that he perform penance (C.1 q.7 d.p.c.4), thus bearing the punishment for his sin. Many early Church texts, including from the Council of Nicaea, however, said that such individuals were "irreparably condemned," but Gratian clarified that condemnation obtained only "unless the rigor of discipline is sometimes relaxed out of the dispensation of mercy" (d.p.c.4—d.p.c.5). He listed and gave examples of seven reasons why dispensation could be granted in individual cases: *pro tempore* (on account of the times, d.p.c.5—c.6), *pro necessitate temporis*, lest worse scandal occur in the Church (out of necessity to prevent scandal, d.p.c.6—c.7), *pro persona* (on account of the particular qualities of a person, d.p.c.10—c.11), *intuitu pietatis* (out of considerations of kindness, d.p.c.11—c.12), *intuitu necessitatis* (out of considerations of necessity, d.p.c.12—c.13), *intuitu utilitatis* (out of considerations of what is most useful, d.p.c.16—c.17), and *pro euentu rei* (because something occurred and it would be more trouble to reverse it, d.p.c.17—c.18). Thus, for instance, Gratian cited Pope Hilary (465) permitting in mercy (*ad veniam*) a bishop who was wrongfully ordained without the knowledge of his metropolitan to remain in office with a view to the "necessity of the times" (c.13). Gratian's treatment provided a basis for future reflections on when laws can legitimately be relaxed in light of higher purposes or what future thinkers in the West would refer to as the "common good."

Procedure

At the end of C.1, Gratian indicated a transition in his text; whereas he had briefly discussed matters of dispensation or the softening of discipline, now he was going to turn to the severity of discipline that the Church was prepared to render. Matters pertaining to judicial procedure now came to the fore. Drawing from Roman law and longtime ecclesiastical concerns for basing judicial decisions on the best possible determination of the truth, the development of procedural norms in the jurisprudence of the second half of the twelfth century for use in ecclesiastical courts constituted one of the most significant legal contributions of the Church to the Western legal tradition.[16] Gratian's treatment of procedure was once again colored by his reading of scripture and had particular application in the context of ecclesiastical discipline. We will look briefly at three issues: (1) the necessity for charges and conviction prior to punishment, (2) the number of witnesses needed, and (3) the ability of subordinates to accuse their superiors.

Gratian cited biblical examples and texts to argue that a condemnation can follow only upon a charge or accusation (*nominatio* or *accusatio*) and proper judgment involving an investigation leading to a conviction. A person can accuse himself—that is, confess to having done something wrong—but if he does not, someone must bring charges and make the case that the person is guilty. Gratian cited a sermon by Augustine (although the more likely author is Caesarius of Arles), saying, "We cannot render a sentence against anyone unless he has either been convicted or voluntarily confessed" (C.2 q.1 c.1),[17] and then he quoted Pseudo-Gregory the Great, saying, "No charge may be made against anyone without a legitimate and suitable accuser. For even our Lord Jesus Christ knew that Judas was a thief, but, because he was not accused, he was not cast out" (c.4). No one else knew what Jesus knew, and thus there was no one to bring charges; therefore, even Jesus could not render judgment against Judas. Gratian later quoted more extensively from the Pseudo-Augustinian sermon to argue that, even if an act were manifest and known to the judge, he could still not proceed in judgment without an accusation by someone else and an investigation, since no one can assume roles of both accuser and judge.

The lengthy text expounded passages in Paul's first letter to the Corinthians. In the Church at Corinth, a case of incest was widely known: a man had taken his stepmother as wife. Other disciplinary problems detracted from the Church's unity. The writer of this sermon referred to a section of the epistle where Paul referenced both nomination and judgment (1 Cor. 5:11–13). While there may be those in the Church who are acting wrongly, sometimes they have to be tolerated if there is no confession and if no proper accusation and judgment are possible. When Christ comes again, all will be made clear; no evil deeds will remain hidden. But, in the meantime, the Church must operate with procedural correctness to ensure that justice advances and that no one is condemned "by the judgment of suspicion or also by some extraordinary, usurped judgment, but rather by the law of God according to the order of the Church, whether confessed of one's own accord or accused and convicted" (C.2 q.1 c.18). Gratian allowed that an investigation could be bypassed in one type of situation, namely, if the person gave evidence by obstinately displaying his crime in a public way, even if verbally denying it, such that the continued act itself functioned as a public confession (*quando opere publico crimen suum confitetur*). Implicitly following the threefold correction of Matthew 18, Gratian said that, after a second and third correction, the incorrigible man could be condemned without investigation (d.p.c.20). Later in the *Decretum*, in the question already discussed about whether a family could be excommunicated because of a parent's sin, Gratian appealed to the same text from Corinthians (1 Cor. 5:11) and the same procedural norms: members of the *familia* could not be condemned unless they personally were first accused and convicted (C.24 q.3 d.a.c.1).

Gratian also considered the number of witnesses necessary to convict someone. The question pertained in particular to a bishop (C.2 q.4), but Gratian did not give any special privilege to bishops on account of their rank. Certain texts from the tradition gave extraordinarily high numbers of witnesses, up to seventy-two, to convict a bishop, but Gratian dismissed these texts as perhaps naming a special privilege of clerics of the Roman Church or being necessary under certain circumstances when dishonest individuals were maliciously accusing bishops. When the witnesses were reputable, however, the standard of Jewish law (Deut. 17:6), repeatedly mentioned in scripture, applied. Gratian himself referred to Jesus's own citing of this standard in John 8, Paul's appeal to the standard (2 Cor. 13:1), and the reference to it in Hebrews (Hebrews 10:28) (C.2 q.4 d.a.c.1). Therefore, *anyone*, including bishops, could be convicted and condemned by the testimony of two or three valid witnesses (d.p.c.3). This also meant, of course, that an accusation and testimony from a single witness would not be sufficient to convict anyone.

Gratian also dealt with the question of whether a subordinate or even a layperson could be the accuser in a case against a bishop. His lengthy treatment cast him back into numerous Old Testament examples, some of which he had discussed in other cases, such as Miriam's grumbling against Moses (Numbers 12) and the curse of Ham (Genesis 9). Yahweh cursed Ham and his son Canaan because Ham had seen his father Noah's nakedness when Noah had become inebriated and, unlike his brothers, did not cover Noah out of respect but instead turned his father into an object of ridicule. A forged decretal of Pope Anacletus had suggested that the story condemned those who pointed out the guilt of their superiors (C.2 q.7 c.12). Gratian narrowed the application of the biblical story: it did not forbid subordinates from accusing their superiors, with valid evidence and with corroboration of other witnesses, but rather forbade subordinates single-handedly betraying their superiors without proof and corroboration, seeking only to put their superiors' failures on display for ridicule (d.p.c.27).

Gratian did not take his reading of Genesis 9 from the *Glossa ordinaria* on the Bible, but he did draw on the *Glossa* for his reading of Miriam's grumbling about Moses's Ethiopian wife. Since Yahweh approved of Moses and punished Miriam with leprosy for her complaint, one might argue, Gratian conceded, that no subordinate (Miriam) is to accuse their superior (Moses). But as Miriam's complaint centered on the fact that Moses had taken a non-Hebrew wife, of which Yahweh approved, the *Glossa ordinaria* read Miriam allegorically as the Jewish people or "the synagogue," Moses as the Lord, and the Ethiopian wife as the Church, gathered from the nations into marriage with him.[18] Gratian presented this as one interpretation of the Numbers 12 narrative, suggesting, "through Miriam is understood the synagogue, which grumbled against Moses, that is against Christ, because he joined himself to the Ethiopian, that is the church, from the nations" (C.2 q.7 d.p.c.27). The point, for Gratian, was that the biblical story did not support the idea that subordinates could not accuse prelates, and, in fact, he then offered patristic texts and biblical passages and figures to support the idea that those not living out their ecclesiastical dignity with appropriate conduct and teaching were to be chided and rebuked, lest they bring destruction upon others (cf. c.28—d.p.c.42).

In short, for Gratian, any reputable person could bring an accusation and serve as a witness, but more than one witness was needed to convict. Such procedural norms protected prelates and anyone else from malicious, unsubstantiated accusations and helped further standards of proofs and notions of a fair trial in Western jurisprudence. Gratian's treatment also advocated for equality before the law, at least among clerics and free persons; higher officials were not to get special treatment.

Conclusion

Gratian's textbook contributed much for the development of Western jurisprudence, both canonistic and secular. His own arguments sometimes conveyed refined ideas and terminology; at other times they did not. Nevertheless, his treatise on law, his questions about clerical qualifications, and his casebook gathered together learning and concepts from the Christian tradition together with bits of Roman law, argued persuasively for what was the judicious answer on many points, and advanced issues of principle joined to questions of practice in such a way that a full-fledged canonistic jurisprudence could emerge. What appears over and over again in the *Decretum* is Gratian's determination to find biblical and patristic support for his arguments and to correct possible wrong exegesis that would ultimately promote a misuse of power or misapplication of justice. Also striking is the extent to which Gratian advanced or raised for the first time significant issues of legal jurisprudence within the context of ecclesiastical administration and discipline. The institutional Church formed the milieu of which Gratian was a part and for which he was primarily concerned. His influence in the history of Western jurisprudence should be understood in terms of this milieu, for he and his commentators and students for centuries after him ultimately viewed their work as finding the correct or best way to implement God's justice for God's mystical bride, the Church, in its earthly, institutional manifestation.

Notes

1 Condorelli; Noonan; Winroth, "Where Gratian Slept."
2 Landau, "Neue Forschungen zu vorgratianischen Kanonessammlungen."
3 Larson, *Master of Penance*, 271–312; also Larson, "The Influence of the School of Laon."
4 For primary examples of the different views, see (long view) Pennington, "The Biography of Gratian," esp. 680–81, and (short view) Winroth, "Where Gratian Slept."

5 An overview of these debates is found in Eichbauer.
6 This does not necessarily mean that R2 was not suitable for teaching. See Dusil, "Learning from Gaius?" On the terminology of R1 and R2, see Larson, "Gratian's *De penitentia*."
7 Larson, "The Reception of Gratian's *Tractatus de penitentia*."
8 All texts from Gratian are translated from *Decretum magistri Gratiani*, ed. Friedberg. The first twenty distinctions are translated in *The Treatise on the Laws (Decretum DD. 1–20)*, trans. Thompson.
9 See Genka.
10 See Duggan; and Pennington, "Decretal Collections 1190–1234," in Hartmann and Pennington, *History of Medieval Canon Law in the Classical Period*, 246–317.
11 Helmhoz, "The Qualifications of the Clergy: Ordination of the Unfree," in idem, *The Spirit of Classical Canon Law*, 61–87, esp. 61–5.
12 The term appears in both an interlinear gloss and a marginal gloss attributed to Rhabanus Maurus in the *Glossa ordinaria* (ed. Rusch, 1.309a). Texts from the *Glossa ordinaria* are taken from *Biblia latina cum Glossa ordinaria.*
13 See Descamps; Kéry; Larson, "Killing a Career."
14 Lefebvre-Teillard, 14.
15 Ivo's Prologue is translated in Somerville and Brasington, *Prefaces*, 132–58.
16 On these developments, see Brasington, *Order in the Court*; and Hartmann and Pennington, *History of Courts and Procedure.*
17 Sermo 351 is often cited by Gratian, usually under the title of a "Homily on Penance." It is printed in PL 39.
18 *Glossa ordinaria* ad Numbers 12 (ed. Rusch, 1.303b—304a).

Bibliography

Biblia latina cum Glossa ordinaria: Facsimile Reprint of the Editio princeps, Adolph Rusch of Strassburg, 1480/81. Introduction by Karlfried Froehlich and Margaret T. Gibson. Turnhout: Brepols, 1992.

Brasington, Bruce C. *Order in the Court: Medieval Procedural Treatises in Translation.* Medieval Law and Its Practice. Leiden/Boston: Brill, 2016.

Condorelli, Orazio. "Graziano." In *Dictionario biografico dei giuristi italiani, XII–XX secolo.* Vol. 1, 1058–61. Bologna: Il Mulino, 2013.

Descamps, Olivier. "Quelques remarques sur la distinction entre homicide volontaire et homicide involontaire en droit canonique médiéval." In *Der Einfluss der Kanonistik auf die europäische Rechtskultur.* Vol. 3: *Straf- und Strafprozessrecht.* Edited by Mathias Schmoeckel, Orazio Condorelli, and Franck Roumy, 107–34. Cologne: Böhlau, 2012.

Duggan, Charles. "Decretal Collections from Gratian's *Decretum* to the Compilationes *antiquae*: The Making of the New Case Law." In *The History of Medieval Canon Law in the Classical Period, 1140–1234: From Gratian to the Decretals of Pope Gregory IX.* Edited by Wilfried Hartmann and Ken Pennington. Washington, DC: CUA Press, 2008.

Dusil, Stephan. "Learning from Gaius? Different Layers in Gratian's *Decretum* and Research on Roman Law." *Zeitschrift der Savigny-Stiftung für Rechtsgeschichte: Kanonistische Abteilung* 104 (2018): 151–81.

Dusil, Stephan. *Wissensordnungen des Rechts im Wandel: Päpstlicher Jurisdiktionsprimat und Zölibat zwischen 1000 und 1215.* Mediaevalia Lovaniensia, Ser. I, Studia 47. Leuven: Leuven University Press, 2018.

Eichbauer, Melodie H. "Gratian's *Decretum* and the Changing Historiographical Landscape." *History Compass* 11/12 (2013): 1111–25.

Genka, Tatsushi. "Hierarchie der Texte, Hierarchie der Autoritäten: Zur Hierarchie der Rechtsquellen bei Gratian." *Zeitschrift der Savigny-Stiftung für Rechtsgeschichte: Kanonistische Abteilung* 95 (2009): 125.

Gratian. *Decretum magistri Gratiani. Corpus iuris canonici.* Edited by Emil Friedberg. Vol. 1. Leipzig: B. Tauchnitz, 1879; Reprinted Graz: Akademische Druck und Verlagsanstalt, 1959.

Gratian. *The Treatise on the Laws (Decretum DD. 1–20).* Translated by Augustine Thompson, O.P. *With the Ordinary Gloss.* Translated by James Gordley. Studies in Medieval and Early Modern Canon Law 2. Washington, DC: Catholic University of America Press, 1993.

Hartmann, Wilfried, and Kenneth Pennington, eds. *The History of Courts and Procedure in Medieval Canon Law.* History of Medieval Canon Law. Washington, DC: Catholic University of America Press, 2016.

Hartmann, Wilfried, and Kenneth Pennington, eds. *The History of Medieval Canon Law in the Classical Period, 1140–1234: From Gratian to the Decretals of Pope Gregory IX.* History of Medieval Canon Law. Washington, DC: Catholic University of America Press, 2008.

Helmholz, RichardH. *The Spirit of Classical Canon Law.* Athens: University of Georgia Press, 1997.

Kéry, Lotte. "Non enim homines de occultis, sed de manifestis iudicant: La culpabilité dans le droit pénal de l'Église, à l'époche Classique." *Revue de droit canonique* 53/2 (2003): 311–36.

Landau, Peter. "Gratian and the *Decretum Gratiani.*" In *The History of Medieval Canon Law in the Classical Period, 1140–1234: From Gratian to the Decretals of Pope Gregory IX.* Edited by Wilfried Hartmann and Kenneth Pennington, 22–54. History of Medieval Canon Law 6. Washington, DC: The Catholic University of America Press, 2008.

Landau, Peter. "Neue Forschungen zu vorgratianischen Kanonessammlungen und den Quellen des gratianischen Dekrets." *Ius commune* 11 (1984): 1–29. Reprinted in Landau, Peter. *Kanones und Dekretalen: Beiträge zur Geschichte der Quellen des kanonischen Rechts.* Bibliotheca eruditorum, Internationale Bibliothek des Wissenschaften 2, 177–205. Goldbach: Keip, 1997.

Larson, Atria A. "Gratian's *De penitentia* in Twelfth-Century Manuscripts." *Bulletin of Medieval Canon Law* 31 (2014): 57–110.

Larson, Atria A., ed. and trans. *Gratian's* Tractatus de penitentia*: A New Latin Edition with English Translation.* Studies in Medieval and Early Modern Canon Law 14. Washington, DC: Catholic University of America Press, 2016.

Larson, Atria A. "The Influence of the School of Laon on Gratian: The Usage of the *Glossa ordinaria* and Anselmian *Sententie* in *De penitentia* (*Decretum* C.33 q.3)." *Mediaeval Studies* 72 (2010): 197–244.

Larson, Atria A. "Killing a Career: Homicide and the Development of Medieval Clerical Discipline." *The Jurist* 74/2 (2014): 247–70.

Larson, Atria A. *Master of Penance: Gratian and the Development of Penitential Thought and Law in the Twelfth Century.* Studies in Medieval and Early Modern Canon Law 11. Washington, DC: Catholic University of America Press, 2014.

Larson, Atria A. "The Reception of Gratian's *Tractatus de penitentia* and the Relationship between Law and Theology in the Second Half of the Twelfth Century." *Journal of Religious History* 37 (2013): 457–73.

Lefebvre-Teillard, Anne. "Les origines: la dispense en droit canonique." *Droits: Revue française de théorie, de philosophie, et de cultures juridiques* 25 (1997): 11–18.

Noonan, John T., Jr. "Gratian Slept Here: The Changing Identity of the Father of the Systematic Study of Canon Law." *Traditio* 35 (1979): 145–72.

Pennington, Kenneth. "The Biography of Gratian, the Father of Canon Law." *Villanova Law Review* 59/4 (2014): 679–706. Expanded version: "La biografia di Graziano, il Padre del diritto canonico." *Rivista internazionale di diritto comune* 25 (2014): 25–60.

Pennington, Kenneth. "Gratian, Causa 19, and the Birth of Canonical Jurisprudence." In *"Panta rei": Studi dedicati a Manlio Bellomo*. Edited by Orazio Condorelli. Vol. 4, 339–55. Rome: Il Cigno, 2004.

Somerville, Robert, and Bruce Brasington, eds. *Prefaces to Canon Law Books in Latin Christianity: Selected Translations, 500–1245*. New Haven: Yale, 1998.

Wei, John C. *Gratian the Theologian*. Studies in Medieval and Early Modern Canon Law 13. Washington, DC: Catholic University of America Press, 2016.

Weigand, Rudolf. *Die Naturrechtslehre der Legisten und Dekretisten von Irnerius bis Accursius und von Gratian bis Johannes Teutonicus*. Münchener Theologische Studien, Kanonistische Abteilung. München: Hueber, 1967.

Winroth, Anders. *The Making of Gratian's* Decretum. Cambridge: Cambridge University Press, 2000.

Winroth, Anders. "Where Gratian Slept: The Life and Death of the Father of Canon Law." *Zeitschrift der Savigny-Stiftung für Rechtsgeschichte: Kanonistische Abteilung* 99 (2013): 105–28.

3 Azo (ca. 1165 to ca. 1220/30) and Accursius (1182/5 to ca. 1263)

Emanuele Conte

Azo of Bologna and his best-known student, Accursius, were the two most prominent figures of the school of civil (that is, Roman) law in Bologna during the first half of the thirteenth century. Legal historians refer to this as the heyday of the "school of glossators," stressing the slow and progressive compilation of a set of short commentaries written in the margins of the books carrying the actual text of the Justinian compilation. While Azo's work would influence generations of jurists, Accursius—the most famous among the many lawyers who had been students of Azo—achieved his own immortality by publishing the definitive compilation of glosses, called the *Apparatus ordinarius*, or the "Ordinary Gloss." Published in manuscripts shortly before the mid-thirteenth century, the *Apparatus* continued to be copied regularly in every manuscript of the Codex, of the three parts of the Digest, of the Institutes, and of the *Authenticum* until the invention of the printing press. Since the late fifteenth century, the *Apparatus* has been printed in every edition of the *Corpus Iuris Civilis*, spreading its influence for centuries.

Azo

Scholars presume that Azo was born before 1170, probably around 1165, in Bologna, where he spent his whole life. His family was not rich; some sources give him the name *Porcus* (that is, "pig" in colloquial Italian) or *Portius*, but in legal literature he is always mentioned simply as Azo. His name appears for the first time in a document dated 1190, in which he already bears the title of *legis doctor*, meaning that he already had received his doctorate and was authorized to teach at the university level.

Azo's main teacher in Bologna was Joannes Bassianus, who was, in turn, a direct student of Bulgarus. Legal historians have stressed this academic genealogy, defining the line from Bulgarus to Joannes Bassianus to Azo to Accursius as the orthodox school of the Bolognese glossators.[1] These glossators have been described as particularly rigorous in the interpretation of Roman law and relatively suspicious towards local legislation, feudal law, and canon law, following Accursius's statement that "everything can be founded in the *Corpus* of Justinian's law" (*omnia in corpore iuris inveniuntur*).[2]

At any rate, in 1191 Azo was already a professor of Bologna, and he quickly became one of the most successful among the faculty there. Some sources report his extraordinary success in attracting students, who numbered so many that he once was forced to change the room where he taught.[3] Odofredus, a law professor who had been his pupil and taught in Bologna a few years later, reports that Azo was so devoted to teaching that he never got sick during teaching time and even died during holidays.[4] The extraordinary success of Azo as a professor is also shown by the fact that a large number of important jurists of the thirteenth century were his direct students: in addition to Accursius, some of the most important professors of civil law, such as Iacobus Balduini, Martinus de Fano, Roffredus Beneventanus, and Odofredus, claimed to have attended his lectures. Among the canonists, his students included Sinibaldo Fieschi (later Pope Innocent IV), Johannes Teutonicus, and Goffredo da Trani.

Besides this intense teaching activity, Azo was also engaged as a counselor of the Commune of Bologna and a lawyer in court: the sources preserve memories of two of his pleadings, to which we will return in a moment. As a lawyer, he served the interests of ecclesiastic litigators in 1190, 1200, 1204, and 1217.[5]

The sources do not agree about the date of his death. Alberic of Trois-Fontaines, a French monk who wrote a chronicle in a Belgian monastery around 1241, declares that Azo died in Bologna in 1220, when he was at the height of his celebrity and was considered the best "interpreter and renewer" of the civil law.[6] However, in his *Lectura codicis* Azo seems to refer to the service of his former pupil Iacobus Balduini as *podestà*, or chief magistrate, in Genoa in 1229, so that Friedrich Carl von Savigny suggested dating Azo's death in 1230. Other clues seem to confirm this later date as more plausible.[7] For instance, 1220 would be too early for Azo to have taught some of his students, given their dates of birth, or for parts of his works to be quoted in the writings of other scholars at certain dates. On the other hand, the documentary evidence mentions Azo as living only until 1219.

Azo as a renewer of the Bolognese tradition: from the glossae *to* summae, brocarda, *and* quaestiones

Azo was a prolific and influential author. Following the tradition of the Bolognese school, he composed and published sets of glosses to the books of Justinian's compilation: to the three parts in which the Digest had been divided since it reappeared in the early twelfth century; to the first nine books of the Code (books 10 through 12, called *Tres Libri*, traditionally were kept separate and seldom taught in the Bolognese curriculum); and to the Latin version of the collection of the *Novellae*, called *Authenticum*. The only part of the Justinian laws for which no apparatuses by Azo are preserved are the *Tres Libri*: as far as we know, Azo never composed a full set of glosses to them.

The apparatuses of Azo are extremely rich in content. His original glosses are many, but they include a vast number of glosses originally written by other jurists, from Irnerius to Bulgarus, Joannes Bassianus, Placentinus, and many others.

Composed to serve more the law professors than the law students, the apparatuses of Azo offer a very large choice of interpretations, often disagreeing about the meaning and the possible use of the original texts. The medieval reader could also find allegations, quoting parallel texts, as well as *distinctiones*, coordinating the passages from different legislative compilations in applying norms, solutions of contradictions, and so on. The apparatus to the *Codex*, which we know better thanks to the research of Gero Dolezalek, was ready probably around 1210, when Azo was already considered the most important professor of Roman law in Bologna.[8]

If Azo had limited himself to the gathering and writing of glosses, however, he would not have deserved the definition of "renewer" given to him by Alberic of Trois-Fontaines. Actually, Azo devoted himself to other genres of legal writings: *summae* to the Code, and to the Institutions, and some titles of the Digest; *quaestiones*, or points of debate or dispute; and *brocarda*, or legal maxims emerging from the opposition of contrasting norms. On top of this, one of his students, Alexander de Sancto Aegidio, drew up a set of notes on Azo's lectures on the Justinian Code which had a certain diffusion in manuscript and was then printed in 1577 and 1596.

Azo owes his fame much more to the collection of his *summae* and *brocarda* than to his apparatus of glosses, which, despite their initial success, were later absorbed in the *Apparatus ordinarius* by Accursius. In contrast to the glosses, the three *summae* (*Codicis*, *Institutionum*, and *Digestorum*, to which the *Brocarda* were often added) formed a collection which very quickly gained a very broad diffusion and became a necessary reference for every lawyer in Italy and abroad. The high number of manuscripts still preserved today (around eighty) witnesses to the broad circulation of this book even before the age of printing. The first printed edition dates from 1482, followed by many others, for a total of thirty-nine editions between 1482 and 1610. This impressive legacy explains the famous motto, *chi non ha Azzo non vada a Palazzo*: "whoever does not own a <book of the *Summae* by> Azo cannot enter the court," and the provisions of some cities (Milan, Verona, and Padua) where the possession of a copy of the *Summae* was a condition to be part of the local college of advocates.

Unlike the apparatuses of glosses, the *summae*, the *brocarda*, and the collections of *quaestiones* were literary genres less used in Bologna than elsewhere. The *summae* were not summaries but complex treatises on Roman law that followed the order of the titles of the Code or of the Institutions, but they also largely quoted the Digest and the Novellae. This form of legal writing had been developed mainly in the centers of legal education that arose quickly in southern France and northern Italy just after the birth of the school of Bologna. The apparatuses of glosses were copied always in the margins of the medieval edition of the compilation of Justinian, which included five large manuscript volumes in folio and was extremely expensive and slow to produce. Smaller teaching centers developed a lighter way to disseminate the results of legal learning. The most successful was the *summae*, which followed the systematic arrangement of the Code and the Institutions but did not include the ancient text.[9] After the first *Summa Codicis*, composed in Provence by Geraudus (the so-called Summa Trecensis),

Rogerius, an Italian professor who moved to southern France, composed a new, similar work of the same genre. After him, another Italian, Placentinus, whom Azo called "enlightened and famous" (*praeclarus et famosus*), offered a large and original survey of Roman law by publishing his two *summae*—one on the Codex and one on the Institutions—around 1180. These two works also went together in the mind of Azo, who mentions his predecessor with respect but offers some sharp criticism as well.

Unlike Placentinus, who taught in different cities between Italy and southern France and only briefly in Bologna, Azo was already the most important law professor at his alma mater when he decided to devote himself to a "foreign" genre, which the *summa* was. Introducing his two *summae*, Azo explains that, already at his age, the number of glosses written to the Roman texts were so many that it became very difficult to find what one was looking for. His aim was to write a "lucid" text, where "nothing obscure, nothing doubtful, nothing contradictory" was to be found.[10] This was a bold statement for a glossator, the author of the most-used sets of glosses of his age and the master of Accursius, the author of the ordinary gloss.

The contemporary grammarian and master of composition Boncompagno da Signa, himself probably a law student of Azo, claimed to have written the prologue for the work of Azo.[11] Writing shortly after the death of Azo, Boncompagno explains much more clearly the need for a renovation of methods in his "Invectiva contra glossatores," which opens the tenth book of his *Rhetorica novissima*, composed over a period of twenty years and published in Bologna in 1235. The natural simplicity of the law, says Boncompagno, has been converted into duplicity, fraud, ambiguity, deception, fallacy, sophism (and more) by the evil of the glossators. They have turned good wine into sludge by adding unnecessary commentaries to very clear laws, so that "nothing is certain in civil law" any more. The glosses, continues Boncompagno, "grow like the locusts of the Pharaoh, and fall over the text like hail and storm."

The invective of Boncompagno is, of course, something exaggerated, an example of the rhetorical proficiency he taught. But it reflects the common feeling of the first decades of the thirteenth century, when many law professors tried to renew their legal writing in search of clarity. This was the case with Azo, who decided to follow the example of Placentinus and committed himself to clear writing in his *summae*.

As noted, the two *summae* by Azo were destined to become one of the most successful legal writings of all ages. Together they formed a book that took the name of *Summa aurea*, being the "golden," or best, companion to every aspect of Roman law. To cover the issues not considered in the systematic of the Code and the Institutions, Azo decided to add a collection of *summulae* (that is, small treaties on particular themes) inspired by some titles of the Digest. These *Summulae Digestorum* were ascribed for a long time to Ugolinus Presbyteri, but they are certainly the work of Azo.[12]

Azo followed this same path of renovation when he decided to compose another original work: a collection of *brocarda*. *Brocarda* was a very peculiar literary genre which originated in the Anglo-Norman environment in the second half of the twelfth century. Following the quick reception of the use of legal arguments in the disputes, the Norman learned clergy started to compose lists of texts of Roman and canon law to be used in favor of or contrary to a certain general statement. The lists of those contradictory citations were arranged under *rubricae* and included the general abstract problem to be discussed with the support of the opposing authoritative texts. That is why *brocarda* were also called *generalia*, referring to the general propositions which formed the titles of each collection of contrary quotations. The *brocarda* were introduced in Italy by the glossator Otto Papiensis, who was acquainted with Anglo-Norman legal literature and took an older English compilation as the basis for his collection. In turn, Azo built on the foundation of Otto's work to compose a very rich and useful collection of arguments, which were often copied in the manuscripts and later printed in the books that contained his *summae*.

The composition of the *summae* and the *brocarda* shows how intensively Azo was committed to introducing Bologna to new forms of literary production besides the traditional writing of glosses that had made Bologna the very center of the study of Roman law from the university's foundation. On the other hand, Azo kept close to local tradition by composing his apparatuses and publishing a set of *quaestiones*. Since the age of Irnerius and Bulgarus, law professors in Bologna had grown accustomed to discussing cases in school to train their students to frame real life in legal categories, and to argue in favor of the plaintiff and the defendant by mobilizing the norms of Roman and canon law books as arguments.

The *quaestiones* of Azo did not share the same extraordinary editorial fortune of his *summae*, because the editors of the fifteenth and sixteenth centuries did not publish them as a printed book. However, Azo made a rather intense use of this genre, discussing cases that were already popular in the school, and adding new cases that he sometimes derived from his personal practical experience. Fourteen manuscripts collecting his *quaestiones* have been discovered so far, and modern editors have published some forty highly interesting texts.[13]

Azo: Roman law and social change

The *quaestiones* reflected a way to confront legal knowledge with real cases arising from social and economic life, so we can turn our attention to some cases Azo discussed to gain an idea of his attitudes towards the Christian society in which he—as everyone in his age—lived.

Azo has been considered a proud defender of the strict logic of Roman law against the influences of literature, theology, and even canon law. His *quaestio* 10 (edited by Landsberg) opens with a sharp remark against one of his students, the Frenchman Bernardus Dorna, who proposed a case inspired by the *Noctes Atticae* by Aulus Gellius and introduced the discussion declaiming some verses and quoting Ovid. Azo replied with a general remark about the method to be adopted by lawyers, which is also a statement for the authority of the law and the function of the jurist as its interpreter. He called for a bold rejection of the traditional rhetorical arts, including classical literature, because "we have to admire the poets, but not believe them." The jurist, proclaims Azo, shall rely only on the laws of Justinian.[14]

Azo is proudly aware of the great power given to the jurist by the force of the law he is called to interpret and apply to social reality. Sometimes the authority of the civil lawyer could empower attempts to change the balance of socioeconomic relationship. In particular, Azo engaged in seeking to loosen the very strong bonds of feudal society by calling for more liberty of property and less restrictive feudal, ecclesiastical, and seigneurial bonds. An example of his approach is found in a case involving the relationship of dependence between two ecclesiastical bodies. Despite the adoption of Roman law by ecclesiastical institutions, the economic relationships between churches were still marked by a hierarchy based on customary rules that hardly matched Roman private law criteria. A case in the *Quaestiones* offers a good example of how Azo struggled against these strongly rooted customs.

Around 1200, Azo proposed to his students for scholarly debate a case that (as we know from other sources) he had actually faced in court. In the narrative he offered for discussion in the *Quaestiones*, he reshaped the case slightly to better serve the needs of a scholastic exercise, but thanks to documentary and literary sources, we are able to reconstruct the facts pretty clearly.[15] Every year, for a long time, the bishop of Bologna used to receive a wagon laden with food and wine from the monks of St. Stephen. This homage was clearly a sign of subjection; but one year, the monks refused to pay this tribute, saying that it was not due, because until then they had given it only out of kindness (*caritative*). The question that arose from the case was whether the bishop could make a claim against the monks by possessory procedures. To deal with this question, it was necessary to ask whether the longstanding practice of receiving services or benefits could be framed at law as a form of possession. This was also a crucial issue for acquisitive prescription, or acquiring property by continuous possession, once the glossators had established on the basis of Roman law that this method of acquiring property applied only to assets of which one had lawful possession.

Azo strongly maintained that homage paid by giving or doing something was a pure act; as such, it lacked the characteristics of property rights and could not be possessed. He was perfectly aware that, on the contrary, some scholars were inclined to consider periodical giving as an atypical form of property. He mentions that such performances tended to be considered as a kind of irregular *servitutes*, that is easements, which, as real rights, were fit to be possessed: therefore, if the performance of homage were defined as easements, they could be defended with possessory procedures and acquired by the simple lapse of time. Azo rejected this argument:

> Why are we discussing real servitudes? I think that this provision (*procuratio*) is not a servitude but a periodical payment. . . . And there is not any servitude in the world which is not due by a corporeal thing, and that is why for real servitudes it is given a real action like the "confessoria" or other actions *in rem*. Indeed, the action *in rem* is naturally coupled with the possessory

> procedure, so that the one who can act at law for a property can also claim possession. But this payment is not due by a corporeal thing, and therefore it cannot be claimed with an action *in rem*, and then not even with a possessory remedy.[16]

In his final *solutio*, Azo concludes that a *procuratio* is a "very personal" relationship, and therefore cannot be treated under the law of possession.

In feudal society many relationships were based on personal bonds whose origins were very often quite ancient. The legal proofs of the ancient establishment of these relationships were usually lost, so that the lapse of time, the *vetustas* of the personal submission, had become the only proof of its existence, and that fact alone became the reason for the legal personal obligation. Treating these situations as involving purely personal obligations meant tying them to an original contract, excluding the lapse of time from the possible legal causes of their establishment.

But even though in his scholarly *quaestio* Azo concluded that a sharp distinction existed between real and personal rights—and, thus, that possessory remedies for recovery of services on the basis of a relationship of personal dependence were excluded—in the real trial discussed in court, things went the other way. Despite all his influence, Azo failed in supporting his position. His struggle to narrow the range of easements to the small number of types provided by Roman law was unsuccessful. Because the parties were ecclesiastical persons, the case had to be discussed before an ecclesiastical tribunal, and because the bishop of Bologna was one of the parties, the person who stepped in as judge was the bishop of the nearby city of Ferrara. Quite remarkably, the bishop of Ferrara was at that time the greatest of the contemporary canonists—Huguccio.

A former student of Azo, Roffredus Beneventanus, reports that Huguccio did not follow Azo's reasoning and ruled against him. Huguccio's reasoning was simpler but effective: if there is a difference between a possessory action and a petitory one, it is because in a possessory trial one has to prove only the fact and not the legal ground. In dealing with duties rather than goods, one cannot talk of a proper *possessio* but we must use the term *quasi possessio*. The logic of the procedure remains the same: if I claim by *quasi possessio* someone else's duty, the defendant cannot ask me for proof of the legal constitution of my right, because the possessory procedure deals only with the facts. Therefore, because the fact of the periodical performance of homage was proved, Huguccio ordered the *quasi restitutio* of it to the bishop.[17]

Some five years later, in 1205, Azo was engaged again in a dispute between two ecclesiastical bodies, and again he took the defense of the weaker against its superior.[18] Again, the core of the question concerned the legal institutions of *dominium* (*utile* and *directum*), possession, prescriptions, and real or personal rights in a way that was not strictly based on the sources of Roman law. In this case, Azo pleaded in behalf of the small church (*canonica*) of Mosciano, which had been subject to the large abbey (*badia*) of Settimo but wanted to protect some of the church's lands from the abbey's claim. We do not know how this case ended, because we only have the text of the *consilium* written by Azo to defend his client; but again, Azo tried to introduce elements of Roman legal reasoning into the hierarchical relationships between ecclesiastical bodies.

Azo defended the strict logic of the particular Roman law under consideration not as an expression of purely abstract scientific positions. On the contrary, the Roman law offered the best instrument to affirm some new values which were typical of the new Italian urban society. One of those values was personal freedom. After the death of Azo, yet while his pupil Accursius was still influential in Bologna, the city issued a statute, the famous *Liber Paradisus*, with which in 1257 the city ordered the freedom of no fewer than 5,682 rural serfs. Forty years earlier, however, the Bolognese city law was not so favorable to the peasants. The local customary law established that someone who had behaved as a dependent peasant for thirty years acquired a permanent *status*, which also affected his heirs, even if he did not express his will to be tied by a permanent bond.

In one of his *summulae*—in fact a very important treaty on the discipline of Roman colonates, or peasants—Azo mentions this earlier custom of Bologna as an evil one.[19] From his position of absolute prominence as the most distinguished law professor in the university, Azo openly declares that the custom of Bologna is "false" because there is a general rule in the Justinian Code that requires a double act to achieve a severe effect such as the worsening of one's personal condition and loss of liberty. In fact, a constitution of Justinian of 531 (C. 11.48.22) states that more than a single constitutive act is required to prove a worsened personal condition in order to avoid the risk of considering free men as serfs. Borrowing the very words of Justinian to criticize the Bolognese statute, Azo interprets the phrase as a "general rule," in order to apply it also to the case of proof based on a long period of time. If it is necessary to have more than one declaration for a permanent reduction of liberty, the simple lapse of time could not be sufficient either to create or to prove the personal condition of an alleged dependent peasant. Azo's logic goes further. If we need two elements to establish a dependent personal condition, and if the lapse of time can be only one of them, we need a second element, such as a written contract or at least testimony of an oral engagement. This engagement must precede the beginning of the prescribed time of thirty years.

Now, what Azo asked of the landlords of the Bolognese countryside was almost impossible: the personal condition of non-free peasants was not usually written down in any official contract, nor was it easy to obtain testimony of an unwritten agreement between lord and peasant which had taken place more than thirty years before the dispute about the peasant's status. By rejecting the proof of the personal condition based only on the lapse of time, the statement of Azo and of many other lawyers created many troubles for the landlords. Azo was using the authority of Roman law to defend a particular point of view: he wanted to provide good arguments to the peasants who came to the city seeking to avoid their lords' orders to recall them.

We know from different sources—Roffredus, Iacobus Balduini, and Martinus de Fano—that this argument was in fact used, and that communal judges tended to accept it in court. This is why we find the first written contracts of personal bondage shortly after 1200: the courts had started to reject the proof of bondage based only on the passage of time, so the masters asked their new serfs to sign a document as an additional proof of their status.

All of this demonstrates that the personal freedom to move and leave the land of the master, which quickly became a goal of the statutes of different Italian communes, began a bit earlier than we usually assume. And this process began with a different and unsuspected method: the use of Roman law. In the case of the liberation of peasants in Bologna, the statutes promulgated between the statement of Azo and the proclamation of the famous *Liber Paradisus* show a continuous trend towards favoring peasants' liberty.

Accursius and the medieval publication of scholarly writings

The large diffusion of Azo's writings was assured by the general spread of a particularly ingenious procedure adopted in Bologna to answer the increasing demand for scholastic texts by the growing number of students and practitioners.[20] Since about 1200, Bologna had developed a very effective system to reproduce manuscript books serially.[21] A selection of the most popular legal writings was held by a specialized dealer in his shop, called a *statio*. These texts were designed to serve as models for producing new manuscripts and were called *exemplaria*. They were not bound; rather, their pages were collected in loose booklets, which were rented to professional copyists, so that the same book could be copied by several copyists at the same time using different booklets. The customer paid the copyists for the production of a book, while the copyists rented the necessary *exemplaria* one booklet after the other. As various copyists were copying from different booklets of the same text, or *exemplar*, it was possible to produce many copies at the same time.

This new system of book production plays a significant role in this history, because Accursius, the author of the *Magna Glossa* and the most famous of Azo's pupils, was personally involved in the process. He held a rather large collection of *exemplaria* and probably began a very profitable business by establishing his own *statio*, where he rented out his own apparatuses along with the *exemplaria* of the writings of others, including the *summae* of his master, Azo. Exploiting his academic influence, Accursius managed to establish his own apparatus as the necessary companion for the actual text of all the parts of the *Corpus Iuris Civilis*. This was a difficult task, given the fact that he had to overcome the competition of another set of apparatuses, compiled by his colleague Hugolinus Presbyteri. Frank Soetermeer has convincingly suggested that Accursius was successful in this endeavor thanks to his own business as dealer of *exemplaria*: a statute of Bologna dated 1250 seems to refer to him as it prohibits book dealers from "exalting" one new apparatus over the others by refusing to lend some legal works to benefit a particular text.[22]

Accursius was born in the territory of Florence between 1182 and 1185. He moved to Bologna to study law in the school of Azo, but probably he received his *licentia docendi* under the supervision of Iacobus Balduini, who began teaching in 1213. This means that Accursius was around thirty when he became *doctor legum*. From then on, he taught for about forty years in Bologna, where he died almost certainly in 1263.[23] Among his students, only a few had successful careers: one was the canonist and future pope Sinibaldo Fieschi (Pope Innocent IV). Accursius married twice, having four known sons, three of whom earned law degrees: Franciscus, born around 1230 from the first marriage; and Cervottus (born in 1240 or 1241) and Guilelmus (1246) from the second. All three received their doctorates very early, between eighteen and twenty years old, and took advantage of the academic prominence of their father.

Some ten years after the death of Accursius, however, his three sons had to leave Bologna because of the increasing hostility between the two political parties—the Ghibelline Lambertazzi party (to which the family of Accursius belonged) and the Guelphic Geremei party. Accursius's eldest son, Franciscus, moved to England to serve King Edward I and remained for a while to escape the persecution of the Ghibellines by the victorious Guelphs. But in 1282 he returned to Bologna, changed his political party to that of the winners, and was restored to his chair and his position in the city. This unscrupulous turnaround bought him a place in the *Inferno* of Dante (canto 15, v. 110), among the sodomites.[24]

Franciscus's political about-face was not his only sin, however. In 1291, Pope Nicholas IV answered a supplication of forgiveness sent by Franciscus for himself and for the soul of his father Accursius. They had committed the sin of usury by lending money to students and had received money in exchange for favorable treatment on exams.[25]

To take an exam with Accursius must indeed have been a rather scary experience. One of his students, Guido de Cumis, tells a couple of stories about the fury of the famous professor against Guido and another student during the exam. Having been brave enough to criticize one of Accursius's glosses, Guido was rejected, although he later became a law professor in Orléans. His colleague, on the contrary, was so disappointed that he became a Franciscan friar.[26]

Accursius's writings comprise a variety of genres. As a prominent lawyer, Accursius gave legal opinions to the city of Bologna and to private and ecclesiastical clients, and a few of these opinions are preserved.[27] Apart from his major work, the *Magna Glossa*, Accursius published at least one other scholarly writing: a *summa* of the *Authenticum* published usually in the collection of *summae* by Azo. As for Accursius's apparatuses, his *summa* also uses an existing work as a basis; the introduction is certainly the work of Joannes Bassianus, and we cannot judge how much of the rest is actually the work of Accursius. This use of parts of works written by other masters was relatively accepted in the context of medieval scholarship. But in the Bologna of Accursius, some voices began to raise complaints against this form of exploitations of others' work. Boncompagno, in his previously mentioned *Invectiva contra glossatores*, blames the glossators for compiling apparatuses using someone else's existing glosses: they commit theft, says the rhetor.[28] We cannot know if Boncompagno's main target was Accursius, but Accursius certainly had no scruples in including large parts of others' work in his own.

This general historical and biographical framework sheds a rather prosaic light on the greatest achievement of the scientific engagement of Accursius, namely the composition of his gigantic compilation of glosses to the *Corpus Iuris Civilis*.

However, we should not overlap the contingent situation that determined the extraordinary success of the work with the actual historical role it played for future generations. On the contrary, the overbearing academic power of the author lent authority to the gloss even beyond its function of explaining and coordinating the massive composition of Justinian. For example, it was Accursius who determined the inclusion in the medieval edition of the *Corpus Iuris* of the *Libri feudorum*, originally an account of feudal customs written by Obertus de Orto, on which Pillius de Medicina wrote a *summa* and an *apparatus* while teaching in Modena. Accursius decided to include the text among the collection of the *Novellae* of Justinian, as if it were new imperial legislation, and he used the apparatus by Pillius to compose his own, merely adding some new glosses. He worked in the same way on the other parts of the *Corpus*, using mainly Azo's apparatuses as a basis but reworking the existing glosses, adding some new ones, and giving a very uniform shape to the whole. In this way, Accursius determined the triumph and the accomplishment of the so-called school of glossators: after his apparatus, no other scholar attempted to substitute it with a new compilation of glosses to the whole of the *Corpus Iuris Civilis*, and his gloss remained the starting point for every new commentary.

Boncompagno and Dante are only two of the many intellectuals who raised sharp criticisms against the Roman law professors, often represented by the central figures of Accursius and his sons. However, opposition to the rapid and aggressive climb of the social class of jurists was inevitable. Azo and Accursius are among the first European intellectuals of the Middle Ages who were not clerics but lay people. In addition, they did not belong to noble families but had relatively humble origins. Their intellectual achievement and the substantial improvement of their social condition testify that in their time the study of law had already become a powerful social elevator.

In the meantime, the new culture based on the ancient legislation of Justinian provided powerful arguments to challenge some of the established social balances of power, as we have seen in the cases discussed by Azo. He was a contemporary of St. Dominic (born in 1170), while Accursius was nearly the same age as St. Francis of Assisi (born in 1181). Azo and Accursius, then, lived through the substantial social changes that led to the birth of mendicant orders, which were designed to address the new lay population of the growing cities and a new social class that was later called the bourgeoisie. This class was building a new moral and legal paradigm of life, based on the one hand on the new everyday morality quickly developed by the new theologians of the mendicant orders, and on the other hand on the new legal culture, largely influenced by the interpretation of Roman law. Azo and Accursius, beyond every possible criticism, made a fundamental contribution to this extraordinary change in Western culture.

Notes

1 Bellomo, *Common Legal Past*, 168; Cortese, *Il diritto nella storia medievale*, 177–9.

2 One of the most quoted glosses from Accursius's apparatus observes that a lawyer does not need to be an expert of theology, because everything can be found in the *Corpus Iuris Civilis*. Among the many scholars who have cited this gloss, see Kantorowicz, 123; and Bellomo, *Common Legal Past*, 180.
3 Savigny, *Geschichte des Römischen Rechts im Mittelalter*, vol. 5, 1–44.
4 Ibid., 9 footnote *g*, quoting Odofredus.
5 See Fiorelli; Fried, 64–6.
6 See Pertz and Hiersemann, 910–11: "Apud Bononiam civitatem Italiae Azo legum interpres optimus et renovator, cum esset apud legistas opinione celeberrimus hoc anno (i.e., 1220) decessit: non magister appellatur, sed dominus legum."
7 Lange, 258–9. See also Conte, *Servi medievali*, 259–75.
8 Dolezalek.
9 Lange, 124–9.
10 Azo (or maybe Boncompagnus: see next note), in the *Prooemium* to his *Summae*, offers his work to the students with these words: "Suscipiatis itaque amabiles et preclarissimi socii lucidum et favorabile munus quod mihi diutius postulastis. Tenetes quod nihil obscurum, nihil dubitabile, nihilque contrarium legibus invenietis." The prologue is found in the editions of the *Summae* of Azo printed in the fifteenth and sixteenth centuries, many of which are now freely readable online.
11 Boncompagni *Rhetorica novissima*, lib. 10 *de invectivis*, 1. *Invectiva contra glossatores*: "dum glosa glosam requirit, lumen queritur a tergo, sententia spernitur et in amphibologie mergitur laberinthum " (I quote from the new edition by Paolo Garbini, now in progress). Actually, the prologue in the printed editions of the *Summa* by Azo reads: "cum ad erudiendum super dubitabilibus patrocinium glossam requirit, lumen reperit a tergo, unde in erroris cadit sepissime labyrinthum." However, it is not quite certain that Boncompagno actually wrote the prologue for Azo: maybe "dixi" means that he only commented on it in school: see Goldin, 36, note 58.
12 See Weimar.
13 Landsberg; Belloni.
14 Azo, *Quaestio X*, ed. Landsberg, 73–4. Cfr. Cortese, *Il* Rinascimento, 39–40.
15 I have dealt at large with the sources about this case in Conte, "Vetustas," 62–8.
16 Landsberg, 75–82 (quaest. XI):

> *Item quare disputamus circa servitutes? Dico quod ista procuratio non est servitus, sed annua quaedam praestatio. . . . Nec aliqua servitus est in mundo quae non debeatur ex certo corpore et ideo data est propter servitutes realis actio sive confessoria aut actiones in rem. Actionem autem in rem naturaliter comitatur possessorium, ut qui rem potest vindicare ad eius possessionem possit aspirare. . . . Sed haec procuratio ex nullo certo corpore debetur, ideo non datur pro ea actio in rem, nec ergo possessorium.*

17 Roffredus, fol. 32va:

> *Et sententiam suam defendit tali modo Ugo: 'Nonne differt petitorium a possessorio? Certe sic: in petitorio oportet probare que dicit dominus meus* (sc. Azo), *sed in possessorio sufficit si probo me possedisse, et vim mihi illatam esse, ut superius dictum est. Unde ex quo probata est quasi possessio illius iuris, etsi non probem mihi constitutum, nihilominus est facienda quasi restitutio,' et ita dicit Ugo, et eum hodie multi sapientes sequuntur.*

18 This is the only preserved original document carrying a *consilium* by Azo. It was discovered in the Florence Archive and edited by Chiappelli and Zdekauer.
19 Critical edition of the *Summula de agricolis et censitis* in Conte, *Servi medievali*, 259–78.

20 Bellomo, *Saggio sull'Università*, 109–28.
21 Soetermeer, *Utrumque ius in peciis*, 183–95.
22 Ibid., 192. Frati, vol. 2, 28.
23 Fiorelli.
24 Full bibliography on the life and works of Franciscus in Soetermeer, "Recherches sur Franciscus Accursii"; and Menzinger.
25 Colliva, 448–9.
26 Gualandi; Brundage, 258, with further literature.
27 Colliva, 406–30; Bellomo, "Consulenze professionali e dottrine."
28 Boncompagni, lib.10 § 25:

> *Sunt autem quidam qui iuramenti vinculo se astringunt, quod facient apparatus. Unde antequam iurent videntur esse periuri. Verumtamen si iurarent quod furtum committerent absque nota periurii remanerent latrones, quoniam aliorum compilationes addendo vel minuendo aut enormiter variando sicut fures depilant, et depilatio nihil est aliud quam furtiva subtractio alieni laboris.*

Bibliography

Azo. *Un consulto d'Azone dell'anno 1205, ora per la prima volta pubblicato*. Edited by Luigi Chiappelli and Ludovico Zdekauer. Pistoia: Fratelli Bracali, 1888.

Bellomo, Manlio. *The Common Legal Past of Europe*. Washington, DC: Catholic University of America Press, 1995.

Bellomo, Manlio. "Consulenze professionali e dottrine di professori. Un inedito 'consilium domini Accursii'." In *Inediti della giurisprudenza medievale*, edited by Bellomo, 47–62. Frankfurt am Main: Klostermann, 2011.

Bellomo, Manlio. *Saggio sull'Università nell'età del diritto commune*. Rome: Il Cigno, 2004.

Belloni, Annalisa. *Le questioni civilistiche del secolo XII. Da Bulgaro a Pillio da Medicina e Azzone*. Frankfurt am Main: Klostermann, 1989.

Boncompagno, da Signa. *Rhetorica novissima*. Edited by A. Gaudenzi. *Bibliotheca iuridica medii aevi*. Vol. 2. Bologna, 1892.

Brundage, James A. *The Medieval Origins of the Legal Profession: Canonists, Civilians, and Courts*. Chicago/London: The University of Chicago Press, 2008.

Colliva, Paolo. "Documenti per la biografia di Accursio." In *Atti del convegno internazionale di studi accursiani*. Vol. 2, 381–458. Milano: Giuffré, 1968.

Conte, Emanuele. "Lapse of Time in Medieval Laws: Procedure, Prescription, Presumptions, Custom." In *Limitation and Prescription a Comparative Legal History*. Comparative Studies in Continental and Anglo-American Legal History, 33. Edited by D. Ibbetson, E. Schrage, and H. Dondorp, 69–89. Berlin: Duncker and Humblot, 2019.

Conte, Emanuele. *Servi medievali. Dinamiche del diritto comune*, 259–75. Roma: Viella, 1996.

Conte, Emanuele. "Summa Aurea." In *The Formation and Transmission of Western Legal Culture: 150 Books That Made the Law in the Age of Printing*. Edited by Serge Dauchy, et al., 22–4. Cham: Springer, 2016.

Conte, Emanuele. "Vetustas. Prescrizione acquisitiva e possesso dei diritti nel Medioevo." In *Uso, tempo, possesso dei diritti. Una ricerca storica e di diritto positivo*, edited by Emanuele Conte, et al., 49–128. Turin, Giappichelli, 1999.

Cortese, Ennio. *Il diritto nella storia medievale*. Vol. 2. Roma: Il Cigno, 1995.
Cortese, Ennio. *Il Rinascimento giuridico medievale*. 2nd revised ed. Roma: Bulzoni, 1996.
Dolezalek, Gero. *Repertorium manuscriptorum veterum Codicis Iustiniani*. Vol. 1, 499–503. Frankfurt am Main: Klostermann, 1985.
Fiorelli, Piero. "Accorso." In *Dizionario biografico degli italiani*. Vol. 1, 118–20. Roma: Enciclopedia Italiana, 1960.
Frati, Luigi, ed. *Statuti di Bologna dall'anno 1245 all'anno 1267*. Vol. 2. Bologna: Regia Tipografia, 1869.
Fried, Johannes. *Die Entstehung des Juristenstandes*. Köln: Böhlau, 1974.
Goldin, Daniela. *B come Boncompagno. Tradizione e invenzione in Boncompagno da Signa*. Padova: Centrostampa Palazzo Maldura, 1988.
Gualandi, Giovanni. "Un gustoso episodio della vita di Accursio e la data di composizione della Glossa Magna al Digestum Vetus." In *Atti del convegno internazionale di studi accursiani*. Vol. 2, 459–92.
Kantorowicz, Ernst. *The King's Two Bodies: A Study in Medieval Political Theology*. Princeton: Princeton University Press, 1957; Reprinted 1997.
Landsberg, Ernst. *Die Quaestiones des Azo*. Freiburg: Mohr, 1888.
Lange, Hermann. *Römisches Recht im Mittelalter*. Vol. 1: *Die Glossatoren*, 258–59. München: Beck, 1997.
Menzinger, Sara. "Francesco d'Accursio." In *Dizionario Biografico dei Giuristi Italiani*. Vol. 1, 900–1. Bologna: Il Mulino, 2012.
Morelli, Giovanna. "Accursio." In *Dizionario Biografico dei Giuristi Italiani*. Vol. 1, 6–9. Bologna: Il Mulino, 2012.
Pertz, Georgius Heinricus. *Monumenta Germaniae historica. Scriptorum*. Vol. 23: *Chronica aevi suevici*. Leipzig: MGH, 1925–33.
Roffredus. *Libelli iuris civilis*. Avignon, 1500; Reprinted Turin: Erasmiana, 1968.
Savigny, Friedrich Carl von. *Geschichte des Römischen Rechts im Mittelalter*. 2nd ed. Vol. 5 (1850), 1–44. Heidelberg: Mohr, 1834–51.
Soetermeer, Frank. "Recherches sur Franciscus Accursii. Ses Casus Digesti Novi et sa répétition sur la loi Cum pro eo (C. 7.47 un.)." *Tijdschrift voor Rechtsgeschiedenis* 51 (1983): 3–49.
Soetermeer, Frank. *Utrumque ius in peciis. Aspetti della produzione libraria a Bologna fra Due e Trecento*, 183–95. Milano: Giuffré, 1997. German tr. Frankfurt am Main, 2002.
Weimar, Peter. "Zur Entstehung der Azoschen Digestensumme." In *Satura Roberto Feenstra sexagesimum quintum annum aetatis compienti ab alumnis collegis amicis oblata*, edited by Hans Ankum, et al., 371–92. Fribourg: Éditions Universitaires, 1985.
Wijffels, Alain. "Glossa ordinaria or Glossa magna." In Dauchy, et al., *The Formation and Transmission of Western Legal Culture*, 24–8.

4 Sinibaldo Fieschi (Pope Innocent IV) (1180/90–1254)

Kathleen G. Cushing

Introduction

Sinibaldo de Fieschi (in Latin: Sinibaldus Fiescus) was born in Genoa sometime between 1180 and 1190.[1] The son of Count Hugh of Lavagna—the first to bear the name Fieschi on account of his office, which controlled the financial affairs of the German emperor—Sinibaldo was part of one of the most influential and wealthy noble families in northern Italy, which had connections in both the imperial government and the Church. Sinibaldo first studied law at Parma under the patronage of his uncle, Bishop Obizo of Parma. By 1213, Sinibaldo appears to have moved to Bologna to continue his legal studies, and it seems that he was awarded a degree in law, as a letter of Pope Honorius III in 1223, conferring a canonry at Parma on Sinibaldo, refers to him both as *magister* and as a papal subdeacon.[2] By 1226, Sinibaldo had been appointed as an *auditor litterarum contradictarum* in the papal Curia.[3] Following Honorius III's death in 1227 and the elevation of Cardinal Ugolino of Ostia as Pope Gregory IX, Sinibaldo was appointed in 1227 as vice chancellor of the Roman Church and was made cardinal priest of San Lorenzo in Lucina. His career in the Curia soon reaped further rewards, and in 1234 Sinibaldo became governor of the March of Ancona. It was during this time, and especially from 1238, that relations between the papacy and Emperor Frederick II became increasingly strained (see the following). Following Gregory IX's death in August 1241, Cardinal Goffredo of Sabina was elected as Celestine IV, but he died after a pontificate of just fifteen days. There followed a long vacancy until June 1243, when Sinibaldo was elected pope, taking the name Innocent IV.

During a pontificate dominated by the ongoing bitter struggle with Frederick II, which involved a lengthy absence from Rome between 1243 and 1250, and facing a serious financial shortfall as well threats from the Mongols, problems with the Eastern Church, and the frustrated attempts of the crusades to recover the Holy Land, Innocent IV wrote over an extended period an extremely influential commentary on the *Liber extra* promulgated by Gregory IX in 1234. Innocent's work, completed c. 1250–51, is titled the *Apparatus in quinque libros decretalium*, the transmission of which was both immediate and long enduring. Innocent's *Apparatus* was cited by contemporary jurists, and the commentary continued to be consulted up to the seventeenth century.[4] Innocent also continued the tradition of being a lawmaking pope and prepared three collections of his own decretals, collectively known as the *Novelle*. The first of these included twenty-two decrees from the First Council of Lyon, in 1245, that Innocent sent to the universities in August of that year. A second collection of twelve decrees was issued in 1246 and largely comprised parts of his decretal *Romana ecclesia*. Innocent finally confirmed the twenty-two decrees from Lyon and the twelve from 1246 and added eight further decrees in 1253.[5] In addition, he wrote commentaries on his *Novelle*, notably a commentary *Ad apostolicae dignitatis apicem* on the deposition decree against Frederick II promulgated at the Council of Lyon. Innocent died on December 7, 1254.

Major themes and contributions

Sinibaldo de Fieschi's career, and especially his pontificate as Innocent IV (1243–54), was extremely important in both ecclesiastical and legal terms for any number of reasons, although much of the historical focus has been concerned with the struggle with Fredrick II. His pontificate witnessed the removal of the pope and the Curia from Rome to France for seven years and the convening of the first General Council of Lyon, in 1245, which saw the emperor excommunicated *in absentia*, and which introduced important canons for the reform of ecclesiastical law and administration. But Innocent's pontificate is equally noteworthy in terms of his refinement of policies on crusade, the papally sponsored mission to the Mongols, and his own legal works, in which he justified his policies and profoundly shaped canonistic commentary for centuries, including through the incorporation of his decretals into the *Liber sextus* promulgated by Pope Boniface VIII in 1298. Although Innocent IV's pontificate has often been characterized as one where spiritual matters were almost completely subordinate to political concerns, his pontificate and legal commentaries profoundly shaped ecclesiastical law and administration, offering a justification for papal authority and jurisdiction, even over non-Christians, that surpassed even the ecclesiological visions of his predecessor and namesake, Innocent III, and his patron, Gregory IX. Innocent IV's decisive moves against Frederick II fundamentally altered the balance of political power in Western Europe, removing central Italy and the papal states from the jurisdiction of the emperor, and Innocent ultimately paved the way for French control of southern Italy until the end of the fifteenth century. This chapter addresses key aspects of his pontificate and his contribution to canon law thematically rather than chronologically.

The papacy and emperor Frederick II

During Sinibaldo's time in the Curia, the relationship between the papacy and the emperor deteriorated dramatically, although the origins of this dispute went back to the early thirteenth century. For much of his pontificate, Pope Innocent III (1198–1216) had supported the claims of the Hohenstaufen Otto IV to the imperial throne. Yet in 1210, after quarreling about imperial territorial claims in Italy, Innocent III turned to support the sixteen-year-old prince Frederick II, son of Emperor Henry VI and king of Sicily by hereditary right. One problem with Frederick was that his promotion to the imperial throne would have potentially given him the ability to rule the whole of Italy, something that the papacy could not countenance. Innocent III persuaded Frederick to make oaths that the two crowns would not be united, and that Frederick would abdicate as king of Sicily before being crowned emperor. This assurance was not kept, and in 1220 Frederick persuaded Innocent's successor, Pope Honorius III, to crown him as emperor without relinquishing the kingdom of Sicily. Thereafter Fredrick devoted the remainder of his life to the cause of uniting all of Italy under his rule. It was left to Gregory IX and Innocent IV to frustrate those ambitions.

Frederick's ambitions of unifying the kingdom of Sicily with the empire intensified conflicts that had lasted the previous thirty-odd years over the territorial integrity of the papal lands, including the Duchy of Spoleto and the March of Ancona, which Sinibaldo had overseen before his elevation. Gregory IX excommunicated Frederick for the first time in 1227 for failing to set out on crusade, although peace was agreed to after lengthy negotiations in 1230. Gregory condemned Frederick again in a letter of October 1236 for determining to proceed against the Lombards, and Gregory excommunicated him a second time in March 1239.[6] In the winter of 1239–40, Frederick advanced on the papal states, effectively imprisoning the pope in Rome; despite Gregory IX's attempts to summon a council in 1241, a Sicilian fleet attacked convoys bringing bishops to Rome and captured a number of them as well as two cardinals. When Gregory died in August 1241, the college of cardinals was reduced to nine in Rome plus the two in captivity and one, John Colonna, who was with the emperor.

When Sinibaldo was elected in June 1243, Frederick agreed to negotiate about the outstanding matters. The long negotiations resulted in Frederick's agreeing, in 1244, to restore the papal states, and Frederick met with the pope at Easter at the Lateran. But by July 1244, it was clear that continued mistrust remained over the emperor's intentions in Lombardy, and Innocent IV declared that peace was not achievable. Clearly recognizing the threat of physical coercion that the emperor employed as a tactic against a papacy established in Rome, Innocent secretly left Rome, first for Genoa and then to Lyon—technically within the empire but in practicality beyond the emperor's jurisdiction—where he reestablished the papal Curia. He would not return to Italy until after Frederick's death on December 13, 1250.

The first ecumenical council of Lyon (1245) and *Eger cui lenia* (*levia*)

Once established in Lyon, where he could call upon the protection of King Louis IX of France, Innocent convened a general council that sat from June 26 to July 17, 1245, which was attended by 150 clerics from France, Italy, and Spain as well as the Latin emperor of Constantinople, Baldwin II, among other laymen and a legation from Frederick II headed by Thaddeus of Suessa. The council was intended to deliberate on a wide variety of matters, including the schism between the eastern and western churches, plans for a new crusade to the Holy Land, the religious life, and the invasions of the Mongols (see ahead). While the *Constitutions* published by Innocent IV in August 1245 and sent to the law schools in Bologna and Paris reflected these issues, along with some important procedural rulings for the regulation of the appeals and canonical procedure, the main business of the council was the condemnation and deposition of the emperor, Frederick II.

Frederick II was charged at Lyon with a number of crimes: perjury for not relinquishing the kingdom of Sicily as he had sworn to do; violation of the peace; suspicion of heresy; the sacrilege of capturing and holding two cardinals; theft of church property in Sicily; and threatening and seizing papal territories in Benevento, the Marches, Tuscany, and Lombardy. The seizure of territory was likely among Innocent's gravest concerns. Although Thaddeus of Suessa offered an effective defense, it is clear from the sentence of excommunication and deposition promulgated by the council, and from the lively detailed account provided by Matthew Paris in his *Chronica majora*, that the principal business for Innocent IV was the condemnation of Frederick; the result was a foregone conclusion.[7] At the third session of the council, on July 17, the pope read a lengthy denunciation of Frederick and induced the council to depose the emperor *in absentia* while absolving his subjects from their oaths of fidelity. In his sentence, while reserving to the papacy and the cardinals the disposition of the kingdom of Sicily, Innocent called on the princes in Germany to elect a new emperor.[8] Frederick responded with renewed attacks in Italy and sent a letter to the rulers of Western Europe in which he protested against the sentence of deposition *in absentia*, challenged the pope's jurisdiction to depose an emperor, radically condemned the clergy's greed for power and wealth, and called for a radical reform that would strip the Church of its temporal wealth. His response was for naught. Frederick's death, on December 13, 1250, left Innocent IV the victor, if only by default.[9]

Sometime around 1246, Innocent issued the decretal *Eger cui lenia* (*levia*) in response to the protests made in Frederick's letter to the western rulers. It remains unclear whether Innocent was in fact the author of this decretal, given the extent to which it contained ideas about papal authority that differed significantly from the more moderate and nuanced position expressed in his *Apparatus* (see below), and authorship is sometimes attributed to Cardinal Rainer of Viterbo. In any event, *Eger cui lenia* (*levia*) was significant in that it offered a new interpretation of the Donation of Constantine, a text which—apart from Gregory IX's earlier letter condemning Frederick in 1239—had figured surprisingly little in debates about the relationship of ecclesiastical and secular power, and especially the temporal authority of the papacy. Already by the time of Gregory's letter, lawyers were questioning not so much the authenticity of the document itself as the legality of Constantine's grant, in that it presented an emperor conceding temporal authority to the papacy, a concession that some worried could be revoked, as Frederick II in fact had seemed to threaten in his letter of 1246. Drawing on the work of canonist Alanus Anglicus and Innocent III's decretals,

Eger cui lenia (*levia*) argued that, from the beginning, the pope, as the vicar of Christ, had inherited royal and priestly powers and "act[s] as a general legate on earth of the king of kings." Moreover, when Constantine conceded the empire to Sylvester, he did not bestow temporal or regal authority upon the pope but rather restored a power that the popes had always had. In this way, the decretal contended that Constantine himself received from the vicar of Christ and successor of Peter a duly ordered power of sacral rulership which thereafter he used legitimately. In very stark terms, *Eger qui lenia* (*levia*) claimed that the Church lawfully possessed the two swords because "the power of the material sword is implicit in the church but is made explicit through the emperor, who receives it from the church, and this power which is merely potential when enclosed in the bosom of the church becomes actual when it is transferred to the prince."[10]

On balance, many historians have argued that the Council of Lyon set a rather disturbing new tone for papal councils. Despite canons aimed at reforming canonical procedure and administrative practice and the management of Church debt,[11] no significant legislation addressed the reform of the Church, its spiritual welfare (apart from within the crusade provisions), and its pastoral life, and perhaps surprisingly the council profferred no condemnation of heresy. The *Constitutions* of Lyon, much like the accounts in Matthew Paris's *Chronica majora* and the *Brevis nota*, gave the impression that at Lyon, Innocent IV put secular political concerns over ecclesiastical ones. That he supported successive anti-kings Henry Raspe and William of Holland in Germany, used the mendicants to preach a crusade against Frederick II, and continued seeking to restore the kingdom of Sicily to the papal territory would, in part, support such an evaluation.

Crusade and the Mongols

By the middle of the thirteenth century, Latin Christendom's assumptions that Christianity and Islam occupied most of the world had been challenged by the discovery that a network of Nestorian Christians and others existed in Asia, although the West really did not become aware of the precise geographical extent and nature of this network until the time of the Fifth Crusade (1218–21) when the first reports of Chinggis Khan's (d.1227) campaigns of conquest reached Latin Christendom. Initially, the Mongols had been mistaken for a Christian army of a "King David," purportedly a relative of Prester John who had come from India and overrun Persia; this idea gained widespread currency through letters of Pelagius, the papal legate at Damietta, and Pope Honorius III. By 1223, however, Queen Rusudan of Georgia and King Bela of Hungary were reporting attacks by a strange and barbarous people who had come from the east. It was not until 1236 that a more precise understanding of the nature of the threat from the Mongols, or Tartars as they were known in the West, became apparent, when the Great Khan Ögödei (c.1186–1241) dispatched a large army westward to complete the subjugation of the western steppes, consequently sending refugees into Hungary and Romania. The Mongols inflicted devastating attacks on cities in Rus', capturing Kiev in December 1240, and subsequently defeated western armies in Hungary, Bohemia, Poland, and Silesia in April 1241. Although King Bela of Hungary received no help from his neighbors despite his pleas, by June 1241 Pope Gregory IX was calling for a crusade for the defense of Bohemia and Germany. In the spring of 1242, however, in a baffling turn of good fortune for Eastern Europe, the Mongols unexpectedly withdrew eastward, leaving Western Christendom to speculate on the likelihood and imminence of their return.[12]

The Mongol invasion of Eastern Europe had both an immediate impact and longer-term consequences. In the short term, it created chaos in Hungary and Poland while inducing fear and bewilderment across Latin Christendom, and the political re-alignments in Eastern Europe and the Middle East in the following decades would have far-reaching effects. The Mongol invasion also confronted a Latin Catholic world that already was in conflict with various schismatic and pagan neighbors and sharply divided by the clash between the papacy and the empire. With the death of Gregory IX in August 1241 and the long vacancy after Celestine's fifteen-day pontificate, it fell to Innocent IV to deal with these new forces from the east, both in practical terms and, more discursively, in understanding the nature of these invaders and their intentions.

Innocent IV seems initially to have sought to collect information about the invaders provided by letters from Bela of Hungary, reports from a refugee cleric from Rus' named Peter, who attended the Council of Lyon in 1245, and from other informants, from whom he learned that the Mongols received embassies favorably and did not mistreat them. Although one of the major purposes in calling the Council of Lyon in 1245 was "to find a remedy against the Tartars," it is clear that the intelligence Innocent received encouraged him to send ambassadors to the Mongols. It is, moreover, a measure of the significance he attached to the Mongol threat that he did not wait for the council in June but already in March and April sent three embassies of mendicant friars to the Mongols, the most celebrated of which was headed by Giovanni di Pian di Carpine.[13] Innocent appears to have given each embassy two letters addressed to the Mongol "king" and peoples: *Cum non solum* (March 13, 1245), in which he appealed for them to stop their attacks on Christians and other peoples; and *De patris immense* (March 5, 1245), in which he gave an exposition of the Christian faith and encouraged the Mongols to accept baptism. Giovanni's embassy left Lyon in March 1245 and arrived in Mongolia in July 1246, in time to be present at the election of the new khan, Güyüg (1206–48). Although the great khan sent a hostile reply in which he demanded papal recognition of his supremacy and claimed that kings who resisted him were guilty of opposing God's will, it is clear from Giovanni's detailed report that Innocent IV was above all interested in gaining intelligence about the nature of the Mongol enemies.[14] The extent to which he also planned for a crusade while undertaking diplomatic missions underlines the vision he would expound in his *Apparatus in quinque libros decretalium*, that the pope had jurisdiction over non-Christians and could even punish them (see ahead). Although in 1245–46 the battles against Frederick and the Eastern

Church as well as Louis IX's departure on crusade appear to have outweighed all other military preparations, Innocent continued to monitor the Mongol threat and arranged for a crusade to be preached in the spring of 1253 in Bohemia and Moravia and in 1254 in Estonia, Livonia, and Prussia.

Innocent IV as jurist

Innocent IV's legal training and expertise in canon and Roman law underpinned many of the decisions and policies he undertook as pope. He clearly saw himself as a lawmaking pope, a role shaped by Innocent III and Gregory IX, but also one that had been underlined in the mid-twelfth century by Gratian's emphasis on the papacy's role as supreme judicial authority in the Church. Although Gratian's *Decretum*[15] had harmonized the law of the Church in the mid-twelfth century, new ecclesiastical law continued to be promulgated, chiefly in the form of decretal collections that were derived from appeals to Rome and were quickly collected into what has been called private collections. By the 1170s, more systematic and thematically organized decretal collections were being compiled, the most important of which was the *Brevarium extravagantium* or *Compilatio prima* of Bernard of Pavia (c.1188–92), which became a model for most subsequent decretal collections and the first of five collections used in the law schools and the courts before 1234, the *quinque compilationes*, which in turn generated significant canonistic commentary.[16] These collections were eclipsed (and became known as the *quinque compilationes antique*) in 1234 by the *Liber extra*, which was also known as the *Decretals* of Gregory IX, a misleading term because it largely contained decretals from his predecessors from the *quinque compilationes*. The pope's chaplain, Raymond of Peñafort, was given discretion to edit the material as he saw fit, but *Liber extra* also contained some two hundred of Gregory IX's decretals, some of which had been specifically drafted for the new collection. In this respect, Gregory IX underscored a more self-conscious role for the pope in making definitive and authoritative collections. The rapid transmission of *Liber extra* was revealed in the writing of commentaries on it within a few years of its promulgation by Vincentius Hispanus (c.1236), Goffredus of Trano (d.1245), and especially Bernard of Parma, who drafted a marginal gloss on *Liber extra* in 1239 that he continued to revise until his death in 1261. Bernard's gloss became *ordinaria*, or standard, by the middle of the thirteenth century and is found in almost every manuscript of the collection. The most influential commentaries on *Liber extra*, however, were those written by Innocent IV and Cardinal Henricus de Segusio, or Hostiensis, who wrote a *summa* around 1252 and an extensive commentary before his death in 1271.[17]

However historians have evaluated and however we might evaluate Innocent IV as pope, there can be no underestimation of his brilliance as a jurist and of the significance of his contribution to canon law, in terms of both the codification of his own decretals and, especially, his commentary on *Liber extra*, the *Apparatus in quinque libros decretalium*, on which he seems to have worked over many years, completing it around 1250 or 1251.[18] In the first place, Innocent IV's laws were glossed by Bernardus Compestallanus junior before 1253 and by "Abbas antiquus" in 1260, and although Bernardus's gloss seems to have been regarded as *ordinaria*, Innocent IV's own gloss on his *Novelle*, which he included in his *Apparatus*, was equally influential.[19]

Any assessment of Innocent IV needs to take into account the articulation of papal authority and other concerns in his *Apparatus in quinque libros decretalium* and in his gloss on the *Novelle*, both of which offer a very different image of the pope's legal ideas than those revealed by his actions in the political events of his pontificate and especially by the decretal *Eger cui levia* (*lenia*), which we can assume was not his own work. Innocent's legal opinions, moreover, complicate the image of a pope infamously renowned for making an unequivocal claim for papal theocracy, for exploiting papal provisions to benefices (the papal right to nominate candidates to vacant benefices throughout Western Christendom), and perhaps especially for his establishment of the inquisition as a permanent institution in Italy, when he combined all earlier papal and imperial enactments in the decretal *Ad extirpenda* (May 15, 1252), which permitted torture of suspected heretics in cases of extreme contumacy.

Throughout his decretals and *Apparatus*, Innocent IV revealed the extent to which his canonistic thinking had been influenced by Innocent III. Some of his most significant contributions to the refinement of ideas about papal authority and legitimate political authority are found in his commentaries on Innocent III's decretals. Innocent IV in fact often offered more precision and even restrictions than Innocent III had done. An interesting example is found in his comments on the decretal *Novit* of 1204, written by Innocent III in light of the dispute between King John of England and King Philip Augustus of France regarding the latter's invasion of Normandy. Innocent III's attempts to intervene were challenged by French bishops, who claimed that the pope had no right to intervene in a feudal dispute tried in the king's court. Innocent III had claimed that he was not attempting to undermine the king's jurisdiction but was rather judging Philip regarding sinful conduct that had led to war. While accepting the validity of this argument, Innocent IV turned the case on its head by noting that any king who sought to bring a feudal case before the papal court on the pretext of the involvement of sin would face considerable difficulties, in procedural terms, in proving the sin.[20]

This concern with technical provisions, perhaps a reflection of his experience as an *auditor* in the papal Curia, can also be seen in Innocent IV's commentary on the decretal *Licet* of 1206 to the bishop of Vercelli, in which Innocent III ruled that appeals from secular courts to the papacy were to be received only in cases where the secular judge had been negligent, especially if an imperial vacancy meant that the appeal could not be heard by the emperor. Innocent IV, however, cautioned that this kind of appeal was permissible only in cases that pertained to the emperor's jurisdiction, given that, as had already been established, the empire was held from the papacy. He then produced a list of all the exceptional cases in which ecclesiastical courts could hear cases that normally pertained to the jurisdiction of secular courts, as when the empire was vacant (as Innocent III had noted), when a judge neglected to do justice to widows, in cases of sacrilege, and when judges disagreed.[21] It was, moreover, at the end of the exceptions that Innocent IV set out his position on the historical origins of legitimate political authority, arguing for transmission of authority in all spiritual and temporal matters from God, through Noah, and thence to the rulers of the Jewish people until Christ established his vicar in the pope. Here, while acknowledging that the offices and governing powers of the world were distinct, Innocent argued with reference to Innocent III's *Per venerabilem* that whenever it was necessary, recourse had to be made to the pope, because no superior judge existed.[22] From this reasoning it was a natural step to claiming, in his commentary on Innocent III's *Quod super his* of 1199, the pope's authority over non-Christians. While noting that it was not licit for the pope or the faithful to take away belongings, faith, lordships, or jurisdiction from infidels, Innocent IV argued that the pope had power not only over Christians but also over infidels *de iure* if not *de facto* as exceptions, which implied that legitimate government could exist among infidels.[23]

As significant as the previous positions were, one of the most far-reaching of Innocent IV's contributions to canon law involved the question of collective guilt and punishment. In his decretal of c.1245, *Romana ecclesia ceterum*, he cited Roman law in justifying the prohibition of collective excommunication, namely the excommunication of organized communities. Accepting the principle of Roman law that only individuals could face criminal proceedings and punishment, he argued that excommunication as a penalty for canonical crimes could not be applied to communities. It is evident from his own comments in the *Apparatus* that he was concerned about punishing innocents like infants and absent members of the community. As Peter D. Clarke has argued, Innocent IV limited the sentence to the guilty members of a community, and although this had been a longstanding tradition in canon law, it now had the force of law and, moreover, seemed to negate ideas of collective guilt.[24] Clarke further underscored the very careful juristic definition that Innocent had in his understanding of a community, not as a collective of individuals who could collaborate in doing something wrong, but rather as something beyond its members as the right to association. An organization could of course be liable for its actions, but Innocent drew an important distinction between collective and individual responsibility and the sanctions appropriate for each.[25]

An epitaph on the tomb of Innocent IV, originally in the basilica of Santa Restituta in Naples but now in the thirteenth-century cathedral that absorbed it, honors Innocent as the pope who laid in the dust the serpent Frederick II, the enemy of Christians. The contest with Frederick II was clearly a significant event in Innocent IV's pontificate, and one which no doubt informed the development of his legal thinking on papal authority. But to understand his pontificate solely in light of this is to underestimate the contribution he made to the canon law of the

Church. In the end, Innocent IV was a gifted jurist whose pontificate witnessed significant, and in the case of the Mongol invasions, unprecedented challenges. To see him as a pope who simply put political interests ahead of spiritual ones, however, would be a serious mischaracterization.

Notes

1 A complete list of Innocent IV's works in manuscripts and printed editions, together with a detailed bibliography of secondary literature, can be found in Pennington, *Bio-Bibliographical Guide to Medieval and Early Modern Jurists*, Report No. a276. For an excellent biographical overview, see Pennington, "Innocent IV, Pope."

2 *Regesta Honorii III*, 4592. Although it was held that this was evidence, *inter alia*, that Sinibaldo taught at Bologna before entering the papal Curia, it is difficult to reconcile this with Sinibaldo's presumed age along with conflicting theories that he served as secretary to Cardinal Ugolino (future Gregory IX) from 1217. See Sayers, 40–1.

3 Potthast, 7610.

4 Innocent IV, *Apparatus in quinque libros decretalium*.

5 First Council of Lyon (1245), in Tanner, 275–301 (English and Latin text]; another edition is available online at www.papalencyclicals.net/councils/ecum13.htm See also Kuttner; Kuttner, "Die Konstitutionen," no. XI, with "Retractationes," at 11–12; and Pennington, "Introduction to 'Concilium Lugdunense I.'"

6 With significant reference to the Donation of Constantine, Gregory argued that while the emperor received the power of the world at his coronation, the pope did not surrender the substance of his jurisdiction: Potthast, 10255.

7 First Council of Lyon (1245), in Tanner, 275–301. Paris, iv. 410–15, 419–20, 430–79. See also Pennington, "Introduction to 'Concilium Lugdunense I,'" 207–11 and Lunt, 72–8.

8 Sentence of Deposition, First Council of Lyon (1245), ed. Norman Tanner, SJ, *Decrees of the Ecumenical Councils* (as n.5), 275–301.

9 Frederick II, letter to the kings of Christendom (1246).

10 *Eger cui lenia*, 696–8. See Maffei, 78–82.

11 First Council of Lyon (1245), Tanner, 275–301.

12 This is a very simplified narrative. For fuller details and analysis, see Jackson.

13 See Giovanni di Pian di Carpine.

14 On Güyüg's perception of Innocent IV's letters and the nature of the embassies, see Jackson, 89–91.

15 See Atria Larson, "Graziano," Chapter 2 in the present volume.

16 *Quinque Compilationes antiquae nec non collectio canonum Lipsiensis*, ed. Emil Friedberg (Leipzig, 1882), 1–65.

17 See Kenneth Pennington, "Enrico da Susa, Hostiensis (1210–1270)," Chapter 5 in the present volume.

18 The nature of the *Apparatus* has led some to suggest that it may have begun as lectures in the schools in Bologna, and has been used as evidence that he taught at Bologna before entering the papal Curia.

19 Innocent IV, *Apparatus*.

20 On decretal 2.1.13 Novit, *Apparatus*, 194.

21 On decretal 2.2.10, *Apparatus*, 197–8.

22 Ibid., 198.

23 On decretal 3.34.8, *Apparatus*, 430.

24 Clarke, 26.
25 This was a position which, as Clarke shows, was widely accepted by his contemporary Hostiensis and later commentators; ibid, 27–8. For Innocent IV's contribution to the development of the notion of a juristic person or corporation, see Cortese, vol. 1, 236–40.

Bibliography

Clarke, Peter D. *The Interdict in the Thirteenth Century: A Question of Collective Guilt.* Oxford: Oxford University Press, 2007.

Cortese, Ennio. *Il diritto nella storia medieval.* Vol. 1. Rome: Il Cigno, 1995.

Eger cui lenia. Edited by Eduard Winkelmann. *Acta imperii inedita*, II, 696–98. Innsbruck: Wagnerischen Universitäts-Buchhandlung, 1885.

Frederick II. "Letter to the Kings of Christendom (1246)." In *Historia Diplomatica Friderici Secundi*, edited by Jean-Louis-Alphonse Huillard-Bréholles. Vol. 1, 391–3. Paris: Henricus Plon, 1860.

Giovanni di Pian di Carpine. *Ystoria Mongalorum.* Edited by Enrico Menestò, et al. *Giovanni di Pian di Carpine. Storia de Mongoli.* Spoleto: Biblioteca Centro studi medievali-Universita di Perugia, 1989; English translation by Christopher Dawson. Toronto: MART, The Medieval Academy Reprints for Teaching, 1980.

Innocent IV, Pope. *Apparatus in quinque libros decretalium* (Frankfurt, 1570). Available at https://works.bepress.com/david_freidenreich/46/

Innocent IV, Pope. *Les Registres d'Innocent IV.* Edited by Elie Berger. 4 vols. Paris: Ernest Thorin, 1884–1920.

Jackson, Peter. *The Mongols and the West, 1221–1410.* Harlow: Pearson, 2005.

Kantorowicz, Ernst. *The King's Two Bodies: A Study in Medieval Political Theology.* Princeton, NJ: Princeton University Press, 1957.

Kuttner, Stephan. "Decretalistica." *Zeitschrift der Savigny-Stiftung für Rechtsgeschichte, Kanonistische Abteilung* (1937): 436–70.

Kuttner, Stephan. "Die Konstitutionen des ersten allgemeinen Konzils von Lyon." *Studia et documenta historiae et iuris* 6 (1940): 70–131. Reprinted in his *Medieval Councils, Decretals and Collections of Law.* Collected Studies Series 126, no. 11. London: Ashgate, 1980.

Lunt, William Edward. "The Sources for the First Council of Lyons, 1245." *The English Historical Review* 33/129 (1918): 72–8.

Maffei, Domenico. *La donazione di Costantino nei giuristi medievali.* Milan: Giuffre Editore, 1964.

Melloni, Alberto. *Innocenzo IV. La concezione dell'esperienza della cristianità come "regimen unius personae."* Genoa: Marietti, 1990.

Melloni, Alberto. "Sinibaldo Fieschi (Innocenzo IV, papa)." In *Dizionario biografico dei Giuristi Italiani*, edited by Italo Birocchi, Ennio Cortese, Antonello Mattone, and Marco Nicola Miletti. Vol. 1, 1872–4. Bologna: Il Mulino, 2013.

Paravicini Bagliani, Agostino. "Innocenzo IV, papa." In *Dizionario Biografico degli Italiani.* Vol. 62, 435–40. Rome: Istituto della Enciclopedia Italiana, 2004. Available at www.treccani.it/enciclopedia/papa-innocenzo-iv_(Dizionario-Biografico)/

Paris, Matthew. *Chronica majora.* Edited by Henry Richard Luard. Roll Series. London: Longman, 1877; Reprinted Cambridge: Cambridge University Press, 2012.

Pennington, Kenneth. "Bio-Bibliographical Guide to Medieval and Early Modern Jurists." *a276*; with an extensive bibliography. Available at http://amesfoundation.law.harvard.edu/BioBibCanonists/HomePage_biobib2.php

Pennington, Kenneth. "Innocent IV, Pope." In *The New Catholic Encyclopedia*. Vol. 7, 473–6. Farmington Hills: Gale Publishing, 2002. Available at http://legalhistorysources.com/InnocentIVBiography.htm

Pennington, Kenneth. "Introduction to 'Concilium Lugdunense I (1245)'." In *The Medieval General Councils: From Constantinople IV (869/870) to Basle-Florence-Rome (1431–1445)*, edited by Alberto Melloni, 207–11. Corpus Christianorum Conciliorum Oecumenicorum Generaliumque Decreta 2. Turnhout: Brepols, 2013.

Piergiovanni, Vito. "Innocenzo IV legislatore e commentartore. Spunti tra storiografia, fonti e istituzioni." In *Gli inizi del diritto pubblico. 2. Da Federico I a Federico II.* Atti del Convegno, Trento, 20–22 settembre 2007, edited by Gerhard Dilcher and Diego Quaglioni, 195–222. Bologna/Berlin: Il Mulino, Duncker & Humblot, 2008.

Potthast, August. *Regesta pontificum Romanorum inde ab anno post Christum natum MCXCVIII ad annum MCCCIV.* Vol. 1. Berlin: Rudolf der Decker, 1874.

Regesta Honorii III. Edited by Pietro Pressuti. 2 vols. Rome: Ex Typografia Vaticana, 1888–95.

Sayers, Jane. *Papal Government and England during the Pontificate of Honorius III (1216–1227).* Cambridge: Cambridge University Press, 1984.

Tanner, Norman, SJ. *Decrees of the Ecumenical Councils.* Washington, DC: Georgetown University Press, 1990. (English and Latin text); Another edition is available at www.papalencyclicals.net/councils/ecum13.htm

5 Enrico da Susa (Cardinal Hostiensis) (ca. 1200–1271)

Kenneth Pennington

Introduction

Enrico da Susa (Latin: Henricus de Segusio)—later called Hostiensis after being named cardinal of Ostia—was born around 1200 in the small town of Susa in the Piedmont area of Italy, about fourteen miles (twenty-three kilometers) from the modern French border. Although biographers have connected him to the de Bartholomeis family, there is no contemporary evidence that he was a part of that family. He had a broad humanistic education before he studied law. In his works he quoted or cited Virgil, Horace, Ovid, Seneca, and Cicero, revealing his learning and interest in the classics. He also must have been introduced to philosophy. Salimbene de Adam (d. ca. 1287) praised him for his learning, his singing, his poetry, and his playing of the viol.[1] Rolandino da Padua (d. 1277) described him as learned in theology, natural science, and the Old and New Testaments as well as canon and Roman law.[2] He studied Roman law in Bologna with Jacobus Balduinus and Homobonus. Johannes Andreae wrote in his *Additiones* to Guillelmus Durantis's *Speculum iudiciale* that Enrico studied canon law with Jacobus de Albenga, but Enrico never named a particular master in his works.[3] He did refer often to a *dominus meus*, who scholars have assumed was Pope Innocent IV but on very tenuous evidence.

Like two other important late thirteenth-century French canonists, Guillelmus Durantis and Johannes Monachus, Enrico pursued advancement in the ecclesiastical hierarchy, not in a law school classroom. His career centered in northern France, England, and, particularly, southeastern France. Perhaps unknown family connections and affiliations influenced his advancement up the ranks in the French church. In any case, Enrico was a jurist who worked between two cultures.

He never seems to have taught at Bologna, but he did teach at Paris for a time.[4] Although a number of modern authorities state that the passage of his commentary in which he mentioned teaching is datable to 1239, no evidence supports that claim. Certainly after he became bishop of Sisteron in 1244, he held offices that would have normally precluded a teaching career. Nevertheless, because of his status, his connections to the universities must have been close throughout his life. The masters at Bologna sent a *quaestio* for him to resolve after he became cardinal, and he took great care in his testament to have corrected copies of his *Lectura* on the Decretals sent to Bologna and Paris after his death.

Career

After studying at Bologna, Enrico became the prior of the cathedral church of Antibes in Savoy sometime during the 1230s. The first datable reference to his holding this office is 1239. He made a number of references to the Savoy region in his works. His horizons soon expanded far beyond the Duchy of Savoy. Although his movements are very difficult to trace with certainty, by 1240 he had acquired benefices in England and had become archdeacon in Paris. During this time, he must have taught canon law in Paris. He had also begun his *Summa* on the Decretals. He mentions the year 1239 in the text of his *Summa* as being the current year in one passage, and, since he mentions that an early draft was destroyed by fire in a colophon appended to the *Summa*, he must have already begun a second draft by this time. He referred to a teaching career in Paris in many glosses, citing French theologians Hugh of St. Cher, William of Paris, and Phillip of Aix, who were active in the 1230s.

In 1244 Enrico became provost of Grasse. On December 6, 1244, Bertrand, bishop of Grasse, and his provost issued new statutes governing the diocese. These statutes granted the provost and cathedral chapter significant authority in diocesan affairs. In his legal commentaries, Hostiensis emphasized the rights of cathedral chapters and of the Roman cardinals to share authority with their respective prelates, bishop, and pope. These statutes seem to have been an extension of his thought into the real world of ecclesiastical government. During the time that Hostiensis was prior, and then provost of Antibes and Grasse, he made several trips to England.

In 1243 the bishop of Avignon, Zoën Tencararius—a canonist who wrote an important apparatus of glosses on *Compilatio quinta*, the last major canonical collection before Pope Gregory IX's decretal collection replaced all earlier collections—appointed Enrico bishop of Sisteron. He also became a papal chaplain at this time, and in 1250 he was translated to the larger and more prosperous archbishopric of Embrun. Pope Urban IV promoted him to cardinal bishop of Ostia in May 1262. Because of the title attached to his new office, later jurists and modern historians normally refer to him as Hostiensis. We do not know much about his role within the papal curia after he became cardinal. We may assume that the references he made to court cases in the second recension of his *Lectura* are quite likely those in which he may have been involved. His long discussion of the case of the royal abbey Notre-Dame of Jouarre, for example, is probably due to his participation in the case,[5] but he gave no indication what his role might have been.

Hostiensis participated in the long papal conclave in Viterbo after Clement IV's death in 1268, but withdrew from the proceedings because of illness. He wrote an extensive discussion of a cardinal's right to renounce his electoral rights in the second recension of his *Lectura* and mentioned his personal circumstances.[6] Even though Hostiensis was not present when the cardinals finally elected Pope Gregory X on September 1, 1271, the cardinals solicited his assent to their choice. By this time he was gravely ill. On October 29, 1271, he drew up his testament in Viterbo. He died shortly afterwards, on either November 6 or 7, 1271.

Hostiensis's testament is a valuable guide to his last wishes and to his personal relationships at the end of his life. He requested that if he died at or near the Roman Curia, his body should be buried in the nearest Dominican church. If far from the Curia, he wished to be buried in the metropolitan church of the province. Several modern authorities state that he died in Lyon and was buried there in the Dominican convent. Not only is there no evidence for this, but it is completely improbable that a dying man would have undertaken such a long journey. The papal Curia was not in Lyon. If he was buried in accordance with his wishes, we do not know with certainty where. Thomas Diplovatatius reported that Hostiensis was buried in the cathedral church of St. Lawrence in Perugia. If so, when the Romanesque church was replaced by the present structure (1345–1490), the monument did not survive. Perugia is an exempt bishopric subject only to the Holy See. If Hostiensis was buried in Perugia, he may have died there on the way to wherever it was that he wished his final resting place to be.

Works

Hostiensis's first systematic work was his *Summa* on the *Decretals of Pope Gregory IX* finished around 1252/1253, while he was archbishop of Embrun.[7] Although modern authors often refer to it as the *Summa aurea*, this name was not given to it until the Roman edition of 1477 (Hain 1860). Other early editions simply call the work *Summa*.[8] The manuscripts refer to it as *Summa* or *Summa copiosa* or *Summa copiosa, siue caritas*.[9] In his testament, Hostiensis called it simply "my *Summa*." The later extended titles are almost certainly the product of others.

Hostiensis had worked on his *Summa* since the 1230s. In a colophon, he wrote that he began the *Summa* while in *minori officio* and completed it in *officio maiori*. The texts of the printed editions confuse Hostiensis's statement slightly and have misled historians. The following passage is based on the readings in two reliable, early manuscripts—Munich, Staatsbibl. 14006 and 15707:[10]

> Although I have had many issues and also difficult and diverse affairs that have distracted me, with the help of Him in whom I have always hoped and who has instilled in me power to write this difficult and almost impossible work that I had begun in minor office, then it was destroyed by fire, and while I was in a higher office I took up the task again and finally I finished it, thanks to the Lord.

The reference to his having held a minor office probably is not an allusion to the priorship of Antibes, which he would not have considered minor, but could refer to an earlier period when he was called a simple *clericus* in a document from the court of Raymond Berenger dating, most likely, before 1234. Most modern authorities have assumed that references in the *Summa* to Hostiensis's teaching career in Paris and to the current year being 1239 must be parts of the *Summa* that survived the fire. The implication of the colophon is that nothing survived. A more likely explanation is that these passages are from after the fire. Since the *Summa* is cited in his *Lectura* to the *Novellae* of Innocent IV and since he does not mention any events or legislation after Innocent's pontificate, a date of 1253 for the *Summa* is probable.

Placentinus's and Azo's *Summae* of Roman law, and Goffredus de Trano's *Summa* of canon law provided the primary models for Hostiensis's *Summa*, which examines the topics and subjects of canon law by discussing each subject area, and not by explicating each decretal. Since many legal issues in canon law were also important in Roman law, he sometimes borrowed from Azo almost word for word. Hostiensis wanted to cover all aspects of canon law in his *Summa*, and to do this he had to add fifty titles to his *Summa* that were not in the *Decretals*.

In his introduction to his *Summa*, Hostiensis quoted a poem that should give guidance to any beginning law student:[11]

> *Si quis forte cupit iurisconsultus haberi*
> *Continuet studium velit quocumque doceri.*
> *Invigilet nec vincat eum tortura laboris,*
> *Fortior insurgat cunctisque recentior horis,*
> *Nam labor improbus omnia vincat.*
> (Who wishes to be considered a jurist
> Should seek knowledge under someone learned.
> Beware that the burden of his studies conquer him,
> Let him arise stronger than ever,
> For magnificent labor conquers all!).

His last line was a quotation from Virgil's *Georgics* (Book 1, line 147), and the poem was quoted often by later jurists. Hostiensis may have been the poem's author. He then turned from poetry to philosophy by citing Aristotle to justify his conviction that Abelard's methodology of constant doubt was a guidepost for him:[12]

> *Studiosus vero debet dubitare de singulis; hoc enim non est inutile secundum Aristotilem, ergo nihil debet negligere.* (Indeed, a scholar must doubt in all things; this doubt is not useless according to Aristotle, therefore nothing should be overlooked).

The maxim reflects Hostiensis's methodology: a thorough and expansive exploration of legal issues characterized his work. He was also a prescient textual critic and warned his readers about ten pitfalls when they studied, read, or practiced law. He labeled these "hasty conclusions," and most of them are as relevant today as they were in the thirteenth century.[13]

> First, a jurist should never judge before he understands the issues of a case. Second, a jurist should read the evidence again and again before he decides fault. Third, documents should be carefully examined for errors. For example, "is" is very different from "is not," but a scribal error can easily change one into the other. Do not accuse the author for a mistake of the scribe. Fourth, do not condemn the writings of others from envy. Fifth, a jurist should always carefully cite the opinions of others and should name the authors of contrary opinions. We read works in order to know them, some works so that we do not ignore them, and some works to reject them. Sixth, a jurist should consider the mind of the writer and whether he advocates the strict rigor or the spirit of the law, and whether the law in question is positive or customary law. He should also consider the persons, reasons, places, times, and other circumstances. Seventh, the jurist should never hold his own grand opinion rather than the truth. Eighth, the jurist should never reject the opinions of prior jurists and texts without considering the new law (*ius novum*) carefully. Ninth, the jurist who attempts to delete superfluous words can eliminate texts that are necessary and useful. As my lord used to say, they cannot easily transform difficult and complex passages into brief texts because when I am brief I am obscure. Tenth, a jurist should avoid clinging to the strict wording of a text rather than the intent and truth of it.

His ninth hasty conclusion was reflected in his work. In his discussion of crusader vows, Hostiensis took to task the compiler of Pope Gregory IX's *Decretals*, Raymond de Peñafort, for deleting words from Pope Innocent III's decretal.[14] An even more dramatic example of his rejecting Raymond's editing was his commentary on *Ad liberandum*, Innocent III's conciliar decree that summoned Christendom to enlist in a new crusade. Raymond had radically shortened the decree. With a not-so-subtle but tacit rebuke of Raymond's editorial skills, Hostiensis inserted the entire decretal into his *Commentary* on the *Decretals* and glossed the parts that Raymond had omitted extensively.[15]

Unlike Azo and other jurists, there is no manuscript evidence that Hostiensis revised or inserted *additiones* to his *Summa* after 1253. After he had become cardinal, however, he did respond to a request from Bologna to clarify a statement that he had made under the title *De sententia excommunicationis* about the responsibility of a cleric to obey a command of his prelate. He wrote a *quaestio* discussing the problem at length and sent it to Bologna. From the number of French manuscripts that contain it, we may infer that he probably also sent it to Paris. Some university scriptoria appended it to manuscripts of his *Summa*; others incorporated it into the title in which the question had first arisen. All the printed editions contain this third stage of the *Summa*'s text.[16]

Hostiensis's *Summa* enjoyed enormous popularity. Almost one hundred manuscripts are extant. It remained a standard text of canon law until the early modern period. It was printed for the first time in Rome, in 1473 (Hain 8959), and many other editions followed. It is quite misleading, however, to assume on the basis of the manuscripts and the printed editions that the *Summa* was much more influential than the *Lectura*. First, Martin Bertram has compiled an extensive list of manuscripts (more than fifty) of the *Lectura* that survive. Second, one cannot evaluate the influence of a work by simply counting manuscripts. Every canon lawyer and Roman lawyer who wrote after Hostiensis knew his *Summa* and his *Lectura* and used them both extensively.

Shortly after completing his *Summa*, he wrote a commentary on Innocent IV's new legislation and the First Council of Lyon conciliar canons that were called *Novellae*. He did not comment on the final version of the *Novellae*, but the one that P.J. Kessler calls the Collection of 37 chapters, plus *Novella* 40 and three *extravagantes* (*Is qui*, *Sane quia*, and *Ad perpetuam*). Bertram has discovered many more manuscripts (twenty-five) than were previously known. Thus the work was more influential than historians have assumed. Since all these texts were included in Pope Boniface VIII's *Liber Sextus*, there was no longer much point in copying this work after the *Sextus* was published. Hostiensis's commentary on the *Novellae* was widely used and disseminated. In two printed editions—Paris 1512 and Venice 1581—the printers appended his work to Book 5 of his *Lectura*, which is the same arrangement found in many manuscripts.

Hostiensis's most important work was his *Lectura* on the *Decretals of Gregory IX*, or if we adopt the name he gave it in his testament, *Commentum super decretalibus*.[17] He labored on this commentary over a long period, finishing it definitively only at the end of his life. He wrote two versions of the work. The first, which survives in only one manuscript, was finished sometime before the pontificate of Pope Clement IV (1265), whom he does not mention. The text is almost completely preserved as a marginal gloss in an Oxford manuscript, New College, 205. The Oxford manuscript lacks Hostiensis's commentary on *Rex pacificus*, which, from references to it later on in the text, was part of the original.

He refers to several datable events in the text of the Oxford manuscript that establish, if only roughly, a *terminus a quo*. He mentions that he currently held the office of archbishop of Embrun and that Innocent IV was dead. When he discussed the proper calculation of the indiction in a dating clause, he chose the year 1262 as his example. That was quite likely the year in which he wrote the passage. Thus, it seems that this version of his *Lectura* was probably completed between 1262 and 1265. The care that Hostiensis took when he stipulated in his testament that copies of his final version of the *Lectura* be sent to Bologna and Paris indicates that he wished to ensure that his earlier text was replaced.

In the last recension, completed at the end of his life, Hostiensis expanded the text in the Oxford manuscript considerably, doubling its size. He did not delete material from the Oxford manuscript but added much. These additions range from sentences and phrases inserted into earlier glosses to the addition of entirely new glosses and writing additional glosses to texts that he had already discussed (that is, creating doublets to some lemmata). He also wrote new glosses to words he had not commented on before. Hostiensis began revising his *Lectura* during the pontificate of Clement IV. The later recension of his text included many references to court cases and decisions that are omitted from the earlier. The famous passage in which he discussed a cardinal's right to renounce his participation in a conclave and his own difficulties at Viterbo may have been a late addition to a work that was already substantially completed.[18] Although the text of the *Lectura* is preserved in many manuscripts, there were only three editions: Paris 1512, Strasbourg 1512, and Venice 1581. Although the Venice edition was chosen to be reprinted in 1965, the Paris and Strasbourg editions are far superior to it.

Three minor works may be attributed to him, two with certainty and one with doubt. Hostiensis wrote a tract on conducting an episcopal election using one of the three procedures employed for ecclesiastical elections: compromise. The tract begins with a text that outlined the procedure to be used for an election by compromise. It may be connected to an unknown election in which he played a part. The tract has glosses that have the sigla of Hostiensis in some manuscripts. The evidence points to the tract having been written between 1253 and 1262.[19] He also prepared an abbreviation of his *Lectura* titled *Diamargariton*.[20] This manuscript contains excerpts from his *Summa* and his *Lectura* but is not of great juristic interest. Although the prologue makes Hostiensis's authorship fairly certain, the text must still be examined to determine whether it includes any passages from the second recension of his *Lectura*. If any were found, they would cast serious doubt on his authorship, as he very likely could not have finished an abbreviation of his *Lectura* in the short time that remained to him after its completion.

We do not know if Hostiensis attended the First Council of Lyon. His name is not in any of the attendance lists we have and does not appear in any of the narrative sources. It is possible but not certain that he did. Nevertheless, John A. Watt has argued that he wrote a short tract written at the council supporting the deposition of Emperor Frederick II.

Hostiensis's testament reveals how carefully he planned to have his juristic legacy live on in the schools and in the courts. He gave copies of the second recension of his *Lectura* to the University of Bologna, the cathedral church of Embrun, the University of Paris, the vice chancellor of the Roman curia, and the new pope. He gave copies of his *Summa* to the vice chancellor and to Paris.[21]

Jurisprudence

In his *Prologue* to his *Summa*, Hostiensis presented his views on the relationship of law to human beings, of law to theology, and of law to society. He lived in a time when positive law began to replace customary law. Consequently, he extolled written law and reminded his readers of the weaknesses of customary law, even the customary law of the Roman Curia:[22]

> I counsel whoever would have a perfect understanding and knowledge of law to adhere to the written law rather than to the customs of the Roman

> curia, although some argue that her customs should be preferred. I say this, however, because custom is weak and uncertain and varies frequently, today it is a white precious stone and tomorrow a black piece of coal.

After he had outlined in the *Prologue* to his *Summa* the ten hasty conclusions that every lawyer and student should avoid, he followed in the footsteps of Gratian and placed human rights in the center of the legal universe. He explained the importance of natural law and reminded his readers that natural law consisted of two principles. The first he captured by a couplet:[23]

> What you wish be done to you, do to me;
> Do not what you do not want for yourself;
> Then you may live on earth according to the justice of heaven (*ius poli*).

The origins of this couplet are not clear. Bernardus Parmensis had inserted it into his *Ordinary Gloss* to the *Decretals of Pope Greogry IX*, from which Hostiensis may have taken it.[24]

Hostiensis's second principle went to the heart of social justice in a society:

> Natural justice dictates that no one should become richer to the detriment of others. The Roman law jurists say this is a principle of the law of nations (*ius gentium*); however, they should consider this truth: according to the law of nations who is stronger is richer.

He argued that human beings created the law of nations with customary usages. This law created a society burdened with inequalities in social status and wealth because human laws created and permitted injustice. Human laws do not always conform to divine justice, but laws that are justly promulgated are based on natural law. Natural reason must be rendered through just laws. Human reason played a central role in law. Hostiensis made the relationship clear:[25]

> In the time before Mosaic law, there were three laws, namely common natural law, rational natural law, which is nothing other than natural reason (of human beings), and the law of nations.

As the human race multiplied, Mosaic law was promulgated, then Athenian and Roman laws. In the end, canon law encompassed all law, divine, public, and private human law.

Canon law, Hostiensis argued, is not completely theological or civil but both. It can be called the *scientia scientiarum*, the science of sciences or the "queen of all knowledge." Although civil law (Roman law), he wrote, makes that claim for itself, canon law reigns over all spiritual and temporal matters and must be received and obeyed by everyone. One can perceive through natural reason that canon law is worthier and superior to all other laws. To prove his point, Hostiensis made an intriguing comparison between a mule, a horse, and a donkey to demonstrate canon law's superiority. Scholars have debated what he meant by his comparison.[26] Isidore of Seville's *Etymologies* was the probable source for what Hostiensis knew about mules; id est "mules;" Isidore had repeated what Pliny the Elder had observed about mules being the infertile offspring of two different species. When Hostiensis wrote his *Summa* in the 1250s, he thought this product of the natural world might resemble the birth of canon law in the medieval academic and intellectual world:

> Just as what is created by nature has more dignity and is greater than all others, so too our field surpasses all others. . . . Indeed, theology is the knowledge of the spiritual person, Roman law of the human person, thus canon law can be said and ought to be acknowledged by men who have adopted it as being above the others. Is the species of the mule greater and more worthy than the horse and donkey? It is clear because the horse represents theological knowledge and the donkey the knowledge of Roman law you could compare them, but I do not want to come to a conclusion.

Years later, in his *Lectura*, Hostiensis repeated his tentative analogy but came to a firm conclusion; the change is an example how his thought evolved as he aged:[27]

> Does it follow by the power of that analogy (that is, horse, donkey, and mule) that Roman law is a donkey and canon law a mule? It is not appropriate that we compare the human genus to beasts.

He did not waiver in his conviction that theology and Roman law were the foundations of canon law; however, canon law elevated both to a higher level.

How may we think of human beings and their relationship to human laws? Hostiensis had a simple answer. Justinian's codification, Lombard law, and feudal law established fundamental principles that he called "legal wisdom which does not permit men to live in poverty nor to suffer the fear of death."[28] In conclusion, he wrote that there are two jurisdictions, although one is greater than the other, and everyone shall be judged by his own law. Both jurisdictions, however, must obey the ecclesiastical canons. The Holy Trinity confirms that there are three genera of men—lay, secular clergy, and religious. These three genera are united in the sacred communion of the Church and the Catholic faith.[29]

Unlike most of his contemporary jurists, Hostiensis wrote his works over a long period of time and revised his *Lectura* in the last years of his life. The Oxford manuscript of his *Lectura* is invaluable because one may now trace changes in Hostiensis's thought between his first and last recensions. Hostiensis changed his mind about many issues. One of the most interesting and profound changes for later jurisprudence was his opinion whether non-Christians could possess legitimate sovereignty. Three centuries later, the legitimate dominium (sovereignty) of "infidels" became a vigorously debated question in the Age of Exploration, especially in Spain. Many jurists rejected or embraced his views on the legitimate dominium of infidels, but none ignored them. Modern scholars have also given extensive attention to his thought as a touchstone for measuring and understanding the European conscience of conquest. None of them knew that he decided only late in life that non-Christians did not possess just dominium, perhaps reflecting renewed enthusiasm for crusades in the late 1260s and early 1270s. In his first recension of the *Lectura*, he wrote a gloss to an old conciliar canon (*Canonum statuta*) promulgated at the Council of Meaux-Paris in 845/846 that had nothing to do with just dominium but did treat the jurisdiction of canonical statutes. Hostiensis expanded the question to include non-Christians:[30]

> *Aliis etiam quam subditis non potest lex imponi, ut C. de incest. nup. Neminem* <Cod. 5.5.2> *et pagani et infideles non sunt subiecti, infra de diuort. Gaudemus, respon.* i. <X 4.19.8> *ideo nec par astringitur, ut infra de elect. Innotuit* <X 1.6.20>, *ff. de arbit. Nam magistratus* <Dig. 4.8.4>. (A law cannot be imposed on anyone who is not a subject . . . Pagans and infidels are not subject [to the pope] . . . their sovereignty cannot be compromised by an equal).

This is a good example of how the canonists did not limit themselves to the narrow boundaries of the subject of the text when they commented on canonical case law. Here Hostiensis noted that the pope could not issue laws binding peoples who were not subject to him, and he specifically exempted pagans and infidels from papal sovereignty. Hostiensis cited Innocent III's decretal *Gaudemus* as a proof that infidels had their own law, which bound them even after they became Christians and even if their law violated canonical precepts.

Hostiensis changed his mind completely when he revised his *Lectura*. In his second recension, he wrote a long gloss to a decretal of Pope Innocent III, *Quod super his*, in which he argued that the pope had jurisdiction *de iure* (as a right) over all infidels.[31] At the birth of Christ, all honor, *principatus, dominium, et iurisdictio* was translated to Christians. When he revised his commentary, Hostiensis did not edit his comments on *Canonum* to bring them into agreement with those at *Quod super his*. The early manuscripts of his second recension of *Canonum* have the same wording as in the Oxford manuscript.[32] Jurists noticed the discrepancy. In later manuscripts, and in the printed editions, the crucial passage in *Canonum* was revised to conform to his views expressed in his remarks on *Quod super his*. The passage then reads, with interpolations in roman:

> *Et pagani et infideles non sunt subiecti spiritualiter, infra de diuort. Gaudemus, respon.* i. <X 4.19.8> nam temporaliter subsunt, quod dic ut plene not. Infra de uoto, Quod super his § Rursus <X 3.34.8>. Aliis igitur quam subditis non potest quis legem imponere, *ideo nec par astringitur, ut infra de elect. Innotuit.* <X 1.6.20> (Pagans and infidels are not subject to the spiritual realm . . . but they are temporally subject as I have noted fully in my commentary on *Quod super his*. . . . No one can impose a law on others, only on subjects, because an equal may not infringe upon the rights of an equal.)

Hostiensis's authoritative opinion became especially relevant in the sixteenth century, when jurists and theologians debated the rights of natives in the New World.[33]

The extent and limits of political power were a central theme in Hostiensis's writings. He conceived of papal power in grand terms and established the terminology of power that was adopted by every Roman and canon law jurist who wrote after him. He conceived of papal absolute power (*potestas absoluta*) as a transcendental authority. He defined the pope's highest power as his freedom to abrogate or derogate positive canon law but also to perform judicial acts that previously had been outside the competence of human rulers, even the pope. Hostiensis now argued that the pope could dispense from divine law because he was the vicar of Christ and represented divine authority on earth. Hostiensis employed the term *potestas absoluta* to describe the pope's authority to dispense from the laws of marriage, from the monastic vow, and from the *status ecclesiae*, the constitution of the Church that Christ established, even though these elements of canon law were established by divine law, not human law. Jurists before Hostiensis believed that the pope or bishops could not dispense from these laws. Under certain circumstances, he argued, the pope's *potestas absoluta* permitted him to exercise power previously denied to humanity.

Hostiensis placed the pope's *potestas absoluta* into the mainstream of Western political thought. Jurists quickly attributed *potestas absoluta* to secular princes as well. The pope's *potestas absoluta* did not, however, grant him unlimited power. Hostiensis created a vocabulary of papal authority that was firmly placed in thirteenth-century political and juridical thought. The prince might possess *potestas absoluta*, but he must also act with cause. Hostiensis left the pope and other rulers little space for arbitrary actions.[34]

A primary focus of Hostiensis's discussion of papal power was within the Church. When he wrote about the structure of the Church, he attributed enormous power to the pope. Papal fullness of power (*plenitudo potestatis*) permeated every crack and crevice of the ecclesiastical polity.[35] Hostiensis tempered his thought, however, by a strong sense of collegiality. The thirteenth-century canonists struggled with the issue of collegiality when they debated the role of bishops in the Church. Hostiensis thought of collegiality in the Church as being primarily between the pope and the cardinals. The importance of the cardinals for the governance and constitution of the Church was established already in the eleventh century.[36] His descriptions of the role and place of the cardinals in the Church were new. The cardinals shared plenitude of power with the pope and participated with him in the governance of the universal Church. Hostiensis very cleverly reinterpreted 1 Corinthians 6:3 "Do you not know that we will judge angels?"[37]

> It is not said "you will judge (*iudicabis*)" in the singular but "you will judge (*iudicabitis*)" in the plural in order that not only the pope but also the cardinals should be included in the expression of the fullness of power.

Hostiensis argued that the cardinals and the pope derived their authority together from Saint Peter and jointly represented the Roman Church. He repeated several times in different places his claim that the cardinals shared in papal fullness of power.

The contradictions in Hostiensis's thought that scholars have debated are resolved in large part by the Oxford manuscript of the first recension of his *Lectura*. None of the passages in which Hostiensis gave cardinals a share in papal fullness of power occur in the Oxford manuscript. Consequently, in his *Summa* and the first recension of his *Lectura* Hostiensis presented a unitary vision of papal power centered on the person of the pope that contradicted his corporate vision of the *Romana ecclesia* in the final revision of his *Lectura*.[38] As in the case of the legitimate dominium of non-Christians, he did not carefully edit all his contradictory earlier glosses. A rise to higher office may make the man and also shape his thought.

Hostiensis, however, never abandoned his episcopal roots. In his conception of the relationship between the pope and the cardinals, he relied on the model of the bishop and his cathedral chapter that reflected his experience as bishop of Sisteron and Embrun. He always supported corporate governance. In order to constitute a corporation (*universitas*), the jurists insisted that a cathedral chapter must have a common treasury (*archa communis*) and must consist of certain other officials (procurator, syndic, and others). The corporate community of the bishop and his cathedral chapter provided the juridical foundation for ecclesiastical governance on the local level; later, Hostiensis applied episcopal governance to the pope and cardinals. This aspect of his ecclesiology is especially important for understanding his conviction that the cardinals played a central role in the governance of the Church. A bishop had the authority to make decisions without his chapter in some cases but had to obtain the consent of his canons in other cases. An example of when a bishop must have the consent of his chapter is when the bishop wanted to alienate ecclesiastical property or to transfer property rights from one church to another. Hostiensis returned again and again to the corporate nature of ecclesiastical government in his *Lectura*.[39]

The sixteenth-century historian of law Diplovatatius wrote that Baldus alleged that Hostiensis favored a bishop's rights in a court case because of a bad conscience and faulty knowledge.[40] Later historians have repeated this assertion. An examination of Baldus's consilium reveals that he meant no general appraisal of Hostiensis's thought in the passage. Baldus had only noted that in the particular case he was discussing, he thought Hostiensis's support of episcopal rights was wrong.

The work of Hostiensis had great influence on the development of canonical jurisprudence and was used extensively by later jurists until well into the seventeenth century. Dante mentioned him in his *Commedia*, not to praise him but to contrast him and other jurists to the Franciscan and Dominican theological traditions: "Not in the world in which they strive for wealth and fame by reading Hostiensis" (Non per lo mondo, per cui mo s'affanna di retro ad Ostiense, *Paradise* 12.82–85). For his readers, Dante had only to use the cardinal's titular name to remind them of the role of lawyers and wealth in the fourteenth-century Church and society. For us, however, it is a signpost for Hostiensis's fame and importance for the medieval and early modern legal tradition.

Sources

For the earlier literature, see Kenneth Pennington, "Enrico da Susa, detto l'Ostiense (Hostiensis, Henricus de Segusio o Segusia)," *Dizionario bibliografico degli Italiani* 42 (Roma: Istituto della Enciclopedia Italiana, 1993), 758–63, slightly revised in English as "Henricus de Segusio (Hostiensis)," in *Popes, Canonists, and Texts 1150–1550*, Collected Studies Series 412 (Aldershot: Variorum, 1993), article XVI. An extensive bibliography of manuscripts, editions, and literature can be found online:

http://amesfoundation.law.harvard.edu/BioBibCanonists/Report_Biobib2.php?record_id=a266

The Munich Bayerische Staatsbibliothek's digitalization project has made color Pdf files of Hostiensis's *Summa* (Augsburg 1477, Venice 1480) and his *Lectura* (Strasbourg 1512) available for download. Book 1 of the *Lectura* and the *Summa* manuscripts are also available (Clm 13015 and Clm 14006) at www.muenchener-digitalisierungszentrum.de/ The tract on elections is printed by Giulietta Voltolina, "Decretum per formam compromissi: Edizione critica," *Ephemerides iuris canonici* 53 (2013) 337–374. Hostiensis's testament is printed in Agostino Paravicini Bagliani, *I testamenti dei cardinali del duecento*, Miscellanea della Società Romana di Storia Patria 25 (Roma: Presso la Società, 1980), 19–22, 133–41; A *consultatio* he may have drafted at Lyon is discussed by John A. Watt, "Medieval Deposition Theory: A Neglected Canonist 'Consultatio' from the First Council of Lyons," *Studies in Church History*, vol. 2, ed. G.J. Cumming (London: Nelson, 1965), at 207–10.

Notes

1 Salimbene, 322–3; Hauréau, 498.
2 *Rolandini Patavini Cronica marchie trivixane*, 151–2.
3 (Basel: 1574), 3 s.v. *Bern. Parm.*)
4 Most manuscripts of his commentary read "legens Parisiis in decretalibus"; however the oldest text in Oxford, New College 205, fol. 11r states that he taught the *Decretum*: "legens Parisiis in decretis."
5 *Lectura* to X 2.22.10 s.v. *tantum venditio*.
6 *Lectura* to X 1.9.10 s.v. *humiliter obedire*.
7 Soetermeer, 5.
8 E.g., Hain 8959, Rome 1473, Hain 1861, Augsburg 1477 and Hain *8963, Venice 1480.
9 Soetermeer, 7–18.
10 Pennington, "Henricus de Segusio (Hostiensis)," xvi (p. 6 for Latin text).
11 On the poetry in Hostiensis and other jurists, see Black, 378, 384–93.

12 *Summa* (Augsburg 1471), fol. 2v.
13 "temeraria reprehensio." For detailed discussions of Hostiensis's critical comments, see Gallager, 66–7; and Reno, 264–72.
14 Reno, 270.
15 Blumenthal, 89–122.
16 Soetermeer, "Summa," 18–25.
17 On the term "Commentum" as a technical description of a legal work, see Soetermeer, "Une catégorie de commentaires peu connue."
18 Munich, Staatbibl. 28152, fol. 56r-56v, labels this entire text an "additio."
19 The text and glosses are edited by Voltolina, "Decretum per formam compromissi."
20 Leipzig Universitätsbibl. 993.
21 Agostino Paravicini Bagliani printed Hostiensis's testament in *I testament dei cardinali del duecento*; see Bagliani, 133–41.
22 Hostiensis's text was quoted often by later jurists.
23 Hostiensis, *Summa* fol. 4r:

> *"Quod tibi vis fieri, mihi fac; quod non tibi noli;*
> *Sic potes in terris vivere iure poli.*
>
> *Ex hac lege etiam procedit quod nemo fiat locupletior cum alterius detrimento . . . licet domini legum exponant illud de iure gentium. Sed minus subtiliter considerant veritatem, cum de iure gentium qui fortior est locupletior fiat."*

24 X 1.1.1 s.v. *ordinatissimam.*
25 Hostiensis, *Summa* fol. 3ra: "Sic tempore ante legem mosaycam fuerunt tres leges, scilicet naturalis communis. Item naturalis rationalis que nihil aliud videtur quam naturalis ratio. Item ius gentium."
26 Some have argued that Hostiensis was indulging in humor with this comparison. I see no humor, just a reliance on natural history of the animal kingdom to make his point.
27 Hostiensis, *Lectura* (Strasbourg 1512) fol. 4rb, X 1.1.1 s.v. *quasi communem*: "Nam constat quod theologia tanquam dignior equina dicetur, numquid ergo ipsa vi sequitur quod civilis dicatur asinina et canonica mulina? Sed non est decens quod omnia genera hominum puris bestiis comparemus." The 1581 edition is corrupt at this point.
28 Ibid., fol. 4v s.v. *per moysen.*
29 Hostiensis, *Summa*, fol. 3va.
30 X 1.2.1 (*Canonum statuta*), Oxford, New College 205, fol. 4r.
31 X 3.34.8 (*Quod super his*) s.v. *pro defensione.*
32 Munich, Staatsbibl. 28152, fol. 4r, Paris, B.N. 3999, fol. 4v, Paris, B.N. 8927, fol. 4v. This passage is an important piece of evidence for separating the earlier from the later manuscripts. These three manuscripts appear to be particularly good witnesses of the *Lectura*'s text.
33 See Muldoon.
34 See Pennington, *Prince and the Law*, 48–75.
35 See Pennington, *Pope and Bishops*, especially 63–74, 110–14, 128–9, 176–7, 187–9.
36 Watt, "Hostiensis on 'Per venerabilem.'"
37 Brian Tierney, "Hostiensis and Collegiality," 403.
38 For what follows, see especially Grison. Grison has demonstrated that Hostiensis elevated the role and position of the cardinals in the final recension of his *Lectura*.
39 On medieval corportate theory, see Tierney, *Foundations of the Conciliar Theory*, 98–120 and passim.
40 Baldus, *Consilia*, Milan, 4.500; Venice, 2.166.

Bibliography

Bagliani, Agostino Paravicini, ed. *I testament dei cardinali del duecento.* Miscellanea della Società di Storia Patria 25. Rome: Presso la Società, 1980.

Baldus, de Ubaldis. *Consilia.* Milan, 1489; Venice, 1491.

Bertram, Martin. "Handschriften und Drucke des Dekretalenkommentars (*Lectura*) des Hostiensis." *Zeitschrift der Savigny-Stiftung für Rechtsgeschichte*, Kan. Abt. 106 (1989): 177–201.

Black, Winston. "Teaching the Mnemonic Bishop in the Medieval Canon Law Classroom." In *Envisioning the Bishop*, edited by Sigrid Danielson and Evan Gatti, 377–404. Turnhout: Brepols, 2014.

Blumenthal, Uta-Renate. "A Gloss of Hostiensis to X 5.6.17 (*Ad liberandum*)." *Bulletin of Medieval Canon Law* 30 (2013): 89–122.

Gallagher, Clarence. *Canon Law and the Christian Community: The Role of Law According to the "Summa Aurea" of Cardinal Hostiensis.* Analecta Gregoriana 208. Rome: Università Gregoriana, 1978.

Grison, Roberto. "Il problema del cardinalate nell'Ostiense." *Archivum historiae pontificiae* 30 (1992): 125–57.

Hauréau, Barthélemy. "Arnauld de Villeneuve, médecin et chimiste." *Histoire littéraire de la France* 28 (1881): 26–126.

Kéry, Lotte. *Gottesfurcht und irdische Strafe: Der Beitrag des mittelalterlichen Kirchenrechts zur Entstehung des öffentlichen Strafrechts.* Konflikt, Verbrechen und Sanktion in der Gesellschaft Alteuropas, Symposien und Synthesen 10. Köln: Böhlau, 2006.

Muldoon, James. *The Americas in the Spanish World Order: The Justification for Conquest in the Seventeenth Century.* Philadelphia: University of Pennsylvania Press, 2015.

Muldoon, James. *Popes, Lawyers, and Infidels: The Church and the Non-Christian World 1250–1550.* Philadelphia: University of Pennsylvania Press, 1979.

Pennington, Kenneth. "An Earlier Recension of Hostiensis's *Lectura* to the Decretals." *Bulletin of Medieval Canon Law* 17 (1987): 77–90.

Pennington, Kenneth. "Henricus de Segusio (Hostiensis)." In id., *Popes, Canonists, and Texts 1150–1550.* Collected Studies Series 412. Aldershot: Variorum, 1993.

Pennington, Kenneth. *Pope and Bishops: The Papal Monarchy in the Twelfth and Thirteenth Centuries.* Philadlephia: University of Pennsylvania Press, 1984.

Pennington, Kenneth. *The Prince and the Law 1200–1600: Sovereignty and Rights in the Western Legal Tradition.* Berkeley: University of California Press, 1993.

Pennington, Kenneth. "A 'Quaestio' of Henricus de Segusio and the Textual Tradition of His 'Summa Super Decretalibus.'" *Bulletin of Medieval Canon Law* 16 (1986): 91–6.

Reno, Edward Andrew, III. "The Authoritative Text: Raymond of Penyafort's Editing of the Decretals of Gregory IX (1234)." PhD diss., Columbia University, New York, 2011.

Rolandini Patavini Cronica marchie trivixane. Raccolta degli storici italiani 8.1. Città di Castello Bologna: S. Lapi, 1905.

Salimbene. *The Chronicle of Salimbene de Adam.* Medieval and Renaissance Texts and Studies 40. Binghamton, NY: Center for Medieval and Early Renaissance Studies, 1986.

Soetermeer, Frank. "*Summa archiepiscopi alias Summa copiosa:* Some Remarks on the Medieval Editions of the Summa Hostiensis." *Ius commune* 26 (1999): 1–25.
Soetermeer, Frank. "Une catégorie de commentaires peu connue: Les 'commenta' ou 'lecturae' inédits des précurseurs d'Odofrède." *Rivista internazionale di diritto comune* 2 (1991): 47–67.
Tierney, Brian. *Foundations of the Conciliar Theory: The Contribution of the Canonists from Gratian to the Great Schism.* Studies in the History of Christian Thought. Leiden: Brill, 1998.
Tierney, Brian. "Hostiensis and Collegiality." In *Proceedings of the Fourth International Congress of Medieval Canon Law, Toronto*, edited by Stephan Kuttner, 401–9. Monumenta Iuris Canonici, Series C 5. Vatican City: Biblioteca Apostolica Vaticana, 1976.
Voltolina, Giulietta. "Decretum per formam compromissi: Edizione critica." *Ephemerides iuris canonici* 53 (2013): 337–74.
Watt, John A. "Hostiensis on 'Per venerabilem': The Role of the College of Cardinals." In *Authority and Power: Studies on Medieval Law and Government Presented to Walter Ullmann*, edited by P. Linehan and B. Tierney, 99–113. Cambridge: Cambridge University Press, 1980.
Watt, John A. *The Theory of Papal Monarchy in the Thirteenth Century: The Contribution of the Canonists.* London: Nelson, 1965.

6 Thomas Aquinas (1225–1274)

Charles J. Reid Jr.

Introduction

Quentin Skinner identified the mid- and late-thirteenth century as a turning point in the history of Italian thought on government, justice, and law. The northern Italian city-states, which Skinner characterized collectively as the *Regnum Italicum*, required a fresh way of explaining the origins and purposes of government. These city-states—communities such as Venice, Genoa, Florence, Pisa, Siena, and others—were compact, vigorous, prosperous, and outward looking. They were active participants in the economic life of the Mediterranean and creative, even experimentalist, in their forms of government.

Thomas Aquinas, Skinner asserted, was among the first and the most influential figures in developing a new vision of government, justice, and law for the benefit of these political communities. He plainly aimed to supplant an older Augustinian model, even if he never directly said as much. That model saw politics as a sordid, albeit necessary, feature of fallen humanity. The wicked, it taught, shall always be with us, so the chief end of government must be the enforcement of coercive law against stubborn, recalcitrant sinners. This vision was no longer sustainable in a century that looked out at the world with promise and optimism. Something new, something hopeful, was called for.

Thomas Aquinas was prepared to meet the fresh demands of his age. He broke decisively with this older conception of government and its purpose. Still, he was no radical. His vision had little in common with someone like Marsiglio of Padua, who wrote a half-century later and sought to carve out a position of municipal independence from Church and empire. But while Thomas worked within the traditional boundaries of philosophy and theology, he was deeply original in his own synthetic sort of way.[1]

As with any exploration of Aquinas's thought, this chapter must be selective in its scope and the sources it employs. The chapter therefore is largely—but not completely—limited to examining the three works that Skinner identified as having the largest impact on northern Italian thought. These include the *Commentary on Aristotle's Politics*; the *De Regno* (which Skinner prefers to its alternate title, *De Regimine Principum*); and the so-called *Treatise on Law*, found at *Summa Theologiae*, Ia IIae, *quaestiones* 90–97.

The first two of these works pose textual issues to which we must be sensitive. When Thomas commented on Aristotle's *Politics*, he did not have the Greek text in front of him. Indeed, Thomas most likely did not know any Greek at all. Rather, he worked from William of Moerbeke's translation, which, however—unlike most of his translations—was based on the original Greek and not an intermediate Arabic version. That said, Moerbeke's translation was elliptical, faulty, and even sometimes misleading.[2] Thomas, furthermore, did not complete his *Commentary*, finishing work on only the first two books and a portion of the third.

The *De Regno* poses problems of attribution. This work consists of a single book within a larger text in four books known as the *De Regimine Principum*. It is certain that the final three books of the *De Regimine* were authored by Ptolemy of Lucca, a disciple of Thomas's, and not the master himself. Several scholars have even doubted Thomas's authorship of the first book, the *De Regno*, although James Blythe, whose work represents the most recent and definitive study of the question, is not prepared to do so.[3] We shall therefore treat the arguments of the *De Regno* as reflecting the genuine Thomas. Certainly, the medieval readership of the *De Regno* received it as an authentic work.

De Regno focuses on the convergence of three themes that would have made Aquinas's work so particularly useful in the context of the northern Italian cities. These are the interrelated subjects of government, justice, and law. In different ways, Thomas's *Commentary on the Politics*, the *De Regno*, and the *Treatise on Law* are each concerned with these topics. In the *Commentary*, Thomas explored the foundation of government and law and recommended the establishment of a constitutional state. In the *De Regno*, on the other hand, Thomas argued forcefully for kingship as the best type of government, but, again, concluded in favor of a constitutional regime. In the *Treatise on Law*, finally, at least insofar as we are concerned, Thomas articulated an elastic, flexible theory of law that seems aimed at giving further support and sustenance to the experiments in governing occurring in the mid-thirteenth century. What emerges is a three-dimensional portrait of Thomas's vision of a smoothly running state. He sought a government that was dedicated to the common good; that promoted the welfare of those subject to it; and that was elastic, within limits, on the means to accomplish those objectives.

Aquinas's adaptation of Aristotle (*Commentary on the Politics*)

Introductory thoughts

One might begin with the model Thomas Aquinas sought to move beyond, and that was St. Augustine's conception of the political order. Few have written about Augustine's political thought more compellingly than Robert Markus, who summarized the Augustinian paradigm well when he wrote, regarding Augustine's pessimism: "Like illness and distress political authority, in claiming a man's obedience, cannot claim to 'perfect' him in any immediately obvious sense."[4] The analogy to illness and disease says it all. Government cannot make persons good, improve their lot in life, or obtain positive benefits for the governed. As Jean Bethke Elshtain summarized it, the earthly city was flawed by "the disobedience of the first man."[5] Conflict was unresolvable, and enmity was intractable. The idea that the state might ameliorate humankind's broken condition or promote the happiness and blessedness of the people entrusted to its care was too much to hope for.

Thomas, to be sure, never identified Augustine as a foil. He never wrote of his predecessor in such unvarnished terms. Thomas, after all, was a synthetic thinker who borrowed and adapted to his own purposes all of the best of what was already a twelve-hundred-year-old intellectual tradition, which he filtered through an Aristotelian prism. Naturally, Thomas reserved only the highest praise for this revered Church father. But his understanding of politics and, by extension, his legal theory, moved decisively in a different direction.

The insights Thomas gleaned from Aristotle were a principal reason why his political theory differed so greatly from what had gone before. It is therefore helpful to begin this investigation with a review of Thomas's *Commentary on Politics* to see how he blended these fresh insights into his philosophy. In examining the *Commentary*, one must always bear in mind that Thomas is explicating a text—Aristotle's *Commentary*—and is not writing on a *tabula rasa*. He means at points to summarize Aristotle, to clarify obscurities, to expand on his teachings, and, ever so carefully, to criticize the master. He borrows from Aristotle but simultaneously imprints on the original the markings of his own keen intellect.

With these admonitions in mind, a careful reading of the *Commentary* reveals four constituent elements that together comprise his thought on government, justice, and law. These include human sociability, human reason, the political community, and the common good. Thomas begins with the insight that virtually every human being has a sociable character, and that the formation of political regimes is therefore in some respect natural; that these states, furthermore, are to be directed by a human reasoning capacity that reigns supreme in the physical world; that the forms governments take are varied and adapted to circumstance; but that every form of government must have as its end and proper purpose the common good.

Human sociability

For Thomas Aquinas, sociability is a defining aspect of human existence and the cornerstone of all subsequent speculation on political and legal arrangements. He sought to prove this point through what might loosely be characterized as several anthropological insights. First, consider the way human beings are born: naked and tiny and needing years of nurture and support to achieve adulthood. But adulthood, for Aquinas, did not mark entry into independence. For we remain dependent on others for the whole of our lives. Many animals have natural coats of fur; human beings do not. Humans, rather, require specialists to gather raw material, produce fabric, manufacture cloth, and knit and tailor clothing suitable for one another's use. Similarly, many animals forage for food, track and hunt down game, or scavenge for detritus. Human beings, on the other hand, require agriculture, domestication, and adequate food preparation in order to nourish ourselves.[6]

Our sociability is further evinced in our biology. Relying on the crude botany of his day, Aquinas distinguished human beings from many species of plants, which purportedly did not require another plant to reproduce. Human beings, in contrast, can reproduce only in pairs. Persons, in other words, need one another for this indispensable act, since if human beings did not reproduce, the species would die.[7] Sociability, therefore, is a matter of biological necessity, not free choice.

Similarly, human beings use speech to communicate. Speech, furthermore, can occur only in social settings. Words mean something only because their definitions have been shaped and formed by social interaction.[8] Many species of animals can emit "vocal sounds."[9] But through speech, human beings are capable of great abstractions and can converse on topics like "justice and injustice."[10] One modern writer has connected these insights to Thomas's larger belief structure. *Logos* is the creative and redemptive force that guides and governs the world, and its root is the Word, spoken in common with others.[11] It was only logical for Aquinas to borrow from Aristotle to conclude that anyone who did not live within society was likely a monster, although he made two exceptions—for John the Baptist and St. Anthony, the famous desert hermit.[12]

For all of these reasons, Thomas argued, we are sociable creatures. Thus, any theory of politics and law must begin with and build upon these premises. Thomas, however, did not believe that human relationships were egalitarian. Paraphrasing Aristotle, he noted that "there is something ruling and something ruled in everything constituted out of many things."[13] No surprise, then, that Thomas perceived God, the universe, and all within it as existing in an almost endless series of hierarchical relationships. Indeed, hierarchical ordering was so deeply embedded within his thought-world that he was likely unconscious of it.

Thus, tracking Aristotle, Thomas observed that there was a hierarchy to nature. Plants constituted the base of the hierarchy and provided food for other creatures. Among animals, he distinguished between wild and domesticated kinds. Both types of animal served the needs of human beings—we might use the skins of wild animals for warmth, while harvesting countless benefits from domesticated creatures. At the top of the pinnacle came human beings. The entirety of this natural hierarchy existed to serve human needs. "[I]t is clear that God made animals and plants for the sustenance of human beings."[14]

There was also a hierarchy within the human being itself. Consider the body in relation to the intellect and soul. In making this comparison, Thomas was no dualist. He did not accept the sharp division between body and soul of someone like Plato. That said, he still viewed the soul as "the first principle of life."[15] Thus he maintained that the *anima*—the soul—must lead and the body must follow.[16] The soul, thus understood as the intellect, was the incorporeal force which allowed human beings to know and understand the world around them.[17]

He similarly rejected egalitarianism as a form of political organization when he turned to Aristotle's recapitulation of Plato's suggestion that wives and property should be held in common. In addressing this commentary, we must bear in mind that Thomas was working neither directly from Plato's text nor from Aristotle's, but from Moerbeke's translation of Aristotle. Thomas viewed Plato as proposing an essentially propertyless society (something for which Plato had not advocated). Having erected that strawman, Aquinas demolished it.

Thomas argued, rather, for a natural class structure to human society. There were ranks and orders within society, and these distinctions had to be preserved. Thus, he argued that, yes, social goods should be distributed according to merit. But Thomas simultaneously insisted "that those of higher status, by virtue simply of their status, rightfully receive more of the goods which society has to offer."[18] So also, an injury inflicted on one of greater status must be punished with greater severity.[19]

Thomas explained himself by saying that he stood for "proportional equality."[20] Only through the maintenance of social and class boundaries might good order be preserved. There must be rulers in society, and there must be subjects. If the "lower classes" knew to obey their rulers and understood who was to lead and who was to follow, then, and only then, was it possible to achieve "the friendship in the political community that should prevail between rulers and subjects."[21]

Similarly, when Thomas perceived human relationships, he understood them, at least in substantial measure, in terms of the legally defined power disparities among them. At the apex were fully developed adult males. They were the heads of households and the owners of property. Over their wives, they exercised matrimonial power, over their sons paternal power, and over their slaves despotic power.[22] These power arrangements depended, furthermore, on a hierarchical ranking of reasoning capacity. Adult males enjoyed the highest level of reasoning. Women, in contrast, were weak in their reasoning, and sons were undeveloped. Slaves, finally—at least natural slaves—were by definition inferior in their reasoning.[23]

It is, indeed, an unfortunate fact that Thomas in his *Commentary on the Politics* accepted slavery as an institution, even though he modified Aristotle's justification for its existence.[24] Nor was this a merely academic point. Slavery was a lamentable reality in swaths of thirteenth-century Europe. To facilitate the trade in slaves, city-states like Venice and Genoa sought "direct control over Black Sea ports and shipping routes."[25] Their citizens—and the citizens of other northern Italian city-states—frequently owned slaves; their markets, finally, formed a vital hub in the trading networks that transshipped prisoners from eastern regions to North Africa.[26]

Reason

Thomas opened his Prologue to the *Commentary on the Politics* with an ode to human reason. It is capable of cognition, abstraction, learning, and memory. The human intellect is the source of all skills. Furthermore, the human intellect bears a kind of likeness to the divine intellect, from which originated the entire natural world *(principium rerum naturalium)*. Indeed, the human intellect is brightened by the divine mind's "intelligible light" (*intelligibile lumen*),[27] which allows the human person to observe and learn from nature. And as we observe, we categorize and create discrete bodies of knowledge known as the sciences.

The sciences, as Thomas understood the term, were disciplined fields of inquiry. A scientist was not a mere passive collector of data but an actively engaged investigator. It was the responsibility of the scientist, furthermore, not only to categorize knowledge, but to derive from this knowledge skills adaptable to human use. Science, in other words, was both theoretical and practical.[28] Thus the physician, through an awareness of biology, might develop a new course of treatment for some illness, or the ship's captain, through a knowledge of astronomy, might devise new techniques for celestial navigation.

Among the scientific disciplines that interested Thomas was the field known as political science. Indeed, the term "political science" figures recurrently in his *Commentary on the Politics.* The word "political," of course, was derived ultimately from Aristotle's *politikon zoon* ("political animal"). The political animal, as Aristotle used the expression, referred to the human ability to live together in community. Such arrangements, according to Aristotle, could be made and sustained only through the exercise of human reason. Thomas's *Commentary on the Politics* is precisely an investigation into the phenomenon of political community. It follows, therefore, that in asking himself how the human person is capable of such communal existence, Thomas was drawn back, again, to the centrality of human reason.

Reason, Aquinas insisted, was a creative force. It was constructive. It is because of reason that the craftsman knew how to design objects and to execute those designs. All of the practitioners of the constructive arts—architects, engineers, the builders of bridges, the founders and leaders of political communities—succeeded because they followed the steady guide of human reason.[29]

Reason was also a distinctively human characteristic, but it was unevenly distributed. Differences in reasoning capacity were discernible from birth. "We perceive that there is a distinction regarding human beings from their very birth, such that some are fit to be subjects and others fit to rule."[30] There is much packed within this sentence. It reinforces hierarchy, privilege, and the status quo. It serves as a pretext for the maltreatment of groups of people deemed suitable only for subjugation. One might try—unpersuasively—to domesticate the text by claiming that it is really about the natural aptitude (or lack thereof) of persons to learn. While all of this was implicit within the text, and ripe for exploitation, Thomas's main point, however, was that he viewed as the natural leaders of the community those who possess reason. Thomas drove the point home by quoting Proverbs 11: 29: "the stupid shall serve the wise."[31]

Human reason, Aquinas asserted, had led to the creation of whole new institutions. He thus gave the example of long-distance trade. Originally, trade was local and aimed at the exchange of "mutually necessary things." But as communities expanded in size and organization, and as the taste for a greater variety of goods kept pace, there was a need "to make exchanges with remote persons as well as neighbors."[32] Out of this practice human reason invented money as a medium of exchange.[33] But money posed its own set of threats, foremost among them something that Moerbeke, in his infelicitous translation of the *Politics*, called *campsoria*—interest on a loan. Aristotle had not meant to denounce usury at this point in the *Politics*, but Moerbeke made it look like he had.[34] Thomas certainly took the opportunity to issue his own condemnation of usury.[35] But he did not stop there. He went on to discuss the relationship of reason and virtue as a means of restraining wealth acquisition within natural, normal limits. King Midas must not become our model in household management or in the conduct of state affairs.[36] After all, he died of starvation because everything he touched turned to gold. Unlimited appetite thus became a parable of self-destruction. On the contrary, reason and its twin manifestations, prudence and wisdom, must operate to restrain our appetites.[37]

If human reason could be counted to conjure into being a social practice like trade, and to restrain our appetites in the quest for unlimited riches, it might also serve as the means by which human societies governed themselves. The community, Thomas asserted, should thus ensure the selection of rulers who enjoyed proper reason. These were governors "who by power of intellect can foresee what things are appropriate for preservation (e.g., by procuring beneficial things and repelling harmful things)."[38]

Significantly, Thomas did not call for rule by the best and the brightest. He was not a revolutionary like Plato, who longed for the inspired rule of philosopher-kings. What Thomas really sought in a ruler was someone with reason, yes, but a reason that manifested itself primarily in administrative skill. To reinforce this point, Aquinas borrowed a metaphor from Aristotle. The ruler, he said, should be a "master-builder," "for as the chief craftsman directs and commands his assistants . . . so the ruler directs his subjects."[39] Such a ruler knows how to enact and enforce reasonable laws. Indeed, Aquinas added, the absence of reasonable laws might be symptomatic of larger issues within a political community, such as the society's relative "barbarism," and the crude and uncultivated minds of those who govern.[40]

Thus, Aquinas asserted, regarding reason and the political community: *Est enim civitas principalissimum eorum, quae humana ratione constitui possunt* ("The political community is constituted most principally by the use of human reason").[41] The superlative *principalissimum* carries most of the weight of this sentence. Its force is hard to reproduce in English, but we can give it a try: The political community is not just principally constituted by reason. It is most emphatically, chiefly, without equivocation or cavil, governed by human reason.

Political community

In his choice of nouns to describe the political community, Aquinas followed Moerbeke, who rendered Aristotle's *polis* into the Latin *civitas.* He could have chosen otherwise. Roman law had spoken of the *status rei Romanae* to signify the empire and its affairs. The medieval glossator Accursius used the expression *status* to convey the meaning of "state," and Aquinas himself had used that term in other contexts.[42] Did he mean something different by *civitas*? Hard to say at our chronological distance, although the choice of words certainly would have resonated in *civitates* like Venice and Genoa.

What, moreover, did Thomas say about the political community? A great deal, actually, hence the need to be selective in what we identify as important. Let us begin, therefore, with definitions. What exactly did Thomas mean by the expression "political community" as he used the term in his *Commentary*?

Following Aristotle, he understood the political community as emerging from a dense network of smaller human associations. There was, at the microcosmic level, the family, consisting of a married couple and their immediate, unemancipated offspring. A little larger than the family was the household. As Aquinas used the term (Latin, *domus*), the household was conceived to serve two vital functions. The first consisted of what he called "daily human needs," which included those things necessary for survival—food, drink, heat in the winter months. But the household was meant to serve larger purposes also. Here, Aquinas spoke of the household as an economic unit. The household so conceived included slaves and retainers, and aimed at production of merchandise that was not only personally useful, but marketable.[43] Even poor families, Aquinas added, might qualify for household status if they owned an ox or some other beast of burden that facilitated the production of a surplus that might be exchanged at market.[44]

Next, there was the village, which consisted of a group of households. Like the family, the village was a "natural" institution—by which Aquinas meant that it was to be expected that over time human reproductive processes alone should ensure that one household might turn into several. The village was constituted by the "interaction" (*communicatio*) of its constituent households. Aquinas distinguished households and villages on the basis of the intensity of their interactions. Households must cooperate on a daily basis to see to all of the necessities of life. Villages, on the other hand, had no need for such intense, ongoing cooperation and might come together less often for *exterioribus actibus*—an almost untranslatable expression that excluded familial intimacy but included matters of interest common to the community.[45]

At the macrocosmic level, finally, there was the *civitas*, the political community. Like the village, the political community was "natural," in that it was the fulfillment of the "natural drive" of "all human beings [for] the association of the political community."[46]

Thomas added that the political community was the "the most perfect" (*perfectissima*) form of human association. By "perfect," Thomas meant "complete." It was perfect, he added, for two reasons. First, it was formed by a large number of persons who come from "different ranks and orders."[47] Thomas was particularly insistent on this point. A state that was too homogeneous, he feared, ceased to be a genuine political community and assumed, rather, the character of a large, agglomerated household.[48] Such a political community was like a chorus capable of singing only one note. Life in community demanded harmony, Thomas declared, and that required not monochromatic unity but the coming together of different voices and talents.[49]

Second, the political community had to be large enough to provide through its own resources what was needed for human life.[50] It had to be large enough, in other words, to see to the defense of the community, to ensure self-sufficiency, and to promote the common good.[51]

But while the political community comprised the largest and most self-sufficient form of human existence, this did not mean that it thereby absorbed smaller units within itself. Subsidiary units enjoyed, in their own right, a kind of completeness. Thomas gave the example of a wall. A wall is complete in itself. But it usually helps to form part of a larger structure. It supports the roof on a house, say, or provides shelter from wind and rain.[52] The implication is clear: the vitality of the community depends on the vitality of its parts. A house without walls cannot stand, and neither can a political community long survive when its subsidiary associations have withered and died.

This and other arguments Thomas advanced regarding the centrality of subsidiary social units to the health of the community have been identified by Nicholas Aroney as a key to understanding Thomas's constitutionalism. In a world of multiple, competing forms of government, Thomas stressed that they must share in common a commitment to small-scale social institutions. Borrowing from the vocabulary of modern Catholic social thought, Aroney sees at work in Thomas's texts the first stirrings of the principle of subsidiarity.[53]

We should keep these ideas in mind as we analyze Thomas's treatment of "regimes" (Latin, *respublicae*). Thomas had a simple definition for regimes. A regime was the government, its offices, its allocation of responsibilities, and its essential character. So understood, regimes might come in different types. There were "good" regimes: these included monarchy, provided the king was wise; aristocracy, that is, government of the few for the benefit of the community; and polity, by which Aquinas meant a public-spirited form of popular rule. But there were also the perversions of these forms: tyranny, that is, the capricious and destructive rule by one; oligarchy, namely, the rule of the wealthy and well-situated for their own benefit; and democracy, the unbridled freedom of the great mass of people to do as it pleased.[54]

Which regime did Aquinas favor? As usual, he was circumspect in addressing this question. At points, he spoke warmly of kingship. It was the oldest form of government, and it constituted a kind of natural outgrowth from households. "[I]t is clear that the rule of a king over a political community or a people developed from the rule of the senior man in the household or village."[55] Where the king was good, kingship might even be the best form of government.[56] But Thomas also retained misgivings about entrusting this much power to a single individual. Following Aristotle, Thomas asserted that "it was better that kings be chosen not from a single bloodline, but from among the virtuous citizens" (*quod melius esset, quod regese non acciperentur, ex uno solo genere, sed ex quibuscumque virtuosis*).[57]

Thomas, in other words, at least nodded in the direction of elective monarchy. The practice of elective kingship, in fact, was a reality throughout thirteenth-century Europe. The Holy Roman Emperor was elective; the doge of Venice was elected; Polish rulers were often elected. And, of course, the popes were routinely elected during Thomas's lifetime by the college of cardinals. Thomas would have therefore been familiar with this form of monarchy.

But Thomas saved his most favorable comments for mixed forms of government. "Those who blend the organization of the political community out of many regimes," Aquinas affirmed, "do far better."[58] Developing this point, Aquinas devoted considerable space to Aristotle's treatment of Solon's reform of the Athenian government. Fearing that government was the monopoly of the wealthy few, Solon abolished the oligarchy. He established a judiciary that depended on a large number of citizen-judges and created structures that allowed for some popular participation in government. Still, Solon was parsimonious in the degree to which he allowed the people to participate in municipal rule, which was a decision Aquinas supported.[59] Did he mean by his favorable comments to anoint Solon's constitution as the best form of government? Not likely. He was far too careful to tip his hand decisively in any one direction.

Every human association, finally, was organized to achieve some purpose, or to accomplish some good. For Thomas, it made no sense to speak of a community lacking all purpose. This was true of smaller, subsidiary associations, such as a craft guild organized within a city's boundaries, and it was true of the political community taken as a whole. Indeed, Thomas declared that the *civitas*, "the supreme association," was "necessarily [directed to] seek the supreme human good."[60] Thus it is we shall turn next to the common good.

The common good

What was the "supreme human good," as Aquinas understood it? We should begin with the term Aristotle used to encapsulate this concept, and that was the Greek noun *eudaimonia*. This term is commonly translated as "happiness," but to leave the translation at that would be seriously misleading. One scholar has described *eudaimonia* as "involv[ing] not just the activity of the theoretical intellect, but the full range of human life and action, in accordance with the broader excellences of moral virtue and practical wisdom."[61] Life in community mattered greatly as a measure of one's happiness. Thus, *eudaimonia* often included political participation.[62] It entailed, as well, the exercise of responsible, ordered freedom in all of one's endeavors.[63]

Aquinas substituted the Latin nouns *felicitas* and *beatitudo* for the Greek *eudaimonia*. A contemporary scholar has defined Thomas's *felicitas* as the near equivalent of "flourishing." To experience *felicitas*, in Thomas's universe, was to thrive emotionally and spiritually consistent with the virtues.[64] Like *eudaimonia*, *beatitudo* has also been commonly translated as "happiness." Again, however, more must be said. It is not "just the psychological condition of feeling happiness," though joy can certainly constitute a part of what *beatitudo* encompasses.

It is also "the actualization of human nature's potentials, thus making a person satisfied."[65]

We must, however, always be sensitive to the religious dimension of Thomas's concept of *beatitudo*. After all, Thomas never lost sight of the Christian predicates of his own worldview, even when he was commenting on Aristotle's texts. Thus he distinguished, in his *Commentary on the Nichomachean Ethics*, between happiness as experienced in a purely human sense and happiness in a transcendent, religious sense.[66] Along these lines, it has been noted that "[t]here are many well-known texts of Aquinas that baldly state that ultimate human beatitude, and the virtues that allow us to attain it, is twofold, the perfect or the imperfect, or, equivalently, the supernaturally infused and the humanly acquired."[67]

There are implications embedded in these insights for the ways in which Thomas explained the specifically Christian *civitas*. To be sure, Thomas did not intend to place the Christian *civitas* under the command of the Church. Indeed, he largely steered clear of conflicts between popes and secular rulers, even though his career spanned some of the most tumultuous controversies of the medieval period (such as the struggle between Pope Innocent IV and Emperor Frederick II). When Thomas spoke of terrestrial government, it was to make it clear that it was to remain in the hands of secular rulers who enjoyed real and substantial autonomy.[68]

Still, this autonomy was not absolute. Its limitations were most clearly manifested in Thomas's commentary on heresy and the responsibility of secular rulers to see to its suppression. He encompassed by the words "heresy" and "heretic" ostensible Christians who harbored grave errors regarding Christian belief. (In a narrow legal sense, the term "heretic" did not apply to Jews, although Muslims were sometimes denounced juridically as heretics.[69]) Thomas also did not mean to embrace by the term "heretic" those who inadvertently made some blunder about the faith but were willing to acknowledge their mistake when corrected.[70]

But pertinacious heretics, those who propagated and clung to their errors even when admonished, sinned gravely. And if they rejected the opportunity to amend their lives, they were to be dealt with severely. They were to be excommunicated from the Church and handed over "to the secular tribunal to be exterminated thereby from the world by death."[71] This was a solemn obligation, from which no political community could gain exemption. Although Thomas did not expressly draw the connection, his position on the persecution of heretics followed logically—but not necessarily—from the premise that the political community was obliged to ensure the spiritual well-being of its members as its supreme obligation. In so writing, Thomas contributed in significant ways to a burgeoning medieval literature on Christ as "persecutor."[72]

We should, however, also consider other aspects of the common good, as articulated in the *Commentary on the Politics*. Thomas wanted a society that was free of crime and disorder. But he realized that such a goal was achievable only within a system that attacked the root causes of crime. "The most deliberate injustices in the community," Thomas wrote, "happen because of love of honor and money."[73] Elsewhere, he stressed that he sought a "system [in which] the just by nature . . . do not want to act covetously."[74] The system, in other words, mattered. He recognized a system as just when those factors that impel criminal activity have been remedied. In part, this might be accomplished by inculcating the virtues. But he also argued that whatever system was adopted, it should prevent "the injustices which provoke human beings to harm others."[75] In other words, Thomas recommended the creation of a political order that foresaw and forestalled those harms and injuries that gave rise to human resentment and the criminal wrongdoing that sometimes followed in its wake.

Thomas also argued for a legal order that saw to a just division of property and resources. Without doubt, as already shown, he believed in a hierarchy that proportionately gave a greater share of goods to those near its top. Still, he acknowledged that disparities of property, and disagreements over its distribution, were a frequent source of rebellion.[76] But for Thomas, the solution was not the total equalization of property holdings. Rather, it was the enactment of just laws mandating that "citizens share their goods with one another."[77] He understood that "in well-regulated communities" "some things are *ipso facto* common regarding use."[78] He cited with approval Solon's restrictions on landownership.[79] There was, in other words, a social character to private property, which Thomas acknowledged when he wrote: "[H]ow the use of private property can be common belongs to the providence of the good lawmaker."[80]

What we have learned so far? Thomas was a flexible thinker regarding the forms of government. He was open to a great deal of variety and even experimentation, provided certain basic threshold considerations were observed. Above all else, the government must suppress threats to the community's religious faith; but the government must also be zealous in maintaining good order. This meant, simultaneously, that government should ensure the preservation of traditional social hierarchy but also take care that disparities of wealth and power not grow too great. Finally, his defense of slavery revealed Thomas at his worst. He understood that there were compelling arguments against slavery, yet he took the expedient course by justifying its continued utility, albeit in a milder, softer form than that urged by Aristotle.

De Regno

Introductory thoughts

Thomas's *Commentary on the Politics* considered carefully the constitutive parts of government, justice, and law. Government, Thomas argued, was natural. It arose from the nearly universal impulse to human sociability. Our capacity for self-government, furthermore, was unique in all of the created order because of human reason. We know how to ascertain the virtuous, and the just, and to incorporate these insights into the forms we impart to government. Finally, we are capable—indeed, obliged—to govern with respect to the common good. The mandate to ensure the common good stands at the heart of Thomas's theory of government and justice. At the very least, rulers must always look to the advantage of the entire community. A ruler who seeks purely private advantage, or who aims to benefit only a small ruling clique, or who wants to punish some disfavored group, stands always and everywhere condemned as an unjust ruler and an opponent to the common good.

In the *De Regno*, on the other hand, we encounter not an analysis of all forms of government, but a narrower discussion focused on a single form of government, kingship. The *De Regno* purports to be a portion of a letter addressed to the King of Cyprus. Cyprus, at the time Thomas wrote, was a crusader kingdom, established by King Richard I of England. Governed by a succession of monarchs of uncertain abilities, the regime was also sustained by the strong presence of religious military orders.[81] Still, one makes a mistake reading too much into the dedication. James Blythe cautions that we remain unsure whether the dedication to the king actually formed a part of the original text. Blythe further notes that the text bears strong resemblance to the mirror-of-princes literature, but also departs from the genre's expectations in certain key respects, especially in the way it advocates for constitutional restraints.[82]

Our own approach is to focus on three key elements in this text: Thomas's justification for kingship ("why kingship"); his analysis of tyranny as the worst form of government; and the desirability of situating the monarch within a broader constitutional order. A review of these three elements will reveal, from a somewhat different angle than the *Commentary on the Politics*, some of Thomas's main ideas about government, justice, and law.

Why kingship?

Kingship, like the other forms of government, has its origin in the intersection of human sociability and human reason.[83] But why should human beings prefer kingship to other forms? Thomas offered a series of explanations for kingship, but it might be best to focus on the final justification he provided, since it seems to be the most all-encompassing. That justification consisted of a series of analogies between the created order and what we know of God and God's role in divine order. If we did that, Thomas proposed, we would recognize at once that there are two types of government, analogous one to the other. The first type is universal government, which consists of God's beneficent rule over the universe and all within it. Through divine reason, God brought the universe into being, sustains it in all of its bounty and goodness, and, at a moment of his choosing, will bring it to its end.[84] God can thus be said to exercise real governance over all "corporeal creatures and all spiritual virtues."[85]

It is here where Thomas draws his first analogy between God and the earthly king. For there is on earth an analogue to God's universal government, and that is particular government—the geographically determined territories and principalities over which rulers have charge. These rulers were tasked with using their reason in the governance of their realms in the same way God employed divine reason to rule over the universe. Thus Thomas declared: "in a certain way reason holds the same place in the human species as God does in the world. . . . [B]ecause . . . a person is naturally social and lives in a multitude, something similar to divine government is found among humans."[86] Notice the steps in the analogy: God in his perfect wisdom superintends the divine order. Human rulers, exercising their albeit imperfect reason, have responsibility over the political entities assigned to them.

The analogies did not stop there. God, Thomas continued, exercises creative power over the world. God brought into being the earth and all within it—"diverse species of things . . . stars in the sky, birds in the air."[87] A king, however, is also creative. One sees the king's creative power at work most clearly at the founding of cities or kingdoms. Thomas thus pointed to Ninus—a mythical Assyrian figure—as the founder of Nineveh, and Romulus as the founder of Rome. Like the God who designed creation, the founder-king must establish villages, castles, administrative centers, great universities for study, and so forth.[88]

Then there are the responsibilities of governance. God, it goes without saying, has care of the universe. But so does the king within the boundaries of the kingdom. God sees to the "healthfulness" of humankind, God ensures "fruitfulness," God promises "pleasantness" and "protection."[89] Kings must perform the same roles in their realms.

Also, just as God lights the path to salvation, so kings are duty-bound to ensure that their kingdoms' laws satisfy the preconditions required for virtuous living. One modern scholar, looking at this succession of analogies and the creativity and powers they confer on kings, has compared the royal role to that of the artist. The king judges, establishes, designs, creates, and foresees needs in the way an artist approaches work on a fine sculpture, say, or a beautiful, intricate painting.[90]

An obvious question occurs: aren't these the responsibilities of any form of government? Why are kings unique? Again, Aquinas answers with an analogy to God and God's relationship with the created order: like God, the king is one. So, Thomas insisted: "[L]et the king know that this is the office that he has taken up, that he in his kingdom is as the spirit in the body and God in the world."[91]

God, furthermore, favored unity. Thomas tried to prove this assertion with a series of examples drawn from nature. There is in nature an unmoved mover, which is God. Similarly, one finds analogues on earth. There is one unmoved mover of the human body, and that is the heart which circulates the blood. We see similar arrangements in the animal kingdom. There is an unmoved mover of the beehive, the king bee that rules the hive (yes, Thomas called the queen bee the king of the hive).[92] These analogies were meant to demonstrate the preferred status of kingship vis-à-vis other forms of government. One God. One ruler. As it is in heaven, so is it on earth.

But Thomas did not stop with nature. Unity, he further claimed, can be empirically proven as essential to the health of the state. For evidence, he turned to the fall of the Roman Republic. For sure, the Roman Republic experienced growth during its final years, but it was also torn by nearly continuous civil wars and conflicts. Eventually, the many competing factions of the republic lost power, as rule was consolidated in the hands of emperors, some of whom, Thomas noted, "procured the common good faithfully."[93] Unity was good, division was pernicious, was the lesson Thomas taught.

Tyranny

What, then, of tyrants? Thomas feared that government could become corrupt. It was a persistent concern of his, voiced in numerous of his writings. And in his taxonomy of bad governments, Thomas assigned the worst place to tyrants. Tyrants were rulers with a monopoly of power. They were, in a sense, analogues to kings and yet their opposite. To borrow from physics, if kings were matter, then tyrants were antimatter. Where kings ruled for the public benefit and the common good, tyrants exploited the people and sought their own enrichment. Indeed, the more a tyrant retreated from the common good, the greater the tyranny.[94]

Insightfully, Thomas probed the harmful effects of tyrants. To be sure, they plundered the public purse. But this was not close to the worst a tyrant could do, for tyrants had the power to destroy the very humanity of those subjected to their misrule. Where citizens and subjects sought peace and cooperation, tyrants brought strife and discord. They feared human association. They might prohibit marriage or "common meals, and other similar things that generate familiarity and trust among human beings."[95]

Tyrants instinctively knew that their rule required the destruction of social trust. And so tyrants adopted policies aimed at shattering harmony. Where there was trust, they sowed suspicion. A tyrant's rule depended on fear, and so they adopted policies that instilled fear in ordinary people. Furthermore, since tyrants were always threatened by the rise of competing centers of power, they eagerly destroyed the kinds of social organizations that might challenge their rule.[96] In all of this, Thomas revealed himself to be a sophisticated student not only of the misuse of power, but of its psychological effects on victims.

Tyrants must also be innately suspicious of others. And their suspicion destroyed the possibility of the friendship between ruler and ruled that good government required:

> Although tyrants desire the good of friendship, they cannot get it. Since they do not seek the common good, but their own, there is little or no communion between them and their subjects, but all firm friendships depend on some communion.[97]

Indeed, tyrants destroyed even the capacity for human love since, in all that they did and said, they despised the very idea of love.[98]

What, however, was to be done about the tyrant? A youthful Thomas Aquinas, writing in his *Commentary* on the *Sentences* of Peter Lombard, recommended tyrannicide, at least in cases where a tyrant had illegally seized power. The lack of legal title to rule was sufficient to establish the case to kill the tyrant, Thomas reasoned. On the other hand, where the tyrant had acquired power through legal means, the constitutional authority to forcibly remove him was missing and tyrannicide was correspondingly illegal.[99] In his *Summa Theologiae*, Thomas asserted that the laws of a tyrant were not law so much as a "perversion of law" (*perversitas legis*)[100] and "acts of violence" (*violentiae*),[101] although Thomas equivocated on the actions that those subject to tyrannical rule were empowered to take.[102]

In the *De Regno*, on the other hand, Thomas offered an answer that differed from these other proposals. He distinguished between two types of tyranny: the kind that must be passively accepted, and the kind that required active resistance. Thomas did not so much define the first type of tyrant as describe him. The Hebrew scriptures gave examples of such tyrants. There was Nebuchadnezzar as described in the Book of Daniel, who persecuted the Jewish people in exile. Similarly, there was Ahasuerus in the Book of Esther, who was nearly led by the wicked adviser Haman to murder the Jewish people of Persia. For tyrants such as these, Thomas counseled prayer and patience. Indeed, he noted that through such means both of these oppressive tyrants were made to see the error of their ways.[103]

Finally, there were the Christians of the early Roman Empire. For generations, they suffered under the tyranny of Roman emperors who hunted them down and martyred them for their convictions. But their endurance was munificently rewarded when, in the fourth century, the emperors not only ceased to persecute them but embraced the Christian faith themselves and conferred on the Church a preferred status within the empire.[104]

Much is embedded in these statements. Even the worst regimes, Thomas was convinced, cannot prevail forever. History is providential and will reward those who suffer and wait. Marginalized peoples, furthermore, whether the Jews of Babylon and Persia or the Christians of the early empire, had little choice but to play for time and Thomas meant to assure those facing similar circumstances that their perseverance would not be wasted.

The logic seems compelling: If God's reward for patience is so great, why should we ever resist a tyrant? Yet Thomas was prepared to counsel resistance in certain circumstances. But to understand those circumstances, we must first take up the question of the constitutional monarch.

Kings and constitutional rule

As he did in the *Commentary on the Politics*, Aquinas endorsed elective kingship. In choosing a king, furthermore, he encouraged the elective body to look for a candidate who was unlikely to become tyrannical and then to surround the individual so chosen with constitutional safeguards that make a lapse into tyranny even more implausible.[105]

What, then, were the qualities one should look for in a monarch? A king, Thomas urged, should love his kingdom and should know that only by loving his kingdom will his love be reciprocated by his subjects.[106] A king must be zealous for justice. He has to understand that his duties lie in service to others. He must be ready "to assist the needy, . . . pacify the discordant, . . . [and] snatch the oppressed from the more potent."[107] A king must not seek glory, riches, or honor. A king hungry for these visible tokens of worldly success is likely to become a tyrant.[108] On the contrary, the king must realize that it is God finally who will reward him for a job well done in the world to come, although a monarch who rules with justice and wisdom will be acclaimed also in this world and so merit a genuinely good reputation.[109] Were these criteria ever used in real life? Probably not, but one can at least imagine them resonating with the aristocratic electors of the doge of Venice.[110]

But what if a king has gone bad? What if he has lapsed into tyranny? In the previous section, we indicated that at least for those who lacked official responsibilities, the only recourse was to pray for the tyrant's conversion. But Thomas was prepared to make a large exception to this rule. Where public authorities, and not private parties, determined that action was needed, it was licit for them to remove the tyrant.[111] Thomas did not define what he meant by "public authorities." Still he provided examples of such public authority in action. Tarquin the Proud, the last of the Roman kings, had abused his office. Lucius Junius Brutus, who held high office under Tarquin, summoned other leading citizens and succeeded in deposing and exiling Tarquin. Similarly, the Roman Senate was right to kill the emperor Domitian "when he exercised tyranny."[112] Brutus was an immediate subordinate of a king who had gained power through usurpation. This position was sufficient to constitute Brutus as a public authority entitled to move against the king. The Senate at the time of Domitian retained at least the nominal power to make and unmake emperors. (In reality, at least if one believes Suetonius, the murder of Domitian was far messier, featuring a plot led by his steward, his chamberlain, and possibly some members of the Senate and praetorian guards).[113] In furnishing such examples, Thomas must have had a capacious understanding of public authority.

The examples are also instructive regarding the fates of the two tyrants. Tarquin was removed from office. He was not killed. Domitian, on the other hand, was murdered. Did Thomas implicitly authorize tyrannicide in praising the manner of Domitian's death? Thomas was elusive on this point. He never expressly approved of the death of Domitian, but he praised its beneficial consequences.[114] If that is not an endorsement of tyrannicide, it is very, very close.

Consent, constitutionalism, and kingship

Thomas's constitutional thought as reflected in the *Commentary on the Politics* and the *De Regno* has been subjected to sustained analysis. A review of some recent scholarship suggests a wide divergence of views. Antony Black understands Aquinas as a constitutional thinker but has also argued that the series of analogies he drew between God and king opened the door to absolutist strains of thought. The door was opened to "the omnipotent and omnicompetent sovereign" and "centralising . . . bureaucratic kingship."[115] The historian of British constitutionalism Samuel Beer has gone even farther in his analysis of the authoritarian tendencies in Aquinas's thought. For Beer, the many hierarchies Thomas erected in his thoughts on government and law were decisive. Beer concluded that Thomas was hopelessly hierarchical: "Thinkers in the hierarchic tradition such as Thomas were much concerned to show why the many should and do consent to be ruled by the wise and the holy."[116]

This mode of reasoning has drawn a response, most notably by Brian Tierney. Citing the *Summa Theologiae*, Tierney emphasized the expansive role consent played in Thomas's constitutional thought.[117] Thomas, Tierney noted, wrote that "all should have some share in government; this makes for peace among the people and commends itself to all."[118] Still, in the end, Tierney concluded that what one finds in Thomas is the "co-exist[ence]" of constitutional and hierarchical elements.[119]

James Blythe has also called attention to the jostling of different ideas in Thomas's constitutional order. At times, he "exalts kingship" as the best form of government. In other contexts, "Thomas suggests that ultimate authority rests with the whole people."[120] Blythe's solution to these difficulties is to see Thomas as an advocate "of [a] mixed constitution . . . that denies sovereignty to any one element and in this way avoids the tyranny of either the one, the few, or the many."[121]

On the whole, Tierney and Blythe seem to have the more correct understanding of Thomas's constitutional thought. In his *Commentary on the Politics*, Thomas explored the wide divergences that existed among different forms of government. In the end, he refrained from selecting a favorite. What mattered was not whether the government was a kingship or an aristocracy, or a "polity," so long as it satisfied the robust demands of the common good and proved a good fit for the culture and expectations of the governed. He was commenting on Aristotle but always held in view the political realities of the day in the *communes* of northern Italy and elsewhere.

In the *De Regno*, he retained his commitment to constitutional order. He revealed a preference for kingship, but he was far from uncritically endorsing monarchy as ideal. In fact, he devoted considerable space to the dangers of tyranny and in developing devices for the removal of the king who descended into tyranny. His work, as Tierney and Blythe point out, can sometimes seem eclectic, even contradictory. But that was because he kept his eye steadily on three main points: the real betterment that government can accomplish in people's lives when the common good is the focus of concern; the genuine fear that great power is always open to abuse and must accordingly be checked and balanced by meaningful constitutional authority; and the realistic appreciation that there were numerous routes to the constitutional order he sought.

The Treatise on Law

We are nearly at our conclusion but a more complete grasp of Thomas on government, justice, and law requires a few observations on the arguments he advances in his *Treatise on Law*. The *Treatise on Law* forms a small part of the *Summa Theologiae* but stands as a rich and magnificently complicated work despite its brevity.[122] I have written a study of the *Treatise* for the volume *Christianity and Global Law*.[123] I shall here highlight only two points that I make at greater length in that other essay. First, in keeping with his vision of law as something positive, and as a tool for improving the life of the community, Thomas spoke of law as a plan to be implemented in conformity with perceived usefulness. Second, far from viewing natural law as a restraint on state policy, he viewed it as remarkably flexible. As we shall see in what follows, this was not necessarily a good thing.

Regula, ordinatio, utilitas

These three Latin nouns are customarily translated as "rule," "ordinance," and "utility," or "usefulness." Let us begin our analysis with Thomas's use of *regula*, "rule." We find the following in one of the many definitions Thomas offered of the word law: *Dicendum quod lex quaedam regula est et mensura actuum secundum quam inducitur aliquis ad agendum vel ab agendo retrahitur* ("It must be said that law is a certain rule and measure of acting according to which one is led to act or restrained from acting.")[124] There is a temptation, constantly found in contemporary scholarship, both to see this statement as Thomas's principal definition of law (in fact, he offered numerous and competing definitions throughout the *Treatise on Law*), and to understand the word *regula* ("rule"), in particular, in contemporary legal positivist terms. That is, many readers see *regula* as standing for the word "rule" in H.L.A. Hart's sense of that word, that is, as signifying discrete commands, such as "no vehicles in the park."[125] I have addressed the problems inherent with this reading in the article I have referenced above.[126]

But I should add the following. In medieval Latin, the meaning of the word *regula* was considerably broader than "rule" in a Hartian sense. Consider the definition Gratian excerpted from Isidore of Seville: *Regula dicta est eo quod recte ducit, nec aliquando aliorsum trahit. Alii dixerunt regulam dictam, vel quod regat, vel normam recte vivendi prebeat, vel quod distortum pravumque est corrigat* ("A rule is so called because it leads one rightly, and never pulls in another direction; others say a rule is so-called, because it governs, or reveals the standard for right living, or corrects the twisted or crooked").[127] Isidore's understanding of *regula*, plainly, is not Hart's. It encompasses much more than a rule like "no vehicles in the park." It looks rather to a way of living (*recte ducit*). And it is the case that *regula*, understood expansively as a guide to a way of life, was one standard usage of *regula*.[128] Religious orders followed *regulae*—"rules." The *Regula Sancti Benedicti* governed the Benedictine Order. The *Regula bullata* defined thirteenth-century Franciscan life.[129] Canons regular, meanwhile, were "congregations of clergy living under a monastic rule."[130] The Dominicans, the order to which Thomas belonged, were governed at the time by the Rule of St. Benedict.

In my earlier article, I argued that *regula*, as Thomas used the term, constituted part of a larger understanding of law as a "plan." Thomas's usage of two other terms support this reading, *ordinatio* and *utilitas*. Thus, we find in another of Thomas's definitions of law: *potest colligi definitio legis, quae nihil est aliud quam quaedam rationis ordinatio ad bonum commune.* ("It can be gathered that the definition of law is nothing other than an ordinance of reason directed at the common good.").[131] Again, some contemporary writers understand the word "*ordinatio*" as "rule."[132] Thus there is a tendency to see it in the same category as, say, "the traffic ordinances."

Such a reading, however, is erroneous. The Latin noun *ordinatio* included in its terms much more than what we mean by "rule." For instance, it signified the organization of knowledge. William of Ockham wrote an *ordinatio* on the first book of Peter Lombard's *Sentences*, proposing to systematize theories of God, creation, and human knowledge.[133] Thomas himself, in another place in the *Summa*, spoke of logic as the *ordinatio rationis.*[134] No surprise, then, that we find the word *ordo* used to signify "plan" when Thomas wrote of the community's law.[135]

Finally, there is *utilitas*, "usefulness." Thomas was well aware that legislators were not philosophers and so he declared that their proper concern must be with the *singularia et contingentia*—"the singular and the contingent."[136] They must, in other words, shape the law to match the needs of the communities that they govern. And in so doing, they must keep in mind the place of *utilitas.* Indeed, in yet another definition of law, Thomas wrote: *Finis autem humanae legis est utilitas hominum.* ("The goal of human law must be the utility of persons"). Law, in other words, must serve the needs of persons in the particularity of their lives. How do we weigh and balance the many and competing demands of the public—from meeting the desperate needs of the poor, to negotiating trade routes and treaties with other political communities? Provided they kept to the demands of the common good, Thomas trusted legislators to resolve these questions in a way that met the needs of the communities that they governed.

This understanding of law underscores Quentin Skinner's point that the northern Italian city-states would have found Thomas's legal theory a useful tool both for planning purposes and for rationalizing the morality of the decisions they reached. Law is a plan, it organizes the life of the community, and it meets the needs of the moment. There is yet, however, one other Thomistic idea that warrants careful scrutiny.

Natural law: first principles or legislative discretion?

For Thomas, the universe was law based and hierarchically structured. At the very top was the eternal law, what Thomas called "the Supreme Governor's plan of governance, from which, necessarily, every plan of governance proposed by subordinate rulers is derived."[137] There was also the divine law, in the form of the law handed down to Moses and the new dispensation of Jesus Christ.

Let us leave to one side the divine law and focus on the relationship of the eternal law and natural law. Natural law, like all law, is a manifestation of the eternal law. Natural law is knowable by reason. Indeed, in its first principles it is a branch of theoretical reason and thus can be compared to the theoretical sciences. Like mathematics, its founding axioms are self evident, at least to the well informed.[138] And among the self-evident predicates of the natural law were numbered mandates like "one ought to know the truth about God"; "one must avoid ignorance"; "one should not give offense to others with whom one lives in community."[139] If natural law consisted only of these first premises, Thomas continued, "is there one natural law that governed all?"[140] The answer seemed to be in the affirmative. After all, if the natural law functioned like mathematics, then what is true now has always been true, and it was impossible for any human being to alter this reality.

Law, however, parted company from the principles of mathematics in the sense that it called for the integration of theoretical reason and practical reason. Thomas explained: "[Natural law's] secondary precepts, which we have described as being like particular conclusions close to first principles, though not alterable in the majority of cases, can nevertheless be changed on some particular and rare circumstances."[141] Thomas gave an example: all would agree "that goods held in trust are to be restored to their owners."[142] Yet if we explore particular factual situations, we will soon recognize that there are circumstances where to return the goods "would be injurious and consequently unreasonable."[143]

A second example of this integration Thomas proposed to examine was the case of killing. Thomas acknowledged as a foundational principle the dictum that one must not kill: "For it belongs to God alone to pronounce sentence of death and life, according to Deuteronomy 32: 39, 'I will kill and I will make to live.'"[144] Thomas, however, crafted a number of exceptions to this rule. Publicly constituted authority might inflict the death penalty where it was deemed required to preserve the common good.[145] Private persons must never take human life yet Thomas found it licit to take another's life in the case of self-defense on the basis of the principle of double effect.[146] It was wrong to kill the innocent, but Thomas acknowledged that a judge might sentence to death a defendant he knew to be innocent where the innocence could not be established at trial[147] (an astonishing display of putting the efficiency of the system ahead of human life).[148] To take one's own life was impermissible, but it was not wrong voluntarily to surrender one's life so that another might live.[149] In this latticework of distinctions and exceptions we see Thomas carving a series of exceptions to what seemed like an absolute rule, either to protect the community, or the judicial system, or to meet some other countervailing concern.

It is not a surprise, therefore, that when Thomas came to investigate the intersection of natural and human law, he focused not on the natural law's first principles or prohibitions but on its dynamic character. "To depend on natural law," Thomas wrote, "is of the essence of human law."[150] But each political community must make "a particular determination" (***particularis determinationis***) regarding the natural law's applicability.[151] How much evil should the law prohibit? It is impossible for a community to forbid "all acts of vice," and how much wrongdoing should be tolerated was up to the community to determine.[152] How much virtue ought the community to mandate? Again, since it was impossible to command a community to be perfectly virtuous, choices had to be made, keeping in mind always the preservation of the common good.[153] Still, Thomas hopefully thought that societies and governments would move in the direction of ever more virtuous choices. Thomas believed in progress. Human reason moved steadily to perfection, in the sciences and the arts, and the law should similarly advance where it was possible to attain "some highly important and evident gain."[154]

There is a stunning degree of flexibility in this set of propositions. One might read these proposals optimistically. Thomas seemed genuinely to believe in an upward trajectory to the human species. We have moved from the simple to the complex in our understanding of the world, and this ascent should be reflected in our law. But a more cynical reading is equally possible. Thomas's view of the law was from the top down. Perhaps he trusted the legislators and rulers of states to strike the right balance for their territories and jurisdictions. But perhaps he merely wished to confer on them broad latitude for action without encumbering their consciences overly much.

But Thomas did not stop there. He also developed the idea that human reason might make "additions" to the natural law. We should pay particular attention to his argument. It began with a distinction. There are certain natural-law doctrines, he asserted, that are unalterable. He gave as an example the principle that one must never harm another human being.

So far, so good. But Thomas went on to propose that human reason may alter the natural law in certain respects, at least where "nature does not bid the contrary."[155] He explained this proposition with an analogy. We are born naked. In a sense, then, our natural state is nakedness, yet we wear clothing. This, Thomas claimed, was an instance of an addition to the natural law made by reason for the convenience of human beings.[156]

The next two examples he gave, however, were more problematic. In our natural state, Thomas continued, there was no such thing as private property. All ownership was in common. Yet we have abandoned this way of life in favor of individual ownership of goods. John Locke, it might be recalled, labored long and hard to resolve this problem. Thomas, however, labored not at all when he asserted that private ownership was introduced "by human reason for the usefulness of human existence" (*sed per hominum rationem ad utilitatem humanae vitae*).[157]

Matters grew even worse when Thomas turned to slavery. He conceded that "universal liberty" was a doctrine of the natural law (*de iure naturali*). This meant, Thomas admitted, that slavery was not natural (*non sunt inductae natura*). But it exists today, he concluded, to serve human convenience.[158]

One modern commentator has written:

> Common possession of all things and universal freedom are said to be of the natural law, yet there is no obligation to maintain them. The natural law is thereby stripped of one of the most important characteristics of law, its binding force.[159]

In truth, the cognitive dissonance, if that is the right name for it, is breathtaking. In the same paragraph, Thomas pronounced "no harm to others" as a non-negotiable, proclaimed liberty as a universal principle of the natural law, and then authorized the capture and ownership of slaves to serve larger social needs. For Aquinas, plainly, tragically, the natural law did not pose a serious barrier to administrative and legislative imperatives.

Concluding observations

Some observations are in order.

First, Thomas was innovative in the way he conceived of government, its functions and its responsibilities. His *Commentary on the Politics* brings this aspect of his thought to the fore. So long as the common good was conserved, Thomas was prepared to countenance kingship, aristocracy, or "polity," though he expressed a preference for mixed forms of constitutional rule.

Second, Thomas was also hierarchical. Indeed, his thought was deeply, probably unconsciously saturated with hierarchical relationships. His commitment to hierarchy manifests itself most clearly in the *De Regno*, where he stated the case for kingship as the best form of rule. Even here, however, there were limits. Thomas held an apprehensive, foreboding fear of tyranny and even endorsed the forcible removal of a tyrant in the appropriate circumstances.

Third, Thomas without doubt believed in a common good, which the law should define and enforce. He even articulated a substantive core to this common good, though we would find some aspects of it—e.g., religious persecution—abhorrent today. His vision of the common good has been criticized by some modern scholars as "repressive" in the degree of power and discretion it conferred on rulers.[160] Still, the proposition that a ruler must never govern for his or her private advantage, and should always keep foremost in mind the good of the entire community, remains a compelling vision.

Fourth, in the end, Thomas was far too deferential to the imperatives of state governance. He entrusted too much discretion to legislators and administrators. His natural law doctrines were so filled with qualifications, admonitions, exceptions, distinctions, and advice that they would have proved little match for clever rulers. *Utilitas*—utility—loomed large in Aquinas's thought. We have seen where it overcame both the right to life (in the case of the judge condemning the innocent defendant), and "universal liberty" (in the case of slavery). It is obvious why Quentin Skinner saw Aquinas's constitutional and legal thought as holding such appeal for the northern Italian city-states and their governors.[161]

Notes

1 Skinner, 30.
2 Schütrumpf, 9–25.
3 Ptolemy of Lucca, 3–5.
4 Markus, 86.
5 Elshtain, 305.
6 *Commentary on the Politics*, Bk. I, ch. 6.
7 Ibid., Bk. I, ch. 1.
8 Ibid.

9 Ibid.
10 Ibid.
11 Hibbs, 133. See also Ramos.
12 *Commentary on the Politics*, Bk. I, ch. 1.
13 Ibid., Bk. I, ch. 3.
14 Ibid., Bk. I, ch. 6.
15 *Summa Theologiae*, Ia, Iae, q. 75, art. 1.
16 *Commentary on the Politics*, Bk. I, ch. 3.
17 *Summa Theologiae*, Ia, Iae, q. 75, art. 2.
18 Archibald, 48.
19 *Commentary on the Politics*, Bk. II, ch. 1.
20 Ibid., Bk. II, ch. 3.
21 Ibid.
22 Ibid. Bk. I, ch. 2.
23 Ibid., Bk. I, ch. 10.
24 Franks, 149–50.
25 Barker, 211.
26 See, for example, Balard, 235–54; and Origo, 321–66.
27 *Commentary on the Politics*, Prologue.
28 Carroll, 36.
29 Clark, 69–70.
30 *Commentary on the Politics*, Bk I, ch. 3.
31 Ibid.
32 Ibid., Bk. I, ch. 7.
33 Ibid.
34 Das Neves, 652.
35 *Commentary on the Politics*, Bk. I, ch. 8.
36 Ibid., Bk. I, ch. 7.
37 Ibid., Bk. I, chs. 7–8.
38 Ibid., Bk. I, ch. 1.
39 Ibid., Bk. I, ch. 10.
40 Ibid., Bk. I, ch. 1.
41 Ibid.
42 Goldman, 116.
43 *Commentary on the Politics*, Bk. I, ch. 1.
44 Ibid., Bk. I, ch. 2.
45 Ibid., Bk. I, ch. 1.
46 Ibid.
47 Ibid.
48 Ibid., Bk. II, ch. 1.
49 Ibid., Bk. II, ch. 5.
50 Ibid. I am here paraphrasing the phrase *ad per se sufficientia vitae humanae*.
51 Ibid., Bk. II, ch. 6.
52 Ibid., Bk. I, ch. 1.
53 Aroney, "Subsidiarity, Federalism, and the Best Constitution"; and Aroney, "Subsidiarity in the Writings of Aristotle and Aquinas."
54 *Commentary on the Politics*, Bk. III, ch. 6; and Bk. II, ch. 7.
55 Ibid., Bk. I, ch. 1.
56 Ibid., Bk. II, ch. 7.
57 Ibid., Bk. II, ch. 16.
58 Ibid., Bk. II, ch. 7.
59 Ibid., Bk. II, ch. 17.
60 Ibid., Bk. I, ch. 1.
61 Nagel, 252.

62 Duvall and Dotson.
63 Long.
64 Lisska, 166.
65 Coward, 67.
66 Celano, 220.
67 Bradley, 488.
68 Larkins, 95.
69 To be sure, Thomas did not believe in religious tolerance. He was highly critical of the Jewish faith, doubting its legitimacy and even ascribing to the Jewish people collective guilt for the crucifixion; see Hood, 62–3. In the thirteenth century, Muslims were often denounced as heretics so as to claim jurisdiction over their affairs; see Mastnak, 183. At different places, Thomas labeled Muslims either as "infidels" by which he meant a wholly other non-Christian faith, or as heretics; see Koch, 31.
70 *Summa Theologiae*, IIa, IIae, q. 11, art. 2.
71 Ibid., IIa, IIae, q. 11, art. 3, resp. ad 3.
72 Ames, 1–20.
73 *Commentary on the Politics*, Bk. II, ch. 14.
74 Ibid., Bk. II, ch. 9.
75 Ibid.
76 Ibid., Bk. II, ch. 8.
77 Ibid., Bk. II, ch. 4.
78 Ibid.
79 Ibid., Bk. II, ch. 8.
80 Ibid., Bk. II, ch. 4.
81 Furber, 599–629.
82 Ptolomy of Lucca, 5.
83 *De Regno*, Bk. I, ch. 1.
84 Ibid., Bk. I, ch. 13.
85 Ibid.
86 Ibid.
87 Ibid., Bk. I, ch. 14.
88 Ibid.
89 Ibid.
90 See Bleakley.
91 *De Regno*, Bk. I, ch. 13.
92 Ibid., Bk. I, ch. 3.
93 Ibid., Bk. I, ch. 5.
94 Ibid., Bk. I, ch. 4.
95 Ibid.
96 Ibid.
97 Ibid., Bk. I, ch. 11.
98 Ibid.
99 Reichberg, 123–4.
100 *Summa Theologiae*, Ia, IIae, q. 92, art. 1, resp., ad 4.
101 Ibid., I a, II ae, 96, q. 96, art. 4, resp.
102 Wyllie, 156–7.
103 *De Regno*, Bk I, ch. 7. Cf., Daniel 4: 35–7; Esther 8: 1–4.
104 *De Regno*, Bk I, ch. 7.
105 Ibid.
106 Ibid., Bk. I, ch. 11.
107 Ibid., Bk. I, ch. 10.
108 Ibid., Bk. I, ch. 8.
109 Ibid., Bk. I, chs. 9–10.

110 Stockwell, 138–39.
111 *De Regno*, Bk. I, ch. 7.
112 Ibid.
113 Southern, 118; see also Collins.
114 *De Regno*, Bk. I, ch. 7.
115 Black, 145.
116 Beer, 393.
117 Tierney, "Hierarchy, Consent, and the 'Western Tradition'," 647.
118 *Summa Theologiae* Ia, IIae, q. 105, art. 1, resp.
119 Tierney, "Hierarchy, Consent, and the 'Western Tradition'," 647.
120 Blythe, "The Mixed Constitution," 548.
121 Ibid., 563.
122 *Summa Theologiae*, I a, II ae, qq. 90–97.
123 Reid, Jr., "Thomas Aquinas: Definitions and Vocabulary in His Treatise on Law."
124 *Summa Theologiae*, I a, II ae, q. 90, art. 1, resp.
125 Bix, 52.
126 Reid.
127 D. 3, c. 2.
128 To be sure, another standard usage was as part of the phrase, *regulae iuris*—the "maxims of law," which articulated basic jurisprudential principles and was found in medieval editions of the Roman and canon law.
129 Grieco, 129.
130 Lawrence, 138.
131 *Summa Theologiae*, Ia, IIae, q. 90, art. 4, resp.
132 Brewbaker, 584–5.
133 Pelletier, 11–12.
134 McInerny, 56 and note 3.
135 See, for example, *Summa Theologiae* Ia, IIae, q. 90, art. 3, resp (*Dicendum quod lex proprie primo et principaliter respicit ordinem ad bonum communem*) ("It should be said that law properly, firstly, and principally looks to the ordering of the common good").
136 *Summa Theologiae*, Ia, IIae, q. 91, art. 3, resp. ad 3.
137 Ibid., Ia, IIae, q. 95, art. 2, resp.
138 Ibid., Ia, IIae, q. 94, art. 2, resp.
139 Ibid.
140 Ibid., Ia, IIae, q. 94, art. 4 (*utrum lex naturalis sit una apud omnes*).
141 Ibid., Ia, IIae, q. 94, art. 5, resp. Cf., Boler, 161–204.
142 *Summa Theologiae*, Ia, IIae, q. 94, art. 4, resp.
143 Ibid.
144 Ibid., IIa, IIae, q. 64, art. 5, resp. Cf., Makdisi, 67, 69, and note 10.
145 *Summa Theologiae*, IIa, IIae, q. 64, art. 2, resp.
146 Ibid., q. 64, art. 7, resp.
147 Ibid., IIa, IIae, q. 64, art. 6, resp. ad 3.
148 Noonan, 228–37.
149 *Summa Theologiae*, IIa, IIae, q. 64, art. 5, resp. ad 5.
150 Ibid., Ia, IIae, q. 95, art. 4, resp.
151 Ibid.
152 Ibid.
153 Ibid., Ia, IIae, q. 96, art. 3, resp.
154 Ibid., Ia, IIae, q. 97, art. 2, resp.
155 Ibid., Ia, IIae, q. 94, art. 5, resp. ad 3.
156 Ibid.
157 Ibid.

158 Ibid.
159 Donnelly, 525.
160 Sunderland, 42.
161 A note on the translations: I have utilized for the most part the following translations: Regan, *Aquinas*; Blythe, *On the Government of Rulers*; and the Blackfriars translation of the *Summa Theologiae*. I have supplemented these translations with my own where I thought necessary.

Bibliography

Ames, Christine Caldwell. *Religious Persecution: Inquisition, Dominicans, and Christianity in the Middle Ages*. Philadelphia: University of Pennsylvania Press, 2009.

Archibald, Katherine. "The Concept of Social Hierarchy in the Writings of St. Thomas Aquinas." *The Historian* 12 (1949): 28ff.

Aroney, Nicholas. "Subsidiarity, Federalism, and the Best Constitution: Thomas Aquinas on City, Province, and Empire." In *Aquinas and Modern Law*, edited by Richard O. Brooks and James Bernard Murphy, 419–86. Burlington, VT: Ashgate, 2013.

Aroney, Nicholas. "Subsidiarity in the Writings of Aristotle and Aquinas." In *Global Perspectives on Subsidiarity*, edited by Michelle Evans and Augusto Zimmermann, 9–27. Dordrecht: Springer, 2014.

Balard, Michel. "Slavery in the Latin Mediterranean (Thirteenth to Fifteenth Centuries): The Case of Genoa." In *Slavery and the Slave Trade in the Eastern Mediterranean (c. 1000–1500 CE)*, edited by Reuven Amitai and Christoph Cluse, 235–54. Turnhout: Prepols, 2017.

Barker, Hannah. *That Most Precious Merchandise: The Mediterranean Trade in Black Sea Slaves, 1260–1500*. Philadelphia: University of Pennsylvania Press, 2019.

Beer, Samuel. "The Rule of the Wise and the Holy: Hierarchy in the Thomistic Tradition." *Political Theory* 14 (1986): 391ff.

Bix, Brian. "H.L.A. Hart and the 'Open Texture' of Law." *Law and Philosophy* 10 (1991): 51ff.

Black, Antony. *Political Thought in Europe, 1250–1450*. Cambridge: Cambridge University Press, 1992.

Bleakley, Holly Hamilton. "The Art of Ruling in Aquinas' *De Regimine Principum*." *History of Political Thought* 20 (1999): 575–602.

Blythe, James M. *Ideal Government and the Mixed Constitution in the Middle Ages*. Princeton, NJ: Princeton University Press, 1992.

Blythe, James M. "The Mixed Constitution and the Distinction between Regal and Political Power in the Work of Thomas Aquinas." *Journal of the History of Ideas* 47 (1986): 547ff.

Blythe, James M., trans. *On the Government of Rulers: De Regimine Principum*. Philadelphia: University of Pennsylvania Press, 1997.

Boler, John. "Aquinas on Exceptions in Natural Law." In *Aquinas's Moral Theory: Essays in Honor of Norman Kretzmann*, edited by Scott MacDonald and Eleonore Stump, 161–204. Ithaca, NY: Cornell University Press, 1999.

Bradley, Denis J.M. *Aquinas on the Twofold Human Good: Reason and Human Happiness in Aquinas's Moral Science*. Washington, DC: Catholic University of America Press, 1997.

Brewbaker, William S. "Thomas Aquinas and the Metaphysics of Law." *Alabama Law Review* 58 (2007): 575ff.

Capizzi, Joseph. "The Children of God: Natural Slavery in the Thought of Aquinas and Vitoria." *Theological Studies* 63 (2002): 31–52.

Carroll, William E. "Aquinas, Thomas." In *Medieval Science, Technology, and Medicine: An Encyclopedia*, edited by Thomas F. Glick, et al. New York: Routledge, 2005.

Celano, Anthony J. "The Concept of Worldly Beatitude in the Writings of Thomas Aquinas." *Journal of the History of Philosophy* 25 (1987): 215ff.

Clark, Patrick M. *Perfection in Death: The Christological Dimension of Courage in Aquinas.* Washington, DC: Catholic University of America Press, 2015.

Collins, Andrew W. "The Palace Revolution: The Assassination of Domitian and the Accession of Nerva." *Phoenix* 63 (2009): 73–106.

Coward, Harold. *The Perfectibility of Human Nature in Eastern and Western Thought.* Albany: State University of New York Press, 2008.

Das Neves, João César. "Aquinas and Aristotle's Distinction on Wealth." *History of Political Economy* 32 (2000): 649ff.

Donnelly, Jack. "Natural Law and Natural Right in Aquinas' Political Thought." *Western Political Quarterly* 33 (1980): 520.

Drury, Shadia B. *Aquinas and Modernity: The Lost Promise of Natural Law.* Lanham, MD: Rowman & Littlefield, 2008.

Duvall, Tim, and Paul Dotson. "Political Participation and *Eudaimonia* in Aristotle's *Politics.*" *History of Political Thought* 19 (1998): 21–34.

Elshtain, Jean Bethke. "Augustine and Political Theology." In *Augustine Our Contemporary: Examining the Self in Past and Present*, edited by Willemien Otten and Susan F. Schreiner. South Bend, IN: University of Notre Dame Press, 2018.

Emery, Gilles, and Matthew Levering, eds. *Aristotle in Aquinas's Theology.* Oxford: Oxford University Press, 2015.

Finnis, John. *Aquinas: Moral, Political, and Legal Theory.* Oxford: Oxford University Press, 1998.

Franks, Christopher A. "Aristotelian Doctrine in Aquinas' Treatment of Justice." In Emery and Levering, *Aristotle in Aquinas's Theology*, 139, 149–50.

Furber, Elizabeth Chapin. "The Kingdom of Cyprus, 1191–1291." In *A History of the Crusades*, edited by Robert Lee Wolff and Harry W. Hazard. Vol. 2, 599–629. Philadelphia: University of Pennsylvania Press, 1962.

Goldman, David B. *Globalisation and the Western Legal Tradition: Recurring Patterns of Law and Authority.* Cambridge: Cambridge University Press, 2007.

Grieco, Holly J. "Pastoral Care, Inquisition, and Mendicancy in the Medieval Franciscan Order." In *The Origin, Development, and Refinement of Religious Mendicancies*, edited by Donald S. Prudlo, 117ff. Leiden: Brill, 2011.

Hibbs, Thomas S. *Virtue's Splendor: Wisdom, Prudence, and the Human Good.* New York: Fordham University Press, 2001.

Hood, John Y.B. *Aquinas and the Jews.* Philadelphia: University of Pennsylvania Press, 1995.

Keys, Mary M. "Politics Pointing beyond the Polis and the Politeia: Aquinas on Natural Law and the Common Good." In *Natural Moral Law in Contemporary Society*, edited by Holger Zaborowski, 170–94. Washington, DC: Catholic University of America Press, 2010.

Koch, Bettina. *Patterns Legitimizing Political Violence in Transcultural Perspective: Islamic and Christian Traditions and Legacies.* Berlin: De Gruyter, 2015.

Larkins, Jeremy. *From Hierarchy to Anarchy: Territory and Politics before Westphalia.* New York: Palgrave Macmillan, 2010.

Lawrence, Clifford Lawrence. *Medieval Monasticism: Forms of Religious Life in Western Europe in the Middle Ages*. 4th ed. New York: Longman, 2015.

Lisska, Anthony J. "Right Reason in Natural Law Moral Theology: Thomas Aquinas and William of Ockham." In *Reason, Religion, and Natural Law: From Plato to Spinoza*, edited by Jonathan A. Jacobs, 155ff. Oxford: Oxford University Press, 2012.

Long, Roderick T. "Aristotle's Conception of Freedom." *Review of Metaphysics* 49 (1996): 775–802.

Makdisi, John. "Aquinas's Prohibition on Killing Reconsidered." *Journal of Catholic Legal Studies* 57 (2018): 67ff.

Markus, Robert. *Saeculum: History and Society in the Theology of St. Augustine*. Cambridge: Cambridge University Press, 1986.

Mastnak, Tomaž. *Crusading Peace: Christendom, the Muslim World, and Western Political Order*. Berkeley: University of California Press, 2002.

McInerny, Ralph. *Aquinas and Analogy*. Washington, DC: Catholic University of America Press, 1996.

Nagel, Thomas. "Aristotle on *Eudaimonia*." *Phronesis* 17 (1972): 252ff.

Noonan, John T., Jr. "Masked Men: Person and Persona in the Giving of Justice." *Proceedings of the American Catholic Philosophical Association* 48 (1974): 228–37.

Origo, Iris. "The Domestic Enemy: The Eastern Slaves in Tuscany in the Fourteenth and Fifteenth Centuries." *Speculum* 30 (1955): 321–66.

Pakaluk, Michael. "Is the Common Good of Political Society Limited and Instrumental?" *Review of Metaphysics* 55 (2001): 57–94.

Pelletier, Jenny. *William Ockham on Metaphysics: The Science of Being and God*. Leiden: Brill, 2013.

Ptolemy of Lucca. *On the Government of Rulers: De Regimine Principum*. Edited and translated by James M. Blythe. Philadelphia: University of Pennsylvania Press, 1997.

Ramos, Alice. "A Metaphysics of the *Logos* in St. Thomas Aquinas: Creation and Knowledge." *Cauriensia* 9 (2014): 95–111.

Regan, Richard J., trans. *Aquinas: Commentary on Aristotle's Politics*. Indianapolis, IN: Hackett, 2007.

Regan, Richard J. "Aquinas on Political Obedience and Disobedience." *Thought* 56 (1981): 77–88.

Reichberg, Gregory M. *Thomas Aquinas on War and Peace*. Cambridge: Cambridge University Press, 2017.

Reid, Charles J., Jr. "Thomas Aquinas: Definitions and Vocabulary in His Treatise on Law." In *Christianity and Global Law*, edited by Rafael Domingo and John Witte, Jr. New York: Routledge, 2020.

Schütrumpf, Eckart. *The Earliest Translations of Aristotle's Politics and the Creation of Political Terminology*. Paderborn: Wilhelm Fink, 2014.

Skinner, Quentin. *Visions of Politics*. Vol. 2: *Renaissance Virtues*. Cambridge: Cambridge University Press, 2002.

Southern, Pat. *Domitian: Tragic Tyrant*. New York: Routledge, 1997.

Stockwell, Stephen. "Venice." In *The Edinburgh Companion to the History of Democracy: From Pre-History to Future Possibility*, edited by Benjamin Isakhan and Stephen Stockwell, 131ff. Edinburgh: Edinburgh University Press, 2015.

Sunderland, Luke. *Rebel Barons: Resisting Royal Power in Medieval Culture*. Oxford: Oxford University Press, 2017.

Tierney, Brian. "Aristotle, Aquinas, and the Ideal Constitution." *Proceedings of the Patristic, Medieval, and Renaissance Conference* 4 (1979): 1–11.

Tierney, Brian. "Hierarchy, Consent, and the 'Western Tradition'." *Political Theory* 15 (1987): 646ff.

Tierney, Brian. *Liberty and Law: The Idea of Permissive Natural Law*. Washington, DC: Catholic University of America Press, 2014.

Turner, Denys. *Thomas Aquinas: A Portrait*. New Haven, CT: Yale University Press, 2013.

Wyllie, Robert. "Reconsidering Tyranny and Tyrannicide in Aquinas's *De Regno*." *Perspectives on Political Science* 47 (2018): 154ff.

7 Cino Sinibuldi da Pistoia (ca. 1265–1336)

Giuseppe Speciale

Biographical introduction

Cino Sinibuldi (Sighibuldi, Sigisbuldi) was born between 1265 and 1270 in Pistoia, a city about thirty kilometers south of Florence. His family, of ancient and noble tradition, belonged to the black faction of the Guelph party. His father, Francesco, and his grandfather, Guittoncino, descended from Sighibuldo or Sigisbuldo, consul of Pistoia in the twelfth century; his mother was Diamante, daughter of the renowned doctor Bonaventura di Tonello.

In Pistoia Cino attended lessons of the liberal arts professor Francesco da Colle in the last decade of the thirteenth century, between 1293 and 1301. In Bologna he studied civil law at schools of Dino del Mugello (whom he called *doctor meus*, that is, my lord,[1] as a sign of deference used habitually by students towards their teachers), Francesco d'Accursio, Lambertino dei Ramponi,[2] and Martino Sillimani. It is likely that as a *licentiatus* (a baccalaureate student), between 1297 and 1299, he gave an *extraordinaria lectura de sero* (extracurricular night class); in fact we have a document attesting a loan of twenty-five bolognini (Bologna coin), the sum that the professors of the University of Bologna usually paid as a deposit to assure the students that they would hold regular classes and would respect *puncta taxata* (the most important topics chosen by students and teachers). Cino was able to hear a *repetitio* from Pierre de Belleperche in Bologna when, in 1300, the French jurist came to Italy for the holy year announced by Pope Boniface VIII.[3] We have no certainty about Cino's training in French law schools, of which he could have known method and style through Francesco d'Accursio and other Italian jurists who had taught in schools on the other side of the Alps.

In 1302, back in Pistoia, he married Margherita, daughter of Lanfranco degli Ughi, of the white Guelphs. From the marriage, probably celebrated in a moment of truce between the opposing Guelph factions, five children were born: a son, Mino, who died before Cino, and four daughters, Diamante, Giovanna, Lombarduccia, and Beatrice. Forced into exile by Pistoia in 1303 because he (Cino) was banned by the white faction, he returned there in 1306 and assumed the office of *assessore delle cause civili* (civil justice judge). Following Ludovico di Savoia, ambassador of Henry VII, in 1310 Cino went to Florence to try to gain the political support of the city for the king of Germany and then to Rome in June of the same year. There he held the position of counselor of the imperial tribunal.[4]

After the coronation of Emperor Henry VII, on June 29, 1312, at the Basilica of St. John Lateran, in Rome, Cino followed the emperor to Pisa, but on August 24, 1313, Henry died, perhaps from malaria, in Buonconvento, near Siena. With him died too the hopes of those who, like Cino and Dante, wished for an orderly and peaceful political order guided by the emperor. The death of Henry VII and the death of Selvaggia Vergiolesi, the woman who inspired Cino's poetry, both date to 1313 and plunged Cino into a state of prostration.[5]

The song "Tutto che altrui aggrada" ("(I despise) Everything that Others Appreciate") refers to those events: I despise everything that others like—Cino says—; the world bores me and I despise it. What do you like, then? I answer: I like it when others hurt themselves; I like to see the blows of the sword hurting the faces of others and the sinking ships; I would like a new Nero, and that every beautiful woman would become ugly. Joy and fun disturb me a lot, while I really like melancholy; and I'd like to be crazy all day. And I would like to kill all those I kill every day in my thoughts, in my thoughts of death.[6]

Cino retired from political commitment and devoted himself to the study of law: within a few months he completed his most important and famous work, *Lectura in Codicem*, which he completed on June 11, 1314.[7] A few months later, on December 9, he obtained his degree in Bologna, and shortly, on December 22, he assumed the role of judge in Siena, in the entourage of the Bishop of Bologna, Bartolino da Sala. He held this office through the first half of 1315. In 1317 he was councilor of the municipality of Pistoia for civil cases. For some time, until 1321, he was pontifical officer in Macerata and in Camerino, with Amélie de Lautrec, the papal rector of Marca. As professor, he taught in Siena from 1321 to 1326, with a probable interruption in Florence in 1324. In Bologna in 1324, he appears as witness to an act of sale made by Giovanni d'Andrea: on this occasion, according to some, through Giovanni d'Andrea he met Petrarch, who was a friend of the canonist. Then from 1326 until 1330, Cino was in Perugia, where his students included Bartolo da Sassoferrato.

The conflict between Pope John XXII and the German king Louis IV, the Bavarian, concluded with the excommunication of Louis in 1324 and the election, commissioned by Louis IV, of the antipope Niccolò V in 1328. These developments led Cino to a new assessment of the political context and to move away from pro-Ghibelline positions. On August 15, 1330, Robert of Anjou, king of Naples and papal vicar for Italy, called him to teach civil law in the capital of Campania, where Cino remained only for a year or so. In Naples Cino met Boccaccio but did not enjoy living there and devoted scornful satirical verses to the city: "Deh! quando rivedrò 'l dolce paese" ("Deh! when will I see the sweet country again").[8]

After leaving Campania, Cino went to Florence and then back to Perugia, where he returned to teach between 1332 and 1333. In Pistoia, between August and September 1334, he was *confaloniere*, "vexillifer iustitiae pro porta Guidonis" (that is, deputy of a neighborhood in the city), but he left the office for health reasons. In 1336, on March 31, he was elected to the People's Council of Pistoia; on December 23, he wrote his will, and shortly after the end of December or at the beginning of January, he died.

He is buried in the cathedral of Pistoia dedicated to Saint Zeno: the funerary monument sculpted by Agostino di Giovanni, or at least by someone close to him, perhaps by his son Giovanni or Agostino di Maestro Rosso, depicts Cino in the act of teaching. Cino's tomb leaves to posterity the memory of Cino the jurist.

Cino between poetry and law

Cino was not only a jurist but also a poet, and among the most productive of his time: twenty songs, eleven ballads, and one hundred thirty-four sonnets (without considering twenty lyrics of dubious authenticity). The verses of love are largely dedicated to Selvaggia Vergiolesi (d. 1313), of the noble family of the white faction of Pistoia, wife of Focaccia (Vanni) Cancellieri (d. ca. 1295), a bloody exponent of the white faction who was remembered by Dante in the Caina (*Inferno*, Canto 32, l. 63) among the traitors of the relatives.

When Cino died, Petrarch wrote, "Weep ladies, and may love weep with you": Petrarch invited women, love, and poetry itself to mourn the disappearance of the "master of the amorous strain" and did not hide his bitter grief.[9] Petrarch wrote that women, love, poetry, the citizens of Pistoia all had to cry for the death of Cino, the great poet who sang of women and love. Petrarch was inspired by Cino for the lyrics "Perché la vita è breve" ("Because life is short"), "Gentil mia donna, i' veggio" ("My dear woman, I see"), "Poi che per mio destino" ("Then for my destiny"), known as the "tre sorelle" ("three sisters").[10] These poems clearly echo Cino's song about the eyes of the beloved "Quando Amor gli occhi rilucenti e belli" ("When Love's shining and beautiful eyes").[11] Boccaccio, too, appreciates Cino and makes extensive use in the *Filostrato* of lines from Cino's song "*La dolce vista e'l bel guardo suave*" ("The sweet look and the suave expression").[12]

Undoubtedly, Cino has left an important mark in the poetry of the thirteenth and fourteenth centuries and in general in the poetry of all time: in 1908, in the collection *A lume spento*, Ezra Pound dedicated to Cino a lyric that concludes: "I have sung women in three cities./But it is all one./I will sing of the white birds/ In the blue waters of heaven,/The clouds that are spray to its sea."[13]

Pound's verses recall those that Dante: "Io mi credea del tutto esser partito" ("I thought I was far away"[14]) addressed to Cino after Selvaggia's death. Dante appreciates the poetry of Cino and invites him to be less voluble in his loves. The Pistoiese replied to the Florentine with "Poich'io fui, Dante, dal natal mio sito" ("Dante, since I was exiled"[15]). Cino is not volatile: rather, exiled and away from his beloved, he seeks in other women a reflection of the beauty of Selvaggia.

Luigi Chiappelli wonders if Cino's love is a calm, ideal, and philosophical feeling like that of Dante, or whether it is sensual, classical, and pagan like Boccaccio's, or, again, something of both, like that of Petrarch.[16] Julius Claro, among others, remembers that Cino was, besides *excellens doctor* ("excellent jurist") also *maximus amator* ("skilled lover"). Claro cites the same passage of Cino's *Lectura in Codicem* (C.9.11.1) remembered by Savigny. Claro is impressed by the contrast between the poet animated by pure love and the jurist impregnated with gross, shameless materialism: *crede experto, quod donum magis valet, quam suspirium, imo suspirium nihil valet sine dono, ferrum tamen praeponitur aurum; nam, secundum Juvenalem: ferrum est quod amant. Quod quidam exponent, id est ferreum membrum, propter cuius ferri fortitudinem insignes etiam mulieres servis vilissimis se exponunt, ut hac lege mostratur.*[17]

Between 1302 and 1306, Dante addressed to Cino the Epistle III, "Exulanti Pistoriensi Florentinus exul inmeritus" ("the innocent banished Florentine to the banished Pistoiese")[18] and the sonnet "Io sono stato con amore insieme" ("I have been together with love")[19] in response to the sonnet "Dante, quando per caso s'abbandona" ("Dante, when casually someone abandons desire"),[20] with which Cino had asked him to be comforted in his conviction that a man, once he had exhausted his passion for a woman, could fall in love with another. The structure and style of these sonnets are very reminiscent of the school setting of a *quaestio*.

Dante in several passages of *De vulgari eloquentia*, in which he defined himself as Cino's *amicus*, or friend, exalts the sweetness, depth, and fidelity of the grammar of Cino's poetry (Dve I,10,4) and recognizes Cino, the poet of love (Dve II,2,6), to have experienced the excellence of the vernacular language (Dve I,13,3), which in his songs emerges noble, limpid, perfect, and urbane (Dve I, 17, 3), as in the examples mentioned (Dve II,5,4 "Non spero che giamai per mia salute" ("I do not hope for my health"), Dve II,6,5 "Avegna che io aggia più per tempo" ("It happened that I after a long time"), written to console Dante on the death of his beloved Beatrice, and Dve II,2,8 "Digno sono eo de morte" ("I deserve to die"). However, the name of Cino is not mentioned in *The Divine Comedy*. After 1313 the relationship that binds the two poets, also united in the political project centered on the emperor Henry VII, perhaps cracks. Perhaps Dante does not tolerate the new political positions of Cino or is angry about three polemical sonnets attributed to the Pistoia jurist ("In verità questo libel di Dante";[21] "Infra gli altri difetti del libello";[22] and "Messer Boson, lo vostro Manoello"[23]).

Although Dante does not expressly mention Cino in *The Divine Comedy*, this is not a *damnatio memoriae*. According to some critics, in fact, the dialogue between the two poets continues, albeit in an allusive and veiled way, even in Dante's most famous work. Certainly, Dante did not like some positions taken by Cino after the death of Henry VII: in 1320, Cino supported the persecutions of the Curia against the Ghibellines of the Marche. And the previous year, he had taken part in a council of civil and canonical lawyers, appointed by the inquisitor of Florence, to condemn the Franciscans as heretics.[24]

In the wake of Dante and Guido Cavalcanti, for Cino poetry is an ornament, the beautiful garment of truth or philosophy, "amoroso uso di Sapienza," "a loving use of wisdom," as Dante says (Convito III,12).[25] Artist and scientist, Cino takes care of the precision of concepts as well as the formal perfection of the verse:

Poi che saziar non posso gli occhi miei
Di guardar a madonna il suo bel viso,
Mirerol tanto fiso,
Ch'io diverrò beato lei guardando.
A guisa d'angel, che di sua natura
Stando su in altura
Divien beato sol vedendo Dio,
Così, essendo umana creatura.
Guardando la figura
Di questa donna che tiene il cor mio,
Potrìa beato divenir qui io:
Tant'è la sua virtù che spande e porge,
Avvegna non la scorge
Se non chi lei onora desïando.[26]

Cino and rhetoric between poetry and law

In Cino's works, lyric poetry and rhetoric merge. As De Sanctis said, Cino, like Dante and Guido Cavalcanti, is both a poet and a scientist. For all three, the training in the Bologna university schools plays a very important role. All three use the scientific method of employing rhetoric to link and associate distant concepts through successive approximations. Love, at the center of the poetry of the chivalric tradition, becomes a subject of philosophy and theology. The poet scientist does not stop only at the phenomenal dimension of love, but goes beyond the literal sense, seeks an "over sense," the theological and philosophical sense. Behind and beyond the phenomenon is the meaning; hidden behind the veil of the phenomenon is the essence. The scientist looks beyond the phenomenon in search of essence. So for Cino, Emperor Henry VII is a *forma del bene*, a "form of good," and for the poets of his time the body is a veil of the spirit, while woman is the form of every moral and intellectual perfection. Cino is as much a poet as a scientist: he is accustomed, as a jurist, to distinguish the general from the particular, the abstract from the concrete, and to link seemingly opposing concepts. With a refined rhetoric, when he reasons about law he arrives at analogical or extensive interpretations, and when he writes verses he arrives at suggestive and engaging poetic images. But he also reasons subtly in his verses. According to Domenico De Robertis, Cino is tormented by the worm of reflection and prefers a reasoning path.[27] According to Elisa Benzi, Cino does not describe the figures represented in his poems through the use of attributes and complements, but uses hypotaxis to establish precise hierarchies between the facts and to identify causes and consequences of actions and behaviors enacted and suffered.[28]

He is certainly a poet when he sings his love for Selvaggia, but he is also a scientist when he investigates the most hidden folds of souls: he creates a "rhetoric of love." De Sanctis writes:

> Selvaggia's love made him a poet, but he could not change his mind. Instead of representing his feelings as a poet, he subjects them to analysis, as a critic, and subtly reasons. Placed out of nature and in the field of abstraction, every limit of reality is lost, and that same subtlety that tied together the most disparate concepts and drew arguments and conclusions out of every reality and every common sense, now created a poetic scholasticism, or to put it in his own name, a rhetoric for the use of love, full of figures and exaggerations, where you can see the love-spirits that go around and the sighs that speak. In place of living persons, personifications abound.[29]

In the refined and exaggerated exercise of rhetoric, woman represents salvation, which is an unattainable goal: to the poet who scientifically distinguishes virtues of love, heart, kind spirit, intellect, soul, and sighs, all that remains is to die (*Questa donna che andar mi fa pensoso*—"this woman who makes me pensive").[30]

If we consider Bologna and Florence as the main centers of Italian culture in the second half of the thirteenth century, though the Sicilian school had now entered the scene, Cino is certainly among the protagonists of the cultural life of both cities. As a jurist scientist, he is appreciated in Bologna; as a refined poet, he is esteemed in Florence. As scientist he uses Latin, the language of the learned; as poet, the vernacular, the language of art. Poetry is no longer the spontaneous and popular art of the troubadours; the scientific method that establishes itself and triumphs in university schools extends its shadow and its light on poetry. The verses written for the death of Emperor Henry VII not only evoke the hopes, the illusions, and the tragic condition of exile, but also lucidly and scientifically draw, with a sweet, musical, and clean language, the power of death and the immortality of virtue. Poetry is the beautiful garment of truth or philosophy, a loving use of wisdom, as Dante says in *The Convito.* The artistic consciousness appears in Cino in the technical and exterior qualities of the form. Its main mission is to develop the musical elements of the language and verse. Until that time, the language was not so sweet in any other poet; now it was making images of a beautiful, polished marble, from which all harshness and inequality are removed.[31]

Cino is a jurist scientist and poet-artist. Poet and scientist, in his verses he tries to explain the most complex aspects of spirit and nature. "The less he appears cultured, the more he is an artist," writes De Sanctis.[32]

The humanist Giovan Giorgio Trissino (1478–1550), to whom we owe the recovery of Dante's *De Vulgari Eloquentia*, in his *Poetica* recalls the seven general forms of poetic language and assigns to Petrarch the primacy for greatness and beauty; to Dante, greatness, custom, and artifice; to Guido Guinizzelli, sweetness and acumen; and to Cino, clarity.[33]

Brevity and clarity are also important in the construction of legal discourse, which does not allow for excessive length and must be characterized by precision: Cino is concise in considering the essential points and the principal novelties of law, neglecting to dwell in the exposition of superfluous concepts. Regarding a law, he does not make a long speech repeating the interpretations of ancient and modern doctors: he gives a brief account of the various interpretations, dwelling on some new points.[34]

In the history of literature, Cino is considered the bridge that unites Dante and the great Florentines of the end of the thirteenth century to Petrarch and Boccaccio. In the history of law, the Pistoiese jurist can be considered the bridge between the post-Accursian jurists and the commentators, or the bridge between French schools and Italian schools of law. The monumental *Lectura in Codicem* in which Cino extensively uses the thought of Pierre de Belleperche and Dino del Mugello, remains his main work, and the author continued to update it with *additiones* even after 1314. Additionally, some *consilia* and *quaestiones* (not a complete and "in-form" collection) have come down to us, as have a *Lectura* at the *Digestum vetus* (only up to Dig.2.9); a *Lectura* on the title *De rebus creditis* (D.12.1); an ordinary *Divina lectura* (up to D.1.8.11), attributed to Bartolo before Domenico Maffei proved Cino's real paternity; *additiones* and *apostillae* on various parts of the *Corpus Iuris Civilis*; and *Glossae contrariae*.

Cino between old and new ways

With the *Lectura in Codicem*, Cino aims to offer to legal scholars, trained in the Accursian gloss, the possibility of applying the method of French schools. Thus he summarizes the method he followed in writing the work:

> *In lectura huius legis taliter procedam. Primo dividam legem istam per partes, et ponam casum, et literalia expediam. Secundo signabo quaedam contraria et dissolvam. Tertio formabo quasdam quaestiones, et earum solutiones subiiciam. quarto et ultimo colligam quaedam argumenta, ad haec utilia.*[35]

First of all, Cino reads the text of the normative provision; then he orders and distinguishes the parts that compose it; then he explains the content of the norm and uses concrete examples to make more evident the facts to which the provision applies; finally, he highlights the problems that can arise from the application of the law and the objections that can be moved; and he concludes by exposing the controversial issues that serve to test and verify the understanding of the provision.

From the ability to distinguish analytically and to synthetically compose parts and meanings of the Justinian text derives also the independence of judgment with respect to the tradition that had been solidified in the Accursian Gloss. Cino uses the hypertextual literary structure of the gloss to move and orient himself in the immense landscape of the *Ius commune*. He uses the connections and nodes of Accursius's apparatus to verify the consistency of ancient logical paths and to create new ones. His choices, in the tradition (never abandoned) of the *summae*, are exposed by his adopting not the hypertextual, fragmentary form typical of the *apparatus*, but the linear, flat, discursive form. Cino uses and moves from the gloss while also being attentive to the tradition (and betrayals) of the gloss, but he does not stop at the results achieved by glossators, and he does not rest on the *communis opinio* (that is, the "mainstream") if he has not verified it before.

His method is the forge of the genius of Bartolo[36] and marks the school of commentators. In Cino's work, references to the *ius proprium*, to the city statutes, and to the normative dispositions of particular laws are very frequent. The *ius novum* constituted by *ius proprium* is, by its nature, episodic, punctual, almost never inserted into an exhaustive and autonomous *corpus*, but it is, on the other hand, the response of the legal system to new political, economic, and social issues.[37] Cino, like the other jurists of his time, undertakes to harmonize this heterogeneous normative material by origin and content; he commits himself to bringing the new rules that govern the society of his time back to the principles and the juridical figures of Justinian law. It is a necessary operation for the jurist who cannot operate without a work tool that is as coherent and comprehensive as possible. Thus, Cino undertakes to identify *glossae contrariae*—that is, contradictory glosses within the Accursian apparatus;[38] he is attentive (perhaps owing to the teaching of Francesco d'Accursio) to distinguishing within the ordinary apparatus glosses that have not been included in the selection by Accursio; he frequently reports cases drawn from experience to exemplify the happy and indispensable coordination between *ius civile* and *iura propria*, between *ius vetus* and *ius novum*, between the tested wisdom of the solutions codified by Justinian and the new discipline of ancient and new relationships that particular systems dictate to order the new economic, political, and social arrangements.[39]

Cino's most important work, the *Lectura in Codicem*, completed in 1314, bears explicit traces of his decade-long commitment as a magistrate. The attention to the *ius proprium* and to the issues related to its concrete application is also evident in the countless *additiones* to the Accursian gloss documenting Cino's thought in the manuscripts of Justinian texts circulating in medieval juridical schools.

But Cino can also be considered the bridge between the science of law and other sciences. Illuminating in this respect is an episode well explained by Hermann Kantorowicz in 1906. Cino is called to express his opinion on a question raised by a husband who believes that the son born of his wife in the seventh month of marriage is not his own but rather the son of his brother. Cino does not stop at the letter of the *Septimo mense* law of the *Digesta De Statu hominum* (*Septimo mense nasci perfectum partum iam receptum est propter auctoritatem doctissimi viri Hippocratis, et ideo credendum est eum qui ex iustis nuptiis septimo mense natus est, iustum filium esse* Dig.1.5.12) and not even at the letter from the Accursian Gloss, which considers that the son born after six months and one day after marriage must be considered legitimate. Cino turns to the medical scientist to have safe elements to use in the evaluation of the matter. Gentile confirms the conclusion of Hippocrates but suggests, however, that: "Ergo,

Domine Cyne, quando de his cadit questio inter iurisperitos, accipiant medicos probos, qui, considerata comprexione pueri nati et mulieris, poterunt dicere: sit natus ex marito uel ex fratre" (good doctors must assess the health of the newborn and the mother in order to determine whether the child is the child of the husband or of his brother). Beyond the Hippocratic rules, "good doctors" will assess whether the degree of maturation of the child being born is compatible with the declared duration of gestation, considering the date of the marriage. Cino, a jurist scientist, turns to Gentile, a medical scientist, to learn more about the facts on which he is called to decide. For Cino, it is not enough to know the rule, the formal principle enshrined in the law and confirmed in the *scientia iuris*; he wants to know more and to understand better, he wants to make use of the results of empirical analysis to judge in the wisest and correct way. This openness to methods and knowledge that are not exclusive to legal science is coherent with Cino's training and intellectual profile, he is accustomed to using all the elements of knowledge in the construction of discourse, both poetic and juridical.

Cino's surviving writings allow us to reconstruct his point of view, and possibly also the changes of his point of view, regarding some juridical and political problems. The medieval jurists reproached him for some volatility in interpretations and solutions proposed in his works. On the political level, Cino passes from initial positions decidedly pro-imperial to positions closer to the hierocracy.

About the authentica *Clericus* (C.1.3.33(32)) Cino writes:

> *Praeterea Deus fecit duo luminaria, unum quod praeesset diei, alterum quod praeesset nocti, id est unum quod praeesset secularibus, alterum quod praeesset spiritualibus. . . . Sed alia criminalia quae non respiciunt immediate fidem, ut furta, latrocinia, et similia, illa sunt civilia, tamen, quicquid dicat, Ecclesia sibi usurpavit ratione peccati totam iurisdictionem.*[40]

Cino thus interrupts a long tradition according to which the sun represented the Church and the moon the empire. From the time of Innocent III (with the decree *Solita*, then merged into the *Liber Extra* X.1.33.6), the sun in fact was associated with the papacy, which radiates with its light the moon (the empire). The supremacy of the papacy over the empire was clearly stated, and the relationship between *pontificalis auctoritas* (the pope's authority) and *regalis potestas* (the king's power) was clarified, naturally establishing the preeminence of the *auctoritas* (sun) over the *potestas* (moon). Cino, in his commentary on *Clericus*, reverses the terms of the relationship: the sun is the empire, the moon the papacy.[41]

Similarly, in his verse Cino adopts the metaphor of the sun to indicate the emperor. In "O voi che siete voce nel diserto" ("You who are a voice in the desert"),[42] Cino applies the rhetorical figure of the antanaclasis: in the same period the word "sol" is used twice, with different meanings and in an ambiguous way. "Sol" in Italian can mean "sun" or "alone." If the word "sol" ("s'è de lo sol, che non rende splendore/per la luna che è fatta maggiore": the moon fully or partially hides the sun, as during an eclipse) is used to mean the sun, the recipient of the poem could be just the emperor Henry VII. The sun would be a little dark because of the moon that grows strongly; the power of the sun-empire would be obscured by the power of the papacy-moon. If, however, the word "sol" in the following verses means "only" ("Voi siete sol d'ogni parente fòre;/però 'l contraro che 'l valore ha merto": you are undeservedly exiled, away from your family), the recipient of the poem could be Dante, unjustly exiled.[43] Undoubtedly in another poem written to celebrate the death of Henry VII "Da poi che la natura ha fine posto" ("After nature has finished"), Cino associates the sun with the emperor, whose fame illuminated the world in every part with its sweet light.[44]

Cino's political and ideological itinerary was influenced by the failure of the project of Henry VII to bring unity and order to Italy under the empire; moreover, for Italy's safety Cino considers Louis IV, the Bavarian, the Germanic oppressor, more dangerous than the king of Naples, Robert of Anjou, who acts within the powers conferred upon him by the pope, but by a pope who still lives in Avignon, far from Italy.

An evident and sure trace of the itinerary taken by Cino emerges from the comparison between the known *Lectura super digesto veteri* (the old *lectura*) and the *Lectura super digesto veteri* (the new *lectura*) identified by Domenico Maffei. In the old *Lectura*, Cino does not directly address the issue of the validity of the Constantinian donation as such; rather, following Revigny and Belleperche, he focuses his reasoning on the nature of the goods subject to the Constantinian donation. The jurist distinguishes the prescriptible assets (those that have an eminently economic value) from the imprescriptible ones (those that have an eminently political value, such as the *iurisdictio*, the *census praestatio*, and, in general, the *signa subiectionis*: jurisdictional activity, taxation, signs of public power). The ratio of the imprescriptibility of such goods resides in the need for the system to be governed by a single person. In the *Lectura in Codicem* and in the old *lectura* (completed in 1314 but containing materials collected during the previous years), Cino then reaches these conclusions: the Church legitimately possesses only the prescriptible goods received with the donation (that is, the goods that after donation became prescripted) but not the imprescriptible goods (that is, the *iurisdictio* and the *signa subiectionis*).

In the *new lectura*, however, dating back to a later period (Maffei thinks that Cino wrote it sometime during the last fifteen years of his life) the Pistoian jurist directly addresses the issue of the validity of the donation, not without affirming superiority *propter nobilitatem originis* (because of the nobility of the origins) of the Church on the empire: the Church is in fact directly constituted by God; the empire, instead, directly by the people and only in a mediated way by God. The donation is valid without any doubt, if nothing else on the basis of the words of the Psalmist, "You are my son; ask and I will give you" (Psalm 2:7–8), which may well refer to the *iurisdictio* and to the pope who is the vicar of Christ (Matthew 16:18–19: "You are Peter, and upon this rock I will build my church, and the gates of hell shall not prevail against it: I will give unto you the keys of the kingdom of heaven, and all that you will bind on earth shall be bound in heaven, and all that you loose on the earth will be melted in the skies").[45]

The poetically expressed disappointment of the jurist

In the sonnet "A che, Roma superba, tante leggi" ("O superb Rome, what have your many laws served?"), with the poignant melancholy of the poet, Cino looks to Roman law, to the Italian situation, and to his life as a scholar of law and concludes very bitterly, imploring the piety and mercy of God upon himself. What is the use of Roman law, with its plebiscites, with its senate's law, and with the responses of the jurists? What is the use of having dominated and governed the world with that law if today Rome, Italy, is instead dominated and governed by others? What is the use of spending all his life studying and applying those laws, all unjust and senseless? For that law which has not prevented the death of every glory in Rome today, Cino has neglected the law that God has written in the hearts of men: Cino implores the mercy of God.[46]

Notes

1 Cino, *Lectura in Codicem et aliquot titulos primi Pandectorum tomi*, l. Cum pro eo, C.7.47.1, vol. 2, fol. 458vb: "Doctor meus Dyn. De Mugel, sequitur distinctionem glos."

2 Ibid., l. Ex libris, C.3.33.17, vol. 1, fol. 174rb: "doctor meus dominus Lambertinus Ramponensis de Bononia" (my lord Lambertino de' Ramponi, my professor of law).

3 Ibid., l. Cum pro eo, C.7.47.1, vol. 2, fol. 458va: "Petrus vero dicit quod . . . Ita audivi eum dicentem Bononie, cum peregrinus venit et repetit han legem illo tempore quo indulgentia centesimi anni dominus Bonifacius Papa octavus fecit totum orbem peregrinari Romam."

4 Ibid., *Lectura in Codicem*, l. Debitores, C.2.11(12).11, vol. 1, fol. 75ra: "sicut vidi fieri cum fui con domino Ludovico de Sabaudia domino Vauldi senatore urbis in consilio senatus"; l. Qui bonis, C.7.71.1, vol. 2, fol. 477ra: "Sed cum ego haberem coram me Romae istam quaestionem de facto, cum essem Iudex in Senatu cum domino Ludovico de comitibus de Sabaudia senatore almae urbis."

5 "Io fu' 'n su l'alto e 'n sul beato monte." In *Letteratura Italiana Einaudi*, 30, available at: www.letteraturaitaliana.net/pdf/Volume_1/t8.pdf); Contini; Ciampi, sonetto LXXV, 85. For translation, see Rossetti, 390: "I was upon the high and blessed mound." It is one of the most famous sonnets by Cino, inspired by a visit to the tomb of the beloved Selvaggia.

6 Cino,

> *Tutto ciò ch'altrui agrada a me disgrada," in Contini*, 14; *Ciampi*, 111: *"Tutto ciò ch'altrui agrada a me disgrada,/ ed èmmi a noia e spiace tutto l'mondo. / Or dunque che ti piace? I' ti rispondo: / Quando l'un l'altro spessamente aghiada. / E piacemi veder colpi di spada/ altrui nel volto, e navi andare a fondo; / e piacerebbemi un Neron secondo, / e ch'ogne bella donna fosse lada. / Molto mi spiace allegrezza e sollazzo, / e la malenconia m'agrada forte; / e tutto l'dì vorrei seguire un pazzo; / e far mi piaceria di pianto corte, / e tutti quelli amazzar ch'io amazzo/ nel fèr pensier là dov'io trovo Morte.*

7 *Hic fit finis non solum huius libri sed totius operis lecturae huius libri: quod ego Cynus de Sigisbuldis de Pistorio, posterus forte illius Sigisbuldii consularis viri, de quo habetur mentio infra . . . quasi continue prosequendo, infra biennium terminavi. Currentibus a nativitate Domini nostri Iesu Christi Anno* M. ccc xiiii *die* xi.

mensis Iunii, quo sestum S. Barnabae celebrandum occurrit, ut cum eo terminarem hoc opus, cum quo Paulus Apostolus post Damascum Arabiamque lustratam etiam, instructus post XII *annos Evangelium praedicavit. Ne forte, testante Hieronymo, in vacuum cucurrisset. Sic ego, ne putarer in vacuum totiens lustrasse Bononiam, ubi bona sunt omnia, post revoluta scripta multorum, doctrinam meam predicavi: hoc est, coram dixi. Et ante faciem omnium posui laboris mei fructum, quem si aemuli, detrectatores, et invidi amare contingant, et arcuato vulnere contra me tamquam scorpiones insurgant, vos veritatis amici et virtutis fratres dolcissimi pergustetis, et ab eius sapore cognoscetis, ubi radicis eius arboris fixae sint, sine hospitis coscientia loquor et scribo, atque si pro huiusmodi est debita laus et aequalis, ne obijcere velitis rogo, quatenus obtrectatorum latrantibus refrenandis vox vestra frequens velut lapis validus emittatur. . . . Ubi vero correctione dignum praesens opus videbitis, charitatissimo oculo et sincera mente corrigite, ubinamque vel bene vel satis invenietis.*

(This is the end of all the work of Cino da Pistoia, of the noble family of the consul Sighisbuldo, a work that I finished in two years on June 11, 1314. And I submit the fruits of my work to the judgment of detractors and envious people who like scorpions want to attack me and also of friends who love the truth. Do not hesitate to correct the parts in which you think you have found errors): Cino, *Lectura in Codicem*, finis post C.9.51, vol. 2, fol. 571vb.

8 Cino classifies his verses as "true satire": it is a ferocious satire, sometimes an invective with offensive tones, in which the virtue of communal Italy opposes the vices of the kingdom of Naples and its reservoir of meanness, ignorance, and roughness. Keen, 143–52.

9 Petrarca, "Piangete donne e con voi pianga amore," in Neri, et al., 139:

> *Piangete, donne, et con voi pianga Amore;/ piangete, amanti, per ciascun paese, / poi ch'è morto collui che tutto intese/ in farvi, mentre visse, al mondo honore. / Io per me prego il mio acerbo dolore, / non sian da lui le lagrime contese, / et mi sia di sospir tanto cortese, / quanto bisogna a disfogare il core. / Piangan le rime anchor, piangano i versi, / perché 'l nostro amoroso messer Cino/ novellamente s'è da noi partito. / Pianga Pistoia, e i citadin perversi/ che perduto ànno sí dolce vicino; / et rallegresi il cielo, ov'ello è gito.*

English version by Tomlinson, sonnet LXXI, 150:

> Weep, ladies, weep! Let Love your sorrow share! / And weep, ye lovers too, of every clime! / Since he is dead whose well-instructed rhyme / Due reverence paid to you, while he lived here. / I pray that if I also add a tear, / Our griefs commingled, may not harshly chime; / Nor that my sighs be out of tune or time, / Since to my anguished heart they bring some cheer. / Let many a rhyme and stanza tell our grief, / For Cino, Master of the amorous strain, / So lately taken from us, but too soon: / Pistoia's sons perverse! Mourn ye in chief, / That your sweet neighbour ye ne'er see again, / While there is joy in heaven where he is gone.

10 Petrarca, "Perché la vita è breve," "Gentil mia donna, i' veggio," "Poi che per mio destino," in *Il canzoniere*, LXXI, LXXII, LXXIII, 106–19, in *Rime, Trionfi e poesie latine.*

11 Cino, "Quando Amor gli occhi rilucenti e belli," in Ciampi, canzone I, 15.

12 Cino, "La dolce vista e'l bel guardo suave," in Ciampi, canzone XVI, 91. About relations between Cino and Boccaccio, see Barsella.

13 Pound, "Cino," 1–2.

14 Dante Alighieri, "Io mi credea del tutto esser partito," in *Rime*, sonetto CXIV, 203.

15 Cino, "Poich' io fui, Dante, dal natal mio sito," in Ciampi, Sonetto LXXXVII, 151.
16 Chiappelli, 31.
17 "Believe me, women are worth more with a gift than a sigh; and iron, however, is worth more than gold. According to Juvenal, women love iron and because of the vigor of iron, even distinguished women give themselves to servants of vile condition": Cino, *Lectura in Codicem*, C.9.11.1, vol. 2, fol. 548rb; Claro, lib. V, § Fornicatio, 362; Savigny, 85.
18 Dante, "Exulanti Pistoriensi Florentinus exul inmeritus," in *Il Convito di Dante*, vol. 3, 432–4, and in *Le opere di Dante*, epist. 3.
19 Dante, "Io sono stato con amore insieme," in *Rime*, sonetto CXI, 195.
20 Cino, "Dante, quando per caso s'abbandona," in *Rime*, sonetto CX, 193; Ciampi, sonetto CXXIX, 151:

> *Dante, quando per caso s'abbandona / Il disío amoroso della speme, / Che nascer fanno gli occhi del bel seme, / Di quel piacer, che dentro si ragiona, / I' dico poi se morte gli perdona; / Se poi ella tien più delle duo streme? / L'almo gentil, la qual morir non teme, / Se tramutar si può 'n altra persona? / E ciò mi fa quella, che è maestra / Di tutte cose, e per quel ch'io sent'anco / L'entrata lascio per la ria finestra; / Per lei che'l mio creder non è manco / Che prima stato si o dentro, o estra, / Rotto mi sono orni mie ossa e fianco.*

Translated by Rossetti, 385:

> Dante, whenever this thing happeneth, / That Love's desire is quite bereft of Hope, / (Seeking in vain at ladies' eyes some scope / Of joy, through what the heart for ever saith,) / I ask thee, can amends be made by Death? / Is such sad pass the last extremity? / Or may the Soul that never fear'd to die / Then in another body draw new breath? / Lo! thus it is through her who governs all / Below,—that I, who enter'd at her door, / Now at her dreadful window must fare forth. / Yea, and I think through her it doth befall / That even ere yet the road is travell'd o'er / My bones are weary and life is nothing worth.

21 Cino, "In verità questo libel di Dante," in Ciampi, Sonetto CIX, 114:

> *In verità questo libel di Dante / È una bella scisma di Poeti, / Che con leggiadro e vago consonante / Tira le cose altrui nelle sue reti. / Ma pur tra Gioviali, e tra Cometi, / Riverscia il dritto, e'l torto mette avante, / Alcuni esser fa grami, alcuni lieti, / Com' Amor fa di questo e quello Amante. / Poi che gli essempi suoi falsi e bugiardi / Quai presso pon, quai lungi dal Demonio, / Debbano star sì come voti cardi; / E per lo temerario testimonio, / La vendetta de' Franchi, e de' Lombardi / Si dorrà, qual di Tullio fece Antonio.*

Translated by Rossetti, 394:

> This book of Dante's, very sooth to say, / Is just a poet's lovely heresy, / Which by a lure as sweet as sweet can be / Draws other men's concerns beneath its sway; / While, among stars' and comets' dazzling play, / It beats the right down, lets the wrong go free, / Shows some abased, and others in great glee, / Much as with lovers is Love's ancient way. / Therefore his vain decrees, wherein he lied, / Fixing folks' nearness to the Fiend their foe, / Must be like empty nutshells flung aside. / Yet through the rash false witness set to grow, / French and Italian vengeance on such pride / May fall, like Antony's on Cicero.

22 Cino, "Infra gli altri difetti del libello," in Ciampi, Sonetto C, 110:

> *Infra gli altri difetti del libello, / Che mostra Dante signor d'ogni rima, / Son duoi sì grandi, che a dritto l'estima, / Che n'aggia l'alma sua luogo men bello. / L'un è, che ragionando con Sordello, / E con molt'altri della dotta scrima, / Non*

fe' motto ad Onesto di Boncima, / Ch'era presso ad Arnaldo Daniello. / L'altr'è, secondo che il suo canto dice, / Che passò poi nel bel coro divino, / Là dove vide la sua Beatrice, / E quando ad Abraam guardò nel sino, / Non riconobbe l'unica Fenice, / Che con Síon congiunse l'Appennino. Translated by Rossetti, 395: "Among the faults we in that book descry / Which has crown'd Dante lord of rhyme /Are two so grave that some attaint is brought /Unto the greatness of his soul thereby. /One is, that holding with Sordello high /Discourse, and with the rest who sang and taught, /He of Onesto di Boncima nought /Has said, who was to Arnauld Daniel nigh. /The other is, that when he says he came /To see, at summit of the sacred stair, /His Beatrice among the heavenly signs, / He, looking in the bosom of Abraham, / Saw not that highest of all women there / Who join'd Mount Sion to the Apennines".

23 Ciampi, Sonetto CVIII, 114.
24 Italia, 7.
25 De Sanctis, vol. 1, 47.
26 Cino, "Poi che saziar non posso gli occhi miei," in Ciampi, madrigal III, 123. Translated by Rossetti, 314:

> Because mine eyes can never have their fill / Of looking at my lady's lovely face, / I will so fix my gaze / That I may become bless'd, beholding her. / Even as an angel, up at his great height / Standing amid the light, / Becometh bless'd by only seeing God: / So, though I be a simple earthly wight, / Yet none the less I might, / Beholding her who is my heart's dear load, / Be bless'd, and in the spirit soar abroad. / Such power abideth in that gracious one; / Albeit felt of none / Save of him who, desiring, honours her.

27 De Robertis, "Cino e Cavalcanti," 57.
28 Benzi, 30.
29 De Sanctis, 45–6:

> *L'amore di Selvaggia lo fece poeta, ma non poté mutare la sua mente. In luogo di rappresentare i suoi sentimenti, come poeta, egli li sottopone ad analisi, come critico, e ne ragiona sottilmente. Posto fuori della natura e nel campo della astrazione, ogni limite del reale si perde, e quella stessa sottigliezza che legava insieme i concetti più disparati e ne traeva argomentazioni e conclusioni fuori di ogni realtà e di ogni senso comune, creava ora una scolastica poetica, o per dirla col suo nome, una rettorica ad uso dello amore, piena di figure e di esagerazioni, dove vedi comparire gli spiritelli d'amore che vanno in giro e i sospiri che parlano. In luogo di persone vive, abbondano le personificazioni.*

30 "Questa donna che andar mi fa pensoso," in Ciampi, Sonetto VI, 14.
31 De Sanctis, 49:

> *La coscienza artistica si mostra in Cino nelle qualità tecniche ed esteriori della forma. La sua principale industria è di sviluppare gli elementi musicali della lingua e del verso, né fino a quel tempo la lingua sonò sì dolce in nessun poeta, rendendo imagine di un bel marmo polito, da cui sia rimossa ogni asprezza e ineguaglianza.*

32 Ibid., 49.
33 Trissino, 72.
34 "Quia omnia nova placent, potissime quae sunt utilitate decora, bellissime visum est mihi Cino Pistoriensi propter novitates modernorum doctorum super Codice, breviter utilia scribere, multis superfluis resecatis": Cyni Pistoriensis, *Lectura in Codicem*, vol. 1, fol. 1ra: C.1.1.1. And then: "Circa legem istam posset fieri longus sermo tractando de primo et secundo decreto, qui tractatus a nostris doctoribus antiquis et modernis satis irritatus et revolutus est, ergo breviter pertranseo, aliquas novitates tangendo": Cyni Pistoriensis, *Lectura in Codicem* C.7.72, vol. 2, fol. 477vb.

35 Cino, *In Digesti Veteris libros Commentaria doctissima a Nicolao Cisnero correcta.*
36 Baldi Perusini, *In Digestum Novum Commentaria doctissima*, De verborum obligationibus, L. Quidam cum filius, Dig. 45.132, fol. 25rb; Baldi Perusini, *In usus Feudorum Commentaria doctissima*, Si de feudo fuerit controversia, § Vasallus, fol. 61vb: "Dicebat autem mihi Bartolus quod illud quod suum fabricabat ingenium erat lectura Cyni."
37 Salvemini, 41–42: Cino believes that the Justinian rules governing the privileges of knights cannot be applied *sic et simpliciter* to knights appointed by municipal cities. In fact, these often do not have any skills in weapons and they perform dishonorable jobs (Cino, *Lectura in Codicem, De iuris et facti ignorantia*, l. Quamvis C.1.18, vol. 1, fol. 30ra).
38 Bellomo. Probably Dino taught and suggested Cino to search contradictory glosses inside the *Apparatus* of Accursius.
39 Annotations documenting Cino's teaching are reported, for the Justinian *Codex* manuscripts, by Speciale, s.v.
40 Cino, *Lectura in Codicem,* C.1.3.33, vol. 1, fol. 18vb. Moreover, God created two lights, one to govern the day, the other to regulate the night, that is one that regulates the earthly affairs, the other the spiritual ones. . . . But the church has kept for herself all jurisdiction because of the fact that crimes are also sins, including those that do not immediately refer to faith such as theft, etc.
41 Quaglioni; Condorelli traces the relationships between the church, temporal realities, and political society in the Western world up to the present day, adopting the historiographical categories of dualism and hierocracy and at the same time explaining their limits.
42 "O voi che siete voce nel diserto," in Ciampi, sonetto CXXV, 150.
43 Ferrara.
44 "Da poi che la natura ha fine posto," in Contini, 31; Ciampi, canzone XV, 89.
45 Maffei, *La "Lectura super Digesto Veteri"*, 48–56. Maffei, "Cino da Pistoia e il 'constitutum Constantini'."
46 *A che, Roma superba, tante leggi / Di senator, di plebe, e degli scritti / Di prudenti di placiti e di editti, / Se 'l mondo come pria più non correggi? / Leggi, misera te!, misera, leggi / Gli antichi fatti de' tuo' figli invitti, / Che ti fêr già mill'Affriche et Egitti / Reggere; et or sei retta, e nulla reggi. / Che ti giova ora aver gli altrui paesi / Domato e posto 'l freno a genti strane, / S'oggi con teco ogni tua gloria è morta? / Mercè, Dio! chè miei giorni ho male spesi / In trattar leggi, tutte ingiuste e vane / Senza la tua che scritta in cor si porta.*

Ciampi, cit., Sonetto CXIV, 337.

Bibliography

Barsella, Susanna. "Boccaccio e Cino da Pistoia: critica alla poetica dell'amore nella parodia di 'Filostrato' V e 'Decameron' III 5, X 7." *Italianistica: Rivista di letteratura italiana* 29 (Gennaio/Aprile 2000): 55–73.

Bellomo, Manlio. "'Glossae contrariae' *di Cino da Pistoia.*" *Tijdschrift voor Rechtsgeschiedenis/Revue d'Histoire du Droit/The Legal History Review* 38 (1970): 433–47.

Benzi, Elisa. *Ricerche sintattiche sui sonetti di Cino da Pistoia.* Rome: Aracne, 2008.

Carducci, Giosué. *Rime di m. Cino da Pistoia e d'altri del secolo XIV ordinate da G. Carducci.* Florence: G. Barbera, 1862. Milan: Istituto editoriale Italiano, 1916; and Florence: G. Barbera, 1928.

Chiappelli, Luigi. *Vita e opere giuridiche di Cino da Pistoia, con molti documenti inediti.* Pistoia: Tip "Cino" dei Fratelli Bracali, 1881 [Bologna: Arnaldo Forni editore, 1978].

Ciampi, Sebastiano. *Vita e poesie di messer Cino da Pistoia*. Pisa: Presso Niccolò Capurro, 1813.

Cino Sinibuldi da Pistoia [Cyni Pistoriensis]. *In Digesti Veteris libros Commentaria doctissima a Nicolao Cisnero correcta, et illustrate*. Francofurti ad Moenum: Sigismund Feyerabendt, 1578. Available at https://books.google.it/books/about/Ciny_Pistoriensis_in_Codicem_et_aliquot.html?id=NfH9h0mJB2gC&redir_esc=y), l. Lecta, D.12.1.40, fol. 56va.

Cino Sinibuldi da Pistoia [Cyni Pistoriensis]. *Lectura in Codicem et aliquot titulos primi Pandectorum tomi, id est Digesti veteris, doctissima commentaria a Nicolao Cisnero correcta, et illustrata*. Francofurti ad Moenum: Sigismund Feyerabendt, 1578. Available at https://books.google.it/books/about/Ciny_Pistoriensis_in_Codicem_et_aliquot.html?id=NfH9h0mJB2gC&redir_esc=y)

Claro, Julius. *Pratica civilis atque criminalis*. Francofurti: Typys Anthonii Hummi, 1636.

Condorelli, Orazio. "Le radici storiche del dualismo cristiano nella tradizione dottrinale cattolica: alcuni aspetti ed esempi." *Diritto e Religioni* 12 (2011): 450–86. Available at www.dirittoestoria.it/10/memorie/Condorelli-Radici-dualismo-cristiano-tradizione.htm

Contini, Gianfranco, ed. *Poeti del Duecento*. 2 vols. Milan/Naples: Riccardo Ricciardi Editore, 1960.

Dante Alighieri. *Il Convito di Dante Alighieri e le Epistole*. Edited by Pietro Fraticelli. Florence: G. Barbera Editore, 1862.

Dante Alighieri. *Le opere di Dante*. Edited by E. Pistelli. Florence: Società Dantesca Italiana, 1921.

Dante Alighieri. *Rime*. Edited by Gianfranco Contini. Turin: Giulio Einaudi, 1965.

De Robertis, Domenico. "Cino da Pistoia e la crisi del linguaggio poetico." *Convivium* (1952): 1–35.

De Robertis, Domenico. "Cino e Cavalcanti o le due rive della poesia." *Studi medievali* 18 (1952): 57.

De Sanctis, Francesco. *Storia della letteratura italiana*. Naples: Domenico e Antonio Morano, 1870.

Ferrara, Sabrina. "Dante, Cino, il Sole e la Luna." *L'Alighieri* 25 (2005): 27–47.

Gorni, Guglielmo. *Dante. Storia di un visionario*. Roma Bari: Laterza, 2009.

Italia, Sebastiano. "Dante e Cino da Pistoia. Un dialogo interrotto?" In *La letteratura italiana e le arti*. Atti del XX Congresso dell'ADI—Associazione degli Italianisti (Napoli, 7–10 settembre 2016), edited by L. Battistini, et al. Rome: Adi editore, 2018 [offprint].

Kantorowicz, Hermann. "Cino da Pistoia ed il primo trattato di medicina legale." *Archivio Storico Italiano* V Serie 37 (1906): fasc. 1, 115–28.

Keen, Catherine M. "Deh, quando rivedrò il dolce paese: considerazioni tematiche e formali sulla satira ciniana." In *Cino da Pistoia nella storia della poesia italiana*, edited by R. Arqués Corominas and S. Tranfaglia, 143–52. Florence: Franco Cesati Editore, 2016.

Maffei, Domenico. *La donazione di Costantino nei giuristi medievali*. Milan: Giuffré, 1964.

Maffei, Domenico. *La Lectura super Digesto Veteri di Cino da Pistoia. Studio sui mss Savigny 22 e Urb. Lat 172*. Milan: Giuffré, 1963.

Maffei, Paola. "Cino Sinibuldi da Pistoia." In *Dizionario Biografico dei Giuristi Italiani (XII–XX secolo)*, edited by Italo Birocchi, et al. Vol. 1, 543–6. Bologna: Società editrice il Mulino, 2013, with large bibliographic indications.

Monti, Gennaro Maria. *Cino da Pistoia giurista. Con bibliografia e tre appendici di documenti inediti.* Città di Castello: Casa editrice "il Solco", 1924.

Perusini, Baldi. *In Digestum Novum Commentaria doctissima.* Venetiis, 1586.

Perusini, Baldi. *In usus Feudorum Commentaria doctissima.* Lugduni, 1566.

Petrarca, Francesco. *Rime, Trionfi e poesie latine.* Edited by Ferdinando Neri, et al. Rome: Istituto dell'Enciclopedia Italiana, 2005.

Pound, Ezra. *Early Poems.* New York: Dover Publications, 1996.

Quaglioni, Diego. "'Quanta est differentia inter solem et lunam.' Tolomeo e la dottrina canonistica dei 'duo luminaria'." *Micrologus* 12 (2004) (Il sole e la luna): 395–406.

Rossetti, Dante Gabriele. *The Early Italian Poets from Ciullo d'Alcamo to Dante Alighieri (1100–1200–1300) in the Original Metres together with Dante's Vita nuova.* London: Smith, Elder and Co., 1861.

Salvemini, Gaetano. *La dignità cavalleresca nel Comune di Firenze.* Florence: Tipografia M. Ricci, 1896.

Savigny, Friedrich Carl von. *Geschichte des Römischen Rechts im Mittelalter.* Vol. 6. Heidelberg: F.C.B. Mohr, 1831.

Speciale, Giuseppe. *La memoria del diritto comune: sulle tracce d'uso del Codex di Giustiniano (secoli XII–XV).* Rome: Il Cigno Galileo Galilei, Edizioni di Arte e scienza, 1994.

Tomlinson, Charles. *The Sonnet: Its Origin, Structure, and Place in Poetry with Original Translations from the Sonnets of Dante, Petrarch, etc. Remarks on the Art of Translating.* London: John Murray, 1874.

Trissino, Giovan Giorgio. *La Poética.* Edited by Isabel Paraíso. Madrid: Arco Libros, 2014.

Weimar, Peter. "Cynus Pistoriensis." In *Lexikon des Mittelalters.* Vol. 2, 2089–91. Munich/Zürich: Artemis & Winkler Verlag, 1983.

Zaccagnini, Guido. *Cino da Pistoia. Studio biografico.* Pistoia: Libreria editrice D. Pagnini, 1918.

Other bibliographic indications are available at: www.mirabileweb.it/calma/cinus-pistoriensis-n-1265-1270-m-1336-1337/1146.

8 Giovanni d'Andrea (1270–1348)

Peter D. Clarke

Introduction

Known as Iohannes Andreae in Latin, Giovanni d'Andrea was one of the most renowned and prolific jurists of the later Middle Ages. His reputation was founded upon his long career of teaching canon law at the University of Bologna, spanning almost half a century (1302–48). Like many successful professors, he lived to see some of his pupils become famous professors themselves, including his adopted son, Giovanni Calderini and Paolo dei Liazari, both of whom also taught canon law at Bologna.[1] Giovanni d'Andrea's lasting fame rested on his voluminous output of writings in various juristic genres which circulated widely in manuscripts; several of his works were printed, some many times over between the late fifteenth and late sixteenth centuries, thus perpetuating his influence into the early modern period.[2]

His career coincided with two important developments in the history of the Western Church and its canon law, both reflected in his writings. One was that the papacy attained the zenith of its power over the Church, especially during the long residence of the popes at Avignon (1309–76), and the papacy's claims to authority were at their most extensive in this period. Giovanni d'Andrea has long been noted as a staunch defender of those claims and an active supporter of the Avignon papacy.

The other development was that the formation of a definitive body of Western canon law, the so-called *Corpus Iuris Canonici*, was largely concluded in his lifetime with the appearance of three collections of post—1234 papal legislation, the *Liber sextus* (1298), the *Clementinae* (1317), and the *Extravagantes* of Pope John XXII (c. 1325). Giovanni d'Andrea was among the first to write commentaries on the *Liber sextus* and the *Clementinae*. Both of his commentaries became the standard "gloss" (*glossa ordinaria*) on these collections, accompanying them in most manuscripts and printed editions. He thus stood at the head of a long line of canonists who commented on the *Corpus Iuris Canonici* as it appeared and evolved, and who even potentially influenced its content. Giovanni d'Andrea indeed claimed that Pope Clement V (1305–14) had issued on his advice the constitution *Saepe contingit*,[3] "commonly recognized as the most important single piece of medieval legislation in the history of summary judicial procedure."

This canonistic tradition stretched back to the mid-twelfth century, when the foundation stone of the *Corpus Iuris Canonici*, Gratian's *Decretum*, appeared, and Giovanni d'Andrea was also famed for his knowledge of this tradition. It was doubtless for this reason that he became known as *iuris canonici fons et tuba* (the fount and trumpet of canon law), since through his works he transmitted the teachings of earlier canonists who were no longer widely read. Thus, scholars have seen him as the first to trace the historical development of canonistic doctrine,[4] and Giovanni d'Andrea occupied an important position as a bridge between the so-called classical age of canon law and the postclassical canonists of the late medieval and early modern periods.

Biography

Much of what we know about the life of Giovanni d'Andrea comes from his juristic writings, which he was fond of embellishing with autobiographical details.[5] He was born about 1270, the illegitimate son of Andrea—hence Giovanni's appellation d'Andrea—and the latter's concubine, Novella. According to tradition, Andrea and Novella came from Rifredo, near Florence, and moved to Bologna when Giovanni was a child; it is now thought more likely that he was born not at Rifredo but in Bologna, as he was later styled "Bolognese" (*Bononiensis*) and was a citizen of Bologna.[6] By his own account, Andrea became a schoolmaster at Bologna and later a priest, and Giovanni studied grammar first under his father and then Bonocio da Bergamo. Giovanni also said that his father arranged private tutoring for him in canon law before he was ten, and that he studied theology under the Dominican friar Giovanni da Parma. Scholars generally assume that this theological training belonged to his youth, but Padovani has recently argued that it happened after 1315 and that its influence is only evident in Giovanni d'Andrea's works thereafter.[7] His formal legal studies began in 1285 at the University of Bologna, where he acknowledged Martino Sillimani as his teacher in civil law and Egidio Foscarari (d. 1289), Boatino da Mantova, and above all Guido da Baisio as his teachers in canon law.[8] He completed his doctorate in canon law in c. 1298 and alleged that, against his wishes, Guido da Baisio permitted him to graduate without paying the usual fees, owing to poverty.

From 1302, Giovanni d'Andrea taught canon law at Bologna for the rest of his life, except for short periods of teaching at Padua during 1307–09 (when studies at the University of Bologna were suspended) and the summer of 1319. He also served his city and university in other ways. In 1316 he was asked to arbitrate in a dispute between the commune and university rectors, and he drafted the university's statutes in 1317, assisting in their revision in 1347. He was particularly active in promoting Bologna's support for the papacy. Giovanni d'Andrea allied himself closely with Pope John XXII's nephew Cardinal Bertrand du Pouget, who exercised papal lordship over the city from 1327 until forced to flee to Florence in 1334, accompanied by Giovanni d'Andrea. He later dedicated to the cardinal his magnum opus, the *Novella* on the Decretals, and in 1328 he joined an embassy sent from Bologna by Bertrand to John XXII at Avignon. He continued to participate in civic politics until 1338, when he backed Taddeo Pepoli as papal vicar of Bologna, whereas some members of Giovanni d'Andrea's family opposed Pepoli's regime and fled into exile.[9]

Giovanni d'Andrea was a married layman and had a large family. He was "not the first lay professor of canon law" of the Middle Ages, Kuttner observed (attributing "this distinction" to Giovanni's teacher Foscarari), but he was "by far the most renowned and successful."[10] His wife, Milancia, whom he married by 1304, bore two sons and three or four daughters.[11] Giovanni d'Andrea's son Bonincontro also taught canon law at Bologna and later Padua.[12] Giovanni's family was further connected to other Bolognese jurists by marriage. Milancia was daughter of the canonist Bonincontro dallo Spedale, while their daughter Bettina and another daughter, allegedly called Elisabetta, married the canonists Azzone dei Ramenghi and Giovanni di San Giorgio, respectively—the latter also Giovanni d'Andrea's pupil.[13] Their youngest and most famous daughter, Novella, married in 1326 a doctor of civil law, Filippo Formaglini, and another putative daughter whose name is unknown was reputedly wife of Giovanni d'Andrea's adoptive son and pupil Giovanni Calderini.[14] The famous jurist and diplomat Giovanni da Legnano (d. 1383) married Giovanni d'Andrea's granddaughter Novella, who is sometimes confused with Giovanni d'Andrea's daughter Novella but was in fact the daughter of his younger son, Federico.

Giovanni d'Andrea talked affectionately of his family in his writings, and contemporaries likewise told stories about him and them, often fanciful and distorted by later tradition. The most famous tale is that Giovanni d'Andrea's daughter Novella stood in for him to give lectures when he was ill but had to do so from behind a curtain, lest her beauty disturb his students. The sole source for this tale is Cristina da Pizzano's *Livre de la Cité des Dames* (Book of the City of Ladies), finished in 1405, which celebrated female contributions to society. Although Schulte deemed this source "reliable," and Rossi argued that Cristina might have learned this story through her father, who was an academic contemporary of Giovanni d'Andrea at Bologna and still in contact with his family in 1351, other scholars, notably Savigny and Kuttner, have doubted the story's veracity.[15] Better grounded is the claim that Giovanni d'Andrea sometimes asked advice from his wife on legal questions, since he tells us so himself, although her opinions reported by him suggest common sense more than legal learning.[16]

One episode in Giovanni d'Andrea's life even occasioned juristic controversy.[17] On his return from the embassy to Avignon in 1328, opponents of Bologna's pro-papal stance captured Giovanni d'Andrea and held him hostage near Pavia. He was released after eight months on his payment of a ransom of 4,000 florins, and his captors apparently also stole from him manuscripts and other goods worth 1,285 florins. He sought compensation for these losses from Bologna, which sought legal advice on his claim. Contemporary jurists, notably the celebrated Bartolo da Sassoferrato (d. 1357), reported that his claim was rejected, so it became a *cause célèbre* on the legal question of whether clients ought to indemnify their agents for damages. Palmieri, nevertheless, found that Bologna in fact compensated Giovanni d'Andrea, although the claim that John XXII awarded him an estate near Ferrara to make good his losses sounds less plausible.

Other evidence, however, exists that he was highly esteemed by his city, his university, and John XXII. He also accumulated considerable personal wealth, including property in Bologna.[18] Giovanni d'Andrea reportedly used some of this wealth for pious and charitable purposes, notably his endowment to help establish a Carthusian monastery at Bologna in 1333. He also had a reputation for ascetic piety in his last years.[19] He died in his seventies of the Black Death on July 7, 1348, and was buried in the Dominican church at Bologna. His striking tomb, attributed to Jacopo Lanfrani and built at the expense of his adoptive son, Giovanni Calderini, now stands in the Museo Civico Medievale of Bologna. The tomb's inscription characterized him as "famous across the world" (*notissimus orbe*) and "teacher of teachers" (*rabbi doctorum*).[20]

Principal writings

Novella *on the Decretals of Gregory IX*

This monumental commentary is doubtless Giovanni d'Andrea's most famous work. In 1234, Pope Gregory IX had issued an authoritative collection of his own and his predecessors' decretals—papal letters ruling on lawsuits or responding to legal queries that had long been treated as a new source of canon law supplementing Gratian's *Decretum*. Many decretal collections had circulated since the late twelfth century, notably the *Quinque compilationes antique* (c. 1190–1226), widely used for teaching canon law, until Gregory IX's compilation superseded these while drawing on them. In the same way, Giovanni d'Andrea designed his commentary as a *novella compilatio glossarum* (new compilation of glosses), synthesizing the opinions of past canonists on rulings in Gregory's collection.[21] Giovanni d'Andrea's commentary drew not only on post–1234 juristic literature, notably the standard commentary (*glossa ordinaria*) on Gregory's collection by Bernardo da Parma (d. 1266), but also on earlier canonistic interpretations of those rulings in the *compilationes antique* which passed into that collection. This was a massive undertaking, which Giovanni d'Andrea pursued gradually from the early years of his teaching career until 1338.[22] He named the work after his daughter Novella, born around April 20, 1312, and his mother, who died about this time, and a poem attributed to him shows that he was already drafting the work then. Pennington argues that two or possibly three earlier drafts, known as *Additiones* (to Bernardo da Parma's *glossa ordinaria*) and written by Giovanni d'Andrea prior to 1317, circulated before he expanded these into the final revised version. According to Kuttner, Giovanni d'Andrea modelled the *Novella* on his teacher Guido da Baisio's *Rosarium* (1300), a commentary on the *Decretum* that similarly surveyed early canonistic doctrine.[23]

Glossa on the Liber Sextus

Undoubtedly one of Giovanni d'Andrea's first works, he wrote this gloss on Pope Boniface VIII's compilation of post–1234 papal legislation before Boniface's death (1303).[24] Other early glosses on the *Liber sextus* were written by the French canonist Jean Lemoine (c. 1301) and Guido da Baisio (c. 1306), and all three glosses accompanied the legal text in some manuscripts, but Giovanni d'Andrea's generally enjoyed the distinction of being *ordinaria*. By Giovanni d'Andrea's own admission, Guido's teaching influenced his gloss, which also drew from other commentators on post–1234 papal rulings.

Glossa on the Clementinae

Clement V issued many constitutions, including *Saepe contingit*, most notably at the council of Vienne (1311–12), and he planned to promulgate a collection of these;[25] his successor, John XXII, eventually published this in 1317, and it was called *Clementinae*, after Clement V. Giovanni d'Andrea was the first canonist to write a gloss on this collection, and his commentary quickly became recognized as *ordinaria*. Although he completed his gloss in 1322, he added revisions, known as *apostillae* or *additiones*, between 1324 and 1330, citing juristic works that appeared after his gloss.[26]

Novella *on the* Liber Sextus

Giovanni d'Andrea found that his gloss on the *Liber sextus* rapidly became outdated by legal changes introduced in the *Clementinae* and by new juristic works, including his own subsequent writings. Like other canonists, he continued revising his works throughout his career.[27] He thus wrote *additiones* to this gloss as well as to his gloss on the *Clementinae*. As Schulte noted, he followed the example of Bartolomeo da Brescia, who made additions (c. 1245) to Giovanni Teutonico's *glossa ordinaria* to the *Decretum* (c. 1215). Like his additions to Bernardo da Parma's *glossa ordinaria*, Giovanni d'Andrea's additions to his own gloss on the *Liber sextus* were a forerunner to an entirely separate work also called *Novella*—not, as Savigny explains, to signify a continuation of his *magnum opus* but to denote his *new* commentary on the *Liber sextus*.[28] He completed this work between 1336 and 1339 while finishing his eponymous work on Gregory IX's Decretals.

Quaestiones mercuriales

Neither Giovanni d'Andrea's gloss nor his *Novella* on the *Liber sextus* treated the last section or "title" of Boniface's collection, headed *de regulis iuris* (on the rules of law).[29] Giovanni d'Andrea instead arranged his *Quaestiones mercuriales* under the individual rules of law and likewise titled this collection *de regulis iuris*.

This work has long been assumed to report the *quaestiones disputatae*, formal university debates on legal questions, in which Giovanni d'Andrea took part with students and colleagues, and *mercuriales* supposedly alluded to the convention that they were held on Wednesdays (*dies Mercurii*). Some of Giovanni d'Andrea's *quaestiones* refer to such disputations on specific dates as far back as

1310, although not all fell on Wednesdays, and Rosen suggests that his *quaestiones* generally reported "classroom discussions."[30] Rosen also argues that Giovanni d'Andrea compiled an earlier version of his *quaestiones* under the "titles," or subheadings, found in decretal collections early in his career,[31] and later revised this into its present form between 1324 and 1338, when his *Novella* on the Decretals and *Novella* on the *Liber sextus* refer to the *quaestiones.* But Condorelli has suggested a longer period of gestation, arguing that Giovanni d'Andrea began to collect his *quaestiones* before 1298 and continued to work on the final version of them, the *Novella in titulum de regulis iuris*, alongside his other writings in the last decade of his life.[32]

Additiones to the *Speculum*

Giovanni d'Andrea's last known work, probably completed by early 1347, was a commentary on the *Speculum iudiciale* of French canonist Guillaume Durand (d. 1296), the most important manual on Romano-canonical procedure from the later Middle Ages. Giovanni d'Andrea's *additiones* were so valued that they accompanied most manuscripts and early printings of the *Speculum.*[33] As Schulte argued, they expanded significantly on certain points made briefly by Durand and surveyed a vast procedural literature and its doctrinal development.

Hieronymianus

This largely non-juristic work, written between 1334 and 1346, was a treatise on the life, teachings, reputation, and works of St. Jerome and reflected Giovanni d'Andrea's personal devotion to the saint. He revered Jerome (d. 420) as author of the Latin Vulgate translation of the Bible and deplored his fellow Italians' neglect of Jerome's cult; this tract helped to spread the cult internationally, even as far as Bohemia.[34]

Many shorter juristic works are also attributed to Giovanni d'Andrea, including two treatises about marriage which circulated widely.[35] One summarized marital law in Book 4 of the Decretals; Schulte considered it a reworking of the Paduan canonist Giovanni Anguissola's commentary on this book (c. 1275), which Giovanni d'Andrea prepared for his students (c. 1309–13). The other tract, also an early work by Giovanni d'Andrea, discussed the degrees of kinship within which canon law prohibited marriage. Another tract credited to him on procedural law in Book 2 of the Decretals is now considered an early thirteenth-century German work.[36] Attribution of other writings to Giovanni d'Andrea has also been judged erroneous, notably the *Suffragium monachorum*; doubtless further minor tracts in his name are spurious and sought to exploit his fame, but their authorship awaits investigation.

Major contributions

Scholars have long agreed that Giovanni d'Andrea's writings display an unrivalled encyclopaedic knowledge of past jurists. These included medieval commentators on not only canon law but also Roman or civil law.[37] He was fond of introducing his commentaries with apparently exhaustive surveys listing these writers.[38] He doubtless had an extensive personal library, and his familiarity with juristic literature ranged beyond major commentaries to obscure opuscula.[39] As Kuttner remarked: "what he had not quoted did not seem worth quoting to later generations." His deep learning led some scholars to dismiss Giovanni d'Andrea as a mere compiler of other writers' opinions, however.[40] Savigny even accused him of extensive plagiarism, especially in his *Additiones* to the *Speculum*. Schulte deemed this charge unfair but held that Giovanni d'Andrea had no original views of his own, although Schulte conceded that he treated others' views critically. Savigny valued Giovanni d'Andrea's works for transmitting this earlier jurisprudence to posterity, but Schulte held that rather than encouraging its rediscovery, Giovanni d'Andrea's thorough discussion of this jurisprudence made future reference to it redundant. However, Kuttner and others have reacted against such criticisms, not least for judging later medieval scholastic writings by anachronistic standards, and they have identified several of Giovanni d'Andrea's original contributions to juristic doctrine.[41]

One major area to which he contributed was ideas of power, especially papal power. Even Schulte recognized this, although his rejection of the nineteenth-century doctrine of papal infallibility led him to dismiss Giovanni d'Andrea as a papal apologist.[42] In his exalted vision of the pope's monarchical and divinely ordained authority as "lord of the world", Giovanni d'Andrea was very much a man of his time and certainly among his fellow fourteenth-century canonists.[43] Admittedly, Watt and Tierney argued that Giovanni d'Andrea sometimes borrowed heavily from other writers on questions of papal authority, notably the canonist Hostiensis (d. 1270) and even the Dominican polemicist Jean (Quidort) de Paris (d. 1306).[44] Nevertheless, he was prepared to disagree with others' views and put forward his own on this and other topics. In his *glossa ordinaria* on the *Liber sextus* and *Novella* on the Decretals, for example, he repeated Hostiensis's views on the role of the cardinals during a papal vacancy but rejected them in his *glossa ordinaria* on the *Clementinae*. His view that cardinals did not succeed to papal authority during a vacancy "found general acceptance among canonists before the Great Schism [1378–1417]", according to Tierney.[45]

Even when Giovanni d'Andrea accepted others' views, he sometimes was unusual in doing so and applied their ideas in innovative ways. Pennington, for example, argued that Giovanni d'Andrea was one of the few canonists to adopt Hostiensis's definition of the pope's absolute power and possibly the first to suggest that this permitted the pope to disregard due process, as regulated in canon law by Clement V's constitutions *Pastoralis cura* and *Saepe contingit*, issued during Giovanni d'Andrea's lifetime. Giovanni thus remarkably argued that a prince was above the law, and elsewhere he wrote even more strikingly that the prince might change the law at will and in accordance with the common good of his subjects, which Pennington considered "new ideas" at the time. These views on power again influenced later jurists, notably Panormitanus. Pennington noted likewise that Giovanni d'Andrea influentially rejected Hostiensis's definition of canon law as divine law and held instead that it was human, positive, and mutable: "later canonists adopted Johannes's opinion, rather than Hostiensis's."[46]

Scholars also credit Giovanni d'Andrea with influential innovations on other legal issues. Trexler, for example, identified his "creative" contribution to juristic debate on the bishop's portion. This was a bishop's claim to a share, usually a third, of all testamentary bequests for pious causes, a lucrative right pursued especially by late medieval Italian bishops. Giovanni d'Andrea's creative view was that all bequests for the good of the soul (*pro anima*) belonged to the poor as a general body, which effectively denied bishops any share of these. His view became central to subsequent jurisprudence and practice on this issue in Italy, where bishops had to find a way around it by claiming to be the "father of the poor," allowing them still to benefit by managing bequests to institutions for the poor.[47] Likewise, Helmholz lauded Giovanni d'Andrea's intervention in juristic controversy on prescription. This was a claim to property rights based on long usage, but jurisdiction over prescription was subject to conflicting claims between Roman and canon law, and canonistic attempts to resolve this conflict had themselves proved problematic, so "a different approach" was needed, as Helmholz argued: "The most sophisticated such approach to harmonizing the Roman and canon laws of prescription was written by Joannes Andreae."[48] Stelling-Michaud also noted Giovanni d'Andrea's ingenious attempts to relate Roman and canon laws on other questions, including custom and foreign ignorance of local statutes.

Moreover, historians have seen the beginnings of humanism in Giovanni d'Andrea's writings.[49] He was a friend of Francesco Petrarca (Petrarch, 1304–74), sometimes considered the founder of early humanism. Although Petrarca shared with Dante a disdain for contemporary canonists, he studied law at Bologna from 1323 to 1326, and although it is uncertain whether Giovanni d'Andrea taught him, he remained in contact with Giovanni after 1326 through letters that show his esteem for the canonist. These letters and Giovanni d'Andrea's own writings indicate that Giovanni shared the humanist's passion for classical literature, including the writings of Pliny the Elder and Pliny the Younger, although Petrarca criticized Giovanni's literary tastes, notably his predilection for Valerius Maximus.[50]

In his juristic works, Giovanni d'Andrea also displayed a humanistic concern with how the process of textual transmission could change the original version of an authority. He was aware that compilers of canonical collections had edited the texts that they selected. For example, as Vodola noted, Giovanni d'Andrea recognized that the canon *Quia periculosum* of Pope Innocent IV (1243–54) originally had been longer (when it circulated in the "definitive" collection of Innocent's legislation, the so-called *Novelle*) than the version of it redacted in the *Liber sextus* (VI 5.11.4); Giovanni d'Andrea observed in his *glossa ordinaria* and his *Novella* on the *Liber sextus* that part of the text had been excised there.[51] Likewise, Condorelli has observed that the fourth and longest part of the *Hieronymianus* also shows humanist tendencies in its catalogue *raisonné* of works attributed to Jerome.[52] This is evident in Giovanni d'Andrea's extraordinary concern to distinguish authentic writings of Jerome from spurious ones, his thorough search for original texts as opposed to extracts in *florigelia*, and his extensive correspondence with other scholars on questions of attribution. Giovanni d'Andrea concluded the *Hieronymianus* with a critical analysis of texts attributed to Jerome in Gratian's *Decretum*, correcting errors and lacunae in these and identifying others misattributed or quoted without acknowledgement by Gratian. Condorelli added that humanist scholars subsequently referred to this work in preparing the famous "Editio Romana" (1582) of the *Decretum*.[53]

Giovanni d'Andrea also had a remarkable tendency to refer to events from his personal and local experience (and not just about his family) in his juristic works, notably in his *Additiones* on the *Speculum*.[54] This inclination parallels to some extent Dante's use of history as "memorable experience" to support his arguments empirically in *De monarchia* (c. 1312–17).[55] Whether or not this was a humanist tendency specifically, it certainly humanized Giovanni d'Andrea's writings. For example, he illustrated from experience the dangers of excommunication and interdict, although he believed that the Church authorities' use of these sanctions was justified. He argued on the basis of corporation theory, for instance, that an interdict—the collective sanction of suspending worship and closing churches in a given locality—might still bind a community if it had not been lifted after a hundred years, since the community remained notionally the same even if its actual members had changed. Nevertheless, he recognized the spiritual perils that might arise in practice from such long-lasting sanctions, noting that he had heard of a place in the Marche region of Italy which fell under interdict for so long that when it was lifted, people there in their thirties and forties had never heard mass and derided priests who resumed celebration of it. He therefore welcomed Boniface VIII's constitution *Alma mater* (1298), which allowed mass in interdicted places on the four main annual feasts.[56] Similarly, as Vodola noted, Giovanni d'Andrea used another example from personal experience to illustrate the problem of excommunicates proving their absolution: so many were excommunicated for trading with Ferrara, an Italian city rebelling against papal rule (c. 1317), that religious had to confer collective absolutions; "hence individuals had no proof of absolution." Vodola also observed that Giovanni d'Andrea's experience of married and family life influenced his remarkably affectionate discussion of excommunicates' familial relations, which concluded that an excommunicate could "ask his wife to tell his children how much he loves his family or ask his children to say the same things to his wife."[57]

Conclusion

Giovanni d'Andrea made distinctive contributions to Christian jurisprudence, as recent scholarship has increasingly recognized. He did so on the basis of both personal experience and his peerless erudition in juristic literature. He is generally recognized as the first Christian jurist to trace the historical development of canonistic doctrine and to relate the works of individual canonists to each other and the wider spectrum of canonistic opinion in such a comprehensive manner. He constantly revised and rethought his commentaries to take into account the latest papal legislation and juristic views and thus make his interpretation of decretal collections as complete as possible. In his compilation of juristic opinions, he followed in the footsteps not only of Raimundo de Peñafort and other compilers of decretal collections but also Gratian, who had harmonized contradictory legal authorities in the *Decretum* two centuries earlier. In likewise synthesizing juristic opinions, Giovanni d'Andrea reflected the fact that by his time, these had become almost as important an authority as canon law itself.[58] Boniface VIII's constitutions written for the *Liber sextus*, for example, sought to settle canonistic controversies and even transformed canonistic opinions into law, notably those of Innocent IV and Hostiensis. By the fourteenth century, jurists, including Giovanni d'Andrea, were highly solicited and remunerated by clients for their *consilia*, or scholarly advice on actual lawsuits.[59] Giovanni d'Andrea's achievement, therefore, was to provide a critical, arguably protohumanist, summation of the canonistic tradition going back to the late twelfth century, incorporating his own original and independent views. He thereby laid jurisprudential foundations on which later canonists built, establishing his formidable international reputation by the fifteenth century.[60]

Notes

1 Schulte, 246–53; another famous pupil was d'Andrea's son-in-law Giovanni di San Giorgio, who taught canon law at Bologna and Padua.
2 See Bio-Bibliographical Guide to Medieval and Early Modern Jurists, http://amesfoundation.law.harvard.edu/BioBibCanonists/Report_Biobib2.php?record_id=r339 (Johannes Andreae) for a recent list of known manuscripts and printed editions of his works.
3 Included in the *Clementinae* at Clem. 5.11.2. Kuttner, "The Date of the Constitution 'Saepe'," 427 (quotation), 430–2; idem, "Joannes Andreae," 397; Pennington, *The Prince and the Law*, 189–90.
4 Savigny, *Geschichte*, vol. 6, 100; Schulte, 227; Kuttner, "Joannes Andreae," 399 (where he credits Italian jurist Baldo degli Ubaldi (d. 1400) with inventing this epithet), 406–7; Pennington, "Johannes Andreae's *Additiones*," 345: "If he lived today, he would have made a first-rate historian of medieval canon law."
5 For relevant quotations and citations, collected by Diplovatatius (1468–541) and later historians, see Savigny, 98–100; Schulte, 205–7; Kuttner, "Joannes Andreae," 395, 398.
6 Tamba, 667; Glöckner, 118. Cf. Savigny, 101; Schulte, 205; Stelling-Michaud, 89.
7 Padovani, esp. 273–7, 282–7, notes that he referred little to theology in his early work, the *glossa ordinaria* on the *Liber sextus*, but in his later *Novella* on the Decretals cited the *Summa theologiae* of Dominican theologian Thomas Aquinas (d. 1274) extensively, unsurprising given Giovanni d'Andrea's Dominican teacher; more remarkably, he sometimes preferred the opinions of Franciscan theologian Duns Scotus (d. 1308) contrary to those of Aquinas.
8 On his teachers, see esp. Kuttner, "Joannes Andreae," 398 and 398R.
9 Tamba, 669–70.
10 Kuttner, "Joannes Andreae," 395.
11 Bartocci, 1008.

12 He had to flee Bologna after participating in a failed conspiracy against Pepoli in 1338 and was apparently executed on his return in 1350. Schulte, 242–3; Caprioli.
13 Schulte, 243.
14 Rossi, 1473–81; after Novella and her husband fell foul of the Pepoli regime, they fled to Padua, dying there in c. 1340.
15 Schulte, 211; Rossi, 1463–73, 1481–6, who observed that Cristina's family was of Bolognese origin, and that her father Tommaso graduated in medicine at Bologna and held a chair in astronomy there in 1344–56. Cf. Savigny, 109, who likens her account to "a fable" (*Märchen*); Kuttner, "Joannes Andreae," 396 n. 9.
16 Rossi, 1486–1502, who acknowledges this but dismisses four *responsa* or *consilia* attributed to Milancia as eighteenth-century fabrications and a claim that Giovanni d'Andrea's daughter Bettina taught canon law at Padua as a sixteenth-century invention based on the Novella story.
17 Palmieri. Cf. Savigny, 106–7; Schulte, 209.
18 Schulte, 208–10; Tamba, 668–9, 670.
19 Savigny, 110–11; Schulte, 212.
20 Tamba, 670; Murano, 45–6; Savigny, 100, reproduces the inscription.
21 Besides decretals, these rulings comprised the canons of church councils convened by popes, notably the four Lateran councils of 1122–1215.
22 Gillmann.
23 Pennington, "Johannes Andreae's *Additiones*," esp. 330–2, thus rejecting Gillmann's view ("Zur Frage der Abfassungszeit," 267–72) that the *additiones* in one manuscript was a version of Giovanni d'Andrea's lectures on Gregory IX's Decretals reported by a student; Kuttner, "Joannes Andreae," 403–6.
24 Schulte, 213–14; van Hove, 474–5.
25 Clement's death in April 1314 delayed this plan; Kuttner, "The Date of the Constitution 'Saepe,'" 429.
26 Kuttner, "The Apostillae."
27 Bernardo da Parma continued working on his *glossa ordinaria* on Gregory IX's Decretals from the late 1230s until his death in 1266, and it circulated in at least four redactions during his lifetime; Kuttner and Smalley, "The Glossa Ordinaria."
28 Schulte, 218–19; Savigny, 116–18.
29 Giovanni d'Andrea's gloss was usually supplemented by Dino Mugellano's commentary on this title in manuscripts and early editions of the *Liber sextus.*
30 See notes 31 and 46 herein; Rosen, 109, 112–13, says that *mercuriales* may refer to private classes that Giovanni d'Andrea held for his own students on Wednesdays, when he disputed his own or other masters' questions.
31 This earlier version is not known to survive, but its existence is indicated by some of Giovanni d'Andrea's *quaestiones* transmitted with those of other jurists in a fourteenth-century manuscript (Cesena, Biblioteca Malatestiana, cod. S.II.3) described by Mesini, who notes his *quaestiones* at pp. 286 (disputed at Padua), 287 (dated 1310), 290–1 (dated 1311 and 1312, with his poem about the *Novella*), 292, 293 (disputed at Padua in 1317), 367, 371–2 (dated 1313), 373, 374, 375–6, 377, 381, and other opuscula of his at 281–4, 376–7 (see note 59 herein). This Cesena collection was probably compiled between 1306 and 1316 and is now thought to have been used by Giovanni d'Andrea, since it contains annotations and other additions in his hand; Murano, 46–8.
32 Condorelli, "Dalle 'Quaestiones Mercuriales'," esp. 132, 138, 143–9, for a fuller analysis of the evolution and manuscript tradition of the *quaestiones* with a description of nine manuscripts containing them (notably the Cesena codex) at 150–71.

33 Savigny, 120–2; Schulte, 221–2; Stelling-Michaud, 91.
34 Fedele, 211–12; Kejř, 87–8; Condorelli, "Giovanni d'Andrea e dintorni," 57–73 (discussed further ahead). Giovanni d'Andrea even had scenes from Jerome's life painted in his home, apparently also wrote a poem, a hymn, and prayers in Jerome's honor, and adopted the soubriquet "de S. Hieronymo" that stayed in his family (Savigny, 100).
35 Savigny, 123–4; Schulte, 214–15.
36 Stelling-Michaud, 91, 92; Hove, 492. On other minor juristic works assigned to Giovanni d'Andrea: Savigny, 125; Schulte, 223–4. As Kuttner remarked long ago ("Joannes Andreae," 399): "In the absence of modern manuscript research, it is not possible to draw up a reliable catalogue of Joannes Andreae's writings."
37 Sorrenti, for example, indexed references to *quaestiones* on Roman law found in Giovanni d'Andrea's *Additiones* to the *Speculum* and attributed to civilians from the twelfth century to his own time; see esp. 11, 16–17, 19, 21–33.
38 Kuttner, "The Apostillae," 197–200, analyzes one prefacing Giovanni d'Andrea's *glossa ordinaria* on the *Clementinae*, identifying the authors listed.
39 Elze, for example, notes that Giovanni d'Andrea reported in his *Novella* on the *Liber sextus* a little known *quaestio* of Bolognese canonist Stephanus Polonus (c. 1270) now found in a single Vatican manuscript. Giovanni d'Andrea apparently owned a collection of other *quaestiones*, including his own, now extant at Cesena (see note 31 herein), and other manuscripts of his must have passed into the extensive library of his adoptive son Giovanni Calderini, since its inventory lists at least one autograph manuscript of his, the original exemplar of the *Speculum iudiciale* with his *additiones*, from which Calderini had copies made; Murano, 46.
40 Kuttner, "Joannes Andreae," 406–8 (quotation from 406); Savigny, 100, 113, 122; Schulte, 220, 222, 227–9.
41 Cf. Stelling-Michaud, 91–2; Tamba, 671.
42 Schulte (1827–1914) was an opponent of the First Vatican Council (1869–70), which proclaimed this doctrine, and together with another German opponent, theologian Ignaz von Döllinger (1799–1890), he founded the Old Catholic movement in 1871–72; his subsequent publications, as this example illustrates, contained polemic against the papacy and papal claims to power; see Weitlauff.
43 Tierney, *Foundations*, 199–200 (*Apostolicus totius orbis est dominus*, borrowing the emperor's usual epithet).
44 Watt, 148–51; Tierney, *Foundations*, 164, 217–18; on Hostiensis see Chapter 5.
45 Tierney, *Foundations*, 210–14; cf. Watt (as note 44 herein).
46 Pennington, *The Prince and the Law*, 53, 87–8, 116–17, 190–1, 224; on Panormitanus, see Chapter 12. Mesini noted that Giovanni d'Andrea also disagreed with Hostiensis on another issue: Honorius III's decretal *Super specula* (1219) had excluded religious from university courses in Roman law, but Giovanni d'Andrea argued in a *quaestio* of 1311 that religious might still study Roman law privately (in line with recent papal privileges) which Hostiensis had denied; "De clericorum" (with an edition of this *quaestio* at 131–46).
47 Trexler, 419–20, 422, 423–4, 431, 434–7.
48 Helmholz, 194–8 (quotation at 196–7). Stelling-Michaud, as note 41 herein.
49 Kuttner, "Joannes Andreae," 406–7; Tamba, 671 (citing Calasso).
50 Fedele, (reproducing the two letters at 213–25); Petrarca similarly reproved him for preferring Jerome to Augustine among the Church Fathers.
51 Vodola, 153–4.
52 Condorelli, "Giovanni d'Andrea e dintorni," 63–73.
53 Condorelli also noted that Giovanni d'Andrea used the "Collection in Seven Books," a canon law compilation predating the *Decretum*, in identifying and correcting attributions to Jerome in the *Decretum*; ibid., 68.
54 Schulte, 222.

55 Canning, 67, 75.
56 Clarke, 78–9, 174; cf. also ibid. 67, 175. *Alma mater*: VI 5.11.24.
57 Vodola, 67, 101 n. 143.
58 See Chapter 2; Raimundo de Peñafort compiled the Decretals of Gregory IX.
59 One of his *consilia* was noted in the Cesena codex by Mesini, 376–7. For other *consilia* of his found in manuscripts and early printed editions: Murano, 49; Bartocci, 1010–11.
60 On the latter: Bartocci, 1011.

Bibliography

Bartocci, Andrea "Giovanni d'Andrea (*Johannes Andreae de Bononia*) (Bologna?, 1271 ca.-ivi, 7 luglio 1348)." In *Dizionario Biografico dei Giuristi Italiani (XII–XX secolo)*, edited by I. Birocchi, et al., 1008–12. Bologna: Il Mulino, 2013.

Canning, Joseph P. *Ideas of Power in the Late Middle Ages, 1296–1417.* Cambridge: Cambridge University Press, 2011.

Caprioli, Severino. "Bonincontro di Giovanni d'Andrea." In *Dizionario Biografico degli Italiani.* Vol. 12. Rome: Istituto della Enciclopedia Italiana, 1970.

Clarke, Peter D. *The Interdict in the Thirteenth Century: A Question of Collective Guilt.* Oxford: Oxford University Press, 2007.

Condorelli, Orazio. "Dalle 'Quaestiones Mercuriales' alla 'Novella in titulum de regulis iuris'." *RIDC* 3 (1992): 125–71.

Condorelli, Orazio. "Giovanni d'Andrea e dintorni. La scuola canonistica bolognese nella prima metà del secolo XIV." *RIDC* 21 (2012): 91–145; Reprinted with updates in *Petrarca e il diritto. Atti del Convegno Internazionale di Studi, Padova 10–11 marzo 2011.* Accademia Petrarca di Lettere Arti e Scienze di Arezzo, Studi Petrarcheschi, Nuova serie xxviii–xxix, 29–73. Rome/Padua: Antenore, 2015–2016 (2018).

Elze, Reinhard. "Stephanus Polonus und Johannes Andreae. Eine Bologneser Quaestion von 1270 und ihre Wiedergabe in der Novella in Sextum." *Studia Gratiana* 12: *Collectanea Stephan Kuttner* 2 (1967): 293–308.

Fedele, Pio. "Francesco Petrarca e Giovanni d'Andrea." *Ephemerides iuris canonici* 30 (1974): 201–25.

Gillmann, Franz. "Zur Frage der Abfassungszeit der Novelle des Johannes Andreä zu den Dekretalen Gregors IX." *AKKR* 104 (1924): 261–75.

Glöckner, Hans P. "Johannes Andreae." In *Dictionary of the Middle Ages*, edited by J.R. Strayer. Vol. 7, 118. 13 vols. New York: Charles Scribner's Sons, 1982–89.

Helmholz, Richard H. *The Spirit of Classical Canon Law.* Athens: University of Georgia Press, 1996.

Kejř, Jiři. "Ioannis Andreae 'Hieronymianum opus' a jeho ohlas v českých zemích." *Studie o rukopisech* 12 (1973): 71–86; 87–8. (French résumé: "Ioannis Andreae Hieronymianum opus et son retentissement dans les pays tchèques").

Kuttner, Stephan. "The Apostillae of Johannes Andreae on the Clementines." In *Études d'histoire du droit canonique dédiés à Gabriel Le Bras*, edited by G. Vedel, 195–201. Paris: Sirey, 1965; Reprinted with *retractiones* in his *Studies in the History of Medieval Canon Law.* Aldershot: Variorum, 1990, XVII.

Kuttner, Stephan. "The Date of the Constitution 'Saepe,' the Vatican Manuscripts, and the Roman Edition of the Clementines." *Mélanges Eugène Tisserant* 4: 427–52, Studi e Testi 234 (1964); Reprinted with *retractiones* in his *Medieval*

Councils, Decretals and Collections of Canon Law. 2nd ed. Aldershot: Variorum, 1992, XIII.

Kuttner, Stephan. "Joannes Andreae and His *Novella* on the Decretals of Gregory IX." *The Jurist* 24 (1964): 393–408; Reprinted with *retractiones* in his *Studies in the History of Medieval Canon Law*. Aldershot: Variorum, 1990, XVI.

Kuttner, Stephan, and Beryl Smalley. "The Glossa Ordinaria to the Gregorian Decretals." *English Historical Review* 60 (1945): 97–105; Reprinted with *retractiones* in his *Studies in the History of Medieval Canon Law*. Aldershot: Variorum, 1990, XIII.

Mesini, Candido. "De clericorum, doctoratu et professoratu in iure civili ex Ioanne Andreae." *Antonianum* 32 (1957): 109–46.

Mesini, Candido. "De codice iuridico N. 3, Pl. II, l. S. bibliothecae Malatestianae (Cesenae)." *Antonianum* 26 (1951): 271–94, 367–85.

Murano, Giovanna. "Giovanni d'Andrea (1271–1348)." In *Autographa. I.1. Giuristi, giudici e notai (sec. XII–XVI med.)*, edited by G. Murano, G. Morelli, and T. Woelki, 44–50. Centro inter-universitario per lo studio delle università italiane, Studi 16. Bologna: Clueb, 2012.

Padovani, Andrea. "La cultura teologica di Giovanni d'Andrea." *BMCL* (new series) 35 (2018): 255–87.

Palmieri, Arturo. "Un episodio della vita di Giovanni d'Andrea ed una vecchia questione di diritto." *Atti e memorie della Regia Deputazione di storia patria per le provincie di Romagna*, ser. 3, 25 (1907): 1–15.

Pennington, Kenneth. "Johannes Andreae's *Additiones* to the Decretals of Gregory IX." *ZRG, KA* 74 (1988): 328–47; Reprinted in his *Popes, Canonists and Texts, 1150–1550*. Aldershot: Variorum, 1993, XIX.

Pennington, Kenneth. *The Prince and the Law, 1200–1600: Sovereignty and Rights in the Western Legal Tradition*. Berkeley/Los Angeles: University of California Press, 1993.

Rosen, Cyprian. "Notes on an Earlier Version of the 'Quaestiones Mercuriales'." *BMCL* (new series) 5 (1975): 103–14.

Rossi, Guido. "Contributi alla biografia del canonista Giovanni d'Andrea (L'insegnamento di Novella e Bettina, sue figlie, ed i presunti responsa di Milancia, sua moglie)." *Rivista trimestrale di diritto e procedura civile* 11 (1957): 1451–502.

Savigny, Friedrich Carl von. *Geschichte des Römischen Rechts im Mittelalter*. Vol. 6. 2nd ed. Heidelberg: Mohr, 1850. See especially pages 98–125.

Schulte, Johann Friedrich von. *Die Geschichte der Quellen und Literatur des Canonischen Rechts von Gratian bis auf die Gegenwart*. Vol. 2. Stuttgart: Ferdinand Enke, 1877. See especially pages 205–29.

Sorrenti, Lucia. *Testimonianze di Giovanni d'Andrea sulle "quaestiones" civilistiche*. Studi e ricerche dei "Quaderni Catanesi" 2. Catania: C. Tringale, 1980.

Stelling-Michaud, Sven. "Jean d'André." In *Dictionnaire de droit canonique*. Vol. 6, col. 89–92.

Tamba, Giorgio. "Giovanni d'Andrea." In *Dizionario biografico degli Italiani*. Vol. 55, 667–72.

Tierney, Brian. *Foundations of the Conciliar Theory: The Contribution of the Medieval Canonists from Gratian to the Great Schism*. Cambridge: Cambridge University Press, 1955.

Trexler, Richard "The Bishop's Portion: Generic Pious Legacies in the Late Middle Ages in Italy." *Traditio* 28 (1972): 397–450.

Van Hove, Alphonse. *Prolegomena: Commentarium Lovaniense in Codicem iuris canonici*. Vol. 1, t. i. Malines/Rome: H. Dessain, 1945.

Vodola, Elisabeth. *Excommunication in the Middle Ages*. Berkeley/Los Angeles: University of California Press, 1986.

Watt, John Anthony. "The Constitutional Law of the College of Cardinals: Hostiensis to Joannes Andreae." *Mediaeval Studies* 33 (1971): 127–57.

Weitlauff, Manfred. "Schulte, Johann Friedrich von." *Neue Deutsche Biographie* 23 (2007): 689–90.

9 Bartolo da Sassoferrato (1313/14–1357)

Orazio Condorelli

Biographical introduction

Bartolo of Sassoferrato spent his short life within the geographically narrow horizon of some of the most important communal cities of central Italy. The merits of his work as a jurist, however, quickly overcame the borders of the Italian peninsula and earned him a universal and imperishable fame.[1]

Bartolo was born in Venatura, a village near Sassoferrato, in the Marche, in 1313 or 1314. His father was probably a small landowner and had the foresight to indulge his son's inclination for studies. In a famous autobiographical passage, Bartolo remembers with emotion and gratitude his first teacher, Friar Petrus of Assisi, called Pietro della Pietà because he had established a hospice for foundlings in Venice.[2] For Bartolo, Petrus was not only a teacher in his primary education ("me primas literas docuit") but also a model of religious piety. Another Franciscan friar was Guido of Perugia, whom Bartolo remembers as his master in geometry in the preamble of his treatise *de fluminibus*. Bartolo's bond with the Franciscan order therefore arose in his early youth and was consolidated and strengthened over the years.

Thanks to his first education from Friar Petrus, at the age of thirteen or fourteen Bartolo began to attend courses in civil law in the *Studium* (University) of Perugia, at the school of Cinus from Pistoia.[3] According to Baldus de Ubaldis, Bartolo acknowledged that Cinus's magisterium, especially his *Lectura Codicis*, had "modeled his genius."[4] Cinus had put to good use the techniques experimented with by the "post-Accursian" jurists, and he introduced into Italy the method of the jurists of Orléans. Cinus's teaching thus expressed a methodological and doctrinal depth that marked the phase of transition from the school of the gloss to that of the commentary. The new method favored the systematic construction of legal science and, through the research and identification of the juridical grounds and reasons of Justinian's laws (*rationes*), prepared the tools to apply the categories and principles found in the *Corpus Iuris Civilis* to the facts of medieval life and to the interpretation of local and particular laws.

When Cinus left Perugia, Bartolo continued his studies in Bologna, where he had Jacobus Bottrigari as a teacher. In the cradle of legal studies, Bartolo was able to get to know other important masters such as Jacobus de Belviso, Rainerius

Arsendi, and Petrus de Cernitis in civil law, and Johannes Andreae and Johannes Calderini in canon law. In the passage noted earlier, Bartolo reports having graduated at twenty-one; according to the document of his doctoral degree, the solemn public ceremony took place in the cathedral of Bologna on November 10, 1334.[5]

For a few years after the doctorate, Bartolo was engaged in judicial activity: he was assessor (judge) of the *capitano del Popolo* in Todi and of the *podestà* in Cagli (Umbria), then assessor of the *podestà* in Pisa in 1339. While discussing the responsibility of the judge, Bartolo tells of a sad episode that happened probably in Todi: when he was a criminal judge, he tortured an accused, who died unexpectedly, although Bartolo was convinced that he had applied only a moderate violence commensurate with the physical constitution of the accused.[6]

In 1339 Bartolo began teaching at the University of Pisa, where he remained until he moved in the autumn of 1343 to Perugia, continuing to teach there uninterruptedly until his death. In 1348, recognizing the merit of the services that he had rendered to the city, and to keep him in Perugia in the face of invitations from other universities, the commune conferred citizenship on Bartolo and his brother Bonaccursius. In 1355 the city sent Bartolo as ambassador to the Emperor Charles IV in Pisa, to obtain the confirmation of ancient privileges and the concession of the *Studium generale*. On that occasion, the emperor appointed the famous jurist counselor and member of the "imperial family" and conferred on him the privileges of granting the *venia aetatis* (a license of greater age) to people under twenty-five and of legitimizing his illegitimate students.

In Perugia, in the convent of San Francesco in Prato, on May 14, 1356, Bartolo dictated his own will, in which he elected the church of San Francesco in Perugia or in Sassoferrato as his place of burial, and left pious bequests for Franciscan institutions (those two churches and a hospital). Feeling the conclusion of his earthly days approaching, Bartolo wanted to consecrate the ties with the Franciscan order that had been formed in his youth.

Bartolo died in 1357, at the age of forty-three or forty-four years; his body rests in San Francesco al Prato in Perugia. Thomas Diplovatatius, his biographer, informs us that he left a large library of fifty-four volumes, thirty-four of them in theology.[7]

Works and major themes

In a life as brief as it was intense, Bartolo left a copious number of writings: they are the result of a very refined theoretical reflection, but at the same time the expression of an approach that responds to practice and was close to the facts of life. His great pupil Baldus de Ubaldis affirmed that his master was a man very adherent to the practice (*fuit homo multum inherens practice*).[8]

Bartolo's universal fame grows primarily out of his *Commentaria* on the *Corpus Iuris Civilis*, which reflect the teachings dictated in the universities of Pisa and

Perugia.[9] They were printed starting from 1470 and then included in the numerous editions of his *Opera omnia*, up to the Venice edition of 1615.[10]

As was clear to scholars as early as the fifteenth century, not everything attributed to Bartolo was in fact the fruit of his work. The commentaries on the first book of the *Digestum Vetus* have been subtracted from its authorship, with the exception of the *repetitio* on the l. *Omnes populi* (D.1.1.9). In the *Digestum Infortiatum*, the commentary on D.27.1 is the work of Nicolaus Spinelli from Naples. The *Commentaries* on the *Institutiones* have been traced back to authors of the school of Orléans (Jacques de Revigny and Raoul d'Harcourt). Bartolo's authorship of the *Commentaria* on the *Authenticum* is also doubtful, while in the *Commentaria* on the *Tres libri Codicis* (C.9–12) Bartolo's hand stopped at C.11.35, and the work was continued by Conte Saccucci from Perugia (with the exception of the commentary on C.12.1.1, which belongs to Bartolo).

The numerous *repetitiones* inserted in the body of the *Commentaria* are also connected to his didactic activity, as are the twenty-two *quaestiones disputatae* that in the editions are collected next to his *consilia* and *tractatus*. The richest editions contain as many as 405 *consilia*, but several *consilia* remain unpublished.[11] They reveal the very intense activity of Bartolo as a consultant jurist who dealt with the most varied practical aspects of the life of medieval Italian communes, connecting the sources of the *ius commune* with the cases regulated by local laws.

Bartolo's *tractatus* stand out for their doctrinal value. They are monographic treatises that deal systematically with themes more or less directly connected with the Justinianic sources, which could not be examined in depth during the *lectura*, or that scientifically develop themes that required a broader examination. Some editions of the *tractatus* contain writings that are either certainly spurious or of dubious bartolian authorship. The treatises on tyranny, on the government of cities, and on the Guelphs and Ghibellines, on which I will dwell later, are recognized masterpieces of Western legal and political thought.[12]

The *Liber Minoricarum decisionum* deserves special mention, as Bartolo here examines the theme of the capacity of succession of the Friars Minor.[13] The patrimonial regime of the order was based on the collective renunciation of property,[14] which raised theoretical doubts and judicial conflicts about the validity of donations or testamentary bequests in favor of the Franciscans.

Due to the extent and depth of his work, there are no aspects of civil life that escaped Bartolo's attention. For his well-deserved fame, his name ended up denominating the juridical method of commentators ("bartolism"), and this identification made Bartolo one of the main targets of the criticism that humanistic jurisprudence moved against the method of medieval jurists and more generally against the *mos italicus iura docendi* (the Italian method of teaching law).

Nevertheless, Bartolo's authority grew to the point of receiving official recognition in the laws of some states. This happened in Spain and Portugal between the fifteenth and seventeenth centuries. The *Ordenações Filipinas* (Ordinations of Philip I) published in Portugal in 1603 (and hence in force also in Brazil) provide that, when a case is not regulated in the established sources (including the *Magna glossa* of Accursius), the judge should refer "to the opinion of Bartolo, since it is commonly the most consistent with reason" (Book 3, title 64).

Law, theology, and ethics

In the epistemological and practical horizon of Bartolo, law maintains a very close relationship with ethics and theology. The distinction of the scientific fields of the various disciplines—law, theology, philosophy—had matured in the twelfth century from the trunk of the liberal arts. The differentiation of the areas was perceived as a distinction that started from the methods and contents (that is, the texts) of the different sciences, but not as a separation that implies the incommunicability among the different spheres, because no separation can exist in the unity of the human person. From this perspective, Bartolo appears closer to the convictions of Irnerius and the jurists of the first half of the twelfth century than to the positions of Accursius. The latter, radicalizing an idea of his master Azo, had stated with proud presumption that the jurist should not study theology, since "everything is found in the body of law" (*omnia in corpore iuris inveniuntur*: gloss in D.1.1.10, v. *notitia*): basically, the jurist should find the fullness of the contents and methods of his own science in Justinian's *leges*. Bartolo's perspective is different and is clearly outlined in the sermon pronounced for his brother Bonaccursius's degree.

Bartolo, in the footsteps of Ulpian, defines the science of civil law as *civilis sapientia* and *res sanctissima* ("civil wisdom," "an extremely sacred thing": D.50.13.1.5), and this brings the function of the jurist closer to that of the theologian because—as Bartolo states in his *Tractatus testimoniorum*—wisdom is a "speculative habit which takes into consideration the highest causes" (*habitus speculativus considerans causas altissimas*), which is the province of the theologian and of the metaphysical philosopher.[15] In the doctoral sermon, Bartolo uses the criterion of perfection to demonstrate the superiority of the science of civil law over other sciences. Some sciences are less perfect, since they presuppose other sciences: thus, philosophy presupposes logic, medicine presupposes philosophy, and canon law requires the support of civil law, without which it would be a "widow" science.

From this perspective, strictly speaking, the *civilis sapientia* is not a perfect science either, because—Bartolo states—it is submitted (*supposita*) to theology.[16] Equally close is the relation between law and ethics. In a well-known fragment enclosed in the first title of the Digest (D.1.1.10), Ulpian had pulled together *iustitia*, *ius*, and *iuris prudentia*, placing justice in the sphere of will (*constans et perpetua voluntas ius suum cuique tribuendi*: "constant and perpetual will to give to everyone his right"), and *iuris prudentia* in the sphere of knowledge (*divinarum atque humanarum rerum notitia, iusti atque iniusti scientia*: "knowledge of divine and human affairs, science of what is just and what is unjust"). The Ulpianic combination of justice and prudence was a moment of contact between the world of law and that of ethics. This relationship, declared in the debut of

Justinian's laws, becomes for Bartolo the subject matter of in-depth reflections. But for Bartolo, theological and moral reflection is never an end in itself, but rather is aimed at a deeper understanding of juridical matters in view of the concrete action of people in the world of law: Bartolo does not contradict his reputation as a "man very adherent to practice."

The *Tractatus testimoniorum*, unfortunately unfinished, concerns the issue of the probative value of testimonies. The treatise is characterized by an imposing and uncommon use of theological-philosophical categories in the legal sphere. An Aristotelian–Thomistic approach is evident. Here Bartolo carries out a wide and articulated reflection on the theme of moral virtues (*prudentia*, *iustitia*, *fortitudo*, and *temperantia*), and today's reader should not overlook the function of this reflection in treating the problem of how to prove the moral qualities of a person: this proof is required, first of all, when the testimony concerns the life and habits of a person. The discussion therefore shifts towards an in-depth reflection on the virtue of prudence, a reflection aimed at analyzing fundamental categories of legal reasoning, such as those of malice (*dolus*), guilt (*culpa*), diligence (*diligentia*), and negligence (*neglegentia*). Ultimately, the continuity between the theological-moral approach and the juridical approach constitutes an operation at the highest theoretical level that moves from a unitary vision of the human dimension.[17]

These connections were further strengthened in the context of a Christian vision of life and implied concrete consequences in the interpretation of human actions. Saint Paul had stated that it is necessary to be subject to the governing authorities "not only because of the wrath but also because of conscience" (Romans 13:5). The question of the moral obligation of human laws, which was familiar to theologians and jurists, revolves around these words.

Just human law obliges the conscience, and therefore disobedience to a just law entails a sin: Bartolo shares this conviction with the jurists and theologians of his time,[18] in particular with Thomas Aquinas, who had lucidly treated the problem in the *Summa theologiae* (Ia–IIae q.96, art.4). This principle regulates the relations between the external forum and the forum of conscience, and such an approach implies the need to evaluate the justice of human law. In a passage handed down in Gratian's *Decretum*, Isidor of Seville had enumerated the qualities that the law (*lex*) must have in order to deserve its name: it must, first of all, be "honest and just" (D.4 c.2: *Erit autem lex honesta, iusta*), that is, it must direct people towards morally honest behaviors that result in acts of justice. Isidor implicitly left open the possibility that there may be positive laws that lack such qualities and are therefore intrinsically invalid.

In Bartolo's doctrine, these ideas do not fluctuate in an empyrean detached from human experience but are applied to the treatment of practical problems of medieval society. A very evident example is found in the *Tractatus represaliarum*, which Bartolo completed in 1354.[19] The preface offers evidence of Bartolo's political conceptions, in which the empire is seen as the supreme institution guaranteeing justice. The weakness or evanescence of the imperial political presence had caused, especially in the Italian communal cities, the impossibility of having recourse to a higher authority capable of correcting injustices. Hence the customary practice of reprisals arose. Bartolo refers to the customs and statutes in force in Italian communes, which, in case of obligations not fulfilled or of a crime committed by a foreigner, allowed the injured person to retaliate against a fellow citizen, however innocent, of the debtor or offender. Justinian had forbidden and severely punished this practice (*pignorationes*: *Novella* 52); Emperor Frederick I had forbidden it with specific reference to students and condemned it as perverse custom (constitution *Habita*, 1155);[20] the second Council of Lyon (1274) had deemed the custom contrary to natural equity and had forbidden it with regard to ecclesiastical persons (*Liber Sextus* 5.8.1).

Bartolo's interpretative horizon is immediately highlighted: in the beginning of the treatise, the author places himself in the perspective of moral theology, wondering if reprisals are lawful in the forum of conscience. The discussion starts from the analogy of reprisals to war. Bartolo discusses the question with rapid incisiveness, referring to the authority of St. Augustine—who had identified the conditions in which a war can be considered just—and to the thought of Thomas Aquinas, who had placed these conditions in a lucid theoretical framework (*Summa theologiae*, IIa—IIae q.40 art.1).

There are circumstances in which wars (and therefore reprisals) are licit from the moral point of view (*in foro conscientiae*): in a nutshell, this happens when it is impossible to resort to a higher political authority for the correction of injustices. A further condition is *iusta et recta intentio*, that is, the just and honest intention to restore justice rather than to harm others in the spirit of revenge. Bartolo believes that this condition is irrelevant in the civil forum and concludes that on this question, it is necessary to adhere to the teaching of theologians.

The next step is to understand whether reprisals are lawful in the legal forum. Although civil and canonical provisions prohibit reprisals, for Bartolo the lawfulness of reprisals depends on the same conditions that theologians had laid out for the forum of conscience, except that the *iusta et recta intentio* would not apply. In conclusion, for Bartolo reprisals find a legitimation in the light of positive divine law (Augustine quoted in *Decretum Gratiani*, C.23 q.2 c.2), and are a reality recognized by the law of nations (*ius gentium*: D.1.1.5) because they derive from the natural faculty of defending one's person from unjust offenses by others (D.1.1.3).

The system of law (*ius* and *lex*)

The complexity of Bartolo's interpretative approach is consciously adequate to the complexity of the legal system. As we have seen in the brief references concerning the right of reprisal, the concrete texture of a juridical institution depended on the plurality of sources that concurred in regulating the reality of life. Medieval Christian jurists could not disregard the conviction that at the height of the juridical system was the divine law, through which God the "legislator" addressed commands to humankind (*ius divinum positivum*): this conviction made it impossible to separate the sphere of law from those of religion and ethics, and for this reason Bartolo speaks of a subjection (*suppositio*) of *civilis sapientia* to theology. The sources of Church law (*ius commune canonicum*) stood beside the sources of Justinianic law (*ius commune civile*). The Justinianic texts themselves postulated the existence of distinct spheres of regulation of human relations: from higher systems, represented by natural law (*ius naturale*) and the law of nations (*ius gentium*), one descends to the laws of different peoples, which par excellence were represented by the laws of the *populus Romanus* enclosed in the *Corpus Iuris Civilis*. But the complexity of the system did not end in these spheres. Medieval European jurists were confronted with the new law: innumerable local customs, laws of the kingdoms, city statutes—in short, all the norms that flowed from the life of the various political communities. These local or particular laws were generally qualified, in the wake of a phrase of Gaius (D.1.1.9), through the category of *iura propria* (the laws particular to each *civitas*, or political community), dialectically linked to the category of *ius commune* (*civile et canonicum*) consisting in the *Corpus Iuris Civilis* and the universal laws of the Latin Church.

The framing of particular laws in the system of law passed through two steps. First, it was necessary to legitimize the existence of the *iura propria* in a system that seemed to reserve to the *princeps* (the emperor) the power to make laws (*leges condere*: C.1.14.12). The second step required identifying the rules that governed the interpretation of particular laws. The *Corpus Iuris Civilis* offered the theoretical tools through which jurists could perform these tasks.

In November 1343, Bartolo held a famous *repetitio* on the *lex Omnes populi* (D.1.1.9), that is, the fragment of the Roman jurist Gaius, handed down in the Digest, which was the classical place for the discussion of this fundamental theoretical question.[21] Bartolo summarizes the meaning of this passage with the following words: "every people that possesses a power of government (*iurisdictio*) has the permission to establish its own law, which is called *ius civile*."[22] According to Bartolo, this norm recognized in general and in advance the power of the particular communities to produce legal norms. In Bartolo's view, this power springs from a more general function of government (*iurisdictio*), which belongs to communities located on various levels: from the kingdoms to the communal cities to the feudal lands and so on, until reaching the minimum nucleus that is family, in which the *paterfamilias* has the power to establish norms that regulate the life of his own household.

The second theoretical moment concerns the problem of the interpretation of particular laws (*iura propria*). Lawmakers of all times have always claimed to ensure the precise application of laws by imposing their "literal" interpretation. In Bartolo's times, in Italian communes this claim was condensed into the maxim that a statute must be interpreted *prout littera iacet* ("according to the literal meaning of the words"). Bartolo, and more generally the jurists of his time, unmasks the fallacy of this claim. Interpretation of the statute (more generally, of the norms of particular laws) is "naturally necessary" (*naturaliter necessaria*) and can be made only through the principles and juridical categories that spring from the *ius commune*. Bartolo defines this procedure as an "extensive passive interpretation" of the statute (*intepretatio extensiva passiva*). In the common language of that time, it was usually repeated that "the statute is interpreted according to *ius commune*" (*statutum interpretatur secundum ius commune*).

Bartolo himself offers his students several examples of this process. If, for instance, a statute imposes a *munus personale* on a citizen (a personal service to be performed for the public utility), then all the Justinianic *leges* referring to the *munera personalia* extend to the case ruled by the statute—that is, the *leges* cannot but be used to interpret the statute and apply it to special cases.[23] Bartolo's *commentaria*, and even more massively his *quaestiones disputatae* and *consilia*, offer innumerable demonstrations of this necessary coordination between the principles and categories of the *ius commune* and the facts of life regulated by particular norms (statutes, customs, etc.). Baldus de Ubaldis illustrated his teacher's doctrine by using some metaphors. The *ius commune* "gives form to the statutes and dresses them," but does not take form from them and is not dressed by them: this happens because the *ius commune* exercises a "force of attraction" (*virtus attractiva*) on particular laws.[24]

Jacobus de Belviso, one of the masters whom Bartolo met in Bologna, had explained this phenomenon by saying that "common laws" (*iura communia*, civil and canonical) are laws "that are communicated to all legal problems" (*iura communicativa omnibus quaestionibus*).[25] This view explains why for many centuries, until the nineteenth-century codifications, the university training of jurists was essentially based on the study of the laws of Justinian and the collections that made up the *Corpus Iuris Canonici.* They were depositories of principles and juridical categories that had to be used to interpret and apply the particular laws in force in various political systems. This also explains the truly international dimension of legal science, which made jurists an intellectual élite that crossed the borders of nations.

Upstream from the need to use the tools of interpretation offered by the *iura communia*, Bartolo believes that jurists cannot avoid evaluating the positive norms—whoever their author is—under the ethical-religious profile: "the law and the statute must be holy and honest."[26] The absence of these qualities would lead to the loss of the very substance of *lex.*

Roman civil law and canon law: *utrumque ius*

In the sermon for the graduation of his brother Bonaccursius, Bartolo emphasized the superiority of civil law science (*civilis sapientia*) over the science of canon law, which is less perfect because it needs the support of the first. Not even the canonists doubted this, and such a conviction was consolidated in the maxim that "the legist without the canons is worth little, but the canonist without the law is worthless."[27]

Nevertheless, Bartolo's statement captured only one aspect of the relationship between civil law and canon law. In medieval Christendom, in fact, the law of the *Corpus Iuris Civilis* was not merely one of the historical forms of secular law; it also concurred with the universal law of the Church (mainly produced by the Roman pontiffs and general councils) in regulating the life of the members of the

Christian society: they were at one and the same time citizens of a political community (*cives*) and the faithful of Christ (*Christifideles*). The very same sources of the *Corpus Iuris Civilis* invited interpreters to link the problem of the relations of the two laws with that of the relations between the two universal institutions, *Imperium* and *Ecclesia*, of which the *iura communia* were the ideal projection in the *societas christiana* and in the life of the *cives* and *fideles*.

In the preface of *Novella* 6, Justinian had spoken of the *Sacerdotium* and the *Imperium* as divine gifts, institutions from the collaboration of which that "good consonance" (*consonantia*, *symphonía*) derives which brings every utility to humankind. The idea of consonance did not contradict the principle arising from the words of Christ, "Render unto Caesar the things that are Caesar's, and unto God the things that are God's," but rather aligned itself with the dualistic thought of Pope Gelasius I (492–96). He had identified the royal power and the priesthood as the two pillars on which the world stands, the two institutions that respectively preside over the temporal dimension and the spiritual dimension of human life.[28] In spite of some belated hierocratic disorientation, Bartolo remained substantially faithful to the dualistic conception of relations between Church and empire, which postulates the need for their collaboration for the good of society.[29]

The distinction of the two different spheres of competence, the temporal and the spiritual, was clear only in theory, because intersections were multiple in the historical reality and often generated conflicts between *leges* and *canones*, between the jurisdiction of civil authorities and the jurisdiction of the Church. Heresy, schism, or apostasy were ecclesiastical crimes against the Catholic faith, but the Roman emperors had already guaranteed the assistance of civil power in the repression of these crimes, which therefore also became public crimes in the secular order (an example of the consonance of which Justinian had spoken). The appointment of a bishop can be considered a merely ecclesiastical act only in theory, because political power has consistently shown an interest in meddling in the choice of bishops, as they exercised a spiritual jurisdiction over the faithful who were also citizens of a political community. A contract is indeed an act of a secular nature, but if its execution implies the commission of a sin (for example usury, permitted by the Justinian law but forbidden by canon law), or if it is confirmed by an oath, or if it is connected with a sacrament (as dowry is connected with marriage), then a contract is inevitably drawn into the spiritual sphere and into the ecclesiastical jurisdiction.

In the wake of a long scholastic tradition, Bartolo also worked to specify the rules for resolving conflicts between *leges* and *canones*. By the time of Bartolo, the Church had already completed the building of the normative system of classical canon law. From the *Decretum* to the *Liber Extra*, from the *Liber Sextus* to the *Clementinae* and to the additional collections of *Extravagantes*, canon law imposed solutions in every sector of social life, even in temporal matters regulated by the norms of *Corpus Iuris Civilis* and local laws. The concurrence of the two laws in the regulation of the same facts of life could be resolved in the *consonantia* advocated by Justinian but could also result in an apparently irreconcilable conflict. Bartolo proposes an articulated solution based on the criterion of sin (*ratio peccati*).[30] If the matter is spiritual or pertains to faith, canons must be followed. If the matter is temporal, it is necessary to distinguish whether the controversy occurs in lands subject to the Church or in those subject to the empire. If it occurs in the lands subject to the temporal sovereignty of the Roman pontiff, no doubt canons prevail. If, on the other hand, the conflict takes place in lands subject to the jurisdiction of the empire, it is still necessary to distinguish. If the application of civil law entails a sin, then canons must be observed. If, on the other hand, the application of civil law does not involve a sin, secular laws can prevail without difficulty.

But it would be simplistic to think of the relations between civil law and canon law only in terms of conflicts between laws. Roman-Justinianic law was an ancient law, which the jurists of the twelfth century had repurposed as the source of their own science. Medieval canon law was a new law, which often corrected ancient law by making its contents more suited to the needs or sensibilities of the new times. The relationship between the two laws was sometimes read in the view of the dialectic between "rigor of law" (*rigor iuris*) and equity (*aequitas*). For instance, Roman law contained strongly discriminatory provisions concerning spurious children, a category that included children born *ex damnato coitu* ("from a condemned union"), such as those born from adultery or incest. Justinian had stated that such children are "unworthy of every substance," so that the father can leave them nothing by donation or testament: such unworthiness goes so far that they have no right to receive even basic sustenance (*alimenta*).[31] If this was the "truth" of civil law, Bartolo emphasizes that medieval canon law had given a different orientation, which he had endorsed in his consultancy activity.[32] A decretal contained in the *Liber Extra* of Gregory IX (X.4.7.5), in fact, obliged both parents to provide the necessary sustenance to children born from adultery. Tradition attributes to Bartolo a *Tractatus de alimentis*, but there are doubts about his authorship: Thomas Diplovatatius suspected that the work could have been written by Nicolaus d'Alessandro from Perugia, Bartolo's son-in-law. In any case, the work clearly reflects Bartolo's teaching. The treatise explains the reasons why the solution of canon law must be preferred. All children, even spurious ones, have the right to sustenance "for the sake of nature or blood."[33] The right of children and the corresponding obligation of parents, therefore, are rooted in natural law, which inspires the solution dictated by canonical equity (*ex aequitate canonica*).

From this perspective, civil law and canon law are considered parts of a single legal system. Bartolo calls this system the "body of both laws" (*utriusque iuris corpus*), with an expression that in itself carries the sense of the organic connection between parts with different but complementary functions.[34]

Bartolo's political thought

Bartolo's political thought is a fundamental aspect of the doctrinal motives that undergird the presence and authority of this great author in the Western juridical tradition. His political reflection arises primarily from the issues of public law found in the *Corpus Iuris Civilis* and therefore pervades his *commentaria* widely. But this reflection also infuses some political treatises concerning specific themes on which Bartolo concentrated his interests in the last three years of his life, and it is also found in his comments on Henry VII's constitutions on summary procedure and on the notion of "rebels of the empire."

The political thought of Bartolo revolves fundamentally around the thematic nucleus of the relationships between the ideals of universal breadth represented by the institutions of the empire and the Church, and the historical reality of the communal cities of central-northern Italy in which Bartolo lived. While the presence of the Roman pontiff in the life of the Latin Church was extremely widespread, the imperial institution was greatly weakened but reemerged occasionally with unrealistic assertions of authority aimed at restoring the political order of the empire.

Bartolo, together with Dante Alighieri, belongs to the ranks of intellectuals who appealed to the ideal and authority of the universal empire as a supreme example of an institution capable of guaranteeing peace and legality in the context of Italian society in the first half of the fourteenth century: this theme emerges with evidence in the proemium of the *Tractatus represaliarum* (1354).[35]

The emperors who occasionally materialized on Italian territory were the *principes* whose powers the *Corpus Iuris Civilis* outlines. Ulpian had transmitted to medieval thought the image of the *princeps legibus solutus*, that is, released from the observance of his own laws and the laws of his predecessors (D.1.3.31.1).[36] The prince's powers appeared further strengthened by the principle that his will has the force of law (D.1.4.1: "quod principi placuit legis habet vigorem"). And yet this freedom from the bonds of positive law (*lex*) does not entail absolute freedom of action in the field of law (*ius*): the action of the *princeps*, like the action of any other legislator, is conditioned by higher laws (positive and natural divine law, the law of nations that reflects the principles dictated by natural reason), by ethical-religious precepts, by the categories of juridical thought emerging from the texts of the *ius commune*. It is up to jurists to evaluate the adequacy of the *lex* (of the prince or of any other legislator) with respect to the bonds emerging from the system. The commentary on Henry VII's constitutions offers a magnificent demonstration of how Bartolo understood the role of the jurist with respect to the role of the legislator.

In 1313 Henry VII issued two constitutions in Pisa which would allow him to condemn Robert of Anjou, king of Naples, as a rebel of the empire. The constitution *Ad reprimendum* required the adoption of the summary procedure in trials for the crime of lèse-majesté. The constitution *Quoniam nuper* defined the juridical figure of the "rebels and infidels of the empire" (*rebelles et infideles imperii*).[37] The two constitutions, accompanied by Bartolo's commentary, were incorporated among the texts of the *Corpus Iuris Civilis*, as the eleventh *collatio* of the *Authenticum* (*Novellae*).

If we look at Bartolo's commentary on the first of the two constitutions, we see that for him, the summary procedure outlined by the legislator (that is, by political power) to punish the accused of lèse-majesté more quickly, cannot escape the constraints of legal interpretation. To what extent can a process be simplified without losing the substance of a fair trial? What rights should be guaranteed to the person who is subject to the judgment? The jurist is entitled to give an answer to these questions: his doctrine must serve as a guide for the legislator and as an unavoidable interpretation of the law. The meaningful analysis of Bartolo follows and deepens some interpretative cues given by Johannes Andreae:[38] it is necessary to distinguish the "substantial elements of judgment" (*substantialia iudicii*), introduced by natural law or by the law of nations, from some formalities introduced by the civil law. The *substantialia iudicii* (for example, the summons) cannot be eliminated from the summary process without its losing the "substance of the judgment."[39] This interpretative line leads to a fundamental theoretical insight, namely, that the right of defense is a power deriving from natural law: an entitlement that any citizen can assert against the abuses of political power.[40]

The three famous political treatises of Bartolo reveal that his concrete concerns were about the government of the Italian communal cities and the transformations connected to the affirmation of the city lordships.[41] Bartolo conducts a fine political reflection in the wake of the thought of the Church Fathers (Gregorius the Great, Isidor of Seville) and of ancient and medieval philosophers (Aristotle, Thomas Aquinas, Egidius Romanus). But in his thinking the theoretical models inherited from the past become instruments of interpretation of the events and political turns of his time. Bartolo devotes the *Tractatus de guelphis et gebellinis* to the study of the factions (*affectiones*, *partialitates*) that troubled the life of Italian communes. At the time of Bartolo, the two denominations (Guelphs and Ghibellines) continued to qualify the factions that conditioned the life of the cities, but had lost their original connections respectively with the party that supported the Church and the pro-imperial party. Bartolo is consistent with his methodological principles, which required verifying whether the existence of divisions in the political body of the city could have an ethical justification. Following the teaching of Thomas Aquinas (*Summa theologiae* IIa—IIae q. 42 a.2), Bartolo discusses the question in the light of the criterion of "just and due purpose" (*iustus et debitus finis*): factions are lawful if they pursue the public good in the function of the just and peaceful governance of the city. Seditions or insurrections are also justified when they are directed at restoring justice against a tyrannical regime.[42]

In the *Tractatus de regimine civitatis*, Bartolo examines the different systems of government (*modi regendi*) in light of Aristotelian schemas and through the mediation of Egidius Romanus.[43] Bartolo does not limit himself to analyzing the *modi regendi* but assesses their adequacy with respect to the size of the political communities, which he distinguishes in three orders (*civitas seu gens magna*, *maior*, *maxima*). Bartolo believes that the monarchy is an adequate form only to the *civitas maxima* (the empire or a kingdom) and excludes its applicability in the context of Italian communal cities. The aristocratic government "of a few rich, good, and prudent men" is instead appropriate for medium-sized cities (Venice and Florence). Bartolo shows an open predilection for popular government (*regimen ad populum*), in which the power of government resides in the people. The *populus* is an entity that in any case does not include people of the most humble condition and could even exclude some magnates who, because of their arrogance, would risk oppressing others; in concrete terms, the government is entrusted to certain people with systems of recurring shifts. The *regimen ad populum* is suited to the cities of the first order of magnitude (*civitates magnae*), for instance Perugia, which—Bartolo states—thanks to this regimen grows and prospers "in peace and unity."[44]

But each of these forms of government—Bartolo warns—risks degenerating into a perverse regime, which with a single name can be called tyranny. The tyrant who hovers in the background of the treatise *de regimine civitatis* becomes the protagonist of the *Tractatus de tyranno*.[45] Following the teaching of Gregory the Great in *Moralia in Job* (XII.38), which a few years earlier had been collected by Johannes Andreae,[46] Bartolo defines the tyrant as "one who rules a whole commonwealth unlawfully" (*qui in communi republica non iure principatur*): where the word *iure* evokes the complex legal system in which human laws and actions must relate to superior laws and are to be evaluated in their congruity with ethical-religious precepts. Nonobservance of law (*ius*) characterizes a regime that tends not to the common good (*bonum commune*) but to the tyrant's personal utility.

This common imprint unites the different types of tyrant that Bartolo describes: a manifest, veiled, or occult tyrant; a tyrant *ex defectu tituli* (whose power lacks a legitimate title) or *ex parte exercitii* ("by virtue of his conduct"), who governs with tyrannical acts; or even a tyrant *propter titulum* ("because of his title"), but going beyond his *iurisdictio*. With his eyes turned to the tyrants of his time, and absorbing the teachings of Aristotle and Egidius Romanus from a legal perspective, Bartolo proposes an admirable analysis of tyrannical acts (*tyrannica opera*). His insight goes beyond the boundaries of juridical-political science to elevate itself to a psycho-anthropological analysis of universal phenomena. "Today Italy is full of tyrants,"[47] he writes.

This phrase, probably not written by Bartolo himself, closes the *Tractatus de regimine civitatis* in part of the manuscript and printed tradition. It echoes a famous exclamation by Dante Alighieri (*Purgatory* VI.124–25) and an opinion of Johannes Andreae. Whoever the author is, the sentence captures Bartolo's concerns in the face of the institutional transformations that were threatening the freedoms of Italian communal cities. In the political horizon of Bartolo the higher authorities (emperor and pope) would have the task of protecting the city freedoms by deposing tyrants; yet—Bartolo notes—emperors, popes, and papal legates had rather legitimized lords that they knew to be tyrants, giving them the titles of imperial or papal vicars (as had happened in Bologna, Lombardy, and the Marche). Although Bartolo tries to indicate the possible justifications for this policy, the jurist's concerns about the crisis of the municipal institutions are evident in the pages of the treatise: the solution, in Bartolo's eyes, still resided in the responsibility of the two supreme universal institutions.[48]

Conclusion

The historical figure of Bartolo of Sassoferrato cannot be understood except within the cultural and religious coordinates of the time in which he lived.

Bartolo certainly brought to fruition the juridical tradition that preceded him, but he was never a mere repeater of other people's doctrines. Paradoxically, the universal fame he enjoyed in later centuries, as well as his becoming the target of critique that humanists aimed at medieval jurisprudence, entails the risk of placing Bartolo out of time and harming the understanding of the historical meaning of his work. For this reason, two different historiographical problems must be distinguished, which touch respectively on the understanding of his historical figure and the contents of his legacy to the modern world.

Bartolo's political doctrines are nurtured by an ideal of a universal Christian empire that was dissolving precisely as it was being evoked by intellectuals such as Bartolo or Dante, who clearly sensed the direction of the institutional transformations of their time. The microcosm of the Italian communal cities was the terrain in which Bartolo elaborated, in the wake of the masters who had preceded him, theoretical models that allowed for coordinating the novelties of history (particular medieval laws) with the legacy of Roman law and with the common law of the Catholic Church: that is, with the two laws (*utrumque ius*) that would remain the foundation of the education of jurists in continental Europe and later in the New World until the age of codifications. This teaching was destined to great fortune: multiple generations of jurists of the late medieval and modern age attributed to Bartolo's opinions, not wrongly, the merit of expressing a fair and reasonable understanding of the laws and the facts that laws were going to regulate. In this activity Bartolo was moved by a faith in law as a necessary regulatory dimension of human life. The human person is at the center of the law and of *civilis sapientia*. And the unity of the human person requires, for Bartolo, that the sphere of law be constantly connected to the ethical dimension nourished by the Christian religion. It is inevitable that this connection of law and ethics, at the time of Bartolo as always, take place within the framework of the changing historical awareness of human rights and duties.[49]

Notes

1 For biographical details, see the works by van de Kamp, Calasso, Lepsius, and Treggiari, listed in the bibliography.

2 Bartolo, *Commentaria* in D.45.1.132, fol. 49vb—50va, n.8. My quotations, unless otherwise indicated, are taken from the edition printed in Venice, apud Iuntas, 1585, divided into ten volumes, the last of which includes a *repertorium*.

3 According to Diplovatatius, *Liber de claris iuris consultis*, 280, Bartolo began his legal studies in the thirteenth year of life, an age that can be read in Diplovatatius's edition of Bartolo's, *Commentaria* (see bibliography). Other editions indicate the age of fourteen.

4 Baldus de Ubaldis, *In Feudorum Usus Commentaria*, *Si de feudo fuerit controversia*, *§ vassallus*, n.1, fol. 55va.

5 The document is in Treggiari, *Le ossa di Bartolo*, 156–9, who also reports the document relating to the granting of the citizenship of Perugia (160–71), the privileges of Charles IV (172–7), Bartolo's will (178–85), cited below in the text. The four documents had been published by Lancellotti (see bibliography).

6 Lepsius, "Bartolus' Auseinandersetzung mit dem *Digestum Novum*," 622–6. The episode is told by Bartolo, *Commentaria* in D.48.18.7, fol. 179rb.

7 Diplovatatius, *Liber*, 286, however, gives a contradictory account, saying that Bartolo left fifty-four volumes—thirty *in iure civili* and thirty-four *in sacra theologia*. See Colli.
8 Baldus, *Commentaria* in C.9.1.1, fol. 193va n.29.
9 For Bartolo's works, see Lepsius, "Bartolus de Saxoferrato," in *C.A.L.M.A. Compendium*; Treggiari, "Commentaria."
10 The edition prepared by Diplovatatius is particularly valuable: see Cortese.
11 Treggiari, "Sulle edizioni."
12 See Cavallar, "Personaggi in cerca di 'editore'."
13 Bartocci.
14 Bartolo, *Liber Minoricarum decisionum*, proemium: "Minorum fratrum sacra religio fuit a Christi confessore Francisco in altissima paupertate fundata et a multis summis pontificibus approbata" ("The order of the Friars Minor was founded by Francis, confessor of Christ, in the greatest poverty, and approved by many high Pontiffs"), in *Consilia, quaestiones, et tractatus Bartoli a Saxoferrato*, fol. 106rb.
15 Edition in Lepsius, *Der Richter und die Zeugen*, 280. Cf. Quaglioni, "Il pensiero di Bartolo," 77f.; Treggiari, "La laurea del giurista."
16 *Sermo domini Bartoli tempore doctoratus domini Bonaccursii fratris sui*, in *Consilia, quaestiones, et tractatus*, fol. 184ra—va. Quaglioni, "Diritto e teologia." Bartolo's terminology is ancient: the word *suppositio* appears, for instance, in the *Exordium Institutionum* (twelfth century), edited by Hermann Fitting, *Juristische Schriften des früheren Mittelalters* (Halle: Verlag des Buchhandlung des Waisenhauses, 1876), 147, from ms. Leipzig, UB, Hänel 14, § V.10: the *ius civile* (concretely, Justinian's *Institutiones*) is "subjected to ethics" ("supponitur ethice") as well as to logic ("loice"), inasmuch as it deals with interpretation of words.
17 Bartolo, *Tractatus testimoniorum*, ed. Lepsius, *Der Richter*, 278–328; Condorelli, "Prudentia in iure," 155–60.
18 Bartolo, *Commentaria* in D.46.1.57, fol. 72vb, n.9. Condorelli, "Le origini teologico-canonistiche," 56–9.
19 Bartolo, *Tractatus represaliarum*, in *Consilia, quaestiones, et tractatus*, fol. 119vb—120ra, n.1–7. Cortese, *Il diritto nella storia medievale*, 431–3. Jacobus de Belviso had discussed this case in a *quaestio* disputed in Perugia, which he later inserted in his *Lectura authenticorum* (Lugduni: per magistrum Jacobum Sachon, 1511), fol. 36vb—37ra, *collatio* V, *Ut non fiant pignorationes*. Bartolo knew that *quaestio* through the *Lectura authenticorum*.
20 It is inserted as *authentica* in *Codex*, post 4.13.5.
21 Bartolo, *Repetitio* in D.1.1.9: it is inserted in the first volume of his *Commentaria*, fol. 9rb—14vb. Condorelli, "*Ius* e *lex*," 61–76.
22 "Omni populo iurisdictionem habenti ius proprium statuere permittitur, quod ius civile vocatur": *Repetitio* in D.1.1.9, fol. 9rb.
23 *Repetitio* in D.1.1.9, fol. 13va, n.60 and fol. 14ra, n.65.
24 Baldus de Ubaldis, *Super Decretalibus, Commentaria* in X.1.2.1, *de constitutionibus*, c. *Canonum statuta*, fol. 11rb—va, n.15.
25 This sentence appears in a *quaestio* by Jacobus de Belviso: it has been discovered and given value by Bellomo, *I fatti e il diritto*, 633–44f.
26 Bartolo, *Repetitio* D.1.1.9, fol. 11ra, n. 26: "lex et statutum debent esse sancta et honesta." In the allegations Bartolo highlights the agreement of Roman law (D.1.1.10.1; C.1.14.9; D.1.3.3, but this is probably an error for D.1.3.2) and canon law (Isidor of Seville in Gratian's *Decretum*, D.4 c.2) about this principle.
27 Pennington, "Legista sine canonibus parum valet."
28 Condorelli, "Le radici storiche."
29 Condorelli, "Bartolo e il diritto canonico."

30 Bartolo, *Commentaria* in C.1.2.12, fol. 13va, n.2.
31 *Novella* 89 § 15 = Auth. *Ex complexu*, post C.5.5.6.
32 Bartolo, *Commentaria* in Auth. *Ex complexu*, post C.5.5.6, fol. 160vb. Cf. Condorelli, "Bartolo e il diritto canonico," 542–5; Cavallar, "Due consulti di Bartolo."
33 Bartolo, *Tractatus de alimentis*, n. 7–8 and 17, in *Consilia, quaestiones, et tractatus*, fol. 126va.
34 Bartolo, *Apparatus* on Henry VII's constitution *Ad reprimendum* (1313), v. *habenis*, in *Consilia, quaestiones, et tractatus*, fol. 95ra.
35 Above, note 19.
36 Condorelli, "*Ius* e *lex*," 39–53, with the literature cited therein.
37 Schwalm, *Constitutiones*, IV.2, respectively n. 929, pp. 965f.; n. 931, pp. 966f.
38 Johannes Andreae, *Apparatus Clementinarum*, 5.11.2, constitution *Saepe*, *de verborum significatione*.
39 Bartolo, *Apparatus* on the constitution *Ad reprimendum*, in *Consilia, quaestiones, et tractatus*, fol. 94va—102va, esp. v. *et figura*, fol. 99ra—va.
40 Pennington, *The Prince and the Law*, 165–201; Condorelli, "*Ius* e *lex*," 53–60.
41 Editions and introductory study by Quaglioni, *Politica e diritto nel Trecento italiano*.
42 Edition in Quaglioni, *Politica e diritto*, 129–46.
43 Ibid., 147–70.
44 Ibid., 163f.
45 Edition in Quaglioni, *Politica e diritto*, 171–213. English translation by Julius Kirshner, in Cochrane and Kirshner, *University of Chicago Readings in Western Civilization*, vol. 5, 7–30.
46 Johannes Andreae, *Apparatus Clementinarum*, 3.15.1, *de baptismo*, c. *Presenti*, v. *regum*.
47 Quaglioni, *Politica e diritto*, 23f., and 170.
48 Ibid., 59–69. Cf. Quaglioni, "Il pensiero di Bartolo," and Pio, "Il pensiero politico di Bartolo."
49 This is why today we consider it an irreconcilable contradiction that the ideals of Christian charity coexist with unacceptable practices such as judicial torture (recalling Bartolo, who, while a criminal judge, involuntarily killed an accused he had subjected to torture), the repression of religious dissent, slavery, the death penalty, etc. But neither can we be sure of how our times and actions will be judged by those who will come after us.

Bibliography

Andreae, Johannes. *Apparatus Clementinarum*. Rome: in aedibus Populi Romani, 1582.

Ascheri, Mario. "Bartolo da Sassoferrato: introduzione a un giurista globale." In *Mundos medievales: espacios, sociedades y poder: homenaje al Prof. J.A. García de Cortázar y Ruiz de Aguirre*. Vol. 2, 1029–40. Santander: Ediciones de la Universidad de Cantabria, 2012.

Baldus de Ubaldis. *In Feudorum Usus Commentaria*. Venetiis: apud Iuntas, 1580.

Baldus de Ubaldis. *In primum, secundum et tertium Codicis libros commentaria*. Venetiis: apus Iuntas, 1577.

Baldus de Ubaldis. *Super Decretalibus*. Lugduni: Claudius Servanius, 1551.

Bartocci, Andrea. "'Minorum fratrum sacra religio.' Bartolo e l'Ordine dei Minori nel Trecento." In *Bartolo da Sassoferrato nel VII centenario*, 351–71.

Bartolo da Sassoferrato. *Commentaria*. Venetiis: apud Iuntas, 1585.

Bartolo da Sassoferrato. *Commentaria*. Edited by Thomas Diplovatatius. Venetiis: De Tortis, 1520; Reprinted in 1527/30, now available in anastatic reprint, Rome: Il Cigno, 1996–98.

Bartolo da Sassoferrato. *Consilia, quaestiones, et tractatus Bartoli a Saxoferrato*. Venetiis: apud Iuntas, 1585.

Bartolo da Sassoferrato. *Studi e documenti per il VI Centenario*. Edited by Danilo Segoloni. 2 vols. Milano: Giuffrè, 1962.

Bartolo da Sassoferrato nella cultura europea tra Medioevo e Rinascimento. Edited by Victor Crescenzi and Giovanni Rossi. Sassoferrato: Istituto internazionale di Studi Piceni "Bartolo da Sassoferrato," 2015.

Bartolo da Sassoferrato nel VII centenario della nascita: diritto, politica, società. Edited by Enrico Menestò, President of the Centro Italiano di Studi sul Basso Medioevo—Accademia Tudertina. Spoleto: Centro Italiano di Studi sull'Alto Medioevo, 2014.

Bartolo da Sassoferrato a Siena nel VII centenario della nascita. Manoscritti, incunaboli, cinquecentine. Edited by Enzo Mecacci and Maria Alessandra Panzanelli Fratoni. Siena: Società Bibliografica Toscana—Accademia Senese degli Intronati, 2014.

Bellomo, Manlio. "Bartolo da Sassoferrato." In Bellomo Manlio, *Medioevo edito e inedito*. 3. *Profili di giuristi*, 179–93. Il Cigno: Roma, 1998.

Bellomo, Manlio. *The Common Legal Past of Europe 1100–1800*, 149–202. Washington, DC: The Catholic University of America Press, 1995.

Bellomo, Manlio. *I fatti e il diritto tra le certezze e i dubbi del giuristi medievali (secoli XIII–XIV)*. Rome: Il Cigno Galileo Galilei, 2000.

Calasso, Francesco. "Bartolo da Sassoferrato." In *Dizionario biografico degli Italiani*. Vol. 6, 640–69. Roma: Istituto della Enciclopedia Italiana, 1964.

Cavallar, Osvaldo. "Due consulti di Bartolo sui figli nati 'ex damnato coitu' e una 'ardua quaestio' posta dagli statuti di Perugia." In *Bartolo da Sassoferrato nel VII centenario*, 373–401.

Cavallar, Osvaldo. "Personaggi in cerca di 'editore'. Una proposta di lettura per alcuni degli ultimi trattati bartoliani." *Rivista internazionale di diritto comune* 25 (2004): 97–142.

Cochrane, Erich, and Julius Kirshner, eds. *University of Chicago Readings in Western Civilization*. Vol. 5: *The Renaissance*. Chicago: The University of Chicago Press, 1986.

Colli, Vincenzo. "La biblioteca di Bartolo. Intorno ad autografi e copie d'autore." In *Bartolo da Sassoferrato nel VII centenario*, 67–107.

Condorelli, Orazio. "Bartolo e il diritto canonico." In *Bartolo da Sassoferrato nel VII centenario*, 463–557.

Condorelli, Orazio. "*Ius* e *lex* nel sistema del diritto comune (secoli XIV–XV)." In *Lex und Ius. Lex and Ius. Beiträge zur Begründung des Rechts in der Philosophie des Mittelalters und der Frühen Neuzeit*, edited by Alexander Fidora, Matthias Lutz-Bachmann, and Andreas Wagner, 27–88. Stuttgart-Bad Cannstatt: Frommann-Holzboog, 2010.

Condorelli, Orazio. "Le origini teologico-canonistiche della teoria delle 'leges mere poenales.'" In *Der Einfluss der Kanonistik auf die europäische Rechtskultur*. Vol. 3: *Straf- und Strafprozessrecht*, edited by Mathias Schmoeckel, Orazio Condorelli, and Franck Roumy, 55–98. Köln/Weimar/Wien: Böhlau, 2012.

Condorelli, Orazio. "Le radici storiche del dualismo cristiano nella tradizione dottrinale cattolica: alcuni aspetti ed esempi." *Diritto e Religioni* 12 (2011): 450–86.

Condorelli, Orazio. "Prudentia in iure. La tradizione dei giuristi medievali (prime ricerche)." In *Phronêsis—prudentia—Klugheit. Das Wissen des Klugen in Mittelalter, Renaissance und Neuzeit. Il sapere del saggio nel Medioevo, nel Rinascimento e nell'età moderna. Matthias Lutz-Bachmann zu seinem 60. Geburtstag*. Edited by Alexander Fidora, Andreas Niederberger, and Merio Scattola, 137–201. Porto: Brepols, 2013.

Conversazioni bartoliane in ricordo di Severino Caprioli. Edited by Ferdinando Treggiari. Sassoferrato: Istituto Internazionale di Studi Piceni "Bartolo da Sassoferrato," 2018.

Cortese, Ennio. *Il diritto nella storia medievale*. Vol. 2. Roma: Il Cigno, 1995.

Cortese, Ennio. "Intorno all'edizione di Bartolo curata dal Diplovatazio e alla sua ristampa anastatica." In *Iuris Historia. Liber Amicorum Gero Dolezalek*, edited by Vincenzo Colli and Emanuele Conte, 369–85. Berkeley: The Robbins Collection, 2008.

Diplovatatius, Thomas. *Liber de claris iuris consultis. Pars Posterior*. Edited by Fritz Schultz, Hermann Kantorowicz, and Giuseppe Rabotti. Bologna: Institutum Gratianum, 1968.

García Garrido, Manuel J. "Bártolo de Sassoferrato." In *Juristas universales. 1. Juristas antiguos*, edited by Rafael Domingo, 524–30. Madrid/Barcelona: Marcial Pons, 2004.

Lancellotti, Giovanni Paolo. *Vita Bartoli*. Perusiae: apud Petrumiacobum Petrutium, 1576.

Lepsius, Susanne. "Bartolo da Sassoferrato." In *Dizionario Biografico dei Giuristi Italiani (XII–XX secolo)*, edited by Italo Birocchi, Ennio Cortese, Antonello Mattone, and Marco N. Miletti. Vol. 1, 177–80. Bologna: Il Mulino, 2013.

Lepsius, Susanne. "Bartolus' Auseinandersetzung mit dem *Digestum Novum*: zwischen *lectura* und *commentum*." In *Bartolo da Sassoferrato nel VII centenario della nascita: diritto, politica, società*, 601–29.

Lepsius, Susanne. "Bartolus de Saxoferrato." In *C.A.L.M.A. Compendium Auctorum Latinorum Medii Aevi (500–1500)*. Vol. 2.1, 101–56. Firenze: Sismel-Galluzzo, 2004.

Lepsius, Susanne. *Der Richter und die Zeugen. Eine Untersuchung anhand des "Tractatus testimoniorum" des Bartolus von Sassoferrato, mit Edition*. Frankfurt am Main: Klostermann, 2003.

Murano, Giovanna. "Bartolo da Sassoferrato." In *Autographa*. I.1. *Giuristi, giudici e notai (sec. XII–XVI med.)*, edited by Giovanna Murano, 66–71. Bologna: Clueb, 2012.

Pennington, Kenneth. "Legista sine canonibus parum valet, canonista sine legibus nihil." *Bulletin of Medieval Canon Law* 34 (2017): 249–58.

Pennington, Kenneth. *The Prince and the Law, 1200–1600: Sovereignty and Rights in the Western Legal Tradition*. Berkeley: University of California Press, 1993.

Pio, Berardo. "Il pensiero politico di Bartolo." In *Bartolo da Sassoferrato nel VII centenario*, 171–98.

Quaglioni, Diego. "Diritto e teologia: temi e modelli biblici nel pensiero di Bartolo." In *Bartolo da Sassoferrato nel VII centenario*, 333–50.

Quaglioni, Diego. "Il pensiero di Bartolo. Tra Medioevo giuridico e modernità politica." In *Giornate di studi bartoliani 29 e 30 giugno 2011*, edited by Ferruccio Bertini and Stefano Troiani, 73–82. Sassoferrato: Istituto Internazionale di Studi Piceni, 2012.

Quaglioni, Diego. *Politica e diritto nel Trecento italiano. Il "De tyranno" di Bartolo da Sassoferrato (1314–1357). Con l'edizione critica dei trattati "De guelphis et gebellinis," "De regimine civitatis" e "De tyranno"*. Firenze: Olschki, 1983.

Rossi, Giovanni. "Bartolo da Sassoferrato." In *Il contributo italiano alla storia del pensiero. Ottava appendice. Diritto*, 51–4. Roma: Istituto della Enciclopedia Italiana, 2012.

Schwalm, Jakob, ed. *Constitutiones et acta publica imperatorum et regum*. Vol. 4.2. Hannover/Leipzig: Hahn, 1911.

Stein, Peter, 1980. "Bartolus, the Conflict of Laws and the Roman Law." In Peter Stein, *The Character and Influence of the Roman Civil Law: Historical Essays*, 83–90. London: Hambledon Press, 1980.

Treggiari, Ferdinando. "Commentaria (*Commentaries on Civil Law*) 14th Century, *ed. pr.* 1470, Bartolus (a Saxoferrato) (Bartolus de Saxoferrato) (1313/1314–1357/1358)." In *The Formation and Transmission of Western Legal Culture: 150 Books That Made the Law in the Age of Printing*, edited by Serge Dauchy, Georges Martyn, Anthony Musson, Heikki Pihlajamäki, and Alain Wijffels, 40–3. Cham: Springer, 2016.

Treggiari, Ferdinando. "La laurea del giurista. Le orazioni dottorali di Bartolo da Sassoferrato." In *Lauree. Università e gradi accademici in Italia nel medioevo e nella prima età moderna*, edited by Anna Esposito and Umberto Longo, 97–111. Bologna: Clueb, 2013.

Treggiari, Ferdinando. *Le ossa di Bartolo. Contributo alla storia della tradizione giuridica perugina*. Perugia: Deputazione di storia patria per l'Umbria, 2009.

Treggiari, Ferdinando. "Sulle edizioni dei 'Consilia, quaestiones et tractatus' di Bartolo da Sassoferrato." *Rivista internazionale di diritto comune* 27 (2016): 159–84.

Van de Kamp, Josephus L.J. *Bartolus de Saxoferrato, 1313–1357. Leven-Werken-Invloed-Beteekenis*. Amsterdam: H.J. Paris, 1936. Reduced Italian version in *Studi Urbinati* 9.1–2 (1935).

Weimar, Peter. "Bartolus de Saxoferrato." In Peter Weimar, *Zur Renaissance der Rechtswissenschaft im Mittelalter*, 339–50. Goldbach: Keip, 1997.

Woolf, Cecil N.S. *Bartolus of Sassoferrato: His Position in the History of Medieval Political Thought*. Cambridge: Cambridge University Press, 1913.

10 Baldo degli Ubaldi da Perugia (1327–1400)

Julius Kirshner

Biographical introduction

After the death of his teacher Bartolo da Sassoferrato, in 1357, Baldo degli Ubaldi da Perugia emerged as the foremost Italian jurist of his generation.[1] He was a leading exponent of the medieval *ius commune*, a transnational and protean body of civil and canon law principles, methods, and jurisprudence. Endowed with a brilliant mind, strong sense of self, and contrarian spirit, Baldo was constitutionally disinclined to accept conventional wisdom and categorical thinking unquestioningly. Nor did he accept at face value Roman law as embodied in the compilation known as the *Corpus Iuris Civilis*, which was promulgated by the Emperor Justinian (527–65). Justinian's *Corpus*, together with its nearly 100,000 glosses gathered and organized by Accursio in the early twelfth century, became the primary source of civil law in medieval Italy and southern Europe. Yet the fractious political landscape of fourteenth-century Italy—a world of self-governing cities, small towns, and rural communes ravaged from 1348 onward by the Black Death and social and political upheavals—was starkly different from the hegemonic Roman Empire. For Baldo, engaging contemporaneous realities on the basis of an unsystematic collection of laws bequeathed by an imperial civilization that, as he pointed out, had long passed away, was problematic. That is why he admonished contemporaries to avoid slavish devotion to the customs, laws, and institutions of ancient Rome as a guide for managing their own legal affairs. Instead, he advised lawmakers and jurists to rely on their own talents and resources.[2]

Time and again, and always in response to specific circumstances, Baldo applied and interpreted Roman law in the light of local customs and practices, many of which were enacted as statutes (*iura propria*). Just as often, he invoked the *ius commune* to validate or restrict local customs and practices. This dialectical procedure was a core feature of his jurisprudence. At the same time, he was adamant that any custom or practice running afoul of the precepts of natural law, the *ius gentium*, and divine law was unlawful. More than any other jurist of his day, Baldo adopted philosophical terminology and concepts from Aristotle and Thomas Aquinas to advance singular approaches and solutions to a wide array of new as well as old questions.[3] The corpus of works he produced between the 1350s and 1400 left an indelible imprint on European jurisprudence.

Born in Perugia in 1327, Baldo was a member of a reputable family. His father, Francesco di Benvenuto, was a physician, and his younger brothers, Pietro and Angelo, were, respectively, a canon lawyer and a civil lawyer. Baldo began studying civil law at the University of Perugia with Giovanni Pagliaresi da Siena in the early 1340s, and then with Bartolo, who joined the faculty in 1343. His teacher of canon law was Federico Petrucci da Siena, an esteemed canonist, who left the university in 1343 to become a Benedictine monk.

Baldo's seemingly fraught relationship with Bartolo has captured the attention of succeeding jurists and modern historians. With gratitude, he acknowledged that Bartolo (*doctor meus*) had a profound influence on his development as a budding jurist, and he followed Bartolo's lead on numerous points of law. Baldo's reverence for his teacher did not inhibit him, however, from expressing disagreement frequently, and sometimes vehemently and sarcastically, with Bartolo's views. For this, he was chided by gossipy jurists for being envious of Bartolo's fame, a rebuke recycled by modern scholars. Attributing Baldo's criticisms of his teacher's views to personal pique and professional envy betrays an atrophied understanding of their intellectual propinquity. Baldo was an independent-minded jurist with little patience for lazy habits of speech and mind. He consistently grounded his agreements and disagreements, not simply with Bartolo but equally with all other jurists, in first principles and reasoned arguments. Sorting out the opposing and tangled views of Bartolo and Baldo posed a daunting challenge for later jurists,[4] who understood that the acceptability of their own arguments was inextricably linked to the authority of these two towering figures.

After receiving his doctorate in civil and canon law, around 1346–47, Baldo lectured on civil law alongside Bartolo at his alma mater. He then taught at Pisa (1357–58) and Florence (1358–64), with a starting annual salary of 250 florins, climbing to 300 florins in 1360, substantial sums at the time. Florence also recruited his younger brother Pietro, who arrived in Florence in 1361/62 to teach canon law. Baldo's years in Florence were personally and professionally fruitful. He married Landa, daughter of Vanni (who belonged to a noble family hailing from Collemedio near Perugia). Landa and Baldo had twin sons, Francesco and Giovanni Zenobio, who, not surprisingly, followed in their father's and uncles' footsteps and became jurists. In 1359, Baldo was granted Florentine citizenship, a privileged status that extended to his male descendants. The grant of citizenship was intended as a reward for teaching in Florence and as an incentive for the jurist to remain teaching there.

During these years, Baldo wrote legal opinions (*consilia*) on citizenship, taxation, dowries, and inheritance.[5] In addition to his ordinary lectures, he presented lengthy reviews (*repetitiones*) of laws in Justinian's *Digest* and *Codex*, including the lex *Iusiurandum speciem* (Dig. 12. 2. 2) and lex *Cunctos populos* (Cod. 1. 1. 1). *Cunctos populos* was the first law of Justinian's *Codex*, which took its name from the opening words of the imperial decree ordering all the peoples within the Roman Empire to observe the Christian faith. By implication, those living outside the empire (*non subditi*) would not be bound by Justinian's decree. In the Middle Ages, *Cunctos populos* was the starting point for tackling the vexed question of whether a city's statutes could be enforced beyond its territorial jurisdiction against foreigners as well as citizens. Was a last will valid everywhere or only in the place where it was drafted or only in the citizen's hometown? Which jurisdiction was looked to in a dispute over a contract when it was concluded in one place, payment made in another, and the parties citizens of different cities? And were the statutes of a city enforceable against a foreigner who committed a crime within its jurisdiction but afterward fled to his hometown or elsewhere? These are but a sample of the questions that arose daily with which Baldo grappled in his noteworthy *repetitio.*[6]

In 1364, Baldo returned to teach at Perugia, where, apart from a three-year stint at the University of Padua (1376–79), he remained until 1390. During the 1360s, Baldo and his brothers were all teaching at the university—a remarkable fraternal accomplishment during the University of Perugia's golden age. Baldo himself held various public offices and was sent as a legate on diplomatic missions. The city relied on his negotiating and oratorical skills in managing its stormy relationship with the papacy. Unlike the self-governing cities of Pisa and Florence, Perugia was located in the Papal States and subject to the temporal authority and onerous taxation of the papacy. In 1370, Baldo headed a diplomatic mission that halted the conflict between Perugia and Pope Urban VI.

Perugia was inevitably drawn into the broader conflicts between the papacy and its enemies when the seat of the papacy resided in Avignon, France (1309–76); and into the conflicts engendered by rival claimants to the papal throne during the Great Schism (1378–1417). Who was the right pope—the Roman claimant, Urban VI, elected on April 8, 1378, or the French claimant, Clement VII, elected September 20 of the same year? The supporters of Clement charged that the cardinals who elected Urban acted out of blinding fear of the Roman mob. Since Urban's election did not conform to canon law procedures, it should be annulled. Baldo addressed the validity of the papal election in two *consilia.*[7] In the first (1378), he took it upon himself to defend the legitimacy of the election. In the second (1380), written at the behest of Urban, he, along with the canonist Giovanni da Legnano (d. 1383), held that the election was canonical. Baldo argued that while fear of the Roman mob was palpable, it remained doubtful that such fear was so great (constant and uninterrupted) that the disaffected cardinals had no other choice but to elect Urban. Furthermore, a doubtful election of the pope could not be resolved by law. "We have neither a law nor an instrument of law [hierarchical superior]," Baldo famously stated, "to resolve this dispute." In effect, even "a doubtful pope is the true pope" (*Dubius papa est verus papa*). The opinions of Baldo and Giovanni constituted cornerstones of the Romanist position throughout the Schism, which came to an end, after considerable turmoil, at the Council of Constance (1414–18).

In 1385, Coluccio Salutati, the chancellor of Florence, invited Baldo—then at the peak of his career—to return to the University of Florence. Salutati appealed to the Perugian authorities to allow the jurist to return to Florence to help restore the city's cultural prominence in Tuscany, which he traced back to the Etruscans and Romans. The request was swiftly denied on the grounds that

Baldo's departure would result in the University of Perugia's utter ruin. Star academic jurists like Baldo were treated as valuable public assets. He attracted a steady stream of foreign students to the city, participated in the operation of the city's legal and political institutions, and enhanced the city's cultural reputation. Indeed, Baldo was made to swear an oath on the Bible that he would not leave the city without the government's express permission.

In 1390, however, Baldo accepted an invitation personally extended by Giangaleazzo Visconti of Milan to teach civil law at the University of Pavia. Giangaleazzo was the overlord of an expansive territorial state, including Pavia, and invested with the title of duke by Holy Roman Emperor Wenceslaus in 1395. The circumstances surrounding Baldo's move to Pavia are murky. It is certain that Perugia's priors would have objected to Baldo's departure, as they had in 1385, and it is possible that Giangaleazzo prevailed on them to permit the jurist to leave for Pavia. It is not clear why Baldo, relatively old at the age of sixty-three, left his hometown, which was the seat of his private affairs and where he was a prominent public figure. Was it the lure of a hefty monthly salary of 100 florins and the opportunity to engage the most powerful ruler of northern Italy? Relations between Baldo and his family and Giangaleazzo were cordial, and they benefited from the prince's patronage.

Recruiting Baldo to Pavia is today's equivalent of a university landing a Nobel laureate. Baldo, as Paul Grendler observes, "was the most famous scholar to teach there during the first forty years" of its history.[8] The years in Pavia were highly productive. Baldo's commentary on feudal customs (*Lectura super usibus feudorum*), dedicated to Giangaleazzo, was published in 1393, together with his standard gloss on the *Peace of Constance* (*Commentum de Pace Constantie*).[9] Although no record exists that Baldo taught canon law, he left an incomplete commentary (*Lectura decretalium*) on the first two books (and the beginning of the third) of the *Decretals* of Pope Gregory IX. This commentary was composed after 1393. He also penned hundreds of *consilia* in this period, a few of which, because they concern the authority and powers wielded by Giangaleazzo, have been dissected by scholars assessing Baldo's support for the prince's political projects.[10] Baldo died early on the morning of April 28, 1400, at the age seventy-two, attempting to complete what would be his final *consilium*. Numbering among Baldo's disciples who became renowned jurists were Pietro d'Ancarano (d. 1415), Francesco Zabarella da Padua (d. 1417), Giovanni Nicoletti da Imola (d. 1436), and Paolo di Castro (d. 1441).

Works of Baldo

In taking the measure of Baldo's works, researchers face four interrelated challenges. First is the sheer quantity. In addition to his commentaries on the decretals and feudal law, he produced extensive but incomplete commentaries on Justinian's *Digest* and *Codex*, *repetitiones*, tracts (e.g., on public notaries (*De tabellionibus*)), and abstracts from the works of leading canonists: Pope Innocent IV, Guido da Baiso, Guillaume Durand, and Giovanni d'Andrea. Of special importance are *consilia* dedicated to the resolution of single cases. These contain a wealth of detail about the activities and relationships of ordinary women and men and the critical role *ius commune* jurists played in the administration of local laws. On the subjects of the legal status of Jews, citizenship, and remarriage of widows, for instance, the *consilia* offer more probing treatments than those found in his commentaries. Over his career, Baldo produced about four thousand *consilia*, with some two thousand preserved in twelve manuscript volumes now housed in the Vatican Library. The volumes, which contain fair copies prepared by Baldo's personal scribes as well as autographs, originally formed part of the jurist's library. Another two thousand *consilia* are found in other manuscripts and early printed editions. Vincenzo Colli estimates that more than 10 percent of all juridical works printed in Italy before 1500 carry Baldo's name as the author.[11]

The second challenge lies in false and uncertain attributions. For example, a commentary on Justinian's *Institutes*, whose author was Bartolomeo da Novara, was mistakenly attributed to Baldo. Likewise, a tract on witness testimony (*De testibus*), was authored by Bartolo.[12] Baldo's authorship of other works published under his name, including tracts on torture (*De tormentis*) and prisons (*De carceribus*), remains uncertain.

The third challenge in assessing Baldo's contributions is the lack of searchable, digitized editions. Only a sliver of Baldo's oeuvre has been critically edited. The manuscripts and early printed editions are characterized by variant readings, omissions, errors, and mistaken conjectures. Basing a discussion of Baldo's views on passages found in a single manuscript or early printed edition is likely to result in misleading and incorrect interpretations.

Finally, textual mutability presents a challenge. Baldo admitted that he was not ashamed of having changed his mind in the service of truth and justice when he thought of a better opinion. In fact, Baldo often reworked and updated his *consilia* and commentaries before and after publication, transforming them into dynamic textual artifacts. Thus, even an autograph or fair copy of his work should not be taken, without a confirmatory investigation, as the jurist's final word on the subject at hand.

Christian moral philosophy

Imbued with a Christian moral philosophy, rooted in the fertile soil of Aristotelian-Thomistic thought, Baldo saw God as the summit of being from which subordinate existence originates. "For the first cause is God," he declared, "and every first cause is greater and nobler than its effect."[13] What separates human beings from animals—beyond their dual spiritual and corporeal natures—is the brain, "a divine organ in which human consciousness and understanding operate,"[14] and free will, which, when exercised with a clear conscience, results in morally correct behavior. Behaving morally, however, is often impeded by misunderstanding and confusion. As a social being, one necessarily is restricted in exercising free will. For Baldo, as Walter Ullmann states:

> human society moulds the individual's will by the promulgation and application of the laws, gradually promoting a habit which implies a real modification

> of man's character. This habit of acting justly is a moral quality which is a virtue of the highest order. His whole doctrine was based on the acceptance of the fundamental idea of Christian moral philosophy that man is God's creature and is born for a destined end.[15]

Baldo foregrounded his Christian moral philosophy in a series of polished orations that he delivered on the occasion of awarding doctoral degrees at the University of Pavia.[16] Having passed the required examinations, the doctorand would give a speech in which he expressed his humility and devotion to his teachers and requested the conferral of the doctorate. His sponsor would reply with a formal speech blessing the candidate or with an oration (*oratio pro doctoratu*) lauding the candidate's perseverance and scholarly excellence, but more importantly depicting the superiority of law (over medicine) as a field of knowledge. Weaving together citations from the Bible and Aristotle, Baldo in his *orationes* trumpeted the idea that law is rooted in moral philosophy. Echoing Ulpian, he celebrated law as a true philosophy constituting a rational and universal system of knowledge that enabled jurists to understand the deepest causes of things human and divine. Lofty professional aspiration served as a rebuttal to vocal critics of the legal profession, like Petrarch (d. 1374), who vilified jurists for their pettifoggery and greed.

Baldo conceived of habit (*habitus*) and custom (*consuetudo*) as artifacts of nature and justified by natural law. In viewing nature as the source of feudal customs, Baldo, Canning states, "is seeking to express the profound point that this whole body of law emerged gradually as the legal expression of the natural development of this form of human relationship, that it was not, in his eyes, instituted by God or a ruler."[17] Canning's reading strikes me as anachronistic. True, for Baldo feudal customs were neither brought about by a ruler nor directly emanated from God. It is always possible that Baldo's view on the origin of feudal customs was a theoretically conceivable exception to his general conception of natural law, derived from Thomas Aquinas, as inseparable from divine or eternal law. But he assumed, as every other jurist did (and as Canning himself recognizes) that natural law itself was created by God—and therefore, by extension, God is the ultimate source of feudal customs.

Baldo was a devoted son of the Church. "I am still in this pitiful body devoted to the Holy Roman Church," he professed, "because through the church I have hope in God."[18] Baldo's allegiance to the Church was not, however, synonymous with blind obedience. He was well aware of the dangers of the Church's overreach into temporal affairs. An apt illustration concerns an episcopal ordinance threatening excommunication for women wearing dresses with low-cut necklines revealing their breasts. Baldo affirmed Giovanni d'Andrea's distinction that the ordinance applied to single women. Married women wearing seductive dresses at the direction and pleasure of their husbands were exempt from the ordinance, for their apparent transgression was sanctioned by lay customs. Needless to say, any woman (single or married) would be excommunicated should she wear clothing exposing her breasts to public view in church or on holy days.[19] It was widely understood that if every case was classified, without qualification, as a sinful act automatically falling within the exclusive jurisdiction of Church courts, then the Church's monopoly *ratione peccati* would drive secular courts into extinction. To avert this outcome, Baldo maintained that cases should be adjudicated in Church courts *ratione peccati* only when they were specifically subject to ecclesiastical jurisdiction or expressly mentioned in canon law. A major exception was cases of usury, which, from beginning to end, were the exclusive preserve of Church courts.

Baldo adhered to the mainstream position in canon law that, in view of its autonomous jurisdiction and immunities, the Church's acquisition, administration, and preservation of ecclesiastical property were exempt from civil laws. The immunity was not absolute, however, particularly in regard to the ability of secular authorities to impose taxes on Church properties in the name of prevailing public interest (*utilitas publica*) and to declare a state of emergency. He began one *consilium* with the observation that it is an old complaint of the laity that because of the Church's tax exemption, it grows richer day after day, while laypersons are crushed by taxation. Despite the exemption, and threatened with interdicts and excommunication, city governments and territorial princes sought to fill their depleted coffers by taxing ecclesiastical properties. Along with other jurists, Baldo limited civil taxation to properties that had been subject to taxes (*collecta*) before they were donated and bequeathed to the Church. The funds raised would be dedicated to the construction and repair of bridges, roads, and walls. He advised that the bishop should compel Church entities in his diocese to pay legitimate taxes to provide for the welfare of local churches and military defense of the state, which benefited all members of the general community.[20]

Between civil and canon law

The preposition "between" is not a figure of speech but is intended to suggest that each domain of the *ius commune* simultaneously (1) *shared* elements with the other—for example, regarding contracts and obligations, testamentary succession and disinheritance, and the procedural rules by which trials were conducted; (2) stood *apart* from the other—for example, regarding oaths, good faith in acquiring a prescriptive title to property, ecclesiastical jurisdiction and privileges, and heresy; and (3), depending on the matter and circumstances at hand, took *precedence* over the other—for example, regarding marriage (canon law), dowries (civil law), usury (canon law), domicile and citizenship (civil law), and so on. A salient characteristic of Baldo's jurisprudence was a dazzling ability to balance the internal tensions of the *ius commune* in crafting solutions that went beyond the letter of the law.

Take the question of whether a wife is bound to provide support (*alimenta/alimonia*) from her own goods, beyond the dowry, to an impoverished husband. The issue was raised in a dispute while Baldo was teaching at the University of Florence.[21] A wife named Caterina petitioned for reimbursement from her late husband's heirs for the fruits (rents and income) generated by her nondotal goods. She claimed that he had consumed the fruits without first obtaining her consent, which was legally required. Caterina had been legally a minor when she married at the age of thirteen, and thus had been incapable of giving consent. Furthermore, she asked for spousal support from the husband's estate. Francesco Albergotti da Arezzo (d. 1376), Baldo's colleague at the University of Florence, opined that the wife was entitled to receive spousal support. He dismissed the heirs' counterclaim that the husband had a reciprocal right to spousal support from the fruits of the nondotal goods. Simply put, it is unnatural for a wife to support and nourish her husband, a view anchored in the *Digest* and Accursius's *Glossa*. In dissent, Baldo rejected Caterina's claim for reimbursement. He stressed that a wife is morally and naturally obligated to furnish spousal support to her husband from her own goods when he suffers misfortune. This especially holds when the wife is well off and the husband impoverished, unless the husband's misfortune results from unlawful activities. Baldo's holding is animated by the conception of the wife and husband as partners of a divine and human household. They are united together in one flesh, a reflection of the incarnation of Christ, and thereby mutually duty-bound to shoulder each other's burdens.

A related question concerned an obligation of reciprocal support among brothers. Roman law imposed a reciprocal maintenance obligation on parents and children and other ascendants and descendants, but not upon brothers and other collaterals (cousins, nephews, nieces, uncles, and aunts). With the approval of Accursius's *Glossa*, a reciprocal support obligation among collateral kin quickly entered into the *ius commune* and continues to be enforced today under Italy's Civil Code. A dispute on which Baldo was asked his opinion related to the fraternal support obligation of a certain Paolo, hailing from Norcia, whose brother Bartolomeo had been disinherited by their late father.[22] In his last will, the father instituted Paolo as universal heir, with the condition that if Paolo willingly supported Bartolomeo from the inherited goods, he would forfeit the inheritance. The disinherited Bartolomeo, in accordance with the *ius commune*, had no claim to support from his father's estate. The question was whether Paolo could be legally compelled to support his brother, despite the testamentary condition. Baldo resolved that Paolo could be compelled, reasoning that it is against natural law for a father to impede a brother's mandatory support obligation. Baldo's unprecedented affirmation of a disinherited son's claim to support from a wealthy brother became the generally accepted view (*communis opinio*).

In another case, a father disinherited a daughter whom he accused of behaving immorally and dishonorably. He left a small bequest, intended as a token of her disgrace, which the daughter immediately claimed. It seems that the heirs objected on the grounds that a disinherited child is not entitled to support from her father's estate. Yet moved by the daughter's plight, Baldo approved the bequest, explaining, "I think it is more humane that the bequest he left be enforced in consideration of human kindness, compassion, and paternal love."[23]

Oath-taking was a daily fact of medieval life, and breaking an oath was a grave sin, violating the eighth commandment and blaspheming God. Baldo's oath not to leave Perugia without official permission was just one of countless oaths he took during his lifetime. As a jurist, he was confronted with the conundrum of squaring the Roman imperial constitution *Non dubium* (Cod., 1. 14. 5), which prohibited taking an oath to "make a contract that the law prohibits," with opposing canon law doctrines. A prime example was the Roman law prohibition, inherited by medieval jurists, against gifts made between husbands and wives.[24] In upholding the customary prohibition, the Roman jurist Ulpian related that it had been instituted to prevent married couples, prompted by the force of mutual love, from wastefully draining their resources by making immoderate gifts. It was also feared that husbands would abuse affluent but stingy wives, and wives would refuse to have sex with penny-pinching husbands. Canon lawyers upheld the validity and irrevocability of interspousal gifts, as long as the donor took an oath confirming that the gift was made by mutual agreement and without either party being forced to do so. Initially opposed to the canonists, civil lawyers had no choice but to acquiesce after the confirmatory oath was validated by Popes Innocent III (1198–1216) and Boniface VIII (1294–1303).[25]

Baldo's pronouncements on this issue varied, exposing his difficulty in either rigidly upholding *Non dubium* or reluctantly accepting the authority of the papal decretals. In the Florentine *repetitio* devoted to *Cunctos populos*, he stated that where a prohibition was not absolute, as the prohibition of interspousal gifts was not, an oath confirming the gift was valid. Where a city's statute expressly stated that the oath was not valid, then the statute should be enforced. By the time he reached Pavia in 1390, he had revised his view, holding that the confirmation of interspousal gifts by oath was unlawful. In support, he cited a rule of law found in the decretal collection (*Liber sextus*) issued in 1298 by Pope Boniface VIII (VI (5. 13) 58), which stated that an oath taken against venerable customs is invalid. Furthermore, Baldo denied that oaths necessarily took precedence over civil laws. If oaths took precedence, civil laws would not be worth the parchment on which they were written. He conceded that an oath has precedence in cases specifically mandated by law.

The core issue facing Baldo was whether a donor could be released from observing a confirmatory oath already taken. Facing the penalty of mortal sin, an oath-taker had to perform what was promised in God's presence. Alternatively, the oath-taker could petition the diocesan bishop to be released from a strict enforcement of the oath in accordance with natural equity.[26]

Modern scholars single out Baldo as a champion of wealth accumulation, commercial enterprise, and freedom of contract against the encroachments of the medieval ecclesiastical prohibition against usury.[27] It is certainly true that Baldo held merchants in high regard, so much so that he placed them on the same pedestal as doctors of law. As traveling merchants were not treated as a privileged and protected class (like, for instance, clerics, pilgrims, professors, and students), either by Roman law or ever-changing local statutes, it was up to the Church, Baldo urged, to provide them with effective, lasting protection. Under canon law, merchants were granted similar protections as pilgrims and in theory came under the universal jurisdiction of the Church.[28] Baldo wanted the Church to use its power of excommunication to deter and punish offenders who assaulted merchants and stole their goods.[29]

His observation that "the world cannot survive without merchants,"[30] even if unexceptionable, was made in recognition of the indispensable public service they performed. Striving for riches was not in itself a mortal sin, so long as merchants acted according to established commercial norms and rules and with a clear conscience.[31] Yet it is inappropriate to recast Baldo as hostile to economic regulation and the usury prohibition. Witness his traditional stance against excessive merchant profits and in favor of the ability of communities to lawfully fix maximum prices for food, clothing, and rent for lodging, which are necessary for human life.[32] His commentary was cited as justification for regulating the prices of woolen cloth in the official gloss of the statutes of Alvignano in the region of Campania.[33]

Italy's prosperity from the twelfth century onward was owing, in large measure, to booming trade in commodities and luxury goods enabled by an expansion of credit and financial innovation. Medieval theologians and jurists approached the regulation of the medieval market economy not as economists but as moral authorities assisting the laity with spiritual and ethical guidance. With great ingenuity and forensic zeal, they scrutinized commercial and financial innovations, including partnership agreements, marine insurance contracts, bills of exchange, international banking, and public debts in order to ascertain whether they violated the usury prohibition. Merchants deserved to be rewarded with reasonable profits for their labors and the genuine risks they bore. Usurers, in contrast, deserved to be denounced and punished as sinners for disobeying the Old and New Testament prohibitions against usury.

By Baldo's time, the definition of usury included several integral elements. According to the classic definition by Saint Ambrose, cited in Gratian's *Decretum* (ca. 1140), "whatever is added to the principal is usury" (*quodcumque sorti accedit usura est*).[34] This definition, which focused on observable behavior, referred to anything demanded or accepted beyond the principal of a loan (*mutuum*). In addition, usury was forbidden because it is a sin against justice. The usurer was denounced as a thief and his profits treated as stolen goods that had to be returned to the parties from whom they were exacted. Usury could also be committed mentally (*usura mentalis*), that is, by merely intending to profit from a loan in disobedience to Christ's command to "Lend freely hoping for nothing thereby" (Luke 6:35). This command became an element of the composite definition of usury after it was cited in the decretal *Consuluit* of Pope Urban III (X 5. 19. 10). A philosophical element was derived from Aristotle, who treated money as a means of exchange. By definition, according to the philosopher and the theologians and jurists who endorsed his view, money has zero intrinsic value, is essentially sterile, and cannot be a source of natural fruits and legitimate profits. To profit from a loan of money contravened natural law.

Although Roman law permitted moderate usury (what we call interest), the medieval prohibition was absolute, without gradations. This tenet could not be modified by human law. Secular legislators—whether the Roman emperor, a lesser ruler, or cities like Todi—might wish to permit usury, but according to Baldo they lacked the power to enact laws contravening divine law.[35]

Baldo identified three types of usury. The first was *usurae punitoriae*, which should not be translated as "punitive damages," or damages assessed beyond actual damages as a means of punishing the offender. Rather, it meant compensatory damages, called *interesse*, on account of the borrower's delayed payment or breach of contract. Absent fraud (when the parties mutually agreed to impose a penalty for delayed repayment in order to disguise usurious interest), the exaction of damages was considered lawful and morally permissible. Canonists and theologians applied this moral logic to the system of interest-bearing government loans in Venice, Genoa, and Florence.[36] There was broad agreement that if citizens were forced to lend to the city and repayment of the loan was postponed to a distant future, which occurred in times of protracted warfare, then the citizens were entitled to receive *interesse*, typically amounting to 5 to 10 percent per annum. If their loans were made voluntarily, then the city could legitimately reward citizen-lenders with an interest payment called a gift (*donum*), provided that gift was made out of benevolence and the creditors made loans without any expectation of being rewarded. This was an implausible scenario featuring moral heroics rather than the converging pressures of a city in dire fiscal straits obligated to satisfy the demands of interest-seeking creditors.

With firsthand knowledge of the system of government loans in Florence, called the *monte comune*, and the moral controversy ignited by the *monte*'s operations, Baldo had no difficulty in picking apart the tried-and-true subterfuges employed by the government to mask the payment of usurious interest to its creditors. For Baldo, the certainty of the interest payment, variously called *interesse*, *donum*, *lucrum*, and *paghe*, smacked of usury. To be sure, a common rate of damages fixed by statute awarded to creditors waiting for repayment of their forced loans was permissible, but any amount of damages exceeding the principal of the loan he condemned as usurious. Creditors were deceiving themselves if they believed that verbal subterfuges would protect them from inducement to sin. They should take the safer road and desist from investing in the *monte comune*.[37] Negative assessments of the *monte comune* also were made by Baldo's brother Angelo and by Bartolomeo da Saliceto (d. 1411).[38]

Elsewhere, Baldo approved a statute providing a fixed annuity of 10 percent to citizens who laid out money to the city. At first, he censured the public annuity as usurious because of its general similarity to an interest-bearing loan and implied similarity to the *monte comune*. Shifting gears, however, he called the annuity a *census*, an arrangement by which the city pays an annuity to citizen-investors from its general revenues. In this arrangement, the city is likened to a seller, the citizen to a purchaser. Yet, as a matter of strict law, the *census* was neither a contract of sale nor a loan. It was unclassifiable (*innominatus*) under the Roman law scheme of contracts, for which there was no specific remedy. Not wishing to impoverish their citizens, said Baldo, farsighted and solicitous legislators provide them with an annuity, as they would provide for their own children. The justification for the *census* resides in the twin principles that all the citizenry's resources are subject to the fisc and that the city has the legitimate power to make laws serving its own interest.[39]

The second form of usury, *usurae recompensatoriae*, referred to compensation to creditors who suffer losses owing to fluctuations in the value of currency and regional variances between currencies. Losses resulted when a difference in value existed between newly minted coinage and older coinage in effect when a contract was concluded, or when there was a difference in the exchange rate between local and foreign currencies. Indemnification for such losses, Baldo determined, was equitable and necessary to prevent one party from unjustly enriching himself at the expense of the other party.[40] In this connection, he approved of the bill of exchange (*lettera di cambio*), "an informal letter by which one merchant ordered his agent-banker in some other city to make payment on his behalf to another merchant in that distant city."[41] The question before Baldo was whether the fee charged by the agent-banker for extending credit was tantamount to usury. Earlier canonists deemed bills of exchange usurious for allowing bankers to evade the usury prohibition by concealing interest charges in exchange-rate adjustments. Baldo disagreed, arguing that the bill of exchange was categorically different from a loan in that the agent-banker's profit was uncertain and contingent on the ups and downs of the market, therefore, making it morally permissible.[42] Recent quantitative research confirms Baldo's insight, made over six hundred years ago, into the difference between lending at interest and bills of exchange.[43]

The third form of usury, *usurae lucratoriae*, referred to usurious profits that were manifestly sinful and associated with public moneylending. The Third Lateran Council (1179) had excommunicated public moneylenders and denied them Christian burial, while the Second Council of Lyon (1274) voided the last wills of manifest usurers who failed to provide full restitution. The decree *Ex gravi* of the Council of Vienne (1311–12) barred the public licensing of moneylenders and declared that anyone who persisted in believing that usury is not a sin would be punished as a heretic. Usury was feared as an existential threat, a spiritual disease infecting everyone it touches. For Baldo, "The usurer is similar to a leper who infects others through his contagious disease. Therefore, usurers are lepers and should be removed from the company of healthy persons, for bad customs are to be rooted out from states."[44]

Strictly speaking, the usury prohibition applied to Jewish moneylenders. Yet they were permitted by the Fourth Lateran Council (1215) to lend at interest, provided that the interest was not excessive. The Church's repression of Christian moneylenders created a credit vacuum that was filled by Jewish moneylenders and pawnbrokers, who arrived in northern Italian cities by government invitation in the fourteenth century. Baldo underscored the beneficial role played by the Jewish community of Perugia in extending credit, via interest-bearing loans secured by pawns of movable property, to poor and hungry Christians. A Perugian statute prohibited artisans from keeping their shops open or practicing their craft on Christian feast days. Baldo was asked to submit a *consilium* on "whether on these days Jews can receive pawns, lend money, return pawns to debtors who satisfied their loans, and keep their shops and storerooms open, notwithstanding the tenor of the said statute."[45] As Baldo recognized, strict enforcement of the statute against Jewish moneylenders and pawnbrokers was unwarranted and would inflict grave damage. The statute, he explained, is not binding on Jews, for they are excused by civil and canon law from observing Christian rituals, including feast days. Moreover, exceptions to a literal application of the law are permitted in cases of exigent circumstances, since consumption credit was at risk of flatlining—an outcome that Perugia's legislators assuredly did not intend. "It is necessary for the poor to find usurers, and especially Jews," Baldo seriously quipped, "since there is no respite from eating and, on top of that, one eats more on feast days." His *consilium* exemplified a quietly tolerant approach to the legal capacity of members of the Jewish community to receive the doctorate, work as notaries, serve as witnesses in Christian tribunals, and be regarded as citizens.

Death with a clear conscience

Baldo was determined to meet his death with a clear conscience before God. In his last will, drafted on October 26, 1399, he sought to relieve his conscience for any ill-gotten gains and property obtained from persons unknown (*tam pro incertis quam male ablatis*), by providing an annual offering for twenty years to the Order of the Friars Minor of Perugia, consisting of two baskets of wheat, two large barrels of wine, and a cape for a friar presbyter.[46] Shortly before this, Baldo had experienced scruples over the purchase of property in the village of Carestello, about five miles from Gubbio and on the border dividing Gubbio's territory from Perugia's. In the 1390s, Baldo acquired adjacent properties in Carestello to create a fortified family compound.[47]

A remarkable sequence of *consilia* and informal notes recently brought to light by Osvaldo Cavallar reveals that Baldo harbored moral doubts about the purchase of one of the properties.[48] The property in question was originally bequeathed to a Benedictine monastery (Santa Maria di Valdiponte) and burdened with an obligation to pay the donors an annual rent in perpetuity. In the early fourteenth century, the property was acquired through a middleman by a nepotistic bishop and member of the Gabrielli family of Gubbio. Afterwards, the bishop transferred the property to his kinsmen, from whom Baldo eventually purchased it. Rumors had circulated that the bishop used church money for the transaction. His kinsmen predictably asserted that the money was their own. Whatever may have transpired, it was no longer possible to establish with certainty the money's provenance. Worried that his purchase was morally tainted because the property had belonged to the church, Baldo asked the jurists Gualterino Zazzi, a canon lawyer, and Cristoforo Castiglioni, a civil lawyer, colleagues at the University of Pavia, for *consilia* to resolve his doubts.

They concluded that the purchase stood on solid moral grounds. For Zazzi, the rumors should be dismissed as unreliable. For Castglioni, the church of Gubbio had a potential claim on the money used in the transaction, but the claim was no longer tenable because the church had not attempted to recover the property, which was now subject to the jurisdiction of Perugia. Having held the property for at least three generations, moreover, the kinsmen could claim ownership by continued use or prescription.

The *consilia* failed to assuage Baldo, who wrestled with nagging doubts, specifically over what a bishop could do with the resources of the church entrusted to his care. In a batch of notes, written for himself, he returned to the issue of the annual rent due to the donor who had bequeathed the property to the monastery. For more than fifty years, the monks had failed to fulfill the obligation they assumed when they received the gift—though they knew of the obligation. He also returned to his doubts in his commentary on the decretal *Vigilanti*,[49] keenly aware that the legislation of Pope Alexander III and the Fourth Lateran Council had altered the rules of prescription established by Roman law.[50] Not only had the rules been changed, but a legal issue also had been turned into a moral quandary in which conscience played a paramount role. In the end, Baldo believed that he had acquired the parcel in good faith and had paid a just and fair price.

Baldo's struggle to resolve his own internal moral conflict through the medium of *consilia*, as Cavallar points out, was unique in the annals of medieval jurisprudence. Jurists employed *consilia* to resolve third-party disputes, not conflicts between their own acts and their moral values and innermost beliefs. In view of Baldo's definition of the term "conscience," his resort to *consilia* is not as surprising as it seems at first glance. "Keep in mind that the term 'conscience' (*conscientia*) derives from the act of inquiring about conduct (*consilio*), which requires performance (*voluntati*), and knowledge (*scientia*), which in turn requires intellectual discernment (*intellectui*)."[51] Having concluded his own extraordinary inquiry, with his conscience unburdened and all legal doubts settled, he saw the way clear to transmit the patrimonial properties in Carestello to his heirs—and, as a devout Christian, to continue his journey "as a spiritual man, a pilgrim on his way between this world and the eternal life."[52]

Notes

1 For bio-bibliographical profiles of Baldo, see Lange and Kriechbaum's fastidiously thorough "Baldus de Ubaldis"; Murano, "Baldo degli Ubaldi"; Cortese, "Baldo degli Ubaldi." Two volumes of studies were published on the occasion of the sixth centenary of Baldo's death: the first in the journal *Ius commune* 27 (2000), Vincenzo Colli, ed.; the second, Frova, et al., *VI centenario della morte di Baldo degli Ubaldi 1400–2000*. NB: All references to Baldo's *Commentaria* on the *Corpus Iuris Civilis* are to the eight-volume edition published in Venice (apud Iuntas) in 1599; on the *Decretals* to the edition published in Venice (apud Iuntas) in 1595; and to his *consilia* published in six volumes in Venice (apud Hieronymum Polum) in 1575.

2 Baldo to Dig. 1. 3. 31, *Princeps legibus*, 22vb, nu. 78.

3 Kriechbaum, "Philosophie und Jurisprudenz."

4 For an anonymous compilation of issues on which Baldo and Bartolo disagreed, see Paris, Bibliotèque Nationale de France, MS Lat. Nouv. Acq. 1700, 240r—263r.

5 See, for example, Kirshner, "*Ars imitatur naturam*"; Id., "Baldo degli Ubaldi's Contribution."

6 Baldus de Ubaldis, *Tractatus duo de vi et potestate statutorum.*
7 Cable, 107–11; Pio, 41–76.
8 Grendler, 83.
9 Baldo degli Baldeschi, *Commentaire sur la Paix*—a useful translation based on an early printed edition.
10 Canning, 221–5; Pennington, "The Authority of the Prince"; Conetti; Black.
11 On the manuscripts and early printed editions of Baldo's works, see the pioneering and exacting studies of Colli, *Giuristi medievali*, 68–297; and his "Le opere di Baldo."
12 Lepsius.
13 Baldo, *Commentaria super primo Decretalium*, *Proemium*, 2ra.
14 My translation is from the text cited by Padovani, 35.
15 Ullmann, quote at 389.
16 See note 14, above.
17 Canning, 83.
18 My translation is from the text cited by Padovani, 31, note 14, above.
19 Lally, ii, 304–5.
20 Baldo, *Consilia*, iii, cons. 246, 69va; Canning, 136–8.
21 Kirshner and Pluss.
22 Kirshner, "Baldus de Ubaldis on Disinheritance."
23 Ibid., 173–4.
24 Laurent-Bonne.
25 Condorelli.
26 Baldo to X 2. 24. 28, *Cum contingat*, 258v, nu. 8; *Consilia*, v, cons. 471, 126ra—b.
27 For example, Wood, 49, 218.
28 Piergiovanni, "Il mercante e il diritto canonico medievale," in id., *Norme, scienza e pratica giuridica*, 617–34.
29 Piergiovanni, "La 'peregrinatio bona' dei mercanti medievali: A proposito di un commento di Baldo degli Ubaldi a X. I. 34," in id., *Norme, scienza e pratica giuridica*, 595–604.
30 Baldo to X 1. 22 (*super rubrica*), 311vb, nu, 1.
31 Baldo to X 1. 2. 4, *Nam concupiscentiam*, 12v, nu. 6.
32 Langholm, 181.
33 Baldo to Cod. 1. 4. 1, *Negotiatores si qui*, 60va, nu. 3; Gamba, *Comunità e statuti*, 237.
34 For overviews and bibliography on the medieval usury prohibition, see Armstrong, "Usury"; Barile, "Credito, usura e prestito a interesse." Still eminently valuable, albeit dated, is McLaughlin.
35 For Baldo's views on usury, see McLaughlin, 90–4; Quaglioni, 169–91 and 229–34; Gamba, *Licita usura*, 193–210.
36 Armstrong, *Usury and Public Debt*; Barile, "Il dibattito."
37 Baldo to Dig. 12. 1. 2. 4, *Mutuum*, § *In mutui datione*, 6ra; to Dig. 12. 1. 11. 1, *Rogasti me*, § *Si tibi*, 13ra—b.
38 Kirshner, "Angelo degli Ubaldi."
39 Baldo to X 2. 24. 1, *Ex administrationis*, 247va, nu. 14.
40 Grossi, 185–7, 259–63, 364–5.
41 Munro.
42 De Roover.
43 Bell, Brooks, and Moore.
44 Baldo, *Consilia*, iii, cons. 449, 131, nu. 2. We now know that in actual fact leprosy, or Hansen's disease, is not highly contagious.
45 Quotes are from his *consilium*, edited and discussed by Quaglioni, 232–3.

46 Baldo, *L'opera di Baldo*, 329.
47 Monacchia.
48 Cavallar, "La coscienza del giurista."
49 Baldo to X 2. 26. 5, *Vigilanti*, 270v—71r, nu. 4–5.
50 Helmholz, 174–99.
51 Baldo to X 2. 18. 1, *Cum monasterium*, 196rb, nu.2; Horn, 105–08.
52 Kuttner, 46.

Bibliography

Armstrong, Lawrin. "Usury." In *The Oxford Encyclopedia of Economic History*, edited by Joel Mokyr. Vol. 5, 183–5. New York: Oxford University Press, 2003.

Armstrong, Lawrin. *Usury and Public Debt in Early Renaissance Florence: Lorenzo Ridolfi on the Monte Comune*. Toronto: Pontifical Institute of Mediaeval Studies, 2003.

Baldo degli Baldeschi. *Commentaire sur la Paix de Constance (1183)*. Translated by Dominique Gaurier. Limoges: PULIM, 2016.

Baldo degli Ubaldi. *L'opera di Baldo, per cura dell' Università di Perugia nel V centenario dalla morte del grande giureconsulto*. Edited by Oscar Scalvanti. Perugia: Tipi della Unione cooperativa, 1901.

Baldus de Ubaldis. *Tractatus duo de vi et potestate statutorum (Repetitio super lege Cunctos populos, C. 1. 1. 1)*. Edited by E.M. Meijers. Haarlem: H. D. Tjeenk Willink & Zoon, 1939.

Barile, Nicola Lorenzo. "Credito, usura e prestito a interesse." *Reti medievali* 11/1 (2010): 475–505. Available at www.rmojs.unina.it/index.php/rm/index

Barile, Nicola Lorenzo. "Il dibattito sul prestito a interesse negli ultimi trent'anni tra probabilisti e rigoristi. Un bilancio storiografico." *Nuova rivista storica* 92 (2008): 835–74.

Bell, Adrian R., Chris Brooks, and Tony K. Moore. "*Cambium Non Est Mutuum*: Exchange and Interest Rates in Medieval Europe." *Economic History Review* 70/2 (2017): 373–96.

Black, Jane. *Absolutism in Renaissance Milan: Plenitude of Power under the Visconti and the Sforza 1329–1535*. Oxford: Oxford University Press, 2009.

Cable, Martin John. *Real and Personal Obedience: Pluralism, Sovereignty and "Communis Error" in the Great Western Schism (1378–1417)*. Morrisville: Author, 2006.

Canning, Joseph. *The Political Thought of Baldus de Ubaldis*. Cambridge: Cambridge University Press, 1987.

Cavallar, Osvaldo. "La '*benefundata sapientia*' dei periti: Feritori, feriti e medici nei commentari e consulti di Baldo degli Ubaldi." *Ius Commune* 27 (2000): 215–82.

Cavallar, Osvaldo. "La coscienza del giurista: Gli scrupoli patrimoniali di Baldo degli Ubaldi." In *Proceedings of the Fourteenth International Congress of Canon Law: Toronto, 5–11 August 2012*, edited by Joseph Goering, Stephan Dusil, and Andreas Thier, 421–32. Città del Vaticano: Biblioteca Apostolica Vaticana, 2016.

Colli, Vincenzo. *Giuristi medievali e produzione libraria. Manoscritti—autografi—edizioni*. Stockstadt am Main: Keip, 2005.

Colli, Vincenzo. "Le opere di Baldo. Dal codice d'autore all'edizione a stampa." In Frova, et al., *VI centenario della morte di Baldo degli Ubaldi*, 25–85.

Condorelli, Orazio. "Alcuni casi di giuramento confirmatorio in materia di dote e di diritti successori. Contributo alla storia dell' "utrumque ius" (secoli XII–XV)." In

"Panta Rei": Studi dedicati a Manlio Bellomo, edited by Orazio Condorelli. Vol. 1, 491–565. Rome: Il Cigno 2004.

Conetti, Mario. "Baldo e la politica viscontea. Appunti a *questiones* e *consilia.*" In Frova, et al., *VI centenario della morte di Baldo degli Ubaldi*, 473–522.

Contino, Elvira. "*Societas* e famiglia nel pensiero di Baldo degli Ubaldi." *Rivista di storia del diritto italiano* 82 (2009): 19–92.

Cortese, Ennio. "Baldo degli Ubaldi." In *Dizionario biografico dei giuristi italiani (XII–XX secolo)*, edited by Italo Birocchi, et al. Vol. 1, 149–52. Bologna: Il Mulino, 2013.

Danusso, Cristina. *Ricerche sulla "Lectura feudorum" di Baldo degli Ubaldi.* Milan: Giuffrè, 1991.

De Roover, Raymond. "*Cambium ad Venetias*: Contribution to the History of Foreign Exchange." In *Business, Banking, and Economic Thought in Late Medieval and Early Modern Europe*, edited by Julius Kirshner, 251–2. Chicago: University of Chicago Press, 1974.

Fredona, Robert. "Baldus de Ubaldis on Conspiracy and *Laesa Maiestas* in Late *Trecento* Florence." In *The Politics of Law in Late Medieval and Renaissance Italy.* Edited by Lawrin Armstrong and Julius Kirshner, 141–60. Toronto/Buffalo/London: University of Toronto Press, 2011.

Frova, Carla, Maria Grazia Nico Ottaviani, and Stefania Zucchini, eds. *VI centenario della morte di Baldo degli Ubaldi 1400–2000.* Perugia: Università degli Studi, 2005.

Gamba, Carlo. *Comunità e statuti della Terra di Lavoro.* Rome: Viella, 2006.

Gamba, Carlo. *Licita usura. Giuristi e moralisti tra Medioevo ed Età moderna.* Rome: Viella, 2003.

Gilli, Patrick. "Les *consilia* de Baldo degli Ubaldi et l'élévation ducale de Gian Galeazzo Visconti: un intellectuel au service du prince?" In *Droit, humanisme et culture politique dans l'Italie de la Renaissance*, 193–209. Montpellier: Presses universitaires de la Méditerranée, 2014.

Gordley, James. "The Achievement of Baldus de Ubaldis (132?—1400)." *Zeitschrift für Europäisches Privatrecht* 8 (2000): 820–36.

Grendler, Paul F. *The Universities of the Italian Renaissance.* Baltimore/London: Johns Hopkins University Press, 2002.

Grossi, Paolo. *Ricerche sulle obbligazioni pecuniarie nel diritto comune.* Milan: Giuffrè, 1960.

Helmholz, Richard H. *The Spirit of Classical Canon Law.* Athens: University of Georgia Press, 1996.

Horn, Norbert. *Aequitas in den Lehren des Baldus.* Cologne/Graz: Böhlau, 1968.

Kirshner, Julius. "Angelo degli Ubaldi and Bartolomeo da Saliceto on Privileged Risk." *Rivista internazionale di diritto comune* 14 (2003): 83–117.

Kirshner, Julius. "*Ars imitatur naturam*: A *Consilium* of Baldus on Naturalization in Florence." *Viator* 5 (1974): 289–331.

Kirshner, Julius. "Baldo degli Ubaldi's Contribution to the Rule of Law in Florence." In Frova, et al., *VI centenario della morte di Baldo degli Ubaldi*, 313–64.

Kirshner, Julius. "Baldus de Ubaldis on Disinheritance: Contexts, Controversies, *Consilia.*" *Ius Commune* 27 (2000): 119–214.

Kirshner, Julius. "Between Nature and Culture: An Opinion of Baldus of Perugia on Venetian Citizenship as Second Nature." *Journal of Medieval and Renaissance Studies* 9 (1979): 179–208.

Kirshner, Julius, and Jacques Pluss. "Two Fourteenth-Century Opinions on Dowries, Paraphernalia and Non-Dotal Goods." *Bulletin of Medieval Canon Law* 9 (1979): 65–77.

Kriechbaum, Maximiliane. "Philosophie und Jurisprudenz bei Baldus de Ubaldis: 'Philosophi legum imitati sunt philosophos naturae'." *Ius Commune* 27 (2000): 299–343.

Kuttner, Stephan G. *Harmony from Dissonance: An Interpretation of Medieval Canon Law*. La Trobe, PA: Archabbey Press, 1961.

Lally, Patrick J. "Baldus de Ubaldis on the 'Liber Sextus' and 'De Regulis Iuris': Text and Commentary." 2 vols. Ph.D. diss. University of Chicago, Chicago, 1992.

Lange, Hermann, and Maximiliane Kriechbaum."Baldus de Ubaldis." In *Römisches Recht im Mittelalter*. Vol. 2: *Die Kommentatoren*, 758–95. Munich: C. H. Beck, 2007.

Langholm, Odd. *The Merchant in the Confessional: Trade and Price in the Pre-Reformation Penitential Handbooks*. Leiden/Boston: Brill, 2003.

Laurent-Bonne, Nicolas. *Aux origines de la liberté de disposer entre époux*. Issy-les Moulineaux: LGDJ, 2014.

Lepsius, Susanne. *Von Zweifeln zur Überzeugung der Zeugenbeweis im gelehrten Recht ausgehend von der Abhandlung des Bartolus von Sassoferrato*. Frankfurt am Main: Vittorio Klostermann, 2003.

Martín, Antonio Pérez. "La recepción de la obra de Baldo en España." *Anales de derecho* 25 (2007): 265–309.

McLaughlin, Terence P. "The Teachings of the Canonists on Usury." *Mediaeval Studies* 1 (1939): 81–147; ibid., 2 (1940): 1–22.

Monacchia, Paola. "Vicende patrimoniali degli Ubaldi a Perugia tra Tre e Quattrocento." In Frova, et al., *VI centenario della morte di Baldo degli Ubaldi*, 101–14.

Munro, John H. *The Bill of Exchange, Draft, or Acceptance Bill*. Available at http://www.economics.ca.munro/5

Murano, Giovanna. "Baldo degli Ubaldi (1327–1400)." In *Autographa I.1: Giuristi, giudici e notai (sec. XII–XVI med.)*, edited by Giovanna Murano, 103–8. Bologna: Clueb, 2012.

Nico Ottaviani, Maria Grazia. "La presenza di Baldo nella vita politica di Perugia." In Frova, et al., *VI centenario della morte di Baldo degli Ubaldi 1400–2000*, 87–100.

Padovani, Andrea. "Sette *orationes* pavesi *pro doctoratu* di Baldo degli Ubaldi." In *L'Università in tempo di crisi. Revisioni e novità dei saperi e delle istituzioni nel Trecento, da Bologna all'Europa*, edited by Berardo Pio and Riccardo Parmeggiani, 27–61. Bologna: Clueb, 2016.

Pennington, Kenneth. "The Authority of the Prince in a Consilium of Baldus de Ubaldis." In *Studia in honorem eminentissimi cardinalis Alphonsi M. Stickler*, edited by Rosalio José Castillo Lara, 483–515. Rome: LAS, 1992.

Pennington, Kenneth. "Baldus de Ubaldis." *Rivista internazionale di diritto comune* 8 (1997): 35–61.

Piergiovanni, Vito. *Norme, scienza e pratica giuridica tra Genova e l'Occidente medievale e moderno*. Genoa: Società Ligure di Storia Patria, 2012.

Pio, Berardo. *Giovanni da Legnano. Un intellettuale nell'Europa del Trecento*. Bologna: Bononia Universty Press, 2018.

Quaglioni, Diego. "Questione ebraica e usura in Baldo degli Ubaldi (c. 1327–1400)." In *Civilis sapientia: Dottrine giuridiche e dottrine politiche fra medioevo ed età moderna. Saggi per la storia del pensiero giuridico moderno*. Rimini: Maggioli, 1989.

Ullmann, Walter. "Baldus' Conception of Law." *Law Quarterly Review* 58 (1942): 386–99.

Wahl, James A. "Baldus de Ubaldis: A Study in Reluctant Conciliarism." *Manuscripta* 18 (1974): 21–30.

Wood, Diana. *Medieval Economic Thought.* Cambridge: Cambridge University Press, 2002.

11 Paolo di Castro (1360/62–1441)

Susanne Lepsius

Biography and major works

Paolo di Castro (in Latin Paulus de Castro) was one of the most renowned professors of civil law of the fifteenth century. Together with Bartolo da Sassoferrato and Baldo degli Ubaldi, he is considered as one of the most prominent jurists of the so-called school of commentators. Despite lasting fame, his biography cannot be entirely reconstructed, and entire years in his career show gaps,[1] deserving clarification through further investigation.

Born in Castro—a town in the northern part of Lazio eradicated entirely in the seventeenth century on command of Pope Innocent X after a war against the Farnese family—Paolo was drawn academically and professionally from early on to the northern Italian city republics, particularly to Florence. He was also orientated to Avignon, where the papal curia had resided since 1305 and where—after the so-called Great Schism of the Latin Christian Church—the French-supported popes, beginning with Clement VII in 1378, kept their residence.

Paolo began his civil law studies in Perugia, where Baldo degli Ubaldi was one of his teachers. He made friends with Baldo's two sons and became their private tutor. He also served as Baldo's scribe and was known for his very neat handwriting.[2] Paolo moved on to study at the university of Pavia and then to Avignon. He went to Avignon probably with the patronage of the Florentine cardinal Petrus Corsini, who had adhered to the French pope Clement VII since 1381. In Avignon, Paolo received his doctorate in 1385 in civil law and probably in canon law as well, since in all printed editions of his works he is referred to as *doctor utriusque iuris.*[3]

He taught civil law in Avignon, where he came into contact with, among others, the famous canonist Gilles de Bellemère, bishop of Avignon since 1392. Most importantly, Paolo became *auditor* of the Florentine cardinal Petrus Corsini, who was a member of the papal Rota, the highest appellate court in all ecclesiastical affairs. As *auditor*, Paolo later wrote, he found almost all lawsuits assigned to Corsini from the papal Rota crossing his desk first.[4] From early on, Paolo combined his activity as professor of civil law with practical functions as judge, legal consultant, or legal administrator in church service. His commentaries on almost all books of the *Corpus Iuris Civilis*[5] are replete with practical insights into the functions of church courts, as well as into Italian statutory laws and real court cases in the secular jurisdiction of Italian cities.

Paolo di Castro remained eighteen years in Avignon, teaching and consulting, interrupted by stays in Siena, Pavia, and other towns. Afterwards, he taught civil law in Florence (1401–03, 1413/14, 1422–23), Siena (1404–06), Bologna (1424–29), and finally Padua (1429–41). He was among the very highly paid law professors of his age.[6]

In 1403, he married the granddaughter of the renowned professor of canon law Pietro da Ancarano (ca. 1333–1416); with her he had two sons and one daughter, all of whom reached adult age despite the waves of plague in those years. Because of his marital status and as a layperson, he needed dispensations for his appointments in 1403 as *podestà* in Viterbo (a town in the papal *patrimonium Petri*) and in 1411 as vicar in spiritual matters of the Florentine bishop Amerigo Corsini. Paolo needed the dispensations because he took his wife with him to Viterbo, although bringing one's wife was forbidden for a *podestà* because of fears of private contacts to the local population. A vicar in spiritual affairs had to be a cleric, i.e. unmarried. Both appointments attest to his qualifications in secular and spiritual affairs, and the dispensations are an indication to his moral integrity and overall personal esteem. Unfortunately, nothing so far is known of the concrete cases and affairs he had to deal with in those two positions.

Much more can be established about his contributions to statutory law making. In 1414/5 he was called as the only law professor along with two judges into a committee to revise the statutes of Florence. There he mainly worked on the sections concerning tax and criminal law,[7] but he discussed of course other parts of the new statutes with his colleagues. Interestingly, he was not always successful in convincing them to follow his proposals when the statutes were enacted in 1415.[8]

In response to a suggestion by San Bernardino of Siena, that city's officials asked Paolo, in 1425, to assist in the revision of the Sienese statutes. Not so clear is whether he also had a hand in revising the statutes of Fermo (1446), in the Papal States. And it is unlikely that he contributed to the redaction of the Lucchese statutes, because no documentary evidence sustains this ancient hypothesis. Quite a number of his *consilia*, however, deal with the communal statutes of Lucca.[9]

When Paolo died on May 30, 1441, he was buried in the Basilica of Santa Maria dei Servi in Padua, where his grandson had a monument erected for him in 1492. Unlike his famous predecessors Bartolo da Sassoferrato and Baldo degli Ubaldis, Paolo had no affiliation with the Order of the Friars Minor or its Third Order. Paolo firmly was a layperson, devoutly committed to the offices and ranks of the Church, personally connected to the highest ranks within the Church.

As a professor, Paolo wrote extensive commentaries on the core pieces of Roman law as taught in the universities of his days—that is, the entire Digest, but only on books 1 to 4, 6 and 7 of the Justinian *Code*. Throughout his long career as a professor, he seems to have revised his lectures several times, and significant differences exist between the printed editions, on which all scholars draw when referring to the content of his teachings, as well as to the manuscripts of his lectures. The extant manuscripts of his works have yet to be analyzed in depth and concrete detail.[10] His commentaries belong to the earliest legal standard textbooks printed in the incunabula era, starting in 1478 (Brescia: Henry of Cologne—Lecture on the Sixth Book of the *Code*). They were reprinted up to the Venice 1610 edition,[11] attesting to his audience all over Europe well into the early modern period of the *ius commune* age. Besides these works, he authored several comprehensive treatments (*repetitiones*) of single laws of the *Corpus Iuris Civilis* and hundreds of opinions (*consilia*) for the parties to a lawsuit or for judges requesting his opinion. Indeed, of his *consilia* there seem to survive more manuscripts than of his commentaries. In most print editions used today by scholars of the *ius commune*, his legal opinions are collected in three books.[12] Which of the printed *consilia* actually were penned by Paolo himself remains to be carefully studied, and it is likely that further unpublished *consilia* might be found in manuscripts that did not find their way into the published editions.[13] The printing press helped to sustain and even foster the Continent-wide fame Paolo di Castro had enjoyed among his contemporaries.

With Raffaele Fulgosio (d. 1427), Paolo was commissioned in 1407 by cardinals loyal to the Roman pope, Gregory XII, to render a legal opinion on how to end the schism (see ahead, para. 'pope(s), cardinals')—a remarkable request in view of Paolo's affiliation with Avignon.[14] In this incident, as in many others when he was asked to render a *consilium*, Paolo carefully avoided the trap of merely confirming with legal arguments the desired result of the commissioning party. This discretion earned him great respect for his impartiality and the titles *doctor veritatis* and *doctor excellentissimus*, making him one of the most sought-after consultors of his age. Aeneas Silvio Piccolomini, later Pope Pius II, observed that Paolo "filled almost all of Italy with his legal opinions" (*omnem Italiam consiliis implevit, cum frequentes ad eum litigantes concurrerent et iudices eius auctoritati multum tribuerent, cuius doctrina solida et sine dolo esset*).[15] In his teachings, too, he proved to be independent minded. One famous story is that he corrected an obvious error that Bartolo had made and rebuked his contemporary colleagues for having slavishly followed the opinion of the Perugian master.[16] His style was succinct, always pointing out to students the most relevant principles. He was one of the very few Italian medieval jurists who escaped the harsh criticism that French humanist jurists persistently uttered against the *mos italicus*. Indeed, François Cujas even recommended that his students sell their shirts and buy instead the commentaries of Paolo di Castro if they did not yet possess his texts.[17]

Characteristic teachings and opinions

As a medieval jurist and renowned law professor of his time, Paolo di Castro was a baptized Christian and was well versed in the teachings of the Catholic Church. His treatment of the standard topics and legal problems of his day illuminates a distinctive attitude towards the official Church and its institutions, as well as towards the role of faith, religion, and equity in daily life.

Relationship between pope and emperor

Teaching exclusively Roman law for his entire university career, Paolo could find in the ancient law texts, especially the *Code* and the *Authenticum* (i.e., *Novellae*) plenty of passages in which the ancient Roman emperors acted with great self-confidence as patrons of the early Christians and the Church. The early glossators of Roman law in Bologna and elsewhere forged an alliance with the medieval emperors of the Staufer dynasty.[18] Perhaps too much is made of this allegiance in particular by German historiography,[19] but even as late as the early fourteenth century, the civil law professor Cino da Pistoia upheld a clear dualistic political approach, attributing highest power in worldly affairs (*gladius materialis*) to the Roman-German emperors and the highest authority in all spiritual and ecclesiastical affairs (*gladius spiritualis*) to the popes, both being invested with their power directly by God and acting independently from each other. Cino even argued that the Roman-German king could wield the full secular powers of an emperor without having yet been crowned emperor by the pope.[20] Roman law could be used as an argument to carve out a clear autonomous realm of legislation and jurisdiction, at the top of which the *princeps/imperator* of the *Corpus Iuris Civilis* exercised *merum imperium* independently of the pope—and not on command of the latter, as the hierocratic interpretation of the two-swords doctrine would have it.[21] In the major crisis of the Great Schism, the Roman-German King Sigismund of Habsburg even saw it as his task to convene in Constance (1414–18) a general council to overcome the schism, putting himself in the shoes of the Emperor Constantine, who had presided over the council of Nicaea.

Nothing of such argument is to be found in Paolo. To the contrary, Paolo opined, when interpreting the relevant passages of Roman law. He never questioned the Donation of Constantine as a matter of dubious historical foundation (unlike, e.g., Nicolaus of Cusa or Lorenzo Valla). He even countered the pro-imperial argument that the emperor could not have alienated parts of the Empire, just as a tutor may not alienate the property of his ward. Instead, Paolo held that the famous gift of the emperor to the pope and to the Church—which established worldly power of the pope in the *patrimonium Petri*—"was not an (unlawful) alienation, but could be done by law as (honorable) resignation into the hands of the superior, since God is Lord and the pope as his vicar stands above the emperor" (*hoc autem facere non potest nisi in ecclesiam Romanam . . . quia illa non dicitur alienatio sed resignatio in manu superioris, quia Deus est dominus et per consequens eius vicarius super imperatorem est.*).[22]

On another cornerstone of medieval political philosophy, the *lex Regia*, Paolo held that the people of Rome had not renounced their sovereignty for good by transferring it to the emperor.[23] The *populus Romanus* in fact could revoke the authority to legislate which they had transferred to the emperor, but only until the time of Emperor Augustus. The advent of Jesus Christ during his reign had established the Christian Church. From the ancient Roman empire nothing but the name remained. Authority and power were vested in the pope as vicar of Christ, who could depose the emperor, demonstrating that the pope wields both swords and that the Roman people no longer were at the center of political power within the empire.[24] In both respects, Paolo held decidedly hierocratic views, focusing on the pope as the head of Christianity.

Pope(s), cardinals, and the problem of the Great Schism

According to Paolo, this point of view consequently applied within the Church administration as well. On commenting upon the Roman law titles *Law and Decrees of the Senate*, he elaborated on typical features of general laws. One of these was that they would be enacted after the legislator had consulted about the pertinent issues with wise and prudent men—not women, as Paolo was careful to stress. For instance, the pope in general, when having to deal with important issues (*negotia ponderosa*), should do so only after having consulted with his cardinals. But if he should choose not to do so, his ensuing act would nevertheless remain valid, since consultation did not belong to the substance of his act.[25] Likewise, the pope could issue a new constitution, derogating the legislation of a general council and of course also that of a former pope. Theoretically, he should use a derogatory formula in his new constitution. The derogating formula would have to mention expressly the particular decree affected, when a council's decree was to be changed, but could be formulated in general words when a constitution of a pope was abrogated. Nevertheless, Paolo concluded, the pope, because of this greater authority, could change any council decrees, as long as he expressly formulated it and was not bound by such a formality as to spell out which specific regulation he wished to overrule.[26]

In 1407, Paolo was apparently asked to submit a legal opinion by the cardinals of the Roman obedience, that is, of Gregory XII.[27] They wanted to know whether they had to move to Saône (French-Comté) and convene a general council of the Church, even if Pope Gregory had announced that he would not come there himself to resign thereby making way for the election of a new pope. It seems that the Roman *pontifex* had even prohibited his cardinals to go to France,[28] because it was unclear whether the French antipope would also step down from office. Paolo came to the conclusion that indeed the cardinals would have to convene in France, especially because the cardinals acting as a collective entity (*ut collegium*) had promised to do so in an earlier meeting at Marseille. Their promise constituted a vow binding by necessity (*votum necessitatis*), so that not even the pope as a higher authority could release them from their vow or command them to the contrary. The cardinals would also have to travel to Saône to make sure that Pope Gregory would follow his obligations—that is, either step down in person or step down at any other place and make his act public through messengers. If he failed to do so, he would have to be considered (by the College of Cardinals) as a notorious perjurer, whose behavior could not be corrected but would cause scandal for the Church (*esse in notorio periurio et voti fractione et incorrigibilem et ecclesiam ex hoc scandalizari*). Paolo concluded his opinion with a moral appeal to the cardinals that they would even have to go to Saône because of their responsibility towards God and the world; otherwise they would prove to be driven by fear and feebleness, censored for all time.[29]

In this *consilium*, Paolo had to answer precisely the questions posed to him by the Roman cardinals. We cannot know how realistic he thought the chances might be for the Avignonese and the Roman cardinals to act together as one association (*collegium*). Moreover, he did not deal with the intricate questions of conciliarism as to who should represent the Church within the council, and who should be invited to participate in the council. He did clarify though that certain issues could be judged and decided only by the council, not by the association of cardinals. Here he insisted that only the council could judge, whether the excuses Pope Gregory would make for not appearing personally in the assembly at Saône were truthful and convincing or rather dubious. The council had this competency, he argued, because it was a question of fact, not of law.

It seems that Paolo in this opinion conferred upon the associated cardinals more constitutional weight because of the extraordinary crisis of the Great Schism. He was careful, though, not to curb the competencies of the yet-to-be-convoked general council. He refrained from claiming the moral responsibility of every bishop, every prelate, and even every Christian to do everything possible to bring back peace and unity to the *ecclesia christiana*.[30] His tone remained sober in comparison to that of his colleague, the distinguished canonist Antonio da Butrio.

Divine law, both learned laws (the *ius commune*), *ius canonicum, ius civile*—statutory law

Whereas the great political and constitutional issues just described concerned primarily the top ranks of the Church administration, other matters of law, legislative competencies, and their applicability became pivotal for all jurists of the *ius commune* era. These issues touched on questions of formal and substantive qualifications of legislative acts when dealing with the ancient Latin terminology codified in the *Corpus Iuris Civilis*, having to translate these ancient laws into the medieval context (mainly *leges, constitutiones, senatusconsulta*). Many extensive and often-revised statutes enacted by self-confident city republics from the mid-thirteenth century onward had posed intricate questions of legitimacy, applicability, and interpretation. Increasingly in the late Middle Ages, such issues were addressed by jurists in their legal opinions. Quite typical for Paolo is how often he also referred in his lectures, transmitted as commentaries, to these ad hoc opinions.[31]

Divine law stood for Paolo di Castro, as for all medieval jurists, at the top of the hierarchy of legal orders.[32] In a long *consilium* he dealt with the enforceability of a statute establishing that a son born out of wedlock, being a *spurius*, was entitled to inherit something from his (biological) father. Here Paolo drew heavily on sources from the Old and the New Testament to establish a prohibition from divine law, which prevented local statute-makers from introducing such a new, favorable rule. The requisites of divine law found their way into canon law, which Paolo also quoted extensively. Local statutes could be compared to unwritten customs (*consuetudines*) and had to be measured against the standard of rational and time-honored regulations; therefore a *spurius* could never inherit from his natural father, whether the father died testate or intestate, and any statute to the contrary was not binding.[33] The ecclesiastical judge should even intervene when a *spurius* tried to bring his case to the secular court to ask for his share of the paternal goods.

In most cases, the *ius commune* as taught at the universities established general principles that served as reference points for interpreting local statutes. In certain cases, Paolo argued that Roman law (*leges civiles*) should itself be corrected by the standards of canon law. He took this position especially with regard to cases in which obeying the civil law would entail committing a sin. As an example, the question might be whether a possessor had to remain in good faith (the requirement of canon law) during the entire prescription time of thirty years in order to acquire true property, or whether it sufficed if he had been in good faith as to the title of the vendor at the moment when the contract was concluded (the requirement of Roman, civil law). Here Paolo held that the relevant regulations of canon law (X 2.26.20; VI. 5.12.2) should be observed even in the secular court and in the territories of the empire, requiring good faith during the entire period of possession.[34] Since a statute maker would not want to contravene the law, it would have to be interpreted in such a way that the requirements of canon law were fulfilled, asking for good faith for the entire thirty years.

A comparable problem arose over oaths. In a legal opinion, Paolo dealt with the question whether a statute could derogate the medieval imperial constitution *authentica sacramenta puberum* (inserted after C. 2.27(28).1, l. *Si minor annis vigintiquinque, c. Si adversus venditionem*).[35] Emperor Frederick I had ordained that a minor who was older than fourteen years of age and who had sworn an oath to fulfill a contract could not petition the court afterwards for restitution of alienated goods because of the nullity of the contract. The moral-religious obligation of fulfilling a promise bolstered by one's oath was sanctioned by the imperial rescript, setting aside the formal aspect of the case (nullity of the contract because the minor, according to Roman law, should be protected if he had entered a contract without the mandatory consent of this tutor).

The glossators already had disputed this dilemma extensively, asking about the effects of the oath if the contract was void not only because of the minor's age but also for some other reason, or whether as a general principle it might be extended to other types of contracts.[36] In the case in which Paolo was asked for advice, the local statute had changed the *authentica sacramenta puberum* so that persons older than twenty-five who had sworn an oath were bound by their oath.[37] Paolo came to the conclusion that local legislators could indeed limit the effects of the *authentica sacramenta puberum* for their territory so far as civil law was concerned, but that they could not derogate from canon law. Therefore, the oath of a minor, which had been sworn without fear for his or her safety of the soul (*salus animae*), had to be binding. Moreover, judging an oath's validity ought not to belong to secular jurisdiction.[38] As Lange observes, here Paolo upheld the prevalence of canon law over statutory law. Paolo also discussed the issue in his commentaries, rebuking Baldo, who had stressed that a statute could annul an oath, just as a general civil law could do. Paolo underlined again that secular courts were not competent in questions of oaths in general. A law or statute, he continued, could dispose of only such aspects of the oath that the statute or law had conferred in addition to the oath, but not those constituted by divine or canon law, because the inferior law could neither directly nor indirectly abrogate higher law.[39]

Paolo expounded even more profoundly on the entire issue of oaths in his *repetitio* to the *authentic sacramenta puberum*.[40] In this commentary, he dealt with the question from a different angle and more systematically. For example, he asked whether local legislators could legitimately enact a statute eliminating the binding force of an oath. He stated that a statute could not do so, because "in our day" (*hodie*) questions relating to oaths belonged to an ecclesiastical and penitential jurisdiction, not to a secular jurisdiction: *Unde si statutum diceret quod etiam non valeat (sc. contractum, S.L.) si intervenit iuramentum, quantum ad hoc non valet statutum, quod non potest tollere iuramentum, quod est hodie de foro canonico et spirituali, non de foro civili ut in c. fi. de fo. comp. li. vi* (VI 2.2.3). He rebuked Baldo for claiming that the emperor could annul the binding force of an oath in affairs of laypersons in the same way that the pope could annul an oath. Instead, Paolo insisted, with regard to oaths, civil laws were corrected by canon law, and just as the emperor stood beneath the pope, so civil law ought to imitate canon law.[41]

After many other arguments—including an argument about canon lawyers arguing mostly against the teaching of Bartolo—Paolo finally raised the question, whether a minor had to be informed and had to know positively about his right to raise the exception of minor age—which would then allow him to claim restitution had he already fulfilled his own contractual obligation—before he swore the oath to fulfill his obligation in any case. If one were to deny this requirement, swearing the oath meant to renounce to the Roman law exception of minor age without knowing of being protected by such an exception. This question had been controversial among civil lawyers. Paolo himself admitted to having changed his opinion. He first thought the teaching of Dino del Mugello and Cino da Pistoia was convincing—that a *renuntiatio iuris* would be valid only if one had positive knowledge about one's claims and legal status. Arguing against Bartolo da Sassoferrato, Paolo found Bartolo's arguments rather feeble and not convincing. Later, however, Paolo was convinced by canonists such as the archdeacon Guido da Baisio and Giovanni d'Andrea, who agreed with Bartolo. Therefore Paolo—the canonist-informed civilian—argued with the canonists, backing now Bartolo. Paolo held that because of the piety (*religio*) inherent in an oath, it would be a sin not to keep an oath. Anyone had to attribute the fault to himself if he had not informed himself about the exact substance of the oath he was about to swear. Such a person sinned against natural law and would not deserve the protection of the law.[42] Like everyone else, the minor had a moral obligation to inform himself about the possible scope of an oath; otherwise he deservedly cut off his right to legal protection.

In other cases of statutory interpretation, Paolo was willing to presume an intention of local legislators to deliberately regulate certain legal issues contrary to the *ius commune*. In these cases, he said, local statutes should not be interpreted restrictively according to the *ius commune*.[43] The formation of regional states in the fifteenth century—preeminently that of Florence—led Paolo to discuss another layer of normative regulation, namely regional *ius commune* principles. These were not drawn directly from the statutes of Florence itself as the hegemon, but rather were a construct Paolo and other jurists of his generation handled in a refined manner[44] to smooth out normative differences between Florence and some of her newly subordinated, formerly independent cities, such as Arezzo and Pisa.

This last topic refers again to major political and constitutional issues of the early fifteenth century. Paolo, who taught so many years in Florence, took it for granted that Florence did not respect the authority of the emperor—this was one further, keen step in comparison to fourteenth-century ideas about Florence as *civitas sibi princeps* (the city as its own ruler)), when the emperor was absent. The title "emperor of the whole world" (*imperator dominus mundi*) was a title only by law, not political reality. Very prominently, in his commentary on the first law of the *Code*, Paolo astutely mirrors the *de iure/de facto* difference he had observed in the status of Florence:

> The emperor as lord of the world indeed would rule all people . . . but even if he would rule all people according to the law, in practice he did not rule all people. . . . Consequently, imperial laws would not bind Florentines, because they—like several other cities—did not accept the emperor as ruler; yet in practice, they all, including the Florentines, live according to imperial laws.[45]

Test cases of everyday life

The *consilia* of Paolo offer valuable insights into how the abstract problems of conflicting jurisdictions between secular and ecclesiastical courts and between the applicability of civil and canon law mattered in the daily lives and affairs of average Christians in the first part of the fifteenth century.

Usury was a major issue. In the protocapitalist world of the early fifteenth century, with banking houses such as the Florentine Medici bank, Paolo di Castro of course treated the ensuing problems intensely. In his commentaries, he seems not to have made further legal contributions to the established civilian doctrine of the fourteenth century, which obeyed as fundamental the prohibition found in divine and canon law against taking interest on a loan.[46] But several exceptions had been carved out from the general prohibition—for example, between *damnum emergens* (licit) and *lucrum cessans* (normally illicit). These exceptions allowed to take interest in certain circumstances. When it came to daily life and the hard questions of whether a contract or a statute allowing interest-taking in certain cases was valid, Paolo took a surprisingly lenient position. He often supported his view by proposing, for instance, that taking interest might be permissible in order to avoid falling into sin. Such was his argument when discussing the validity of a chapter in the Paduan statutes, allowing interest-taking of one percent when a dowry was not handed over to a husband on the date agreed upon. Paolo upheld the statute, because without the authority to demand their due, men would not marry, thus driving women into prostitution.[47] As far as merchants were concerned, he affirmed that they could demand interest for *lucrum cessans* if they could prove that according to their usual business practices they would have made a certain profit from their capital.[48] In his *consilia*, even when it came to usury that could not be justified in conformity with a title of allowed interest-taking, Paolo demonstrated his pragmatism. For instance, he expressly permitted Jews to exact usurious interest, for local communities were dependent on the credit provided by Jewish pawnbrokers and bankers. By necessity, Christian debtors had to pay the interest they had agreed upon in a written contract and could not seek restitution afterwards.[49]

Apart from the questions of usury, Paolo had several opportunities to deal with legal issues in which Jews were one party. This topic in general deserves further research. In the cases discussed so far, Paolo did not adhere to widespread prejudice against Jews by discriminating against them in his *consilia*. This might be attributed to his commitment to Roman law, which took it as self-evident that Jews were Roman citizens and lived by civil law: *judaei vivunt iure commune Romano*. Mere canonists would have been more likely to justify the many discriminatory regulations against Jews—if they had not participated in drawing up these rules in the first place. For instance, canon law since the Fourth Lateran Council (1215), had established an (in)famous rule requiring Jews to wear distinguishing badges in public.[50]

In a legal opinion which was ignored by tradition, because it did not find its way into the printed editions and was only discovered and edited by del Re,[51] Paolo was asked whether a Jew younger than eighteen who had had sexual intercourse with a Christian prostitute should be punished, and, if so, how severely. Apparently even the death penalty came up in the court proceedings. The legal argument was that the death penalty might be justified if the young man's deed were reckoned as if he had contracted marriage with the woman. Since Jews and Christians were prohibited from marrying one another according to Roman law, he should be treated like an adulterer. Combining thus C. 1.9.6 with C. 9.9.29, the adulterer might even face the death penalty.

To the contrary, Paolo opposed any criminal liability whatsoever for this Jewish adolescent. First, he rejected in stark words the notion that simply having sexual intercourse would constitute an act comparable to marriage or illicit coupling. He called such an argument a stupidity (*fatuitas*)

> evidencing not the least humanity, especially not that kind of humanity all men ought to show towards each according to *ius gentium et naturae*—even more so the humanity that Christians owe towards Jews, because the Church of God tolerated them in order to correct them until they would come to the true cult of God. In the meantime, no cruelty should be committed against them.[52]

Even if such a view of finally converting Jews to Christianity does not align with the modern idea of religious tolerance, it helped him to argue his case that the young man, had he been a Christian, would not have been culpable, because the woman after all was a prostitute. Moreover, the accused had no intent of committing a crime, and thus there was no criminal liability. And finally, even if the court should find the adolescent guilty, he ought to be spared capital punishment because of his young age.

It should be underscored that Paolo did not at least question the prohibition of marriage between Jews and Christians according to canon law. Nevertheless, he upheld the prohibition with arguments from canon law—the only one he referenced in this *consilium* (X 4.19.2 & 7, X 3.32.1)—especially because of the likelihood that in religiously mixed marriages the non-Christian partner (*infidelis*) might convert the other. Even divorce in such cases was possible, as he stressed.[53]

Conclusion

Paolo di Castro was a jurist who reflected profoundly on the challenges the Latin Church and Christian faith had to face in the fifteenth century. Many lines of argument he dealt with in his legal opinions can be found also in his commentaries. On the important political and constitutional issues of the Middle Ages, such as the relationship between pope and emperor, or the authority of the pope within the Church, he entertained a decidedly pro-papal, hierocratic position. Taking into account that he worked in Avignon in the service of the papal court during the most formative period of his life, his pro-papal view is not surprising. More surprising is the frequency with which he touched on questions of canon law and ecclesiastical jurisdiction when commenting on the Roman law in his university lectures. There he stressed that secular (civil) law, especially city statutes, would have to be subordinated to the precepts of canon and divine law. When it came to the questions of daily life and legal problems, he characteristically employed arguments inspired by the terminology of moral theology and the penitential forum. He often referred to considerations such as that "falling into sin has to be avoided," or that something should be permitted in order to avoid greater evil or sin. Interestingly, when discussing the definition of a *permissio*, he put forward three possible definitions, the third of which was that a permission could mean that some lesser evil is permitted to prevent a greater evil. But this, Paolo said, should rather be called a "tolerance, by which the respective act would be neither consented to nor rejected, just as concubinage is permitted by civil law to prevent adultery." Here Paolo quoted exclusively Roman law (D. 25.7.3).[54] He did not refer to the sacramental interpretation of marriage in this context.

In some hard test cases, he also argued in favor of a more lenient, permissive treatment of the parties or a culprit. Apparently, he was willing to attribute much weight to the conscientious decisions of lawyers and judges in individual cases. For instance, he urged judges to use their own mind and judgment and, if necessary, to limit the meaning of a statute and not blindly follow its wording when it came to punishing a culprit, without distinguishing, for example, whether one had acted in bad faith in not paying his fine.[55] Paolo di Castro himself lived up to high ethical standards when arguing thoughtfully and objectively in his legal opinions and thus earned great respect among his contemporaries.

Notes

1 Pieri, 15–17.
2 For Paolo's biography, see Cortese, "Paolo di (da) Castro," 1505–6; Lange and Kriechbaum, 814–18; and d'Amelio, 227–230. Paolo's characteristic handwriting was identified by Tanzini, 284f., and evaluated by Murano, 129–35, in comparison to the handwriting of other jurists of his generation as "almost the hand of a professional scribe," 129.
3 That Paolo received a doctorate in both learned laws (*doctor utriusque iuris*) is taken for granted by most of the historiography; cf. Lange and Kriechbaum, 814. More reticent about Paolo's doctorate in canon law is Cortese, 1505a.
4 Cortese, "Paolo di (da) Castro," 1505b; d'Amelio, 228b. Paolo di Castro in his commentary to authentica post Cod. 3.1.5, *aut. Ad haec, c. de iudiciis*, fol. 113vb n. 2 *in fi.* There Paolo even expressed some qualms about this practice of the Roman *curia*. The commentaries of Paolo are cited in this article from the edition: Venice: apud Iuntas 1582.
5 A survey of which university he lectured at, on which part of the Roman *Corpus Iuris Civilis*, including a list of surviving manuscripts, is to be found in Murano, 130–2. We know more about his lectures in Padua than in Florence or in Bologna, thanks to the research by Belloni, 283–6.
6 The salaries he was paid as a professor reached from 100 to 330 *fiorini* a year; cf. d'Amelio, 229f.; perhaps as much as 800 *ducati* were paid in Padua for one year: Lange and Kriechbaum, 817.
7 Tanzini, 283.
8 Especially on the question of who should inherit the dowry of a predeceased wife, the statutory lawmakers opted for a different solution than Paolo had suggested; cf. Lepsius, "Paolo di Castro as Consultant," 77–105, 82–7.
9 Del Re, "Paolo di Castro, dottore della verità," n. 56.
10 Murano, 131, where she lists also extant manuscripts of his commentaries. See also d'Amelio, 230s.
11 Osler, vol. 2, no. 3897. In the sixteenth century, full sets of Paolo's commentaries were printed twenty-one times in Lyon, another eleven editions in Venice, three more in Milano, and one in Torino. My profound thanks go to Douglas Osler for providing me with this information from his yet-to-be-published survey of sixteenth-century European legal imprints.
12 Belloni, 291. Editions are Torino: apud heredes Nicolai Bevilaqua 1580 and Frankfurt a.M.: apud Sigismundum Feyerabendt 1582. The Frankfurt edition is quoted in this article. In the sixteenth century, Paolo's *consilia* were published six times in Venice; four more editions in Lyon are known, and two early rare editions were printed in Pavia. The first set of *consilia* in three parts was the Venice edition: apud Gasparum Bindonum 1571. Again, I am very grateful to Douglas Osler for this provisional insight into his database and work in progress on early modern European legal imprints.
13 Editions of yet-unpublished original *consilia* by Paolo (mostly on questions of private law) by del Re, *Sei consigli inediti di Paolo di Castro*, 31–53; del Re, "Paolo di Castro," 231–6; and Romano, 605–34, 629–32. Another source for hitherto unpublished *consilia*—but not, of course, autographs—by Paolo is the manuscript tradition of commentaries to the Florentine statutes of 1415, where later jurists such as Tommaso Salvemini or Alessandro Bencivenne referenced original *consilia* of Paolo on the applicability of the Florentine

statutes; cf. Lepsius, "Paulus de Castro als Konsiliator," 61–122, nn. 43, 70f., 86, 90.

14 Pieri, 33.

15 Romano, 620f.

16 Lange and Kriechbaum, 818f. In his commentaries, Paolo did not hesitate to criticize his great predecessors, e.g., in his *repetitio* on the medieval *authentica Sacramenta puborum*; see below n. 41.

17 Lange and Kriechbaum, 820.

18 See Quaglioni, 47–65.

19 Such was the critique of Cortese, "Il tramonto del mito dell'Impero universale," and Gouron.

20 Similar arguments had been raised in 1298 by a *doctor utriusque iuris*, perhaps Johannes de Angusellis, in a *quaestio*, where he referred abundantly to canon law to foster his line of argument. Both texts are edited and interpreted within the context of medieval political doctrine by Lepsius, "Die Legitimierung nichtehelicher Kinder."

21 The allegory of the two swords held either independently from or on behalf of (*de nutu*) the pope was based on Luke 22:38. For a pro-papal interpretation in a famous case, see Pennington, 177, and Walther.

22 Paulus de Castro, *Commentaria in secunda parte Digesti veteris*, in D. 14.2.9, *l. Deprecatio, ff. ad legem Rhodiam de iactu*, fol. 90vb n. 6. See also Maffei, 289, on the context and a comparable *consilium* by Paolo.

23 On the *lex Regia* according to the doctrines of twelfth- and thirteenth-century civilians, see Cortese, *La norma giuridica*, 183–92.

24 *Secundo potest intelligi post adventum Christi et tunc dico, quod Imperium Romanum fuit a populo Romano translatum in ecclesiam et non remansit nisi nomen et dicitur Imperium Christi vel ecclesiae et solus Papa potest ipsum privare, sicut et confirmare et coronare, ut in c. ad apostolice, de re iud., li. 6* [VI. 2.14.2] *et iurat sibi fidelitatem. Nam apud ecclesiam est uterque gladius temporalis et spiritualis et est quintum Imperium de quo prophetavit Daniel, qui vidit lapidem sine manibus scissum cadere ad pedes, qui significabat Romanum Imperium et statuam illa contrivit et destruxit, ut hic notatur per Bartolum in extravagant. ad reprimendum in principio super verbo "totius orbis," nihil concludere potest hodie populus Romanus in Imperio.* [The second can be understood after the advent of Christ. Then, I say, the Roman Empire was transferred from the Roman people unto the church and nothing remained with the people, this was called 'Empire of Christ' or 'of the church' and the pope alone can deprive him (sc. the emperor, S.L.) of his office, just as it is up to him to confirm and to incoronate him, VI. 2.14.2 and he (the emperor, S.L.) swears him an oath of loyalty. Thus, both swords reside with the church, the spiritual and the temporal sword; this is the fifth empire, about which Daniel prophesied of seeing a stone thrown not by any hand, falling to the feet of a statue signifying the Roman Empire. And that statue was thrown over and destroyed, just as Bartolus de Sassoferrato noted in his comment on 'totius orbis' of his tract on Ad reprimendum, that today the Roman people had no competency within the Empire.]

Paulus de Castro, Commentaria in prima parte Digesti Veteris, ad D. 1.3.9, *l. Non ambigitur, ff. de leg. et senatuscons.*, fol. 10rb—va n. 6.

25 Paulus de Castro, *Commentaria in prima parte Digesti veteris*, in D. 1.3.1 no. 5, fol. 9va.

26 *si non haberet clausulam derogatoriam, etiam si nullam faceret mentionem, tolleretur per ultimam, ut in d. c. i de const., lib. vi* [VI. 1.2.1]. *Potest ergo Papa tollere constitutiones factas in concilio, dummodo hoc dicat expresse, quia maior est eius*

authoritas, ut no. in c. significavit, de elect. [X 1.6.4]. Paulus de Castro, *Commentaria in prima parte Codicis*, in C. 1.14.8, fol. 27rb no. 2.

27 This often-quoted *consilium* can be found among others in Paulus de Castro, *Consilia*, Turin 1580, as cons. I.418, fol. 213ra—214ra (also as cons. I.419, in: Id., *Consilia*, Frankfurt 1582, fol. 216ra—217ra]. Paolo's *consilia* were printed even earlier than those of his commentaries, for the first time in an incunabula edition—Rome: Wendelinus de Wyla, Teobaldus Schencbecher, Johannes Reinhard, 1473.

28 Padovani, 433f.

29 Paulus de Castro, *Consilia*, cons. I.418, fol. 213vb n. 3s: *si eos paratos facere quod eis incumbit et sic erunt iustificati apud Deum et mundum. Si vero timore sive pusillanimitate aut aliqua humana gratia torpescant et resiliant, perpetua nota maculabuntur.* On the manuscript tradition of his legal opinion, but only very briefly on its content, see Padovani, 443, n. 47, and Condorelli, 59–157, 93–5.

30 As did Antonio da Budrio, cf. the *consilium* of Antonius de Butrio, which is also printed in Paulus de Castro, *Consilia*, cons. I.419, fol. 214va—215r (cons. I.420, fol. 217ra—218ra]. See also Padovani, 443; Condorelli, 95–97f.

31 Specifically analyzing later passages in his commentaries where he referred to his practical experience as statute maker and consiliator, is Lepsius, "Paulus de Castro als Konsiliator," 78f, 95 n. 78, 98 n. 83. Another important issue in the context of the validity of communal statutes was, of course, the question, whether naturalized citizens would enjoy all the same rights and prerogatives as native-born citizens; cf. Kirshner, "Paolo di Castro on *Cives ex privilegio.*"

32 Important insights into the strata of legal orders were established by Lange, "Rechtsquellenlehre." His observations would need further clarification because Lange worked exclusively with the *consilia* of Paolo without correlating them to his teachings in the commentaries; see, e.g., his n. 23, where he refers to D. 1.3.32, but does not treat Paolo's succinct commentary on the passage. Lange's interpretation of his choice of *consilia* of Paolo is somewhat limited, (1) because he does not make any attempt to contextualize Paolo's interpretation within the specific statutory regulations of the different cities, (2) because he regards exclusively private law cases, and (3) because he does not try to establish the concrete leading case question, which was submitted to Paolo.

33 Lange, "Rechtsquellenlehre," 422–4, interpreting Paulus de Castro, *Consilia,* cons. II.467, fol. 225va—230rb.

34 Lange, 429, referring to Paulus de Castro, *Consilia,* cons. II.258, fol. 127vb—128rb.

35 Paolo even had held a *quaestio disputata* on this topic in Florenz, on March 5, 1422, which is transmitted in a Lucchese manuscript, cf. Belloni, 292.

36 Cortese, *Le grandi linee della storia giuridica medievale*, 264f.; Hallebeek, 73–81.

37 Lange, 430f. At age twenty-five though, the person no longer was a minor, but had full legal capacity. At twenty-five years he had to fulfill all contractual obligations, no matter whether they were supported in addition by an oath to fulfill the promise.

38 Paulus de Castro, *Consilia*, cons. II.53, fol. 27va—28ra.

39 Paulus de Castro, *Commentaria* in C. 1.14.5, *l. Non dubium, c. de legibus et constitutionibus principis*, fol. 27ra n. 11:

> *Ultimo nota in fine quod lex civilis potest annullare iuramentum et eodem modo statutum poterit secundum Baldum, quod non placet hodie, cum non sit de foro laicorum, ut dixi in aut. sacramenta puberum. . . . Licet enim lex civilis vel statutum possint auferre iuramento vires quas ipsa lex, vel statutum ei tribuisset, ut in auth. decernimus, infra de arbit. [?], non tamen potest auferre vires, quas habet de iure divino et canonico, cum inferior legem superioris tollere*

non possit directo vel per indirectum. Has autem vires non posuerunt, nec considerarunt iura civilia, ideo iuramento annullabant.

40 Paulus de Castro, *Commentaria* in *authentica post* C. 2.28.1, *auth. sacramenta, c. si adversus venditione*, fol. 88va—89ra. Probably this long passage resembling more a *repetitio* than a comment is identical with the so-called *quaestio disputata*; see above n. 35.

41 Paulus de Castro, *Commentaria*, in *aut. post* C. 2.28.1, no. d <recte: 11>, fol. 89rb: *Baldus allegat . . . quod ius civile etiam annullare poterat iuramentum et annullabat, sicut hodie potest Papa. Sed hodie non potest annullare, quia in hoc Imperator subest Papa et leges imitantur canones.*

42 Paulus de Castro, Commentaria, in *aut. post* C. 2.28.1, no. 12, fol. 89va n. 12: *debebat enim scire vires iuramenti et nesciendo peccat contra ius naturale et sic sibi non subvenitur.* It is quite interesting that Paolo here speaks of sinning against natural law, not against divine law, if an oath was taken rashly. Perhaps he considered the binding force of oaths overarching even persons of different religious faiths—for example, being binding between Christians and Jews. For a case in which Paolo discussed a promissory oath, confirming a contractual obligation with Jews on both sides, see Quaglioni, "Gli ebrei e il giuramento nell'età del diritto comune," 125–7. Paolo held that if a Christian judge would have to decide an oath between two Jews, only Roman law was applicable, neither canon law nor *ius commune*. Since public necessity (*utilitas publica*) was a concept inherent in Roman law, the judge would then also have to take into account that any stipulation confirmed by an oath could not validate necessary formal requirements which had been neglected in the contract.

43 Lepsius, "Paulus de Castro als Konsiliator," 82–93, for cases in which inheritance rights of children and the husband after the death of their mother or wife were concerned, and in particular when questions of dowry were involved.

44 For this problem, see Lepsius, "Paulus de Castro als Konsiliator," 103–11. Briefly treated also by Lange, 425–7, who considers neither the political aspect of the expanding Florentine regional state nor the substantive law in the different statutes themselves.

45 Paulus de Castro, *Commentaria* in C. 1.1.1, *l. Cunctos populos, c. de summa trinitate*, fol. 3va n. 2: *nam cunctos populos regit Imperator, cum sit mundi dominus . . . quod licet de iure omnes regat, de facto tamen non omnes. . . . Item sequeretur quod leges imperiales non ligarent Florentinos et alios, qui Imperatorem non recognoscunt, sed tamen contrarium servari videmus, quia vivunt legibus imperialibus.*

46 Pieri, 94–6, 102–3, mainly focusing on the question of the aspects of Jews taking interest and the civilian doctrine. Pieri does assess Paolo's position on the issue of usury in his commentaries as more interesting because of what he did *not* expressly treat or repeat from earlier doctrine; Pieri, 126s.

47 Pieri, 129f., referring to Paolo di Castro, *Commentaria* in C. 1.1.1, *l. Cunctos populos.* See on the topic in general Kirshner, *Pursuing Honor while Avoiding Sin*, 9–13.

48 Pieri, 131, referring to cons. II.396 (415] of Paolo.

49 Pieri, 144–51, interpreting specifically cons. II.296s (311s], but also referring to other cases

50 Kisch, 205–7 (illicit sexual intercourse between a Jew and a Christian according to German medieval law books), 275–87, 349–55. Todeschini, 67–107 (not quoting any jurists, however).

51 Del Re, "Paolo di Castro," 233–6.

52 Ibid., 234, l. 25–37:

fatuitas . . . et modicam habet in se humanitatem qui hoc attentaret quam humanitatem communiter omnes homines habere debent de iure gentium seu naturae, D. 1.1.2, maxime christiani etiam contra iudeos quos Ecclesia Dei tollerat ut corrigantur cum ab eorum gente fides et regeneratio emanaverit et verus Dei cultus unde contra eos non delinquentes nihil inhumaniter est exercendum.

53 Del Re, "Paolo di Castro," 235, l. 46–55.
54 Paulus de Castro, *Commentaria* in D. 1.3.7, *l. Legis virtus, ff. de legibus et senatuscons.*, fol. 10ra n. 3.
55 Paulus de Castro, *Commentaria* in D. 1.3.1, *l. Lex est commune, ff. de legibus et senatuscons.*, fol. 10ra n. 10.

Bibliography

Belloni, Annalisa. *Professori Giuristi a Padova nel Secolo XV. Profili bio-bibliografici e Cattedre.* Ius Commune Sonderhefte, Studien zur europäischen Rechtsgeschichte, 28. Frankfurt am Main: Klostermann, 1986.

Condorelli, Orazio. "Antonio da Budrio e le dottrine conciliari al tempo del concilio di Pisa." *Rivista internazionale di diritto comune* 27 (2016): 59–127.

Cortese, Ennio. "Il tramonto del mito dell'Impero universale. Un parere di Oldrado e la sua fortuna in Spagna tra Tre e Quattrocento (da Iacobus Cionis a Petrus Belluga e Rodericus Sancius de Arévalo)." In *"Panta rei". Studi dedicati a Manlio Bellomo*, edited by Orazio Condorelli. Vol. 2, 23–67. Rome: il Cigno Edizioni, 2004.

Cortese, Ennio. *La norma giuridica. Spunti teorici nel diritto comune classico.* Mailand: Giuffrè, 1962.

Cortese, Ennio. *Le grandi linee della storia giuridica medievale.* Rome: il Cigno, 2000.

Cortese, Ennio. "Paolo di (da) Castro (Castro, 1360/62—Padova, 20 Luglio 1441)." In *Dizionario biografico dei giuristi italiani*, edited by Italo Birocchi, Ennio Cortese, Antonello Mattone, and Marco Nicola Miletti. Vol. 2, 1505–7. Bologna: il Mulino, 2013.

D'Amelio, Giuliana. "Castro, Paolo Di." In *Dizionario biografico degli Italiani*, edited by Istituto della Enciclopedia Italiana. Vol. 22, 227–33. Rome: Istituo della enciclopedia italiana, 1979.

Del Re, Niccolò. "Paolo di Castro, dottore della verità." *Studi senesi* 82 (1970): 193–236.

Del Re, Niccolò. *Sei consigli inediti di Paolo di Castro nei codici vaticani latini 8068, 8069, 11605 e Urbinate latino 1132.* Rome: Tip. regionale, 1945.

Gouron, André. "Glossateurs et théories politiques." In *Science politique et droit public dans les facultés de droit européennes (XIIIe–XVIIIe siècle)*, edited by Jacques Krynen and Michael Stolleis, 7–22. Studien zur europäischen Rechtsgeschichte, 229. Frankfurt am Main: Klostermann, 2008.

Hallebeek, Jan. "Actio ex iuramento: The Legal Enforcement of Oaths." *Jus commune* 17 (1990): 69–88.

Kirshner, Julius. "Paolo di Castro on *cives ex privilegio*: A Controversy over the Legal Qualification for Public Office in Early Fifteenth-Century Florence." In *Renaissance Studies in Honor of Hans Baron*, edited by Anthony Molho and John A. Tedeschi, 227–64. Dekalb: Northern Illinois University, 1971.

Kirshner, Julius. *Pursuing Honor While Avoiding Sin: The Monte Delle Doti of Florence.* Studi Senesi. Quaderni, 41. Milan: Giuffrè, 1978.

Kisch, Guido. *The Jews in Medieval Germany: A Study of Their Legal and Social Status.* Chicago: University Press, 1949.

Lange, Hermann. "Die Rechtsquellenlehre in den Consilien Paul de Castros." In *Aktuelle Fragen aus modernem Recht und Rechtsgeschichte. Gedächtnisschrift für Rudolf Schmidt*, edited by Erwin Seidl, 421–40. Berlin: Duncker & Humblot, 1966.

Lange, Hermann, and Maximiliane Kriechbaum. *Römisches Recht im Mittelalter. Bd. 2: Die Kommentatoren*. Munich: C.H. Beck Verlag, 2007.

Lepsius, Susanne. "Die Legitimierung nichtehelicher Kinder als Testfall für die Kompetenzen des römisch-deutschen Königs im späten 13. Jahrhundert." *Zeitschrift der Savigny Stiftung für Rechtsgeschichte* vol. 135—*Kanonistische Abteilung* 104 (2018): 72–150.

Lepsius, Susanne. "Paolo di Castro as consultant: Applying and Interpreting Florence's Statutes." In *The Politics of the Law in Late Medieval and Renaissance Italy*, edited by Lawrin Armstrong and Julius Kirshner. Toronto Studies in Medieval Law. Vol. 1, 77–105. Toronto: University Press, 2011.

Lepsius, Susanne. "Paulus de Castro als Konsiliator: Anwendung, Interpretation und Fortbildung der Florentiner Statuten." *Rivista internazionale di diritto comune* 25 (2014 [2015]): 61–122.

Maffei, Domenico. *La donazione di Costantino nei giuristi medievali*. Mailand: Giuffrè, 1964.

Murano, Giovanna. "Paolo da Castro." In *Autographa I.1: Giuristi, giudici e notai (sec. XII–XV)*, edited by Giovanna Murano, 129–35. Imola: La Mandragora, 2012.

Osler, Douglas. *Jurisprudence of the Baroque: A Census of Seventeenth Century Italian Legal Imprints*. 3 vols. Bibliographica Iuridica, 5; Studien zur europäischen Rechtsgeschichte, 236. Frankfurt am Main: Klostermann, 2009.

Padovani, Andrea. "*Consilia* e *tractatus* dei giuristi italiani negli anni del grande schisma (1405–1409)." *Glossae. Revista de historia del derecho europeo* 10 (2013): 430–56.

Pennington, Kenneth. *The Prince and the Law, 1200–1600: Sovereignty and Rights in the Western Legal Tradition*. Berkeley: University of California Press, 1993.

Pieri, Bernardo. *Usurai, ebrei e poteri della Chiesa nei consilia di Paolo da Castro. Le competenze canonistiche di un civilista*. Monografie, 282. Bologna: Bononia University Press, 2016.

Quaglioni, Diego. "Il diritto comune pubblico e le leggi di Roncaglia. Nuove testimonianze sulla l. 'Omnis iurisdictio'." In *Gli inizi del diritto pubblico. L'età di Federico Barbarossa: legislazione e scienza del diritto/Die Anfänge des öffentlichen Rechts. Gesetzgebung im Zeitalter Friedrich Barbarossas und das Gelehrte Recht*, edited by Gerhard Dilcher and Diego Quaglioni. Annali dell'Istituto storico italo-germanico in Trento/Jahrbuch des italienisch-deutschen historischen Instituts in Trient, Contributi/Beiträge. Vol. 19, 47–65. Bologna/Berlin: il Mulino; Duncker & Humblot, 2007.

Quaglioni, Diego. "Gli ebrei e il giuramento nell'età del diritto comune." *Rivista di Storia e Letteratura Religiosa* 39 (2004): 113–28.

Romano, Andrea. "La giurisprudenza consulente e Paolo di Castro. Alcuni consilia inediti del ms. Venezia, Bibl. Marciana, lat. 2324." In *Studi in memoria di Mario E. Viora*. Biblioteca della Rivista di storia del diritto italiano. Vol. 30, 605–34. Rome: Fondazione Sergio Mochi Onory per la storia del diritto italiano, 1990.

Tanzini, Lorenzo. *Statuti e legislazione a Firenze dal 1355 al 1415. Lo statuto cittadino del 1409.* Biblioteca storica Toscana, 45. Florence: Leo S. Olschki editore, 2004.

Todeschini, Giacomo. *Gli ebrei nell'Italia medievale.* Rome: Carocci, 2018.

Walther, Helmut G. "Das Reich in der politischen Theorie der Legistik und im Umkreis der päpstlichen Kurie." In *Heinrich Raspe, Landgraf von Thüringen und römischer König (1227–1247): Fürsten, König und Reich in spätstaufischer Zeit*, edited by Matthias Werner, 29–52. Frankfurt am Main: Peter Lang, 2003.

12 Niccolò dei Tedeschi (Panormitanus) (1386–1445)

R. H. Helmholz

Introduction

The Christian jurist who is the subject of this chapter was a native of Sicily, and his place of birth meant something to him. His professional career would take him far from home and bring him into contact with the greatest political and ecclesiastical issues of his day. But when he died in 1445, he was back in Sicily, where he was in office as archbishop of Palermo.[1] He is remembered today for his participation in those difficult issues, but among lawyers of earlier centuries he has long been celebrated as one of the greatest of the medieval canonists. Of him, Henry Swinburne (d. 1624), an English ecclesiastical lawyer and author of a book on the law of marriage, once wrote admiringly that he was "the captain of the canonists."[2] High praise! There were many canonists, and Swinburne could not have had a self-interested motive for putting this Italian jurist at the top of his list. Swinburne himself was a Protestant, a lawyer active in the ecclesiastical courts of England. He also wrote almost two centuries after the death of the man he praised so highly. One special circumstance might account for his use of *Commentaria* written by the Italian jurist. In England the medieval canon law of marriage had been retained in the face of the Tridentine decree *Tametsi*, which had reformed the law of the Catholic Church on the subject. The treatment of medieval marriage law found in the *Commentaria* that Panormitanus had written therefore remained immediately relevant to Swinburne's subject.

Even so, Swinburne had a wide choice of medieval canonists to extol. His accolade can be explained only by his special admiration for what he found in the works of this particular jurist—one lawyer admiring and praising the exceptional expertise of another. Today, the comment also raises a legitimate question. Despite Swinburne's considered opinion, the jurist who was its object is not accorded similar recognition in most recent historical accounts of the development of medieval canon law. One modern and useful handbook on the subject, for example, lists and describes the work of many medieval jurists,[3] but Panormitanus is not among them. Although his name and his works do appear in every encyclopedic list of authors of the literature of the *ius commune*,[4] more often than not he is given no special recognition among them.[5] With a few honorable exceptions, nothing like the praise that Swinburne once accorded him appears in the recent literature on the history of European jurists. Nor does such acclaim often appear in general historical works written about the period. This apparent difference of opinion between then and now therefore calls for a closer look. What grounds did Swinburne have for a comment that placed Panormitanus at the very top of his list of jurists? And what has caused the apparent decline in the reputation of the Sicilian jurist? Those questions are among the subjects raised by this chapter. They provide a window through which modern readers can perceive something of the character of the man and the quality of his achievements as a Christian jurist. Both require beginning with a brief biographical account.

Life and career

The future canonist Niccolò dei Tedeschi was born in Catania in 1386.[6] We have no certain knowledge about his family's background, which at best can be described only by conjecture.[7] Indeed, what knowledge we have about any of his activities while a youth is quite small. We do know, for example, that at a young age he assumed the habit of a Benedictine monk in the cathedral church in Catania, but this is because he himself later left a record of the event in his *Commentaria* on the Gregorian Decretals in the course of commenting on a quite different legal issue.[8] He must have shown extraordinary promise as a boy, however, for he was early sent with a bursary to pursue legal studies at Bologna—and again, we know this because he himself remarked upon it incidentally in the *Commentaria* while dealing with a question of the privileges held by universities under canon law.[9] He began a teaching career in Bologna around 1411, subsequently moving to similar positions in Parma, Siena, and Florence. What we have as evidence leaves the exact circumstances of these moves unexplained. Surviving university records are also silent on the moves, but it is safe to assume that he excelled as a teacher. His early reputation so indicates. He attracted students, and he would not have moved to other universities without having been called there. Apparently he was also not immune to the attractions of emoluments that went with moving from one ecclesiastical dignity to another, and also from accumulating more than one position within the Church. In 1421, he was named an auditor of the *Camera apostolica*, and in 1425 he was chosen as abbot of a monastic house in the diocese of Messina. Such accumulation of offices was characteristic of the times.[10] More importantly for us, however, the years he spent as a university lecturer allowed him to write the commentaries and other juristic works upon which his later reputation rests. He himself moved on, but he was at the university in Bologna in 1431 or 1432, when his academic career was interrupted by a quite different sort of call.

That call plunged him into the midst of the great controversy of the day, the struggle over what we now call conciliarism. The issue took him first to the Council of Basel, initially as one of the representatives of Pope Eugene IV and later as a spokesman for King Alfonso V of Aragon and Sicily. His actions at Basel have long been matters of controversy. The council had been assembled to follow through on the actions begun at the earlier Council of Constance; at issue were both the meaning and the implementation of the conciliar decrees which had been accepted there. Panormitanus took a leading role in the Basel proceedings, one vividly described in the account of the council written by Aeneas Sylvius Piccolomini, later Pope Pius II.[11] These events also led to the selection of Panormitanus as archbishop of Palermo by King Alfonso V, a choice confirmed by Pope Eugene IV in 1435. Five years later, Panormitanus was named a cardinal at the behest of the antipope Felix V, a grant that was not confirmed during the lifetime of Panormitanus by any of the other claimants to the apostolic see.[12] However, in 1443, after an appearance as envoy of the Council of Basel at an imperial diet convoked in Frankfurt, one which also confronted the questions of the authority within the Church, Panormitanus returned to his see in Palermo, where he died, probably a victim of the plague.

Panormitanus at the Council of Basel

The role of Panormitanus at the Council of Basel has been the subject of several monographs and scholarly works, most notably a book written by Knut Wolfgang Nörr and published in 1964.[13] Much of the modern commentary, however, is quite disparaging of what appears to critics to have been the willingness of Panormitanus to speak in favor of positions in which he did not believe. He did so, it seems, at the behest of a prince who had sent him, who paid him, and who determined the positions he should take—that is, Alfonso V. Panormitanus might therefore be described—as he has been—as a man who sacrificed principle to self-interest.[14]

At the same time, one should recognize that the subject of his interventions was often complex, not easily reducible to the simple "pope vs. council" dichotomy that so often prevails in modern accounts.[15] For example, the question of who had the right to take part or to be represented in a general council of the Church had not been solved at Constance, and Panormitanus spoke at length to urge a delay so that princes (including his principal, Alfonso V) might be counted among the participants and adequately represented. Moreover, there was then quite respectable canonical authority on the side of the Conciliarists. Its ultimate failure was not a *fait accompli* at the time that Panormitanus spoke. The proconciliar views and the wide net of representation in favor of which he spoke were defensible positions, taking support from established canonical principles, as even hostile critics sometimes granted.[16]

More than that, however, Panormitanus was a lawyer. In their professional lives, lawyers serve clients, not political ideologies. There are limits to how far they may go in defense of those clients. That much is certain. Lawyers must not perjure themselves or advance arguments they know are contrary to firmly established legal principles of justice. But in most legal controversies there is room for reasonable argument on both sides. That was certainly true of the issues raised at Basel.[17] Professor Nörr reminded his readers of the complexity of the issues raised there, adding that some of the speeches that Panormitanus made should "be used with caution as a source for his views on ecclesiastical constitutional law."[18] What this jurist said there was not unlawful or mendacious. In Nörr's considered view, Panormitanus also stood out from many of the partisans on one side or the other of the controversies surrounding conciliarism in that he was "a pure lawyer."[19] This matters. Panormitanus was not a politician with an ideological program to promote. He was not a religious reformer. He was not a political theorist. He was a lawyer. In a less-than-enthusiastic review of Nörr's book on the subject, Walter Ullmann expressed something like an equivalent view of the Italian jurist. But there was an important difference. Ullman used a similar but negative term in describing his subject's character. For him, Panormitanus was "a mere lawyer." His actions at Basel proved this.[20] And he was not to be admired for it. Between these two ways of expressing what amounts at bottom to the same characteristic, there is a real divide, one that has worked its way into the modern scholarship on the subject.

Commentaries on canon law

The great work of Panormitanus was the compilation of his commentaries on the texts in the Decretals. It quickly became a standard point of reference for lawyers throughout Europe, and it retained that elevated status for many years after his death. A standard bibliography lists ten editions of the work printed between 1485 and 1617, the last being the edition used in writing this chapter.[21] The work's influence is made particularly apparent by its popularity far from home, even in England. Ernest Jacob, for example, found sixty-six volumes of this work in the college libraries (including the Bodleian) in Oxford.[22] Another scholar found that "wherever canon law treatises are mentioned in wills of London judges and advocates," the commentaries of Panormitanus "invariably are specified."[23] They were even sometimes cited as authoritative in cases involving ecclesiastical law that were heard in the royal courts in England.[24]

Panormitanus also produced two volumes of *Consilia* and several shorter, occasional works—the *Repetitiones* and *Quaestiones* and the like that were the normal products of academic jurists of the time.[25] So great a reputation did he obtain among contemporaries that works written by other men were attributed to him, seemingly in order to enhance their authority and (probably) also their sales.[26] There are still many things about the composition of these works we do not know. Panormitanus added to his commentaries on the law from time to time, perhaps occasionally even altering his arguments. The history of the transition of his works from manuscript to print is also full of traps and puzzles. Kenneth Pennington has made a brave and promising start at sorting out what can be honestly concluded about these complications.[27]

In the end, however, his reputation among lawyers of his own day and of later times and other places must be focused upon what is found in the printed pages of his great work on the Decretals and similar comments on the medieval Church's laws. His commentaries are marked throughout by a clarity in treatment, a command of the relevant sources, a willingness to entertain views other than his own, and a masterful ability in interpreting the texts of the Roman and canon laws.[28] I know of none better. Examples will illustrate these qualities better than the multiplication of laudatory adjectives, and I have taken three of them, two from the *Commentaria* on the Decretals and one from his collected *Consilia*, in order to illustrate the approach Panormitanus took to legal questions.

Statutory interpretation

The first example comes from the seventh chapter of the title *De constitutionibus* in the first book of the *Commentaria* (X 1.2.7). A northern Italian city had enacted a statute allowing any person facing the likelihood of indigence a legal right to alienate a fief he held, even without the consent of the lord from whom he held it. Presumably this statute was meant to offer a way of helping an impecunious tenant facing financial ruin. The statute "came to the notice" of Pope Innocent III. He wrote to the bishop with jurisdiction over the city and directed him to secure the rights of the Church if they were undermined by the statute. Unless the consent of the proper ecclesiastical official had first been secured, the pope ordered, such alienations were to be treated as null and void.

We should expect that such a statute would raise the issue of conflicts between *regnum* and *sacerdotium*, ancestors of today's clashes between state and Church. The question would also be complicated by the canon law's oft-repeated holding that the Church claimed no jurisdiction over questions of feudal law and by the requirement under feudal law that the consent of the lord was necessary for alienations of land held of him. The question of jurisdiction, however, is not the main tack Panormitanus took in commenting on this decretal. He did record the decretal's holding, raising the incidental but important question of whether it applied to alienation that had already taken place.[29] However, the greater part of his discussion went in a different direction—one that was raised indirectly by this decretal but was more general—the question of how statutes were to be interpreted. It is a lawyer's question. It is one that still plagues lawyers today.

The first legal requisite—then as now—is that the body issuing the statute have authority to do so, a problem Panormitanus illustrated by discussing the parallel powers of universities. They do normally have some power to enact rules; they must, if they are to carry out their proper functions. But did this power extend to grave consequences, as in the imposition of serious penalties? If it did, did it also extend to all students? Some of them would have been in holy orders. The commentary marshaled reasons pro and con, backed by references to treatments of the subject found in works of Baldus, Bartolus, Cino da Pistoia, Hostiensis, Innocent IV, and several lesser lights among the jurists. It then turned to the more general question of the relationship of statutes and the *ius divinum*, the *ius naturale*, and the *ius gentium*. This question was raised by the case because the commune's statute was subject to these laws. In fact, the city had enacted a rule which might, or might not, stand in violation of the Church's interests and perhaps also its law. This was a not uncommon situation. Think, for instance, of the many secular laws allowing a specific amount of interest on a loan; these laws seemingly opposed the prohibition of usury found in canon and divine law. If so, were they enforceable in practice nonetheless?

What Panormitanus offered in his commentaries on this decretal was a way to analyze the problem. For each form of accepted law he offered an example, one his students might have carried away with them. As to the *ius divinum*, the first example was the commandment, "Thou shalt not kill." We must know that positive law limits the effects of this commandment. Human reason and experience supply a justification for those limitations—for instance, a person who kills another is himself rightly executed. However, sometimes no such legitimate dispensation from a commandment exists. A statute allowing a man to marry his mother, for instance, would be invalid from the start; the commandment to honor one's father and mother had never admitted an exception to allow a child to marry a parent. No rational *causa* existed for a statute authorizing such marriage. If there was doubt about the absence of a *causa*, Panormitanus concluded, the normal presumption was in favor of its existence.[30]

Similar discussions involving the other forms of law followed; we need not follow them in detail, except perhaps to note, first, that he held that the pope was bound by the same rules as the emperor,[31] and second, that Panormitanus cited Thomas Aquinas in his discussion of the law of nature and statutes—one of the few canonists to do so.[32] The more important point for appreciating the jurist's high reputation is that he began with a papal decretal on a small point of law but ended with an extended lesson in statutory interpretation. Not that he solved all the problems involved; no lawyer has ever done that. But he gave his students (and his readers) a start and an example of how it should be done properly.

Canonical procedure

A second example of the juristic skill of the man comes from the second chapter of the twelfth title in the second book of the Decretals (X 2.12.2). It contained the answer of Pope Celestine III (d. 1198) to a query concerning procedure to be used by papal judges delegate. Their letter of delegation gave them the power to deal both with the possessory and the propriety rights of the parties involved. The decretal as edited by Raymond of Peñaforte says nothing more about the nature of the claim itself. Whether it concerned real property, an ecclesiastical benefice, or something else we do not know. We do know that, like Roman law, medieval canon law provided two separate remedies for the recovery of property. The possessory remedy required a showing only that the petitioner had been ousted from possession. The petitory required a showing of legitimate title to the property. Thus, a person with good title but without possession who nevertheless took the property by force of arms might lose the possessory action but prevail in the petitory. This was the same basic idea found in English common law that distinguished the assize of novel disseisin from the writ of right.[33] To save the parties from delay and unnecessary expense, the pope's decretal allowed the judges delegate to hear both the possessory and the petitory together (commixtum). The basic problem the decretal raised lay in determining how much leeway was to be allowed judges in dealing with disputes over title to property.

It is this subject on which Panormitanus commented. It was then, and remains today, a lawyer's subject—unrelated to constitutional politics but obviously relevant to the conduct of litigation. Particularly at the time the decretal was dispatched, appeals to the papal court were often delegated to men who could hear and receive the relevant evidence, investigating the facts in the place where the dispute had arisen.[34] The subject must have interested commentators, or at least have been of sufficient importance to warrant considered thoughtful discussion—which is exactly what the Sicilian jurist supplied. Canonical procedure, derived in the first instance from Roman law but modified by the canons, was always a subject of immediate importance to practicing canon lawyers.

In commenting on this decretal, Panormitanus took it as widely significant to canonical procedure. He first noted that the decretal's object was to permit the judges to serve "the utility of private parties" by saving expense and minimizing confusion. Its words should be interpreted in accord with that purpose.[35] Could the judges, on this account, first hear and decide the possessory claim and then pass to the proprietary claim if (as was likely) one of the parties involved was dissatisfied with the result? No, he said, they should not. This interpretation would subvert the point of the decretal, which was to save time and expense for the litigants. The same witnesses and at least some of the same evidence would likely be relevant to both claims, and if the parties were obliged by the judicial decision to split the dispute into two halves, as it would be if the two claims were heard one after the other, they would likely be put to double expenses. They would have to produce the same witnesses twice. That would have the effect of subverting the decretal's true objective. The interpretation Panormitanus offered would have had the result of leaving it up to the litigants and the judges to decide how to proceed, but it also limited that choice. He therefore concluded that if a party addressing the possessory issue wished also to introduce the proprietary question, he could do so "if he was willing to prove it promptly."[36] The judge, therefore, might determine the possessory claim first, but he might receive the evidence on both as part of the same proceedings if it could be done expeditiously.

Panormitanus produced support for this conclusion from texts in both the Roman and canon laws, as well as from the writings of Hostiensis and Innocent IV (who apparently differed on their interpretation of the decretal's true meaning). Students and lawyers were thus given the chance to do the same, consulting the same authorities their teacher had turned to and forming their own opinions.

Criminal law

The skill of Panormitanus as a lawyer is also particularly well illustrated by a third example, one taken from a *consilium* published in the 1617 edition of his works.[37] It contains his response to the case of a man who sought a divorce *a mensa et thoro* (what we would call a judicial separation) and return of the dower rights from his wife. The grounds for this claim were that she had committed adultery with another man and was in fact pregnant with the second man's child at the time of the plea. In defense, she alleged that she had not consented to the adultery. She had been violated by force. She had proved this, it was said, "by sufficient conjectures."

Panormitanus's answer begins with three possible negative answers to her petition, all supported by texts found in canon law. First, "coerced consent does not excuse a person from sin or even from the penalties of sin" (C 32 q. 5 c. 3). Second, only absolute force will excuse a person from sin, not force which leaves the victim with a choice, even if that choice is likely to involve serious injury or perhaps even the loss of one's life (X 1.40.5). Third, Pope Marcellinus (296–304) was deposed after he had sacrificed to the pagan gods under compulsion from Roman authorities; neither his status nor the compulsion excused his fault. (Dist. 21 c. 7). It followed, the *consilium* continued, that under the canons the woman "should not evade punishment because of [her] fear."

The *consilium* went on, however, to arrive at something close to the opposite conclusion. In doing so, Panormitanus did not dispute the authority of these canons. The woman should not be exonerated. She might even be punished. However, he introduced a significant limitation to the import of the canons, concluding that although the woman should not escape *some* consequences of her action, she should escape these particular consequences—that is, the divorce and return of the dower rights. For this distinction and result, he found authority in the Roman laws (Dig. 48.5.40(39); Dig. 48.5.14(13).7; Cod. 9.9.20). They all allowed some punishment to be imposed in such criminal cases, but not the most serious punishments that judges might choose to impose. Thus, voluntary adultery would have warranted, even required, full punishment. However, intention (*dolus*) to commit the crime involved was required before the most serious sanctions were justified. This intent had to be proved, and it had not been proved in this case. It was rather like the role *mens rea* plays in modern criminal law, a requirement of conscious intent that controls many parts of our criminal law. In fact, here the opposite had been shown. The woman had not consented. She had been raped, so she should not lose the important dower rights to which she was otherwise entitled.

It is noteworthy that the only canonical text Panormitanus cited in support of this result was a comment found in the *glossa ordinaria* (*gl. ord.* ad X 4.1.14, v. *metus*) to the effect that, in questions of marriage, a lesser degree of force and fear would excuse a woman rather but not necessarily a man from the consequences of having entered into a contract of marriage. Otherwise, it was the texts of the civil law of crimes that provided the textual support for this result. He ended the *consilium* by citing the example of Lucretia, the Roman noblewoman who was raped by Tarquin and committed suicide in consequence. Its relevance to this case? Lucretia had not suffered any punishment at the hands of the Roman authorities. Neither should the woman whose future was the subject of this *consilium* from the pen of Panormitanus. The case served as a counter to the example of Pope

Marcellinus, effectively excepting the wife from what would have amounted to a heavy penalty.

Uses of the works of Panormitanus

An additional insight into the character and perceived utility of the works of Panormitanus before the modern era comes from investigating their use in practice. This approach will also shed some light on the reasons he was held in such high regard in earlier centuries. To do this fully would present enormous challenges; it would require examining many hundreds of legal works. Here all that is attempted is a brief examination of the ways his work was used by English ecclesiastical lawyers during the sixteenth and seventeenth centuries. A summary of that subject is feasible. It connects the subject to the praise from Henry Swinburne for Panormitanus mentioned at the start of this chapter. Evidence from the uses made of the *Commentaria* of Panormitanus suggests both the reasons for his outstanding reputation in earlier centuries and the lesser value placed on his work in many modern accounts.

In England, the use and authority of most parts of the existing canon law survived the Reformation. Of course, that usage was necessarily selective. Not all of the law of the medieval Church remained acceptable or relevant. Decretals reserving power to the Roman pontiffs and some of the canons concerning the clergy were rejected. Much the greater part of canon law, however, retained its status in the English courts where the civil law was applied. A Parliamentary statute actually mandated that result.[38] This meant that the surviving records and other commentaries on legal practice at the time tell us a good deal about the legal authorities that then mattered. It is revealing how often the works of Panormitanus were cited as authoritative in the works of the English lawyers and in the course of litigation in the English courts.

The ecclesiastical courts were the normal venue for such citation, but the utility of his works was by no means so limited. In an admiralty case from the first decade of the seventeenth century, for example, a technical question regarding the legitimacy of an appeal made in the preliminary stages of the litigation called forth fully fifteen citations to the treatment of the subject found in the works of Panormitanus.[39] The manuscript report of the case contains a long discussion, one containing citation to the works of more than one Continental jurist, but numerically none of them came close to having the relevance (and apparently the authority) of Panormitanus. The case, and others like it, call particular attention to the importance of procedural questions in English litigation—something that was only marginally touched by the Reformation statutes and that raised many disputed questions in practice. With the notable exception of Knut Nörr, Bruce Brasington, and a few others, such questions of procedural law have not attracted the attention of today's historians. If they had, this would have encouraged greater scholarly appreciation for the Italian jurist.

Similar in its use of the works of Panormitanus, but quite different in its subject matter was a case from around 1600 in which the judge in an ecclesiastical cause had earlier issued an admonition to one of the parties. The question on appeal, apparently to the Court of Arches in London, was the admonition's legal status. Was it sufficient to constitute the equivalent of a formal and peremptory citation, in particular a threefold citation to which defendants were normally entitled? Or was it something less? The answers to those questions could determine the outcome of the case, because if the admonition had been sufficient, the party to whom it was issued would be contumacious if he disregarded its terms. Further process in the case would be foreclosed to him. One of the lawyers therefore argued that the admonition was indeed sufficient, and he cited as authorities two discussions found within the *Commentaria* of Panormitanus (X 1.29.24 and X 2.20.2).[40] He cited nothing else—at least nothing more that was recorded in the contemporary Notebook compiled by Thomas Eden, who was then either a student or a young advocate but later was knighted after becoming a distinguished civilian and master of Trinity Hall, Cambridge.

Such use the works of Panormitanus in England's ecclesiastical courts was not limited to procedural subjects. One example is an ecclesiastical case from about 1610 involving the law of defamation. The case was recorded in the contemporary lawyer's notebook. The plaintiff alleged that the defendant had called her a whore. That was actionable under then-current law because a criminal offense had been imputed—what we call extramarital sexual intercourse, which was then an ecclesiastical crime. The open question was whether the defendant could escape liability by proving that the words were true; she wished to show that the plaintiff was in fact a whore. Would this be a legitimate defense? Today it would be, but then it depended on whether there was any legitimate public interest in knowing what the defendant's words had revealed. If so, the defendant had a privilege to say what she did. If not, it was simply a way of injuring a person's reputation, in other words a purely malicious act. In arguing that question in the case, only two authorities were cited. One, for the view that no public interest existed, was a *consilium* of Nicholas Boerius (d. 1539); the other, for the view that it did, was the discussion found in the *Commentaria* of Panormitanus.[41]

Conclusion

The evidence hangs together. As a pure lawyer, Panormitanus had few peers. Among the canonists of his own century and those that followed, his masterful presentation of the law of the Church made his works an invaluable guide even in England. Other lawyers would also have noticed how frequently he presented two sides to the issues he discussed. He normally preferred one over the other, but not in every case, and he was open to the possibility that other solutions might be preferable. To many modern historians of the period, this characteristic can be puzzling, even annoying. For some, it makes lawyers like Panormitanus appear to have been a crowd of "bickering luminaries."[42] It also opens lawyers to the complaint that they acted as "opportunists who sacrificed principle to self-interest."[43]

In some measure, these characteristics may also explain how the reputation of this great Italian lawyer could have declined as it appears to have done in recent years. He has gone from standing tall as "captain of the canonists" to the diminished status of a partisan who had acted in "disregard of the scholar's intellectual, social, and historical responsibility." The very qualities that made him a "lawyer's lawyer" are seen today in a quite different light—a darker light. Only thoughtful lawyers of today will preserve the opinion that today's negative view of the character of this skilled canonist rests on a misunderstanding of the function lawyers serve.[44]

Notes

1 In the historical literature of the law, Niccolò has also been known as *Abbas Siculus* or *Abbas modernus* (because of his position as abbot of the monastery of Santa Maria di Maniace in the diocese of Messina); this chapter refers to him as Panormitanus, the name by which he is now most commonly known among English speakers.
2 Swinburne, 60.
3 Brundage, 206–30. See also Berman; and Ourliac and Gilles.
4 See, e.g., Landau; Schulte, 312–13; Panziroli, 354–7.
5 E.g., Van Hove, 501, 505–6; Smith, 94.
6 Although some account of his life appears in most of the encyclopedic works described here, the most complete account remains Lefebvre; also very useful are Genuardi, 423–6; and Bellomo, 177.
7 He is described as *obscuris natalibus ortus* in Panziroli, Lib. 3, c. 42. However, he was described as *Tudesco sanguine natus* on his tomb in Palermo's cathedral church; see Pennington, "Nicolaus de Tudeschis (Panormitanus)," 9.
8 See his *Commentaria super Decretalium libros* (Venice 1617), ad X 2.1.9, no. 8: naming the church in Catania *ubi ego habitum a pueritia sumpsi sancti Benedicti.*
9 *Commentaria* ad X 3.50.10, no. 3.
10 See, e.g., the many examples discussed in Hallman, 17–65.
11 See *De Gestis Concilii Basiliensis Commentariorum Libri II.*
12 Lefebvre's entry in the *Dictionnaire* (n. 6) states that he wore the clothing and other accoutrements of a cardinal until his death.
13 Nörr, *Kirche und Konzil*; Schweizer; Black, *Council and Commune*, 92–105; Vagedes (I have not been able to consult this work).
14 Watanabe, 217.
15 See the corrective account in Morrissey.
16 See, e.g., Jedin, vol. 1, 94–5.
17 See Black, *Monarchy and Community*, 21–2; also Tierney, *Foundations.*
18 Nörr, "Tudeschis, Nicolaus de."
19 Nörr, *Kirche und Konzil*, 9.
20 The review appeared in *Journal of Ecclesiastical History* 16 (1965): 99–100. It ended by suggesting that Panormitanus had demonstrated "a contemptuous disregard of the scholar's intellectual, social and historical responsibility." A more favorable view of the same subject was expressed by one of Ullmann's students, Brian Tierney, "Canon Law and Church Institutions," 61–2.
21 See Lipenius (d. 1692), vol. 1, 166.
22 Jacob, "Panormitanus," 214–15.
23 Wunderli, 56. The admiration for Panormitanus was not limited to England; see, e.g., Erdö.
24 E.g., Morris v. Webber (CP 1587), 2 Leo. 169, 172, 74 Eng. Rep. 449, 452; Evans & Kiffin v. Ascuithe (1624), Palm. 457, 463, 81 Eng. Rep. 1169, 1172.
25 These are listed and discussed in the cited article from the *Dictionnaire de droit canonique* (n. 6), col. 1202; for Consilia, see Kisch, 82.

26 E.g., Joannes Urbach (fl. 1510), *Processus iudicii* was often ascribed to Panormitanus.
27 See Pennington, "Nicolaus de Tudeschis (Panormitanus)."
28 See Jacob, *Essays in Later Medieval History*, 139–40 (praising Panormitanus because "he thinks out familiar problems in a fresh way and carries them a stage further"). See also Grassi.
29 *Commentaria* ad id, no. 3, taking, it seems, the position that the terms of the decretal letter annulled both.
30 Ibid., no. 9: *Sed si dubitat an subsit; praesumendum est tunc pro lege principis et nota hoc dictum.*
31 Ibid, no. 10: *Et id quod dixi in principe seculari, habet locum in papa respectu iurisdictionis suae.*
32 Ibid, no. 17.
33 Sutherland, 1–42.
34 Pavloff.
35 *Commentaria* ad X 2.7.2, no. 2: *iudex supplet ex officio ad utilitatem privatarum personarum.*
36 Ibid, no. 4: *An autem admittatur volens docere de proprietate; dic quod sic, si incontinenti vult probare.*
37 No. IV.
38 27 Hen VIII c. 15 (1535); 35 Hen. VIII, c. 16 (1543).
39 Case of the Ship Our Lady of the Conception (1604), London Metropolitan Archives, CLC/420/MS11448, fols. 60 et seq. to f. 71 (with breaks).
40 Anon. (No. 46), in Helmholz, 58.
41 MS. Prec. Bk. 11, Borthwick Institute of Historical Research, University of York, fols. 5–5v; the reference was to his *Commentaria* ad X 5.36.5.
42 Makowski, 62.
43 Watanabe, 217.
44 See the discussion in Parker, 10–29.

Bibliography

Bellomo, Manlio. *The Common Legal Past of Europe, 1000–1800.* Translated by Lydia Cochrane. Washington, DC: Catholic University of America Press, 1995.

Berman, Harold. *Law and Revolution: The Formation of the Western Legal Tradition.* Cambridge, MA: Harvard University Press, 1983.

Black, Antony. *Council and Commune: The Conciliar Movement and the Fifteenth-Century Heritage.* London: Burns & Oates, 1979.

Black, Antony. *Monarchy and Community: Political Ideas in the Later Conciliar Controversy, 1430–1450.* Cambridge: Cambridge University Press, 1970.

Brundage, James A. *Medieval Canon Law.* Harlow: Routledge, 1995.

Condorelli, Orazio. "Commentaria in libros decretalium." In *The Formation and Transmission of Western Legal Culture: 150 Books That Made the Law in the Age of Printing*, edited by Serge Dauchy, et al., 49–52. Cham, Switzerland: Springer, 2016.

Condorelli, Orazio. "Niccoló Tedeschi." In *Dizionario Biografico dei Giuristi Italiani (XII–XX secolo)*, edited by Italo Birocchi, et al. Vol. 2, 1426–9. Bologna: Il Mulino, 2013.

De Gestis Concilii Basiliensis Commentariorum Libri II. Edited by Denys Hay and W.K. Smith. Oxford: Oxford University Press, 1967.

Erdö, Péter. "Sull'uso dell'opera del Panormitano nei centri diocesani dell'Ungheria tardomedievale." In Condorelli, *Niccolo Tedeschi (Abbas Panormitanus)*, 89–102.

Genuardi, Luigi. "Canonisti siciliani del secolo XV." In *Studi in onore di Francesco Scaduto*. Vol. 1, 421–32. Florence: Casa Editrice Poligrafica Universitaria, 1936.

Grassi, Giuseppina Nicolosi. "Interesse di Nicola Tedeschi al tema della scomunica nei *Commentaria* alle *Decretales* di Gregorio IX." In *Proceedings of the Eleventh International Congress of Medieval Canon Law*, edited by Manlio Bellomo and Orazio Condorelli, 419–36. Vatican City: Biblioteca apostolica Vaticana, 2006.

Hallman, Barbara M. *Italian Cardinals, Reform, and the Church as Property, 1492–1563*. Berkeley/Los Angeles: University of California Press, 1985.

Helmholz, Richard H., ed. *Three Civilian Notebooks 1580–1640*. London: Selden Society Publications 127, 2010.

Jacob, Ernest Fraser. *Essays in Later Medieval History*. Manchester: Manchester University Press, 1968.

Jacob, Ernest Fraser. "Panormitanus and the Council of Basel." In *Proceedings of the Third International Congress of Medieval Canon Law*, edited by Stephan Kuttner. Vatican City: Biblioteca apostolica Vaticana, 1971.

Jedin, Hubert. *History of the Council of Trent*. Translated by Ernest Graf. St. Louis, MO: B. Herder, 1957.

Kisch, Guido. *Consilia: Eine Bibliographie der juristischen Konsiliensammlungen*. Basel: Helbing & Lichtenhahn, 1970.

Landau, Peter. "Nikolas de Tudeschis (Panormitanus; 1386–1445)." In *Juristen: Ein biographisches Lexikon: Von der Antike bis zum 20. Jahrhundert*, edited by Michael Stolleis, 458–9. Munich: Beck, 1995.

Lefebvre, Charles. "Panormitain." In *Dictionnaire de droit canonique*, edited by R. Naz. Vol. 6, cols. 1195–215. Paris: Letouzey et Ané, 1935–65.

Lipenius, Martin. *Bibliotheca realis juridica*. Leipzig: Joannes Wendlerum, 1757.

Makowski, Elizabeth. *A Pernicious Sort of Woman: Quasi-Religious Women and Canon Lawyers in the Later Middle Ages*. Washington, DC: Catholic University of America Press, 2005.

Morrissey, Thomas. "Radicalism and Restraint in a Late Medieval Canonist." In *Proceedings of the Eleventh International Congress of Medieval Canon Law*, edited by Manlio Bellomo and Orazio Condorelli, 409–17. Vatican City: Biblioteca apostolica Vaticana, 2006.

Niccolo Tedeschi (Abbas Panormitanus) e i suoi Commentaria in Decretales, edited by Orazio Condorelli. Rome: Il Cigno Galileo Galilei, 2000.

Nörr, Knut Wolfgang. *Kirche und Konzil bei Nicolaus de Tudeschis (Panormitanus)*. Cologne: Böhlau, 1964.

Nörr, *Knut Wolfgang*. "Tudeschis, Nicolaus de." In *New Catholic Encyclopedia*. 2nd ed. Vol. 14, 99–100. Detroit, MI: Thomson/Gale, 2003.

Ourliac, Paul, and Henri Gilles. "La période post-classique (1378–1500)." In *Histoire du droit et des Institutions de l'Eglise en Occident*, edited by Gabriel Le Bras. Vol. 13. Paris: Cujas, 1971.

Panziroli, Guido. *De Claris legum interpretibus libri quatuor*. Leipzig: Gleditschius, 1721, Reprinted 1968.

Parker, Christine. *Just Lawyers: Regulation and Access to Justice*. Oxford/New York: Oxford University Press, 1999.

Pavloff, George. *Papal Judge Delegates at the Time of the Corpus Iuris Canonici*. Washington, DC: Catholic University of America Press, 1963.

Pennington, Kenneth. "Nicolaus de Tudeschis (Panormitanus)." In Condorelli, *Niccolo Tedeschi (Abbas Panormitanus)*, 9–36.

Pennington, Kenneth. "Panormitanus: Additiones to Novit ille [X 2.1.13] in His Commentary on the Decretales." In *Ins Wasser geworfen und Ozeane durchquert: Festschrift für Knut Wolfgang Nörr*, edited by Mario Ascheri, et al., 39–51. Weimar-Wien: Böhlau Verlag, 2003).

Schulte, Johann Friedrich von. *Die Geschichte der Quellen und Literatur des canonischen Rechts.* Vol. 2. Graz: Akademische Druck, 1956; Reprint of 1877 edition.

Schweizer, Julius. "Nicolaus De' Tudeschi, Archiepiscopus Panormitanus et S.R.E.: Seine Tätigkeit am Basler Konzil." Diss., Strasbourg, 1924.

Smith, J.A. Clarence. *Medieval Law Teachers and Writers: Civilian and Canonist.* Ottawa, Canada: University of Ottawa Press, 1973.

Sutherland, Donald W. *The Assize of Novel Disseisin.* Oxford: Oxford University Press, 1973.

Swinburne, Henry. *Treatise of Spousals, or Matrimonial Contracts.* 2nd ed. London: Daniel Brown, 1711.

Tierney, Brian. "Canon Law and Church Institutions in the Late Middle Ages." In *Proceedings of the Seventh International Congress of Medieval Canon Law*, edited by Peter Linehan, 49–69. Vatican City: Biblioteca apostolica Vaticana, 1988.

Tierney, Brian. *Foundations of the Conciliar Theory.* Cambridge: Cambridge University Press, 1955.

Vagedes, Arnulf. *Das Konzil über dem Papst?: die Stellungnahmen des Nikolaus von Cues und des Panormitanus zum Streit zwischen dem Konzil von Basel un Eugen IV.* Paderborn: F. Schöningh, 1981.

Van Hove, Alphonsus. *Prolegomena ad Codicem Iuris Canonici.* Mechlin and Rome: Dessain, 1945.

Watanabe, Morimichi. "Authority and Consent in Church Government: Panormitanus, Aeneas Sylvius, Cusanus." *Journal of the History of Ideas* 33 (1972): 217–36.

Wunderli, Richard. *London Church Courts and Society on the Eve of the Reformation.* Cambridge, MA: Medieval Academy of America, 1981.

13 Thomas Cajetan (1469–1534)

Wim Decock

Biographical introduction

Thomas Cajetan (Tommaso de Vio Gaetano, alias Cajetanus or Cajetan) was born as Giacomo de Vio into a family of landowners in Gaeta, Italy, in February 1469.[1] His hometown, Gaeta (Latin Cajeta), a seaport and archiepiscopal see halfway between Rome and Naples, gave de Vio his additional surname, Cajetan(us)—the name by which he is referred to in legal and theological literature in the early modern period. Giacomo adopted the first name Tommaso when entering the Dominican convent in Gaeta in 1484. After initial training at study houses run by the Dominicans in Naples, Bologna, and Padova, he obtained his master's degree in theology in 1494 at the University of Padova, where he started teaching metaphysics the same year. This work deepened his knowledge of Aristotle, which would form the basis for subsequent research and writings on philosophical subjects: *In Isagogen Porphyrii*, *In Predicamenta Aristotelis*, *De nominum analogia*, *De infinitate primi motoris*, *De subjecto naturalis philosophiae* and *In tres libros Aristotelis de anima*. From 1497 through 1499 Cajetan went on to teach theology at the University of Pavia, south of Milan, where he was asked to use Thomas Aquinas's writings as the starting point for his lectures. It was the beginning of a profound and influential engagement with Thomism, years before other famous Dominicans such as Pierre Crockaert (d. 1514) and Francisco de Vitoria (d.1546) reinvigorated the study of Thomas Aquinas at the Universities of Paris and Salamanca, respectively.

The renewed attention to the *doctor angelicus* in Cajetan's teaching was characteristic of a broader shift in scholastic knowledge culture at the turn from the fifteenth to the sixteenth century.[2] Previously, like most theology professors, Tommaso de Vio had been lecturing on the basis of a much more traditional text book, namely, Peter Lombard's *Sententiae*. A manuscript copy of Cajetan's commentaries on the *Sentences*, delivered at the Dominican School of Saint Augustine in Padova in 1493, has been preserved in the Bibliothèque Nationale in Paris.[3] While Lombard's *Sententiae* remained popular with scholastics in the early modern period,[4] Cajetan's decision to teach theology at Pavia on the basis of Thomas Aquinas's writings nevertheless turned out to be a watershed moment in the renewal of scholastic learning across the Catholic world. Compared to earlier engagements with Thomas's *Summa theologiae* in the late fifteenth century—for instance, at German and Spanish universities—Cajetan's commentaries were unique in their depth and comprehensiveness.[5] They were published in four volumes between 1508 and 1523 and rapidly gained the status of a reference work, not in the least among theologians belonging to the School of Salamanca, such as Francisco de Vitoria, Domingo de Soto, and Tomás de Mercado. Through their incorporation into the Leonine edition of the *Summa theologiae* (1888–1906), named after Pope Leo XIII, who commissioned the edition, they continue to influence the interpretation of Thomistic theology to this day.[6]

Cajetan did not have to wait for posterity, though, to be recognized as an exceptional figure. His superiors in the Dominican order noticed his extraordinary intellectual prowess early on, and also discovered his great organizational talent. Before long, he was appointed to major administrative positions. Beginning in 1501 he was charged with the office of procurator of the Dominican Order, meaning that he represented the order in the Roman Curia and had to preach in the Sistine Chapel at the beginning of Lent and Advent. A mere six years later, on August 10, 1507, Cajetan was appointed general vicar of the order, eventually leading to his election as the thirty-eighth master general (*magister generalis*) of the Dominican Order on June 10, 1508.[7] He exercised this function for ten years, during which the reinforcement of the intellectual formation of the Dominican friars was a priority of his mandate. Cajetan wanted to prepare the Dominicans for careers as preachers and confessors in a world that had profoundly changed following the discovery of the Americas, the rise of international trade, and the encounter with indigenous peoples. However, Cajetan's promotion to cardinal by Pope Leo X on July 1, 1517, meant that his energy was increasingly drawn elsewhere, especially into the fight against Martin Luther and the Ottoman threat in the Balkans and the Mediterranean. On July 6, 1517, he received the title of cardinal priest of the Basilica of San Sisto Vecchio—an honorific title frequently mentioned on the title page of his printed works; on February 8, 1534, just months before he died in Rome on August 10 of the same year, Cajetan was also granted the title of cardinal priest of Santa Prassede. Moreover, Cajetan had been nominated archbishop of Palermo on February 8, 1518, before receiving the archiepiscopal see of his hometown Gaeta a year later.

These various administrative and honorific functions led Cajetan to encounter some of the most famous protagonists on the religious and political scene at the outset of the Reformations. Cardinal Oliviero Carafa played a major role in brokering all of Cajetan's appointments in the administration of the Dominican Order. Popes Alexander VI and Julius II assisted to at least five of his sermons in Rome, which were published afterwards and included in his *Opuscula*. While Cajetan was still a procurator for the Dominican Order at the Roman Curia, Pope Julius II ordered the start of the construction of Saint Peter's Basilica, offering special indulgences to finance this monumental project. When Cardinal Giovanni de' Medici rose to power as Pope Leo X, he fully endorsed the practice of selling indulgences. He found a special ally in Albert of Brandenburg, Archbishop of Mainz and Magdeburg. The archbishop considered the sale of special indulgences as an opportunity to facilitate the reimbursement of a loan contracted with the Fugger bankers to purchase his ecclesiastical offices. To promote the sale of the indulgences, he called upon Johann Tetzel, a Dominican friar named inquisitor of Poland and Saxony in 1509 by Cajetan.

Tetzel's aggressive marketing practices scandalized Martin Luther, then provincial vicar of Saxony and Thuringia in the Order of Augustinian friars. After a preliminary investigation by Silvester Mazzolini Prierias,[8] the great Dominican theologian and master of the Sacred Palace, Pope Leo X called upon the *magister generalis* of the Dominican order to further examine the matter. And thus it happened that Cajetan occupied center stage in the conflict between Rome and Luther that began the Reformation.[9]

As a papal legate to the imperial diet of Augsburg in mid-1518, Cajetan had a twofold mission: to persuade the emperor and the estates to support a crusade against the Turks, and to investigate the heretical character of Martin Luther's views. After three meetings with Luther in mid-October 1518, Cajetan tried to arrive at a "differentiated judgment," but Luther showed little interest in compromise.[10] Much later, after Luther's condemnation, Cajetan advised Pope Clement VII to concede to the Lutherans' practice of clerical marriage and communion under both forms—to no avail. But Pope Clement VII gave in to another of Cajetan's wishes. He granted him free time to study the holy scriptures.[11]

It is not unlikely that Cajetan's encounters with Luther further stimulated his investigation of the Bible, but his interest in the scriptures predated the Lutheran Reformation.[12] Drawing on the original Greek and Hebrew texts, and using Erasmus's *Annotationes*, Cajetan devoted the last decade of his life, until his death at the age of sixty-five, to translating and commenting on various biblical texts, becoming a protagonist of "biblical Thomism."[13] Thanks to Dominican friars at the College of St. Thomas in Alcalá de Henares, these impressive commentaries were posthumously published together in five volumes in Lyon in 1639.[14]

Despite his recognition of the importance of scripture for the purpose of "Catholic reform,"[15] Cajetan did not adhere to any of Luther's doctrines. Throughout his life, he remained a staunch defender of papal power and the Aristotelian-Thomistic tradition. Against the spiritualization of Christianity propagated by the Lutheran reformers, he advocated a literal reading of the Bible that protected the jurisdictional interests of the Roman Catholic Church—for instance, regarding the personal and real transfer of the power of the keys to Peter and his successors in Rome. It is fitting that Cajetan, a brilliant theologian at the service of the Roman pontiffs, was buried in the Eternal City. His small tomb is contained in the floor of the vestibule of the Santa Maria Sopra Minerva—the Church of the Order of Preachers where the magnificent tombs of the Medici popes Leo X and Clement VII, whom Cajetan served loyally, are also located.

Major themes and contributions

The defense of papal power

Cajetan's life and career coincided with the reign of some of the most powerful and (in)famous Roman pontiffs the Catholic Church has ever known—Alexander

VI, Julius II, Leo X, Adrian VI, and Clement VII. As the master general of the Dominican order between 1508 and 1518, Cajetan spent a decade defending papal power in theory and practice against attacks both from within and from outside the Church. Despite the apparent victory of the papalists against the conciliarists following the Council of Basel (1431–37), the Council of Florence-Ferrara (1438–45), and the condemnation of conciliarism by Pope Pius II in his bull *Execrabilis* (1460), conciliarist views continued to circulate. At the beginning of the sixteenth century, conciliarism witnessed a major revival. It is often associated with the works of John Mair and Jacques Almain, professors of theology at the University of Paris.[16]

Nevertheless, against the background of increased royal resistance against papal power, the revival of conciliarist ideas was in fact a much wider phenomenon, attested to very clearly not only in France but also in the Spanish empire.[17] Believing that the ultimate authority in the Church lay not with the pope but with the community of the faithful and the bishops assembled in a general council, the conciliarists questioned the supreme jurisdictional power of the Roman pontiff from within the Church.[18] At the same time, Martin Luther launched an assault on the papacy, first from within, then eventually as the leader of a schismatic reform movement wholly outside the Catholic Church.[19] Cajetan was at the forefront of combatting both dissonant voices, leading to the publication of three major writings on the question of papal power: *De comparatione auctoritatis papae et concilii* (1511), *Apologia de comparata auctoritate Papae et Concilii* (1512), and *De divina institutione pontificatus totius Ecclesiae* (1521).[20] While the last treatise was the product of his encounter with Luther, the first two writings were the fruit of his opposition to the French conciliarists.

A major starting point for the so-called silver age of conciliarism was events in France and Italy from 1510 to 1512. At that time, King Louis XII provoked Pope Julius II by convincing French cardinals to convoke a general council in Pisa in May 1511, despite the canonical prohibition against summoning a general council without papal consent (see the bull *Execrabilis*). In reply, Julius II convoked his own, rival council—which came to be known as the Fifth Lateran Council (1512–17)—[21]and appealed to Cajetan to combat the dissident cardinals gathering at the "alleged council" in Pisa—designated pejoratively in Latin with the word *conciliabulum*. Threatening any member of the Order of Preachers with excommunication if they dared to attend the Council, Cajetan organized resistance to the conciliarists from the monastery of the Dominicans in Pisa, urging the rebel cardinals to leave Pisa for Milan. Moreover, the master general of the Dominicans went on to demonstrate the illegitimacy of the *conciliabulum* in his *De comparatione auctoritatis papae et concilii*.

Published in October 1511, this treatise prompted immediate reaction from the French king, who requested a refutation of Cajetan's work by the theologians of the University of Paris. Charged with this daunting task, the young Jacques Almain developed an intelligent apology for the Council of Pisa in his *Libellus de auctoritate Ecclesiae*, urging Cajetan to refine some of his arguments in his *Apologia*, a second treatise on the relationship between the Roman pontiff and the council published in November 1512. As Hubert Jedin has observed, the conflict between Cajetan and the dissident cardinals at Pisa was "a momentous event," illustrating the sheer brilliance and energy of early modern ecclesiological debates.[22] It had a lasting impact on debates about the Catholic Church's ecclesiology, not the least through the reception of Cajetan's ideas in Francisco de Vitoria's teachings on the subject of ecclesiastical power in the 1530s at the University of Salamanca.[23]

Undoubtedly one of the strongest apologists of the supremacy of papal power within the Catholic Church at the outset of the sixteenth century, Cajetan argued emphatically that the bishop of Rome, in his capacity as the successor to Peter, was the sole person to have received immediate jurisdictional power (*potestas iurisdictionis*) from Christ to govern the Church.[24] The other bishops, as successors to the other apostles, could receive jurisdictional power only through the hands of the pope, viz. mediately. Therefore, their authority as leaders of the Church was inferior to that of the pope. Although Cajetan admitted that the power of order, namely the capacity to dispense the sacraments (*potestas ordinis*), had been granted immediately to all the apostles, the power of jurisdiction could be transmitted to them only by the pope.

Cajetan based this idea of papal supremacy on the metaphor of the two keys which Christ had given to Peter (Matthew 16:19). Cajetan's exegesis of the transfer of the power of the keys followed the interpretation of Matthew 16:19 by twelfth-century decretists such as Huguccio. They claimed that while one key, symbol of the power of order, had been conveyed to all the apostles, the other, representing the jurisdictional power, had been given to Peter alone.[25] Cajetan was very clear about the necessity to adhere to this view, which he based on several canons and on Thomas Aquinas's *Summa contra gentiles*:[26]

> You must pay careful attention to the following proposition, to close the door to opponents who talk about a royal form of government (*regale regimen*) instituted by the senate or the free people: It is not through the church, the Christian people, or any kind of universal council that the ecclesiastical government (*Ecclesiae regimen*) was instituted, but through the living and reigning Christ directly, so that Peter is not the vicar simply of the church but of Jesus Christ.

The conciliarists obviously opposed these views. They argued that the power of jurisdiction originally lay with the whole community of the faithful, or at least with the general council of bishops as the representatives of the community. The power of both keys, including the key of governance, had been transferred to all apostles, not just to Peter. As a result, the pope could not claim to be superior to the general council of bishops. Moreover, by using the terminology of Aristotelian and Thomistic political philosophy (*regimen*, *respublica*), Cajetan unwittingly played into the conciliarists' hands, as Elliot van Liere has rightly pointed out.[27] Almain used the analogy between the Church and the civil community (*respublica*) to construct his argument that the origins of ecclesiastical jurisdiction had to be the same as those of civil power, namely, the community's original power to govern itself. Even if the political community could transfer its original authority to a monarch, it retained the unalienable right to safeguard its own well-being, especially when the monarch risked destroying the community. Following other conciliarists, Almain emphasized the close parallelism between the ecclesiastical and civil polities (*regimen*).[28] As a consequence, the power of the community of the faithful, represented through the general council of bishops, was superior to that of the pope. The universal Church could even decide to depose a pope if the latter exercised his power destructively, just as a political community could repeal a tyrant from his office.

Cajetan rejected the far-reaching analogy between the civil and ecclesiastical *regimen*. With James Burns one can observe that he was "concerned to make as absolute a distinction as he can between civil and ecclesiastical authority, so as to undermine the conciliarist exploitation of their supposed similarity."[29] Cajetan clarified in his *Apologia* that the nature of civil and ecclesiastical power was so different that one could not reason from one to the other. While a political community naturally needs an authority to take care of the common good—an authority which, in the civil polity, lies with the people, who can decide to confer this power upon a small elite (in an aristocracy) or, in the best of circumstances, upon a king (in a monarchy)—the Church has authority merely because it received it directly from Christ, and Christ decided to give it solely to Peter as His vicar, not to the community of the faithful. By virtue of its specific nature, the ecclesiastical community is not free when it comes to choosing its leader. The right to determine the supreme ecclesiastical leader, the *ius principatus*, belongs solely to Jesus Christ, the Church's Lord by nature, whom the ecclesiastical community serves.[30]

Cajetan nevertheless acknowledged that, under extreme circumstances, a heretical pope could be deposed by an inferior authority. Cajetan did so by drawing a subtle distinction between the papal office in the abstract, the specific human person occupying that office, and the conjunction of the two through the human process of election. Should the universal Church or the general council depose a heretical pope, it would merely be unwinding that process of combining the office with the specific person, without laying claim to jurisdictional supremacy.[31]

While the conciliarist threat gave Cajetan an early opportunity to explicate his views on papal supremacy, less than a decade later he was forced to make his argument about the authority of the pope even more forcefully in light of the Lutheran threat. His *De divina institutione pontificatus totius Ecclesiae* (1521), published shortly after the excommunication of Martin Luther by virtue of the papal bull *Decet Romanum Pontificem*, offers an unprecedented apology of papal power. Rather than concentrating on papal decretals or conciliar documents, his argument is principally based on the exegesis of key phrases in Matthew 16:18 (*tu es Petrus*), Matthew 16:19 (*tibi dabo claves*), and John 21:17 (*pasce oves meas*). He interprets these passages as saying that Christ gave the power to lead the Church to Peter alone, and that He wanted Peter to have successors—the popes—to whom alone that power would be transmitted. Compared with earlier attempts to justify papal claims on supremacy against Luther—for instance in Johann Eck's *De primatu Petri*—which drew heavily on arguments from tradition, the biblical turn in Cajetan's argumentation is remarkable. It is often considered indicative of a shift towards a more theological and less canonical understanding of ecclesiology in the early modern Catholic Church.[32] The juridical nature of the arguments presented in Cajetan's *De divina institutione pontificatus* should not be overlooked, however. In the introduction to his treatise, Cajetan explains that, by clarifying the *ius principatus*, he wants to protect it as belonging to Peter and the Roman pontiffs—a right of princely rulership which he says "is shining thanks to the sun of the Gospel" (*evangelico sole fulgens*) but has been acquired over the centuries "through peaceful possession" (*tranquilla possessione*)—a subtle reference to the acquisition of ownership by means of acquisitive prescription.[33]

The morality of the marketplace

Cajetan was a formidable theologian indeed—familiar not only with the biblical sources of the Roman Church's ecclesiology but also with Aristotelian-Thomistic moral philosophy and the Romano-canon legal tradition. The many requests for practical advice submitted to Cajetan throughout his life—ranging from the morality of banking practices in southern Germany to the legitimacy of the marriage between Henry VIII and Catherine of Aragon—urged him to master a technical, philosophical, and legal vocabulary sophisticated enough to deal adequately with the big issues of his day. Those issues not only concerned the attacks on papal authority following the revival of conciliarism, the rise of increasingly powerful secular princes, the emergence of the Lutheran reform movement, and the imminent schism between Rome and the Anglican Church. They were also related above all to profound changes in the economic structure of Europe at the threshold of the sixteenth century, which was increasingly characterized by the intensification of cross-continental and cross-maritime trade and finance. Although Cajetan's work makes little reference to the discovery of the Americas,[34] there is no denying the paramount importance of reflections on the morality of the marketplace in several of his works as a consequence of the rise of cities such as Milan, Lyons, and Antwerp as major hubs in international trade and banking.

Cajetan's activity as a moral adviser in economic affairs took off during the years he taught theology on the basis of Thomas Aquinas's *Summa theologia* in Pavia. On July 13, 1498, he delivered (negative) advice on the Mounts of Piety (*De monte pietatis*), which formed the basis of his (unsuccessful) attempt to have those public pawnshops condemned at the Fifth Lateran Council.[35] His rejection of the Mounts of Piety was followed by a more lenient report, which he finished in Milan on December 9, 1499, on the practice of money exchange (*De cambiis*).[36] The following year saw the composition of his advice on moneylending and usury (*De usura*), which he finished writing on April 18, 1500.[37] Brief statements about the morality of the market are also included in Cajetan's *Summula peccatorum* of 1523, an alphabetically ordered manual for confessors that features brief entries on sale and usury. Along with his more extended commentaries on articles 77 (about sale) and 78 (about usury) in Thomas's *Secunda secundae*, published in 1522, the *Summula peccatorum* became a standard reference work among theologians and jurists belonging to the School of Salamanca dealing with similar topics.

Cajetan's engagements with economic subjects nevertheless lacked the depth, comprehensiveness and clarity that characterized later scholastic treatises on the subject, especially by the Jesuits. In comparison with the subsequent economic ethics of Luis de Molina, Leonardus Lessius, and Juan de Lugo, Cajetan is rather moderate in promoting the values of economic prudence and industry (*industria*).[38] Nor did Cajetan bother about establishing a general theory of contract or a systematic overview of all specific contracts—despite contemporary attempts to that effect by the Tübingen theologian Conrad Summenhart (see his *Opus septipertitum de contractibus*, ca. 1500).[39]

Much more research is needed on the content and development of Cajetan's economic ideas, but some basic elements stand out. First of all, it is important to realize that Cajetan's assessment of the morality of the market is not based merely on abstract reasoning. He endeavors to combine Aristotelian and Thomistic wisdom with empirical insights from practice.[40] In this manner he prepared the "empirical turn" that would become the hallmark of Jesuit economic thought about a century later.[41] Cajetan wanted to know how banking worked in practice, and he inquired among professionals to get empirical evidence about the functioning of money exchange and markets for goods. In the introduction to his work on money exchange, Cajetan clearly states that his work is the product not only of silent meditation and the reading of authors but also of consultation with practitioners.[42] His actual work abounds with references to the practice of money exchange in cities such as Bruges, Genoa, London, Lyons, and Milan. As John T. Noonan and Raymond de Roover have observed, Cajetan's work on money exchange provides an important step towards the legitimation of the profession of the money exchanger and, as a consequence, of modern banking practices.[43]

Cajetan's sensitiveness to practice also shows up in his treatment of some of the more traditional principles of scholastic economic thought, such as the doctrine of the just price. In discussing the traditional prohibition on charging a higher price in a credit sale, he argues that the rule that considerations of time should not influence the just price "should be taken with a grain of salt" (*est tamen hic grano salis opus*):[44] first of all because, in practice, the just price covers a range of prices (*latitudo*) and is not just a specific and exact, indivisible price; and second because, in practice, there is uncertainty about the future value of goods, and the merchant may well have wanted to sell his goods later at a higher price.

A second element that deserves mentioning besides Cajetan's sensitivity to economic reality is that he formulated many seminal economic insights such as the rule that "absent money is less worth than present money"—which foreshadows similar notions in Lessius (*carentia pecuniae*) and modern economics (liquidity preference).[45] Another truly innovative element that has attracted scholarly attention is Cajetan's willingness to recognize that market prices are formed according to a logic of their own that ignores subjective characteristics of the buyers and sellers involved, such as their need.[46] It is not the subjective intent or reason (*causa*) motivating people to enter into a transaction which determines the justice of the price, but rather the specific circumstances of the sale and the mode of selling (*modus vendendi*). For example, at auction the price of a certain good may be totally different from the price the same good is sold at in an individual transaction. Moreover, if a seller offers that same good for sale on his own initiative, he must expect to get less for it than if he is requested by the buyer to sell. According to a famous principle articulated in Cajetan's commentary on the *Secunda Secundae*, and taken up by subsequent scholastic theologians such as Lessius, "merchandise offered spontaneously decreases in value" (*merces ultroneae vilescunt*). In other words, the specific modalities of the exchange have a decisive impact on the formation of the just price. On account of insights like these, Odd Inge Langholm has affirmed that "Cajetan's doctrine represents a first step toward the depersonalization of economic ethics that characterizes post-scholastic thought."[47]

Cajetan's economic ideas were not always as forward looking and innovative, however, as these examples suggest. His views on interest and usury remained rather conservative, and he argued against the Mounts of Piety.[48] Moreover, his willingness to accept new commercial and financial techniques was subject to great hesitation. In 1515, the famous German Dominican theologian Johann Eck delivered a groundbreaking defense of the so-called triple contract—the legal backbone of commercial capitalism and the practices of the Fugger banking industry.[49] Yet in April of the same year, Cajetan delivered an almost entirely negative advice about the practice after Conrad Köllin, Dominican friar in Ulm, had solicited his opinion on this investment technique, which was very popular in southern Germany.[50]

Often, Cajetan is more interesting because of his restatement of traditional economic ideas than because of his allegedly protoliberal thought.[51] A good example is his brief but compelling explanation of the typically scholastic prohibition on market abuse through monopolies.[52] Even legal monopolies, Cajetan argues, are not to be allowed if they are merely intended to increase prices at the expense of the buyers. Robbery (*rapina*) is forbidden, even if allowed by the government. "That kind of monopolies," Cajetan explains in his *Summula peccatorum*,[53] "not only damages individual citizens but also violates the freedom of the whole community (*communis libertas*); as a consequence, it should not be tolerated."

General appraisal and influence

A brilliant theologian, prolific writer, and clever administrator within the Order of Preachers, Cajetan was a major actor on the academic, religious, and political scene at the threshold of the modern period. As a papal legate at the Diet of Augsburg in October 1517, he incarnated the modern Roman Church's pope-centered ecclesiology in confronting, both literally and figuratively, an Augustinian friar who dared challenge the authority of the Roman pontiff: Martin Luther. It turned out to be a watershed moment in the history of Christianity—and Cajetan was at the center of it. Two decades before, Cajetan had also been at the forefront of another revolution, albeit one of a more silent, slow, and intellectual nature: the revival of the study of Aristotle and Thomas Aquinas as the basis of philosophical and theological teaching at universities and religious schools. Combined with his humanist bent for biblical exegesis and his sharp insight into the realities of economic life, Cajetan thus contributed to laying the foundations of the renaissance of a highly hybrid and effective Thomistic theology across sixteenth-century universities and religious orders. His fundamental impact on major Spanish theologians belonging to the School of Salamanca—such as Francisco de Vitoria, Domingo de Soto, and Tomás de Mercado—may not come as a surprise, given that they belonged to the same Dominican order. But he was equally seminal in shaping the theological, political, and economic thought of great Jesuits such as Robert Bellarmine, Francisco Suárez, and Leonardus Lessius. In the literature, however, the intimate connection between Cajetan and the early modern scholastic tradition needs further emphasis and recognition. The continuity between the ecclesiological and economic-legal viewpoints of Cajetan, on one hand, and those of later Dominican and Jesuit theologians, on the other, often goes unnoticed, as Martin Grabmann was already sorry to observe.[54]

Although admired by many intellectual historians as the leading Thomist of his generation,[55] over the past decades Cajetan has suffered from neglect by scholars of his own trade. There are several reasons for that, some of which are more justified than others. In a letter to Henri de Lubac, the Jesuit father who initiated the influential movement of the "Nouvelle Théologie" of the mid-twentieth century, the French Thomistic philosopher Étienne Gilson, who has had a profound impact on historiography, rejected Cajetan for being the initiator of a "corrupt" tradition of Thomism.[56] Interestingly, Gilson's revulsion against Cajetan and other scholastic theologians of the early modern period may seem like a late echo of the rejection which the then master general of the Dominican Order suffered by French conciliarist theologians at the Sorbonne. Jacques Almain and Tommaso de Vio were never going to be friends. In addition, on account of his loyalty to the Roman pontiffs at such a delicate moment in the history of the Catholic Church, Cajetan has also suffered from the contempt often expressed at the public and private vices associated with pontiffs such as Alexander VI, Julius II, and Leo X. There is a long history to that story line as well.

Moreover, on account of his role in opposing Luther, Cajetan became a favorite target of critics on the Protestant side—for instance in Ulrich von Hutten's satirical dialogue "The Observers" (*Inspicientes*, 1520).[57] In addition, as Cathy Curtis has recently recalled, Cajetan became the subject of parody even earlier, immediately following his confrontation with the French conciliarists. He is ridiculed in one of the most widely circulated satires of the sixteenth century, "Julius Excluded From Heaven" (*Julius exclusus e caelis*, 1514)—often attributed to Erasmus but more likely the work of the humanist cleric Richard Pace, a friend of Thomas More and counselor to Henry VIII.[58] As a result of these polemics, an enormous amount of scholarship remains to be undertaken to fully understand and appreciate the lasting impact Cajetan has had—through his more than 115 writings—on early modern ecclesiology, biblical exegesis, neo-Aristotelian philosophy, neo-Thomistic moral theology, and economic thought.

Notes

1 The factual information about dates and places in this article largely draws on Eckehart Stöve's excellent contribution on Cajetan in *Dizionario biografico degli Italiani*.
2 For example, strong Thomistic currents of thought were already present in Salamanca long before Francisco de Vitoria started teaching there in 1526, see Belda Plans, 64–73.
3 Bibliothèque nationale, ms. Lat. 3076.
4 See Lanza and Toste.
5 Grabmann, 608.
6 The Leonine edition is available online at www.corpusthomisticum.org/repedleo.html.
7 Mortier, 141–230.
8 See Fabisch and Iserloh.
9 Wicks, *Cajetan Responds*; Wicks, *Cajetan und die Anfänge der Reformation*; Fabisch and Iserloh, 37–240; Morerod.
10 Wicks, "Cajetan."
11 O'Connor, 59.
12 Tanoüarn, 83.
13 See Vijgen.
14 Cajetan, *Opera omnia quotquot in Sacrae Scripturae expositionem reperiuntur*.
15 O'Connor, 63.
16 Oakley, 673–90; Oakley, *Watershed of Modern Politics*, vol. 3, 242–51.
17 See Tubau.
18 See Oakley, *The Conciliarist Tradition*.
19 See Witte.
20 The first two treatises are available in English translation; see Burns and Izbicki, 1–133 and 201–84.
21 See Minnich.
22 Jedin, vol. 1, 114.
23 See Elliot van Liere; also Tutino.
24 See Horst.
25 Tierney, 30.
26 Cajetan, *De comparatione authoritatis Papae et Concilii*, in *Opuscula omnia*, vol. 1, tract. 1, f. 1v: *Et tu valde notabis assumptum, scilicet quod Iesus Christus instituit tale regimen [sc. Ecclesiae regimen], ut claudas ora opponentium de regali regimine instituto a senatu seu populo libero: non enim ecclesia aut populus Christianus aut concilium aliquod universale, sed Christus ipse, qui vivit et regnat, instituit tale regimen sic, ut Petrus non ecclesiae, sed Iesu Christi vicarius esset.*
27 Elliot van Liere, 605–7.
28 Burns, "Scholasticism: Survival and Revival," 150–1.
29 Ibid., 153; compare Izbicki, 81–9.
30 Cajetan, *Apologia de comparata authoritate Papae et Concilii*, in *Opuscula omnia*, vol. 1, tract. 2, f. 20r: *In ecclesia ex sua natura natus est ordo talis ut ius principatus sit non in se sed in domino suo naturali.*
31 Oakley, "Almain and Major," 676.
32 Armogathe, 172; Jedin, 114.
33 Cajetan, *De divina institutione pontificatus totius ecclesiae*, in *Opuscula omnia*, vol. 1, tract. 3, f. 32r.: *Ea propter Petri, successorumque eius Romanorum Pontificum principatus (tot aetates, tempora, atque aevitates tranquilla possessione obtenti) ius evangelico sole fulgens, impetitum argumentationibus involventibus exercitatos parum in sacris literis tueri, tenebris exuere atque in medium proferre sic intendimus, ut veritas haec omnibus luceat et propriis splendoribus universae creaturae penetralia attingat.*

34 Izbicki, "Cajetan on the Acquisition of Stolen Goods in the Old and New Worlds."
35 See Muzzarelli.
36 A translation of this text has been offerred by Brannan; see his "Thomas De Vio Cardinal Cajetan, on Exchanging Money (1499)."
37 For a modern edition of the aforementioned *opuscula*, see De Vio Cardinalis Caietanus, *Scripta philosophica, Opuscula oeconomico-socialia.*
38 On this point, see Decock, *Le marché du mérite*. For Cajetan's discussion of the value of reputation, which is less influenced by concerns about individual freedom and industry than is the case with later authors, see Schwartz, 78–99.
39 A limited set of specific statements by Cajetan did have an impact, though, on subsequent debates about the bindingness of vows and promises or, for that matter, debt relief; see, e.g., Decock, *Theologians and Contract Law*, 180, 199, 433, and Decock, "Law, Religion, and Debt Relief," 131–2.
40 This point is worthwhile emphasizing, see Neri Reese, 351. But whether the introduction of this empirical method was really "innovative" can be questioned. It suffices to think of the practical engagement with economic problems by medieval scholastic theologians such as Pierre Jean de Olivi, whose lectures on the morality of the market, delivered in Narbonne around 1293–5, reflect his empirical observations of commercial practice in the Mediterranean; see Piron.
41 See Decock, "Knowing Before Judging."
42 Cajetan (trans. Brannan), *On Exchanging Money*, 211.
43 Noonan, 317–27; de Roover.
44 Th. Cajetanus, *Summula peccatorum*, Antverpiae, In aedibus Petri Belleri, 1575, s.v. *venditio*, 544–5.
45 De Roover, "Cardinal Cajetan on 'Cambium' or Exchange Dealings" (repr. in *Journal of Markets and Morality*), 202.
46 Langholm, 113–16; Martinat, 60–7.
47 Langholm, 116.
48 For further explanation, see Noonan, 250–5, 296–9.
49 See Birocchi; Decock, "In Defense of Commercial Capitalism."
50 Cajetan, *Responsio XI*, in *Opuscula omnia*, vol. 2, tract. 3, f. 95r. Noonan nevertheless observes that Cajetan's opposition to the triple contract was "not intransigent," since he preferred this practice to loans at manifest usury; see Noonan, 211–12.
51 See Rothbard's chapter "Cardinal Cajetan: Liberal Thomist," in his *Economic Thought Before Adam Smith*, rightly criticized in Neri Reese.
52 Höffner; Decock, *Le marché du mérite*, ch. 7 ("Monopoles et industrie").
53 Cajetanus, *Summula peccatorum*, s.v. *venditio*, p. 544: *Est enim monopolium huiusmodi non solum in privatorum hoc damnum, sed communis libertatis offensivum, et ideo non est tolerandum.*
54 Grabmann, 610–13.
55 E.g., Burns, "Scholasticism: Survival and Revival," 137.
56 Tanoüarn, 15, 36.
57 Becker, 68–9.
58 Curtis, 108–10.

Bibliography

Arici, Fausto. "Potestas sine ordine: Tommaso de Vio, detto il Gaetano (1468–1534): teologo della politica e del diritto." In *Silete theologi in munere alieno: Alberico Gentili e la seconda scolastica*, edited by Marta Ferronato and Lucia Bianchin, 223–38. Padova: Cedam, 2011.

Armogathe, Jean-Robert. "L'ecclésiologie de Cajétan et la théorie moderne de l'État." In *Rationalisme analogique et humanisme théologique. La culture de Thomas de Vio "Il Gaetano"*, edited by Bruno Pinchard and Saverio Ricci, 171–82. Naples: Vivarium, 1993.

Becker, Arnold. "Hutten's Polemical Dialogues: Literary Positioning and Its Impacts." In *Forms of Conflict and Rivalries in Renaissance Europe*, edited by David A. Lines, Marc Laureys, and Jill Kraye, 61–78. Göttingen: Vandenhoeck & Ruprecht, 2015.

Belda Plans, Juan. *La Escuela de Salamanca y la renovación de la teología en el siglo XVI*. Madrid: Biblioteca de Autores Cristianos, 2000.

Birocchi, Italo "Tra elaborazioni nuove e dottrine tradizionali. Il contratto trino e la 'natura contractus'." *Quaderni fiorentini per la storia del pensiero giuridico moderno* 19 (1990): 243–322.

Bondolfi, Alberto. "Zur Almosenlehre des Kard. Thomas de Vio (Cajetan)." In *Wirtschaftsethik und Recht*, edited by Kurt Seelmann, 97–111. Stuttgart: Franz Steiner, 2001.

Brannan, Patrick T. "Thomas De Vio Cardinal Cajetan, on Exchanging Money (1499)." *Journal of Markets and Morality* 10 (2007): 209–52.

Burns, James H. "Scholasticism: Survival and Revival." In *The Cambridge History of Political Thought, 1450–1700*, edited by J.H. Burns, 132–55. Cambridge: Cambridge University Press, 1991.

Burns, James H., and Thomas Izbicki, eds. *Conciliarism and Papalism*. Cambridge: Cambridge University Press, 1997.

Cajetan, Thomas de Vio. "On Exchanging Money (1499)." Translated by Patrick T. Brannan. *Journal of Markets and Morality* 10 (2007): 209–52.

Cajetan, Thomas de Vio. *Opera omnia quotquot in Sacrae Scripturae expositionem reperiuntur*. Lyons, 1639; Reprinted Hildesheim: Georg Olms Verlag, 2005.

Cajetan, Thomas de Vio. *Opuscula omnia*. Antwerp: Ioannem Keerbergium, 1612.

Cajetan, Thomas de Vio. *Scripta philosophica, Opuscula oeconomico-socialia*. Edited by P.P. Zammit. Rome: Apud Institutum Angelicum, 1934.

Curtis, Cathy. "'The Best State of the Commonwealth': Thomas More and Quentin Skinner." In *Rethinking the Foundations of Modern Political Thought*, edited by Annabel Brett, James Tully, and Holly Hamilton-Bleakley, 93–12. Cambridge: Cambridge University Press, 2006.

Decock, Wim. "In Defense of Commercial Capitalism: Lessius, Partnerships and the Contractus Trinus." In *Companies and Company Law in Late Medieval and Early Modern Europe*, edited by B. Van Hofstraeten and Wim Decock, 55–90. Leuven/Paris/Bristol, CT: Peeters, 2016.

Decock, Wim. "Knowing before Judging: Law and Economic Analysis in Early Modern Jesuit Ethics." *Journal of Markets and Morality* 21 (2018): 309–30.

Decock, Wim. "Law, Religion, and Debt Relief: Balancing above the 'Abyss of Despair' in Early Modern Canon Law and Theology." *American Journal of Legal History* 57 (2017): 125–41.

Decock, Wim. *Le marché du mérite. Penser le droit et l'économie avec Léonard Lessius*. Brussels: Zones Sensibles, 2019.

Decock, Wim. *Theologians and Contract Law: The Moral Transformation of the Ius Commune (c. 1500–1650)*. Leiden/Boston: Brill/Nijhoff, 2013.

De Roover, Raymond. "Cardinal Cajetan on 'Cambium' or Exchange Dealings." In *Philosophy and Humanism: Renaissance Essays in Honor of Paul Oskar Kristeller*, edited by Edward P. Mahoney, 423–33. New York: Columbia University Press, 1976. Reprinted as a preface to the translation provided by Brannan in *Journal of Markets and Morality*.

Doherty, Dennis J. *The Sexual Doctrine of Cardinal Cajetan*. Regensburg: Pustet, 1966.

Elliot van Liere, Katherine. "Vitoria, Cajetan, and the Conciliarists." *Journal of the History of Ideas* 58 (1997): 597–616.

Fabisch, Peter, and Erwin Iserloh, eds. *Dokumente zur Causa Lutheri, 1517–1521, Vol. 1: Das Gutachten des Prierias und weitere Schriften gegen Luthers Ablassthesen (1517–1518)*. Münster: Aschendorff, 1988.

Felmberg, Bernhard Alfred R. *Die Ablasstheologie Kardinal Cajetans (1469–1534)*. Leiden: Brill, 1998.

Giers, Joachim. *Gerechtigkeit und Liebe: Die Grundpfeiler gesellschaftlicher Ordnung in der Sozialethik des Kardinals Cajetan*. Düsseldorf: Mosella-Verlag, 1941.

Grabmann, Martin. "Die Stellung des Kardinals Cajetan in der Geschichte des Thomismus und der Thomistenschule." In *Mittelalterliches Geistesleben: Abhandlungen zur Geschichte der Scholastik und Mystik*. Vol. 2, 603–13. Hildesheim: Georg Olms, 1984 [1956].

Henning, Gerhard. *Cajetan und Luther: Ein historischer Beitrag zur Begegnung von Thomismus und Reformation*. Stuttgart: Calwer Verlag, 1966.

Höffner, Joseph *Wirtschaftsethik und Monopole im fünfzehnten und sechzehnten Jahrhundert*. Jena: Fischer, 1941.

Horst, Ulrich. *Juan de Torquemada und Thomas de Vio Cajetan: zwei Protagonisten der päpstlichen Gewaltenfülle*. Berlin: Akademie-Verlag, 2012.

Izbicki, Thomas M. "Cajetan on the Acquisition of Stolen Goods in the Old and New Worlds." *Rivista di Storia del Cristianesimo* (2007): 499–509.

Izbicki, Thomas M. "Cajetan's Attack on Parallels between Church and State." *Cristianesimo nella storia* 20 (1999): 81–9.

Jedin, Hubert. *A History of the Council of Trent*. London/New York: Nelson, 1957.

Langholm, Odd Inge. *The Legacy of Scholasticism in Economic Thought: Antecedents of Choice and Power*. Cambridge: Cambridge University Press, 1998.

Lanza, Lidia, and Marco Toste. "The Sentences in Sixteenth-Century Iberian Scholasticism." In *Mediaeval Commentaries on the Sentences of Peter Lombard*, edited by Philipp W. Rosemann. Vol. 3, 416–503. Leiden/Boston: Brill, 2015.

Martinat, Monica. *Le juste marché: le système annonaire romain aux XVI et XVIIe siècles*. Rome: École française de Rome, 2004.

Minnich, Nelson H. "Luther, Cajetan and *Pastor Aeternus* (1516) of Lateran V on Conciliar Authority." In *Martin Luther in Rom: Die Ewige Stadt als kosmopolitisches Zentrum und ihre Wahrnehmung*, edited by Michael Matheus, Arnold Nesselrath, and Martin Wallraff, 187–204. Berlin: De Gruyter, 2017.

Morerod, Charles. *Cajétan et Luther en 1518: Edition, traduction et commentaire des opuscules d'Augsbourg de Cajétan*. 2 vols. Fribourg: Éditions universitaires, 1994.

Mortier, Daniel Antonin. *Histoire des maîtres généraux de l'Ordre des Frères Prêcheurs, vol. 5 (1487–1589)*. Paris: Alphonse Picard, 1911.

Muzzarelli, Maria Giuseppina. "Il Gaetano ed il Bariani: per una revisione della tematica sui Monti di pietà." *Rivista di storia e letteratura religiosa* 16 (1980): 3–19.

Neri Reese, Philip. "Cajetan's Economic Treatises: A Critique of Rothbard's Proto-Austrian Portrayal." *Journal of Markets and Morality* 18 (2015): 349–71.

Noonan, John Thomas. *The Scholastic Analysis of Usury*. Cambridge, MA: Harvard University Press, 1957.

Oakley, Francis. "Almain and Major: Conciliar Theory on the Eve of the Reformation." *The American Historical Review* 70 (1965): 673–90.

Oakley, Francis. *The Conciliarist Tradition: Constitutionalism in the Catholic Church 1300–1870.* Oxford: Oxford University Press, 2003.

Oakley, Francis. *The Watershed of Modern Politics.* Vol. 3: *Law, Virtue, Kingship, and Consent (1300–1650).* New Haven/London: Yale University Press, 2015.

O'Connor, Michael. *Cajetan's Biblical Commentaries: Motive and Method.* Leiden/Boston: Brill, 2017.

Pirón, Sylvain, ed., and Ryan Thornton, trans. *Peter of John Olivi: A Treatise on Contracts.* St. Bonaventure, NY: Franciscan Institute Publications, 2016.

Rothbard, Murray. *Economic Thought before Adam Smith.* Aldershot: Elgar, 1996.

Schwartz, Daniel. *The Political Morality of the Late Scholastics: Civic Life, War and Conscience.* Cambridge: Cambridge University Press, 2019.

Schweigmann, Ambrosius. "De meritis Caietani in iure canonico." *Angelicum* 11 (1934): 533–88.

Stöve, Eckehart. "De Vio, Tommaso." In *Dizionario biografico degli Italiani.* Vol. 93, 567–78. Rome: Istituto della Enciclopedia italiana, 1991. Available at www.treccani.it/enciclopedia/tommaso-de-vio_%28Dizionario-Biografico%29/

Tanoüarn, Guillaume de. *Cajétan. Le personnalisme intégral.* Paris: Cerf, 2009.

Tierney, Brian. *Foundations of the Conciliar Theory: The Contribution of the Medieval Canonists from Gratian to the Great Schism.* New, enlarged edition. Leiden/New York/Köln: Brill, 1998.

Tubau, Xavier. "Hispanic Conciliarism and the Imperial Politics of Reform on the Eve of the Council of Trent." *Renaissance Quarterly* 70 (2017): 897–934.

Tutino, Stefania. "Ecclesiology/Church-State Relationship in Early Modern Catholicism." In *The Oxford Handbook of Early Modern Theology, 1600–1800*, edited by Ulrich L. Lehner, Richard A. Muller, and A.G. Roeber, 150–64. Oxford: Oxford University Press, 2016.

Vijgen, Jörgen. "Biblical Thomism: Past, Present and Future." *Angelicum* 95 (2018): 371–98.

Wicks, Jared. "Cajetan." In *The Oxford Encyclopedia of the Reformation*, edited by Hans J. Hillebrand, 233–4. Oxford: Oxford University Press, 1996.

Wicks, Jared. *Cajetan Responds: A Reader in Reformation Controversy.* Washington, DC: Catholic University of America Press, 1978.

Wicks, Jared. *Cajetan und die Anfänge der Reformation.* Münster: Aschendorff, 1983.

Witte, John, Jr. *Law and Protestantism: The Legal Teachings of the Lutheran Reformation.* Cambridge: Cambridge University Press, 2002.

14 Andrea Alciato (1492–1550)

Alain Wijffels

Not a man "inclined to speculate about heavenly matters"

Legal history is not a court of conscience. Even sources which occasionally appear to document a jurist's inner motives can only be handled by the historian *in foro externo*. The selection of jurists in this series merely considers whether the names who earned an entry belong objectively to what may be regarded as a Christian legal tradition. Andrea Alciato lived in an era that witnessed the outbreak of one of the most deep-rooted schisms in the history of the Christian religion. Only a few ripples reflecting that storm may be recognized in his scholarly output. More private documents provide at most a hint of how those events affected the scholar, but their interpretation remains inevitably speculative, and beyond the province of legal history. Thus, around 1518, at the start of Alciato's intellectual and professional career, he admonished a friend who had decided to become a friar: "No one will ever persuade me that a man, whatever his qualities, could be inclined to speculate all day long about heavenly matters. For man's forces are fragile and quite liable to be deluded by demons" .[1] That remark of the young Alciato may then be compared with the censorious comment of someone who claimed to have witnessed the jurist's lifestyle during his final years:

> One thing I shall certainly not conceal: Alciato did not die as if (as it says in the Adage) what comes later is for the better, but on the contrary it was for the worse. During the last years of his life, he indulged so much in his craving for eating and drinking that, unrestrained by any reasonable considerations, he would insist that he could pander to all his appetites. So it happened that not only did he bring about his own death by such boundless gluttony and voracity, but that it had long before become clear that such was the course of action he had decided upon. In addition, even worse was that when he was about to depart from life, he signalled that he had become much estranged from the Christian religion.[2]

History may well record such sources, but ultimately, they are only evidence of their author's practical strategies at a given time.

Life and career

Andrea Alciato (commonly known as Andreas Alciatus or Alciati) was born in Milan on May 8, 1492, and died in Pavia during the night of January 11–12, 1550.[3] During his lifetime, Alciato's academic and intellectual itinerancy was far less straightforward than suggested by the proximity of his birthplace to the city where he died. His early education prepared him for the more historically and philologically conscious approach to the classical *bonae* (or *humaniores*) *litterae* which historiography associates with humanism during the transition from the Middle Ages to the early modern period.[4] Among some famous humanist teachers whose lectures he is said to have attended are Aulo Giano Parràsio and Janus Lascaris. In 1508, Alciato began studying law at Pavia, where his teachers included Giasone del Maino and Filippo Decio. From 1511 until 1514, he pursued his law studies in Bologna, and he obtained the doctor's degree *in utroque* at Ferrara on March 18, 1516.

Alciato's professional academic career began in 1518, when he was invited to teach at Avignon. He appears to have taught law following the traditional legal methods for the regular curriculum, but he used more innovative humanist methods for extracurricular lectures. In 1521, he was granted the title of papal count palatine, an honor that may have allowed him to grant doctorates. The following year, he returned to Milan, where he was involved in advocacy and scholarly writing.[5] Possibly because of the military and political developments in Lombardy, which lay on the geostrategic fault line between royal French and Habsburg politics, he returned to Avignon in 1527. His second stay at Avignon lasted until 1529, when, as a mark of his reputation as a prominent figure of the new legal scholarship, he was appointed to teach in Bourges.[6] There he seems to have switched rapidly from traditional teaching to a resolutely humanist register of lecturing, at the behest of his audience.[7]

Alciato's years at Bourges, from 1529 to 1533, definitively confirmed his fame as a humanist legal scholar. His lectures were attended by students who would later become eminent humanist jurists themselves, and even the French king François I arranged to hear him teach. Alciato's scholarly work at the time reinforced his agenda of incorporating historical sources into a proper understanding of the ancient Roman law texts, while also developing a command of Latin that matched that of the ancient Roman jurists. While he asserted more strongly the humanist agenda and raised the stakes with regard to its scholarly demands, his approach became controversial and the focus of polemics from jurists who favored traditional learning.

In 1533, after failed negotiations to secure a position at Padua, Alciato accepted a position at the university of Pavia and was made a senator in Milan. His teaching at Pavia lasted until 1537, when he was given the teaching position formerly held by Pietro Paolo Parisio at Bologna. In Bologna, his interest in the revision of Roman law texts brought him in contact with main figures of legal humanism, such as Antonio Agustín and Jean Matal. He was recalled to Pavia in 1541 but left there in 1542 for Ferrara, where he taught until 1546. That same year, he was made a protonotary by Pope Paul III and prevailed upon to return to teach in Pavia, where he remained in office until his death.[8]

During his lifetime, Alciato was involved in the inevitable polemics of his day, whether because of personal and professional rivalries or more fundamental issues about scholarly opinions and methods.[9] The historical sources providing insight into Alciato's character need to be assessed with the usual caution. Aspersions about greed, presumption, and opportunism may have been supported to some extent by some of his career moves or correspondence with printers and associates but should also be viewed against the backdrop of professional academic prospects at the time and the need to find patronage. In his inaugural lecture at Ferrara, Alciato himself countered the criticism of inconstancy based on his recurrent changes from one university to the other, which he explained by referring to the political instability and the effects of warfare in northern Italy. Biographers have highlighted episodes from his life which may have suggested a high degree of concern for securing his own career and welfare. Thus, his correspondence expresses his serious worries when he feared that Erasmus, who he was told had come into possession of the antimonastic argumentation which Alciato had written as a young man, might publish this argument at a time when Alciato was seeking ecclesiastical preferment. Another episode which has clung to his reputation is the publication of his treatise on weights and measures, which contained some criticism of Budé. Alciato appears to have considered publishing this work until his appointment at Bourges made him more dependent on patronage and protection in France; nevertheless, the treatise did appear in print, and Alciato embarked on a sustained epistolary damage-control, particularly in his relationship with Budé.[10]

Works

A definitive bibliography and calendar of Alciato's works are not yet available. Moreover, a census of the printed works does not always reflect the time when a particular work was begun or written, and because Alciato revised or continued working on many of his works throughout his life, a proper critical edition of his works would also require a reconstruction of the variations from one printed version to the next. Douglas Osler, whose PhD dissertation on Alciato triggered a new era in the history of early-modern legal bibliography, called already in the 1980s for editorial work—on Alciato and other contemporary jurists—which would apply to printed works the same stringent rules that prevail for editing manuscript sources. Meanwhile, an indispensable bibliographical tool for Alciato studies can be found in the introduction by Jochen Otto in the 2004 reprint of the *Opera omnia*, including a very useful analysis of the successive editions of Alciato's *opera omnia*, which were not all published according to the same principles.[11] That introduction may serve here for a general (though not comprehensive) survey of Alciato's editorial and doctrinal production. Works published under Alciato's name but commonly believed to be apocryphal attributions by publishers are not taken into account in this brief survey.

Alciato's reputation in legal history is mainly owing to his early contribution to a neoclassical renewal of legal methods. That contribution was already the main reason for his fame and success in his own lifetime. However, legal historians may have overstated the significance of the polemics at the time between the defenders of the traditional methods and those scholars who, like Alciato, paved the way to a new approach to Roman law sources. In addition, one should not overlook Alciato's position in a period of transition, when the innovations that Alciato and others proposed were not presented, whether for strategic reasons or otherwise, as a clear-cut break with tradition. Alciato's work reflects that transitional stage: some of his contributions were almost entirely new, with no major precedents, and he emphasized his own view of their significance by using book titles which were unconventional in legal literature. Other works, conversely, appeared with titles and general formats more recognizable to lawyers steeped in conventional learning. In general, Alciato's contributions to Roman law tend to provide important new insights into both methods and substance. His works on canon law are usually not identified as innovative scholarship.

Early publications

Among Alciato's earliest works, written when he was still pursuing academic degrees, are contributions which show how the young scholar was using his classical education to understand and emend Roman law texts. Both the *Annotationes in tres posteriores libros Codicis* (1515) and the *Opusculum quo graecae dictiones fere ubique in Digestis restituuntur* can be traced to 1514 and earlier.[12] The first work dealt typically with a collection from the medieval *Volumen* (the last volume of the *Corpus Iuris Civilis* in its medieval appearance), which had received comparatively less attention in the main commentaries, but which contains a hoard of information on Roman and Byzantine institutions and regulations of general public interest.[13] The second work was a driving factor behind the historical and philological restoration of the most prestigious compilation of Roman law, which would culminate shortly after Alciato's death in the 1553 Torelli edition of the Florentine manuscript of the Digest. The reincorporation of Greek texts into the Digest (later also into the Code of Justinian) was a decisive step in undermining the very foundation of late-medieval legal scholarship, which, as either the ubiquitous Accursian gloss or the increasing number of commentaries, followed the *ordo legalis* according to the vulgate ("Bolognese") version of the main compilations.

Another work thought to be from Alciato's early years is a long-term project on ancient epigraphic material in Milan, which would provide materials for a history of the ancient city published in the seventeenth century (*Rerum patriae libri IIII.*, Milan, 1625). Alciato also provided annotations to Filippo Beroaldo's edition of Tacitus's *Annales*.[14] In 1518, Alciato published his *Paradoxa* (at the time, six parts, or "books") and *Dispunctiones* (*LIB. IIII.*),[15] together with some of his earlier and other works: *In Tre*[i]*s Lib. Cod.* (*LIB. III.*), *De eo quod interest,*

Praetermissorum (*LIB. II.*), and a model disputation in classical Latin, *Declamatio*. With updates and additions, this series of works was later republished on several occasions. In 1519, his commentaries on *De verborum obligationibus* (D.45.1) were published in Lyons, reflecting some of his teaching during the early years of his career at Avignon. A treatise dating from perhaps 1518 characteristically deals with technical aspects of ancient Roman life which were relevant as an auxiliary science for legal studies: *Libellus de ponderibus et mensuris*, published at Hagenau in 1530, apparently against the author's will, as it included some criticism of Guillaume Budé's work.

Bourges and the mature scholarship

The *editio princeps* of Alciato's commentary *De verborum significatione libri quatuor* (D.50.16) is dated 1530 and was published by S. Gryphius, who published several other works by Alciato the same year.[16] *De verborum significatione* is perhaps Alciato's most successful legal commentary.[17] It was reprinted several times during the following years and was included in the *Opera omnia*; some publishers insisted on having that commentary in the first volume of the collected works because they thought it was the most likely to attract a broader readership.

The work consists of two parts. Alciato began drafting the second part, in the form of a commentary, in the early 1520s in Avignon and derived it from his teaching; he wrote the first part, in the form of a treatise, at Bourges in 1528. The layout of the commentary may seem to follow a traditional format, but only at first glance: at the center of the page, the reader finds the *lex* of D.50.16, which is surrounded by Alciato's commentary—thus, the presentation is not that of standard commentaries but resembles lengthy glosses. In addition, references to authorities appear in the margins—that is, they are not included in the commentary itself, as in traditional legal works. The treatise, in a theoretical way, and the commentary, in its more specific focus on particular *leges*, offer an extensive overview of principles and cases of legal interpretation.[18] The method of interpretation had been one of the defining features of late-medieval civil law scholarship. This method served to construe not only the Roman law texts themselves but also the rules of particular laws and, beyond that, terms in contracts, testaments, and other legal documents. Civil law doctrines and principles of construction were therefore a powerful tool in maintaining the grip of civil law science over legal authorities and legal instruments in everyday practice. Now, Alciato used this title of the Digest, which had been somewhat disregarded by many commentators, as the key for a nascent theory of interpretation and for displaying the benefits of including a wide range of classical learning borrowed from nonlegal sources for a proper understanding and interpretation of legal phrases. Although Alciato dismissed many readings by previous authors, he stressed the positive contribution and continuing importance of the more penetrating late-medieval authors. His *De verborum significatione* appealed therefore both to more scholarly minded lawyers, who were keen to catch up with the neoclassical learning, and to practitioners, who looked for fresh ways of argumentation and counterargumentation.

In 1529–30 Sebastian Gryphius printed and reissued commentaries on several civil law titles and texts[19] which Alciato had selected for their relevance in showing the need and advantages of a historically and philologically founded reading of Roman law texts. In key areas, this method of reading Roman law could affect the use of civil law in the practice of public administration and the courts. These commentaries included *De quinque pedum praescriptione liber unus*, *De magistratibus civilibus et militaribus officiis liber unus*; and in a separate imprint *Ad rescripta principum commentarii: De summa trinitate, De sacrosanctis ecclesiis, De in ius vocando, De pactis, De transactionibus.*

In 1529 Alciato wrote a work that he dedicated to François I, capturing the interest of a probably aristocratic audience after it was first published in Latin (Paris, 1541) and then translated into French: *De singulari certamine liber seu duello tractatus.*[20]

In 1531 the first edition of Alciato's *Emblemata* came out. This work consists of allegorical images accompanied by neo-Latin verses, often conveying a moral message. Most of the emblems are inspired by ancient mythology and history. The *Emblemata* were exceedingly successful, published by famous printing houses in both Roman Catholic and Protestant Europe (and beyond). The success also inspired a genre of Western illustrated literature. Some 170 editions have been identified, including translations in various languages.

After the somewhat troublesome years of teaching at Pavia in 1533–37, Alciato published new works in 1537–38: *In Digestorum sive Pandectarum librum XII, qui de rebus creditis primus est, rubric. Si certum petatur, commentarius* (Basel and Lyons, 1537). Alciato also resumed his old propensity to launch new genres under original (and in legal literature, unusual) titles with the publication of his *Parergon iuris libri III* (Lyons, 1538),[21] soon followed by new editions, and augmented in 1540 with *Parergon libri VII posteriores* (Lyons, 1544), consolidated into *Parergon iuris libri X* (Basel, 1543), and finally, in the posthumous edition of Lyons (1554), augmented with *Parergon iuris libri XI. et XII.* In the *Parergon*, which Alciato appears to have started in Milan before moving to Bourges, the author collected useful obiter dicta from various (nonlegal) sources that he considered useful in interpreting Roman law texts. He obviously continued collecting such *parerga* throughout his later reading.[22]

At the same time, he published the more conventionally titled, but for practitioners valuable, *De praesumptionibus* (Lyons, 1538, and later editions); from his earlier teaching, *Commentaria in iure canonico* (Lyons, 1538); and later more canon law commentaries. From the late 1540s, *opera omnia* and collected works under various titles and arrangements appeared. Giunta in Lyons, for instance, collected under separate titles the commentaries on parts of the *Infortiatum* and the *Digestum Novum* (1551).

Responsa

A substantial collection of legal opinions reflecting Alciato's continuing implication in legal practice was published posthumously: *Responsa, nunquam antehac excusa* (Lyons, 1561, followed by later editions in Venice and Basel). The belated publication is partly owing to Alciato's unwillingness to have his opinions published, although the manuscript circulation and the printed versions of *consilia* (or *responsa*) had been a prominent feature of civil and canon law literature, first in Italy, then all over Western Europe. In his *Parerga*, Alciato had criticized the publication of vast collections of *consilia*, mainly, it seems, because they all too often defended opportunistic arguments which contradicted principles extolled in the commentaries or even in other opinions by the same author: Alexander Tartagnus's popular seven-volume collection of opinions was a prime example.[23] In the latter part of the sixteenth century, Tiberio Deciani countered Alciato's objections in his *Apologia pro iuris prudentibus qui responsa sua edunt imprimenda* (1579), which prompted a wider debate about the merits of each position. The posthumous publication of Alciato's *Responsa* had been carried out under the aegis of Alciato's nephew and executor of his literary legacy, Cardinal Francesco Alciato.[24] The *Responsa* deal with a broad diversity of legal topics and social and economic interests. Although the work may not reflect Alciato's scholarly humanist agenda, some of the more politically sensitive opinions betray the growing difficulty of weighing traditional civil law learning against the emerging new balance of power in the early modern polity.[25]

Alciato's standing in early legal humanism

Although some of the features conventionally attributed to legal humanism in mainstream historiography may be recognized as early as the works of Lorenzo Valla (1407–57) and Angelo Poliziano (1454–94), such authors were still mainly representatives of a strong neoclassical current which stood for the restoration of classical culture and language as the means to improve political and social culture in general. The more systematic implementation of that agenda in the field of legal studies started somewhat later, at the beginning of the sixteenth century. By then, the French political and military involvement in Italy had gained momentum and contributed to a more intensive reception of Italian humanistic learning and arts in France.

The development of legal humanism was two-edged. On one hand, humanist scholars seeking information about ancient Roman institutions, economic and social life, and a wide range of specialized language discovered that the Roman law compilations included a mass of information not readily available in the literary genres they had usually considered. At the same time, these scholars were appalled (though also delighted) to discover how corrupt and incomplete the textual tradition of the compilations had been in medieval scholarship. Here was a field where humanistic philological and historical expertise could restore on a vast scale an important corpus of ancient texts and discredit the traditional learning.[26]

On the other hand, the call *ad fontes* for Roman law texts was not obvious: the main compilations available—those promulgated by Justinian—had appeared relatively late in the development of Roman civilization. In the Digest especially, an older layer, soon considered more valuable (and still regarded in present-day Roman law studies as the era of classical Roman law), could be detected through the fragments of works by jurists from earlier centuries; some legal scholars were quick to realize that the humanistic agenda would be better served by focusing on that golden age of ancient Roman jurisprudence. That realization, however, meant that beyond the historical and philological critical review of the compilations' textual tradition, aiming to restore the "authentic" text of the compilations, a more formidable task loomed: a conceptual reconstruction of Roman law not at the time of Justinian and Tribonian, who had produced the compilations, but at an earlier stage of its development, when it was supposed to have reached its classical high-water mark. The realization of that agenda was gradual and not uncontroversial, whether for ideological or methodological reasons. In any event, whether a scholar wanted to reconstruct the law at the time of Justinian on the textual basis of his compilations, or the classical Roman law of the first centuries CE, for which Justinian's textual basis provided only indirect evidence, a different intellectual exercise was required than the historical and philological review of texts. The approach required a conceptual reconstruction of Roman jurisprudence—that is, the ancient jurists' way of reasoning and arguing, whether in the classical era or in Justinian's Eastern Empire ruled from Constantinople. At that point, historical and philological expertise became ancillary and subordinated to jurisprudential expertise and escaped the skills of grammarians and other masters of classical literature, history, and language.[27]

The early years of the sixteenth century thus coincided with the assertion of lawyers as humanist experts in the area of legal studies. The historiographical cliché presenting the dawn of legal humanism with the triumvirate of Ulrich Zäsy (Zasius, 1461–1535), Guillaume Budé (1467–1540), and Andrea Alciato may be somewhat oversimplified by focusing exceedingly on figureheads (who conveniently represent different national backgrounds), and thus may obfuscate the much broader current of humanistic learning which supported the new agenda. As a simplification, however, it compellingly represents that wider cultural change in legal studies, precisely during the generation of lawyers active in the first half of the sixteenth century. Even so, the whole legal-humanistic movement never prevailed and never became the new mainstream paradigm of jurisprudence. In the legal practice of the courts, the traditional late-medieval (scholastic) approach of the so-called *mos italicus* continued to dominate in all countries. Accordingly, the book market followed, and late-medieval authors continued to be reprinted until the end of the sixteenth century, even until the first quarter of the following century for the most prominent authorities. By the second half of the sixteenth century, a new paradigm of jurisprudence emerged, borrowing elements from the medieval heritage and from legal-humanistic learning, but with a distinct agenda and its own characteristics. That new paradigm eventually (more or less by the mid-seventeenth century) became the new mainstream approach in jurisprudence, whereas the true successors of early sixteenth-century legal-humanistic studies were somehow forced to seek refuge in the respectable academic niche of antiquarian studies.

Andrea Alciato stood at the beginning of those legal-humanistic developments. Not only a transition figure, he was one of the most prestigious and influential scholars of his day who advanced the cause and the methods of legal humanism. Alciato was at the tail end of the medieval teaching tradition which ran from Bartolo da Sassoferrato (1314/4–1357), Baldo degli Ubaldi (1327–1400), Paolo di Castro (1360/2–1441), and Alessandro Tartagni (1423/4–1477, though it is no longer certain whether he attended di Castro's lectures), to Alciato's master Giasone del Maino (1435–1519)—a tradition which then and now has been styled as that of "bartolist" jurisprudence, and has often been used as such in contrast to sixteenth-century legal humanism.[28] In spite of that tradition's reliance on defective texts and lack of historical interest, Alciato acknowledged the legal acumen of its most prominent representatives and their contribution to legal developments. Alciato's own work continued to refer to that tradition without systematically rejecting its achievements and doctrines. The increasing number of emendations of texts and corrections of traditional opinions—together with the transformation of the textual tradition of Roman law compilations in the contemporary editions of the *Corpus Iuris Civilis*—was nevertheless bound to undermine in the long run the very authority of that traditional heritage. In that sense, Alciato's work stands on the modern side of the fault line between medieval and early-modern jurisprudence.

Jurisprudence, public governance, and legal humanism

The object of teaching and learning at medieval law faculties was not the law as it came to be understood in early-modern and modern times. The purpose of medieval jurisprudence was primarily education about the art of governance, for which a scholarly and practical expertise in justice was required. Roman law texts provided the building stones for such an education. After the Gregorian reform, the Church leaders' foremost concern was to provide the Church at all levels of its management, throughout Latin Christendom, with skilled directors. They recognized the potential of civil law studies for the Church's corporate governance and adjusted Roman law so as to fit the ideological and political agenda of the Church. By the time of the *Quinque compilationes*, canonists were able to fill many of the executive offices and to produce a specialized science of ecclesiastical government based on a normative system produced by the Church's own governance and relying on the canonistic scholarship of governance. The Church governance remained nonetheless reliant on the further developments of the general science of government worked out in the civil law faculties. The achievements of ecclesiastical governance and the need of Italian city-states to consolidate their commonwealth on a rule of law ensured that canon lawyers and civil lawyers found employment in their administrations. Territorial princes followed suit and started appointing legal experts in their councils, in addition to the traditional members of the higher nobility and clergy. By the end of the Middle Ages and the beginning of the sixteenth century, the prevailing model of governance in the Church and secular polities came increasingly under fire. The essential efficiency and justice which any political authority was expected to foster through its governance were found wanting. The resulting criticism inevitably also affected jurisprudence as the core science of governance.

Late-fifteenth-century reform movements were not homogeneous. Moreover, political and social actors were aware that any shift in the balance of power might also affect the interests they supported or depended upon. The need to reform or modernize governance also varied from one country to another. Insofar as a wind of change with respect to the standards of governance reached late-fifteenth-century elites, a revival of the ancient classical (Greek-Roman) was the hallmark of progressive intellectuals. The quest for a historically authentic command of ancient classical expertise was for some elites—among whom were also conservative forces who did not necessarily challenge the established authorities—the platform for a new culture of governance. Legal humanism was in that respect a project aiming at a new—both better performing and therefore more legitimate—art of governance founded on a historically substantiated science of Roman law.

However embedded the late-medieval Italian art of governance was in a religious environment where the Roman Catholic Church remained a powerful actor, this governance was essentially secular in outlook. In contrast to Christian ecclesiology and ecclesiastical corporate governance, the end of Italian governance was the economic and social welfare of the polity and its citizens in the present world. In that respect, legal humanism, drawing largely from classical sources and therefore pre-Christian, Roman law, further strengthened the secular features of law as a science of governance. On the other hand, the humanists' historization of Roman law may have helped emphasize a paradigm of legal reasoning severed from contemporary issues of policy and governance.

Alciato's contribution to legal humanism

As a major figure of early legal humanism, Alciato enjoys a reputation based on the quality and quantity of his emendations and reinterpretations of Justinian's compilations. In addition, he contributed to introducing on a vast scale the humanist note of (neoclassical) Latin in legal scholarship, together with an approach no longer relying systematically on the accumulation of doctrinal interpretations, distinctions, and exceptions characteristic of some late-scholastic legal literature.

While his work touches on a broad range of topics allowing emendations and fresh interpretations (an approach Alciato also developed in his commentary on D.50.16), several of his other civil commentaries tend to select titles closely linked to governance and procedure. This focus serves as a reminder that late-medieval legal scholarship already had made procedural law a matrix for principles of due process of law when public authorities and their executive agents were making decisions. Alciato occasionally refers to the well-established late-medieval doctrine of *potestas absoluta*, which assumed that the ordinary exercise of political power would follow the rule of law.[29] Alciato's success and reputation beyond the more resolute circles of humanists may be explained partly by his determination to take into account (and recurrently commend) authorities of the bartolist tradition. In that sense, the polemics with Pierre de l'Étoile[30] and Jean Longueval[31] were not so much a symptom of a mere opposition between reactionary bartolists and progressive humanists, but rather an episode reflecting scholarly and personal rivalries within the wider community of more or less committed humanist scholars.

Most of Alciato's work on the text of the Digest, for which he relied partly on Lodovico Bolognino's collation of Angelo Poliziano's study of the *Florentina*, was bound to become obsolete after the 1553 edition of the Florentine manuscript. By then, however, even standard editions of the *Corpus Iuris Civilis* had reflected for more than a generation the transition between the Vulgate and the late-medieval doctrine which had relied on that translation. The transitional period was continued during the second half of the sixteenth century, and later on through so-called antiquarian studies, but by the latter half of the sixteenth century even the new concept of a commentary which Alciato had proposed and started to work out was largely abandoned for still another legal method, which succeeded in merging late-medieval and humanist legal doctrines and scholarship in a more systematic arrangement by subject matter. By the mid-seventeenth century, this new legal literature had replaced much of the late-medieval and sixteenth-century legal works as standard references. The Frankfurt edition of Alciato's *opera omnia* in 1616–17 coincides with the last reprints of the major authorities of the *mos italicus* during the first quarter of the seventeenth century, the relative paucity of new editions of Alciato's legal works after the sixteenth century probably signals that, notwithstanding his reputation as a modernizer of legal science, the interest in his work for early-modern mainstream legal literature and legal practice had faded.

Law and religion

Perhaps around 1518, Alciato addressed in writing an older friend who had joined the Franciscan order and whom Alciato wanted to persuade to return to secular life.[32] This epistle has drawn the attention of historians because of his repeated attempts to prevent its publication, when his career and a hoped-for benefice depended on the support of ecclesiastical authorities. Similar reasons may explain why Alciato's initial sympathies for Lutheran ideas quickly dwindled. According to some sources, he later may even have suggested some anti-Lutheran gibes in his commentaries as a bargaining chip for ecclesiastical preferment.[33] Alciato's religious ideas have often been conveniently dubbed Erasmian, suggesting a critical and reformist, yet loyal, adherence to Roman Catholic doctrines. On the other hand, Alciato's enduring connections with Bonifacius Amerbach and other Basel printers may also reflect his concern to maintain a readership north of the Alps and in the Holy Roman Empire as well as a Protestant audience. The implication is that he would tread cautiously around, or avoid altogether, divisive religious issues.

The address includes several themes of antimonastic literature. The general argument is that monastic orders (and the Franciscan order is particularly targeted) have developed entirely against Christian values and have turned around the original ambitions of the first monks, of Saint Augustine and Saint Benedict, and even of Saint Francis himself. Conversely, Alciato argues to his friend that a committed Christian life as an active member of society has greater value in God's eyes than the unsociable lifestyle of most members of a religious order. Only in a few obiters does Alciato in his address refer to the law. Thus, he criticizes the greed of monks who will sue beyond reason their own benefactors.[34] The most explicit reference to the law, however, occurs when Alciato applies his familiarity with the *Tres Libri* and quotes at length the constitution C.10.32.26 to emphasize that even a Christian emperor like Justinian had included the constitution in his code in order to condemn the solitude and idleness of monks.[35] More important, however, is the passage where Alciato wants to highlight how early Church fathers were well acquainted with classical culture and letters and were therefore able to circumvent the emperor Julian's attempt to weaken Christianity by forbidding (by law: *legem tulit*) Christians to read the original "humane letters."[36] The message, it seems, is that during the early centuries, Christians had been able to strengthen their position and belief by their very familiarity with the style and substance of classical pagan literary and historical sources. That message was clearly a call for a renewal of that proficiency in Alciato's own time.

The primary interest of legal humanism was the secular governance, law, and institutions of pre-Christian Rome and its Greek cultural background. The literary and historical sources were in that respect mainly sought among "pagan" literature. The religion of classical antiquity (in contrast to biblical antiquity) was relevant insofar as it provided background information on legal practices or legal phrases. There was some assumption that the moral code underpinning ancient culture could also assist Christians, although that code had inevitably to be read selectively. Some of Alciato's statements, for instance, may have been inspired by Stoic attitudes. Whether or not his scholarship may be said to belong to a Christian tradition depends primarily, as for most scholars of the civil law tradition, on the direct and above all indirect influences the Christian religion may have had on the anthropology which supported legal thinking. Apart from some fault lines where a tension between religious and secular interests proved irrepressible, civil law scholarship had been able to develop fairly independently from the religious sphere. Canon law was a religious law, and the Church had been keen to extend the province of its jurisdiction, but conflicts of laws and jurisdictions were more general issues which medieval legal science had characteristically tackled as issues of governance.

Imperial legislation from the Christian era of the Roman Empire (especially in the east) constituted an area of mixed jurisdiction. The first book of Justinian's Code contained some clusters of imperial constitutions touching on ecclesiastical governance. Those were precisely some of the titles which Alciato discussed in some of his extracurricular teaching. Apart from offering him an opportunity to apply humanist learning in his comments, however, religion provided rather a cultural and institutional background of his treatment.[37] As in most of his other legal works, more explicit references to religious topics or issues creep in only occasionally and are attended to with the equanimity generations of civil law scholars before Alciato had become used to.

For example, when the issue of usury turns up in his commentary *De verborum significatione* (ad C.50.16.12), Alciato states that if the creditor is no merchant or has not suffered any damage by a belated payment, interest may not be due, "cum usurae hodie omnino sint prohibitae."[38] Similarly, when he comes upon the terms *divortium* and *repudium* while discussing lex 101 of the same title, he observes that "hodie iure pontificio neutrum permittitur, sed solum separatio ex certis causis," with a prohibition to marry again.[39] In the civil law commentaries, Alciato refers often to canon law. In some cases, the reference is about the authority of canon law. Thus, in his comment of C.1.2.11, Alciato points out that Church canons prevail over civil law in spiritual matters; as a subsidiary authority when civil law is silent and canon law provides an explicit rule; and whenever secular laws contradict Christ's law, however slightly.[40] In the comment on D.12.1.1, Alciato discusses a variety of authorities admitted in law, including nonlegal authorities or private opinions. In the same passage, he explains that Greek and Roman authors are sometimes quoted as authorities by civil lawyers, and that canon lawyers may refer to sacred authorities, including the writings of Church fathers whose opinions, when corroborated by both the Old and the New Testaments, should be preferred to any other law, even the pope's.[41] The commentary on *De pactis* offers numerous other opportunities to include references to or comparisons with canon law: the canon law enforcement of a *nudum pactum* is a recurrent topic,[42] as is enforcement of an oath[43] and the sanction of bad-faith parties,[44] emphasizing the concerns of canon law *ratione peccati*. Prescription (*usucapio*), though not a main theme in his commentaries, is another topic on the fault line between civil and canon law,[45] as are the formal requirements for testaments.[46]

Alciato also discusses several of his principal themes in his canon law commentaries. In the context of commentaries *in utroque*, all such remarks were well anchored in the scholarly tradition. Similarly, Alciato very occasionally uses the phrase *Christiani* for establishing a universally valid principle, though in contrast to what non-Christians may profess. In the *Tractatus praesumptionum*, on the presumption of a person's link with his country of origin, he quotes Baldus on one's association with a *patria* and a province, and hence the rule that someone who moves from his place of origin to another place in the same province may retain the residence of his place of origin. Alciato adds: "quod potest esse verum de iure Romanorum, sed de iure Christi, quilibet Christianus nascitur universae Christianitati, ut habetur in Actibus apostolorum, quia omnes in Christo sunt fratres, xii. q. iii. c. ad mensam [*Decr. Grat.* C.11.q.3.c.24]."[47]

Universal brotherhood also appears in his commentary on D.50.16.118, where he discusses the term *hostes*. Referring to the general grant of citizenship in the Roman Empire, he infers that all Christians in his day form the *populus Romanus*: "quo iure exciderunt, qui in Asia, Aphrica'ue, caeterisque provinciis fidem CHRISTI non agnoscunt: hi enim hostes populi Romani sunt, et civitatis Romanae ius amiserunt."[48] The practical effect is that postliminium rules apply in wars against non-Christians, and that prisoners of war belong to their captors. Such principles of the law of war, however, do not apply among Christians.[49] In the commentary on D.50.16.215, Alciato returns to the grant of Roman citizenship to all residents in the empire, which was transferred to all Christians: thus, in Alciato's argument, the French, whose king may not regard himself subordinated to the emperor, are still part of the Roman Empire and live under Roman laws.[50]

French and imperial political interests, however, were not the only factors Alciato had to handle as an itinerant scholar; pontifical political interests also demanded their toll. In a famous *parergon*, he tackled the issue of Constantine's Donation. In that short essay, he bypassed Lorenzo Valla's argument as if the latter's scholarly evidence of a forgery were irrelevant: instead, he points out that the early medieval rulers who had bestowed gifts of cities and territories on the Church had in any event established the pope's claims. He further buttresses that counterargument by a reference to Boniface VIII's ("Pontifex, idem et Iurisconsultus acutissimus": "a pontiff, who was also a most penetrating jurist") theory of the two swords under the pope's authority.[51]

Conclusion

Alciato's niche in legal historiography remains that of a scholar who ensured the breakthrough of humanist scholarship and methods in legal studies. Recent studies may emphasize the extent of the continuity of much of his work with traditional methods and doctrines, and his somewhat conventional and perhaps opportunistic adherence to the Roman Catholic Church and its doctrines by the time he had launched his career as an academic teacher. He certainly did not pursue his early humanist agenda to the point of making *tabula rasa* of late-medieval learning, but he did contribute to bringing down that learning's standing as a paradigm of legal science. At the same time, Alciato's positive assessment of the medieval learning's strength and its significance for the jurisprudence of his time also made him an influential intermediary in the transfer of much of that learning to later, early-modern legal scholarship. Humanist learning was supposed to provide a sounder basis for good governance, but Alciato seems to have realized that the philological and historical quest for authenticity could not replace the unique role of jurisprudence in public governance. For the same reason, the injection of classical studies in legal scholarship by legal humanism did not directly contribute to a large-scale secularization of legal scholarship. Late-medieval political governance was already characterized by a high degree of secular self-sufficiency. Legal humanism contributed to strengthen the neoclassical features of that legal science as an art of governance, as humanist studies in general contributed to give a neoclassical outlook and foundation to the Christian medieval heritage.

Notes

1 "Mihi quidem persuadebit numquam aliquis posse hominem, quantumvis optimum, integrum diem caelestium speculationi incumbere. Fragiles enim humanae

vires sunt et daemonum illusionibus multum obnoxiae" (*Andreae Alciati contra vitam monasticam epistula*, 61).

2 "Illud unum minime reticebo, decessisse Alciatum non (ut in Adagio est) posterioribus melioribus, sed plane deterioribus. Is siquidem postremis aetatis suae annis tanto edendi bibendique desiderio tenebatur, ut nulla ratione adhibita quicquid valde libuisset, idem sibi licere assereret. Quo factum est, ut ea edacitate atque ingluvie non tantum sibi mortem consciuerit, sed et se ita facturum longe pridem statuisse visus sit. Deinde illud gravius, quod è vivis excessurus non mediocriter se a Christiana religione alienum esse indicavit."

(September 20, 1553): Giacomo Mandello, letter to Bonifacius Amerbach, quoted by Jenny, 99, Fn. 85.

3 Biographical information follows the (largely corresponding) entries in *Dizionario biografico degli Italiani*, vol. 2 (1960), 69–77, read on www.treccani.it/enciclopedia/andrea-alciato_(Dizionario-Biografico) and by Belloni and Cortese; Russell (mainly on the *Emblemata*). See also the entry by S. Lepsius in Dauchy, et al., 76–80 (especially on *De verborum significatione libri quatuor*). A recent collection of essays offering a *status quaestionis* on various aspects of Alciato and his work is Rolet and Rolet. For an older monograph, still often referred to, see Viard. The fundamental work of reference is now Belloni, *L'Alciato e il diritto pubblico romano.*

4 In legal studies especially, the progress of legal humanism during the first half of the sixteenth century should not be viewed entirely in opposition to the traditional "Italian" *mos docendi*: see, in the context of Alciato (and providing much information about the backdrop of legal teaching in France and Italy at the time, as well as useful information about the international circle of Alciato's pupils), Belloni, "L'insegnamento giuridico in Italia e in Francia."

5 Legal scholarship and practice converged somehow in the literary enterprise of a Latin play, *Philargyrus*, which contains a critical parody of litigators' dilemmas: Alciato, *Filargiro.*

6 Maclean, "Le séjour d'Alciat à Bourges."

7 Thus at least the version of events reported by Alciato himself in his often-quoted address to the reader preceding his civil law commentaries (*Opera omnia, ed. cit. infra*, III, ante col. 178).

8 On descriptions of Alciato by contemporaries, and his funeral monument, Grünberg-Dröge, 15–16.

9 Much information about Alciato's academic and professional networks, as for other (humanist) contemporaries, may be found in his correspondence and in his correspondents' letters, among whom Bonifacius Amerbach, his former pupil at Avignon and later agent and printer in Basel, stands out; see Barni; also Abbondanza.

10 On the latter episode, Gueudet; this may be supplemented with Penguilly (read on books.openedition).

11 Alciato, *Opera omnia*, V—L. The reprint is based on the edition (in four vols.) of Basel 1557–1558. In this chapter I shall always refer to that reprint. Unfortunately, research facilities at this stage have not yet reached the point where Dr. Osler's demanding (but legitimate) specifications for checking any reference in (at least) as many different editions as possible can be met. See also: Rolet and Rolet, "André-Alciat (1492–1550): quelques repères bio-bibliographiques," in Rolet and Rolet, *André Alciat (1492–1550)*, 33–49. Tung deals with the *Emblemata* only. For a critical survey of the sixteenth-century Lyonese editions of Alciato's work: Mouren.

12 Maclean, "Les premiers ouvrages d'Alciat."

13 A historical reconstruction of the ancient Roman offices was one of Alciato's main interests in some of the extracurricular lectures he gave at Avignon and Bourges.

That interest also matched Alciato's early investigations into the municipal law of Milan under Roman rule. Annalisa Belloni has highlighted those contributions to Roman public law; see, e.g., Belloni, "Contributi dell'Alciat," in which several examples drawn from private Roman law touch in fact on issues of public interest and law. Belloni has now richly documented and further developed that contribution by Alciato in her fundamental monograph: Belloni, *L'Alciato e il diritto pubblico romano* (*cit. supra*)

14 Claire.

15 Osler offers examples of Alciato's at times opportunistic and strategic changes, from one edition to the next, in his proposed readings, whether based on conjectures or textual sources. Throughout the three editions of the *Dispunctiones* published in Alciato's lifetime, Osler observes an increasing cautiousness and conservatism.

16 Méniel.

17 Leveleux-Teixeira and M. Bassano.

18 Drysdall, "A Lawyer's Language Theory," emphasizing Alciato's agenda to retain a specificity of semantics in legal studies.

19 On Alciato's publications of new and older works during his years at Bourges (1529–33), see Maclean, "Le séjour d'Alciat à Bourges," 273–4.

20 Grünberg-Dröge, "The *De singulari certamine liber*"; Grünberg-Dröge provides the political background of the work and its printing history as well as an analysis of the contents of the treatise.

21 Rossi; see also Guerrier.

22 Drysdall, "Alciato and the Grammarians"; Drysdall notes that Alciato also proved adept at intervening in the methods of "grammarians" beyond concerns of legal scholarship. The *Parergon* was dedicated to Alciato's former pupil Otto Truchsess, who later became bishop of Augsburg, and as such a key figure in the opposition to the spread of Protestantism in Bavaria.

23 *Parerga* XII.12 (*Opera omnia*, II, col. 489–94).

24 Barni, "L'attività consulente," records that Alciato's approach to the question was closely associated to the issue of the public interest (*publica utilitas*) of publishing *consilia* (p. 38); Vaccari, "I consulti dell'Alciato"; also Cavina.

25 Mearns, "A Consultation by Andrea Alciato."

26 Osler, "Andreas Alciatus (1492–1550) as philologist"; Osler draws a sharp distinction between humanist philology and modern philology, the former blurring the lines, in Osler's view, between manuscript (i.e., textual) criticism and conjectures. That may be an excessive projection of present-day scholarly standards onto the earlier stages of philological studies. As Osler acknowledges (p. 2), most of Alciato's conjectures (however they may have been construed) were both intelligent and wrong. One may as well envy those early generations of humanists (in the same way as one may envy, *mutatis mutandis*, the first generations of glossators a few centuries earlier) for the intellectual freedom and leeway they enjoyed in considering their canonical texts, unbound by more rigorous methodological strictures. Later methodology may perhaps demand a more authentic reading and interpretation, but a much-needed creativity in legal thinking is lost along the way.

27 The issue has been approached from a different vantage point by Troje, who points out that the more groundbreaking changes in Alciato's works appeared at the beginning of his career, while later commentaries may have been more in line with traditional features. However, the long-term contribution of Alciato would have been to reduce the primary importance of the main *mos italicus* authorities (such as Bartolus and Baldus), and to destroy forever the canonical authority of the textual foundation of legal doctrine.

28 The same sequence of authors is also remembered in the verses Alciato included in his *Parerga* II.42 (*Opera omnia*, II, col. 244).

29 For example, in *Opera omnia*, III, col. 297 (commentary *De in ius vocando*: arguing, however, that the *plenitudo potestatis* is not acknowledged "in our law" (*in iure nostro*); see also *Tractatus de praesumptionibus*, Reg. III, pr. 8 (*Opera omnia*, IV, col. 728 ff.), Reg. III, pr. 11 (col. 739 ff.), Reg. III, pr. 36 (No. 9, col. 795–6). Alciato uses the phrase *potestas absoluta* in the context of the prince's power to grant legitimate status to a bastard (on D.45.2.2, *Opera omnia*, IV, col. 172. Vaccari, "Andrea Alciato e la 'plenitudo potestatis.'"

30 Monheit.

31 *Andreae Alciati iurisconsulti, in Stellam & Longovallium LL. Doctores defensio, Aurelio Albucio autore* (Basileae, In officina Frobeniana, 1529). Jean Longueval had published the year before in Paris *Nova et facilis Declaratio ad l[egem] Imperium. ff. de jurisd[itione] om[nium] judi[cum] & ad multas alias leges.* On Alciato's "allograph," see J. Köhler.

32 References hereafter are to the modern edition by D.L. Drysdall, who provides a *status quaestionis* on the scholarship around this work. See also Enenkel; and Bénévent.

33 See the well-documented narrative by Belloni, "Andrea Alciato fra simpatie luterane," esp. 124–5, on Alciato's commentary *De summa trinitate et fide catholica*. Whereas Alciato's correspondence testifies that he was inclined to nurture favorable opinions on some of Luther's criticism during the years 1520 to 1522, by 1521 he had nevertheless become more cautious and preferred to sit on the fence (by that time, he had been granted the privilege of count palatine): ibid., 118–24. See Barni, "Andrea Alciato giureconsulto milanese."

34 *Contra vitam monasticam epistula*, 55 *infra*. Further on, perhaps not entirely consistently, Alciato argues that his friend's civil law expertise will be of no use to his order (111).

35 *Contra vitam monasticam epistula*, 81 and 83. Alciato had discussed the same text in *Andree Alzati Mediolanensis in tres posteriores Codicis Iustiniani Annotationes* . . . (Strasbourg, 1515), p. 2r.

36 *Contra vitam monasticam epistula*, 113, 115.

37 For example, on C.1.4.5 in his *Dispunctiones* (III.18), on the phrase "Archigerontes," quoting the Gospel of Matthew, correcting Accursius and other jurists, but attacking more particularly the *grammatici*.

38 *Opera omnia*, I, col. 142 ("since interests are nowadays altogether prohibited").

39 *Opera omnia*, I, col. 258–9 ("today, according to pontifical law, neither is allowed, but only a separation on certain grounds"), including brief references to opinions by Saint Ambrose and Erasmus (in the latter's comment on 1 Corinthians). The conclusion appears to be that on such matters, the pope may impose a different rule from the civil law. Both interest and divorce are discussed together in the *Parerga*, VI. 20 ("Defensus Iustinianus, quod divortium permiserit, et tractatum usurarum non aboleverit"), ending with the cautious conclusion "Sed haec Pontificiis Theologisque relinquamur" (*Opera omnia*, II, col. 356–7).

40 *Opera omnia*, III, col. 216 ("Idem in his quae adversus legem Christi peccantur, etiamsi venialiter . . .").

41 *Opera omnia*, III, col. 579. Alciato draws examples of ancient authors from both literature and nonfiction (e.g., medics, historians, philosophers), and, remembering his early research at Milan, he also mentions epigraphic sources.

42 See, e.g., on C.2.3 (*Opera omnia*, III, col. 307: "Hodie tamen iure pontificum ex pacto agi posse receptum est," asking whether the *ratio peccati* and the breach of trust may not be regarded in civil law courts).

43 E.g., on C.2.3.13 (ibid., col. 362: several authors maintain that an action arises if a *nudum pactum* is confirmed by an oath, "idque hodie ita observandum esse, propter ius pontificium, certissimum est: iure enim civili non videtur regulariter ea religione pactum confirmari").

44 E.g., on C.2.3.27 (ibid., col. 422: civil lawyers reject the validity of a waiver of prescription "Sed cum hac in materia hodie ad ius canonicum attendamus, videtur nulli praescriptioni locum esse, cum deficiat bona fides").

45 E.g., on C.2.3.20 (ibid., col. 396, discussing the acquisition of property through prescription; when dealing with a long period, but mala fide possession, ownership is said not be transferred, but the possessor may have a defense; however, "iure autem pontificum nec exceptio quidem conceditur, idque propter eius delictum, qui malae est fidei").

46 E.g., on C.1.2.13 (ibid., col. 222, on the validity of a testament witnessed by two persons in canon law; Alciato's discussion here seeks a justification in the Gospel: "Ego crediderim secundum Evangelicam regulam illud intelligendum, ut videlicet in foro conscientiae compellatur unusquisque ad observationem huiuscemodi voluntatis, si de intentione testatoria sit certus. . . . His accedit, quod et regula Evangelica (qua ratione canon nititur) proprie ad conscientiae forum refertur: nec enim verisimile est Christum de iudiciariis strophis loquutum").

47 *Opera omnia*, IV, *Tractatus praesumptionum*, Reg. 137, col. 644 ("which may be true according to the law of the Romans, but according to the law of Christ, any Christian is born to the whole church, as it says in the Acts of the Apostles, because all are brethren in Christ").

48 "from which are excluded by law those in Asia, or Africa, or in other regions, who do not uphold the faith in CHRIST: those are indeed enemies of the Roman people, and have lost the right of Roman citizenship".

49 *Opera omnia*, I, Commentary *De verborum et rerum significatione*, col. 274: the words are almost verbatim the same ("cum enim ex lege CHRISTI omnes sint fratres"), including the reference to the *Concordia*. On Alciato's indebtness to Bartolus with regard to the law of war, see Mearns, "The influence of Bartolus de Sassoferrato," esp. at 24 on the issue of *postliminium*.

50 *Opera omnia*, I, Commentary *De verborum et rerum significatione*, col. 400.

51 *Opera omnia*, II, *Parerga*, VII.19, col. 380–1.

Bibliography

Abbondanza, Roberto. "Alciato (Alciati), Andrea." In *Dizionario biografico degli Italiani*. Vol. 2, 69–77. Roma: Istituto della Enciclopedia Italiana, 1960. Available at www.treccani.it/enciclopedia/andrea-alciato_%28Dizionario-Biografico%29/

Abbondanza, Roberto. "A proposito dell'epistolario dell'Alciato." *Annali di Storia del Diritto, Rassegna internazionale* 1 (1957): 467–500.

Alciato, Andreas. *Andreae Alciati contra vitam monasticam epistula. Andrea Alciato's letter against monastic life. Critical Edition, Translation and Commentary by Denis L. Drysdall.* Leuven: Leuven University Press, 2014.

Alciato, Andrea. *Filargiro. Commedia.* Latin text edition and Italian translation by Raffaele Ruggiero; introduction by Giovanni Rossi. Torino: Nino Aragno Editore, 2017.

Alciato, Andreas. *Opera Omnia von Andreas Alciato, mit einer Einleitung von Dr. Iur. Jochen Otto.* Ius Commune, Rechtstradition der Europäischen Länder, Legistische Literatur, 2. Frankfurt am Main: Vico Verlag, 2004.

Alciato, Andreas. *Responsa nunquam antehac excusa, ediert von Franciscus Alciatus.* Ius Commune, Rechtstradition der Europäischen Länder, Forensische Jurisprudenz, 1. Frankfurt am Main: Vico Verlag, 2005.

Barni, Gian Luigi. "Andrea Alciato giureconsulto milanese e l'idea della riforma protestante." *Rivista di Storia del Diritto Italiano* 21 (1948): 161–209.

Barni, Gian Luigi. "L'attività consulente dei giureconsulti in un'opinione di Andrea Alciato." In *Studi in onore di Carlo Castiglioni Prefetto dell'Ambrosiana*, 33–45. Milan: Giuffrè, 1957.

Barni, Gian Luigi. *Le lettere di Andrea Alciato Giureconsulto.* Firenze: Felice Le Monnier, 1953.

Belloni, Annalisa. *L'Alciato e il diritto pubblico romano, I Vat. Lat. 6216, 6271, 7071.* 2 vols. Città del Vaticano: Biblioteca Apostolica Vaticana, 2016.

Belloni, Annalisa. "Andrea Alciato fra simpatie luterane e opportunismo politico." In *Margarita amicorum. Studi di cultura europea per Agostino Sottili*, edited by F. Forner, C.M. Monti, and P.G. Schmidt. Vol. 1, 117–43. Milano: Vita e Pensiero, 2005.

Belloni, Annalisa. "Contributi dell'Alciat all'interpretazione del diritto romano e alla sua storia." In *I classici e l'università umanistica*, edited by L. Gargan and M.P. Mussini Sacchi, 111–60. Messina: Centro Interdipartimentale di Studi Umanistici, 2006.

Belloni, Annalisa. "L'insegnamento giuridico in Italia e in Francia nei primi decenni del Cinquecento e l'emigrazione di Andrea Alciato." In *Università in Europa. Le istituzioni universitarie dal Medio Evo ai nostri giorni. Strutture, organizzazione, funzionamento. Atti del Convegno Internazionale di Studi Milazzo 28 Settembre—2 Ottobre 1993*, edited by Andrea Romano, 137–58. Soveria Mannelli: Rubbettino, 1995.

Belloni, Annalisa, and Ennio Cortese. "Alciato (Alciati), Andrea." In *Dizionario biografico dei Giuristi Italiani (XII–XX secolo)*, edited by Italo Birocchi, Ennio Cortese, Antonello Mattone, and Marco Nicola Miletti. Vol. 1, 29–32. Bologna: Società Editrice Il Mulino, 2013.

Bénévent, Christine. "Erasme, Alciat et le contra uitam monasticham." In Rolet and Rolet, *André Alciat (1492–1550)*, 225–40.

Cavina, Marco. "Indagini intorno al 'mos repondendi' di Andrea Alciato." *Rivista di Storia del Diritto Italiano* 57 (1984): 207–51.

Claire, Lucie. "Les *In Cornelium Tacitum annotationes* d'André Alciat." In Rolet and Rolet, *André Alciat (1492–1550)*, 85–96.

Daly, Peter M., Daniel S. Russell, and John Manning, eds. *Emblematica: An Interdisciplinary Journal for Emblem Studies* 9/2 (1995) [special issue: *Alciato's Emblems and Their Context*]: 239–400.

Dauchy, Serge, et al. *The Formation and Transmission of Western Legal Culture: 150 Books That Made the Law in the Age of Printing.* Studies in the History of Law and Justice 7. Cham: Springer Verlag, 2016.

Drysdall, Denis L. "Alciato and the Grammarians: The Law and the Humanities in the Parergon iuris libri duodecim." *Renaissance Quartely* 56/3 (2003): 695–722.

Drysdall, Denis L. *Hieroglyphs, Speaking Pictures, and the Law: The Context of Alciato's Emblems.* Glasgow: Glasgow Emblem Studies, 2013.

Drysdall, Denis L. "A Lawyer's Language Theory: Alciato's *De verborum significatione.*" *Emblematica: An Interdisciplinary Journal for Emblem Studies* 9/2 (1995): 269–92.

Enenkel, Karl A.E. "Alciato's Ideas on the Religious: The Letter to Bernardus Mattius." *Emblematica, An Interdisciplinary Journal for Emblem Studies* 9/2 (1995): 293–313.

Geonget, Stéphan, ed. *Bourges à la Renaissance, hommes de lettres, hommes de lois.* Paris: Klincksieck, 2011.

Grünberg-Dröge, Monika. *500 Jahre Andreas Alciatus (1492–1550). Jurist, Humanist, Emblematiker. Eine Ausstellung aus Beständen der Universitätsbibliothek Bonn, des Instituts für Römisches Recht und des Kunsthistorischen Instituts der Universität Bonn, Mai-August 1992.* Bonn: Rheinische Friedrich-Wilhelms Universität Bonn, 1992.

Grünberg-Dröge, Monika. "The *De singulari certamine liber* in the Context of Its Time." *Emblematica: An Interdisciplinary Journal for Emblem Studies* 9/2 (1995): 315–41.

Guerrier, Olivier. "Fantaisies et fictions juridiques dans les *Parerga*." In Rolet and Rolet, *André Alciat (1492–1550)*, 165–76.

Gueudet, Guy. "Une lettre inédite de Budé à Alciat." *Moreana, Bulletin Thomas More* 19–20 (1968): 70–90.

Jenny, Beat Rudolf. "Andrea Alciato e Bonifacio Amerbach: nascita, culmine e declino di un'amicizia fra giureconsulti." *Andrea Alciato, umanista europeo. Periodico della Società Storica Comense* 61 (2000): 83–99.

Köhler, Johannes. "Alciato's Shadow: Aurelio Albucio." *Emblematica: An Interdisciplinary Journal for Emblem Studies* 9/2 (1995): 343–67.

Leveleux-Teixeira, Corinne, and Bassano, Marie. "Alciat, le *De verborum significatione* et la morphologie du droit." In Geonget, *Bourges à la Renaissance*, 283–309.

Maclean, Ian. "Le séjour d'Alciat à Bourges, vu à travers sa correspondance et ses préfaces berruyères." In Geonget, *Bourges à la Renaissance*, 263–81.

Maclean, Ian. "Les premiers ouvrages d'Alciat: les *Annotationes in tres posteriores Codicis Iustiniani*, et l'*Opusculum quo graecae dictiones fere ubique in Digestis restituuntur* (1515)." In Rolet and Rolet, *André Alciat (1492–1550)*, 73–84.

Mearns, James. "A Consultation by Andrea Alciato on the Laws of War." *Tijdschrift voor Rechtsgeschiedenis* 82 (2014): 100–40.

Mearns, James. "The Influence of Bartolus de Sassoferrato on Andrea Alciato's Discussion of a Legal War." *Studi Umanistici Piceni* 34 (2014): 1–26.

Méniel, Bruno. "La sémantique d'un juriste: la réflexion d'André Alciat sur le titre *De uerborum significatione*." In Rolet and Rolet, *André Alciat (1492–1550)*, 131–44.

Monheit, Michael L. "Guillaume Budé, Andrea Alciato, Pierre de l'Estoile Renaissance Interpreters of Roman Law." *Journal of the History of Ideas* 58 (1997): 21–40.

Mouren, Raphaële. "André Alciat et les imprimeurs lyonnais." In Rolet and Rolet, *André Alciat (1492–1550)*, 257–92.

Osler, Douglas J. "Andreas Alciatus (1492–1550) as Philologist." In *A Ennio Cortese*, edited by D. Maffei, et al. Vol. 3, 1–7. Rome: Il Signo Galileo Galilei, 2001.

Osler, Douglas J. "Developments in the Text of Alciatus' *Dispunctiones*, *Ius commune*." *Zeitschrift für Europäische Rechtsgeschichte* 19 (1992): 219–35.

Penguilly, Thomas. "Le juriste et le philologue. Enjeux des rivalités entre André Alciat et Guillaume Budé à travers leurs correspondances." In *Conflits et polémiques dans l'épistolaire*, edited by E. Gavoille and F. Guillaumont, 467–83. Tours: Presses Universitaires François Rabelais, 2015.

Rolet, Anne, and Stéphane Rolet, eds. *André Alciat (1492–1550), un humaniste au confluent des savoirs dans l'Europe de la Renaissance*. Turnhout: Brepols, 2013.

Rossi, Giovanni. "Alciato, Andrea." In *Enciclopedia italiana. Il contributo italiano alla storia del pensiero. Ottava appendice*. Roma: Istituto della Enciclopedia Italiana, 2012. Available at www.treccani.it/enciclopedia/andrea-alciato_%28Il-Contributo-italiano-alla-storia-del-Pensiero:-Diritto%29/

Rossi, Giovanni. "La lezione metodologica di Andrea Alciato: filologia, storia e diritto nei *Parerga*." In Rolet and Rolet, *André Alciat (1492–1550)*, 145–64.

Russell, Daniel S. "Alciato (Andrea) (1492–1550)." In *Centuriæ Latinæ. Cent une figures humanistes de la Renaissance aux Lumières offertes à Jacques Chomarat*, edited by Colette Nativel. Vol. 1, 51–5. Genève: Droz, 1997.

Troje, Hans Erich. "Alciats Methode der Kommentierung des 'Corpus iuris civilis'." In *Der Kommentar in der Renaissance*, edited by A. Bück and O. Herding, 47–61. DFG Kommission für Humanismusforschung, Mitteilung 1. Bonn/Bad Godesberg: Deutsche Forschungsgemeinschaft, 1975.

Tung, Mason. "Towards a New Census of Alciati's Editions: A Research Report That Solicits Help from the Scholarly Community and Curators of Rare Books and Special Collections." *Emblematica* 4/1 (1989): 135–76.

Vaccari, Pietro. "Andrea Alciato e la 'plenitudo potestatis' del principe." *Rivista di Storia del Diritto Italiano* 24 (1951): 161–4.

Vaccari, Pietro. "I consulti dell'Alciato." *Rendiconti dell'Istituto Lombardo di Scienze e Lettere* 84 (1951): 84–92.

Viard, Paul. *André Alciat 1492–1550.* Paris: Recueil Sirey, 1926.

15 Robert Bellarmine (1542–1621)

Lorenzo Sinisi

Biographical introduction

Of all the emblematic figures of the Roman Catholic Church during the Counter-Reformation, Robert Bellarmine is without a doubt among the most noteworthy. He is considered the most strenuous defender of Catholic orthodoxy against the doctrines of the reformers, and the primary controversialist theologian.

Bellarmine (christened Roberto Bellarmino but known in the English-speaking world by his Anglicized name) was born in Montepulciano, in the territory of Siena, on October 4, 1542. His parents were Vincenzo, from a noble but impoverished family, and Cinzia Cervini, a deeply religious woman and the sister of Marcello, an important figure in the ecclesiastic-humanist realm, who became a leading character at the Council of Trent and was elected pope in 1555, serving under the name of Marcellus II for only twenty-two days until his death.[1] The influence of Bellarmine's mother and his uncle's example were the basis of the young Bellarmine's early religious vocation, which, in contrast to his father's wishes for him to become a doctor, led to his entrance into the Society of Jesus in 1560. This step coincided with the start of his education at the Collegio Romano, where he attended philosophical courses under important professors, including Francisco de Toledo, Pedro Parra, and Benito Pereyra. In 1563 Bellarmine earned the title of *magister*, and in 1581, at a more mature age and for purely formal reasons, he added the title of *doctor theologiae*.[2] This gap in academic milestones occurred because he was unable to complete his later studies regularly owing to poor health and to the demands on his time as an extraordinarily talented and sought-after preacher and teacher.

From 1564 to 1569, living in Florence, Mondovì, and Padua, young Father Bellarmine gained a reputation as a "a master and disciple of himself," leveraging his natural and uncommon talent for deep comprehension, meditation, and rapid memorization of an ample quantity of texts, in particular patristic and scholastic texts, which were the foundations of his lessons. With his in-depth humanistic body of knowledge and solid preparation in the sacred sciences, he could fully demonstrate his oratorical and didactic skills in Louvain, the farthest Catholic outpost in northern Europe, where the Reformation had already made its mark. Once he arrived in Flanders with an assignment as a preacher, he was ordained as a priest and taught scholastic theology, in which he became an expert. He also studied in-depth the doctrines of Luther, Calvin, and the other reformers for the purpose of being better able to debate their ideas and demonstrate their faults. This newly acquired skill, together with his profound knowledge of patristics and ecclesiastical history, were the foundations for his appointment in 1576 in Italy as a teacher of controversial theology at the same Collegio Romano where he had studied.[3]

During his twelve years of teaching theology, Bellarmine on the one hand acquired authority and prestige as a strenuous defender of orthodox Catholicism and enjoyed significant success among his students, to whom he provided more effective weapons for combating heresy. On the other hand, he laid the foundations for drafting his "magnum opus", the *Disputationes de controversiis*, published for the first time between 1586 and 1593, and acknowledged from a theological perspective as the most representative work of the Counter-Reformation.

Despite his abandoning of the classroom in 1588, the fame and prestige he had acquired through teaching led this gifted Jesuit priest to take on even more commitments: in addition to his studies, which he never strayed from, he was often involved as a consultant for various committees in the Holy See and for the pope on various political and doctrinal issues. After serving as the theological consultant for cardinal Caetani in a delicate diplomatic mission to France, which was heavily impacted by religious wars, Bellarmine was named on his return to be the rector of the Collegio Romano and the provincial of the Jesuit Order in Naples. Once back in Rome, in light of his skill as a theologian, he became a member of the Sacred Congregation of the Index (1587) and ten years later a member of the Holy Office. Chosen by pope Clement VIII as his most trusted theological consultant, the fifty-year-old Bellarmine brilliantly fulfilled Clement's assignment to draft an official catechism in vernacular for teaching and learning the Christian doctrine. This work successfully accompanied *Cathechismus ad parochos* by Pius V and was translated into many European and non-European languages.

In 1599, despite some reluctance, Bellarmine accepted the red hat to become the second Jesuit cardinal, after his former professor Francisco de Toledo. In his role as cardinal, Bellarmine participated in the congregation instituted by the pope to resolve a bitter theological dispute between the Jesuits and Dominicans about the relationship between divine grace and free will. Probably due to a contrast with the pope, in 1602 Bellarmine was sent as a pastor to the archdiocese of Capua, where he resided for three years and gained notice for his scrupulous implementation of the decrees of the Council of Trent. He was recalled to Rome by the new pope, Paul V, and dealt in rapid succession with some very sensitive issues, including the defense of the position of the Holy See in the "trouble" with the Republic of Venice (1606–07), and therefore also in the violent doctrinal diatribe with King James I of England regarding the power of the pope over temporal matters (1608–10). Despite age and poor health, he spent the last decade of his life studying and writing theological-ascetic works and continuing to serve the Church and the pope.

Known for his irreproachable morality and modest, frugal lifestyle, cardinal Bellarmine passed away, famous for his sanctity, on September 17, 1621, on the threshold of eighty. Even though the canonical process for the recognition of sainthood was initiated early, it was strenuously objected to and only reached its conclusion in 1930 with his canonization seven years after beatification. He was proclaimed a doctor of the Church in 1931

An overview of Bellarmine's works

Reviewing a well-known bibliography of writers belonging to the Society of Jesus makes immediately evident the extensive quantity and variety of the works that Robert Bellarmine produced, even though he was often forced to be apart from his beloved studies to fulfill important roles in service to the Church.[4] Long ago an attempt was made to classify this large quantity of works into distinct groups according to type and subject. The groups include "controversial works," such as the *Disputationes de controversiis Christianae Fidei adversus huius temporis haereticos*; the more in-depth analyses of subjects he previously studied or barely touched-upon elsewhere, such as the *De exemptione clericorum* (1599) or *De indulgentiis et Iubilaeo* (1599); and strenuous defenses of the Holy See against specific attacks during the first decade of the seventeenth century, such as the *Risposta al trattato dei sette teologi di Venetia sopra l'Interdetto* (1606) and the *Tractatus de potestate Summi Pontificis in rebus temporalibus adversus Guliemum Barclaium* (1610). There are also "exegetical and catechetical works" like the *In omnes Psalmos dilucida expositio* (1611) and the *Copiosa dichiaratione della dottrina cristiana* (1598), and finally "spiritual and ascetical works," especially from the last stage of his writings, including, *De ascensione mentis in Deum* (1615), *De aeterna felicitate sanctorum* (1616), and *De arte bene moriendi* (1620).[5]

Among these works and many others are no specifically legal-canonical texts because, of course, Bellarmine was essentially a theologian. Nevertheless, just as he dedicated most of his intellectual energy to learning theology, in which he was essentially self-taught, some of his works and a passage from his autobiography can lead one to deduce that he also was largely self-taught in canon law, a subject on which he accumulated a solid body of knowledge while reading on his own "almost the whole *corpus canonicum*."[6]

The interdependence of these two sacred sciences was so strong that no good canonist could do without sufficient preparation in the theological field (even more so then than now), just as no good theologian could do without adequate knowledge of canon law. In the specific case of Bellarmine, one should note that through many of his works he was able to offer significant contributions to the development of canon law doctrine in several subjects, the first of which concerns the constitution of the Church and the discipline governing relationships between the Church and the State.[7]

Leaving the *Controversiae* and issues related to ecclesiology aside until later sections of this chapter, it is evident how a certain familiarity with the use of legal texts, not only of canon law, emerges among the works in *De indulgentiis et*

Iubilaeo. Written at the specific request of the pope for the upcoming Jubilee of 1600, the work presented an issue defined by Bellarmine himself in the preface as "the very first of all controversies of our time," clearly alluding to one of the main themes of the Lutheran theses of 1517; the editor's rush to publish his larger work, where it should have appeared, resulted in the later publication *De indulgentiis* as a freestanding work.[8]

In contrast to the writing style prevalent in *Controversiae*, Bellarmine dedicated only the second part of *De indulgentiis* to a rebuttal of the doctrines of the reformers. The first part he developed as an essay, similar in format to legal treatises, beginning with the original meanings of the words "indulgences" and "jubilee," then moving on to their contemporary definitions and a treatment of themes these institutions were based on. These themes included the spiritual wealth of the Church owing to the merit of Christ and the saints, and the power of the pope and bishops to distribute this wealth by means of indulgences for the salvation of the souls of penitents. Bellarmine reflects on the nature of indulgences, their usefulness, the various types practiced in the Church, the sensitive theme of how the indulgences are achieved, and their applicability "by suffrage" on behalf of the dead. By dealing with the themes in this first section, the Jesuit theologian demonstrates his total familiarity not only with the *ius decretalium*, represented by the numerous legislative measures of the popes issued up to that time, but also with the doctrine of the "interpreters of canon law," represented above all by Giovanni d'Andrea, Panormitanus, and Martin Azpilcueta. These *auctoritates* meld with those of patristic and scholastic theology to substantiate a natural reciprocal integration between canon law and theology. This integration cannot be omitted in such a complex subject as indulgences, for which Bellarmine provided a contribution that would remain significant up to the mid-twentieth century.

A similar methodology, though applied to a different kind of work, can be found in a controversial response Bellarmine wrote after he had been appointed cardinal. Paolo Sarpi and six other theologians had published an essay defending the positions of the Republic of Venice in a bitter dispute with the Holy See over ecclesiastical immunity. Arising around 1606, the dispute culminated in the proclamation by Pope Paul V of an interdict sanction against the Republic.[9] In his preface, the new cardinal dismantled the foundations of his adversaries' essay with lawyer-like finesse, demonstrating that the authors had not even made a minimal effort to prove the injustice of the pope's order they were lamenting, and therefore were not vested with a principal duty clearly stated by the well-known Roman law maxim, "the burden of proof lies on the accuser";[10] he then goes on to refute one by one the nineteen propositions offered by the Venetians in support of their theses. He demonstrates from the start his expert knowledge of canon law sources (from both a legal and a doctrinal standpoint), of theological texts (both patristic and scholastic), and of ecclesiastical history.

An example of his approach is his response to his adversaries' first proposition, which asserts the inefficacy of the pope's interdict because it was not published. Bellarmine, after recognizing that Roman and canon law sources (which he specifically cites, in contrast to his adversaries) support the need for publication of a law for it to be enacted and observed; he then demonstrates, citing Giovanni d'Andrea and Panormitanus in addition to the *ius decretalium*, that in this case the publication occurred via solemn posting of the order in the usual venues in Rome, a formality that traditionally also triggered the wider spread of the news of its having been issued. Bellarmine offers as authoritative examples the decrees of the Council of Trent, which he claims "obligate all of Christianity, solely with publication in Rome by Pope Pius IV." The nonobservance of these decrees in some places was owing to obstacles interposed by political power, obstacles that have little effect on an order that establishes a spiritual penalty like an interdict.

Continuing to concentrate more specifically on observance of the interdict by the ecclesiastics under Venetian dominion when faced with the dilemma of whether to obey the pope or the "secular prince," Bellarmine concludes that those who "obey the temporal prince instead of the spiritual prince in merely spiritual matters demonstrate that they believe that the supreme leader of the Church is the temporal prince, whose belief coincides with the heresy of Henry VIII of England."[11] Thanks also to the contribution of the scholarly cardinal, who took a firm stance on doctrine while nevertheless favoring a peaceful solution to the dispute through diplomacy, the two sides reached an agreement after about a year. Bellarmine thus helped avert a much more serious threat with respect to the reshaping of ecclesiastical immunity, represented by a new schism that would have had disastrous consequences for the Italian context.

The *Disputationes de controversiis adversus huius temporis haereticos*: genesis, characteristics, and contents

As previously mentioned, the most important and far-reaching work by Bellarmine is *Disputationes de controversiis*, which saw the light for the first time in Ingolstadt, the stronghold of Catholicism in Bavaria, from 1586 to 1593. What was probably one of the best and most complete systematic expositions of Catholic doctrine—achieved through a close dialectic confrontation with the ideas of the reformers, criticizing and refuting them without excessively aggressive controversy but by use of the immense wealth of doctrine of the Roman Catholic Church—was a long time in coming. If the early origins of this work were identified in his preaching activity in a frontier land like Louvain, when he first came into close contact with the Protestant world, his scrupulous research and redrafting for the preparation of his lectures while holding the chair of controversial theology at the Collegio Romano from 1576 to 1588 were the foundations of this work. His fear of unauthorized publication of his teachings, which were circulated as manuscripts because of the great admiration of his students, induced Bellarmine to prepare an edition for publishing, which was immediately destined for great success. The overriding reason for this success, which would have an impact not only on Catholics but also on Protestants, was Bellarmine's wealth of doctrine, his clear presentation, his forgoing of a violent, offensive style in examining the positions of his adversaries, and above all his original and functional systematic approach.

The first edition was published in three volumes. The first concentrates initially on sources of divine revelation and on Christ, the Incarnate Word and the head of the Church, then moves on to the figure and prerogative of the Church's vicar, the supreme pontiff and successor to the Apostle Peter. The first volume thus takes into consideration the Church in its hierarchical construction and triple manifestation as "militant," "suffering," and "triumphant." The second volume is dedicated to the sacraments, and the third to sensitive topics ranging from grace to justification. From this monumental work, the success of which gave way to several more editions up to the latter half of the nineteenth century, this chapter focuses on the themes presented for the most part in the first volume, in which Bellarmine reflected on the Church and its prerogatives with respect to secular power, while also offering an important contribution in canon law.

Major themes and contributions: the definition of Tridentine ecclesiology

The main theme of all of Bellarmine's ecclesiology, which was destined to become a longstanding doctrine of reference on the constitution of the Church, is without a doubt represented by the figure and prerogative of the Roman pontiff, to whom the third *Controversia generalis* in the first volume of *Disputationes* is dedicated. What stands out in this *Controversia*, which for its size and systematic approach resembles an authentic monographic treatise, is that Bellarmine starts off from afar, unfolding his exposition with a reflection about which of the three classic forms of governance—monarchy, aristocracy, and democracy—could be the best and therefore the form chosen by Christ for his Church. His response to this question, in the wake of great Dominican theologians like St. Thomas Aquinas and Juan de Torquemada, is that the system of governance established by God for the Church is a "mixed" form of a "tempered" monarchy with the addition of some aristocratic and democratic elements.[12] Once he identifies this "regime," he moves on to identifying the "highest president and priest" of the Church as the Roman pontiff, the successor of the Apostle Peter and by divine institution the visible head of the Church and vicar of Christ. It is therefore the pope—the true ecclesiastical monarch at the apex of the hierarchical-pyramid structure of the Church—who possesses the prerogatives of total apostolic power over the world, supremacy over all bishops (well demonstrated in the right to receive appeals "from all parts of the Christian realm" and in the fact that the pope cannot be judged by anyone on earth), and above all the charisma of infallibility, considering that "when he proposes teachings on faith to the Church he cannot in any way be in error."[13]

The affirmation that the pope is the head of the "militant Church," namely the Church that exists and struggles on earth to save as many souls as possible, does not exempt Bellarmine from reaffirming the doctrine of the absolute supremacy of the sovereign pontiff over the ecumenical council and rejecting the heretical and conciliarist theses, in his usual stringent and articulated manner covering the various opinions on these topics. The reflection on the councils, regarding not only general ones but also the more particular and not less necessary councils "to the good governance of the Church," precedes his reflection on the Church overall, where he provides a definition of the Church which was destined to be taken up in canon law manuals until at least the mid-twentieth century: for Bellarmine the Church is nothing more than "a society composed of persons united with one another in the sole and identical profession of Christian faith and communion of the sacraments under the jurisdiction of legitimate pastors, and mainly the Roman pontiff, the only vicar of Christ on earth."[14] This "perfect society" was represented since the apostolic era as a body whose head is united to all of its members, including clerics, monks, and laypersons. Bellarmine takes inspiration from this image to delineate the hierarchy that characterizes the clerical order, obedient to the pontiff, as guardians and upholders of the truths of the faith and responsible for their transmission to laypersons, not yet acknowledged as subjects with any active function within the life of the Church. But since clerics and laypersons are also citizens of a temporal State, Bellarmine takes this occasion to reflect on the origins of political power and the need of every entity that exercises it to be governed by laws. If, as the scriptures and the holy fathers teach, the origin of all political power must necessarily be traced back to God, the creator of humanity and nature and therefore also the source of natural law, by which the State exercises its power, the consent of the people is necessary for the selection of a form of governament, which can also be changed for legitimate cause by the will of the people.[15] This concept, according to which it is therefore possible to "pass from a monarchial government to an aristocratic or democratic government and vice versa," can be viewed with some foundation as a preconception of the principle of popular sovereignty which lies at the basis of modern democracies.[16]

An intermediate solution for governing the relationships between the Church and the State: the *potestas indirecta in temporalibus*

The start of the sixteenth century brought not only the consolidation of western Europe into the first modern nation-states ruled by absolute monarchies but also the affirmation of the Protestant Reformation, which put an end to the religious unity that had reigned through the Middle Ages as "Respublica Christianorum." These developments spawned a conflict between two doctrines with opposing views of the power of the Church in temporal affairs. On one hand was the medieval doctrine of *plenitudo potestatis* of the Roman pontiff, who—as the indisputable head of the Church according to divine law—had supreme power over the entire world in both political and ecclesiastical matters. On the other hand was the doctrine, reinforced by the political and religious reforms of the era, that tended to refuse the pontiff and the Church any power over temporal matters.

In light of this conflict, and aware of the anachronism of the doctrine of total power of the pope in spiritual and temporal matters, Bellarmine drafted (especially in the wake of works by Juan de Torquemada and Francisco de Vitoria) an intermediate solution. According to his doctrine, the pope, by divine institution, would have no direct power over temporal matters outside of his state territories; temporal matters instead would be the responsibility of secular rulers. But as the bearer of unlimited and universal power in the spiritual sector, indisputably far superior to the temporal sector, the pope could take exception and extend his power indirectly, especially if spiritual matters of absolute importance were under threat. As an example, Bellarmine stated that, on the basis of indirect power over temporal matters, the vicar of Christ could intervene in the internal affairs of states and even depose a ruler and nominate a replacement "if this was necessary for the salvation of souls." This position is especially significant in view of Bellarmine's reflection on laws, which he often considered to be tools for implementing policies hostile to the Church and to its primary mission from Christ: if "the pope cannot ordinarily establish a civil law, or confirm or invalidate the laws of secular princes," nevertheless, even though his principality is not of a political nature, he can "do everything necessary if a secular law is required for the salvation of souls and the kings do not want to establish it, or in the case that another law is harmful to the saving of souls and the kings do not want to abolish it."[17] Interestingly, Bellarmine backs up these affirmations with clearly legal concepts and makes specific reference to authoritative legal sources of both canon and Roman law, once again demonstrating his familiarity with the world of *utrumque ius*.[18]

This doctrine, which Bellarmine conceived of in Louvain around 1570, then developed fully during his Roman teaching period and published for the first time in 1586, would soon need defending from violent attacks from different sources. The first, particularly intense and harmful, came from the reigning Roman pontiff, Sixtus V, who, advocating the total power of the pope over temporal affairs, intended to insert the entire volume into the Index of Forbidden Books, exposing the reputation of one of the most important consultants of the Congregation of the Index to grave danger.[19] The unexpected death of the pope in 1590 squelched this threat, but opposition from those on the other side, who insisted on the absolute reign of the State and negated any say of the pope in temporal affairs, was just as arduous. This was especially true of King James I of England, who, through controversial writings and policies aimed at affirming his own divine right of supremacy over his subjects, including with regard to religion, disputed any power of the pope over temporal matters. James arrived at the point of forcing Catholics to swear their allegiance to the English crown and renounce their faith in the prerogatives of the pope.[20]

Even more important than Bellarmine's controversial writings against the English king, in which he defended his theory of indirect power, it is necessary to mention the essay by which the cardinal refuted his adversaries' theses point by point. These theses were then presented in a work by the Scottish jurist William Barclay, a Catholic who immigrated to France and adhered to Gallican theories. In his treatise commissioned by Pope Paul V, even more than in the *Controversia de Romano Pontifice*, Bellarmine relies heavily on legal doctrine to support the theory of the pope's power to depose rulers where it is necessary to defend a superior spiritual good. Here Bellarmine demonstrates an in-depth knowledge of the juridical literature of both canon and Roman law, not only in Italian sources but also in Spanish, French, and German.[21] For example, he quotes the French civil lawyer Jean Faure, according to whom it was legitimate for the pope to intervene in temporal affairs when "the saving of souls and the people" was in play; in these cases he "can and should act and if necessary even depose any king," even though both in the mind of the fourteenth-century French jurist and in that of Bellarmine, this was considered a totally exceptional event.[22]

Despite hostility from Protestants as well as from Catholics supporters of absolute regalism or papal theocracy, Bellarmine's doctrine later became dominant and remained so until only a few decades ago as the doctrine on which the Church stood in its dealings with modern nations.[23]

The inseparability between the matrimonial contract and the sacrament

Bellarmine's intervention with regard to holy matrimony was also significant, in particular his views on the separability or inseparability between the matrimonial contract and the sacrament.

Thanks to St. Thomas, who identified consent as the efficient cause of matrimony, the principle of identity between the contract and the sacrament was already affirmed in the thirteenth century and widely agreed upon among theologians. Nevertheless, dissenting opinions subsequently emerged that would be resumed in the work of an important Dominican theologian, Melchior Cano, published posthumously in Salamanca in 1563. His opinions were not based on knowledge of the Tridentine canons, which made pronouncements on matrimony only three years after his death. In fact he supported the idea that not every legitimately contracted marriage between Christians was also a sacrament, but only those celebrated with the solemn words by a sacred minister. The words with which the spouses express their consent were therefore only the basis of the matrimonial contract; those spouses were ministers only of the contract and certainly not of the sacrament, whose minister was the priest called upon to preside over the rite of marriage.[24]

The authority of Cano and the fact that the Tridentine canons had not specifically made pronouncements on the relationship between the contract and the sacrament in matrimony created a situation of uncertainty, which could be overcome only thanks to Bellarmine, who intervened in the question in the second volume of his *Disputationes de controversiis*. Starting from a strong affirmation of the Tridentine dogma of the sacramentality of marriage in response to various contrary Protestant texts, he demonstrated to his Catholic adversaries that the sacramentality of marriage involved all the methods for implementing the marriage contract between baptized Christians, which was therefore inseparable from the sacrament.[25] In Catholic marriage, therefore, the contract and the sacrament are inseparable, the origin of this concept being the central idea of Bellarmine's view of matrimony, namely, the elevation of the contract to sacrament through the hand of Christ.[26] It is worth noting that in this essay, as in the rest of the second volume, the cited sources are almost exclusively theological, a choice that Bellarmine explained as follows: "in all that involves divine law, like the sacraments, more trust must be placed in theologians, who are the true experts in divine law, as opposed to canonists, who focus mainly on human laws."[27]

Bellarmine's theory according to which the matrimonial contract and sacrament are absolutely inseparable was greeted by rapid, widespread appreciation and made a significant contribution to reformulating and almost eliminating the controversies in this area. Adopted by the most important matrimonial doctrinal statements, beginning with the *De sancto Matrimonii sacramento* by Thomas Sanchez (1602), this theory was also implemented in papal teachings over the course of the nineteenth century and encoded into canon 1012 §. 2 of the *Codex* of 1917 as the official theological-legal doctrine of the Church.[28]

The intervention regarding ecclesiastical immunity

Some of the prerogatives that the Church defended most strenuously against the aggressive policies of modern states were related to the Church's fiscal and legal immunity from secular authority. In truth, Bellarmine had already intervened on this thorny issue in his first volume of *Disputationes de controversiis*, taking a very moderate position against the ideas generally supported by canonists. Starting from the assumption that Christ, whose "Kingdom was not of this world," had never exercised power on earth over temporal matters, he denied that exempting clerics from the jurisdiction of secular courts was by divine law. Moreover, clerics, independently of their *status*, were still "citizens and part of a political State," and therefore the immunity that they enjoyed, whether personal or real, could certainly not constitute an original right, but instead was a right introduced by human law through concession from the states.[29] A less-accommodating stance by the Holy See towards the more aggressive state policies restricting the "liberties of the Church," manifested under Gregory XIV and reconfirmed up to the early years of the reign of Pope Clement VIII, caused Bellarmine to revisit his position on the matter in his *Disputatio de exemptione clericorum*, published for the first time in 1599. In this work, Bellarmine considered the relevance of the topic from a legal and theological standpoint, referring to the texts of the two *corpora iuris*, as well as to those of experts who interpreted and based their positions on these texts. Referring, for example, to the position by which the "clerics and their property" would be exempt by divine law "from the power of secular princes"—a position found in the first part of *Decretum* by Graziano (D. 96, c. 11) and in a decretal by Boniface VIII in the *Sextus* (VI, 3. 20. 4)—he takes into consideration the doctrine developed in relation to these texts starting from the respective *Glossae Ordinariae* and arriving at two commentators on the Boniface passage, Domenico da San Giminiano and Pietro d'Ancarano. After highlighting a second position sustained by, among others, Francisco de Vitoria and Diego Covarruvias, according to which the clerics would have been exempt in ecclesiastical and spiritual cases by divine law and in other cases by human law, Bellarmine then presents his new thesis, in which he repudiates the human origin of exemption of clerics. Having recourse to the concept of "natural divine law," he traces the origin of this privilege to the Roman law category *ius gentium*. Therefore, based on this "natural secondary law" regarding living subjects in the same order but belonging to different communities, while admitting that clerics could be subject to their secular princes "in those things that relate to the good government of the public sphere," he concludes that it is necessary to repudiate as improper that they can be corrected and punished in a secular court because this would negate "all of the reverence that common people must necessarily have for their priests" in consideration of their sacred office.[30] This solution was essentially a compromise, which was however destined to have a more reduced consequence than that of the *potestas indirecta in temporalibus*.[31]

Conclusion

All the most important figures have a destiny in common, that of having as many opponents as they have supporters. Robert Bellarmine did not escape this fate, and among the various accusations that were made against him, one of the most frequent was his supposed lack of originality. On one hand, it is evident that this claim is not without merit, as many of the doctrines that he developed in his works, including those from the *potestas indirecta in temporalibus*, were certainly not new. On the other hand, it should also be conceded that this criticism does not hit home, because Bellarmine did not have the ambition to be original, but instead aimed to successfully present the doctrines of the Catholic faith, perhaps also enhancing and explaining them more effectively. That he was successful is demonstrated in the indisputable role assigned to him for his writings in the cultural context of the Counter-Reformation.

His works, ranging from *Disputationes de controversiis* to the shorter controversial/apologetic pamphlets, were born not as a mere intellectual exercise but as an instrument for the triumph of truth over heresy and as a contribution to the primary mission assigned by Christ to his Church: the saving of souls. It can also definitely be said that his entire life and all of his works were characterized by constant reference to the idea of saving souls. This was true in Louvain, where he was a preacher, and in Rome, where he was a teacher and writer. It was also true, perhaps even more so, in Capua during his brief but fruitful experience as a bishop. There he demonstrated a zeal that he held in common with the greatest pastors, who in the wake of Carlo Borromeo designed their diocesan governance on the faithful application of the Tridentine decrees; Bellarmine in fact resided constantly in his episcopal see, acting as a talented preacher to the faithful, personally visiting the parochial churches in his diocese many times, and celebrating a provincial council and three diocesan synods.[32] As he also stated specifically in some of his minor writings, from the perspective of an acute observer of certain common phenomena, it was really the nonobservance of the Council of Trent's wise decrees on the duties of bishops that could cause serious damage to the souls of the faithful.[33] Throughout a long life marked by the coherence of what he wrote with what he did, he faced not a few conflicts, sometimes finding himself taking on positions that were not perfectly aligned with those of the Curia, and even with those of some of the popes; he nevertheless managed to defend his positions courageously and effectively, as in the case of the doctrine of indirect power of the pope over temporal affairs. This doctrine, which prevailed over time and waned only with the affirmation of the "substantially separatist" doctrine of the pastoral constitution *Gaudium et spes* of the Second Vatican Council, is perhaps the contribution that had the greatest influence on Bellarmine's fame as an emblematic figure of the Counter-Reformation, in both a theological and a legal sense.[34] Influential as Bellarmines's doctrine was, it was only part of the significant legacy of "saint and scholar" cardinal to the Church and its law.

Notes

1 For more detailed information about Bellarmine's family environment, education, and subsequent events that characterize the biography of Pope Marcello's nephew, refer to the works of Le Bachelet, Brodrick, Motta and the essays published in the book *Bellarmino e la Controriforma.*

2 Le Bachelet, 436–7.

3 On the teaching of *Controversiae* the Jesuit Collegio Romano, see García Villoslada, 72–3.

4 Sommervogel, 1151–254; to this datum, already significant on its own, regarding the edited works listed in this repertoire that attempts to take a census of the various editions of the single works, should also be added what emerges from the notable collection of unpublished writings in Bellarmine, *Auctarium Bellarminianum.*

5 For an old example of classification of the works of the Jesuit cardinal, see von Eggs, 230.

6 Bellarmine, *Vita ab ipso conscripta anno 1613*, in Le Bachelet, *Bellarmin avant son cardinalat*, XLII, 464.

7 It is therefore not by chance that the historical treatises on the canon law sources as well as the encyclopedic and bio-bibliographic works regarding the law of the Church give attention to this figure; see, for example, Schulte, 459–62; Jombart, 287–96; Blanco, 646–8; Costigane, 203–14.

8 Bellarmine, *De indulgentiis.*

9 On this issue and the ensuing "war of writings," in which Bellarmine, on behalf of the pope, played a central role in defending the positions of the Holy See, cf. Bouwsma, in particular 167–377.

10 Bellarmine, *Risposta*, I, 5.

11 Ibid., VII, 22.

12 Bellarmine, *Disputationes de controversiis*, t. I, *III Controversia generalis de Summo Pontifice*, lib. I *De Romani Pontificis Ecclesiastica Hierarchia*, chap. I–III, 596–607.

13 Ibid., lib. IV *De potestate spirituali Summi Pontificis*, chap. III, 957–65.

14 Bellarmine, *Disputationes de controversiis*, t. I, pars II, *IV Controversia generalis de Conciliis et Ecclesia militante*, lib. III *De Ecclesia militante*, chap. II, 147.

15 Ibid., *V Controversia generalis de membris Ecclesiae militantis*, lib. III *de laicis*, chap. VI, 638–9.

16 See Rager.

17 Bellarmine, *Disputationes de controversiis*, t. I, *III Controversia generalis de Romano Pontifice*, lib. V *de potestate Pontificis temporali*, chap. VI, 1070.

18 In particular, a reference to a *casus* added to the *Glossa Ordinaria* of Giovanni d'Andrea at the II *regula iuris* in the *Liber Sextus,* which reads: "when with regard

to the same subject there are imperial and papal laws that contradict one another, in the case in which the subject of the law is something that could cause danger to the souls, the imperial law is abrogated in favor of the papal law" (*Liber Sextus decretalium . . . cum suis glossis . . .* (Venetiis: apud Socios Aquilae Renovantis, 1605], 533, gl. *Possessor* ad VI, 5, *De regulis iuris*, 2) as well as an exemplative reference to VI, 2. 13. 2 which prevailed in the case of conflict C. 7. 39.
19 Godman, 100–1.
20 See Bourdin.
21 Bellarmine, *Tractatus*, 3–21; among the jurists cited (all cited firsthand, as is clear from the precision in the citation description), the Italians Bartolo da Sassoferrato, Baldo degli Ubaldi, Pietro d'Ancarano, Nicolò de Tedeschi "Panormitano," Giovanni d'Anagni, and the then-living colleague Cardinal Domenico Toschi; the Frenchmen Guillaume Durand, Jean Faure, and Gilles de Bellemere; the Spaniards Ramon de Penyafort, Diego Covarruvias, and Martin de Azpilcueta; and the German Conrad Braun.
22 Cf. Bellarmine, *Tractatus*, 13, and Faure, *In Iustiniani Imperatoris Codicem*, 2.
23 Even though there was dissent in the Catholic realm that persisted through the seventeenth century (Tutino, 7 and *passim*), subsequently this doctrine was the basis for the creation of "a consent no less unanimous and constant of Catholic doctors," so much so that at the beginning of the 1960s it was affirmed that it was "constantly confirmed in the practices of Catholic life" (Ottaviani, 139).
24 Cano, *De locis theologicis*, lib. VIII, 275–9.
25 Bellarmine, *Disputationes de controversiis*, t. II, *De matrimonii sacramento*, lib. I, chap. VII, 1264–7.
26 Corecco, 1014–16.
27 Bellarmine, *Disputationes de controversiis*, t. II, *De matrimonii sacramento*, lib. I, chap. V, 1256.
28 Jemolo, 70. The §. 2 of can. 1012 of CIC 1917 has been faithfully reproduced in the text of §. 2 of can. 1055 of current CIC 1983.
29 Bellarmine, *Disputationes de controversiis*, t. I, pars II, *De clericis*, lib. 1, chap. 28, 410.
30 Bellarmine, *Disputatio de exemptione clericorum*, 53–4.
31 Frajese, 308–9.
32 On Bellarmine's episcopate in Capua, see Iodice, "I principi ispiratori della pastorale riformatrice del Bellarmino a Capua," 311–62.
33 Cf. Bellarmine, "De officio primario Summi Pontificis ad Clementem VIII," *Auctarium Bellarmininanum*, 514–18; "Admonitio Cardinalis Bellarmini ad episcopum theanensem nepotem suum quae necessaria sint episcopo qui vere salutem suam aeternam in tuto ponere velit," *Auctarium Bellarminianum*, 639–55.
34 De Bernardis, 563–4.

Bibliography

Bellarmine, Robert. *Auctarium Bellarminianum: Supplementum aux Oeuvres du Cardinal Bellarmin*. Edited by Xavier-Marie Le Bachelet. Paris: Beauchesne, 1913.

Bellarmine, Robert. "Disputatio de exemptione clericorum." In *Opuscula quae disputationibus Roberti Bellarmini . . . in editione veneta ab eodem auctore adiuncta fuerunt*. Venetiis: apud Minimam Societatem, 1599.

Bellarmine, Robert. *Disputationes de controversiis Christianae Fidei adversus huius temporis haereticos*. Ingolstadt: ex officina typographica Davidis Sartorii, 1588.

Bellarmine, Robert. *Risposta del cardinal Bellarmino al trattato dei sette teologi di Venetia sopra l'interdetto della Santità di nostro Signore Papa Paolo Quinto*. Rome: appresso Guglielmo Facciotto, 1606.

Bellarmine, Robert. *De indulgentiis et iubileo libri duo*. Coloniae Agrippinae: apud Antonium Hierat, 1599.

Bellarmine, Robert. *Tractatus de potestate Summi Pontificis in rebus temporalibus adversus Gulielmum Barclaium*. Romae: Bartolomeo Zannetti, 1610.

Blanco, María. "Belarmino, Roberto." In *Diccionario general del derecho canónico*, edited by Javier Otaduy, Antonio Viana, and Joaquín Sedano. Vol. 1. Pamplona: Universidad de Navarra: Thomson Reuters Aranzadi, 2012.

Bourdin, Bernard. *The Theological: Political Origins of the Modern State: The Controversy between James I of England and Cardinal Bellarmine*. Translated by Susan Pickford. Washington, DC: Catholic University of America Press, 2010.

Bouwsma, William J. *Venezia e la difesa della libertà repubblicana*. Bologna: Il Mulino, 1977.

Brodrick, James. *Robert Bellarmine Saint and Scholar*. Westminster, MD: Newman Press, 1961.

Cano, Melchior. *De locis theologicis libri duodecim*. Salmanticae: excudebat Mathias Gastius, 1563.

Corecco, Eugenio. "L'inseparabilità tra contratto matrimoniale e sacramento alla luce del principio scolastico 'Gratia perficit, non destruit naturam'." *Strumento internazionale per un lavoro teologico: Communio* 16 (1974): 1010–23.

Costigane, Hellen. "Robert Bellarmine." In *60 Porträts aus dem Kirchenrecht: Leben und Werk bedeutender Kanonisten*. Edited by Philipp Thull. Sankt Ottilien: Eos, 2017.

De Bernardis, Lazzaro Maria. "Le bolle alessandrine: San Roberto Bellarmino e la 'potestas indirecta in temporalibus'." In *Atti del III Convegno Internazionale di Studi Colombiani, Genova 7–8 ottobre 1977*, 547–64. Genoa: Civico Istituto Colombiano, 1979.

De Maio, Romeo, et al., eds. *Bellarmino e la Controriforma: Atti del Simposio Internazionale di Studi, Sora 15–18 ottobre 1986*. Sora, IT: Centro di Studi sorani "Vincenzo Patriarca", 1990.

Eggs, Georg Josef von. *Purpura docta*. V–VI. Monachi: Remy, 1714.

Fabbri, Enrica. *Roberto Bellarmino e Thomas Hobbes: Teologie politiche a confronto*. Rome: Aracne, 2009.

Faure, Jean. *In Iustiniani Imperatoris Codicem Breviarium*. Lugduni: excudebat Balthazares Arnoulletus, 1550.

Frajese, Vittorio. "Regno ecclesiastico e Stato moderno. La polemica fra Francisco Peña e Roberto Bellarmino sull'esenzione dei chierici." *Annali dell'Istituto storico italo-germanico in Trento* 14 (1988): 273–339.

García Villoslada, Ricardo. *Storia del Collegio Romano dal suo inizio, 1551, alla soppressione della Compagnia di Gesù, 1773*. Rome: Pontificia Università Gregoriana, 1954.

Godman, Peter. *The Saint as Censor: Robert Bellarmine between Inquisition and Index*. Leiden: Brill, 2000.

Iodice, Antonio. "I principi ispiratori della pastorale riformatrice del Bellarmino a Capua." In *Roberto Bellarmino arcivescovo di Capua, teologo e pastore della Riforma Cattolica: Atti del Convegno internazionale di studi, Capua 28 settembre—1 ottrobre 1988*, edited by Gustavo Galeota. Capua: Arcidiocesi di Capua, 1990.

Jemolo, Arturo Carlo. *Il matrimonio nel diritto canonico*. Milan: Vallardi, 1941.

Jombart, Emile. "Bellarmin (Saint Robert)." In *Dictionnaire de droit canonique*, edited by Raoul Naz. Vol. 2. Paris: Letouzey et Ané, 1937.

Le Bachelet, Xavier-Marie. *Bellarmin avant son cardinalat, 1542–1598: Correspondence et documents.* Paris: Beauchesne, 1911.

Motta, Franco. *Bellarmino: Una teologia politica della Controriforma.* Brescia: Morcelliana, 2005.

Ottaviani, Alfredo. *Institutiones iuris publici ecclesiastici.* Vol. 2. *Ecclesia et Status.* Vatican City: Typis poliglottis vaticanis, 1960.

Prodi, Paolo. *Il sovrano pontefice. Un corpo e due anime: La monarchia papale nella prima età moderna.* Bologna: Il Mulino, 1982.

Rager, John Clement. *Democracy and Bellarmine: An Examination of Blessed Cardinal Bellarmine's Defense of Popular Government and the Influence of His Political Theory upon the American Declaration of Independence.* Shelbyville, IN: Qualityprint, 1926.

Schulte, Johann Friedrich von. *Die Geschichte der Quellen und Literatur des canonischen Rechts.* III/1. Stuttgart: Enke, 1880.

Sommervogel, Carlos. *Bibliothèque de la Compagnie de Jésus. Bibliographie*, I. Brussels: Schepens-Picard, 1890.

Tromp, Sebastian. "De evolutione doctrinae potestatis indirecte R. Pontificis circa res temporales in controversiis S. Roberti Bellarmini." In *Acta Congressus iuridici internationalis: VII saeculo a decretalibus Gregorii IX et XIV a codice iustinano promulgatis: Romae 12–17 novembris 1934.* Rome: Pontificium Institutum Utriusque Iuris, 1936.

Tutino, Stefania. *Empire of Souls: Robert Bellarmine and the Christian Commonwealth.* Oxford: Oxford University Press, 2010.

16 Alberico Gentili (1552–1608)

Giovanni Minnucci

Biographical introduction

Alberico Gentili was born in San Ginesio on January 14, 1552. He enrolled at Perugia University in 1569 and graduated in civil law on September 23, 1572. He was appointed judge in a civil law court and then served as a lawyer for the San Ginesio municipality. In 1579, because of his endorsement of Reformed theology, he was forced to flee with his father and brother, Scipione. At first he took refuge in Ljubljana, then he went to Germany and reached London in 1580. There he came into contact with the political and cultural élite of the royal court, particularly Robert Dudley, First Earl of Leicester, and Sir Francis Walsingham, the secretary of state. On January 14, 1581, he was co-opted as a civil law pundit at Oxford University and qualified as a lecturer on March 6, 1581. Between 1583 and 1585, Gentili came into contact with Giordano Bruno, and their relation continued during Gentili's brief sojourn in Wittenberg in 1586. Thanks to Dudley's and Walsingham's recommendations, he was appointed Regius Professor of Civil Law by royal decree from Elizabeth I on June 8, 1587. Between 1588 and 1589 he married Esther De Peigny, with whom he would have five children. In 1602–1603 the Sacred Congregation of the Index listed his books in the *Index Librorum prohibitorum*. In 1605 he retired from lecturing to devote himself to law practice. He served as a lawyer for the Spanish embassy at the High Court of Admiralty, in charge mainly of piracy and war-looting cases. He died in London on June 19, 1608 and was buried there at St. Helen's Bishopsgate.

The first works

Historians have established that Italian intellectuals were held in grave suspicion by certain parties in England in the 1580s, condemned for defects, real or imaginary, in their "customs." This is shown in a letter dated January 29, 1583, from the English theologian William Watkinson to Jean Hotman, in which the English theologian, to defend Alberico, stated that Gentili, though Italian, was different than his compatriots: he was not—according to Watkinson—"a fake and a dissembler." If this was the cultural milieu in which Gentili found himself after his long flight across Europe, it is hardly surprising that he spent his first years in England trying to establish his professional credentials as a jurist of distinction.

As such, he would be, from a strictly religious viewpoint, untainted by any papist influence.[1]

On the academic side, accordingly, Gentili could represent himself as a civil lawyer, or civilian, with his *De iuris interpretibus dialogi sex* and with the *Lectiones et Epistolae* which appeared shortly after.[2] This reputation would facilitate a prestigious career at Oxford, where there was still a strong attachment to the teaching of civil law along traditional lines:

> Like Gentili, in short, English civilians refused to believe that history or philology had anything to do with the science of law. . . . This guild mentality, with the compulsive utilitarianism accompanying it, constituted perhaps the major obstacle to historical and comparative study.[3]

At the same time, consider the writing and the subsequent publication of a work like *De papatu Romano Antichristo*, preserved in a single autographed manuscript at the Bodleian Library of Oxford and recently edited. The first draft is dated to the five years between 1580 and 1585. From a religious perspective, this text could have been the concrete demonstration that, despite being Italian, Gentili's approval of the Reformation and his antagonism towards the pope were absolutely unquestionable.[4] In fact, it is worth noting that Gentili described himself on the title page as Italian (*Italo auctore*), information which he never specified in the titles of his other works.[5] In a hostile atmosphere, Gentili thus chose these projects to demonstrate his competence as a jurist. He also thus offered the essential proof that, although Italian, he was absolutely committed to the reformed faith and correspondingly and implacably opposed to the Roman papacy.

If this was Gentili's aim, however, he was very much hindered in achieving it. His *Dialogi* in particular, which had appeared in 1582 and were closely followed by the *Lectiones et Epistolae* (1584), attracted significant opposition in humanist circles. Jean Hotman had been a friend to Gentili and to his father, Matteo, when they first arrived in England, but he now mounted a veritable crusade against Alberico. The full and extensive correspondence which he now addressed to other London and Oxford intellectuals (for example, Henry Cuffe, and Thomas Savile), describing the unsuspecting Gentili in the most aggressive and intemperate terms, was only one part of this assault. Hotman also managed what amounted to an effective propaganda campaign, which reached, directly or indirectly, the most prominent jurists of Continental Europe. For example, Hotman wrote directly to Bodin, and Jacques Cujas was sent a copy of Gentili's *Dialogi*.

By 1585, the forces opposing Gentili came not only from Jean Hotman's sphere of influence but also from the more dangerous Puritan side. This is demonstrated by a letter of February 8, 1594, in which Gentili reminded John Rainolds of the events which had unfolded when his appointment as Regius Professor of Civil Law had been mooted in the mid-1580s.

Gentili claimed that Rainolds and his supporters had found an argument against his appointment by accusing him of *italica levitas* which can be translated as Italian fickleness and unreliability.[6] Using Gentili's foreignness against him and alleging that the dedication of his *Legalium Comitiorum Oxoniensium Actio* was written in vaunting and flattering language, Rainolds and his supporters charged him with *levitas* in order to underline the flirtatiousness and the inconstancy of Italian people.[7]

Gentili may have waited ten years after the event to make this assertion about Rainolds,[8] but there is no need to disregard it even if we can identify further grounds for the Puritan party's hostility: namely, Gentili's appreciation of the work of Niccolò Machiavelli and his beliefs concerning the interrelationship of law, theology, and religion. These themes and problems are apparent in *De legationibus libri tres* (1585),[9] a work published in precisely the period of the mid-1580s when Rainolds and other Puritan thinkers began to voice their antagonism towards Gentili.

De legationibus, it is true, is a far less influential text than *De iure belli*, which appeared thirteen years later. Nevertheless, relevant passages of *De legationibus* can be emphasized here to demonstrate that Gentili's scholarly output over time featured a logical thread and a unity of ideas on the interrelationship of law, theology, and religion. It would certainly be impossible for Rainolds to condone the bald assertion that religious law governs only human relations with God and not human dealings with each other,[10] a theme which Gentili would develop in later years.[11] Also significant is Gentili's acknowledgement of the importance of historical knowledge in the formation of diplomats (3.8: "Magna in legato historiarum cognitio requiritur" (A wide knowledge of History is required in the Ambassador)) and of human activity in politics generally. With explicit allusion to Aristotle's *Rhetoric* and Machiavelli's *Discourses*, Gentili asserts that an ambassador cannot dispense with knowledge of the past, whether of recent history or of antiquity: without this resource, the ambassador is in fact incompetent to exercise the diplomatic office. At the beginning of the next chapter (3.9. "Quatenus philosophia legatum deceat" (To what Extent is Knowledge of Philosophy suitable for the Ambassador?)), Gentili makes an even starker reference to Niccolò Machiavelli, showing himself fully cognizant of the accusations of impiety and lack of moral integrity addressed against the Florentine, because Gentili refers to them directly and designates the *Discorsi* ("aureas in Livium Observationes" [Observations in Livy]) as the methodological model for treatment of ethical and political problems.[12]

It was hardly to be expected that Gentili's unambiguous stance on this point would go unnoticed, especially among the most determined opponents of Machiavelli's ideas. One of the major proponents of anti-Machiavellianism, which was widespread in England, was John Rainolds himself. Rainolds was particularly harsh in his assessment of Machiavelli's ideas on political realities, declaring them absolutely and incontestably antithetical to the precepts of Christian doctrine.[13]

Although the works which Gentili published between 1582 and 1585 were received with approval and appreciation in England's scholarly and political milieus, they also provoked strong and significant opposition. This was perhaps the true cause of Gentili's early difficulties in developing his academic career according to plan. It was the opposition of Puritan and humanist thinkers, reacting mostly to the content of his early works, which endangered his ambition to succeed Griffin Lloyd as Regius Professor of Civil Law. This is most likely why he accompanied Orazio Pallavicino on a journey to Germany in the spring of 1586, intending to leave England permanently. As we now know, however, events took a turn at this point which confounded his opponents. On June 8, 1587, supported by Walsingham and Leicester, who among others remained on excellent terms with him, and by members of the Anglican hierarchy, Gentili was named Regius Professor of Civil Law.

The jurist and the theologian: Gentili and Rainolds

By this time, the quarrels which had developed between Gentili and the theologians in the mid-1580s seemed to have subsided, but they would soon be revived in all their complexity. As evidenced by the source material preserved in England and as demonstrated by copious research, the theater controversy between William Gager and John Rainolds had its origins in the early 1590s. Given that women were not permitted to appear on stage at this time, the question at issue was whether it was acceptable for actors to assume feminine roles and costumes in spite of the prohibitions of Deuteronomy (Deut. 22:5).[14] This controversy would come to a head in 1592, in public, with Queen Elizabeth's visit to Oxford. Gentili, considering her his most powerful and influential patron, dedicated a sonnet in Italian to the Queen on this occasion.[15] During her visit, she attended performances of the works of William Gager, whom John Rainolds had opposed in his polemics on theater. On September 28, she gave clear voice to her displeasure with Rainolds on this account: "Elizabeth schooled Dr. John Rainolds for his obstinate preciseness, willing him to follow her laws, and not run before them."[16]

Nonetheless, the theater controversy flared up again after a lull of several months, in 1593–94, and this time it was Gentili himself who emerged as Rainolds's opponent. Gentili published his *Commentatio ad legem III. Codicis de professoribus et medicis* in June 1593.[17] One of the questions addressed in *Commentatio ad legem III* was the central problem of the Gager-Rainolds controversy. Not only did Gentili offer implicit support for Gager's position, he also queried the legitimacy of theologians' claim to intervene on the key question of the controversy. He arrived at the conclusion that, while religious thought could not but be informed by theological arguments, these arguments could not be granted comparable influence *in re morali et politica* (in moral and political matters).[18] It was already clear from Gentili's earlier publications, from *De legationibus* (1585) to *De iure belli Commentatio prima* (1588), that he differentiated *ius religionis* very clearly from *ius humanum*, founding the distinction between the two kinds of law on the different relations which they governed. From this perspective, it was only the relations between God and humanity which were covered by *ius religionis*; for human relations, one must look for guidance to *ius humanum*. The watchful Rainolds had not failed to notice that Gentili had been promoting this assessment of law, theology, and religion for quite some time, and he was well aware of the content of Gentili's earlier scholarship, to which Rainolds made reference in the course of the controversy.[19] It took very little to stir the smoldering embers back into flame, and the controversy between Gager and Rainolds, in which Gentili quickly became embroiled, did much to spark a veritable war of words, with the two battling it out in private correspondence. A total of eight manuscript letters are extant, starting with a letter from Gentili to Rainolds on July 7, 1593, and finishing (at least where correspondence is concerned) with a missive from Rainolds to Gentili on March 12, 1594.

Scholars have already examined the epistolary controversy between Gentili and Rainolds. While their exchange started from issues and problems concerning theatrical performance, it developed to include the question of the *officiosum mendacium* (a dutiful or useful lie). The substance of the debate, however, turned upon the roles and competence of the theologian and the jurist, respectively. This debate will not be examined at length here. Nevertheless, it merits further investigation, especially in light of the unpublished letters preserved at Corpus Christi College Oxford (O.C.C.C., *ms. 352*), which have been the subject of some discussion elsewhere.[20] It is sufficient for now to note that Gentili did not consider the interpretation of scripture the sole prerogative of theologians: he asserted, in his letters to Rainolds from July 1593 onward, that it was fully permissible for jurists to study the Bible as well. Scripture was therefore a resource which scholars from both fields held in common, with the proviso that jurists must be acknowledged to have greater authority to deal with precepts governing relations between persons.[21]

Gentili would maintain this position, remaining totally convinced of his justification, through new lines of argument developed as his correspondence with Rainolds progressed. His starting point was the division of the Ten Commandments across the two Tables of the Law, the first being inscribed with God's precepts for human relations to God (divine law), and the second with God's precepts for human beings' relations with each other (human law).[22] Thus, theologians as interpreters of scripture must be granted the competence to study and to interpret the divine precepts on relations between humanity and God. Jurists, however, *ratione subiecti* (because of the focus of their discipline: on human behavior) and *ratione finis* (because of the ultimate end of their discipline: to perfect human law), must be considered competent to interpret the norms regulating human interactions, and then, guided once more by scriptural precepts, to define these issues in terms of the law.

It was not to be imagined that Rainolds could condone this position. In fact, having accused Gentili of *immodestia* and of *impietas* (the latter term having been applied to Machiavelli, though refuted by Gentili in his own defense), he asserted that the interpretation of scripture must remain the exclusive prerogative of theology, the only discipline which could be considered a guide to faith and life (*fidei et vitae magistra*). The Ten Commandments were of course part of scripture, and for Rainolds it was essential to discuss them in terms of theology.

It was God's will that theologians should serve as *praecipui interpretes*, charged by virtue of their function as interpreters with explaining the commandments on both the first and the second tablets to church and people.[23]

Gentili's correspondence with Rainolds had gone beyond a straightforward exchange of letters and had become more widely known among Oxford's academic community. This can be deduced from Gentili's conclusion to his letter to Rainolds of February 8, 1594,[24] in which he contended that Rainolds had broadcast part of their correspondence, making the text of his letters to Gentili public (and thus of course offering a selective account of their quarrel). He accused Rainolds of trying to damage his reputation by passing copies of these letters directly or indirectly to such an influential personage as Toby Matthew; since his arrival in England, Gentili had developed a close friendship with Matthew, who was now Bishop of Durham.[25] Gentili therefore had no option but to defend himself by making his position public, making the case for *iurisprudentia* and its practitioners to those members of the university who had become party to the correspondence without his knowledge.

Gentili made his defense in a discourse addressed to the *nobilissimi auditores oxonienses*,[26] which contains an autobiographical reference confirming that it was produced after March 12, 1594. The discourse was developed after the pattern of Pomponius's *Liber singularis enchiridii* ("De origine iuris et omnium magistratuum et successione prudentium"; Dig. 1.2.2.36–53), with the addition of a final section referring to the great Roman jurists Papinianus and Ulpian and to the contribution of humanist literature such as Bernardino Rutilio's *Iuris consultorum vitae*, which drew on classical scholarship to expand Pomponius's account of Roman jurist consults as transmitted in the Justinian Digest: proof evident for Gentili of the stature and importance of jurists throughout time. He recalled how law had originated in ancient Greece and was developed in Rome. After the Roman Empire fell to the invading Germanic tribes, Roman law had effectively disappeared. But, Gentili emphasized, it had reasserted itself after the medieval rediscovery of the *Corpus Iuris Civilis* of Justinian: the law of a conquered people thus regaining its unquestionable and universal authority by its own force alone.

Gentili had other motives for making a public statement. The text of his discourse was designed not only to demonstrate the worth of *iurisprudentia* and its scholars over the centuries, but also to defend himself from the accusation that he was an "Italian intriguer, Machiavellian, and atheist," and against the view that he was still, in spite of his long sojourn in England and his appointment to such a prestigious chair, a foreigner. The true cause of the hostilities to which he was subjected was the fact of his being "foreign and Italian," since his unnamed accuser was ignorant of the principles of hospitality and of the whole concept of a natural law guaranteeing refuge to strangers—a law which Gentili showed by explicit reference to *Iovis hospitalis* to have its foundation in classical antiquity. In responding to Rainolds around the same time, on February 8, 1594, Gentili asserted that he had been ostracized in the mid-1580s, when his appointment as Regius Professor was first mooted, on these same grounds of being foreign and Italian. From this assertion, it is clear that Rainolds himself was Gentilis's main persecutor, and that the discourse in defense of jurisprudence was designed to inform *academici oxonienses* of the true impetus for Rainolds's attack. Gentili turned to them in part in order to offer his opinion on the virtue of jurisprudence—which had political value too. Gentili also wished to reveal the motives underlying the current dispute, of which they had only partial knowledge from Rainolds's letters: a long-running dispute founded not only on legitimate academic differences (as amply demonstrated in the correspondence between the two) but also on the refusal to accept a foreign scholar in the chair of civil law at the ancient and prestigious University of Oxford.

At the conclusion of his text, in order to prove the accusations against him unfounded and to demonstrate his academic credentials, Gentili could not refrain from a rhetorical call to witness, citing those who had supported him on various occasions. These included Queen Elizabeth, the now deceased Robert Dudley, Earl of Leicester (d.1588), and the professors at Oxford who had welcomed him, so that he could say with Aeneas's emissaries their words to the king of the Latins (Aen., VII.231), "we will not bring dishonor upon the kingdom" (*non erimus regno indecores*). As a foreigner, then, he had been appointed Regius Professor at the ancient University of Oxford and had taught there over many years. In spite of adversity, he still considered himself fully integrated not only into English society but also into the service of the realm.

Some ten years later, Gentili would refer again to this issue of not being considered a citizen of England, in very different terms but from essentially the same position, in his *Laudes Academiae Oxoniensis.* Here, Gentili would defend his claim to be English in clear and forthright language and in a combative tone, on the basis that he had now lived more than twenty years in the country and had taught there for so long ("and get you gone, you who would deny me anything that you would concede to an Englishman: since I am certainly English by virtue of having dwelt here full twenty-four years, an English citizen with the right to teach and to hold this chair here").[27] He invoked once again, as in 1594, the name of Elizabeth (who had died in March 1603), submitting himself to her indisputable authority, asserting metaphorically that he could only find final rest in the light of her judgment: "Hail you who reign in the heavens with your Christ, with our Christ, Hail O Queen Elizabeth. Here I submit myself to your judgment, in your most holy name, most holy of names for me eternally."[28]

Gentili's search for peace of mind is attested by the verb *conquiescere* (to find rest),[29] which he used both in the discourse of 1594 and in the *Laudes Academiae Oxoniensis*, as if to demonstrate that even at the beginning of the next century he still suffered a measure of antagonism.

Alberico Gentili between law, theology, and religion: a brief summary

The drama of Gentili's relations with Puritan circles and with Rainolds in particular seems to have abated for the three years between 1595 and 1598. However, the two scholars were soon at odds again, even if they did not come into direct conflict at the turn of the century as they had in earlier years. This contention can be seen especially in the publication of a series of works by Gentili which elaborated on questions the two had previously debated. These works can be considered his public proclamation, developed along academic lines, of the conclusions he had reached during the years of his controversy with Rainolds. While the themes of these works have already been discussed, it is necessary to consider the timing of their appearance in order to understand fully why some of them were published.

In 1598, Gentili revisited and expanded significantly on the ideas already expressed in the *Commentationes De iure belli*. Augmenting the work with a considerable quantity of *auctoritates*, he published the *De iure belli libri tres*, a work which confirms, in at least some of its passages, his perspective on the interrelationship of law, theology, and religion as previously expressed in *De legationibus* and *De iure belli Commentatio prima*. Here he argues that quarrels of religion cannot constitute a legitimate cause of war: one cannot define a law in accordance with one's own religious faith and impose it on those who, by virtue of their religion, believe differently. Religious affairs pertain to relations between God and humanity (whether considered as individuals or in community); relations between persons, on the other hand, are regulated by human law.[30] In light of Gentili's assertions in his correspondence with Rainolds, divine law (intended to regulate relations between God and humanity) and human law (relative to relations between persons), come within the remits of the theologian and the jurist, respectively. This helps to elucidate the very famous phrase which appears at the end of Book 1, Chapter 12 of *De iure belli*: *Silete theologi in munere alieno* (Silence, theologians, where you do not belong!).[31]

This point merits far more than the very restricted space it can be allocated here, but it might reasonably be understood to refer exclusively to theologians claiming that difference of religion (*diversitas religionis*) could justify war, since Gentili placed it at the end of a series of chapters (1.9–12) dedicated to the problems of war and religion. However, his earlier assertions on the subject indicate that it applied in fact to all theologians wishing to intervene on questions which he would reserve to human law, like the relationships of person to person, which was the proper context for discussion of just causes for war. The interpretation of human law, as in the case of just war, was the exclusive preserve not of theologians but of jurists or, in Gentili's terminology, jurisconsults. He had already discussed these issues extensively in his earlier works and in his correspondence with Rainolds and would tackle them again three years later in the first book of *De nuptiis*.

In 1599, Rainolds, as if to confirm his marked dissent from Gentili's ideas, had part of the correspondence between the two printed: the letters exchanged between July 7 and August 5, 1593.[32] The controversy, it will be recalled, had arisen from the dispute between Rainolds and Gager on theatrical performance and had developed after Gentili's intervention to include the problem of *officiosum mendacium*, before coming finally and inevitably to the underlying problem of distinguishing between the jurist's and the theologian's fields of competence.

At almost the same time, and certainly in the same year when Rainolds published this selection from their correspondence, Gentili had a work printed in which he expanded his position on the points which had triggered the controversy: *Disputationes duae:* I. *De actoribus et spectatoribus fabularum non notandis.* II. *De abusu mendacii* (Hanoviae 1599).

But it is the work which followed shortly after, *Disputationum de nuptiis libri VII* (Hanoviae 1601), that can be considered, from Gentili's perspective, as the conclusion of a debate which had begun as long ago as the publication of *De legationibus* (1585) and reached its full development through his correspondence with Rainolds. In this work on the institute of marriage, Gentili developed and extended the arguments he had used in his epistolary controversy with Rainolds in an academic forum. He held firmly in his convictions about the relationship of law, theology, and religion. This was the subject of much of Book 1, which purported to illustrate the role of the interpreter of law.[33] Gentili proved to have reached the definitive conclusion that the jurist cannot fulfill his interpretative function by relying on Justinian alone. Instead, in the humanist spirit, the jurist must draw on knowledge from other disciplines to historicize the study of law, to discover the rational spirit which produced intelligent understanding and treatment of norms and of the legal system as a whole in various times and places. An examination of Book 1 of *De nuptiis* can facilitate a fuller understanding of the development of Gentili's thought on this theme: the evolution of his conception of the jurist and of the interrelationship of law, theology, and the religion.

Alberico Gentili *iuris interpres*

Book 1 of *De nuptiis* features a chapter on the authority of theologians.[34] The discussion is composed on the classical model of the *disputatio*, an interpretative methodology which, as the title indicates, Gentili adopts for the work as a whole. Here, the question is, who has competence to interpret the precepts contained in the second tablet of the Decalogue, which is inscribed with God's commandments regulating human relationships. To counter the assertions of an unnamed theologian, doubtless John Rainolds, Gentili makes significant and very explicit changes to his previous assertions in *De iuris interpretibus Dialogi sex.* He offers a very reductive summary of that work, recalling that he had argued there that the jurist had no need of deep acquaintance with Latin and Greek, nor of dialectic nor history nor any of the other arts and sciences;[35] tools which, according to his interlocutor, counted in fact among theologians' essential cultural equipment. According to the theologian, the jurist's lack of substantial knowledge in these disciplines disqualified him from pronouncing on any of the precepts of the Ten Commandments.[36]

In a hypothetical dialectical dispute between jurist and theologian, Gentili the author of the 1582 *Dialogi* would be defeated. But Gentili the author of the 1601 *De nuptiis*, having changed his position substantially, could usefully demonstrate his competence to interpret divine precepts regulating human interactions. One further point must be emphasized. The title that Gentili gave his

Dialogi in 1582, *De iuris interpretibus Dialogi sex*, seems to promise a systematic reflection on the function of the *interpres iuris*. However, in writing his *Disputationes* on matrimony in 1601, Gentili felt the need to specify in Book 1 (*Qui est de interprete*), that he had acted twenty years earlier as an interpreter of Justinian law (*et de iuris Iustinianici interprete illic egi*). Now, however, he acted as *interpres iuris*. If we take Gentili at his word here, the title of his first work should in fact have been *De iuris Iustinianici interpretibus Dialogi sex*. Without disowning what he had written in the *Dialogi*, Gentili represented that text as no more than a straightforward description of the responsibilities of a jurist who relied on the *Corpus Iuris Civilis* of Justinian, responsibilities which could now be fulfilled only by drawing on much wider knowledge.

This meant that he was no longer merely an interpreter of Justinian law, he was now fully armed and equipped as a true *interpres iuris*. Having acquired wide and deep expertise in many disciplines, Gentili, who made significant progress towards the humanist ideal of encyclopedism, could now grant the jurist his proper role of seeking out the principles governing human relations, using for this purpose not only the dictates of the *Corpus Iuris Civilis* but also all of the relevant knowledge available from careful reading in ancient and recent jurisprudence as well as in those disciplines (history, philology, philosophy, and theology) which he had considered superfluous in the not too distant past. It seems to have been no accident that in comparing these two phases of his methodology, he transformed himself from "*interpres iuris Iustinianici*" to "*simpliciter interpres iuris*." He wished perhaps to emphasize with the use of the adverb *simpliciter* that the jurist, who obviously had a key role in interpreting the law, must find new approaches in order to fulfill this role, drawing on contributions from all of the other disciplines to achieve unity of interpretation.

The expert in jurisprudence, as conceived of by Gentili in *De nuptiis* in contrast to the *Dialogi*, was no longer simply a commentator on the normative corpus. Nor was he an interpreter treating the *Libri legales* through the prism of juristic sources alone (which Gentili had now come to consider "an improper practice of our discipline"). He was an intellectual who, by virtue of the breadth of his knowledge, reigned as high priest of justice (*sacerdos iustitiae*).[37] For Gentili, the guiding principles of human actions were now to be derived not only from the *Corpus Iuris* of Justinian but also from works developed in jurisprudence and in every other discipline without exception down through the years with the aim of separating *aequum ab iniquo, iustum ab iniusto* (justice from injustice, right from wrong), and thus discovering the foundations on which to build human justice. This role could no longer be entrusted to the canon or the civil lawyers, a division of labor which was obsolete in an age of political and religious divisions. Rather, it was to be assigned to the *iurisperitum*, the expert in jurisprudence.[38]

In constructing the first book of *De nuptiis*, Gentili thus presented himself as heir to the universal tradition of *ius commune* and, accordingly, as the portal for the renewal of jurisprudence for a new age. The quest for justice would not be fulfilled through developments in the interpretation of Justinian law, but through the hermeneutic efforts of the jurist who, thanks to an encyclopedic range of knowledge, could in effect be considered the only intellectual capable of formulating principles of justice.

Notes

1 The most recent account of Gentili's early years in England is Minnucci, *Silete theologi in munere alieno*, 26–82. For an account of Gentili's printed and unpublished works see Maclean.

2 Gentili, *De iuris interpretibus dialogi sex*; see on this work Astuti; Gentili, *Lectionum et epistolarum*.

3 Kelley, 46.

4 Gentili, *De Papatu Romano*. Its layout shows that it was already prepared for printing, but numerous deletions, insertions, and marginal annotations (until 1591) demonstrate that it was then revisited and subjected to major revision.

5 Ibid., 7: *De papatu Romano Antichristo Assertiones [ex uerbo Dei et SS. Patribus] Alberico Gentili Italo auctore*. Gentili later altered the title by scoring out the words placed in square brackets above.

6 See Oxford, Corpus Christi College, *ms. 352*, 277–8 (February 8, 1594): "Et Jtalica tamen, Jtalica leuitate tantum peccaui isthic, ut indignissimus fuerim hoc loco, quem apud uos teneo, imo quem apud uos occupo, ut tu clarius uis semper. Et tu de illis fuisti, qui humanissimæ genti uestræ | labem illam aspersam uoluerunt inhumanitatis, dum, extero homini patere locum apud uos, indignum uociferabantur." For a fuller version of the text, see Minnucci, "Un discorso inedito di Alberico Gentili," 217 n. 14.

7 See on this point Panizza, 51; Feingold, "Giordano Bruno," 333–4: "Gentili vigorously canvassed his candidacy and, for his troubles, was charged with *Italica levitas* when his opponents turned against him the flattery and boastful expressions he had used in the dedication of his *Legalium Comitiorum Oxoniensium Actio* (1585) to Lloyd.

8 See Minnucci, "Un discorso inedito", 234–41.

9 On this work see most recently Feingold, "What's in a Date?".

10 Rainolds's rejection of this position is expressed in his correspondence with Gentili, 1593–4, on which see Minnucci, "Un discorso inedito", 215–22 and the references cited there, as well as *infra*, endnote 23 and related text.

11 Gentili, *De legationibus libri tres*, 2.11, 63:

> *Secundum argumentum, quo ego in istam definitionem inclino, illud est: quia religionis ius hominibus cum hominibus non est, sed cum Deo. Cum Deo enim communio nobis religione intercedit: nam haec est inter homines, et Deum ratio: quia est religio scientia diuini cultus, et habitus obseruantiae eius, quo habitu nos cum Deo deuincimur et religamur.*

Gentili expressed the same ideas three years later when writing *De iure belli Commentatio prima* (Gentilis, *De iure belli Commentationes duae*, Lugduni Batavorum 1589, *Commentatio prima*, D3i, "Caussa religionis"), which makes explict reference to the text of *De legationibus*.

12 For Gentili's reference to Machiavelli, see *De legationibus libri tres*, 3.8–9, 109.

13 Cfr. D. Joannis Rainoldi, *Orationes duodecim, cum aliis quibusdam opusculis* (Londini 1619), 164; Johannis Rainoldi Angli, *De Romanae Ecclesiae idololatria, in cultu sanctorum, reliquiarum, imaginum, aquae, salis, olei, aliarumque rerum consecratarum, et sacramenti Eucharistiae, operis inchoati Libri duo* (Genevae 1596), 1.6.9, 251.

14 For a full account of this subject, and for bibliographic references, see Binns, "Women or Transvestites."

15 Minnucci, "Una lettera inedita," 10–11, 17, and n. 35.
16 Boas, 266–7. Elizabeth's speech can be found in Plummer, 271–3, and is partially reproduced in Minnucci, "Una lettera inedita," 5 n. 13: "Moneo ego, ut non praeeatis leges; sequamini. Ne disputetis, non meliora possint praescribi; sed observetis, quae lex Divina iubet, et nostra cogit."
17 Critical edition and English translation in Binns, "Alberico Gentili in Defense."
18 "Nam qui histrioniam omnem sublatam esse volunt, hi auctoritate theologorum magis moventur. Ego vero ut theologorum auctoritate in re religionis valde moveor, ita in re morali, aut politica non valde." (see *Commentatio ad l. III Codicis de professoribus*, in Binns, "Alberico Gentili in Defense," 247, and English translation, 269).
19 See, e.g., Gentili and Rainolds, *Latin Correspondence*, 26 n. 18, 28 n. 21. On this correspondence, from which Rainolds printed only a selection in 1599 (the letters in question dating from July 7 to August 5, 1593), published in a critical edition in the last century (see *Latin Correspondence*, 16–135), to which must be added the still unprinted letters preserved in O.C.C.C., *ms. 352* (from November 1593 to March 12, 1594), see the works cited in Minnucci, "Una lettera inedita," 11–12 and n. 35.
20 See Panizza, *Alberico Gentili*, 55–87; Binns, "Women or Transvestites," 95–120.
21 "at moralia, et politica sacrorum librorum aut nostra existimavi, aut certe communia nobis, et theologis"; "Communes sunt sacri libri; et in his, quae spectant ad secundam tabulam, nostri magis, quam vestri." (*Latin Correspondence*, 18, 38).
22 O.C.C.C. *ms. 352*, 283–4, Letter from Gentili to Rainolds, February 8, 1594:

> *Sed | secunda tabula est ius humanum: ergo secundam tabulam sic tractant iurisconsulti, non theologi. Atque assumptionem ita confirmabam, quod est ius inter hominem et hominem, humanum est: sed secunda tabula hoc ius est inter hominem et hominem, ergo secunda tabula ius humanum est;*

Ibid., 284:

> *Si ars, uel scientia theologorum distinguitur ab arte iurisconsultorum, fine distinguitur, subiecto distinguitur. Sed hoc iurisconsultorum est ius humanum, diuinum theologorum: finis iurisconsultorum homini hominem, finis theologorum deo hominem coniungere. ergo extra subiectum, et finem uestrum, et in nostris miscetis uos si in iure humano miscetis;*

similar concepts are expressed in *De nuptiis*, 37, 41.
23 O.C.C.C. *ms. 352*, 304, Letter from Rainolds to Gentili, March 12, 1594: "Ac ego theologorum potius sententiæ credendum esse confirmavi, quod hi sint praecipui secundæ tabulæ interpretes. Praecipui quippe sunt, quos Deus instituit, ut eam ecclesiæ populoque suo publice explicarent."
24 Gentili wrote thus to Rainolds on February 8, 1594:

> *Tu scis, an promeritus sis, qui per academiam triumphabundus de me absente incedebas cum tuis litteris. quas et ad D. Matthaeum miseras. testes habeo, qui eas uiderunt Oxonii in manibus tabellarii. Quis misisset, nisi tu? Quid uoluisti? uirum illum mihi alienum facere, quem unum supra omnes colo, et cupio mihi beneuolentem!*
>
> (O.C.C.C. *ms. 352*, 288)

Gentili was right to complain that Rainolds had subjected him to numerous insults in these earlier letters, another reason for his strong opposition to their circulation: "Tu me immodestum, confidentem, irreligiosum, architectum nequitiae et impietatis Academici dedecoris autorem, impurissimo similem principio dicis: et ego respondere non possum, horum nihil verum esse?" (O.C.C.C. *ms. 352*, 213; s.d. but datable to November 1593).

25 In his response of March 12, 1594, Rainolds denied direct responsibility:

> *At descripsit eas amanuensis meus: nam eius manus illa ad D. Matthaeum, cujus hæc ad te. Demonstratio certior ex fide instrumentorum: nisi in Academia nostra multi scirent (ut ab amico mihi significatum est ex quo accepi tuas) cuius illæ manu, non mei librarii, sint descriptae.*
>
> (O.C.C.C. *ms. 352*, 307)

On this point, see Panizza, *Alberico Gentili*, 74 and n. 39.

26 Minnucci, "Un discorso inedito," 211–51.

27 Gentili, *Lodi delle Accademie*, 80.

28 Ibid., 83.

29 For *Laudes*, see ibid., 82: "Ego in iudicio tuo . . . hic conquiesco"; for the 1594 discourse see Minnucci, "Un discorso inedito," 250, n. 127: "in his penitus, ac totus conquiesco."

30 Gentili, *De iure belli libri III*, 1.9, 64–5:

> *Nunc illa est, si vno religionis obtentu bellum inferri possit. Et hoc nego. Et addo rationem: quia religionis ius hominibus cum hominibus proprie non est: itaque nec ius lęditur hominum ob diuersam religionem: itaque nec bellum caussa religionis. Religio erga Deum est. Ius est diuinum, id est, inter Deum et hominem: non est ius humanum, id est, inter hominem et hominem. Nihil igitur quæritat homo violatum sibi ob aliam religionem.*

31 Ibid., 1.12, 92.

32 Rainolds, *The' Overthrow of Stage-Playes*. Cfr. *supra*, n. 19.

33 On Book 1 of *De nuptiis* see most recently Minnucci, *Alberico Gentili*, 19–60, and the literature cited therein.

34 See Gentili, *Disputationum de nuptiis libri VII*, 88–95: "De auctoritate theologorum. cap. XVI."

35 Ibid., 91–2:

> *Qui mecum aliquando contendebat theologus, is contra me asserebat, quod ante annos plurimos scripsi in dialogis meis* de interpretibus iuris, *Bartolum, Baldum, alios nostros, qui ad ius nostrum ediderunt commentaria, dedisse tamen ad secundam legis Dei tabulam ne litteram quidem. Et illud quoque, bonum esse interpretem iuris sine linguae Latinae exquisitiori, et sine ulla Græce, alteriusve cognitione: absque dialecticis præceptionibus: absque notitia historiarum, aliarum artium, scientiarum, disciplinarum. Quae imo omnia in sacrorum librorum interprete desiderantur. Sed tamen vicisse olim* Albericum Gentilem *non est hinc vincere. Et de iuris Iustinianici interprete illic egi, non simpliciter de interprete iuris. Nam scripsi illico* De legationibus, *et mox alia pro officio quidem interpretis iuris, ut non pro iuris Iustinianici: quæ non sine historiarum multa notitia, disciplinarum et linguarum aliquantulo usu exponi possunt.*

On the theory contained in the *Dialogi* see Astuti, *Mos italicus e mos gallicus.*

36 Rainolds had expressed this opinion in his letter to Gentili of August 5, 1593 (see *Latin Correspondence*, 66–8).

37 *Disputationum de nuptiis libri VII*, 57:

> *Nostra non est ars, recitare quid in libris Iustiniani est constitutum, sed definire explicate, quid in quaque quæstione est iuris. Quemadmodum philosophia . . . non est Aristotelismus, aut Platonismus, sed studium sapientiæ et*

veritatis: ita nostra philosophia Iustinianismus non est, sed 'ars boni et æqui, cuius merito quis nos sacerdotes appellet iustitiam namque colimus, et boni et æqui notitiam profitemur: equum ab iniquo separantes, licitum ab illicito discernentes, bonos non solum metu poenarum, verum etiam præmiorum quoque exhortatione efficere cupientes: veram, nisi fallor, philosophiam non simulatam affectantes' (Dig. 1.1.1). *Corruptus ille est usus disciplinæ nostræ: qui non istam artem æqui, et boni, sed legum Iustinianicarum notitiam solam profitetur.*

38 Ibid., 93: "neque civilistæ, hoc est Iustinianico, competere ius supradictum, neque canonistæ, sed iurisperito. Quem humanarum et diuinarum rerum scientie, ad iusti, et iniusti, æqui et boni interpretationem definio, et definiui."

Bibliography

Astuti, Guido. *Mos italicus e mos gallicus nei dialoghi "De iuris interpretibus" di Alberico Gentili.* Biblioteca della "Rivista di storia del diritto italiano" 16. Bologna: Zanichelli, 1937.

Binns, James W. "Alberico Gentili in Defense of Poetry and Acting." *Studies in the Renaissance* 19 (1972): 224–72.

Binns, James W. "Women or Transvestites on the Elizabethan Stage? An Oxford Controversy." *Sixteenth Century Journal* 5/2 (1974): 95–120.

Birocchi, Italo. "Il De iure belli e 'l'invenzione' del diritto internazionale." In *Ius gentium, ius communicationis, ius belli: Alberico Gentili e gli orizzonti della modernità, Atti del Convegno in occasione delle celebrazioni del quarto centenario della morte di Alberico Gentili (1552–1608), Macerata, 6–7 Dicembre 2007*, edited by Luigi Lacchè, 101–38. Milan: Giuffré, 2009.

Boas, Frederick S. *University Drama in the Tudor Age.* Oxford: Clarendon Press, 1914.

De Benedictis, Angela. "Gentili, Alberico." In *Dizionario Biografico degli Italiani.* Vol. 53, 245–51. Rome: Treccani, 1999.

Domingo, Rafael, and Giovanni Minucci. "Alberico Gentili and the Secularization of the Law of Nations." In *Christianity and Global Law*, edited by Rafael Domingo and John Witte, Jr., chapter 6. London/New York: Routledge, 2020.

Feingold, Mordechai. "Giordano Bruno in England, Revisited." *Huntington Library Quarterly* 67/3 (2004): 329–46.

Feingold, Mordechai. "What's in a Date? Alberico Gentili and the Genesis of De legationibus libri tres." *Notes & Queries* 64/2 (2017): 312–17.

Gause, Artemis. "Gentili, Alberico (1552–1608), Jurist." In *The Oxford Dictionary of National Biography.* Oxford: Oxford University Press, 2004.

Gentili, Alberico. *De iure belli libri III.* Hanoviae, 1598.

Gentili, Alberico. *De iuris interpretibus dialogi sex. Ad exemplar prioris editionis edidit prolegomenis notisque instruxit*, edited by Guido Astuti. Turin: Istituto giuridico, 1937.

Gentili, Alberico. *De legationibus libri tres.* Translated by Gordon J. Laing and Edited by James B. Scott. The Classics of International Law. New York: Oxford University Press, 1924.

Gentili, Alberico. *De Papatu Romano Antichristo recognovit e codice autographo bodleiano D'Orville 607.* Edited by Giovanni Minnucci. Archivio per la Storia del diritto medievale e moderno; Studi e Testi 17. Milan: Monduzzi Editoriale, 2018.

Gentili, Alberico. *Disputationum de nuptiis libri VII*, Hanoviae 1601.

Gentili, Alberico, and John Rainolds. *Latin Correspondence by Alberico Gentili and John Rainolds on Academic Drama*. Translated with an introduction by Leon Markowicz. Salzburg: Institut für Englische Sprache und Literatur, 1977.

Gentili, Alberico. *Lectionum et epistolarum quae ad ius civile pertinent, Libri I–IV*. Londini, 1583–4.

Gentili, Alberico. *Lodi delle Accademie di Perugia e di Oxford*. Latin text with Italian translation and notes, edited by Giuseppe Ermini. Perugia: Libreria Universitaria, 1968.

Helmholz, Richard H. "Alberico Gentili e il Rinascimento. La formazione giuridica in Inghilterra." In *Alberico Gentili (San Ginesio 1552—Londra 1608). Atti dei Convegni nel quarto centenario della morte*. II. *(San Ginesio, 11–12–13 settembre 2008; Oxford e Londra, 5–6 giugno 2008; Napoli l'Orientale, 6 novembre 2007)*, 311–31. Milan: Giuffrè, 2010.

Kelley, Donald R. "History, English Law, and the Renaissance." *Past & Present* 65 (1974): 24–51.

Kingsbury, Benedict, and Benjamin Straumann, eds. *The Roman Foundations of the Law of Nations: Alberico Gentili and the Justice of Empire*. Oxford: Oxford University Press, 2010.

Lavenia, Vincenzo. "'Mendacium officiosum': Alberico Gentili's Ways of Lying." In *Dissimulation and Deceit in Early Modern Europe*, edited by Miriam Eliav-Feldon and Tamar Herzog, 27–44. New York: Palgrave Macmillan, 2015.

Maclean, Ian. "Alberico Gentili: His Publishers and the Vagaries of the Book Trade between England and Germany." In Ian Maclean, *Learning and the Market Place: Essays in the History of the Early Modern Book*, 291–337. Leiden: Brill, 2009.

Minnucci, Giovanni. *Alberico Gentili iuris interpres della prima Età moderna*. Archivio per la Storia del Diritto medioevale e moderno; Studi e Testi 16. Bologna: Monduzzi Editoriale, 2011.

Minnucci, Giovanni. *"Silete theologi in munere alieno." Alberico Gentili tra diritto, teologia e religione*. Milan: Monduzzi Editoriale, 2016.

Minnucci, Giovanni. "Una lettera inedita su questioni teologiche di Alberico Gentili al padre Matteo con un Sonetto inedito dedicato alla Regina Elisabetta I d'Inghilterra (18 settembre [1592?]." *Historia et Ius* 8 (2015): paper 11.

Minnucci, Giovanni. "Un discorso inedito di Alberico Gentili in difesa della iurisprudentia." *Quaderni Fiorentini* 44 (2015): 211–51.

Panizza, Diego. *Alberico Gentili, giurista ideologo nell'Inghilterra elisabettiana*. Padova: Tipografia "La Garangola," 1981.

Petrina, Alessandra. "Ai margini del testo: Alberico Gentili e la circolazione dell'opera di Machiavelli in Inghilterra." In *Alberico Gentili "Responsibility to Protect": nuovi orientamenti su intervento umanitario e ordine internazionale. Atti del Convegno della XV Giornata Gentiliana (San Ginesio, 14–15 settembre 2012)*, edited by Vincenzo Lavenia, 195–214. Macerata: EUM, Edizioni Università di Macerata, 2015.

Plummer, Charles. *Elizabethan Oxford: Reprints of Rare Tracts*. Oxford: Clarendon Press, 1887.

Rainolds, John. *The Overthrow of Stage-Playes*. Middleburg, 1599; 2nd ed. Oxford, 1629.

Van der Molen, Gesina H. J. *Alberico Gentili and the Development of International Law: His Life Work and Times*. 2nd revised ed. Leiden: A. W. Sijthoff, 1968. First published in 1937.

Wijffels, Alain. "Alberico Gentili's Oxford Lectures." In *Inter cives necnon peregrinos: Essays in Honour of Boudewijn Sirks*, edited by Jan Hallebeek, et al., 785–802. Göttingen: V&R Unipress, 2014.

Wijffels, Alain. "Antiqui et Recentiores: Alberico Gentili: Beyond Mos Italicus and Legal Humanism." In *Reassessing Legal Humanism and Its Claims: Petere Fontes?*, edited by Paul J. du Plessis and John W. Cairns, 11–40. Edinburgh Studies in Law 15. Edinburgh: Edinburgh University Press, 2016.

17 Giovanni Battista De Luca (1613–1683)

Italo Birocchi

Introduction

Universally acknowledged as the greatest Italian jurist of the seventeenth century, Giovanni Battista De Luca was born in Venosa, Basilicata, probably in 1613,[1] to a highly religious family (three sisters were nuns, while his father Stefano's brother belonged to the Order of Friars Minor Conventual and taught theology at the Sapienza University of Rome between 1603 and 1639). De Luca carried out his first legal studies in Salerno and always retained fond memories of his master, Pietro Salimbeni, particularly of his teaching method, which provided for discussion in Italian after the dictation of the text. After graduating, possibly in Naples in 1635, during his internship he had the good fortune of meeting a jurist of worth in Fernando Arias de Mesa, who combined theoretical knowledge (he belonged to the Salamanca school and was chair in the capital of the southern kingdom) and practical sensitivity (he was also a magistrate at the Holy Royal Council of Naples).

In 1639 De Luca returned to Venosa, where he received his first tonsure and was appointed vicar general of the bishop while continuing to work as a lawyer. He settled in Rome after 1644 (apparently, contact with the city was occasional at first and staying there was not part of his plans).[2] In the capital of Western Christianity and working for the law firm of a great lawyer, Angelo Andosilla, De Luca became familiar with important names in the Church and civil society—Prince Nicolò Ludovisi, the Panphili family, and the Caracciolo family. For about thirty years he worked as an advocate at a very high level. A collection of *discursus* extracted from court practice, highly selected for the sake of prudence, occupies fifteen thick volumes that constitute his masterpiece, the *Theatrum veritatis et iustitiae* (Rome, 1669–73, to which four volumes were added in 1677–78, as well as the indices in two more volumes, 1680–81). Thus commenced his period of "public commitment" that marked the last part of his life.

Aiming for greater dissemination of the subject matter in the *Theatrum*, he published a compendium in Italian (*Il dottor volgare*, 1673, far from reduced in size) and almost simultaneously launched a campaign fostering the use of the Italian language in legal matter (*Difesa della lingua italiana*, 1675). Invigorated by the publication of a plethora of Italian works, this advocacy of Italian was beset by much controversy, which peaked with the publication of testamentary dispositions in the vernacular. Critical of the methods of teaching law and of exercising the profession of lawyer in general, De Luca published *Dello stile legale* (1674), which in turn elicited lively discussions and controversy in the literary and curial worlds alike. In the same years, he was actively involved in the Academy of Maria Christina of Sweden and produced an array of other works which, all written in Italian and dedicated to figures archetypal of that world (the prince, the bishop, the cardinal, etc.), express his cautiously reforming and moralizing beliefs.

In 1676, having abandoned the legal profession, De Luca entered the priesthood and was summoned by the newly elected Pope Innocent XI to act as auditor and secretary of memorials. De Luca became one of the pope's closest collaborators (in 1677 he was appointed referendary of the two signaturae) and employed his legal expertise in drafting provisions for the moralization of public life, the restriction of personal and familial privileges of the high ecclesiastical hierarchies, the abolition of nepotism, and financial readjustment. Frugal in life, genuinely religious, endowed with a great appetite for work, and financially independent thanks to an inheritance and the revenues generated by his profession—traits largely shared with Pope Innocent, who came from an affluent family and had studied law in Naples at more or less the same time as De Luca—De Luca in his activism must have appeared dangerous among conservative circles. The implementation of reforms proved only partial, however, as various projects set aside at the time were resumed towards the end of the century by Pope Innocent XII (specifically, the one on the abolition of nepotism). On the matter of sovereign rights (*iura regalia)*, which reached its peak during De Luca's active life and resulted in a bitter diplomatic dispute with France, De Luca believed that in ancient times the king had the right to assign vacant ecclesiastical benefits, but he failed in persuading the pope to mitigate his radical opposition to the demands of Louis XIV. Overall, De Luca enjoyed considerable public visibility, although he met with strong curial resistance (particularly by Pietro Ottoboni) and was attacked because of the popular discontent engendered by the decorum-oriented politics and the restriction of expenses. His was a declining star when he was appointed cardinal in 1681. He died on February 5, 1683.

The *Theatrum veritatis et iustitiae*

The principal work of this jurist is also the one less scrutinized by historiography, and the reasons for this are twofold. Indeed, considering its extensiveness, to take possession of its contents requires a systematic project and long labor. Moreover, the work's structure, fragmented into many *discursus* proposing practical cases dealt with by the jurists in court, makes it difficult to master the diverse subjects covered and attain a summary interpretative outcome. The *Theatrum* is divided into fifteen books corresponding to as many major themes, under which the practical cases are arranged. Nevertheless, it is quintessentially case law.[3] The magnificent indices, stemming from the skillful effort of one of De Luca's assistants, Nicola Falcone, greatly facilitate consultation of the volumes and inquiry into the many issues by means of cross-referencing of texts, yet the work does not encourage comprehensive reading of the masterpiece.

The work is a legal encyclopedia, but in a larger sense it is a mine from which to extrapolate biographical information and sociocultural assessments. However, the fragmentation of the treatise does not prevent the reader from grasping the global vision of the jurist. Entirely removed from method-based discourse, De Luca certainly possessed intellectual coordinates that he applied consistently, except for the understandable variations arising from the fact that the collection contained materials produced over a considerable period of practicing law, both as an expert in court proceedings and as a lawyer at the service of a given party.[4]

The *Theatrum* is a critical immersion in the sphere of law. The jurist masters the doctrines, but even more so the spirit behind them. He knows the mentality and the operational mechanisms of judges and lawyers. He is strong enough to observe the distortions of the administration of justice and, while keeping quiet about his sources, he is aware of the main spirited debates in Europe—for example, those relative to the teaching crisis in France in the 1660s—and the proposals advanced. All of this he distilled here and there in the sequence of the *discursus.*

One can argue that everything made known to us by the subsequent educational works of the jurist is essentially already present in the *Theatrum.*[5] The work was directed at "professors," viewed not as lecturers but as those who professed the law, who were legal experts endowed with discernment. The intent was pragmatic, since practice, in De Luca's view, was the highest moment in jurisprudence, as it aimed at applying law in human relationships. The pragmatic guideline did not exclude, and indeed presumed, a high level of legal training, except that in itself the mere command of theory (knowledge of the legislative sources, use of logic, language, and legal categories) was not sufficient to remedy practical problems, always different in their specific nuances or the novelty of situations. On the other hand, that very practical guideline was not to be confused with the simple availability of instruments and ready-made solutions: anyone who relied in court on the fragmented sources of the legal system as an endless arsenal of opportunities (*corpus iuris civilis et canonici*, princely legislation, customary and jurisprudential standards) was, according to De Luca, a pettifogger and not a jurist. Hence, De Luca railed constantly and bitterly against "solicitors," whom he considered instigators of disputes prepared to employ any contrivance, if only to please their clients; he deplored the Scholastic method, by now an empty vessel in the endlessly alternating positions of dialectics; and he deprecated the principle of authority, which replaced solid reasoning with an accumulation of citations.

He extended his denunciation to the state of legal teaching at the university level: first and foremost at the Roman Sapienza University (which at the time, however, boasted admirable professors), but he endowed his criticism with a broader meaning. In the Italian law faculties, people graduated who were not well versed in Latin or in the fundamental texts of Roman and canon law; the exam, essentially a ceremony, was reduced to a chant recited by heart.[6] De Luca leveled his open denunciation with a pragmatic spirit, in the style of the jurist. Indeed, De Luca noted that the doctorate in civil and canon law (*in utroque iure*) achieved without a substantive preparation, did not necessarily lead to social life, given that the selection for practice as a lawyer or magistrate depended on abilities displayed during a practical internship.[7] A university professor enjoyed considerably less prestige than the great lawyers and magistrates. He thus expressed a consolidated idea on the steps required for the training of a jurist: the doctorate was but an initial formal requisite, while his own personal experience demonstrated that a legal internship proved essential.

Overall, these positions were far from original in light of the canons practiced by application of the *Usus modernus Pandectarum* in German areas and the incipient branches of natural law. De Luca lacked an explicit theoretical vision, in contrast (just a few decades later) to Giambattista Vico (1668–1744) and Gian Vincenzo Gravina (1664–1718); it is no coincidence that they received their training in the same circles as De Luca. He also lacked a historical interest that went beyond his relativistic tendency: he was well aware that legal experience was ever-changing in various countries over time, and his pragmatism encouraged him to ascertain the practical impact of varying circumstances. Nevertheless, those attitudes took on unitary significance and modern meaning in the context of his idea of the legal system. It is worth dwelling on how the jurist viewed legal sources and the role of interpretation.

De Luca considered the legal system as circumscribed by the *leges*—those of the twofold compilations (*ius civile* and *ius canonicum*), but especially those of the *ius patrium*, by definition correlated to specific territorial conditions and actual dynamic elements. These laws required an interpreter who could ensure effective compliance with the law in practical cases. Refusing any abstract constructions and the illusory objective of the certainty of law, De Luca particularly relied upon princely legislation, which was pivotal for the system, and on the prudence of the jurist, who had a practical and active role. (De Luca's ideology was never anti-jurisprudential, despite his criticism against pettifoggers, a criticism that intensified in his ensuing works.) The search for justice, as for truth, could lead to only probable results; and practical circumstances proved excessively variable to allow for certain and unalterable rules. In the light of a widespread skepticism resulting from the accumulation of the sources to be handled—each brain ended up searching, in its own way, for the "reason for things"—the prospect of an enlightened sovereign entrusted with the task of making and administering the laws for the common good (*bonum commune*) emerged clearly. This is the reason behind the need for reformed and efficient institutions and jurists who were flexible and God fearing, thus morally sound. This necessity was the creed of Second Scholasticism, espousing the conditions of Christianity and possibly only of the Papal States in the second half of the seventeenth century. Prudence also implied attention to censure, which also resounded in the *Theatrum* itself. (A prosecution was initiated in 1680 and another one after the death of De Luca, in 1689, when one of De Luca's most tenacious adversaries, Ottoboni, was elected pope: in both cases the procedure did not come to an end.) However, from De Luca's perspective prudence was not tantamount to a spirit of conservatism. This absence of spirit of conservatism is proven by the works that the jurist tackled after his masterpiece.

Works in Italian

Following publication of the first fifteen volumes of the *Theatrum*, De Luca commenced a steady wave of works in Italian. Compared to his masterpiece, which used traditional Latin, the transition to Italian appeared to express a need and possibly a conversion of sorts, all the more so since the author drew attention to it to defend himself against criticism as well as to better expound on the reasons for his conviction about the correctness of his choice.

Thanks to his insistence, coherence, intensive efforts, and authority, this period in De Luca's work is referred to rightly as a turning point for Italy, even though the use of the vernacular was not entirely new in law.[8] In the sixteenth century, to suppress early testimonies of the late medieval period, many examples were offered in Germany in the form of Protestant legal literature (Oldendorp, *inter alia*), and in France the humanist streams reaching out towards the affirmation of national law had produced texts in French (such as the *Pandectes* by Le Caron). In Italy, from the late sixteenth century on, works aimed at illustrating procedural rules or at publishing notarial forms appeared in Italian, and Italian was considered a language of habitual use in politics, an area adjacent to, if not partly shared with, public law. All of this, however, does not explain why De Luca, after 1673, decided to launch a crusade in favor of the vernacular, or why his work was perceived as unconventional and met with harsh opposition. His very last will and testament, drawn up in Italian and criticized for that, is the epitaph of this matter.

The use of Italian is associated with the mission that De Luca manifestly felt in those years. He had always been a practical jurist, a prominent lawyer in the Roman society of his time, but at this moment the practical profile was complemented by a political and cultural commitment: he selected his interlocutors from outside the circle of legal professionals, he took part in the Academy of Maria Christina, and he would shortly be immersed in government activity attacking immunity, nepotism, and licentious customs.[9] It seemed that he truly intended to have an impact on civil society. It is emblematic that the first great work of this "crusade"—*Il dottor volgare*—reduced the *Theatrum* to a compendium, but with an important innovation: although the subdivision of topics remained the same one that was adopted for the masterpiece, the case law approach disappeared, and the jurist exposed principles and the articulation of the topic by using the deductive method.

Considerable effort was required to render the wide variety of materials (mostly private law, but also public law) in terms that often needed to be recovered or specially adapted in language foreign to traditional teaching and to available treatises (chiefly in Latin). For this work of linguistic revision, De Luca sought the contribution of Andrea Peschiulli (with further assistance from Eusebio Eusebi) for the presentation of criminal procedure, an area he was unfamiliar with and a topic not found in the *Theatrum*). The result was not only innovative presentation but also evidence of the jurist's method of employing a team of collaborators, some of whom were destined for success in the legal profession (for example, Giovanni Antonio Tomati and Ansaldo Ansaldi).

The explicit revelation of the recipients of the *Il dottor volgare* was extremely indicative of De Luca's intention. They included the active strata of civil society, namely those who, while not jurists, were involved in trade and institutions. According to De Luca, such recipients needed to possess a smattering of law, since to have an active and informed role, they required basic and practical legal knowledge. It was necessary to break away from the vision of law as a sequence of enigmas managed by an isolated caste of jurists, and to encourage the conscious reclamation of law by the actors in the legal system. Hence, the pedagogic and civil purpose of the work emerged. The jurist, however, was a step ahead, even going as far as recognizing the dignity of the Italian language as a means to explain law in technical terms[10] and, in a manual published posthumously, admitting that lecturers and students could also benefit from the use of Italian.[11]

Thus, there emerged an organicistic and historical notion that law ultimately should find its natural expressive form in the national language. Although, as was commonly the case, the origins of the suggestions were concealed for the sake of prudence, a French élan may be clearly perceived. Not only the title and some content of the *Difesa* echo the *Deffence et illustration de la langue françoise* by Joachim du Bellay (1549), but behind De Luca's new activism it is possible to perceive the proposals of the new generation of French masters, who in the various branches of human sciences (philosophy, history, logic) envisaged renewed and simplified models and methods and, within the context of law, summaries or manuals in the vernacular.[12]

De Luca naturally did not copy; he listened or read, pondered, and drew upon what he needed in the situation. His main concern was a practical commitment in which only abstract terms could separate legal matters from religious spirit and ethical preoccupations, and even from the interest in convenience that pervaded economics and politics. The meditations on the summer or autumnal tranquility of Frascati (the *otia tuscolana*), mostly drawn up between 1675 and 1680 in Italian, were a kind of exercise in which the jurist identified an institutional or class-based figure (the prince, the cardinal, the bishop, the dame) active in Christian society but also in the specific pontifical judicial system; he analyzed the characteristics and requirements, tasks and functions, and behavioral guidelines to which each figure should adhere. This effort resulted in a somewhat flexible handbook of duties—with the ever-present warning to appraise practical circumstances and not linger over abstract rules—but above all a social portrait of ordinary figures, in which Christian duty faced the realism of common sense.

With these portraits in mind, it is possible to grasp the autobiographical references on which De Luca dwelt at times. For instance, in *Il vescovo cristiano pratico*, the jurist made use of his experience as a young vicar general to the bishop to reconstruct the requirements and practical duties for sound governance of the Church and of the flock entrusted to him. Aside from the conditions required for the appointment (to profess the Catholic faith, to possess a doctorate in canon law or in theology, to be over the age of thirty, and to be a priest with at least six months' experience), the jurist dwelt on the exercise of the office in relation to which he stressed a general leitmotif of his thought ("theory alone is not sufficient unless combined with practical experience"). And exploring the question whether it was better to operate in a great and powerful bishopric to achieve one's tasks, he conceded that in the abstract the answer had to be yes because of the greater possibility of being respected and obeyed and of performing good deeds and offering alms; however, the realistic angle made the jurist warn against the temptation to abuse usually engendered by great power, so that the analysis was aimed at denouncing luxury, ambition, and the sale of influence that was not uncommon in a bishopric, considered as a fief.[13]

Public commitment between law and politics

The vernacular dissemination of De Luca's thought accentuated the critical aspects already contained in the *Theatrum*, abstracting them from the essentially legal topic and emphasizing them. Typically, De Luca affirms the assertion that only a tenth of the law in force derived from the *ius civile* and the *ius canonicum*. Here the jurist reproduced a cliché brought to the fore by Hotman and then frequently encountered in the German circles of the *Usus modernus*. But he also undertook to review what little of the *ius civile* and the *ius canonicum* remained in use and, in a positive sense, to build a manual comprising the cornerstones of current legislation in an orderly fashion.[14] The project appears innovative in scope. Drafted in Italian, the work was supposed to collect institutional matters in a first volume according to the classical tripartite division (persons, things, actions), but only as regards the parts effectively in use; instead, a second volume was meant to comprise the principal regulations extracted from canon, feudal, and municipal law as currently practiced. Thus, De Luca planned an extremely extensive project that would take into consideration the teaching practices in vogue among lawyers and magistrates, especially in Naples, though opening them to a wide and organic design. The overall project, however, was not accomplished, and only the first volume was published (posthumously) via a manuscript left behind by the author (*Istituta civile*, Pesaro, 1733).[15] During the eighteenth century, six other editions appeared and proved a lasting interest in the book, which cannot be explained by the author's reputation alone, as in that century the *Il dottor volgare* appears to have been published only three times.

Like the *Il dottor volgare*, but targeting different recipients, the manual represented a compendium of law. It was a practical and specific proposal, but at this point the overall structure inspiring the jurist needs to be considered. In the last decade of his life, which coincides with his public commitment, it is possible to glimpse the cultural orientation of his action, which ultimately stemmed from a tortured notion of human society and, hence, of the legal system. It is a scenario suffused with chiaroscuro effects. On one hand, the awareness of human rationality invited the outline of an optimistic horizon, dominated by choices in pursuit of the collective good with a gradual abandonment of all that was no longer aligned with the *bonum commune*; thus customs, which were often the crystallization of power relations and possibly the result of unconscious conduct, needed to be screened by reason, amended, or removed from the laws.[16] On the other hand, human weakness, vices, and earthly passions were equally factors of resistance against innovation; they could not be eradicated but merely constrained by a progressive and prudent action to avoid tensions and upheavals. This situation was framed in a relativistic conception of legal systems constantly changing because of varying human conditions and needs.[17] It was inconceivable, therefore, to talk about a general common law: each state had its own common law consisting of the *ius patrium* and the interpretation specifically deriving from the set of sources according to the history and life of each territorial society. Besides, no jurist could have the knowledge and the means to operate in practical terms beyond his own territory (De Luca himself confessed his inability to act outside the Kingdom of Naples and the Pontifical States). It is easy to understand the refusal to embrace general and mannerist presentations, increasingly abstract and repeated as clichés.

Within this realistic picture, the question of how to govern complexity arose. Skepticism, even if marked, was mitigated by the Christian vision. Thus, notwithstanding the abstract ideal of the good, the jurist circumscribed action to the good that was feasibly attainable, in a given space and in a given time, after assessing the diverse circumstances: "in the things of this world, no entirely perfect good can exist without some evil counterbalance, whereby the predominant part of the greater good should be expected, thus of the lesser evil."[18]

Education played a cardinal role, both with regard to religious principles (evidently considered the heritage of all members of civil society) and in legal terms, to be diffused selectively but with no less care: education in law had to be widespread among the elite that was primarily active in civil society in exchange transactions, in successions, and in concession agreements, whereas different and specific attention had to be paid to the training of the jurist, his style, and interpretative instruments. De Luca hoped for a general reordering of the regulatory system, collecting what was still used from the Roman and canon laws and comprising new legislation according to current jurisprudential use; however, he believed that, at the time, the political conditions were not right for this implementation. Meanwhile, it was possible to compensate for this deficiency with private compendia, and specifically by education about interpretation. In any case, the role of the prince was central: because he was key to maintaining order and energizing the required reforms, it was necessary to rely on his ability to govern and on his law, which had to be clear and effectively coercible (this utilitarian element is manifest in De Luca's conception). The law was meant to express reason-based content, although ultimately it was an order, namely the indication of the wishes of the higher authority,[19] which should be powerful and feared so as to ensure obedience.[20]

Thus, we come to the issue of the bedrock of sovereignty and of the relation that holds between law and politics. De Luca refused the fantastic theory of the social contract, based on which a precise human society would reject the natural status and embrace the "civil" condition. As in the *Theatrum*,[21] and according to a legal and political culture which since the Middle Ages had transitioned to Second Scholasticism, he used the figure of the marriage contract to represent the relation that holds between the prince and the State (*republica*):

> The Prince is a prime minister, or a magistrate, and an administrator of the republic, endowed with greater authority than the other ordinary and subordinate ministers and magistrates; namely and more appropriately, he is the husband, to which the intellectual woman that is the republic, through political marriage, supports the governance of its formal person made up of the people, as if by an implicit reciprocal dowry contract, and grants him the jurisdiction and the powers and those rights of the principality referred to by jurists as regal, as are in particular levies, collections, contributions, taxes . . . . All of this is granted by the republic to the prince as with a dowry, the fruits of which (excepting the capital, that he must keep and faithfully administer just as a good head of the family may do) should go towards sustaining the burdens of this political union. And these include governing the people and freeing them from harassment, burdens, and oppression from enemies, tyrants, thieves, and corsairs and other criminals and imparting justice efficiently by appointing good ministers and workers to this end and safeguarding trade . . . and also preserving and restoring and rebuilding, as appropriate, roads and bridges, and defending and maintaining the arguments and supremacy of the principality and of the people, and recovering any that should be wrongly occupied; and feeding the poor, who are the people themselves.[22]

This relationship existed between the prince and the institution. The action of the former was aimed at the well-being of the subjects (*bonum commune*), considered as a whole and not as individuals; individual rights came into play only by extension. Sovereignty lay with the institution, the holder of the higher power (*potestas in habitu*), whereas the prince was viewed as an administrator, endowed with actual power (*potestas in actu*); except that he, as the holder of the *dominium utile*, enjoyed a position of superiority compared to his wife (the republic), who was bound to him by a duty of obedience. Furthermore, remedies for nonperformance were not provided to individuals per se: these, considered the offspring of this marriage, were responsible for acknowledging the paternal power and exercising obedience.[23] Conversely, the republic, like a woman who in marriage may separate from her husband and take back her dowry, could "elude the prince and elect another," though (as clarified by the jurist) within the limits of the law, in order to avoid rebellions and treasons.[24]

Can this conception be considered a system of legality heralding the rule of law? This does not appear to be the case. According to De Luca, the *leges*, the breach of which authorized separation, were "fundamental" laws and therefore those (few) customary standards considered expressive of the structure of the State (the principle of Catholicism and rules for succession to the throne) or the other standards stemming from divine law; indeed, the jurist put forward the possibility of separation only in the event that the prince should become heretical, or be "adulterous" (that is, favor another state), or commit egregious acts of cruelty. If the offenses were not that serious—for instance poor asset management—no grounds for divorce existed.[25]

In any case, this conception applies only in theory. Realism, or even prudence, prevailed. De Luca scorned those who, as promoters of ideal systems, invoked general rules to settle other conflicts than those between individuals. To assert presumed limits inferred from natural law, or to distinguish between ordinary and absolute power (*potestas ordinaria* and *absoluta*), to investigate the presence of the "right cause" (*iusta causa*): these were all ineffective instruments. In court, the will of the prince was decisive, in that he was not subject to the requisite of the *iusta causa*, nor was he subject to coercive measures.[26] In this sense, De Luca reproduced a consolidated doctrine (one descended, moreover, from medieval elaboration): in favor of power it was necessary to recognize the assumption of reason, which, being by its very nature "varied and uncertain," is determined by who exercises power.[27] Besides, the occurrence of any tyranny in specific cases was preferable to the incitement to disobedience.[28]

Hence, De Luca propounded realism. As Bodin before him, De Luca admitted that the life of legal systems was punctuated with violence and force of arms, and he believed that "there is no enterprise that cannot be made to appear proper by reasons and pretexts and by the authority of writers: hence, the advices and writings of jurists and theologians, and of politicians and other scholars, with respect to all that pertains to the external court are indeed like flags."[29]

The observation that the force of factuality was endorsed through ideologies and the law was ruthless: "the law springs from fact" (*ex facto oritur ius*). And yet, the disenchanted De Luca was far from an inert spectator. Critical of curialist practices but not inclined towards jurisdictionalism, yearning for a sovereign dedicated to the public good, he supported a reform path under his aegis. Leaving aside aspects of modernity such as the separation between the moral judgment of the prince's conduct and the law, or such as the assertion that the prince could not transfer, in whole or in part, the State's territory via a unilateral deed,[30] in general De Luca proposed a consistently critical program and a project for the rationalization of institutional and social life alike. He felt the crisis plaguing the law—a crisis in teaching, study methods, interpretative uses, and the function regulating civil relations—to which he reacted with his cultured mind, which was not pedantic but endowed with common sense. With intrinsic prudence, he intuited a need to expand his circle of interlocutors and not address expert jurists alone, but rather to inform what would be referred to as "public opinion." Baroque prose, rich in metaphors and extremely redundant in expressing its concepts, the detailed and clear indices overall responded to a pedagogic and educational function. As De Luca explicitly stated, in the face of the publication of myriad books, read here and there only as much as was necessary on occasion, his antidote was to repeat himself so as to increase the likelihood that his concepts would be grasped.[31] Thus, De Luca was able to transfer criticism of the world of law from the utopia of political writers to a practical dimension; on the other hand, by preaching the simplification of forms and expository style and relativizing the significance of dogmatic categories, he endeavored to reconcile law to civil life.

In his time, he was *nemo propheta in patria*, as evidenced by a certain difficulty in selling his works on the market according to the testimony of the executor of his will. However, his proposals are considered an underground current that influenced and at times substantiated the reforming action of the governments and the reform-oriented legal thought in the coming decades (assumptions critical of the neo-humanistic currents may be detected, whereas towards the mid-eighteenth century he was the evident source of inspiration for Muratori).

In terms of legal culture, one can affirm that, as a witness to the crisis of the *mos italicus*, he espoused instances of that *Usus modernus* which were shortly to be colored through the prism of the Enlightenment. Nevertheless, De Luca always and intimately lived in the present: indeed, he undertook to reincorporate the instances of *Usus modernus* in the legal system in which he operated.

Notes

1 Although the year of his birth is uncertain, more evidence suggests 1613 than the more traditional 1614. See Lauro, xxxvi–xxxviii.
2 The assumption of a first vicariate towards 1634 is unreliable, as attributed to him by Del Gratta, 7.
3 The fifteen books are dedicated to the following subjects: (1) fiefs; (2) sovereign rights; (3) jurisdiction and competent court; (4) servitude, emphyteusis, and rental; (5) usury and trading contracts; (6) dowry; (7) donations, purchase agreements, contracts in general, and guardians; (8) credit and debt; (9) wills; (10) trusts; (11) bequests and intestate successions; (12) ecclesiastical benefits; (13) right of patronage; (14) marriage, tithes, regulars, and other ecclesiastical subjects; (15) judgements.
4 This circumstance is hardly ever taken into account. Recently, nevertheless, on the matter of property and fiefs, Giancarlo Vallone has encountered fluctuations most likely resulting from De Luca's defense of vested interests; see Vallone, 87.
5 Even the short booklet dedicated to games, *Del giuoco dell'ombre*, published in at least four somewhat rare editions, was discussed in Latin in the masterpiece: *Theatrum veritatis et justitiae*, lib. VII, pars III, disc. XLIX, 97–99.
6 De Luca, *Theatrum veritatis et justitiae*, lib. VII, pars III, disc. XXX, n. 7: ed. cit., 62: "neque *Digestorum*, *Codicis* et *Decretalium* exteriores tabulas viderunt."
7 De Luca, *Theatrum veritatis et justitiae*, lib. II, disc. CLXXVIII, No. 11, 325.
8 Fiorelli, "La lingua giuridica dal De Luca al Buonaparte," 330.
9 A vibrant picture, with reference both to the opposition apparent in the Curia as well as to popular discontent, is presented by Neveu, 597–633.
10 De Luca, *Difesa della lingua italiana*, No. 21: 21.
11 De Luca, *Istituta civile*, lib. I, preface, No. 34, 11.
12 It suffices to mention Gabriel Argou, Jean Domat (who in those very years was planning his principal work), and Claude Fleury (who trained as a practical jurist but was a great teacher), the last of whom surely engaged with De Luca. *Il cavaliere e la dama*, dedicated by De Luca to Maria Christina of Sweden, was translated into French in 1680 by Fleury, who in the preface sang the praises of the Italian jurist. Bruno Neveu detected a French imprint on the culture of the

Roman elite in the second half of the eighteenth century; see Neveu, "Culture religieuse," 38.

13 De Luca, *Il vescovo cristiano pratico*, chap. III, No. 4, 27–33.

14 De Luca, *Difesa della lingua italiana*, No. 33, 35 and 51–67.

15 The volume was published by Sebastiano Simbeni, a nephew of one of De Luca's assistants. In addition to the manuscript, the editor incorporated, with a brief treatise, the fourth book (on actions), as furnished with notes and index by topic.

16 The opposition between custom (likened to nature and chance and often unreasonable) and law (as a guideline chosen by reason) is palpable in De Luca, *Difesa della lingua italiana*, spec. No. 5, 8–9.

17 De Luca, *Lo stile legale*, chap. I, No. 2–4 (in the edition by Mazzacane: 48).

18 De Luca, *Il principe cristiano pratico*, chap. 10, No. 5, 115.

19 De Luca, *Il dottor volgare*, preface, chap. 5, No. 16, 40, and book 2, chap. 21, No. 5–6, 306; and particularly Id., *Il principe cristiano pratico*, chap. 16, No. 10: 200–3.

20 This is a recurring concept in De Luca: for instance, *Il principe cristiano pratico*, chap. 21, No. 16–17, 304.

21 For instance, De Luca, *Theatrum veritatis et iustitiae*, I, de feudis, disc. 3, No. 12 (ed. cit.: 20).

22 De Luca, *Il cavaliere e la dama*, chap. 22, No. 7 (ed. cit.: 378–80). The original version is as follows:

> *il Principe si dice un primo ministro, overo un magistrato, ed un amministratore della republica, con un'autorità maggiore di quel che abbiano gli altri ministri e magistrati ordinarij e subordinati; overo più adattamente si dice il marito, al quale la donna intellettuale della republica, per mezzo del matrimonio politico appoggia il governo della sua persona formale costituita da popoli, onde come per un implicito contratto reciproco dotale, gli concede la giurisdizione e l'imperio, e quelle ragioni del principato, le quali da Giuristi si dicono regali, come particolarmente sono i tributi, le collette, le contribuzioni, le gabelle. . . . Tuttociò dalla republica si concede al Principe come per una dote, con i frutti della quale (salvo il capitale, che deve custodire e fedelmente amministrare da buon padre di famiglia) debba sopportare i pesi di questo matrimonio politico. E questi sono di governare i popoli e liberarli dalle molestie, pesi e vessazioni de nemici, de tiranni, de ladroni e de corsari e degl'altri malfattori e d'amministrar bene la giustizia col deputare a tal effetto de buoni ministri e operarij e di conservare il commercio . . . ed anche nel conservare e ristorare e fare di nuovo, quando bisogni, le strade ed i ponti; e nel difendere e mantenere le ragioni e preminenze del principato e de popoli, e di ricuperare quelle che fossero malamente occupate; e nel dare gli alimenti alli figli poveri, che sono li medesimi popoli.*

23 In particular, De Luca, *Il principe cristiano pratico*, chap. 1, No. 28–30, 13–14; chap. 48, No. 3, 659.

24 De Luca, *Il cavaliere e la dama*, chap. 22, No. 7, 381. For the sake of simplicity, a host of works in which the jurist reiterated these concepts is omitted here.

25 De Luca, *Il principe cristiano pratico*, chap. 48, No. 5–9, 661–4.

26 Nitidissimo De Luca, *Theatrum veritatis et iustitiae*, II, de regalibus, disc. 148, No. 11, 246.

27 De Luca, *Il principe cristiano pratico*, chap. 16, No. 10, 202. Cf. Cortese, vol. 2, 263ff.

28 De Luca, *Il principe cristiano pratico*, chap. 11, No. 7–10, 128–30; chap. 15, No. 3, 183–4.

29 De Luca, *Il principe cristiano pratico*, chap. 9, No. 8–9, 103. The original version is as follows: "non vi è quasi impresa, la quale non si possa coonestare e di fatto non sia coonestata da ragioni e pretesti e dalle autorità degli scrittori: sicché i consulti e le scritture de' giuristi e de' teologi & anche de' politici & altri letterati, per

quel che appartiene all'accennato foro esteriore di fatto sono per appunto come le bandiere." The same concept appears in chap. 12, No. 15–16, 144.

30 De Luca, *Il cavaliere e la dama*, chap. 22, No. 8–9, 382–3.

31 De Luca, *Il principe cristiano pratico*, chap. 48, No. 4, 660. Moreover, by recycling concepts in works targeting different audiences (think about the relation between the *Theatrum* and the texts in Italian), the jurist achieved his goal of spreading his thought in different spheres.

Bibliography

A gamut of reports proving De Luca's activity in the curia have remained in handwritten form. An initial extensive, albeit incomplete, list was offered by Agostino Lauro (see ahead).

Birocchi, Italo. *Alla ricerca dell'ordine. Fonti e cultura giuridica nell'età moderna.* Torino: Giappichelli, 2002.

Birocchi, Italo. "L'Istituta civile di Giambattista De Luca." In *Amicitiae pignus. Studi in ricordo di Adriano Cavanna*, edited by A. Padoa Schioppa, G. di Renzo Villata, and G.P. Massetto. Vol. 1, 87–119. Milano: Giuffrè, 2003.

Birocchi, Italo. "Un finto contrattualismo: il diritto di resistenza in Giambattista De Luca." In *Wissen, Gewissen und Wissenschaft im Widerstandsrecht (16.—18. Jh.)/Sapere, coscienza e scienza nel diritto di resistenza (XVI–XVIII sec.)*, edited by A. De Benedictis and K.-H. Lingens, 351–67. Frankfurt am Main: Klostermann, 2003.

Birocchi, Italo, and Ersilia Fabbricatore. "De Luca Giovanni Battista." In *Dizionario biografico dei giuristi italiani (XII–XX secolo)*, edited by Italo Birocchi, Ennio Cortese, Antonello Mattone, and Marco Nicola Miletti. Vol. 1, 685–89. Bologna: Il Mulino, 2013.

Cortese, Ennio. *La norma giuridica. Spunti teorici nel diritto comune classico.* 2 vols. Milan: Giuffrè, 1964 = Milan, 1995.

Dani, Alessandro. *Giovanni Battista De Luca divulgatore del diritto: Una vicenda di impegno civile nella Roma barocca.* Rome: Aracne, 2012.

Dani, Alessandro. "La figura e le prerogative del giudice nell'opera di Giovanni Battista De Luca." In *La giustizia dello Stato pontificio in età moderna*, edited by M.R. Di Simore, 125–48. Rome: Viella, 2011.

Dani, Alessandro. *Un'immagine secentesca del diritto comune: La teoria delle fonti del diritto nel pensiero di Giovanni Battista De Luca.* Bologna: Monduzzi, 2008.

Del Gratta, Rodolfo. *Giovan Battista De Luca e gli statuti di Piombino.* Naples: Edizioni Scientifiche Italiane, 1985.

De Luca, Giovanni Battista. *Del giuoco dell'ombre.* Rome, 1674.

De Luca, Giovanni Battista. *Difesa della lingua italiana.* Rome: Dragondelli, 1675.

De Luca, Giovanni Battista. *Il cavaliere e la dama.* Rome: Dragondelli, 1675.

De Luca, Giovanni Battista. *Il dottor volgare.* Florence: V. Batelli, et al., 1839–43.

De Luca, Giovanni Battista. *Il principe cristiano pratico.* Rome: Stamperia della Reverenda Camera Apostolica, 1680.

De Luca, Giovanni Battista. *Il vescovo cristiano pratico.* Rome: per gli eredi del Corbelletti, 1675.

De Luca, Giovanni Battista. *Istituta civile.* Colonia: a spese di Modesto Fenzo, 1743.

De Luca, Giovanni Battista. *Lo stile legale.* Edited by Aldo Mazzacane. Bologna: Il Mulino, 2010.

De Luca, Giovanni Battista. *Theatrum veritatis et justitiae*. Venice: apud Paulum Balleonium, 1706.

Fiorelli, Piero. "Introduzione." In De Luca, Giovanni Battista, *Se sia bene trattare la legge in lingua volgare*, 5–20. Florence: Clusf, 1980.

Fiorelli, Piero. "La lingua giuridica dal De Luca al Buonaparte." In id., *Intorno alle parole del diritto*. Milan: Giuffrè, 2008.

Lauro, Agostino. *Il cardinale Giovan Battista De Luca: Diritto e riforme nello Stato della Chiesa (1676–1683)*. Naples: Jovene, 1991.

Mazzacane, Aldo. "De Luca Giovanni Battista." In *Dizionario biografico degli italiani*. Vol. 38, 340–46. Rome: Istituto della enciclopedia italiana, 1990.

Mazzacane, Aldo. "Giambattista De Luca e la 'compagnia d'uffizio'." In *Fisco religione Stato nell'età confessionale*, edited by H. Kellenbenz and P. Prodi, 505–30. Bologna: Il Mulino, 1989.

Mazzacane, Aldo. "Introduzione. Giambattista De Luca avvocato e curiale." In De Luca, *Lo stile legale*, 19–41.

Neveu, Bruno. "Culture religieuse et aspirations réformistes a la cour d'Innocent XI." In *Accademie e cultura. Aspetti storici tra Sei e Settecento*, edited by Centro di Studi Muratoriani, 1–38. Florence: Olschki, 1979.

Neveu, Bruno. "Episcopus et princeps Urbis: Innocent XI réformateur de Rome d'après des documents inédites (1676–1689)." In *Römische Kurie. Kirchliche Finanzen. Vatikanisches Archiv. Studien zu Ehren von Hermann Hoberg*. Vol. 2, 597–633. Rome: Università Gregoriana Editrice, 1979.

Prodi, Paolo. *Il sovrano pontefice: Un corpo e due anime: la monarchia papale nella prima età moderna*, 136–46 and *ad indicem*. Bologna: Il Mulino, 1982.

Rossi, Giovanni. "'Del modo di deferire all'autorità de' dottori.' Scienza giuridica e communis opinio doctorum nel pensiero di Giovanni Battista De Luca." In *A Ennio Cortese*, edited by I. Birocchi, M. Caravale, Emanuele Conte, D. Maffei, and U. Petronio. Vol. 3, 176–203. Rome: Il Cigno, 2001.

Vallone, Giancarlo. "La terra e il potere: il cardinale De Luca." In *Alla riscoperta del cardinale De Luca giureconsulto. Atti del Convegno Nazionale di Studio—Venosa, 5–6 dicembre 2014*, edited by Raffaele Coppola and Ezio M. Lavoràno, 50–91. Venosa: Osanna, 2016.

Zanotti, Andrea. *Cultura giuridica del Seicento e jus publicum ecclesiasticum nell'opera del cardinale Giovanni Battista De Luca*. Milan: Giuffrè, 1983.

18 Giambattista Vico (1668–1744)

Marco Nicola Miletti

Biographical introduction

Giambattista Vico was born in Naples on June 23, 1668, the sixth child of Antonio, a bookseller, and Candida Masullo. From 1679 to 1684 he attended the Neapolitan Jesuit College. He sat through sporadic lectures at university but was disappointed: those by Francesco Verde seemed to him "full of cases on the minutiae of the practice" (*Autob.*, 115). Vico lived most of his life in Naples, at the time the capital of the Spanish viceroyalty, subsequently Austrian (from 1707), and finally capital of the independent Bourbon kingdom. But from 1686 to 1695, as tutor to the sons of Marquis Domenico Rocca, he spent most of the time at Vatolla, in the Cilento. Plato's works, which Vico read in the rich library of the castle, inspired him to "meditate on an eternal ideal law" and immunized him against materialistic epicureanism (*Autob.*, 121–2, 126–8), at the time widespread in Naples and culminating in the "trial of the atheists."[1]

In 1693 or 1694 Vico graduated in both civil and canon law, probably at the University of Naples, where the records show he had matriculated in 1689. Returning from Vatolla, Vico felt a stranger in his native city and quite unknown (*Autob.*, 134): but the image—credited by Croce—of an eccentric and misunderstood genius seems to be contradicted by recent studies.[2]

On October 25, 1698, Vico gave his lecture to obtain the vacant chair of rhetoric. He won the competition, perhaps because of the interference of Viceroy Medinacoeli, who preferred a teacher ideologically kindred to the Curia.[3] On December 2, 1699, Vico married Teresa Caterina Destito, who gave him eight children.

The subsequent competition for Morning Chair of Civil Law (April 1723) had an unlucky outcome. Vico, who trusted in recent publication of his juridical works, chose as the topic for his lesson a law of Papinian contained in the title *De praescriptis verbis* (D. 19.5: *Autob.*, 49–52). But pressures by Viceroy Althann on the committee determined the victory of Domenico Gentile, representative of an antiquarian legal culture; it is unclear whether Vico had withdrawn before the end of competition (so *Autob.*, 164). Some scholars (Gentile, Piovani, Patetta) suspect that Vico deservedly lost the 1723 competition because he was unfit to teach law.[4] Recently, it has been hypothesized that the Austrian government had not appreciated, in Vico's historical reconstruction of ancient Rome, either the references to class inequalities or the contradictory "signals" in *Universal Right* between exaltation of the free role of jurisprudence as civil equity and standardization of case law.[5]

The academic misfortune accentuated Vico's pessimistic and solitary vein. Shortly after the Bourbon dynasty ascended to the throne of Naples, he was appointed (1735) royal historian. Vico dedicated his last years to incessant reworking of *The New Science* and died in Naples on January 23, 1744.

Most significant works

After some occasional writings, between 1699 and 1707 Vico published *Six Inaugural Orations* (annual academic prolusions) and, in 1703, an account of the pro-Austrian conspiracy (so-called of Macchia) suppressed in September 1701.[6] The oration *De nostri temporis studiorum ratione* (*On The Study Methods of Our Times*, October 18, 1708), published in February 1709, was later defined by the author as a "first draft" of *Universal Right* (*Autob.*, 146). This attempt to compare and to balance ancient (rhetorical) and modern (scientific) study methods (*ratio*: *SM*, I, 4–5) is considered the "birth certificate of Vichian philosophy."[7]

De antiquissima Italorum sapientia (*On the Most Ancient Wisdom of the Italians*), edited in October 1710 and dedicated to Paolo Mattia Doria (supporter of a *togated republic* on the Platonic model), challenged Descartes's theory of clear and distinct ideas: Vico argued that true knowledge can start only from things, and that sciences, through their operations (*operatione*), become similar to divine science because the truth is convertible with the made (*verum et factum convertuntur*: *AW*, 16).

After his biography of Antonio Carafa (prepared between 1713 and 1715),[8] Vico focused his work overtly on law in *Diritto universale* (*Universal Right*). In July 1720 it was preceded by an essay later titled *Synopsis of Universal Law*. In September of the same year, he published *The One Principle and the One End*. *The Constancy of the Jurist* came out in August 1721, and in the summer of 1722 the *corpus* was completed by *Notae in duos libros*.[9] The unity of the editorial plan is attested by Vico himself (*Autob.*, *Continuation by the Author* [1731], 192).

The One, a partial development of a (lost) oration of 1719,[10] aimed at a synthesis between philosophy (*verum*) and philology (*certum*), reason and authority (*The One*, *Prologue* [16], 8). The importance of this work has recently been acknowledged.[11] *The Constancy* was divided into two parts: *The Constancy of Philosophy* and *The Constancy of Philology*. The first, much shorter, part summarized philosophical principles of legal history and civilization. The second part, whose first chapter was titled *Nova scientia tentatur* (*A New Science is Essayed*), revived (against Descartes and Malebranche) the relevance of philology, considered indispensable for knowing ancient languages of religion and laws (*Const. Philol.*, ch. 1 [1–2], 329; ibid. [24], 337). "Some were displeased" by the attempt to found a new science; nevertheless, the *Constantia* received plaudits (*Autob.*, 158).[12]

While Croce and Nicolini judged *Universal Right* to be only a step in approaching *The New Science*, jurists (Donati, Betti, Capograssi, and Piovani) reevaluated its scientific autonomy.[13] The three books published in 1720–22 provided a *manifesto* for the ministerial class and judiciary power: not by chance, both parts of it were dedicated to the influential magistrate Francesco Ventura.[14]

In 1723 Vico prepared for print a *New Science in Negative Form*, which examined "the principles of the natural law" through the criticism of the theses of other authors. At the last moment, Vico "decided that this negative form of exposition" was not appropriate for understanding. At the same time, he suffered the denial of financing promised by Lorenzo Corsini (future Pope Clement XII) (*Autob.*, 165–6).

In 1725 Vico published in Naples, at his own expense, *The Principles of a New Science of the Nature of Nations through Which the Principles of a New System of the Natural Law of the Nations Are Discovered*, officially addressed just to Corsini. The text started with an invocation to European academies, which in that enlightened age were severely criticizing "not only the fables and vulgar traditions of gentile history but all the authority" of philosophers (*FNS*, 3): this appeal disappeared in subsequent editions, maybe because the author had the disappointing feeling that he had sent his work to the desert (Letter to Father Bernardo Maria Giacco, October 25, 1725, in *Autob.*, 14).[15]

This edition, named *first* by Nicolini, was organized in five slender chapters. Vico admitted that all his previous works "were devised to win me one of the higher chairs in our university": now he hoped that only this new book would survive him (letter to Giacco [see earlier], in *Autob.*, 15; see also *Epistole*, 113–14). Against Croce and Nicolini, who considered *The First New Science* the point of arrival of a rather linear path, Giarrizzo judged it a solution of continuity from a political dimension to a conservative "isolation."[16] This opinion seems to be confirmed by the chapter which explained that the "jurisprudence of mankind" should have been considered "to be a science of the mind of man ... placed ... in solitude" and devoted to self-conservation (*FNS*, b. II, ch. XII, cpv. 41, 31).

Between 1723 and 1728 Vico elaborated his *Autobiography*. It was commissioned by Count Giovanartico di Porcía, within an ambitious cultural project. In the end, the editorial plan was modified, and Vico's *Life* took its place in the *Raccolta d'opuscoli scientifici e filologici* (1728).[17] Unsatisfied, Vico wrote (1731) an *Aggiunta* (*Continuation*), to which Carlantonio de Rosa Marquis of Villarosa joined some unpublished pages in 1818 (see *Autob.*, 173–200, 200–9).

In the summer of 1730, after various typographical misadventures, the second edition of *The New Science* appeared again in Naples.[18] For the first time, it contained the *Occasione di meditarsi quest'opera*; the *Explanation of the Picture Placed as Frontispiece*; 109 *axioms* or *degnità*. The author was induced by his chronic uneasiness to an incessant reworking.[19] The last edition began to come out in 1743, but the definitive text appeared posthumously (July 2, 1744).

Place in the tradition

Vico's influence on legal culture began to be clearly felt from the late eighteenth century. Francesco Mario Pagano (constituent, then martyr of the Bourbon reaction in 1799) shared Vico's analysis of the historical and natural origins of the power, although he understated their religious roots.[20] Among the southern Italian jurists of the early nineteenth century, the legacy of the *genius loci* was understood as a humanistic and historicist approach to juridical and institutional problems:[21] the "Neapolitan" school (Niccola Nicolini, Pasquale Stanislao Mancini, Giuseppe Pisanelli, Enrico Pessina) was anchored in Vico's ideas about the popular and historical formation of law and the jurists' claim of political centrality.

In the first decades of the nineteenth century, interest in Vico also grew in France, promoted by the free translation of *The New Science* carried out by Michelet.[22] In the German area, Savigny considered Vico—to whom he was linked by evident ideological similarities—a talented exception in the depressed landscape of Neapolitan legal studies.[23] Among well-known references to Vico contained in Marx's writings, a letter to Lassalle (1862) remarked the "philosophical view of the spirit of Roman Law, contrasting with that of the legal Philistines."[24]

In the late Italian Risorgimento, Vico's inheritance, which had become now a symbol of national redemption,[25] was ideologically disputed. Some exponents of the Positivist School saw a presaging of juridical sociology in *The New Science* and identified Vichian providence in the "necessity" of social facts.[26] The editorial enterprise of Croce and Nicolini made Vico a precursor of Idealism.[27] Both this neo-idealistic hegemonic interpretation and the Catholic one, which valued a wholly religious and antiutilitarian Vico,[28] dissuaded jurists from approaching him.[29] However, there were notable exceptions. In 1925 Giuseppe Capograssi, while admitting the anti-modernity of Vichian thought, observed that *The One* could have been "extraordinarily useful" in a period when law had become "either inactive and extraneous to real life, or a mere technique, a flexible utensil at the mercy of the real interests, or a disordered experience without beginning and without end."[30] Emilio Betti considered the "brilliant intuition" engraved in *The New Science* (since "the world of civil society has certainly been made by men," it's possible to find the "principles" of the civil world "within the modifications of our own human mind": *NS 1744*, 96) a founding act of hermeneutics.[31]

Croce's interpretation was questioned by Badaloni (1961), who tried to place Vico in an environment characterized by scientism and power of the courts.[32] But even in 1976 Tarello denied any influence by Vico on legal culture, while he recognized for him a "place of great importance" in the "stories of the philosophy of law."[33]

Meanwhile, after English translations of the *Autobiography* (1944) and *The New Science* (1948), the Anglo-Saxon world has shown a growing curiosity for Vico. Meetings and proceedings promoted by Giorgio Tagliacozzo,[34] essays of Donald Phillip Verene, the activity of the Institute for Vico Studies (1974) and of the review *New Vico Studies* (1983–2009),[35] Berlin's research[36] favored Vico's resurrection. In the last decades, in the wake of Elio Gianturco, Anglo-American literature has begun to look at Vico as jurist. The same trend can be found in recent contributions from France and Spain.[37]

Law between philosophy and philology

Unclear, convoluted, enigmatic: similar adjectives are usually attributed to Vico's thought, which in fact is not suitable for synthesis or systemization,[38] but proceeds from intuitions, breaks, ellipses. Yet it offers the contemporary reader a lot of suggestions, also thanks to a syncopated and compelling style, to the majestic language, to the surprising mastery of humanistic culture. Faced with a boundless literature about him, this chapter will focus only on some aspects of the influence of religion (in a broad sense) on Vico's legal vision.

A preliminary question is: was Vico a jurist? This is a paradoxical question: in fact, the subtitle of *The First New Science* (1725) aims to identify *The Principles of a New system of the Natural Law of the Nations.*[39] He advocated a fully political philosophy, "useful to the human race," unlike that "monastic, or solitary" philosophy of the Stoics and Epicureans (*SN 1730*, lb. I, *Degnità* IV, 95; *NS 1744*, b. I, *axiom* V, cpvv. 129–30, 61–2).

Jurisprudence stood out for this "social function" of intellectual activity.[40] Vico proclaimed it the point of conjunction among moral doctrine, civil doctrine, and moral theology (*HE*, *Oration* VI, § 9, 133). He observed that, while philosophy "considers man as he should be," and therefore benefited only very few who wished to live in the Republic of Plato rather than in the dregs of Romulus, "legislation considers man as he is in order to turn him to good uses in human society" (*SN 1730*, lb. I, *Degnità* V–VI, 93; *NS 1744*, b. I, *axiom* VI–VII, cpvv. 131–3, 62).

The One said that "all jurisprudence depends upon reason and authority": the former is based on natural necessity, while the latter depends on the "will of those who give orders"; "philosophy inquires the necessary causes of things," while history is witness to the will. Therefore, "jurisprudence's nature results from three elements: philosophy, history, and a certain appropriate art of applying" law to facts. According to Vico, the mistake made until his time had consisted in keeping these two principles distinct: it was wrong to think that "authority comes" from "capricious will" (*libido*) and does not contain an element of reason (*The One*, *Prologue* [2 and 16], 4 and 8).

Against authors who had argued for the relative and utilitarian character of law (Epicurus, Machiavelli, Hobbes, Spinoza, and finally Bayle), *The One* aimed to look for *ius aeternum verum* "with the help of metaphysics." In this research, Vico believed he had found the solution in Varro's *formula naturae* (referred in Augustine's *De civitate Dei*), that is, the recognition of one infinite divinity in place of "many deities." Natural law—Vico added—was that *formula*, "the idea of truth, that shows us the true God": God is the principle, "at the same time," of true religion, true law, true jurisprudence. True jurisprudence was the knowledge of divine and human things. Vico declared he had learned that three elements of all divine and human erudition were knowledge (*nosse*), will (*velle*), and power (*posse*), whose unique principle was mind, whose eye was reason, and whose light was God (*The One*, *Prologue* [21–5], 9–10).

On the Most Ancient argued that true and made are interchangeable or convertible (*verum et factum convertuntur*), and that the mind knows things which it has made (*AW*, b. I, ch. I, 16–17; ibid., *Conclusion*, 129).[41] *Universal Right* developed the same insight in the juridical field. Vichian "restless modernity"[42] consisted in confirming the prescriptive character of law, without disregarding its empirical usefulness.[43] The true was generated by "the mind's conformation with the order of things," and the power of *verum* or human reason was justice "so far as it would direct and equalize utilities": "it is the one end of universal right." Unlike Grotius, Vico thought that utility (as well as necessity, fear, and needs, hypothesized by Epicurus, Hobbes, Spinoza, and Bayle) had been the *occasion*, not the *mother*, of human law and sociability after the original sin (*The One*, *Prologue* [31], 35; ibid., ch. 17, 31; ch. 43–6, 37–40).

An immanent providence

"All Vico's writings show the Catholic religion established grave, solid, immovable, as adamantine column in his soul."[44] Croce's peremptory claim has received confirmations, clarifications, corrections. Corsano's studies have highlighted the key points of Vico's religiosity: full acceptance of the dogma of the Fall; the Augustinian idea of religion as the "foundation" and *prius* of politics; and an option for a "vulgar and popular" faith, derived from "common sense."[45] After all, Vico did not hide that he had felt Augustine's charm (*Autob.*, 119).

In opposition to Bayle, Vico was firmly sure of the foundational value of religion (*FNS*, b. I, *ch.* I, cpv. 8, 9; see also *NS 1744*, b. I, *axiom* XXX, cpv. 176, 69). This belief concerned not only anthropology but also law. *Universal Right* placed the religion at origin of the first private law institutions (*The One*, ch. 104 [8–9], 78; *Const. Philol.*, ch. 21 [63], 448) and legislation: after all, had Numa Pompilius not faked having "received his laws from a nymph, so that more easily the feral people would submit to laws because of their religious aurora?" (*The One*, ch. 149, [4], 118–19). Some passages suggest that Vico found the origin of religion essentially in fear (*Const. Philos.*, ch. 6 [4 and 7], 305–6): a providential fear, and therefore different from that described by Hobbes (*SN 1730*, lb. II, 186–7; ibid., lb. I, *Degnità* XXIX, 100; *NS 1744*, b. II, *sect.* III, cpvv. 502–4, 170–1; ibid., b. I, *axiom* 31, cpvv. 177–8, 70).

Interpretation of the role of providence in Vico's thought is not univocal. The most persuasive hypothesis is that it acted as a natural and immanent force,[46] a "divine legislative mind," able to stimulate the self-preservation of humankind (*NS 1744*, b. I, cpv. 341, 101–2), to combine utilities of the passions and justice, to drive wild and lonely beasts towards the civil order and human society (*SN* 1730, lb. I, *Degnità* VI, 93; *NS 1744*, b. I, *axiom* VII, cpv. 132–3, 62).

The insistence on the sociopolitical rooting of providence allowed Vico to label his science as civil theology (e.g., *SN 1730*, lb. I, 128; *NS 1744*, b. I, cpv. 342, 102). *Religio*, considered by Machiavelli to be an *instrumentum regni*, carried out a unifying task between the divine sphere and "effective sociality" in Vico. *Timor*, which according to Hobbes generated an opportunistic social contract, led primitive humankind to eternal truth and founded civil society for the Neapolitan philosopher.[47]

History as revelation of the true

History was the meeting point between the true and the contingent, between the natural and the political orders. Vico was not interested in diligently reconstructing details (*Autob.*, *Continuation by the Author* [1731], 195). Conversely, he proposed an integral history of civilization. Deeds of men and nations proceeded, with constant uniformity, in three ages: of gods, heroes, and men. The tripartition was reflected in three kinds of governments, languages, and natural laws of the *gentes* (*FNS*, b. V, ch. II, cpvv. 402–4, 235–6). Later, Vico added that all special unities of this triadic proceeding were "embraced by one general unity. This is the unity of the religion of a provident divinity" (*SN 1730*, lb. IV, 319; *NS 1744*, b. 4, Introduction, cpv. 915, 335).

The New Science is the fascinating overview of this incessant, nonlinear and noncyclic triadic path: first, and longer, it reconstructed the age of poetic wisdom (*b.* II–III), then the course of the nations (*b.* IV), and finally the recourse of human things and the resurrection of the nations (*b.* V). In the phase of poetic wisdom, which Vico preferred so much as to earn him the nickname "sunrise poet,"[48] knowledge of the laws was guarded through the science of language (*Const. Philol.*, ch. 12 [2], 367; ibid., ch. 13 [20, 25–6], 380–1; see also *Notae in librum alterum* [in *Diritto universale*, ed. 2019], nt. 85*, 447 = *Notes to Const. Philol.*, nt. 131*, 551). From the "vulgar wisdom" of poets, embodied by Homer and expressed through fables and mythologies, humanity moved on to the rational reflection of philosophers (*NS 1744*, b. I, *axiom* LIII, 75). But the recourse dictated by providential order brought back a new "barbarism of reflection." This last formula marked those times in which "the misbegotten subtleties of malicious wits" made men more inhuman beasts than the ancients living in the "generous savagery" of the "barbarism of sense." However, development triggered a providential regression to essential needs and religious values (*NS 1744*, *Conclusion*, cpv. 1106, 424; see already *SN 1730*, lb. V, *Conchiusione*, 375).

Compared to *Universal Right*, which contemplated the chance of redemption, the conclusion of *The New Science* foreshadowed a distressing return to the wild primitivism of the ancients and medievals (*The One*, ch. 34, 35; *Const. Philos.*, ch. 5 [18], 310). The darkness of the *Picture* opening the 1730 and 1744 editions of the *New Sciences* (*SN 1730*, 55; *NS 1744*, cpv. 40, 26) now revealed itself to be invincible. Therefore, the close of Vico's masterpiece acquires a dramatic meaning: "This Science carries inseparably with it the study of piety, and . . . he who is not pious cannot be truly wise" (*NS 1744*, *Conclusion*, cpv. 1112, 426; and already *SN 1730*, lb. V, 378).[49]

Like general history, so too Vico's legal history flowed between the immutable *verum* and the changing *certum*. The law, after descending into the concreteness of *auctoritas* and conflicting utilities, concluded its circle by returning to God, "the One Principle and the One End of Universal Right" (*The One*, *Last*

Chapter, 209). The "jurisprudence of mankind require[d] knowledge of the history of the law uniformly dictated by nature to all the nations" in different times (*FNS*, b. II, ch. CXXXVIII, cpv. 175, 107–8). Unlike Meinecke's, Vico's "legal" historicism was interested not so much in contextualizing past events but rather in illustrating the "classic" age as the humanistic paradigm of civilization.[50]

Roman law: a great poem

In early eighteenth-century Naples, such an archetype could not consist in other than Roman law. Quoting Horace (*Ars Poetica*, 396–9), Vico noted that, while Greeks had assigned to philosophers "the task of teaching the philosophy of law, that is, the theory of the state, of justice," in Rome philosophers "were jurists" (*SM*, XI, 49; *The One*, ch. 183 [7], 167; ibid., *Prologue* [7], 5). Vico imagined the "ancient jurisprudence" as "a kind of poem" (*The One*, ch. 182, 165) and proposed a sumptuous fresco of the five epochs of ***dark time***. According to him, the exit from the lawless state (the "hidden face of modernity")[51] had been favored by the typical institutes of original *ius civile*: marriages, parental authority, wills (*The One*, ch. 102–4, 75–81; *Const. Philol.*, ch. 20, §§ 1–5, 400–17). Under what he termed the theocratic regime, patricians became holders of language, rites, and laws and began to practice clienteles, which Vico compared to feudal protection (*The One*, ch. 104 [11], 78–9; *Const. Philol.*, ch. 21 [1, 3, 32, 42–3, 51, 54–6], 428–9, 438–9, 442–6).[52] In the third epoch, revolts and secessions guaranteed the bonitary dominion of land (the later *possessio* in feudal law) to plebeians: violence gave way to imitations of violence (*Const. Philol.*, ch. 22 [1–6], 450–2; *The One*, ch. 124 [1], 92). Capograssi summarized these passages in the triad ***dominion—liberty—tutelage***.[53] In examining the fourth epoch, Vico severely criticized the traditional thesis about the *Lex Regia*, that is, the phantom provision that would have transferred full legislative power from patricians to a monarch (*Const. Philol.*, ch. 26 [2], 469; *The One*, ch. 140 [3], 107; ibid., ch. 160 [1], 137; see too *Autob.*, *Continuation* 1731, 193).[54] In the fifth and last epoch of dark time, providence used wars to close the divine circle of law from God to God: henceforth, history turned in a reverse direction, from free republics to theocracies; at the end of this double but not identical sequence, God, Eternal Justice, again entrusted the power to better contenders (*Const. Philol.*, ch. 30 [31–4], 494–5; *DC*, II, cap. XXIX, 362).

The passionate diachronic exposure of Roman history attested a providential sense (*Const. Philol.*, ch. 34 [1 and 5], 511–12; *DC*, II, cap. XXXIII, 375–6). Therefore, Vico sincerely admitted that his admiration for ancient Rome rested on different bases from those of Machiavelli, who did not comprehend the complexity of Roman institutions; from Polybius, who was more attracted to misdeeds than to Roman virtue; and from Plutarch, who unjustly attributed to fortune what had instead depended on wisdom (*Const. Philol.*, ch. 35 [1–3], 515; *DC*, II, cap. XXXIV, 378–9).

The Vichian approach to Roman law has received technical objections[55] or has been deemed too influenced by the feudal landscape of modern southern Italy.[56]

However, various original aspects remain remarkable: the interpretation of conflict between patricians and plebeians as a symptom of archaic class struggle;[57] the relevance of agrarian laws (*Const. Philol.*, ch. 34 [17], 515; *DC*, II, cap. XXXIII, 378; *FNS*, b. II, ch. XLV, 112–16); the confutation of the "fabulous" Greek origins of the Twelve Tables (*Autob.*, *Continuation* 1731, 193; *FNS*, b. II, ch. XXXVI, 101–6);[58] and the idea that property relations could condition institutional balances.

Civil equity and the key role of great courts

The Roman law history showed that the *reflected wisdom* allowed jurists to play the role of social intellectual. In a time of legal uncertainty, Vico used the Roman model as a *manifesto* of "centrality of judiciary, and jurisprudence, in the governance of political community."[59] He considered providential the edicts of the praetors and the responses of the best jurists (*Const. Philol.*, ch. 37 [17], 527). In accordance with Pomponius (D. 1.1.2.5), Vico restated that Roman *ius civile* was what "resulted not from custody but from invention" and in an unwritten form: therefore jurisprudence was born in the world only among Romans (*Const. Philol.*, *Last ch.* [2], 530).

Vico's works outlined, with some inaccuracies, a chronology of creativity in Roman jurisprudence. At the time of the Republic and of the Twelve Tables, "the rigorous observance of the law binds citizens like the worship of an unknown God" (*SM*, XI, 51). Under the Principate, jurisprudence aimed not at certainty but at truth, not at civil but at natural equity, called by Varro *formula naturae*: it would equalize all unequal utilities, as the "lesbic rule that adapts itself to the bodies and not the bodies to itself" (*The One*, ch. 187 [10], 178; see also *Const. Philos.*, ch. 4 [2], 305; *NS 1744*, b. IV, cpv. 1045, 393). Instead, emperors, through the *ius respondendi* and Hadrian's Perpetual Edict, transformed jurisprudence "from the science of the just into an art of equity, a technique of the equitable" (*SM*, ch. XI, 54–6).[60]

Vico's attitude towards the equitable interpretation was ambivalent. In *On the Study Methods*, he feared the risks of an increasing equity. Nonetheless, he appreciated the Neapolitan *Sacro Regio Consiglio*, the supreme court of the kingdom, which sometimes "decided contrary" to Roman law, and often preferred the civil to natural equity: he even proposed that this practice be institutionalized (*SM*, XI, 58 and 70). It is evident that Vico, during the transition of the kingdom to Austrian dominion, considered the *Sacro Regio Consiglio* "as a living institutional source of natural law,"[61] and the praetorian model as a possible solution to the crisis of legal order. But he hoped that judges would return to preferring a literal interpretation of the laws and to keeping the public interest, unlike lawyers, whose task was to emphasize the spirit of the law and "to give priority to the private claims" of their clients (*SM*, XI, 59, 69–70).

On the Study Methods encouraged interpretation oriented towards civil equity, which Italians named *giusta ragion di Stato*, a wider concept than natural equity because it aimed not at individual interests but at public weal (*SM*, XI, 66; *The*

One, ch. 179, 163).[62] In *The One*, the prerogative of supreme courts of ruling against law was conceived as functional to a further equality (*The One*, ch. 43, 37).[63] Unlike Bayle, Vico did not think that equity was a typical invocation of the weak and losers (*The One*, *Prologue* [21], 9): on the contrary, he considered it a stronger confirmation of the first law, as well as the way that the secondary natural law (*ius naturale posterius*) relates to the primary (*ius naturale prius*) (*The One*, ch. 85 [1–2], 64).[64]

Vico always preferred a sacral and impenetrable model of legislation. *On the Study Methods* defined as very blessed that *respublica* "where the rigorous observance of the law binds citizens together like the worship of an unknown god" or like "an army" (*SM*, XI, 51). A chapter of *The One* (ch. 174, 161) accentuated "The Benefits of the Arcane Law" in republican Rome. *The New Science* added that the mind of the "sovereign civil person . . . was an order of wise men": without it, states "are so many dead and soulless bodies" (*NS 1744*, b. II, cpv. 630, 237). On these assumptions, Vico defended a wise-men's government, dependent on *arcana iuris* and legitimized by *consensus gentium*.[65]

Natural law: eternal order and common sense

The concept of consensus, or rather of common sense, was an architrave in Vico's thought: it has attracted the attention both of Gadamer and of many Anglo-Saxon scholars.[66] *The New Science* defined common sense as "judgment without reflection, shared by an entire class," people, nation, or the human race. Since his next famous axiom established that "uniform ideas originating among entire peoples unknown to each other must have a common ground of truth," Vico concluded that common sense was the criterion devised by providence to identify what is certain in the natural law of the people (*NS 1744*, lb. I, *axioms* XII–XIII, cpv. 142–5, 63).

Such a statement must be connected to the dual face of natural law: on one hand, an immutable value, the eternal order of things, "wanting the good that was known to be equal" (*The One*, ch. 48 [1], 40; ch. 47, 40);[67] on the other hand, the outcome of historical transition (as usual, illustrated by Roman law) from *primary natural law*, consisting of survival instincts, to *secondary natural law*, protected by the *ratio* (*The One*, ch. 75 [1, 4, 8–9], 57–60; ibid., ch. 117 [4 and 6], 89).

Grotius was an inevitable term of comparison. While writing *The Deeds of Antonio Carafa* (1713), Vico honored the Dutch jurist as his "fourth author" because of the ability to embrace philosophy and philology, history of facts and history of fables "in a system of universal law." But a few years later (about 1717), Vico abandoned the task of preparing notes for a new edition of *De iure belli ac pacis*: he acknowledged "that it was not fitting" for a Catholic "to adorn with notes the work of a heretical author" (*Autob.*, 154–5).[68]

Vico reproached Grotius for numerous misunderstandings:[69] above all, for not having gotten the difference between natural law of the nations and natural law of philosophers (*The One*, ch. 136 [1], 102; *Autob.*, 172); for claiming that natural law system would remain standing even if God did not exist (*FNS*, b. 1, ch. V, cpv. 16, 14); and for believing in a rationality devoid of providence (*NS 1744*, b. II, cpv. 395, 124).[70] Vico rejected abstract, nonhistorical, intellectualistic iusnaturalism (*FNS*, b. I, cpv. 20, 16): according to him, "the natural law of the nations was certainly born with the common customs," and its roots were in religions (*FNS*, b. I, ch. I, cpv. 8, 9; see ibid., ch. V, cpvv. 20–2, 16–18 for dissent from Grotius, Selden, and Pufendorf).

In Vico "iusnaturalism and historicism" were "coupled" into a higher synthesis, not a "cacophonous discord" or "a hybrid monster."[71] As political outcomes of this peculiar synergy, he emphasized the strength of custom (*NS 1744*, b. I, *axiom* 104, cpvv. 308–10, 91) and incited the jurist to shape his constancy on "principles of Christian jurisprudence" (*Synopsis*, § 9, lxxvi). Thus, the Neapolitan philosopher dissociated himself from the challenge of a part of modern natural law to the authority principle.[72]

The legacy: anti-Cartesian spirit

Usually, the least modern side of Vico's thought is ascribed to his anti-Cartesianism. This aspect has not aroused equal attention so far among legal historians—with some brilliant exceptions—[73] although the Vichian epistolary openly denounced the noxious effects of Descartes's method on legal literature (e.g., *Epistole*, 132; ibid., 145–7; see also *Autob.*, 113 and 129).

Among the jurists of the third millennium, reasons for Vico's intolerance towards the *esprit de géométrie* could evoke unexpected similarities with actual trends: a renunciation of using fantasy as an instrument of knowledge (*HE*, *Oration* I, § 6, 42; ibid., § 10, 45–6); the abuse of "analytical methods" and the mortification of the "faculty of soul"; and the contempt for imagination, the "mother of all human error" (*Epistole*, 121).

In *On the Study Methods* (1708), dissent from Descartes invested the crucial question of the method in modern legal science. Vico mantained that "the greatest drawback of our educational methods" was the excessive "attention to the natural sciences and not enough to ethics," especially to "the science of politics": for the latter, variability of human affairs demanded to be measured with a pliant lesbian rule, rather than with a *recta linea* (*SM*, VII, 33–4). Vico mourned a golden age during the which "all arts and disciplines were interconnected and rested in the lap of philosophy." He compared responsibility for the current fragmentation to that of a "tyrannical ruler" who disperses inhabitants of a great, opulent city in order to prevent their rebirth (*SM*, X, 47). Jurists in training also suffered from specialism. They risked finding as masters "a disciple of Accursius" for the Institutions, "a follower of Antoine Favre" for the Digest, a student of Alciato for the Code: this heterogeneity would have made them "extremely learned" in single disciplines, but without consistency on the whole culture, that is, "the flower of wisdom" (*SM*, XIV, 77).[74]

To react to the unnatural disjunction "between arts and sciences" (*SM*, XIV, 76), Vico proposed that young people should be trained in terms of the "totality of sciences and arts." He also asked for enhancing of imagination and memory, *common sense*, and criticism: so students would become "exact in science, clever in practical matters, fluent in eloquence, imaginative in understanding poetry or painting, strong in memorizing what they have learned in their legal studies" (*SM*, III, 14, 19). Today Vico's contribution to studies of *topoi* within legal argumentation theories is recognized without dissent.[75] Viehweg (1953) claimed that he followed Vico's trail, that is, the recovery of reasoning by problems, rather than the Cartesian geometric deductivism.[76] Vico's meticulous care for eloquence (*SM*, III, 15) and for legal language (*The One*, *Prologue* [10], 7) has also become a reference model.

With regard to the organization of educational institutions, Vico suggested "that our professors should so coordinate all disciplines into a single system so as to harmonize them with our religion and with the spirit of the political form ... In this way," they could offer "a coherent body of learning ... according to the genius of our public polity" (*SM*, XIV, 77). To obtain a scientific synthesis, Vico was willing to accept an enforced and authoritarian conformation of the official academic culture.[77]

Vico's crusade against mathematics seems to fade in the *New Science*. A passage of the 1730 edition (omitted in the 1744 edition) announced the use of a "strictly geometric method," that is, of well-founded and well-ordered premises (*SN 1730*, *Idea dell'opera*, 58). In the same work, the author declared himself convinced that his *New Science* proceeded "as mathematics" (*Geometry* in *NS* 1744), which created for itself when it constructed a world of quantity or contemplated that world: but he pointed out that "our science" created "with a greater reality," because human things "are more real than points, lines, surfaces, and figures are"; and because the creative knowledge gave a divine pleasure (*NS 1744*, b. I, cpv. 349, 104–5; with minimal variations, *SN 1730*, lb. I, 132).

Some years ago, an authoritative Vico scholar reflected: "We live in a Cartesian world, a world of scientific research, technology, and gadgets, which invade and condition our lives."[78] Today, the Cartesian world is increasingly altering the shape of legal science. Ahead of his time, Vico denounced the limits of this epistemological paradigm. To contrast it, he suggested traditional, maybe illusory instruments: an unpredictable use of *ingenium* instead of calculation; a methodological blending of physical and humanistic sciences. Those solutions, which had often marked Vico as an antimodern, could prove fruitful in legal postmodernity. De Sanctis's prophecy comes back to mind: Vico embodied "the resistance of Italian culture," but a resistance which, "while searching in the past, finds the modern world"; he "felt and believed himself to be an ancient, but really was a modern; and resisting the new spirit he received it into himself."[79]

Abbreviations of Vico's works

Autob. = *The Autobiography ... translated from the Italian by Max Harold Fisch and Thomas Goddard Bergin* (1944). Ithaca, NY/London: Cornell University Press, 1975.

AW = *On the Most Ancient Wisdom of the Italians. Drawn out from the Origins of the Latin Language*. Translated by Jason Taylor. With an Introduction by Robert Miner. New Haven, CT/London: Yale University Press, 2010.

Critical edition: Giambattista Vico. *De Antiquissima Italorum Sapientia*. Con traduzione italiana a fronte, edited by Manuela Sanna. Rome: Edizioni di Storia e Letteratura, 2005, reprint 2009.

Const. Philol. = *The Constancy of the Jurist, That Is, The Guarding of Divine and Human Institutions* (September 1721), in *Universal Right* (see below), *Part Two*: *The Constancy of Philology*, 327–613.

Critical edition: *DC*, II (see below).

Const. Philos. = *The Constancy of the Jurist, That Is, The Guarding of Divine and Human Institutions* (September 1721), in *Universal Right* (see below), *Part One*: *The Constancy of Philosophy*, 301–26.

Critical edition: *De constantia iurisprudentis. Pars prior*, in *Diritto universale*, edited by Marco Veneziani. Rome: Edizioni di Storia e Letteratura, 2019: 204–22.

DC, II = *De constantia iurisprudentis. Pars posterior*, in Veneziani, ed., *Diritto universale* (see above), 222–392.

Epistole = *Epistole con aggiunte le epistole dei suoi corrispondenti*, edited by Manuela Sanna. Naples: Morano, 1993.

FNS = *The First New Science*, edited by Leon Pompa. New York: Cambridge University Press, 2002 (this edition maintains Nicolini's paragraph enumeration).

Italian (not critical) edition: *Principj di una Scienza nuova (1725)*, edited by Paolo Cristofolini. Pisa: Ets, 2016.

HE = *On Humanistic Education (Six Inaugural Orations, 1699–1707)*. From the definitive Latin Text, Introduction, and Notes of Gian Galeazzo Visconti. Translated by Giorgio A. Pinton and Arthur W. Shippee with an introduction by Donald Phillip Verene. Ithaca, NY/London: Cornell University Press, 1993.

Critical edition: *Le orazioni inaugurali I–VI*, edited by Gian Galeazzo Visconti. 2nd ed. Rome: Edizioni di Storia e Letteratura, 2013.

NS 1744 = *The New Science* ... Revised Translation of the Third Edition (1744). Thomas Goddard Bergin and Max Harold Fisch. Ithaca, NY: Cornell University Press, 1968 (this edition maintains Nicolini's paragraph enumeration).

Critical edition: *La Scienza nuova 1744*, edited by Paolo Cristofolini and Manuela Sanna. Rome: Edizioni di Storia e Letteratura, 2013, repr. 2018.

SM = *On the Study Methods of Our Time*. Translated with an introduction and notes by Elio Gianturco. Preface by Donald Phillip Verene. With a translation of *The Academies and the Relation between Philosophy and Eloquence* by Donald Phillip Verene. Ithaca, NY/London: Cornell University Press, 1990)

CRITICAL EDITION: *DE NOSTRI TEMPORIS STUDIORUM RATIONE*, EDITED BY FABRIZIO LOMONACO. POMIGLIANO D'ARCO: DIOGENE, 2014.

SN 1730 = *La Scienza nuova 1730*, edited by Paolo Cristofolini with collaboration of Manuela Sanna. Naples: Guida, 2013.

Synopsis = *Synopsis of Universal Right*, in Id., *Universal Right* (see below), lxi—lxvii.

The One – *The One Principle and the One End of Universal Right* (September 1720), in Id., *Universal Right* (see below), 1–291.

CRITICAL EDITION: *DE UNIVERSI JURIS UNO PRINCIPIO, ET FINE UNO LIBER UNUS*, IN VENEZIANI, ED., *DIRITTO UNIVERSALE* (SEE ABOVE), 19–198.

Universal Right. Translated from Latin and edited by Giorgio Pinton and Margaret Diehl. Amsterdam/Atlanta, GA: Rodopi, 2000.

CRITICAL EDITION: VENEZIANI, ED., *DIRITTO UNIVERSALE* (SEE ABOVE).

Notes

1 Osbat, *L'inquisizione a Napoli*, 20–1.
2 Croce, *La filosofia*, 223; Sanna, *Vico*, 13 and *passim*.
3 Ascione, *Seminarium doctrinarum*, 36.
4 Catalano, esp. 573–4.
5 Naddeo, *Vico*, 166–9.
6 Vico, *La congiura dei príncipi napoletani*.
7 De Giovanni, "Topica e critica." For cultural context see De Giovanni, "Il 'De nostri temporis studiorum ratione'"; Lomonaco, "La 'politicità'," 54–7.
8 Giambattista Vico, *De rebus gestis Antonj Caraphaei Libri Quatuor* ..., Neapoli, Felix Musca 1716; Id., *Le gesta di Antonio Carafa*, ed. Manuela Sanna (Roma: Edizioni di Storia e Letteratura, 2013^{2}); Id., *Statecraft: The Deeds of Antonio Carafa (De rebus gestis Antoni Caraphaei)*, translated and edited by Giorgio A. Pinton (New York etc.: Peter Lang, 2004).
9 Vico, *Notes and Dissertations* (August 1722), in Id., *Universal Right*, 615–711. For critical edition see now Vico, *Diritto universale*, 393–512.
10 See *Autob.*, 156; Fausto Nicolini, "La prolusione universitaria del 18 ottobre 1719," in Vico, *Versi*, 283–4.
11 Ruggiero, *Nova scientia*, 23; Lomonaco, *I sentieri*, 95.
12 Sina, *Vico e Le Clerc*.
13 E.g., Donati, "I prolegomeni," 256–7.
14 Naddeo, *Vico*, 102–5. See *The One*, *Prologue*, 3; *Const. Philol.*, *Conclusion*, 531.
15 In 1729 Vico published the *Vici Vindiciae*, an answer to a critical review appeared in *Acta eruditorum lipsiensia* (1727): see Verene, "Vico's Reply."
16 Giarrizzo, "La politica di Vico" (1968), 55–6.
17 Verene, *New Art of Autobiography*.
18 See *SN 1730*, *Occasione di meditarsi quest'Opera*, 21–6; *Autob.*, *Continuation 1731*, 191–7.
19 Before the book was distributed, Vico inserted *Correzioni, miglioramenti e aggiunte prime* (*corrections, improvements, and additions*); he eliminated a *Novella letteraria* from the first thousand distributed copies. The second draft (ed. December 1730), dedicated to Corsini (now pope Clemente XII), contained a letter to Francesco Spinelli and *second corrections, improvements, and additions*. Thirth and fourth *corrections, improvements, and additions* are datable, respectively, 1730–1 and 1732–4. See Cristofolini, "Introduzione" to *SN 1730*, 1–4; see *Corrections* ibid., 382–6, 396–404, 405–544, 545–646.

20 Solari, 181.
21 Cospito, *Il "gran Vico"*.
22 Vico, *Principes de la philosophie de l'histoire traduits de la* Scienza Nuova. Vico's penetration in France has been described by Alain Pons, "Vico et la pensée française" (1968), It. tr. "Vico e il pensiero francese," in Id., *Da Vico a Michelet* (2014): 131–57, esp. 143–51.
23 Savigny, "Ueber den juristischen Unterricht in Italien"; Savigny, "Erinnerungen an Niebuhr's Wesen und Wirken, durch seine Briefe veranlasst," in Niebuhr, 348, then in Savigny, *Vermischte Schriften*, vol. 4, 217–18. See also Becchi.
24 Karl Marx, to Ferdinand Lassalle, April 28, 1862, in Marx and Engels, vol. 41, 355–8.
25 See Oldrini.
26 Pio, "Il positivismo di G.B. Vico"; Viazzi, *La modernità e il positivismo di G.B. Vico*, 5–34.
27 Croce, *La filosofia*, 223–7. Croce began collecting the *Bibliografia vichiana* in 1903; see 1947–48 edition in bibliography. The last update is Scognamiglio.
28 Amerio, 357–61.
29 Repetto, n. 2, 295.
30 Capograssi, "Dominio, libertà e tutela nel 'De Uno'," in Capograssi, *Opere*, vol. 4, 9–28, 11–12 (the translation is mine).
31 Betti, "Storia", 115. See also Betti, "Le categorie civilistiche dell'interpretazione," 43.
32 Badaloni, *Introduzione a G.B. Vico.*
33 Tarello, 372 (the translation is mine).
34 First of all, Tagliacozzo and White.
35 See Tagliacozzo, "Gli studi vichiani nel mondo," 7–8; Verene, "Works on Giambattista Vico," and the Supplement of Peone.
36 Berlin, *Vico and Herder*. See also Verene, *Vico's Science of Imagination.*
37 Gianturco, "Vico's Significance," 328; Pons, *Da Vico a Michelet* (2014); Sevilla, *Giambattista Vico.*
38 Gentile, "La prima fase della filosofia vichiana," in Gentile, *Studi vichiani*, 93 disagreed with Donati, "I prolegomeni," 232, who had identified in *The One* a complete philosophy of law.
39 Schaeffer, *Giambattista Vico*, 1.
40 Donati, "I prolegomeni," 225, 227.
41 See Biagio De Giovanni, "'Facere' e 'factum' nel *De antiquissima*." *Quaderni Contemporanei* 2 (1969), *G.B. Vico nel terzo centenario della nascita*: 13–16; Löwith, 81; Scalercio.
42 Piovani, 180.
43 Capograssi, "Dominio," 14.
44 Croce, *La filosofia*, 255. Promptly Catholic scholars challenged Croce for portraying a Vico too Hegelian (Del Gaizo) or philosophically reluctant to accept revelation, although personally respectful of orthodoxy (Lanna).
45 Corsano, esp. 138–40, with specific reference to *De civitate Dei*, VI, 4.
46 Hösle.
47 Lomonaco, *I sentieri*, 127–8.
48 Capograssi, "L'attualità di Vico," in Id., *Opere*, vol. 4, 400.
49 See Vitiello.
50 Gianturco, "L'importance de Vico," 330–7; Naddeo, *Vico*, 136–7. But see Lomonaco, *I sentieri*, 82.
51 De Giovanni, "*In discussione con l'* Italian Thought," 293. See also Carrino, "Colpo di fulmine."
52 Ruggiero, "Vico e la ricostruzione storica," esp. 162–6.
53 Capograssi, "Dominio."
54 See Lomonaco, *Lex Regia*; and Id., *New Studies on Lex Regia.*

55 Momigliano, "Roman 'Bestioni'," 167–72; Mazzarino, *Vico*, 46.
56 Giarrizzo, "La politica di Vico" (1968), 106–7.
57 Momigliano, "Roman 'Bestioni'," 173.
58 Vico also wrote a *Ragionamento primo d'intorno alla legge delle XII Tavole venuta da fuori in Roma*, 1731, added to *SN 1730* and excluded from *NS 1744*: Sanna, *Vico*, 89.
59 Naddeo, *Vico*, 156–7, 123–4.
60 Vico often dealt with Romanistic *fictiones*, even to criticize Justinian who had defined them "fables of the ancient law": *The one*, ch. 182, 164–5; *NS 1744*, b. IV, cpv. 1037, 390.
61 Naddeo, *Vico*, 85.
62 Corsano, "G.B. Vico" (1956), 192 (and the objections of Lomonaco, *I sentieri*, 47); Giuseppe Giarrizzo, "*Aequitas* e *prudentia*: storia di un topos vichiano" (1977), now in Id., *Vico, la politica e la storia*, 174.
63 Naddeo, *Vico*, 125.
64 See Ruggiero, *Nova scientia*, 88.
65 Ajello, "Cartesianismo," 112.
66 Volpi; Schaeffer, *Giambattista Vico.*
67 Vico used an ambiguous lexicon in reading Romanistic sources: e.g., see *Const. Philol.*, last ch. (1), 530.
68 Fassò, *Vico e Grozio*, 28–30, 42–3.
69 E.g. *The One*, *Prologue* (20), 9; ibid., ch. 76 (1), 60; *Const. Philol.*, ch. 30 (47), 498.
70 Corsano, "G.B. Vico" (1956), 230–1.
71 Gianturco, "Vico's Significance," 329.
72 Agnelli, "Motivi e sviluppi," esp. 643, 648.
73 Ajello, "Cartesianismo," esp. 96–8, 111–21.
74 Witteveen, "Reading Vico": 1200 expresses perplexity.
75 Perelman and Olbrechts-Tyteca.
76 Viehweg, *Topik und Jurisprudenz*, intro. and ch. 1.
77 De Giovanni, "Il 'De nostri temporis studiorum ratione,'" 189–91; Ajello, "Cartesianismo," 119–20.
78 Gianturco, "Translator's Introduction," in *SM*, XIX.
79 De Sanctis, 797–8.

Bibliography

Agnelli, Arduino. "Motivi e sviluppi della costanza del diritto in G.B. Vico." *Rivista internazionale di filosofia del diritto* 33/5 (1956): 608–50.

Ajello, Raffaele. "Cartesianismo e cultura oltremontana al tempo dell' 'Istoria Civile'." In *Pietro Giannone e il suo tempo*, edited by Raffaele Ajello. Vol. 1, 1–181. Atti del convegno di studi nel tricentenario della nascita. Foggia—Ischitella, 22–24 ottobre 1976. Naples: Jovene, 1980.

Amerio, Franco. *Introduzione allo studio di G.B. Vico.* Turin: Società Editrice Internazionale, 1947.

Ascione, Imma. *Seminarium doctrinarum. L'Università di Napoli nei documenti del '700. 1690–1734.* Naples: Edizioni Scientifiche Italiane, 1997.

Badaloni, Nicola. *Introduzione a G.B. Vico.* Milan: Feltrinelli, 1961.

Becchi, Paolo. *Vico e Filangieri in Germania.* Napoli: Jovene, 1986.

Berlin, Isaiah. *Vico and Herder: Two Studies in the History of Ideas.* London: The Hogart Press, 1976.

Betti, Emilio. "Le categorie civilistiche dell'interpretazione" (1948). In Id., *Interpretazione della legge e degli atti giuridici. Teoria generale e dogmatica* (1949), edited by Giuliano Crifò. 2nd ed. Milan: Giuffrè, 1971.

Betti, Emilio. "Storia e dogmatica del diritto." In *La storia del diritto nel quadro delle scienze storiche.* Atti del primo congresso internazionale della Società italiana di storia del diritto. Florence: Olschki, 1966.

Capograssi, Giuseppe. *Opere.* Vol. 4. Milan: Giuffrè, 1959.

Carrino, Gennaro. "Colpo di fulmine. Vico e il tempo barbaro." *Il Pensiero* 57/2 (2018): 45–58.

Catalano, Gaetano. "Attualità di Vico 'giureconsulto'." *Il Tommaso Natale* 6 (1978); also in *Scritti in memoria di Girolamo Bellavista.* Vol. 2, 567–83. Palermo: Cartografica, 1978.

Corsano, Antonio. "G.B. Vico" (1956). In Id., *Umanesimo e religione in G.B. Vico (1935) e Giambattista Vico (1956)*, edited by Francesco Paolo Raimondi, 147–280. Edizione coordinata da Giovanni Papuli. Galatina: Congedo, 1999.

Corsano, Antonio, ed. *Omaggio a Vico.* Naples: Morano, 1968.

Corsano, Antonio. "Umanesimo e religione in G.B. Vico" (1935). In Id., *Umanesimo e religione* (see above): 31–146.

Cospito, Giuseppe. *Il "gran Vico." Presenza, immagini e suggestioni vichiane nei testi della cultura italiana pre-risorgimentale (1799–1839).* Genoa: Name, 2002.

Croce, Benedetto. *Bibliografia vichiana. Accresciuta e rielaborata da Fausto Nicolini.* 2 vols. Naples: Ricciardi, 1947–48.

Croce, Benedetto. *La filosofia di Giambattista Vico* (1911). Edited by Felicita Audisio. 1st ed. Naples: Bibliopolis, 1997.

De Giovanni, Biagio. "Il 'De nostri temporis studiorum ratione' nella cultura napoletana del primo Settecento." In Corsano, ed., *Omaggio a Vico*, 141–91.

De Giovanni, Biagio. "'Facere' e 'factum' nel *De antiquissima.*" *Quaderni Contemporanei* (*=G.B. Vico nel terzo centenario della nascita*) 2 (1969): 11–35.

De Giovanni, Biagio. "*In discussione con l'* Italian Thought." Appendice in Id., *Kelsen e Schmitt. Oltre il Novecento.* Napoli: Editoriale Scientifica, 2018.

De Giovanni, Biagio. "Topica e critica." *Il Pensiero* (2002): 31.

Del Gaizo, Modestino. *A proposito dei nuovi studi su Giambattista Vico.* Naples: Giannini, 1911.

De Sanctis, Francesco. *Storia della letteratura italiana.* Naples: Morano, 1870. English translation, *History of Italian Literature.* Translated by Joan Redfern. Vol. 2. New York: Basic Books, 1959.

Donati, Benvenuto. "I prolegomeni della filosofia giuridica del Vico attraverso le Orazioni inaugurali dal 1699 al 1708" (1915). Now in Id., *Nuovi studi sulla filosofia civile di G.B. Vico con documenti*, 165–262. Florence: Le Monnier, 1936.

Fassò, Guido. *Vico e Grozio.* Naples: Guida, 1971.

Gentile, Giovanni. *Studi vichiani.* Edited by Vito A. Bellezza. 3rd ed. Florence: Sansoni, 1968.

Gianturco, Elio. "L'importance de Vico dans l'histoire de la pensée juridique." *Les Etudes Philosophiques* (1968): 327–49.

Giarrizzo, Giuseppe. "La politica di Vico" (1968). Now in Id., *Vico, la politica e la storia*, 53–122. Naples: Guida, 1981.

Hösle, Vittorio. "Vico und die Idee der Kulturwissenschaft. Genese, Themen und Wirkungsgeschichte der 'Scienza Nuova'." Introduction to G.B. Vico, *Prinzipien einer neuen Wissenschaft [. . .].* Hamburg: Felix Meiner, 1990.

Lanna, Domenico. "L'antireligiosità del pensiero vichiano, secondo Benedetto Croce." *Rivista Internazionale di scienze sociali e discipline ausiliarie* 29, 56/224 (1911): 448–63.

Lomonaco, Fabrizio. *I sentieri di Astrea. Studi intorno al Diritto Universale di Giambattista Vico.* Rome: Edizioni di Storia e Letteratura, 2018.

Lomonaco, Fabrizio. "La 'politicità' di Vico nelle *Orationes.*" In *Politica e storia in Vico*, edited by Giuseppe Cospito, 37–57. Como/Pavia: Ibis, 2019.

Lomonaco, Fabrizio. *Lex Regia. Diritto, filologia e fides historica nella cultura politico-filosofica dell'Olanda di fine Seicento.* Naples: Guida, 1990.

Lomonaco, Fabrizio. *New Studies on Lex Regia: Right, Philosophy and Fides Historica in Holland between the 17th and 18th Centuries.* Bern: Peter Lang, 2011.

Lomonaco, Fabrizio. "Vico, Giambattista." In *Dizionario biografico dei giuristi italiani*, edited by Italo Birocchi, Ennio Cortese, Antonello Mattone, and Marco Nicola Miletti, Vol. 2, 2040–44. Bologna: il Mulino, 2013.

Löwith, Karl. "'Verum et factum convertuntur': le premesse teologiche del principio di Vico e le loro conseguenze secolari." In Corsano, ed., *Omaggio a Vico.*

Marx, Karl, and Frederick Engels. *Collected Works.* Vol. 41. New York: International Publishers, 1985.

Mazzarino, Santo. *Vico, l'annalistica e il diritto.* Naples: Guida, 1971.

Momigliano, Arnaldo. "Roman 'Bestioni' and Roman 'Eroi' in Vico's Scienza Nuova" (1966). Now in Id., *Terzo contributo alla storia degli studi classici e del mondo antico.* Vol. 1, 153–77. Rome: Edizioni di Storia e Letteratura, 1966.

Naddeo, Barbara Ann. *Vico and Naples: The Urban Origins of Modern Social Theory.* Ithaca, NY/London: Cornell University Press, 2011.

Niebuhr, Georg, ed. *Lebensnachrichten über Barthold Niebuhr.* Vol. 3. Hamburg: Perthes, 1839.

Oldrini, Guido. "La questione del vichismo meridionale." In *Ricerche sulla cultura dell'Italia moderna*, edited by Paola Zambelli, 201–13. Bari: Laterza, 1973.

Osbat, Luciano. *L'inquisizione a Napoli. Il processo agli ateisti 1688–1697.* Rome: Edizioni di Storia e Letteratura, 1974.

Peone, Dustin. *Works on Giambattista Vico in English from 2009 to 2018.* Atlanta, GA: Emory University, Institute for Vico Studies, n.d.

Perelman, Charles, and Lucie Olbrechts-Tyteca. *Traité de l'argumentation. La nouvelle rhétorique.* Paris: Presses Universitaires de France, 1958. English translation, *The New Rhetoric: A Treatise on Argumentation.* Translated by John Wilkinson and Purcell Weaver. Notre Dame, IN: University of Notre Dame Press, 1969.

Piovani, Pietro. "Il debito di Vico verso Roma" (1969). In Id., *Invito a Vico, con un saggio di Fulvio Tessitore*, edited by Leonardo Pica Ciamarra. Naples: Ispf Lab, Consiglio Nazionale delle Ricerche, 2018.

Pons, Alain. *Da Vico a Michelet. Saggi 1968–1995.* Translated by Paola Cattani. Pisa: Ets, 2004.

Repetto, Giorgio. "Il metodo comparativo in Vico e il diritto costituzionale europeo." *Rivista critica del diritto privato* 27 (2009): 295–334.

Ruggiero, Raffaele. *Nova scientia tentatur. Introduzione al diritto universale di Giambattista Vico.* Rome: Edizioni di Storia e Letteratura, 2010

Ruggiero, Raffaele. "Vico e la ricostruzione storica degli istituti feudali: la giurisprudenza napoletana tra Sei e Settecento." In *The Vico Road. Nuovi percorsi vichiani.* Atti del convegno internazionale Parigi, 13–14 gennaio 2015, edited by Monica Riccio, Manuela Sanna, and Levent Yilmaz, 145–66. Rome: Edizioni di Storia e Letteratura, 2015.

Sanna, Manuela. *Vico.* Rome: Carocci, 2016.

Savigny, Friedrich Carl von. "Ueber den juristischen Unterricht in Italien." *Zeitschrift für geschichtliche Rechtswissenschaft* 6 (1828): 224.

Savigny, Friedrich Carl von. *Vermischte Schriften.* Vol. 4. Berlin: Bei Veit und Comp, 1850.

Scalercio, Mauro. "Verità e politica in Vico. Il 'verum/factum' della 'Scienza nuova'." *Filosofia politica* 2 (2018): 215–32.

Schaeffer, John. *Giambattista Vico on Natural Law: Rhetoric, Religion and Sensus Communis.* Oxford/New York: Routledge, 2019.

Scognamiglio, Alessia. *Nono contributo alla bibliografia vichiana (2011–2015).* Rome: Edizioni di Storia e Letteratura, 2018.

Sevilla, José Manuel. *Giambattista Vico: metafisica de la mente e historicismo antropologico [...].* Sevilla: Servicio de publicaciones de la Universidad de Sevilla, 1988.

Sina, Mario. *Vico e Le Clerc: tra filosofia e filologia.* Naples: Guida, 1978.

Solari, Gioele. "Vico e Pagano. Per la storia della tradizione vichiana in Napoli nel secolo XVIII" (1917). In id., *Studi su Francesco Mario Pagano*, edited by Luigi Firpo. Turin: Giappichelli, 1963.

Tagliacozzo, Giorgio. "Gli studi vichiani nel mondo: situazione attuale e possibilità future." In *Vico e il pensiero contemporaneo*, edited by Antonio Verri. Lecce: Milella, 1991.

Tagliacozzo, Giorgio, and Hayden V. White, eds. *Giambattista Vico: An International Symposium.* Baltimore: Johns Hopkins University Press, 1969.

Tarello, Giovanni. *Storia della cultura giuridica moderna.* Vol. 1: *Assolutismo e codificazione del diritto.* Bologna: il Mulino, 1976.

Verene, Donald Phillip. *The New Art of Autobiography: An Essay on the Life of Giambattista Vico Written by Himself.* Oxford: Clarendon Press, 1991.

Verene, Donald Phillip. "Vico's Reply to False Book Notice: The Vici Vindiciae." In *Giambattista Vico: Keys to the New Science*, edited by Thora Ilin Bayer and Donald Phillip Verene, 85–135. Ithaca, NY/London: Cornell University Press, 2009.

Verene, Donald Phillip. *Vico's Science of Imagination.* Ithaca, NY: Cornell University Press, 1981.

Verene, Molly Black. "Works on Giambattista Vico in English from 1884 through 2009." *New Vico Studies* 27 (2009): 83–304.

Viazzi, Pio. "Il positivismo di G.B. Vico." *Il Pensiero italiano* 6/23 (1892): 412–29.

Viazzi, Pio. "La modernità e il positivismo di G.B. Vico" (1902). Preface to Giambattista Vico, *Principi di una Scienza nuova [. . .] secondo l'edizione del 1725 con annessa l'Autobiografia.* Milan: Sonzogno, 1903.

Vico, Giambattista. *La congiura dei príncipi napoletani. 1701 (Prima e seconda stesura).* Edited by Claudia Pandolfi. Naples: Morano, 1992. For English translation see Giorgio A. Pinton, *The Conspiracy of the Prince of Macchia & G.B. Vico*, 7–125. Amsterdam/New York: Rodopi, 2013.

Vico, Giambattista. *Principes de la philosophie de l'histoire traduits de la* Scienza Nuova *[. . .] et précédés d'un discours sur le système et la vie de l'auteur, par Jules Michelet.* Paris: Chez Jules Renouard, 1827.

Vico, Giambattista. *Versi d'occasione e scritti di scuola con appendice e bibliografia generale delle opere.* Edited by Fausto Nicolini. Bari: Laterza, 1941.

Viehweg, Theodor. *Topik und Jurisprudenz: ein Beitrag zur rechtswissenschaftlichen Grundlagenforschung.* Munich: Beck, 1953. English translation, *Topics and Law: A Contribution to Basic Research in Law.* Translated with a foreword by W. Cole Durham, Jr. Frankfurt am Main: Peter Lang, 1993.

Vitiello, Vincenzo. "Vico nel suo tempo." In Giambattista Vico, *La scienza nuova. Le tre edizioni del 1725, 1730 e 1744*, edited by Manuela Sanna and Vincenzo Vitiello, VII–CLXXII, CLXVIII–CLXXII. Milan: Bompiani, 2012.

Volpi, Alessandro. "Gadamer e Vico: il sensus communis nell'ermeneutica filosofica." *Meta* 10/1 (2018): 122–48.

Witteveen, Willem J. "Reading Vico for the School of Law." *Chicago-Kent Law Review* 83/3 (2008): 1197–223.

19 Cesare Beccaria (1738–1794)

Maria Gigliola di Renzo Villata

Introduction

Cesare Beccaria, jurist, philosopher, and economist, is widely regarded as one of the founding fathers of modern criminal law, as well as one of the most influential representatives of the Enlightment. He contributed to the humanization of criminal law tackling arbitrariness, abuses of power, and, above all, the death penalty and torture. Moreover, he strongly supported the reception of the legality and transparency principles in criminal law so that all citizens could be aware of the rules governing their conduct and foresee the consequences of unlawful behavior. The interest for his main work, *Dei delitti e delle pene* (1764), across three centuries has been impressive; an approximate survey has demonstrated a list of at least two hundred editions and translations throughout the world. Such a masterpiece has spread its influence over very many thinkers, not only jurists, and remains applicable even today.

Biographical information

Cesare Beccaria was born in Milan on March 15, 1738, to the Marquis Giovanni Saverio Beccaria Bonesana (his family had the title since 1711) and Maria Visconti di Saliceto, both from a distinguished Roman Catholic family of longstanding religious tradition. He was the firstborn, with two younger brothers, Francesco and Annibale, and a sister, Maddalena (three other sisters were born after him but did not survive). He was baptized in the Church of St. Eusebio.[1] At the age of eight he was sent to the Jesuit-run school Collegio Farnesiano, in Parma, where he lived unhappily for eight years (his "sentiments of humanity were stifled by eight years of fanatical and servile education," he wrote in a well-known letter to André Morellet, his French translator, on January 26, 1766[2]). Early on he showed an aptitude for mathematics (he picked up the nickname "Newtoncino," little Newton) and for languages, French in particular. After finishing this period of his education, he attended the University of Pavia, where he studied law from 1754 to 1758 and got a doctor of laws degree at the age of twenty: at the time of applying for the license to be admitted to the final exam in 1758, he presented the required certificate *de fide catholica*.[3] Once back in Milan, he was admitted to the Accademia dei Trasformati (Academy of the Transformed), a socially prestigious literary society that included, in those years, the poet Giuseppe Parini and Beccaria's older friend and mentor Pietro Verri.

In 1760 Beccaria fell in love with Teresa de Blasco, a beautiful sixteen-year-old girl who was the daughter of an army colonel of non-elevated social position. Despite his father's obstinate disapproval, Beccaria continued courting Teresa and proposed marriage, at the point that Cesare's father asked and obtained his son's house arrest for three months, hoping to block his son from marrying Teresa: those tactics appeared to weaken Cesare's will, as he then asked Teresa to be released from his promise to marry. However, on February 22, 1761, Cesare and Teresa's marriage ceremony took place without the blessing of Beccaria's father and family, despite Cesare's efforts to obtain his parent's consent. On July 21, 1762, Giulia, the future Alessandro Manzoni's mother, was born at the Beccaria family's home after reconciliation between father and son, thanks to Pietro Verri.

Meanwhile, Pietro and Alessandro Verri, after leaving the Accademia dei Trasformati, formed the Accademia dei Pugni (Academy of Fists), and their closest friends, including Beccaria, followed them.[4] In these years, Beccaria read many books that offered him a wide array of Enlightenment ideas. As he wrote to Morellet in the aforementioned letter, he was largely influenced by a series of authors who shaped his intellectual development: Montesquieu and his *Lettres persanes* (he owed his "conversion to philosophy" to its reading), Helvétius and his *L'esprit* (1758) (which pushed him "powerfully in the direction of the truth and who first awoke [his] attention to the blindness and misfortune of mankind"), Buffon (author of *Histoire naturelle*), Diderot, Hume, d'Alembert, and Condillac, whom Beccaria met in Milan. Like these authors and books, he was influenced also by Montesquieu's greatest masterpiece, *Esprit des loix* (1748), and by Rousseau's *Du contrat social* (*The Social Contract*, 1762), whose influence was stigmatized a few years later by Ferdinando Facchinei.

In those years Pietro Verri and his friends met regularly at the Verri family home, where they conceived and founded *Il Caffè*. This journal demonstrated that the most prominent Italian periodicals in the second half of the eighteenth century participated in international intellectual debates in order to promote and stimulate practical social reforms. In 1764 Beccaria published in *Il Caffè* the following articles: "Il giuoco del Faraone calcolato" (The Calculated Pharaoh's Game) and "Tentativo analitico su i contrabbandi" (An Attempt at an Analysis of Smuggling), both of them testimony to his passion for mathematics, applied particularly to games and smuggling, with repercussions on the public economy. He also wrote "Frammento sugli odori" (Essay on odors), "I piaceri dell'immaginazione" (The pleasures of imagination), and "Risposta alla rinunzia" (Answer to the renouncement), an ironic and playful response to the paper "Rinunzia avanti il Notajo degli Autori del presente Foglio periodico al Vocabolario della Crusca" (Renouncement . . . of the Crusca vocabulary), by Alessandro Verri, who, in a controversy over the rules of the Crusca Academics, claimed the right to invent new words, even foreign ones. Beccaria further published "De' fogli periodici" (On periodical sheets), a rich analysis of the merits of periodical publications.[5]

In the meantime, in 1762, he published his first book, *Del disordine e de' rimedi delle monete nello Stato di Milano* (On desorder and monetary remedies in Milan) about the local monetary system and the need for its reform. Between March 1763 and early 1764, he worked on the manuscript of his main work, *Dei delitti e delle pene* (On crimes and punishments). Questions have often been raised about whether the author of the work actually was Pietro Verri. Pietro, leader of the Academy of the Fists, was older than Beccaria and undoubtedly more authoritative. He indeed proposed Cesare to write about the reform of criminal law, and he continually monitored Beccaria's progress, discussing the work with Beccaria, revising the last draft, and taking care of the publication. But research conducted in the last decades has overcome these doubts and confirmed the Beccarian paternity, without underestimating Pietro's contribution. Finally, on April 12, 1764, *De I delitti e delle pene* was published anonymously, as was widespread custom at the time for works dealing with delicate subjects destined to clash with the powers and to arouse a debate in public opinion. Once it was clear that the government approved of his essay, Beccaria republished it, this time crediting himself as the author.

In 1765 Ferdinando Facchinei, a Dominican monk, in his *Notes and Observations on the Book On Crimes and Punishments*, accused the Milanese writer (and some other enlightened men of the eighteenth century) of "believing the most chimerical facts for real" and of affirming "the most palpable falsehoods," of aspiring to be regarded as "the Rousseau of the Italians." In his opinion the book was "a true daughter of Rousseau's Social Contract"; its author a "socialist,"[6] only capable of destroying an orderly system of hierarchies that were theologically sanctioned by tradition. Facchinei charged Beccaria with heresy, sedition, and impiety. It is worth giving some examples of Facchinei's charges: "He is an enemy of Christianity, a bad man and a bad philosopher"; "He is a declared enemy of the Supreme Being"; "he refuses to consider heresy a crime against God"; "he affirms that heretics are victims of some false linguistic subtleties" (*dopo aver chiamati sottigliezze ed oscurità i dogmi più sublimi del Cristianesimo, anzi dopo averli trattati da semplici opinioni, mal sicure e false*); he writes sacrilegious impostures against the Inquisition;[7] "he states that a monarch has no right to inflict the death penalty."[8] Such charges were expressed in a time still far away from the renewal of the institutions: the Church was still very influential, and Austria, through Pietro Leopoldo, had not abolished death penalty in Tuscany yet.

Soon after the Verri brothers, Beccaria's friends, published a strong defense, *Apology of the Book On Crimes and Punishments*, which gave a point-by-point answer to Facchinei's charges.[9] Their efforts, however, were not sufficient to protect Beccaria' work, because all the ideas in the book led to its being placed on the *Index of Forbidden Books* on February 3, 1766.[10]

Meanwhile, the fifth edition was published in Livorno with a false place of publication (Lausanna): it included for the first time the name of Cesare Beccaria on the title page, the introductory note "To the Reader," and two new chapters, *Del fisco* and *Delle grazie* (On revenue authorities and On pardons). After the condemnation of the Sacred Congregation, Beccaria and his publisher, Aubert, tried to manipulate the fifth version by changing the front page: Beccaria's name disappeared, and the place of the publication was changed to Harlem.

Between 1766 and 1767 the Russian Empress Catherine II invited Beccaria to St. Petersburg to take part in legal reforms she was introducing in Russia, but he refused the invitation. In November 1768 the Count of Firmian, governor general of Lombardy, proposed to Cesare the chair of 'Scienze Camerali' at Scuole Palatine in Milan, one of the first chairs in public economy in Europe: he accepted and began his lectures in January 1769. His short-lived lectures (only from 1769 to 1771), notwithstanding Empress Maria Theresa's insistence, were not published during his life but only, as *Elementi di economia pubblica* (Elements of political economy), after his death, in 1804.[11] In 1770 he also wrote *Ricerche intorno alla natura dello stile* (Research on the nature of style) and conceived another project about a philosophical history of civilization.

In 1771 he began to serve in Lombardy's Supreme Economic Council, a consultative body intended to reform economic and social policies: it was the realization of his wish to devote himself to the practicalities of economic reforms in Milan and Lombardy. Between 1771 and 1773 he was put in charge of monetary reforms, a topic around which he had thought and written in the previous years, and also, in 1771, just before entering service as official, he was entrusted with preparing a plan about a new law on bills of exchange.[12] In 1773, he was in charge of overseeing the food supply. During the years of his commitment to Supreme Economic Council, his work was mainly focused on agriculture, industry, and trade, as well as on education: to mention but a few areas on which he exercised his practical and intellectual skills.

As for his private life, in 1772 Margherita, the couple's fourth child, was born but survived only for a few days, as had the third child, Giovanni Annibale, born in 1767 (the second child, Maria, was born in 1766 and died in 1788, some years before her father's death). The year 1774 was a year of great sadness and happiness: Teresa, his first wife, died on March 14, 1774. Just a few months after her death, Cesare married another woman, Anna Barbò, the daughter of Count Barnaba Barbò, a wealthy man. Cesare Beccaria's successful marriage to Anna Barbò, surely less turbulent than the first one ("an excellent wife, discreet, sweet, virtuous, pious, without intolerance," Pietro Verri wrote of Anna to his brother Alessandro almost two years after the marriage[13]), took place on June 4, 1774. Anna was a devout Catholic and her deep religious beliefs influenced Cesare: from this marriage in the subsequent year Giulio, Cesare's fifth child, was born.

Meanwhile, his career in public administration continued with new assignments. In 1778 he was named the provincial magistrate of the mines. In 1786 he was also called to lead the Department of Agriculture, Industry, and Commerce. In fulfilling this task he had to deal with many tensions in the labor market, between the factory owners and the workers—for instance, challenges linked to the silk crisis of 1787, as well as to unemployment in the textile industry in Como. Later, around the time that Pietro Leopoldo, Grand Duke of Tuscany, succeeded his brother, Joseph II, as Holy Roman Emperor, Beccaria was entrusted with drawing recommendations and rules for work relations in the textile industry.[14]

In 1791 Beccaria was called to participate in a commission aimed at preparing a project for the reform of the penal legislation in Lombardy. On that occasion, in 1792, joined by two other Enlightenment intellectuals, Paolo Risi and Francesco Gallarati Scotti, Beccaria supported the minority position within the commission against the death penalty, adding to the longstanding and well-known reasons for refusing the death penalty yet another reason—the irrevocability of the execution of the punishment.[15]

Beccaria died on November 28, 1794 ("struck by an accident": *colpito da un accidente* is written in the death certificate). He had worked in his last months on issues of public food supply, rice fields, and public health. He had shown himself to be not only "honest, skillful, a man of letters, precise" but also "slightly idle. He works little, he is very weak" (Leopold II); he was known not only to have "mind and knowledge, but he is lacking in energy and activity" (Luigi Cremani). Beyond appearances, he was reflective, ready to listen and to draw the consequences from listening and, ultimately, industrious, animated by a willingness to work.[16]

The works of Cesare Beccaria

Dei delitti e delle pene *(1764)*

As already noted, Beccaria gave his major, best-known, and most-celebrated contributions in criminal law: *Dei delitti e delle pene* (On crimes and punishments)[17] is considered a sort of watershed between a retrospective criminal law and a modern criminal law. Anonymously published in Livorno, it was written in Italian, instead of Latin, which was the language of legal tradition, and its style was accessible, short, and concise. It was immediately translated into French by André Morellet and was praised by Voltaire, Denis Diderot, and Jean-Baptiste d'Alembert, men undoubtedly among the greats of the Age of Enlightenment, giving its author (not only) European fame.

Even if his contribution in the field of economics was not absolutely irrelevant, as Joseph Schumpeter and, later, Peter Groenewegen have emphasized, placing him alongside Turgot and Adam Smith among the great economists of the eighteenth century, his fame remains essentially linked to *Dei delitti e delle pene*. One of his essays as contributor to *Il Caffè*, *Tentativo analitico su i contrabbandi* (A tentative analysis of smuggling), provides an economic and empirical analysis of crime by building an equation based on a merchant's decision. The merchant is in the position to choose between legally spending money on imported goods, with a corresponding tax burden, or smuggling in the goods to avoid paying taxes but with the risk that some of the goods will be confiscated and lost. Therefore Paternoster and Fisher have written that "he initiated economically based studies of criminal behavior that bear a close affinity to current rational choice theory in criminology."[18] He also wrote, as already mentioned, *Del disordine e de' rimedi delle monete nello Stato di Milano* (On desorder and monetary remedies in Milan, 1762)[19] and *Ricerche intorno alla natura dello stile* (Research on the nature of style, 1770), about the skillful use of language, printed in Milan by the royal printer Galeazzi. The *Nature of Style* was not very successful, unlike *Dei delitti e delle pene*. It was translated only into French, by André Morellet, but even in France it did not receive much appreciation. He had already faced the topic for *Il Caffè*, writing a "Fragment on Style"; this subject continued to attract him in the subsequent years. *Dei delitti e delle pene* are often praised for their sober, clean style. In the same years he had also planned to write a philosophical history of civilization (*Ripulimento delle nazioni*), but only a few fragments of the project have remained to us. More over, he also wrote *Elementi di economia pubblica* (Elements of political economy). Beyond his essays, he was a contributor to *Il Caffè* and drafted numerous *Consulte* (Documents of advice), which have been recently published.[20]

Major themes and contributions

The main ideas at the core of this work were separation of powers and safeguarding the rights. The law had to be clear, precise, equal, and leaving no space to interpretation, which at the time was regarded by a growing number of intellectuals as arbitrary handling by jurists and judges. Beccaria's aim was legal certainty, exempt from manipulative intervention. Judges had to submit to the law. In applying the law, they had to apply a simple syllogism:

> The judge should construct a perfect syllogism about every criminal case: the major premise should be the general law; the minor, the conformity or otherwise of the action with the law; and the conclusion, freedom or punishment. Whenever the judge is forced, or takes it upon himself, to construct even as few as two syllogisms, then the door is opened to uncertainty.
>
> (Ch. 4, "The interpretation of the laws")

Beccaria followed Thomas Hobbes in believing that the asocial state was one of war ("a war of all against all") and that fear and the desire for security provided the motivation for uniting to form a society. He was, however, far from sharing Hobbes's ideas of sacrificing all of our freedom to the Leviathan in return for the protection of our security. Instead, he argued that we must give up only the smallest portion of our liberty:

> Thus it was necessity which compelled men to give up a part of their freedom; and it is therefore certain that none wished to surrender to the public repository more than the smallest possible portion consistent with persuading others to defend him. The sum of these smallest possible portions constitutes the right to punish; everything more than that is no longer justice, but an abuse.
>
> (Ch. 2, "The right to punish")[21]

He continued: "it is a matter of fact not of right. Note that the word 'right' is not opposed to the word 'power,' but the former is rather a modification of the latter, that is to say, the species which is of the greatest utility to the greatest number": utilitarianism at its best.

Beccaria contributed significantly to the secularization of criminal law, although he was not an atheist nor did he want to be taken for an atheist. Criminal law, based on his conceptual construction, had to deal with crimes and not with sins. However, in his work he does refer to God and religion, albeit rather rarely. When God and religion come into question, they contribute, on one hand, to emphasize the distinction between crime and sin and, on the other hand, to underscore the value of religion as an inherent necessity linked to human honesty.

Chapter 7 ("Errors in weighting punishments") considers possible errors in weighting punishments. Here Beccaria refers more often to sin, the Divine Being, God, and his omnipotence. The beginning regards his concept of crime and punishment: the true measure of punishment is "the damage done to the nation" (Ch. 7), "namely, harm to society" (Ch. 8 "Classification of crimes"). He expresses at the same time his opinion with regard to the subjective element of crime reducing the relevance of the intent: "therefore, those who believe that the true measure of criminality lies in the malefactor's intention are mistaken" (Ch. 7). Later, almost in accord with that statement, he says:

> The gravity of a sin depends on the inscrutable malice of the heart, which finite beings cannot know without special revelation. How, then, could it be used as a guide for the punishment of crimes? If such a thing were tried, men could punish when God pardons and pardon when God punishes. If men can run counter to the Almighty by blaspheming against him, then they can do also by punishing on His behalf.
>
> (Ch. 7)

For Beccaria it is another opportunity to mark the boundaries between sin and crime, between secular punishment and spiritual punishment. Thus, reflecting on a measurement criterion deduced by the injured party and his status, as had been customary in the past, he can affirm:

> Others measure the seriousness of crimes more by the rank of the injured party than by their significance for the public good. If this were the true measure of criminality, an irreverence towards the divine Being ought to be more harshly punished than the murder of a monarch, the superiority of His nature off-setting infinitely the difference in the offence.
>
> (Ch. 7)

Shortly afterward, in an even more significant matter, in my opinion, he condemns some authors' opinion

> that the gravity of the sin plays a role in measuring the degree of criminality of an action. The fallaciousness of this opinion will be obvious to an impartial student of the true relations among men, and between God and men. The

former are relations of equality. Necessity alone, from the confrontations of emotions and the opposition of interests, has given rise to the idea of *common utility*, which is the foundation of human justice. The latter involves relations of dependence upon a perfect Being and Creator, Who has retained for Himself alone the right to be at the same time Lawgiver and Judge, for He alone can be both without impropriety.

(Ch. 7)

Secularization, utilitarianism, and awareness of the superiority of divine justice intertwine, each in its own role. Beccaria states in a famous passage of his book:

> If He has laid down eternal punishments for those who disobey His Omnipotence, what manner of insect will dare to add to divine justice, will seek to avenge the Being Who is sufficient unto Himself, Who cannot be affected with pleasure or pain by anything, and Who, alone among beings acts without fear of any reaction?
>
> (Ch. 7)

On the other hand, he offers the example of the oath, widely used in trials as a tool to reinforce the truth of the depositions of the accused, an oath condemned by Beccaria. He describes with suggestive words the contradiction between laws and the "natural" sentiments of humanity in the case of oaths used to make the criminal speak the truth. The interests and love of life of those who swear are often inescapably in conflict with their religion, their love of God, "perhaps the only motive of honesty in the greatest part of mankind":

> The motives which religion opposes to the cries of fear and love of life, are too weak because too remote from the senses. The affairs of Heaven are conducted according to laws altogether different from those that govern the affairs of men. Why should the former be confused with the latter? And why should a man be put in the terrible dilemma of being either lost to God or conniving at his own ruin? The law which demands such an oath requires one to be either a bad Christian or a martyr. Oaths slowly become mere formality, thereby sapping the strength of religious feelings which, in most men, are the sole pledges of virtue.
>
> (Ch. 18 "Of oaths")

From his concept of crime and punishment, Beccaria deduces his scale and graduation of crimes. Given all the various sorts of crimes, each different from the other owing to "the differing of circumstances of differing times and places," he believes it is useful to point out the most general principles and to distinguish three categories of crimes with regard to the offended goods. The first category concerns crimes that directly destroy society or its representative. The second includes crimes that undermine "the personal security of a citizen by attacking his life, goods, or honour . . . which run counter to the security of individuals"; the third covers "actions contrary to what each citizen, in view of public good, is obliged by law to do or not do" (Ch. 8, "The classification of crimes"), particularly those which disturb the public peace and the calm of the citizenry, such as brawls and revels in the public street, which "make up one of the main branches of the care of the magistrate, which the French call *police*" (Ch. 11 "Public peace").

The specific and general aims of preventing crimes are clearly stated:

> The purpose of punishment is not that of tormenting or afflicting any sentient creature, nor of undoing a crime already committed. . . . The purpose, therefore, is nothing other than to prevent the offender from doing fresh harm to his fellows and to deter others from doing likewise.

Therefore: "punishments and the means adopted for inflicting them should, consistent with proportionality, be so selected as to make the most efficacious and lasting impression on the minds of men with the least torment to the body of the condemned" (Ch. 12, "The purpose of punishment"). And in another crucial chapter about capital punishment (Ch. 28, "The death penalty"):

> In order to deter citizens from murder it is not the intensity, but the extent of a punishment which makes the greatest impression on the human soul. For our sensibility is more easily and lastingly moved by minute but repeated impressions than by a sharp but fleeting shock. . . . As a general rule, violent passions take hold of men but not for long. . . . For most people, the death penalty becomes a spectacle and for the few an object of compassion mixed with scorn. Both these feelings occupy the minds of the spectators more than the salutary fear which the law claims to inspire. But with moderate and continuous punishments it is this last (i.e., *the fear*) which is the dominant feeling, because it is the only one.

He promoted promptness of punishment as a core value to be achieved on the side of the guilty and on the side of citizens to deter them from committing crimes:

> The swifter and closer to the crime a punishment is, the juster and more useful it will be, I say juster, because it spares the criminal the useless and fierce torments of uncertainty which grow in proportion to the liveliness of one's imagination and one's sense of one's own impotence. Juster because, loss of freedom being a punishment, a man should suffer it no longer than necessary before being sentenced. . . . I have said that the promptness of punishment is more useful because the smaller the lapse of time between the misdeed and the punishment, the stronger and more lasting the association in the human mind between the two ideas *crime* and *punishment*. The former will come to be sensed as the cause and the latter as the necessary, inexorable effect. It is

> proven that the compounding of ideas is the cement which holds together the fabric of the human intellect, and without it pleasure and pain would be unconnected feeling and of no effect. . . . A long delay only serves to separate these two ideas further. Whatever impression the punishment of a crime may make, (it makes less as a punishment than as spectacle, and) it will be felt only after the spectators have half-forgotten their horror at the crime in question, which would have served to reinforce their sense of what punishment is.

The speed of punishment is linked to the speed of justice: "The minimum time should be calculated taking into account both the length of time needed for the trial and the right of those who have been held the longest to be tried first. . . . The trial itself ought to be brought to a conclusion in the shortest possible time": it is a warning that still applies today (Ch.19, "Of prompt punishments").

He advocated a nondiscriminatory criminal law observing that "the punishments ought to be the same for the highest as they are for the lowest of citizens" and that "the laws . . . treat every subject as equally subordinate to them" (Ch. 21, "The punishment of the nobility").

Beccaria would like the same equality in family relationship (the traditional submission to his *paterfamilias* had costed him so many tribulations):

> Such lamentable but authorised injustices were sanctioned by the most enlightened men and implemented by the freest republics, as a result of regarding society as a union of families rather than as a union of persons. . . . When a republic is made up of persons, subordination within the family is not a matter of comand but of a contract; and when the children, having outgrown the natural dependence resulting from their weakness and need for education and protection become free members of the city, they submit to the head of the family in order to share in its advantages, just as free men do in society at large.
>
> (Ch. 26, "The family feeling")

The best-known pages of the work are about the death penalty (Ch. 28): "not a matter of *right* . . . but . . . an act of war on the part of society against the citizen": the crucial point consists in the serious doubts raised in a systematic way about the legitimacy of the death penalty, *de facto* considered as a useless and ineffective punishment for its purpose, through a whole series of arguments still used today by abolitionists all over the world.

> If I can go on to prove that such a death is neither necessary nor useful, I shall have won the cause of humanity. There are only two grounds on which the death of a citizen might be held to be necessary. First, when it is evident that, even if deprived of his freedom, he retains such connections and such power as to endanger the security of the nation, when, that is, his existence may threaten a dangerous revolution in the established form of government. The death of a citizen becomes necessary, therefore, when the nation stands

> to gain or lose its freedom, or in periods of anarchy, when disorder replaces the laws. But when the rule of law calmly prevails, under a form of government behind which the people are united, which is secured from without and from within, both by its strength and, perhaps more efficacious than force itself, by public opinion, in which the control of power is in the hands of the true sovereign, in which wealth buys pleasure and not influence, then I do not see any need to destroy a citizen, unless his death is the true and only brake to prevent others from committing crimes, which is the second ground for thinking the death penalty just and necessary.

I have already mentioned what he wrote about the value of the extent of a punishment rather than of the intensity:

> It is not the terrible but fleeting sight of a felon's death which is the most powerful brake of crime, but the long-drawn example of a man deprived of freedom, who having become a beast of burden, repays the society which he has offended with his labour.
>
> (Ch. 28, "The death penalty")

The reasoning unfolds in many other topics; among other suggestions he adds:

> The death penalty is not useful because of the example of savagery it gives to men. . . . It seems absurd to me that the laws, which are the expression of the public will, and which hate and punish murder, should themselves commit one, and that to deter citizens from murder, they should decree a public murder.

A reference to religion as a lifeline for the condemned is not lacking: "Then, religion comes into the mind of the ruffian, who makes ill-use of everything, and offering an easy repentance and near-certainty of eternal bliss, considerably diminishes for him the horror of the last tragedy."

In 1792 Beccaria (with Francesco Gallarati Scotti and Paolo Risi, all signers of a well-renowned minority report) added a new ground on which the death penalty should have been condemned: it was irreversible and irreparable, and the execution of innocent people in the case of a miscarriage of justice was always possible. The miscarriage of justice could occur due to the unavoidable imperfection of human evidence and to the limits of moral certainty "that, well examined, is only a high probability and nothing more."[22]

At a time when most nations used to find acceptable uses for torture, he condemned it in exciting, passionate, though rational, pages. He described it almost meticulously in its "unjustified" purposes (Ch. 16, "Of torture"):

> The torture of a criminal while his trial is being put together is a cruelty accepted by most nations, whether to compel him to confess a crime, to exploit the contradictions he runs into, to uncover his accomplices, to carry

> out some mysterious and incomprehensible metaphysical purging of his infamy, or lastly to expose other crimes of which he is guilty but with which he has not been charged.

This discussion offered Beccaria the opportunity to affirm the principle of the presumption of innocence: "No man may be called guilty before the judge has reached his verdict," he wrote, adding that "nor may society withdraw its protection from him until it has been determined that he has broken the terms of the contract by which that protection was extended to him," showing Rousseau's influence. His reasoning is stringent:

> By what right, then, except that of force, does the judge have the authority to inflict punishment on a citizen while there is doubt about whether he is guilty or innocent? This dilemma is not a novelty: either the crime is certain or it is not: if it is certain, then no other punishment is called for than what is established by law and other torments are superfluous because the criminal's confession is superfluous; if it is not certain, then an innocent man should not be made to suffer, because, in law, such a man's crimes have not been proven. Furthermore, I believe it is a willful confusion of the proper procedure to require a man to be at once accuser and accused, in such a way that physical suffering comes to be the crucible in which truth is assayed, as if such a test could be carried out in the sufferer's muscles and sinews.[23]

Another absurd ground for torture was the purging of infamy, that is, when a man who had been detained by the law had "to confirm his own testimony by the dislocation of his bones."

The desired decriminalization of suicide offers Beccaria, one more time, the opportunity to disentangle God's law from human law but, contemporaneously, to enhance the role of God and religion in the spiritual existence of the individual. In this regard, Beccaria writes:

> even if it is a sin which God will punish, because only He can punish after death, it is not a crime before men, since the punishment, instead of falling on the malefactor, falls on his family. If it should be urged against me that such a punishment may nevertheless draw a man back from killing himself, I reply that one who calmly gives up the benefits of life, who so hates life here below as to prefer an eternity of sorrow, could hardly be prevailed upon by the less powerful and more distant thoughts of his children or relatives.
>
> (Ch. 32, "Of Suicide")

One of the central tenets of the book is the condemnation of the artificial system of proofs adopted in inquisitorial procedure, according to rules very common at the time. The "pieces of evidence" were divided in two classes, perfect and imperfect; the first ones exclude the possibility of innocence, while the second "do not exclude that possibility." Even a single piece of perfect evidence was sufficient to lead to conviction. On the other hand, if there was not a full proof (*plena probatio*), as many pieces [of imperfect evidence] as were necessary to make up one perfect piece of evidence were needed; that is to say, if, in relation to each of the pieces taken alone, it was possible that a man should be innocent, then, in relation to them jointly, it was impossible that he should be. It may be noted that imperfect evidence against which the accused could exonerate himself could become perfect if he did not do so adequately.

This issue also provides Beccaria an opportunity to reiterate that laws must be "clear and precise"; so the office of the judge becomes merely "to discover the fact" (Ch. 14, "Evidence and forms of judgment").

Beccaria also wrote about "crimes difficult to prove" (Ch. 31, "Crimes difficult to prove"): this offered the chance to fight against torture and its abuse, against legal tradition made by civilians who want to dictate laws beyond law makers: "There are some crimes which are at once common in society and difficult to prove. And in these cases, the difficulty of producing evidence indicates the probability of innocence." These crimes, such as

> adultery and sodomy, which are hard crimes to prove, are precisely those in which, according to the received views, the tyrannical presumptions of the *nearly proofs* and *half-proofs* are admitted (as if a man could be *half innocent*, that is, *half-punishable* or *half-acquittable*), and where, according to the cold and iniquitous teaching of some learned men who presume to offer norms and rules to the judiciary, torture exercises its cruel prerogatives on the body of the accused, the witnesses, and even the whole family of the unfortunate.

The final reflection in the book is reserved for "a very useful general axiom, though it little conforms to custom—the most usual legislator of nations": he wrote: "In order that punishment should not be an act of violence, perpetrated by one or many upon a private citizen, it is essential that it should be public, speedy, necessary, the minimum possible in the given circumstances, proportionate to the crime, and determined by the law" (Ch. 47, "Conclusion").

Conclusion

Beccaria was not an atheist, he was Christian, but he pointed out the deep difference between the religious and laical worlds, between sin and crime. He promoted the abolition of the death penalty, becoming over time—even to the present day—the champion of this battle. He worked in favor of a mild, humanitarian, nondiscriminatory criminal law, of a "due process" which balances the power of the law and protects the individuals' rights against the courts' arbitrariness.

At the time, there were no procedural guarantees or at least very few guarantees: resorting to the increasingly widespread Enlightenment philosophical theories, he developed a preestablished model intended to remedy some of the distortions criticized by the most enlightened intellectuals. The almost immediate diffusion of his ideas throughout the contemporary civilized world of his day did not mean an instant reception of the principles and rules proposed in his writings, but promoted a lively, productive debate among people with different ideas. The sown seeds sprouted over time between moments of progress and others of recrudescence, but some proposals launched by the Lombard writer have proven to be durable or capable of making us reflect and promote a gradual improvement of criminal law.

Notes

1 Beccaria, *Opere* IV, 20. For biographical details see the summary biographies (and the bibliography) by Venturi; Castaldo and Castaldo; Audegean; Bognetti; Pasta; and Birocchi.
2 Beccaria, *Opere* IV, 219–28: 220.
3 Ibid., 20 (from Milano, Archivio Storico Civico, *Famiglie*, cart. 123, fasc. *Beccaria*).
4 See lastly Reinert.
5 See Francioni and Romagnoli, respectively, according to the order of quotation in the text, 18–26, 173–5, 39–46, 476–80, 104–6, 47–50, 411–19.
6 Facchinei, 4, 9, 100–101.
7 Ibid., 92ff.
8 Ibid., 98–136.
9 See Massetto, "Pietro e Alessandro Verri in aiuto di Cesare Beccaria"; and id., "Il Dei delitti e delle pene."
10 See around the events that led to the censorship Pisani, *Cesare Beccaria* e l'Index librorum prohibitorum.
11 See the critical edition by Gaspari, in Beccaria, *Scritti economici*, 197–390.
12 Beccaria, *Riflessioni intorno un piano delle leggi per le cambiali*, 70–84.
13 Greppi and Seregni, eds., 59.
14 See Cartocci, *Cesare Beccaria* and *I lavoratori della seta nella Lombardia austriaca*.
15 Cavanna, *passim*, but see 154.
16 See Massetto, *Beccaria tra diritto penale ed economia* pubblica, 1342.
17 See the Italian critical edition of Cesare Beccaria, *Dei delitti e delle pene*, ed. by Francioni, also providing a description drafted by Luigi Firpo of all the other Italian editions of the same work in *Edizione Nazionale delle Opere di Cesare Beccaria diretta da Luigi Firpo*, vol. 1, 13–129, 369–699.
18 Paternoster and Fisher, 179.
19 See the critical edition by Gaspari, in Cesare Beccaria, *Scritti economici*, in *Edizione Nazionale delle Opere di Cesare Beccaria diretta da Luigi Firpo*, vol. 3, 13–52.
20 Beccaria, *Atti di governo*.
21 Beccaria, *On Crimes and Punishments*, 1–113.
22 Cavanna, 154. See the minority report about death penalty in Cantù, 369–74, 372; also in Romagnoli, ed., Cesare Beccaria, *Opere*, II (Firenze: Sansoni, 1958), 735–41.
23 See Fiorelli, 247–50; also Langbein, 67–68.

Bibliography

Audegean, Philippe. "Cesare Beccaria." In *Il contributo italiano alla storia del pensiero—filosofia*, 350–9. Rome: Istituto della Enciclopedia Italiana, 2012. Available at www.treccani.it/enciclopedia/cesare-beccaria_%28Il-Contributo-italiano-alla-storia-del-Pensiero:-Filosofia%29/

Audegean, Philippe. *La philosophie de Beccaria: savoir punir, savoir écrire, savoir produire*. Paris: Vrin, 2010.

Audegean, Philippe, Christian Del Vento, Pierre Musitelli, and Xavier Tabet, eds. *Le bonheur du plus grand nombre: Beccaria et les lumières.* Lyon: Ens Éditions, 2017.

Audejean, Philippe, and Luigi Delia, eds. *Le moment Beccaria: naissance du droit pénal moderne.* Oxford University Studies in the Enlightment. Oxford: Oxford University Press, 2018.

Beccaria, Cesare. "Atti di governo." In *Edizione Nazionale delle Opere di Cesare Beccaria diretta da Luigi Firpo*, edited by Rosalba Canetta. Vol. 6–16: Serie 1. 1771–1777; Serie 2. 1778–1783; Serie 3. 1784–1786; Serie 4. 1787; Serie 5. 1788; Serie 6. 1789; Serie 7. 1790; Serie 8. 1791; Serie 9. 1792; Serie 10. 1793; Serie 11, January–December 1794 (2 vols: 1. January–August; 2: September–December). Milano: Mediobanca, 1987–2009.

Beccaria, Cesare. *Des délits et des peines. Dei delitti e delle pene.* Introduction, translation, and notes by P. Audegean. Italian text established by Gianni Francioni. Lyons: Ens édition, 2009.

Beccaria, Cesare. *Edizione Nazionale delle Opere di Cesare Beccaria diretta da Luigi Firpo.* Milan: Mediobanca, 1984—.

Beccaria, Cesare. "Elementi di economia pubblica." In Beccaria, *Scritti economici*, edited by Gianmarco Gaspari. *Edizione Nazionale delle Opere di Cesare Beccaria diretta da Luigi Firpo.* Vol. 3, 197–390. Milan: Mediobanca, 2014.

Beccaria, Cesare. *On Crimes and Punishments and Other Writings.* Edited by Richard Bellamy and translated by Richard Davies, Virginia Cox, and Richard Bellamy. Cambridge: Cambridge University Press, 1995.

Beccaria, Cesare. *Opere IV Carteggio (parte 1: 1758–1768).* Milan: Mediobanca, 1994.

Beccaria, Cesare. "Riflessioni intorno un piano delle leggi per le cambiali" (1771). In *Edizione Nazionale delle Opere di Cesare Beccaria diretta da Luigi Firpo*, edited by Rosalba Canetta. Vol. 6, 70–84. Milan: Mediobanca, 1987.

Bessler, John. *The Celebrated Marquis: An Italian Noble and the Making of the Modern World.* Durham, NC: Carolina Academic Press. 2018.

Birocchi, Italo. "Beccaria, Cesare." In *Dizionario Biografico dei Giuristi Italiani (XII–XX secolo)*, edited by Italo Birocchi, et al. Vol. 1, 200–4. Bologna: Il Mulino, 2013.

Bognetti, Giuseppe. "Cesare Beccaria." In *Il contributo italiano alla storia del pensiero—economia.* Rome: Istituto della Enciclopedia Italiana, 2012. Available at www.treccani.it/enciclopedia/cesare-beccaria_%28Il-Contributo-italiano-alla-storia-del-Pensiero:-Economia%29/

Cantù, Cesare. *Beccaria e il diritto penale.* Florence: G. Barbera, 1862.

Cartocci, Fabrizio. *Cesare Beccaria e l'industria serica comasca.* Lipomo (Como): Dominioni, 2014.

Cartocci, Fabrizio. *I lavoratori della seta nella Lombardia austriaca.* Lipomo (Como): Dominioni, 2018.

Castaldo, Andrea, and Maria Elena Castaldo. "Beccaria, Cesare." In *Juristas Universales.* Vol. 2: *Juristas modernos*, edited by Rafael Domingo, 692–5. Madrid: Marcial Pons, 2004.

Cavanna, Adriano. *La codificazione penale in Lombardia. Le origini lombarde.* Milan: Giuffrè, 1975.

Chiodi, Giovanni, and Loredana Flavia Garlati, eds. *Dialogando con Beccaria. Le stagioni del processo penale italiano.* Turin: G. Giappichelli, 2015.

Dezza, Ettore. "Il problema della pena di morte." In *Il Contributo italiano alla storia del pensiero- Diritto* Rome: Treccani, 2012.

di Renzo Villata, Maria Gigliola. “Beccaria e gli altri. Noterelle sulla criminalistica del tardo Settecento.” In *Attualità e storicità del Dei delitti e delle pene a 250 anni dalla pubblicazione*, 41–74. Naples: Edizioni Scientifiche Italiane, 2015.

di Renzo Villata, Maria Gigliola. “Beccaria e gli altri tra ieri e oggi. Alcune riflessioni a margine della relazione Zagrebelsky.” In *Cesare Beccaria: La pratica dei lumi*, 23–47. Florence: Olschki, 2000.

di Renzo Villata, Maria Gigliola. *Beccaria und die Anderen*. Berlin: Lit, 2016.

di Renzo Villata, Maria Gigliola. “Giuristi, cultura giuridica e idee di riforma nell’età di Beccaria.” In *Cesare Beccaria tra Milano e l’Europa*, 225–78. Bari: Laterza, 1991.

di Renzo Villata, Maria Gigliola. “Quale scienza penale? Prima e dopo Beccaria.” In *Dei delitti e delle pene a 250 anni dalla pubblicazione. La lezione di Cesare Beccaria*, 133–62. Milano 3 ottobre 2014 (Centro Nazionale Previdenza e Difesa Sociale 28). Milan: Giuffrè, 2015.

Facchinei, Ferdinando. *Note ed osservazioni sul libro intitolato Dei delitti e delle pene*. Bassano: A spese Remondini di Venezia, 1797.

Ferrone, Vincenzo, and Giuseppe Recuperati. *Il caso Beccaria: a 250 anni dalla pubblicazione del Dei delitti e delle pene*. Bologna: Il Mulino, 2016.

Fiorelli, Piero. *La tortura giudiziaria nel diritto comune*. Vol. 2. Milan: Giuffrè, 1954.

Francioni, Gianni, and Sergio Romagnoli, eds. *Il Caffè. 1764–1766*. Turin: Bollati Boringhieri, 1993.

Garlati, Loredana, and Giovanni Chiodi. *Un uomo, un libro. Pena di morte e processo penale nel Dei delitti e delle pene di Cesare Beccaria*. Milan: Giuffrè, 2014.

Greppi, Emanuele, and Giovanni Seregni, eds. *Carteggio di Pietro e di Alessandro Verri*. Vol. 8. Milan: L.F. Cogliati, 1934.

Langbein, John H. *Torture and the Law of Proof: Europe and England in the Ancien Regime*. Chicago: University of Chicago Press, 1976.

Massetto, Gian Paolo. “Beccaria tra diritto penale ed economia pubblica.” In Massetto, *Scritti di storia giuridica*. Vol. 2, 1249–358.

Massetto, Gian Paolo. “Il Dei delitti e delle pene: Cesare Beccaria sotto accusa (1764–1766).” *Corte d’Assise Rivista quadrimestrale di scienze penalistiche integrate* 3/2–3 (2013): 227–83. Now in Massetto, *Scritti di storia giuridica*. Vol. 2, 1481–514.

Massetto, Gian Paolo. “Pietro e Alessandro Verri in aiuto di Cesare Beccaria: la risposta alle ‘Note’ del Facchinei.” In *Pietro Verri e il suo tempo*. Milano, 9–1 ottobre 1997, edited by Carlo Capra. Vol. 1, 289–351. Bologna: Cisalpino 1999. Now in Massetto, *Scritti di storia giuridica*. Vol. 2, 1359–479.

Massetto, Gian Paolo. *Scritti di storia giuridica*. Vol. 2. Milan: Giuffrè 2017.

Miletti, Marco Nicola. “Beccaria e la fondazione della scienza penale. Origine settecentesca di un equivoco.” *Criminalia. Annuario di scienze criminalistiche* (2013): 179–201.

Pasta, Renato. “Cesare Beccaria.” In *Il contributo italiano alla storia del pensiero—diritto*, 249–52. Rome: Istituto della Enciclopedia Italiana, 2012. Available at www.treccani.it/enciclopedia/cesare-beccaria %28Il-Contributo-italiano-alla-storia-del-Pensiero: Diritto%29/

Paternoster, Ray, and Darren Fisher. “The Foundation and Re-Emergence of Classical Thought in Criminological Theory: A Brief Philosophical Theory.” In *The Handbook of the History and Philosophy of Criminology*, edited by Ruth Ann Triplett. Hoboken, NJ/Oxford: Wiley Blackwell, 2018.

Pisani, Mario. *Cesare Beccaria e l'Index librorum prohibitorum*. Naples: Edizioni Scientifiche Italiane, 2013.
Pisani, Mario. *Cesare Beccaria. Studi*. Milan: Giuffrè, 2015.
Porret, Michel. *Beccaria: le droit de punir*. Paris: Michalon, 2003.
Reinert, Sophus A. *The Academy of Fisticuffs: Political Econmy and Commercial Society in Enlightment Italy*. Cambridge, MA: Harvard University Press, 2018.
Scognamiglio Pasini, Carlo. *L'arte della ricchezza: Cesare Beccaria economista*. Milan: Mondadori Università, 2014.
Venturi, Franco. "Beccaria, Cesare." In *Dizionario Biografico degli Italiani*. Vol. 7, 458–69. Rome: Istituto della Enciclopedia Italiana, 1965.

20 Pietro Gasparri (1852–1934)

Alberto Lupano

Introduction

In the context of the Catholic Church and culture, the important figure of Pietro Gasparri is associated with a historical epoch of extraordinary significance, encompassing the culmination of the temporal power of the papacy in 1870, the First World War, and the reconciliation between Italy and the Holy See in 1929. Such momentous events posed a severe test to the capacities of Gasparri, who hailed from a modest family background but who, after receiving a comprehensive training in theology and law, rose to attain positions at the very summit of the ecclesiastical hierarchy. Equipped with an essentially juridical mind, he was devout in his day-to-day life and was able to succeed in all he undertook, thanks to the combination of his extensive knowledge of doctrine and the personal quality of practical common sense which he brought to bear in the political sphere.

The foundations of Gasparri's learning were laid at the so-called St. Apollinare Seminary, the pontifical Roman seminary devoted to the training of Roman clergy, where a number of future prelates destined for the highest echelons of the Roman Curia and the Church hierarchy were taught. A key contribution in the development of his juridical and diplomatic capacities was provided by the private coaching he received from Cardinal Teodolfo Mertel, who was not only a highly capable legal expert but also, more importantly, a leading statesman in the preceding papal administration.

Gasparri is remembered now for the singular nature of his personality as an academic as well as for his qualities as a governor of the Church, a politician, and a diplomat who faithfully served under four popes: Leo XIII, Pius X, Benedict XV, and Pius XI. Gasparri was the author of works on canon law which have become classics of their kind. He is also considered the principal architect of the project of codification of canon law which occupied him for thirteen years, or even longer if one considers his pursuit in publishing sources of the *Codex iuris canonici* right up until his death.

In his capacity as the Vatican secretary of state, a position he retained until 1930, under the papacy of Pius XI, he was faced with the task of dealing with the immense burden of work brought on the Vatican by the First World War. In this same period Gasparri was also able to initiate, to pursue, and to bring to a successful conclusion negotiations designed to establish concordats with a number of other states, particularly Italy, where the aim was to resolve the difficulties arising from the Roman question, a term used to refer to the issue of Italy's annexation of Rome, formerly the capital of the Papal States. On February 11, 1929, Gasparri himself signed the Lateran Accords in his capacity as the pope's plenipotentiary.

Biographical information

Gasparri the jurist and diplomat in the service of the Holy See

Pietro Gasparri sprang from a patriarchal family of small farmers and herders with deep roots in the Sibillini Mountains. The hard life of this rugged zone encouraged the local people to develop qualities of simplicity and integrity, discouraging vanities and vices, and Cardinal Gasparri retained these virtues throughout his life. He was born on May 5, 1852, in Capovallazza, now in the municipality of Ussita in the Marche region.[1] His mother was sister to Pietro Silj, archpriest of the cathedral of Nepi and vicar general of the diocese. Pietro Gasparri was set on the road to priesthood and, despite hailing from the diocese of Norcia, through the offices of his priestly maternal uncle he pursued his early studies in the seminaries of Nepi and Sutri. Owing to the aftereffects of an accident that injured his face at a tender age, he obtained an exemption from the three years of military service then demanded by the Italian state of members of the clergy. In November 1870, immediately after Rome was annexed to the Kingdom of Italy, he was able to pursue his studies at St. Apollinare, the pontifical seminary there, in keeping with the most hallowed Catholic traditions. His juridical education was directed by two dependable teachers within the curialist tradition, Filippo De Angelis and Francesco Santi. Gasparri received a diploma in philosophy and a degree in theology together with a combined degree in civil and canon law (*in utroque iure*).[2] Ordained as a presbyter in 1875, he became chaplain and secretary to Cardinal Deacon Teodolfo Mertel, for whom he celebrated Holy Mass each day. Mertel was an outstanding jurist and former minister of the interior in the papal administration who continued to hold numerous positions within the Roman congregations and was also prefect of the Segnatura Apostolica. In his own way, he was a mentor to the youthful Gasparri in politics and diplomacy and always took a benevolent interest in the younger man's career.

Gasparri taught sacramental theology in Rome at the St. Apollinare Seminary as well as canon law at the College de Propaganda Fide. From 1880 to 1897, he was teacher of canon law at the Institut Catholique in Paris after being called to that post by Cardinal Benôit-Marie Lamgénieux, the archbishop of Reims, a prelate intolerant of contemporary laicism who was also a personal friend to Pope Leo XIII.[3] In the French capital the young specialist in canon law also performed tireless charity work on behalf of the Benevolent Institute for the Assistance of Destitute Italians. He likewise devoted himself to the activities of the St. Raimundo de Peñafort Academy for the study of canon law, made occasional contributions to the periodical *Le canoniste contemporain*, and explored the question of the validity of Anglican ordinations, then highly debated in the ecclesiastical world in view of a putative reconciliation of the Church of England with the Roman Church.[4] The controversy was definitively brought to an end with the encyclical *Apostolicae curae*, in which Pope Leo XIII decreed the absolute invalidity of Anglican ordinations.

In Paris Gasparri published his treatises on canon law,[5] *De matrimonio*, *De sacra ordinatione*, and *De sanctissima Eucharistia*, which met with considerable success. In these he adopted a methodology by which, abandoning the order of the *Decretals*, he sought to review each subject in a systematic fashion and organized his arguments in accordance with a rigorous juridical technique[6] without following the framework of *theologia casuistica*. His aim was to perform an exhaustive analysis of the theological and juridical character of the various aspects of the sacraments, including their origin, nature, and officiants; the requisites for those administering and receiving them; and the sacramental environment, schedule, and liturgy. He presented his ideas in a rational and overarching manner in the form of a treatise, with the emphasis placed on substantive aspects. The young writer set out the subject matter exhaustively and in detail, taking care to complete the picture in normative terms by including the latest jurisprudence emerging from the courts of the Holy See, together with measures adopted by the Roman congregations and all else that could be constantly updated. In these works, Gasparri displayed no particular appetite for historical description of the institutions, possibly due to his awareness of the risks that this type of historical interpretation could pose to the evaluation of the accepted doctrine of the Catholic Church over the centuries.

The most important of these writings was *De matrimonio*, which was reprinted three times and continued to be used as a standard work on the topic until the years following the Second World War. This work proved to be highly useful in the training of advocates of the Apostolic Roman Rota Court and also of Italian civil advocates, since the latter were on occasion called on to assesses the canonical aspects of matrimonial cases following the recognition, under civil law, of ecclesiastical marriages which had accompanied the Lateran Accords. Gasparri's text provided experts and novices with simple and clear guidance which could serve to resolve issues on all aspects of matrimonial law. The format that Gasparri adopted in writing *De matrimonio* he retained in drafting other treatises, making it the methodological template for his later codification of canon law.

In France Gasparri found the tranquillity to devote himself to his canonical and theological studies and was able to develop his own scholarly personality. He would happily have stayed in a place where he had formed numerous friendships and where he could perform such useful pastoral work. His departure from Paris occurred under singular circumstances which are remembered in the Roman Curia to this day, helping us to understand his individual psychology and at the same time displaying his blunt, not to say rough, manner but also his absolute devotion to the pope. During a holiday visit to Rome in the summer of 1897, he was called by Cardinal Mariano Rampolla del Tindaro, Pope Leo XIII's secretary of state. The cardinal intimated that the pope intended to name

Gasparri as apostolic delegate and special envoy to Peru, Bolivia, and Ecuador. Conscious of the difficulties of a mission to Latin America, a mission which was not exempt from dangers, and being furthermore devoted to his own studies, Gasparri begged to be excused from this mission. In reply to a further letter of insistence, he had the courage to reiterate his absolute commitment to writing an additional treatise on the subject of the sacraments in canon law. Rampolla wrote in reply that he had informed the pope, who desired to speak to Gasparri personally at a private audience. In this audience the pope imposed obedience on him, remarking that Gasparri could equally well pursue his writing while in America.[7] On March 6, 1898, on the eve of his departure for this mission, Gasparri was consecrated in Paris as archbishop of Caesarea in Palestine. In his episcopal coat of arms he included the olive branch, a symbol of peace. The new mission, with all the difficulties associated with the authoritarian and often intransigent Latin American regimes, did not daunt the youthful prelate, who acquitted himself well and was instrumental in drafting concordats governing the relations between these nations and the Holy See.

Recalled to Rome in the spring of 1901, he was appointed secretary to the Congregation for Extraordinary Ecclesiastical Affairs. In this department of the Curia, which handled relations between the Holy See and other states, Gasparri was able to further develop his political and diplomatic skills. In 1904, when Pope Pius X initiated the codification of canon law, he named Gasparri among the members of the Pontifical Commission *Pro Ecclesiae legibus in unum redigendis* (the Pontifical Commission for the compilation of all laws obtaining in the Latin rite of the Roman Catholic Church), in the phrase which was used thereafter. His work in connection with the new code increased again after he was made cardinal in 1907. Gasparri also collaborated with the secretary of state, Cardinal Rafael Merry del Val, to contribute to the sweeping reforms of the Roman Curia conceived by Pius X.

The turning point in Gasparri's ecclesiastical career arrived with Pope Benedict XV's nomination of Cardinal Domenico Ferrata as secretary of state immediately following Benedict's election. Ferrata died just a month later, however, and the pope replaced him with Cardinal Gasparri on October 13, 1914. The new position kept Gasparri busy throughout the First World War in constant diplomatic and constructive assignments, acting as the pope's representative in charitable enterprises for the benefit of those affected by the conflict, particularly prisoners of war and civilians. He was also involved in liaising with the warring parties, particularly Austria and Germany, as well as with those states that had remained neutral. Although the peace initiatives pursued by the Holy See did not bear fruit, owing partly to the hostility of the Italian government, Gasparri showed himself capable of engaging all parties, ranging from papal nunzios to bishops and government representatives from across the spectrum, in a pragmatic conversation, thus making a key contribution to the humanitarian work promoted by Benedict XV and reestablishing contacts with predominantly Catholic countries such as France. Since the passing of the *Loi de séparation* in 1905, relations between France and the Vatican had lapsed. Thanks to Gasparri's behind-the-scenes mediation, normal diplomatic relations were resumed in 1921. He followed a similar approach in the case of the Swiss Federation, with which official relations had been interrupted in 1873. An apostolic delegate was dispatched to China, and attempts were even made to initiate a dialogue with Soviet Russia, the new political entity which initially the cardinal did not view unfavorably.

Gasparri was confirmed in the position of secretary of state by Pope Pius XI when he succeeded Benedict XV in 1922. The pope took a favorable view towards the concordats, which represented in his opinion the best guarantors of the rights of the Church and the person.[8] Thus, the cardinal and secretary of state pursued his diplomatic activities, which led to the signing of a succession of concordats with states across the spectrum of political and juridical traditions, including Latvia, Poland, Romania, Lithuania, Czechoslovakia, Bavaria, Prussia, and Yugoslavia. The formula of the concordat as implemented by Gasparri was designed to safeguard the rights and freedom of action of the Church and was based on the precepts emerging from the codification of canon law, centered once again on the figure of the pope.[9] A further contributing factor was the idea propounded by Eugenio Pacelli, the secretary of the Congregation for Extraordinary Ecclesiastical Affairs, whereby the concordat was not only a form of agreement for the management of relations between the Church and the state but also an embodiment of certain canonical laws.[10] Pacelli, Francesco Borgongini Duca, and Angelo Giuseppe Roncalli as well as many other ecclesiastical figures all placed their expertise at the disposal of the secretary of state. Gasparri's activities allowed the Holy See to resume its place on the international scene with authority.

As far as a path to reconciliation between the Vatican and the Kingdom of Italy was concerned, it should be remembered that at the end of the First World War Pope Benedict XV had already put out feelers, through Gasparri, with a view to a rapprochement. The pope had appointed one of the leading Vatican diplomats, Bonaventura Cerretti, to hold private informal talks with the Italian delegation present at Versailles for the peace negotiations in 1919. This established the basis for the reconciliation which led to an outline agreement to create an independent Vatican State.[11] Cardinal Gasparri himself had exchanges with Francesco Saverio Nitti, the new Italian prime minister in the postwar years, with Baron Carlo Monti (a personal friend of Pope Benedict XV and a high-ranking state official and unofficial go-between for the de facto relations between Italy and the Holy See), and even with Benito Mussolini. The conditions for reconciliation arose out of the favorable political climate and the propitious influence created during Benedict XV's pontificate through the good offices of Gasparri. In 1926 Pope Pius XI decided to initiate direct negotiations intended to resolve the Roman question and come to an agreement with the Italian state. By the will of the pope, and contrary to the normal practice adopted by previous popes in matters of such fundamental moment in the life of the Church, the negotiations were kept completely secret from the Sacred College of Cardinals. Only Cardinal Gasparri, reporting directly to the pope, was personally present at the exchanges taking place between the lawyer Francesco Pacelli, representing the pope, and the member of the Council of State, Domenico Barone, who represented Italy.[12] Every single deed and document in the laborious build-up to the Lateran Accords bore Gasparri's name. Finally, on February 11, 1929, Gasparri signed the accords in his capacity as papal plenipotentiary. The accords were composed of a treaty (with four appendices) placing the Vatican State within the power and jurisdiction of the Holy See, a financial convention, and a concordat, considered a necessary complement to the treaty and having the purpose of regulating the conditions of the Catholic religion and Church in Italy.[13] Even in the aftermath of the accords, when differences emerged over their interpretation by the fascist government, the pope entrusted Gasparri with the task of resolving these issues. In Italy there was no lack of criticism of the accords by members of the old liberal political establishment. Within the Roman Curia, only one cardinal, Bonaventura Cerretti, a leading light of Vatican diplomacy, withheld his support for the pact before the pope, who was notoriously intolerant of dissent. Cerretti objected that it would have been opportune to demand more from a treaty which was intended to continue in force indefinitely, with a view to securing a more favorable juridical position for the Church, while the concordat, by its very nature, could always be revised.

In 1929 Gasparri became the president of the commission of cardinals responsible for the preliminary studies for the codification of the articles of canon law relating to the Eastern Church. On February 11, 1930, he was relieved of the role of secretary of state, and his erstwhile collaborator, Eugenio Pacelli, took his place. The elderly Gasparri returned to private life, bathed in the glow of his fame as an expert in canon law and accomplished diplomat. He was appointed Camerlengo of the Holy Roman Church and decorated by the king of Italy with the Collar of the Order of the Annunziata. He was also inducted into the Accademia d'Italia with the status of member for the juridical disciplines. In the time remaining to him, he was further able to compose and publish his Catholic catechism.[14] He had also planned to write his autobiography, in collaboration with the editor of *Osservatore Romano*, Count Giuseppe Dalla Torre, with whom he had previously made specific arrangements, but he continued to put off this task.[15] He died in Rome on November 18, 1934.

The *Codex Iuris Canonici* and the work of cardinal Gasparri

Gasparri's name is remembered chiefly in connection with the codification of canon law, of which he was considered the principal promoter and guiding spirit.[16] He himself claimed this role publicly in a speech made at the Rome Convention on Ecclesiastical Law, just a few days before his death.[17]

In order to understand fully the importance of the codification of canon law, one should remember that from the sixteenth to the nineteenth centuries the sources for the general canon law of the Roman Church were mainly to be found in the collections comprising the *Corpus Iuris Canonici* and in the decrees of the Council of Trent. Beyond these sources, Church legislation had grown enormously, taking the form of all manner of canonical dispositions, especially in the wake of the Council of Trent. This situation caused difficulties for the study of Church law and uncertainties regarding its application. There were many gaps and repetitions, many elements were considered to have lapsed and doubts arose over which laws were applicable.[18] In most cases of controversy, interpreters tended to identify the applicable law by reference to doctrine.[19] When nation-states began to codify the bulk of their legislation, the idea began to circulate among specialists in canon law that it would be opportune to reorganize Church legislation by likewise adopting the modern technique of codification.

From the time of the preliminary meetings and discussions leading to the First Vatican Council (1869–70), the idea had been mooted of a system of codification for the collection and organization of the vast number of legislative ecclesiastical texts. However, the decision to follow the example of these secular organizations by applying the system of codification to canon law appeared to many to be inappropriate or even impossible, in the light of the particular nature of the ecclesiastical ordinances and of their sheer quantity.[20] Among the advocates of the idea of codification was Cardinal Casimiro Gènnari, an accomplished specialist in canon law,[21] who voiced his support for the desirability of adopting a code for ecclesiastical law. The widely desired project of codification became feasible with the election of Pope Pius X.

Pius X had risen through all the ecclesiastical and pastoral ranks, starting from the bottom, as a simple chaplain, and attaining the position of cardinal patriarch of Venice. During the nine years he spent as chancellor of the bishopric of Treviso, in particular, he had been able to take personal stock of the difficulties of consulting all the provisions of canon law and of applying them correctly without doubts and uncertainties. On being elected to the papal throne, Pius X courageously embarked on the work of codification of canon law with the issue of the motu proprio *Arduum sane munus* on March 19, 1904.

In this text the pope underlined the importance of law in the life of the Church and acknowledged that the various collections of canon law which had been created over the preceding centuries had not resolved all problems. He recalled the preferences which had been expressed from all over the Catholic community in favor of compiling the entirety of the norms of the Roman Church within a single clearly organized body, suppressing lapsed elements and bringing the remainder into line with the times. The pope accepted these requests and set up a special commission of cardinals and a college of advisers to act in consultation with bishops from around the world, with the various congregations of the Curia and with the ecclesiastical universities. However, he as yet expressed no judgment regarding the *form* which the consolidation of canon law should take, other than to express the need for it to meet certain criteria of practical utility.

Pius X appointed Gasparri as secretary of the papal commission entrusted with the task of drafting the code of canon law. In a letter of April 6, 1904, addressed to the Catholic universities, the secretary finally explained the pope's intentions regarding the method to be adopted. The whole body of canon law was to be organized in a logical sequence of canons forming a special code. In a departure from the structure of the collections of *Decretals*, Gasparri's letter drew its inspiration from the systematic review characteristic of the manuals of the institutions of canon law adopted in the universities. These manuals, along the lines of Justinian's *Institutiones*, divided the material into *personae*, *res*, and *actiones*.[22] As stated earlier, Gasparri himself had made use of this division for his lessons in Paris, dispensing with the traditional order of subject matter in the *Decretals*. Having received further briefing from Pius X, the commission worked diligently, ignoring the criticisms of such academics as Francesco Ruffini, who doubted the wisdom or even the feasibility of codifying canon law.

On December 16, 1907, Gasparri was made a cardinal, passing from the position of secretary to the equivalent of rapporteur in the commission. The cardinal supplied even more dynamic guidance thereafter and, while he was possibly too little inclined to delegate, his work proved effective,[23] so that he became what amounted to the coordinator and guiding spirit of the codification. Gasparri directed the working methodology of the various collaborators in the work of codification. He prepared the working schedule and the index of topics, distributed the sections to be prepared, and amassed the material, dividing it among the various collaborators. He determined the system, the methods, and the schedule, streamlining procedures considerably through a process of editing and printing of the sections to be dealt with. It was he who coordinated the relations between the commission and the other bodies involved in the codification. He collected, examined, and selected the various parts, arranging them coherently, while seeking always to strike a balance between theoretical and practical requirements.[24]

Contemporary commentators as well as recent studies have sometimes downplayed Gasparri's role in the great work of codification. However, he always claimed for himself the credit of having suggested the idea of the code to Pius X immediately following his election to the papacy and of having been the architect of the codification of canon law. Recent studies by Carlo Fantappiè have shown that the code of Pius and Benedict emerged from a variety of different types of contribution.[25]

In the period from 1912 to 1914, the commission transmitted the first draft of the code to bishops and religious leaders around the world and invited their comments. The text was then introduced in its revised form to cardinals and prelates within the Roman Curia for further reactions. In 1916 the commission completed its work. The final version of the code consisted of 2,414 *canones* divided into five books. The model for the subdivision drew its inspiration from Justinian. The first book, titled *Normae generales*, lists the sources of canon law and the reckoning of time. The second, *De personis*, is further subdivided into *De clericis*, *De religiosis*, and *De laicis*. The third, *De rebus*, contains the discipline regulating the sacraments, ritual, ecclesiastical teaching, and property. The fourth volume is *De processibus*, and the fifth *De delictis et poenis*.

In the end, the *Codex iuris canonici* was promulgated by Pope Benedict XV on May 27, 1917, with the apostolic constitution *Providentissima Mater Ecclesia* and was published on June 28 of that year in the *Acta Apostolicae Sedis*, the official organ launched in 1909. The *Codex* came into force a year later, on May

19, 1918. Its official title is *Codex iuris canonici Pii X Pontificis Maximi iussu digestus, Benedicti Papae XV auctoritate promulgatus.*

The code is not concerned with liturgical regulations or with relations between the Holy See and other states. The previous legislation contained in the ancient collections is largely incorporated into the *Codex*, but here the precepts making up the text constitute a single entity to be approached as having emanated simultaneously from the paramount legislator.

The pope instituted a dedicated commission for the legitimate interpretation of the new code and named Cardinal Gasparri as its president. Gasparri added a preface summarizing the history of the corpus of ecclesiastical legislation and also an index together with notes specifying sources. The extended version of the *Fontes* of the *Codex iuris canonici* engaged the cardinal until his death. The first six volumes were finalized between 1923 and 1932. The seventh was issued posthumously in 1935, edited by Cardinal Jusztinián György Serédi, who also edited volumes 8 and 9, completing the series relating to sources. This, together with the preface and the index, is accorded the status of a private compilation with no authenticated character.

The *Codex* represented a turning point in the juridical and institutional nature of the Catholic Church, of which it was an agent of modernization, borrowing from the secular states of the time the format together with those elements which were considered compatible with the theological character of an ecclesiastical society, including the organization of codified law. Such a radical departure was made possible by historical circumstances. The nineteenth century brought a change in the national interlocutors of the Holy See. Up to the eighteenth century, absolute rulers had indeed recognized certain privileges for ecclesiastical institutions as well as their public nature, but at the same time they had subjected them to the control and intrusion of the State through the principle of jurisdictionalism. However, in the nineteenth century the Church was forced to contend with the nation-states, which were the product of a new political context, states characterized by representative systems which tended to confine religious matters to the private domain and brought the Church within the scope of positive law like any other private institution. In this historical context, the pope in Rome, the sole surviving element from the collapse of the old regime, reclaimed full dominion over doctrinal and disciplinary matters within the Church with greater vigor than previously. As a result, the Roman Church increasingly closed ranks around the pope and the Roman Curia, the source of power in the ecclesiastical context as well as the place where the future Catholic hierarchy would be trained. Thus, the promulgation of the *Codex*, with its pretensions to the status of indisputable law, contributed to the centralization of the Roman Church, strengthening the jurisdiction of the supreme tribunals, intensifying the hierarchical organization of the Church, and reinforcing the central role of the Roman Curia. The *Codex* brought about the unification of legislation and the simplification of the laws,[26] leading to concrete results which corresponded precisely to the intentions of Pope Pius X in sponsoring the work of codification. The new *Codex* constituted a cultural paradigm which, in combination with other reforms introduced by Pope Pius

X, contributed to the process of universalization of the Roman Church through disciplinary and functional uniformity. The codification should be viewed not as a self-contained juridical reform but in the context of Pius X's other major reforms of the Curia, the dioceses, the seminaries, the catechism, and the liturgy.

Gasparri was likewise appointed president of the commission of cardinals for the codification of canon law applying to the Eastern Church, where he benefitted from the assistance of Luigi Sincero, who later became a cardinal and Gasparri's successor in this same commission. In this context, Gasparri conceived the idea of developing a *Codex Ecclesiae universae*, consisting of the Pius/Benedict *Codex* with the addition of further legal elements specific to the Eastern churches. Pius XI rejected this idea and opted for the creation of a separate code for the Eastern Church, the formula which continues in use today.[27]

Conclusion

Pietro Gasparri's life and works may be viewed in a variety of different ways and from various points of view, resulting in differing interpretations. He was a priest, a university professor, a scholar of theology and of canon law, a diplomat, a cardinal, a secretary of state, and the author of the codification of ecclesiastical law. However, the key element remains the principal events of his life. Gasparri was a man of the Curia, trained for a diplomatic and juridical career, but at the same time he remained a Roman priest possessing a strong faith and good sense, always ready to help anyone who turned to him.

The figure of Cardinal Gasparri as an expression of the Roman Curia of the early twentieth century belongs to the history of the Church and hence the world. The position of secretary of state, which he held under two popes—Benedict XV and Pius XI—a fact which was exceptional for the time, placed him at the center of the political and diplomatic life of the Catholic Church. His experiences as a member of the Curia and as a trusted and respected adviser are reminiscent of other notable prelates who defined an epoch. It would be natural to view Gasparri alongside Cardinal Ercole Consalvi, who was Pius VII's secretary of state during a time of difficulties for the Church. Just as Pius VII's achievements cannot be viewed without reference to Consalvi's contributions, so the historic figures of Benedict XV and Pius XI could not be understood without being viewed together with that of their secretary of state, Cardinal Gasparri.

He was party to the secrets and to the strategies of papal diplomacy and was a faithful interpreter of the aspirations of the papacy for the defense of Catholicism, of peace, and of harmony among nations during the tragic period of the First World War. However, this adept diplomatic activity was never based simply on principles of abstract pacifism but on criteria of law and of justice. It can be said that all of Gasparri's life and works were shaped by a juridical mentality that combined law and diplomacy. On attaining cultural maturity he composed three treatises of canon law which embodied a perfect synthesis of technical competence and innovative methodology. These three treatises brought him renown. In addition, the codification of canon law, which occupied him for thirteen years on top of the heavy responsibilities of his involvement in the political affairs of the Holy See, is considered a monument of juridical expertise. While directing the work on the code of canon law, he was simultaneously occupied in negotiations with other states and, thanks to the trust and the esteem in which he was held, was able to resolve momentous and apparently irreconcilable diplomatic rifts, as in the Holy See's relations with France and Italy. The signing of numerous concordats and other agreements demonstrates the success of Gasparri's diplomatic dealings. These emerged from the vast preliminary work of a prudent negotiator, the tough negotiations, the minute adjustments to the text, and the constant pursuit of formulae of mediation with counterparts.

Gasparri's approach to problems was unfailingly pragmatic. As an interpreter of the traditions of Vatican diplomacy, he was able to show flexibility and understanding both towards civilian authorities and towards the aspirations of the masses, whenever doctrinal principles allowed him to do so. For example, after the First World War, when circumstances were favorable, drawing inspiration from the social doctrine of the Catholic Church, he contributed to the birth of the Italian People's Party, notwithstanding the reservations of some of the bishops. When the political climate changed with the rise of fascism, Gasparri counseled the disbanding of the Italian People's Party to its leaders Don Luigi Sturzo and Alcide De Gasperi, pending more favorable circumstances. In the great controversy over Catholic modernism, Gasparri maintained a neutral stance and took no part in the systematic repression aimed at its proponents, despite not sharing their ideas in any way. His position is further illustrated by the correspondence he maintained with the principal exponent of modernism in Italy, Ernesto Buonaiuti, in an attempt to bring this academic of international scientific renown back within the bosom of the Church.

Gasparri, connoisseur of the Roman Curia and of the world of politics, was shaped by a disposition to diplomacy and government and was an eminent exponent of that party within the Curia who were custodians of longstanding traditions both spiritual and in terms of expertise in international relations accumulated through centuries. No one could have been better suited than Cardinal Mertel to point the youthful Gasparri towards a knowledge of the techniques required to examine specific issues and identify the steps needed to resolve them. Gaining his technical know-how under the benevolent guidance of the aged cardinal, Gasparri became a model of competence within the environment of the Curia, focused on selfless service to the Church.

He succeeded in reconciling the Vatican's relations with the world through dialogue with those in power who were disposed to attend to the Church's message and spiritual strength as an institution working among and on behalf of humankind. This was a Roman Church which combined intransigence over fundamental principles with a willingness to reconsider individual details in agreements with other states, as long as they did not controvert the essential doctrines of the Church itself. In such circumstances, a certain diplomatic elasticity could come into play which Gasparri was able to exploit very adroitly. On the basis of all these qualities, Cardinal Pietro Gasparri is assured of a place in history.

Notes

1 Fantappiè and Astorri, "Gasparri, Pietro."
2 Fantappiè, "La formazione teologica e giuridica di Pietro Gasparri."
3 The *Institutiones iuris publici* dictated in the course of his lessons, were printed only in 1992.
4 Gasparri wrote a separate theological and canonical treatise on this topic, *De la valeur des Ordinations Anglicanes.* See Crivelli; see also Rambaldi.
5 Fantappiè, *Chiesa romana e modernità giuridica*, vol. 1, 417–15.
6 Grossi, 594–5.
7 Dalla Torre, 110.
8 Stella; also Fattorini.
9 Fantappiè, *Chiesa romana e modernità giuridica*, vol. 2, 959.
10 Astorri.
11 This was acknowledged by Vittorio Emanuele Orlando, who was the prime minister at the conclusion of the First World War and Italian plenipotentiary at the Versailles peace conference. See Orlando, 118–44. See also Monti.
12 Pacelli.
13 Del Giudice; Jemolo, 637–70.
14 Cardinal Pietro Gasparri (ed.), *Catechismo cattolico* (Brescia: La Scuola, 1932).
15 Dalla Torre, 112.
16 Feliciani.
17 Gasparri, *Storia della codificazione*, vol. 4, 1–10; Stickler, "La funzione della scienza storica di diritto canonico"; also Baura.
18 Vetulani; Stickler, *Historia iuris canonici latini*, vol. 1, 371–91; Kuttner; Fantappiè, *Chiesa romana e modernità giuridica*, vol. 2.
19 For example, Lucio Ferraris's work *Prompta Bibliotheca canonica iuridica moralis theologica nec non ascetica polemica rubricistica historica* has remained celebrated, having been in print continuously from the time of the first Bologna edition of 1746 to the last edition published in Rome from 1885 to 1898. See Lupano.
20 Feliciani, "Il Concilio Vaticano I"; Feliciani, "Gasparri et le droit de la Codification."
21 Vercellone.
22 The celebrated work titled *Institutiones iuris canonici* (Venetiis, 1563) by Claudio Lancellotti from Perugia had provided the model for the tripartite Justinian structure applied to a manual designed to illustrate the basic elements of canon law for the universities: see Sinisi.
23 Stickler, "La funzione della scienza storica di diritto canonico," 530.
24 Fantappiè, *Chiesa romana e modernità giuridica*, vol. 2, 699–805.
25 Ibid., 906–15.
26 Ibid., 1065–141.
27 Condorelli.

Bibliography

Alesandro, John A. "One Hundred Years since the 1917 Code of Canon Law." *Studia canonica* 51/2 (2017): 357–89.

Astorri, Romeo. "Gasparri, Pietro Giuseppe." In Birocchi, et al., *Dizionario biografico dei giuristi italiani, XII–XX secolo.* Vol. 1, 953–6.

Baura, Eduardo. "Gasparri Pietro." In *Juristas universales*, edited by Rafael Domingo. Vol. 3, 623–26. Madrid/Barcelona: Marcial Pons, 2004.

Birocchi, Italo, Ennio Cortese, Antonello Mattone, and Marco Nicola Miletti, eds. *Dizionario biografico dei giuristi italiani, XII–XX secolo.* Bologna: Il Mulino, 2013.

Condorelli, Orazio. "Gli studi storici sul diritto canonico orientale: appunti sullo stato attuale e sulle prospettive di ricerca." (*Alfons Maria Stickler (1910–2007). In memoriam*). Edited by José Miguel Viejo-Ximénez. *Annaeus. Anales de la Tradición Romanística* 7 (2010): 3–17.

Crivelli, Carlo. "Anglicane ordinazioni." In *Enciclopedia Cattolica*. Vol. 1, 1271–3. Città del Vaticano: Ente per l'Enciclopedia Cattolica, 1948.

Dalla Torre, Giuseppe. *Memorie*. Verona: Mondadori, 1967.

Del Giudice, Vincenzo. *La questione romana e i rapporti fra Stato e Chiesa fino alla Conciliazione, con considerazioni sui Patti Lateranensi e sull'articolo 7 della Costituzione repubblicana*. Rome: Edizioni dell'Ateneo, 1947.

De Luca, Giuseppe. "Discorrendo col cardinale Gasparri." *Nuova Antologia* 1 (1930): 195–205.

De Luca, Giuseppe. "Memoria di Pietro Gasparri." *Nuova Antologia* 1 (1934): 380–4.

Erdö, Péter. *Storia delle fonti del diritto canonico*. Venice: Marcianum Press, 2008.

Fantappiè, Carlo. *Chiesa romana e modernità giuridica*. Vol. 1: *L'edificazione del sistema canonistico (1563–1903)*. Milan: Giuffré, 2008.

Fantappiè, Carlo. *Chiesa romana e modernità giuridica*. Vol. 2: *Il codex iuris canonici (1917)*. Milan: Giuffré, 2008.

Fantappiè, Carlo. "La formazione teologica e giuridica di Pietro Gasparri a Roma nel Seminario dell'Apollinare." *Mélanges de l'École Française de Rome, Italie et Méditerranée* 116/1 (2004): 115–40.

Fantappiè, Carlo, and Romeo Astorri. "Gasparri, Pietro." In *Dizionario Biografico degli Italiani*. Vol. 52, 500–7. Rome: Istituto dell'Enciclopedia italiana, 1999.

Fattorini, Emma. *Diplomazia senza eserciti. Le relazioni internazionali della Chiesa di Pio XI*. Rome: Carocci, 2013.

Feliciani, Giorgio. "Gasparri et le droit de la Codification." *L'Année canonique* 38 (1996): 25–37.

Feliciani, Giorgio. "Il cardinal Gasparri e la codificazione del diritto canonico." In *Studi in onore di Gaetano Catalano*, 563–87. Soveria Mannelli: Rubbettino, 1998.

Feliciani, Giorgio. "Il Concilio Vaticano I e la codificazione del diritto canonico." In *Actas del III Congreso internacional de derecho canónico, Pamplona, 10–15 de octubre 1976*. Vol. 1, 505–38. Pamplona: Eunsa, 1979.

Gasparri, Pietro. *De la valeur des Ordinations Anglicanes*. Paris: F. Levé, 1895.

Gasparri, Pietro. *Institutiones iuris publici*. Bologna: Giuffré, 1992.

Gasparri, Pietro. "Storia della codificazione del diritto canonico per la Chiesa latina." In *Acta congressus iuridici internationalis VII saeculo a Decretalibus Gregorii IX et XIV a Codice Iustiniano promulgatis, Romae 12–17 novembris 1934*. Vol. 4, 3–10. Rome: Pontificium Institutum Utriusque Iuris, 1937.

Gasparri, Pietro. *Tractatus canonicus de matrimonio*, 1–2. Paris/Lyon: Delhomme et Briguet, 1891–92.

Gasparri, Pietro. *Tractatus canonicus de sacra ordinatione*, 1–2. Paris/Lyon: Delhomme et Briguet, 1893–94.

Gasparri, Pietro. *Tractatus canonicus de sanctissima Eucharistia*, 1–2. Paris/Lyon: Delhomme et Briguet, 1897.

Gaudemet, Jean. "Collections canoniques et codifications." *Revue de droit canonique* 33 (1983): 81–109.

Grossi, Paolo. "Storia della canonistica moderna e storia della codificazione canonica." *Quaderni fiorentini per la storia del pensiero giuridico moderno* 14 (1985): 587–99.

Jemolo, Arturo Carlo. *Chiesa e Stato in Italia negli ultimi cento anni*. Turin: Einaudi, 1949.

Kuttner, Stephan. "Il diritto canonico nella storia." *Jus* 18 (1967): 239–54.

Lupano, Alberto. "Ferraris, Lucio." In Birocchi, et al., *Dizionario biografico dei giuristi italiani*. Vol. 1, 846.

Metz, René. "La codification du droit de l'Eglise catholique au début du XXe siècle à la fois résultats et expression du pouvoir pontificale et de la centralisation romaine." In *Diritto e potere nella storia europea. Atti in onore di Bruno Paradisi. Quarto Congresso internazionale della Società italiana di storia del diritto*. Vol. 2, 1069–92. Florence: Olschki, 1982.

Monti, Carlo. *La Conciliazione ufficiosa. Diario del barone Carlo Monti incaricato d'affari del governo italiano presso la S. Sede 1914–1922*. Edited by Antonio Scottà. Città del Vaticano: Libreria Editrice Vaticana, 1997.

Orlando, Vittorio Emanuele. *Miei rapporti di governo con la Santa Sede*. Milan: Garzanti, 1944.

Pacelli, Francesco. *Diario della Conciliazione*. Edited by Michele Maccarrone. Città del Vaticano: Libreria Editrice Vaticana, 1959.

Rambaldi, Giuseppe. *Ordinazioni anglicane e sacramento dell'ordine nella Chiesa. Aspetti storici e teologici a cento anni dalla bolla Apostolicae curae di Leone XIII*. Rome: Pontificia Università Gregoriana, 1995.

Sinisi, Lorenzo. "Lancellotti, Giovanni Paolo." In Birocchi, et al., *Dizionario biografico dei giuristi*. Vol. 2, 1142–3.

Stella, Giordano. *Pio XI. Il papa dei concordati*. Milan: Gribaudi, 2009.

Stickler, Alfons Maria. *Historia iuris canonici latini: Institutiones academicae. Historia fontium*. Vol. 1. Augustae Taurinorum: Pontificium Athenaeum Salesianum, 1950.

Stickler, Alfons Maria. "La funzione della scienza storica di diritto canonico nella codificazione pio-benedettina e per la riforma attuale del diritto canonico." *L'Année catholique* 15 (1971): 525–40.

Vercellone Fagioli, Guido Gregorio. "Gènnari, Casimiro." In *Dizionario biografico degli italiani*. Vol. 53, 114–16. Rome: Istituto dell'Enciclopedia italiana, 2000.

Vetulani, Adam. "Codex iuris canonici." In *Dictionnaire de droit canonique*. Vol. 3, 909–35. Paris: Letouzey et Ané, 1942.

21 Contardo Ferrini (1859–1902)

Rafael Domingo

Every moment is lost that is not a heartbeat of love.[1]

Biographical information

A scholar of great originality and deep spirituality, Contardo Ferrini belonged to an outstanding generation of Italian legal historians of antiquity, who brought to prominence the studies of Roman law just after the establishment of the Kingdom of Italy (1861). Moved by a patriotic feeling and scientific enthusiasm, they tried to wrest intellectual supremacy from Germany. In addition to Ferrini, the most influential representatives of this select group included Vittorio Scialoja, Carlo Fadda, Silvio Perozzi, Salvatore Riccobono, and Pietro Bonfante.

Although Scialoja, not Ferrini, was the leader of the group, Ferrini was a very prominent member of it, the most distinguished expert in Roman Byzantine law and criminal law, and probably the one who more properly embodied the notion of Christian jurist. Ferrini lived in a time of strong tensions between Church and State due to the Roman question.[2] He was a forerunner of the theology of the universal call to holiness, deeply developed decades later by the Second Vatican Council (1962–5),[3] and he contributed to linking Christian love, especially for the poor, with the flourishing of human science.

In the course of an informal conversation in Berlin in August 1902 the historian of Rome, Theodor Mommsen, said to the director of the Etruscan Vatican Museum, Bartolomeo Nogara, that if the nineteenth century might be called "Savigny's century" because of the indelible imprint of the German scholar Friedrich Carl von Savigny on Roman law studies, the twentieth century might be called "Ferrini's century." Thanks to Ferrini, concluded Mommsen, the leadership in Roman studies had passed from Germany to Italy.[4] What Mommsen did not know then was that his student Contardo Ferrini would die just months later at the age of forty three, when the twentieth century was still taking its first steps.[5]

Eugenio Contardo Ferrini was born April 5, 1859, in Milan, the oldest son of Rinaldo Ferrini, a distinguished professor of physics and mathematics at the Polytechnic University of Milan, and Luigia Buccellati, a woman of the Milanese upper-middle class. The family atmosphere, deeply Christian and highly cultured, was decisive in the formation of the young Ferrini. He received his primary education at the Boselli School, and secondary education at the Beccaria High School, where he learned Latin and Greek. The prefect of the Ambrosian Library, Antonio Maria Ceriani, taught him Hebrew and Syriac. Later Ferrini also learned the rudiments of Sanskrit and Coptic. While still in high school, Ferrini started reading an edition of the Hebrew Bible, which he had received as a gift from a family friend. A formative moment of his childhood was the day of his first communion, which marked a "before and after" in his spiritual life, as he himself acknowledged so many times.[6]

In 1876, Ferrini became a law student at the University of Pavia, where his uncle Antonio Buccellati was a distinguished professor of criminal law. He introduced Ferrini to criminal law, as a student and later as a young professor, at a time of intense academic debate in the years prior to the promulgation of the so-called Zanardelli Code (1889), the first criminal code of the Kingdom of Italy.[7] Simultaneously with his law courses, Ferrini was also able to study in the Faculty of Letters and to learn German.

In addition to Buccellati, Ferrini was especially attracted by the intellectual stature of the classic philologist Giovanni Canna, who instilled in Ferrini his passionate love for Greek civilization.[8] Ferrini also established a great friendship with Bishop Agostino Gaetano Riboldi, later a cardinal. Bishop Riboldi appreciated Ferrini's moral, intellectual, and spiritual qualities and helped him discern his vocation as a contemplative scholar living in celibacy in the midst of the academic world. Ferrini also became very close friends with Count Paolo Mapelli and his brother Vittorio, who occupied an important place in Ferrini's personal life. We now know many details of Ferrini's soul and activity thanks the correspondence between these two friends.[9]

In 1880, Ferrini graduated with a dissertation, written in Latin, on the contribution of the poems of Homer and Hesiod to the knowledge of criminal repression in the Greek world.[10] Soon after, and because of the quality of his dissertation, he was awarded a scholarship to conduct research in Roman law in Berlin, then the capital of the German Empire. For a number of reasons—the still-vibrant legacy of Friedrich Carl von Savigny, the overwhelming intellectual strength of Theodor Mommsen as editor of primary Roman texts (e.g., the edition of the Digest of Justinian) and organizer of big projects (e.g., *Corpus inscriptionum Latinarum* (Body of Latin inscriptions)), and the strong impact of the *Zeitschrift für Rechtsgeschichte* (supported by the Savigny Foundation since 1880)—[11]Berlin was the epicenter of the study of Roman law.

In Berlin, Ferrini attended courses taught by Moritz Voigt, Heinrich Dernburg, and Theodor Mommsen, but he was especially mentored by Alfred Pernice and Karl Eduard Zachariae von Lingenthal.[12] With the support of these two scholars, Ferrini undertook one of his great intellectual enterprises: the edition of the so-called *Paraphrasis* of Theofilos.[13] This work of the sixth century, written in Greek, might have been based on notes taken by a student at a course given by the *Corpus Iuris* compiler Theophilos, after the completion of Justinian's *Institutes* (533 CE). Although Ferrini erroneously disputed the attribution of the paraphrasis to Theophilos, Ferrini's edition, enriched with a Latin translation of the Greek text, was the standard edition regularly consulted by scholars and researchers for more than a century until the new edition by J. H. A. Lokin, published in 2010.[14]

From a spiritual point of view, Ferrini's stay in Berlin was crucial.[15] He experienced the vitality of a Catholic minority working with great success under the pressure of the *Kulturkampf*.[16] Ferrini became very close to the botanist Massimiliano Westermajer, a Franciscan tertiary, who invited Ferrini to enroll in the Society of St. Vincent de Paul.[17] Ferrini accepted, and in the fall of 1881, after receiving the Holy Eucharist, he made a permanent vow of chastity that he had made temporarily and renewed monthly for a time. That day, his spiritual joy was profound.[18] Some weeks later, on January 4, 1882, he wrote in a letter to his friend Paolo Mapelli that "the fruitful virginity of Mary" is a "beautiful image of Catholic virginity." He added: "pleasing to God in your brothers, the martyrdom of this immaculate sacrifice of the soul arises, and she does not surrender to the most violent temptations or to the still more fatal languor of certain moments."[19] On January 6, 1886, Ferrini became a lay Franciscan, and one year later he made the profession of the Third Order rule of life.

After his return to Italy in the summer of 1882, Ferrini began his academic career at the University of Pavia teaching Roman criminal law and exegesis of Roman law sources. Soon he was promoted to the rank of extraordinary professor. In February 1887 he was granted a tenured position at the University of Messina (in Sicily), which had been acknowledged two years earlier as an academic institution of the first level. In Messina, Ferrini lived at Villa Macrì with the later political leader Vittorio Emanuele Orlando, then professor of constitutional law.

Ferrini's desire to live closer to his parents' home led him to move in 1890 to the University of Modena, where he was elected dean of the School of Law (1891). There he met his close friend, the international-law professor Luigi Olivi, who later promoted Ferrini's beatification. In 1894, Ferrini was appointed full professor of Roman law at his alma mater, the University of Pavia, and one year later, in 1895, a full member of the Instituto Lombardo in Milan. The proximity between Pavia and Milan allowed him to live with his beloved family. Between these two cities, Ferrini spent the days focused on his teaching, research, and prayers as well as his social work, visiting the sick, which he interrupted only with occasional alpine excursions, many times in the company of his friend Achile Ratti, the future Pope Pius XI.

Affiliated with the conservative Catholic party, in 1895 Ferrini was elected as a member of the city council of Milan. He worked decisively on the commission for tax reform. However, the dramatic events of May 1898, the so called Bava-Beccaris massacre,[20] compelled him to engage more deeply in politics to protect the interests of religion and the country at the local level. He defended a reconciling position between the young Kingdom of Italy, born as result of the unification of Italy, and the Holy See and, therefore, the need for a political agreement between Church and State. Ferrini tried to seek an alliance with the Christian Democrats led by Filippo Meda, but he did not succeed. The Christian

Democrats instead wanted to form an autonomous party totally separate from any political influence of ecclesiastical authority. This was not the case with Ferrini's Catholic party. Discouraged by the result of the elections, which gave the victory to the leftist parties, as well as by the lack of political union among Catholics themselves, Ferrini decided to abandon politics and return to the peaceful academic life.

In 1900, Contardo Ferrini was afflicted with a heart lesion. In the fall of 1902, he went for a rest to his country home in the village of Suna (today part of Verbania), on the shore of Lake Maggiore. Unfortunately, he was stricken there with typhus, and after some days in bed, he died on October 17, 1902. He was buried in Suna in accordance with his will. However, in 1942, at the request of the first president of the Catholic University of the Sacred Heart, the Franciscan Agostino Gemelli, Ferrini's body was reinterred in the chapel of the Catholic University of Milan. Gemelli had a dual purpose. On the one hand, he wanted to propose Ferrini to university students and professors as a model of holiness in the academy. On the other hand, he thought that the transfer would favor the process of beatification. Ferrini's heart was brought back to Suna years later, after his beatification on April 14, 1947, by Pope Pius XII.[21] Ferrini was named the patron of universities, and his remembrance day in the Roman Catholic Church is October 17.

Ferrini's contribution to Roman law

Ferrini's work is characterized by its abundance and thematic variety. In his twenty-one years of scholarly production (1881–1902), Ferrini wrote several books and more than two hundred papers,[22] many of them very short. Ferrini did not seek perfection in writing, but the advancement of knowledge. He was not afraid to rectify his earlier views when he thought they were mistaken, nor to return repeatedly to the same subject when necessary. He was occupied more with the opening of new areas of research, with good intuitions, with interesting projects. In fact, some colleagues and friends, among them Scialoja and Baviera, sometimes complained about his lack of accuracy in quotations.[23]

Many of his contributions are marked by the circumstances of the scholarship of his time, but at no point can his work be considered obsolete in our day. Twenty-seven years after his death, a large selection of his articles was collected in five volumes.[24] Fifty-one years after his death, the fifth edition of Ferrini's *Manuale di Pandette* (Textbook on the Pandects) was edited by Giuseppe Grosso.[25] Sixty-five years after Ferrini's death, his edition of the *Paraphrasis* of Theophilos was reprinted by the German publisher Scientia, in Aalen (1967). Seventy-four years after his death, the Roman publisher L'Erma di Bretschneider reprinted some of Ferrini's works,[26] and more than a century after his death, a Spanish version of his textbook on Roman criminal law appeared.[27] His co-edition of the Digest, the so-called *Digesto milanese*, in collaboration with his Italian colleagues Pietro Bonfante, Carlo Fadda, Salvatore Riccobono, and Vittorio Scialoja, is still a book of great value among the experts.[28] It is the one that I personally used more than thirty years ago at the University of Navarra to begin studying Roman law.

Although it is difficult to classify because of its extreme variety, Ferrini's contribution to the study of Byzantine law, criminal law, and Roman jurisprudence, as well as his research on Roman inheritance and obligations, stand out fundamentally. The most popular of Ferrini's works, and probably the best expression of his scholarly legacy, is his *Manuale di Pandette* (1900). As Francesco Paolo Casavola categorically affirmed: "There was no lawyer, especially in Italy, who had not read his handbook on *Pandects.*"[29] Ahead of his time, Ferrini saw the need for the study of post-Justinian law, which in our day has flourished in a very particular way.[30]

In the field of Byzantine law, Ferrini was primarily involved in the edition and translation of sources. In addition to his edition of the *Paraphrasis*, Ferrini focused on, among others, the edition of many unpublished fragments of Anatolios,[31] a Byzantine compiler and professor of law at Berytus, who wrote a Greek paraphrasis of constitutions of Justinian's Code. Ferrini also edited, with his friend Giovanni Mercati, new fragments of the Basilika,[32] found in the palimpsest Cod. Ambros. F. 106, as a supplement[33] of the edition of the Basilika published and edited by Karl Wilhelm Ernst Heimbach and Gustav Ernst Heimbach.[34] Paul Krüger's book review on Ferrini's supplement for the *Zeitschrift der Savigny-Stiftung für Rechtsgeschichte* was favorable.[35] Relevant for the knowledge of the Basilika was Ferrini's edition, always in collaboration with Mercati, of the first twelve books of the so called Tipucitus, or Tipoukeitos, which lay largely unpublished in the Vatican Library. The Tipucitus is a table of contents of the Basilika, giving the rubrics under each title, and is very important from the point of view of the reconstruction of the lost books of the Basilika.[36] It was probably produced at the end of the eleventh century by a judge named Patzes.

In the field of editing legal sources, Ferrini's Latin translation of the enigmatic Syro-Roman Law Book should be mentioned. The Syro-Roman Law Book is a collection of imperial constitutions enacted by Roman emperors of the fifth century.[37] The original version, written in Greek, was lost, but not the Syriac, Arabic, and Armenian versions. Ferrini's translation, published in 1902, was based on a Syriac version and was revised and corrected by Giuseppe Furlani in 1940, taking into consideration new developments in research.[38]

Ferrini also dealt with Roman criminal law, a research field abandoned in Italy for a long time.[39] In addition to his dissertation and some articles on specific issues (e.g., intent to commit crime, theft, and the Aquilian action), Ferrini published a general theory of Roman criminal law which still remains a point of reference for scholars of the subject.[40] As Ferrini himself recognized, the textbook dealt only with the exposition of those general doctrines with greater relevance for jurists. It is a volume written by a jurist and addressed to jurists. Ferrini used a technical-dogmatic methodology that escapes an excess of historicism. In some sense, Ferrini's methodology opposed the great treatise of Mommsen on criminal law,[41] which appeared some months later. From the first pages of his work, Mommsen made it clear that "criminal law occupies a middle ground between law and history,"[42] and that any scientific treatment of criminal law required considering criminal law and criminal procedure together.[43] Although technically superior to Ferrini's work, Mommsen's monumental handbook did not eclipse Ferrini's talent and research.[44] Mommsen's contribution intellectually stimulated Ferrini, who, after analyzing it, devoted himself to the publication of a new edition of his treatise on criminal law, now titled *Diritto penale. Esposizione storica e dottrinale* (Roman criminal law. Historical and doctrinal exposition). The manuscript, which reflects the intellectual maturity of the author, was published in the first volume of the *Enciclopedia del diritto penale italiano* (Encyclopedia of Italian Criminal Law), edited by Enrico Pessina, leader of the classical school of criminal law after the death of Francesco Carrara.[45] This new edition, which maintains the structure of the previous one, added the great contributions of Mommsen as well as a special section to deal with specific crimes. The Lincean Academy in Rome honored Ferrini posthumously for this magnificent contribution to criminal law in the academy's session of June 7, 1903, which was attended by King Victor Emmanuel III.

In Roman private law, Ferrini became an international expert in the field of inheritance and obligations. Special mention must be made of his volume titled *Teoria generale dei legati e dei fedecommessi* (General theory of legacies and trust law),[46] and his wide and erudite entry on obligations for the *Enciclopedia giuridica italiana* (Italian Legal Encyclopedia) in collaboration with Nicola De Crescenzio, who had died in 1895.[47] Ferrini's minor writings on these Roman law topics were collected in volumes three and four of his works, edited respectively by Emilio Albertario and Pietro Ciapessoni.[48]

Following the example of his mentor Alfred Pernice, author of a valuable work on Labeo,[49] Ferrini focused on the particular analytical study of some of the Roman jurists. The compilers of the Justinian *Corpus Iuris* had no qualms about sacrificing the identity and works on the Roman jurists to favor the main purpose and interest of the great Compilation.[50] Taking an opposite tack, Ferrini tried to recover the nature, identity, and main characteristics of the work of the Roman jurists, their particular doctrines, and their contributions to the development of the legal culture.[51] Ferrini's endeavor started in 1885 with an essay on some Roman jurists[52] and culminated in 1901 with studies on the commentaries of Terentius Clemens, Gaius, Paul, and Ulpian[53] to the *lex Julia et Papia*,[54] and an article on the *Institutes* of Marcian.[55]

Ferrini's spiritual writings

Ferrini did not publish religious writings during his lifetime. A selection of letters and religious papers addressed to his friends from 1879 to 1885 was posthumously edited by Carlo Pellegrini, curator of Ferrini's case for beatification.[56] After Ferrini's beatification, the Catholic University of the Sacred Heart edited a little book of his spiritual thoughts and prayers (*Pensieri e preghiere*) with an introduction by the university's president, Agostino Gemelli.[57]

A hallmark of Ferrini's spirituality was the search for union with God in the fulfillment of daily endeavors.[58] Ferrini tried to experience divine presence in the beauty, order, and consonance of the created world, and in human beings, especially his beloved family, his closest friends, and the poor. For Ferrini, Christian friendship was an expression of the union of souls in Christ.[59] His lifestyle was simple, calm, and austere: his entire day was devoted to intense academic work (which he offered to God as a sacrifice), his contemplative prayer, and his moments of rest and conversation with his friends and family—moments when he took advantage to vivify the presence of God.

In his *Regolamento di vita* (Rules of life),[60] we can see that Eucharistic adoration was at the heart of his spirituality. He was convinced that the daily reception of the holy sacrament, at that time an uncommon practice,[61] was the best way to be transformed into Christ. Devotion to the Virgin Mary also occupied a central place in his life. Contardo committed to recite the rosary and to make a visit to an image of the Virgin Mary every day, to pray the angelus at noon, and, if possible, the Hail Mary and a spiritual communion every hour. He also committed to pray a Hail Mary before every conversation with someone in order to develop the consciousness of the presence of God.[62]

To know Ferrini's spirituality, there is no better writing than the *Programma di vita del giovane cristiano*[63] (Life program of the young Christian.) It is a long letter written to his friend Vittorio Mapelli, in November 1880, before Ferrini left for Berlin. Ferrini found good inspiration for his life program in the letters of Saint Paul, especially Philippians 4:8–9,[64] and in the attitudes and works of Saint Augustine. For Augustine,

> study was a conversation with the Supreme Truth. Augustine thanked the Supreme Truth every step of the way, he submitted to it in every situation, before it he humiliated himself in all the darkness and, from the fruitful results of that multiple work, the Supreme Truth absorbed that soul thirsting for God to the eternal beauty of the True Absolute.[65]

Besides Saint Paul and Saint Augustine, Ferrini professed special admiration for Antonio Rosmini and John Henry Newman,[66] among others. Ferrini learned from Rosmini the importance of humility for spiritual growth, and from Newman the inherent matching and harmonic relationship between faith and science.

According to Ferrini, the end of Christian prayer is personal transformation in Christ.[67] This transformation requires recollection of the spirit, union with God, spiritual wisdom, longing for the eternal good, and purity of heart and humility, which is the only way worth living.[68] Ferrini's soul used to live in contemplative prayer: "How much purity, insisted Ferrini, in those moments when the soul abandons herself in the arms of her Bridegroom, in the embrace of an immense charity, and she rests in his adored Heart."[69]

With regard to the neighbor, Ferrini proposed a program of love that sees Christ in the neighbor.[70] When that happens, dealing with others is courteous, sweet, meek, and full of charity. According to Ferrini, this charity becomes manifest, above all, in the care for the reputation and health of the neighbor. He understood the human being as a creature with thirst for infinity, a "finite being that tends to infinity,"[71] as Ferrini, following Vico, explained in his short work *Un po' d'Infinito* (A little bit of Infinity)[72] probably the deepest of Ferrini's religious papers: "Every intelligent creature," he wrote,

> knows and can rise to infinity. More, there is already a part of infinity in every intelligent being in which the splendor of the face of God is reflected: this thought, which flows from an immortal soul and free child of the spirit, ignores the limits of time and space, and evokes the ages that were, and dreams to come.[73]

Conclusion

Ferrini was above all a Catholic legal scholar, expert in Roman law, who tried to live an intense academic life and scholarship in permanent union with God. His life passed between the modest tranquility of the study, the serene contemplation of nature, and the silent constant dialogue with God. A patriotic man, he contributed in such a way that the study of Roman law achieved worldwide eminence in the newly created Kingdom of Italy. Ferrini deeply understood that law and love are not opposite, and that the reduction of the concept of law to merely positive law was a cultural error. He emerged among the Roman law scholars of his time for the originality of his thought and the vastness of his research. A distinguished publisher of sources from Antiquity, he translated into Latin the Paraphrasis of Theophilos and from the Syriac the Syro-Roman Law Book, and he enriched with a supplement Heimbach's edition of the Basilika. He published in collaboration with Italian colleagues the so-called *Digesto milanese*. His treatises include a handbook on Roman criminal law and the Handbook of Pandects, among others. A man of intense spirituality and deep love of nature and the poor, he became, with his beatification in 1947, the Roman Catholic Church's model of a Catholic scholar.

Notes

1 Letter of Ferrini to Vittorio Mapelli, November 21, 1880, in Ferrini, *Pensieri e preghiere*, 45: "è perduto ogni istante che non sia un palpito d'amore!" The English translations of all Italian texts are mine.

2 The Roman question refers to the dispute between the Holy See and Italy during the Italian Risorgimento regarding the temporal power of Roman pontiffs as rulers of a civil territory. The controversy ended with the Lateran Pacts (1929) between King Victor Emmanuel III of Italy and Pope Pius XI, which established the Vatican City as a sovereign state. See Fiorentino; also, Camaiani.

3 See Paul VI, *Lumen Gentium*, num. 39.

4 See the anecdote with all detail in Pellegrini, 466. Pellegrini provides abundant information about the life of Ferrini. It is still the most complete biography (and hagiography) of Ferrini and the starting point of any reflection on Ferrini's life. For a description of the cultural context and Ferrini's contribution to Roman law, see Mantovani (ed.), *Contardo Ferrini nel I centenario della morte*, with excellent contributions by Bernando Santalucia, Dario Mantovani, Fausto Goria, Renzo

Lambertini, and Antonio Mantello, among others. For the scientific works of Ferrini, see his *Opere* (hereafter *Opere* and the number of the volume).

5 Mommsen and Ferrini died almost at the same time, and both obituaries opened number 23 of the *Savigny Zeitschrift*, which shows the prestige achieved by Ferrini among German scholars. However, this relationship should not be exaggerated. See Die Redaktion, *Zeitschritft der Savigny-Stiftung für Rechtsgeschichte (Romanistische Abteilung)* 24 (1903): v–vi (Mommsen) and vii–viii (Ferrini).

6 See Pellegrini, *La vita del Prof. Contardo Ferrini*, 25–7.

7 Named after Giuseppe Zanardelli, then minister of justice, this code was in force from 1889 to 1930. It unified criminal legislation, abolished the death penalty, and acknowledged the right to strike, among other relevant hallmarks.

8 About the intellectual environment of Pavia University at that time, see Mantovani, *Almum Studium Papiense*.

9 See Ferrini, *Scritti religiosi*.

10 The doctoral thesis was published one year later in Berlin. See Ferrini, *Quid conferat*; see also the publication in *Opere*, vol. 5, 50ff.

11 In 1880 the name of this still-leading journal was changed to *Zeitschrift der Savigny-Stiftung für Rechtsgeschichte*, and it was split into two autonomous series, one for Roman law (Romanistische Abteilung) and the other for German law (Germanistische Abteilung). In 1911, a canon law series was added (Kanonistische Abteilung).

12 See the obituaries written by Ferrini on the death of these two scholars: "Zachariae von Lingenthal," in *Opere*, vol. 1, 461–5; "Alfred Pernice," in *Opere*, vol. 5, 413–16.

13 Ferrini, *Institutionum Graeca paraphrasis*.

14 Lokin, et al.

15 See the chapter "Vita di Berlino," in Ferrini, *Scritti religiosi*, 46–96.

16 *Kulturkampf* ("culture struggle") refers to the bitter struggle by chancellor Otto von Bismarck to submit the Roman Catholic Church to the control of the political power. For an overview, see Gross.

17 The Society of St. Vincent de Paul is an international voluntary Catholic organization founded in 1833 in Paris by Frédéric Ozanam for the sanctification of its members by personal service to the poor.

18 Pellegrini, *La vita del prof. Contardo Ferrini*, 186.

19 Ferrini, *Pensieri e preghiere*, 50.

20 During serious riots prompted by high food prices, General Fiorenzo Bava-Beccaris (1831–1924), commanding troops in Milan, ordered them to open fire against the protesters. The number of victims, never ascertained with precision, was high, in the order of several hundred individuals, due to the indiscriminate use of weapons, including artillery. King Umberto I rewarded the general with the Great Cross of the Order of Savoy. The famous novel *La paura* (1970) by Piero Gadda Conti centers on this massacre. See Colapietra; Caccamo; and Canavero.

21 On the process of beatification, see Xenio Toscani, "La causa de beatificazione di Contardo Ferrini: moventi e strategi," in Mantovani, *Contardo Ferrini nel I centenario della morte*, 203–5; and Michele Mosa, "Il proceso rogatoriale pavese sulla causa di beatificazione di Contardo Ferrini," ibidem, 227–47.

22 For Ferrini's complete scholarly bibliography, see Valerio Marotta, "La bibliografia scientifica di Contardo Ferrini," in Mantovani, *Contardo Ferrini nel I centenario della morte*, 294–309.

23 See Scialoja, at 307; Pellegrini, *La vita del Prof. Contardo Ferrini*, 221; Invernizzi, 93–4.

24 See Ferrini, *Opere*.

25 Ferrini, *Manuale di Pandette*.

26 Ferrini, *Diritto penale romano*; and *Teoria generale dei legati e dei fedecommessi*.

27 Ferrini, *Derecho penal romano*.

28 *Digesta Iustiniani Augusti*, edited by Pietro Bonfante, Carlo Fadda, Contardo Ferrini, Salvatore Riccobono, and Vincenzo Scialoja (Milan: Formis Societatis Editricis Librariae, 1908–1931; reprint, 1960).
29 Casavola, 856.
30 See, in the same vein, Antonio Mantello, "Contardo Ferrini e la Pandettistica," in Mantovani, *Contardo Ferrini nel I centenario della morte*, 177–200, at 192–3.
31 Ferrini, *Opere*, vol. 1, 254–90.
32 The Basilika is considered the most important legal compilation after Justinian. Around 890, Emperor Leo the Wise (r. 886–912) completed an extensive Greek restatement of all of Justinian's codification in sixty books. The collection is grounded on all four parts of Justinian's compilation, although there is little from the *Institutes*. The labor of compilation, however, began under Leo's predecessor, Basil I (r. 867–86). From the eleventh century, the collection was called the Basilika (from *basilikos*, or "imperial" (laws)). The laws were supplemented with explanatory notes (*scholia*) on the manuscript based on law professors' teachings in Justinian's time (old *scholia*) or from the eleventh and twelfth centuries (new *scholia*). On the Basilika, see Domingo, 85–7, with bibliography. The edition of the Basilika edited between 1945 and 1988 by H. J. Scheltema, D. Holwerda, and N. van der Wal is now available at: http://referenceworks.brillonline.com/browse/basilica-online.
33 See Ferrini and Mercati, *Basilicorum libri LX*, vol. 7.
34 Heimbach and Heimbach, *Basilicorum libri LX*.
35 See Krüger.
36 *M. Kritou tou Patze Tipoukeitos*, 5 vols., ed. Contardo Ferrini and Giovanni Mercati (books 1–12] (Rome: Typis Poliglottis Vaticanis, 1914); F. Dölger (books 13–23] (Rome: Typis Poliglottis Vaticanis, 1929); St. Hoermann, E. Seidl (books 24–60] (Rome: Typis Poliglottis Vaticanis, 1943–57).
37 Ferrini knew the edition of Bruns and Sachau. The first critical edition of the Syriac version was published by Selb and Kaufhold. For an overview of the Syro-Roman law book, see Thür.
38 See Ferrini, *Opere*, vol. 1, 397–437; and *Fons Iuris Romani Anteiustiniani, in usum scholarum ediderunt S. Riccobono, G. Baviera, C. Ferrini. Pars altera: Auctores* (Florence: Barbera, 1909), 639ff.; 2nd. ed., 1940 reprint, 1968.
39 For an overview of Ferrini's contribution to criminal law, see Bernardo Santalucia, "Contardo Ferrini e il diritto penale," in Mantovani, *Contardo Ferrini nel I centenario della morte*, 99–110.
40 See Ferrini, *Diritto penale romano*.
41 Mommsen.
42 Ibid., vii.
43 Ibid.
44 Ferrini wrote a book review of Mommsen's *Römisches Strafrecht*, in which the Italian scholar recognized the value of Mommsen's work while criticizing his methodology. Although very short, this book review is a clear expression of Ferrini's talent and temperament. See Contardo Ferrini, "Theodor Mommsen: Römisches Strafrecht," *Archivio Giuridico* 64 (1900): 377–9. This book review was not collected in Ferrini's *Opere*.
45 See Ferrini, "Diritto penale. Esposizione storica e dottrinale."
46 Ferrini, *Teoria generale dei legati e dei fedecommessi*.
47 Ferrini and De Crescenzio.
48 *Opere*, 3 and 4 (1929, 1930).
49 Pernice.
50 Many of Ferrini's works on jurists are collected in volume 2 of his *Opere*.
51 On the contribution of Ferrini to the knowledge of the Roman jurists, see Dario Mantovani, "Contardo Ferrini e le opere dei giuristi," in Mantovani, *Contardo Ferrini nel I centenario della morte*, 129–70.

52 Ferrini, "Saggi intorno ad alcuni giureconsulti romani."
53 Contardo Ferrini, "I commentari di Terenzio"; and "I commentari di Paolo e di Ulpiano."
54 The second statute both supplemented and partly recast the first, eliminating loopholes and relaxing some of the rules. Although they were two different laws, jurists and modern commentators refer to them as one: the *lex Iulia et Papia*, since the second statute (*lex Papia Poppaea*) supplemented and recast the first (*lex Julia de maritandis ordinibus*. On this topic, see McGinn, 70–104.
55 Ferrini, "Intorno alle Istituzioni di Marciano."
56 Ferrini, *Scritti religiosi.*
57 See Ferrini, *Pensieri e preghiere*. The volume has been reedited many times. I use the edition published by Edizioni Radio Spada (Milan, 2014), with a preface of Ilaria Pisa.
58 For an overview of Ferrini's spirituality, see Invernizzi, 95–109.
59 Ferrini, *Pensieri e preghiere*, 85.
60 Ibid., 71–3.
61 Pope Pius X was the great promoter of daily communion. See, among others, the English version of the decree *Sacra Tridentina*, on frequent and daily reception of holy communion, issued and approved by Pius X on December 20, 1905: www.ewtn.com/library/CURIA/CDWFREQ.HTM.
62 Ferrini, *Pensieri e preghiere*, 71–3.
63 Ferrini, "Programma di vita del giovane cristiano," in *Pensieri e preghiere*, 45–53.
64 Philippians 4: 8–9:

> Finally, brothers and sisters, whatever is true, whatever is noble, whatever is right, whatever is pure, whatever is lovely, whatever is admirable—if anything is excellent or praiseworthy—think about such things. Whatever you have learned or received or heard from me, or seen in me—put it into practice. And the God of peace will be with you.

65 Ferrini, *Pensieri e preghiere*, 48.
66 Lodigiani, 24.
67 Ferrini, *Pensieri e preghiere*, 49.
68 Ibid., 51.
69 Ibid., 50.
70 Ibid., 51.
71 Ibid., 9.
72 The full version is in Ferrini, *Scritti religiosi*, 149–204; short version in Ferrini, *Pensieri e preghiere*, 9–22.
73 Ferrini, *Pensieri e preghiere*, 9; and Ferrini, *Scritti religiosi*, 160.

Bibliography

Albertario, Emilio. *Contardo Ferrini: l'uomo e lo scienziato.* Milan: Vita e pensiero, 1928.

Arangio Ruiz, Vincenzo. *Contardo Ferrini. Commemorazione tenuta nella Università di Modena il 15 giugno 1948.* Modena: Publicazoni della Facoltà di Giurisprudenza della Università di Modena, 1948.

Archi, Gian Gualberto, et al. *Miscellanea Contardo Ferrini: conferenze e studi nel fausto evento della sua beatificazione.* Rome: Pontificium Athenaeum Antonianum, 1947.

Archi, Gian Gualberto, ed. *Scritti di diritto romano in onore di Contardo Ferrini pubblicati dalla Regia Università di Pavia.* Milan: U. Hoepli, 1946.

Bona, Ferdinando. “Contardo Ferrini: tra storia e sistematica giuridica.” *Nuovo Bollettino Borromaico* 20 (1982): 33–49.

Bonfante, Pietro. “Prefazione.” In Contardo Ferrini, *Opere*, edited by Vincenzo Arangio Ruiz. Vol. 1, v–xi. Milan: Ulrico Hoepli, 1929.

Bonfante, Pietro, et al., eds. *Digesta Iustiniani Augusti*. Milan: Formis Societatis Editricis Librariae, 1908–1931; Reprinted, 1960.

Bruns, Karl Georg, and Eduard Sachau. *Syrisch-römisches Rechtsbuch aus dem fünften Jahrhundert. Aus den orientalischen Quellen herausgegeben, übersetzt und erläutert. 2. Neudruck der Ausgabe*. Leipzig: Brockhaus, 1880; Aalen: Scientia-Verlag, 1985.

Caccamo, Michele. *1898: Cannonate a Milano*. Paderno Dugnano: Colibrì Edizioni, 1998.

Camaiani, Pier Giorgio. *Il diavolo e la questione romana. Saggi sulle mentalità dell'Ottocento*. Bologna: Il Mulino, 2018.

Canavero, Alfredo. *Milano e la crisi di fine secolo (1896–1900)*. 2nd ed. Milan: Unicopli, 1998.

Casavola, Francesco Paolo. “Ferrini, Contardo.” In *Dizionario biografico dei giuristi italiani*, edited by Italo Birocchi, et al. Vol. 1, 856–7. Bologna: Il Mulino, 2013.

Colapietra, Raffaele. “Fiorenzo Bava-Beccaris.” In *Dizionario Biografico degli Italiani*. Vol. 7, 302–3. Rome: Istituto della Enciclopedia Italiana, 1970.

Domingo, Rafael. *Roman Law: An Introduction*. London/New York: Routledge, 2018.

Fernández de Buján, Federico. “Contardo Ferrrini.” In *Juristas universales*, edited by Rafael Domingo. Vol. 3, 711–15. Madrid: Marcial Pons, 2004.

Ferrini, Contardo. *Derecho penal romano*. Translated by Raquel Pérez Alonso, et al. Madrid: Marcial Pons, 2017.

Ferrini, Contardo. “Diritto penale. Esposizione storica e dottrinale.” In *Enciclopedia del diritto penale italiano*, edited by Enrico Pessina. Vol. 1, 1–478. Milan: Società Editrice Libraria, 1905; Reprinted Rome: L'Erma di Bretschneider, 1976.

Ferrini, Contardo. *Diritto penale romano*. Rome: L'Erma di Bretschneider, 1976.

Ferrini, Contardo. “I commentari di Paolo e di Ulpiano *ad legem Iuliam et Papiam*.” *Rendiconti dell'Istituto Lombardo di Scienze, Lettere e Arti* 34 (1901): 394–405 = *Opere*. Vol. 2, 237–50.

Ferrini, Contardo. “I commentari di Terenzio e di Gaio *ad legem Iuliam et Papiam*.” *Rendiconti dell'Istituto Lombardo di Scienze, Lettere e Arti* 34 (1901): 303–38 = *Opere*. Vol. 2, 251–68.

Ferrini, Contardo, ed. *Institutionum Graeca paraphrasis Theophilo Antecessori vulgo tributa*. 2 vols. Berlin: Calvary, 1884; Reprinted Aalen: Scientia 1967.

Ferrini, Contardo. “Intorno alle Istituzioni di Marciano.” *Rendiconti dell'Istituto Lombardo di Scienze, Lettere e Arti* 24 (1901): 736–41= *Opere*. Vol. 2, 85–90.

Ferrini, Contardo. *Manuale di Pandette*. 5th ed. Edited and expanded by Giuseppe Grosso. Milan: SEL, 1953.

Ferrini, Contardo. *Opere*. 5 vols. Edited by Vincenzo Arangio Ruiz, Emilio Albertario, and Pietro Ciapessoni. Milan: Ulrico Hoepli, 1929–30.

Ferrini, Contardo. *Pensieri e preghiere*. 2nd ed. Milan: Edizioni Radio Spada, 2014.

Ferrini, Contardo. *Quid conferat ad juris criminalis historiam Homericorum Hesiodeorumque poëmatum studium*. Berlin: Calvary, 1881.

Ferrini, Contardo. “Saggi intorno ad alcuni giureconsulti romani.” *Rendiconti dell'Istituto Lombardo di Scienze, Lettere e Arti* 18 (1885): 200–17 = *Opere*. Vol. 2, 11–38.

Ferrini, Contardo. *Scritti religiosi*. Edited by Carlo Pellegrini. Milan: Tipografia e Libreria Pontificia ed Arcivescovile Romolo Ghirlanda, 1911.

Ferrini, Contardo. *Teoria generale dei legati e dei fedecommessi*. Rome: L'Erma di Bretschneider, 1976.

Ferrini, Contardo, and Nicola De Crescenzio. "Obbligazione." In *Enciclopedia Giuridica Italiana*, edited by Pasquale Stanislao Mancini, Vol. 12, part 1. Milan: Società Editrice Libraria, 1900.

Ferrini, Contardo, and Giovanni Mercati, eds. *Basilicorum libri LX*. Vol. 7: *Editionis Basilicorum Haeimbachianae supplementum alterum*. Leipzig: Barth, 1897.

Ferrini, Contardo, and Giovanni Mercati, eds. *M. Kritou tou Patze Tipoukeitos*. Edited by Contardo Ferrini and Giovanni Mercati (books 1–12]. 5 vols. Rome: Typis Polyglottis Vaticanis, 1914.

Fiorentino, Carlo M. *La questione romana intorno al 1870. Studi e documenti*. Rome: Archivio Izzi, 1997.

Gross, Michael B. *The War against Catholicism: Liberalism and the Anti-Catholic Imagination in Nineteenth-Century Germany*. Ann Arbor: University of Michigan Press, 2005.

Grossi, Paolo. *Scienza giuridica italiana. Un profilo storico 1860–1950*. Milan: Giuffrè, 2000.

Guenzi, Pier Davide, ed. *La strada all'infinito e l'umiltà. La lezione spirituale di Contardo Ferrini (1859–1902). Atti del Convegno* (Verbania, 26–27 ottobre 2002). Novara: Interlinea Edizioni, 2003.

Heimbach, Karl Wilhelm Ernst, and Gustav Enrst Heimbach. *Basilicorum Libri LX*. 6 vols. Leipzig: Barth, 1830–1870.

Invernizzi, Marco. *Il beato Contardo Ferrini. Il rigore della ricerca, il coraggio della fede*. 2nd ed. Verbania: Alberti Libraio Editore, 2010.

Krüger, Paul. "Zu den Basiliken." *Zeitschrift der Savigny-Stiftung für Rechtsgeschichte. Romanistische Abteilung* 19 (1898): 192–8.

Lodigiani, Giovanni Angelo. *Contardo Ferrini. Santo e giurista*. Siena: Edizioni Cantagalli, 2007.

Lokin, Johannes Henricus Antonius, et al., eds., Alexander F. Murison, trans. *Theophili Antecessoris Paraphrasis Institutionum*. Groningen: Chimaira, 2010.

López Ortiz, José. "En la beatificación de Contardo Ferrini." *Anuario de Historia del Derecho Español* 18 (1947): 5–14.

Mantovani, Dario, ed. *Almum Studium Papiense. Storia dell'Università di Pavia*. Milan: Cisalpino, 2017.

Mantovani, Dario, ed. *Contardo Ferrini nel I centenario della morte*. Milan: Cisalpino, 2003.

Mantovani, Dario. "Contardo Ferrini nel ricordo di Camillo Golgi. Scienze e fede alla fine dell'Ottocento." In *Almum Studium Papiense. Storia dell'Università di Pavia*, edited by Dario Mantovani, 1249–52. Milan: Cisalpino, 2017.

Martín, Isidoro. *Semblanza del profesor Contardo Ferrini*. Murcia: Real Sociedad Económica Murciana de Amigos del País, 1947.

McGinn, Thomas A.J. *Prostitution, Sexuality, and the Law in Ancient Rome*. 2nd ed. Oxford: Oxford University Press, 2003.

Mommsen, Theodor. *Römisches Strafrecht*. Leipzig: Duncker & Humblot, 1899.

Paul VI, Pope. *Dogmatic Constitution on the Church "Lumen Gentium."* November 21, 1964.

Pellegrini, Carlo. *La vita del Prof. Contardo Ferrini*. 2nd ed. Turin: Società Editrice Internazionale, 1928.

Pernice, Alfred. *Marcus Antistius Labeo: Das Römische Privatrecht*. 3 vols. Halle: Waisenhaus, 1873, 1878, 1892.

Pius XII, Pope. "Discorso in occasione della beatificazione di Contardo Ferrini." Vatican City, April 14, 1947. Available at https://w2.vatican.va/content/pius-xii/it/speeches/1947/documents/hf_p-xii_spe_19470414_singolare-gradimento.html

Scialoja, Vittorio. "Necrologia: Contardo Ferrini." *Bullettino dell'Istituto di diritto romano* 14 (1901): 295–319.

Selb, Walter, and Hubert Kaufhold. *Das Syrisch-römische Rechtsbuch*. Vol. 1: *Einleitung*. Vol. 2: *Text und Übersetzung*. Vol. 3: *Kommentar*. Vienna: Verlag der Österreichischen Akademie der Wissenschaften, 2002.

Thür, Gerhard. "Syro-Roman Law Book." In *The Encyclopedia of Ancient History*, edited by Roger S. Bagnall, et al., 6495–6. Malden, MA: Wiley-Blackwell, 2013.

Università Cattolica del Sacro Cuore, ed. *Scritti in onore di Contardo Ferrini pubblicati in occasione della sua beatificazione*. 4 vols. Milan: Società Editrice Vita e Pensiero, 1947–49.

Vasiliev, Alexander. *History of the Byzantine Empire*. 2 vols. Madison: University of Wisconsin Press, 1958.

22 Luigi Sturzo (1871–1959)

Romeo Astorri

Introduction

Luigi Sturzo was a notable figure in early twentieth-century Italian political history. At first, he occupied an unobtrusive position, mostly as an emerging leader in the Catholic intransigent movement, in particular in the wing known as Christian Democracy. He rose in the period after World War I to become secretary of the Partito Popolare Italiano (Italian People's Party), of which he was a cofounder and which, according to the historian Federico Chabod, constituted "the most remarkable event in twentieth-century Italian history."[1] This phase of Sturzo's life came to a close when, in 1924, he was first forced to resign and then was exiled.

Over the next twenty years, his writings revealed his exceptional historical and political understanding, showing an ability as a political thinker capable not only of leading a party but also of formulating highly original theoretical and programmatic approaches to the Catholic political presence in Italy. The final chapter of his life, after his return to Italy in 1946, was characterized chiefly by isolation.

When describing his personality, one must take into account that the Sicilian priest was above all a man of action, while not diminishing the intellectual efforts that were the focus of his period in exile and only apparently less relevant to his active political life. In an essay on Sturzo, Francesco Traniello called him "a new intellectual."[2] Traniello locates this novelty in the fact that Sturzo was "one of the men who intuited, in an age where intellectual work was primarily thought of in a literary sense, that ideas in and of themselves have political meaning, whether desired or not; that each cultural act is also a political act."[3] This characterization justifies the approach we have chosen to recreate this important figure who "in his political work refers primarily to culture."[4]

This chapter about Sturzo comprises two parts: a biographical study, including an examination of his contribution to the formation and operation of the People's Party in relation to the broader Catholic intransigent movement in Italy; and a second part, examining the most relevant social-political issues he analyzed in his essays and speeches while in exile, with particular attention to his thought on international organizations, the theory of war, democracy in totalitarian states, and finally the relationship between Church and State and, specifically, the Lateran Pacts.

Biography

Luigi Sturzo was born in Caltagirone on November 26, 1871, the fourth of six children of Felice and Caterina Boscarelli. His father was from a noble family, the barons of Altobrando, while his mother, also from that area, came from the middle class. Sturzo attended the Acireale seminary from 1883 to 1886, then the seminary of Noto until 1888, before finishing his studies at the Caltagirone seminary. Upon his ordination in 1894 by the bishop of Caltagirone, Don Saverio Gerbino, he was sent to Rome to pursue theological studies at the Pontifical Gregorian University; he simultaneously enrolled at the Faculty of Humanities at the Sapienza University of Rome. He earned his degree in theology from Gregorian University in 1898. Sturzo's years in Rome were a turning point, partly because they placed him in a world that, according to Gabriele De Rosa, gave him "the nourishment of broad, sophisticated history and culture."[5] More critically, these years put him in touch with a system of thought, the Leonian, which proposed a vision that applied Thomistic theological-philosophical principles to the new public presence of ecclesiastical organizations and sought to bring about a renewal of the Church's structure that would allow it to participate in democratic movements.[6]

On returning to Caltagirone, he taught in the seminary and became involved in Catholic associationism; he founded the diocese's first committee of Opera dei Congressi, which he led for many years. In the first years of the new century, he was an active participant in the town's public life, heading a list of Catholic candidates for the municipal council in 1902 and serving as the deputy mayor of Caltagirone[7] and as a member of the provincial council from 1905 to 1920. He also became active in the Association of Italian Municipalities, serving as vice president from 1915 to 1924. In October 1914, he was recruited to the committee of the Unione Popolare and in the following year, following Benedict XV's reform of Catholic Action, was appointed secretary of the group's executive committee, holding that post until 1917.

On January 18, 1919, he signed, along with other Catholic leaders, a manifesto known as the "Appeal to the Strong and the Free" (taken from its incipit); he subsequently became one of the founders of the Italian People's Party and was appointed its political secretary. He was re-appointed to this post at subsequent party meetings in Bologna (1919), Naples (1920), Venice (1921), and Turin (1923).

The party enjoyed success at the polls beginning in 1919 (winning around 20 percent of the vote and one hundred deputies that year) and continuing in the elections of 1921. The party's deputies formed part of all the many governments formed in those years of political and social turmoil, including the first government led by Benito Mussolini, which was installed after his march on Rome on

October 31, 1922. Debates over the party's relationship with Giovanni Giolitti and Mussolini began to cause internal rifts within the party, which were exacerbated by dissent over the radically majoritarian electoral reform advanced by the Mussolini government. In April 1923, a majority of the party decided that its delegation, including the secretary himself, should resign from the government. Directly thereafter, the political fortunes of the party and its secretary underwent a rapid decline: the former began to fracture while the latter was forced to tender his resignation as secretary to the party's national council on July 10, 1923. On October 25 of the following year, amid the political situation that had developed after the elections of 1924 and the assassination of Giacomo Matteotti, the socialist deputy who had railed against electoral fraud, Sturzo left Italy for London, beginning an exile that would last until 1946. His departure was prompted partly by repeated requests by the Holy See, which was concerned by threats against the Sicilian priest, and partly by pressure exerted by Mussolini, who considered Sturzo's presence an obstacle to his policy of conciliation.

Sturzo remained in the British capital until September 1940, when the bombing of London, together with the British government's decision to intern Italian citizens following Italy's entry into the war, convinced him to depart for the United States, where he arrived on October 3. He returned to Italy on September 6, 1946, despite concerns about his return expressed by the Holy See's representative Don Amleto Cicognani. Sturzo's years in exile were, in general, years of isolation owing to the difficulty of maintaining contact with old friends, both those few who had been compelled to emigrate and those who had remained in Italy, and for the most part he retreated into private life. This period generated his most mature thoughts on a wide variety of topics, including international law, political theory, the history of the relationship between Church and State, and sociology.

On his return to Italy, Sturzo obeyed the canonical and treaty injunctions forbidding priests from enrolling in political parties, and he did not join the Christian Democratic Party, the party that had succeeded his own. Moreover, he expressed serious reservations about the party, in part because of what he saw as the ambiguity in its stance of aconfessionality and therefore in its relationship with ecclesiastical authority, but primarily because of its platform, which called for extensive state intervention in economic and social life. He spoke publicly on many occasions about this latter topic, including on the floor of the Senate.

Sturzo returned to the forefront of Italian politics in the spring of 1952. The People's Bloc, an alliance of the communist and socialist parties, seemed poised to win the administrative elections in Rome, and the president of Catholic Action in Italy, Luigi Gedda, supported by leaders of the Christian Democrats and some Roman clergy, convinced Pope Pius XII to support the creation of an electoral list made up of Christian Democrats and their centrist, republican, liberal, and social democratic allies, as well as right-wing parties, including the successors of fascism. Sturzo's virulent antifascist past and unquestionable orthodoxy led him to be chosen to assess the feasibility of the project and carry it out; for this reason, the maneuver was christened the Sturzo Operation. It was ultimately unsuccessful because of the opposition of Prime Minister De Gasperi and the withdrawal of the secular centrist parties, which caused Sturzo to determine that the conditions to organize the list no longer existed.

That same year, on December 17, 1952, President Luigi Einaudi appointed Sturzo a senator for life. The new senator registered not with the Christian Democrats but with the "Mixed Group" of unaligned officeholders. Sturzo was also a charter member of the Regional High Court of Sicily, established on January 21, 1948, and served until its dissolution in 1955.

The years after his repatriation were also marked by isolation and by his strong criticism of "the degeneration of political conduct and the practice of patronage."[8] Luigi Sturzo died on August 3, 1959.

Luigi Sturzo's thought: between political action and theoretical reflection

The period of Sturzo's education and participation in Catholic organizations

In the years before the founding of the Italian People's Party, Sturzo represented the influence of the Catholic intransigent movement, which used the teachings of Pope Leo XIII as a fundamental point of reference. Sturzo's thought, however, distinguished itself owing to its elaboration of a modern conception of a political party that went beyond the bounds of Catholic intransigence and its criticism of the liberal state. The party was united by a platform that advocated positions derived from its Catholic origins while containing other elements, such as meridionalism (attention to the south of Italy), which attuned it to liberal, not to mention secular, thinkers such as Antonio de Viti de Marco and Gaetano Salvemini.

In a speech at Caltagirone on December 29, 1905, on "the problems presented by national life to Italian Catholics," Sturzo posed the idea of a Catholic party. This topic was already at the center of a debate among Catholics, exemplified by the more or less contemporary contributions of Filippo Meda and Romolo Murri. Meda, in a speech on December 28, 1904, at Rho, "called for the formation of a nonconfessional Catholic party, 'reformist and moderately progressive,' which would not limit itself to defending religious interests and papal rights, but rather proposed a platform of 'religious peace, political liberty, and social justice.'"[9] Murri, meanwhile, proposed "gathering together young, proletarian, conscious and mature forces." In the weekly newspaper that Murri founded and directed, *Cultura Sociale*, the positions of these three thinkers met those of other leaders of the early Christian Democrats. That movement had taken its name from a passage of Leo XIII's encyclical *Graves de communi re*, in which the pope laid out his initial thoughts on the means by which Italian Catholics should participate in national political life, along with his views on the nature of the liberal state.

Sturzo's positions trace their origins to his experience as founder and organizer of socially oriented Catholic organizations in Sicily, within a largely pre-capitalist agrarian society far from the world of Lombardy. In Lombardy, by contrast, agriculture was already affected by capitalism, fostering social associationism in the Milan countryside, and by the textile industry, which led to the first Catholic trade unions, the eventual electoral base of Filippo Meda. The absence of industrial capitalism in Sicily, except in its initial stages, meant that the labor market was determined primarily by the economies of rural villages, which offered little social mobility.[10]

The creation of a party appeared to Sturzo to be a natural consequence of the detachment of Catholics from "the forms of a purely clerical understanding,"[11] with the purpose of addressing "the national problem as a synthesis of all the problems of civil life, from the political to the religious, from the economic to the social, from the educational to the scientific."[12] Starting from the elaboration of a general concept of party and specifically of a party of Catholics, one can see already in 1905 the core of Sturzo's thought. He saw the necessity of moving beyond the hybrid nature of the Opera dei Congressi, which arose "with modestly religious characteristics, to support and unify the actions of parishes and bishops . . . in an effort of necessary expansion or exaggerated invasiveness." It attempted to unify all Catholic associations, while changing "neither their religious . . . nor their ecclesiastical nature."[13] Sturzo proposed removing the millstone from the necks of Italian Catholics with his assertion that the "Roman Question" could be solved only by the papacy and the Italian state, not by a party, even a Catholic party. A national party of Catholics should therefore abstain from taking on not only the Roman Question but also the related question of the monarchy.

Already in 1905, then, Sturzo's analysis allowed for these two questions—whose solution had been widely considered a precondition for Catholic participation in political life—to be dismissed as obstacles to Catholic political action. Furthermore, his reflections demonstrate the criteria by which Sturzo evaluated the content of a Catholic party's platform. In a speech delivered in Milan on November 17, 1918,[14] on the eve of the founding of the People's Party, Sturzo responded to the suggestion of an imminent and necessary palingenesis of society, a goal that was rather far from his way of thinking, but was favored in Italian and international Catholic circles. In the speech, he outlined clearly his ideas about a new Catholic party and the framework in which those ideas should be considered.

The future secretary of the People's Party began by acknowledging the growing polarization between freedom, identified first and foremost with freedom of religion and education, and the constraints imposed by the complexity of the modern state; he criticized the limited model of religious liberty proposed by European states, judging the American system of separatism, even with its shortcomings, as offering "a freedom that admits all legitimate consequences of a moral and religious principle as foundational, essential to the composition of the state."[15] He outlined the policy elements necessary to resolve the predicament of the liberal state: freedom of education, administrative decentralization and respect for municipal autonomy, recognition of workers' organizations, and, finally, essential constitutional amendments to reform the electoral process, including proportional representation in the Chamber of Deputies and indirect election of the Senate by royal appointment.

The party, spurred by a strong policy program, would therefore become a primary foil to the secular state, which Sturzo saw as a precursor to a totalitarian state. In his conception, the party platform preserved aconfessionality while simultaneously providing an ideal to strive for. Sturzo saw the party not only as an institution giving voice to a social movement that was united by an ideal, but also as a factor contributing to the social and political pluralism he had come to embrace during his American exile. A passage from the book *Chiesa e Stato*, although of limited importance within the context of the work, confirms this interpretation. For Sturzo, the originality of the parties of Catholics created immediately after the war, in contrast to their previous incarnations, was the centrality of a serious reflection on the state.[16]

The years of exile

In the two decades he spent abroad, Sturzo's observations were no longer stimulated by the urgency of his political role and underwent an evolution. His new circumstances allowed him to broaden his thinking, which, without becoming purely theoretical or academic, grew more systematic and less scattershot. In fact, during these years he produced works dealing both broadly and deeply with sociology, history, politics, and theology. Because of their objective importance, I examine here some of the themes frequently addressed in these books. One of the most characteristic aspects of Sturzo's way of proceeding is how he makes distinctions without separating the methodological perspectives he uses to approach his topics.

The international community[17]

Sturzo's book on international organizations and the law of war is the fruit of an idea that germinated during his first few years in exile. The Sicilian priest, like the rest of his generation of Europeans, experienced the duality of impotence and anger at the world war, the dramatic arguments over the reasons for its outbreak, and the desire to build an international organization capable of preventing its recurrence. He saw US President Woodrow Wilson's proposal for a League of Nations as a concrete step in the right direction while acknowledging the insufficiency of political theory and moral reasoning to explain the war. Interestingly, Sturzo had already brought up this theme, albeit solely as a suggestion, in a November 1918 speech in Milan,[18] his first after the conclusion of hostilities, in which he cited the collapse of the great powers' imperial ambitions and the influx of the new power of America to conclude that "Wilson's fourteen points, partially reminiscent of the papal proposal of August 1, 1917, contain the palingenetic elements necessary for the future of all peoples."[19] To these thoughts he later added that "the most important event of international politics after the

Great War has been the creation of the League of Nations and the attempt to substitute for war a permanent, organic system to bring about peaceful solutions to disputes between states."[20]

Beyond the immediate meaning of this assertion, it demonstrates that the central focus of Sturzo's assessment is the transcendence of an atomistic conception of international organization, a transcendence made possible by the finality of the triumph of one civilization, Western Christian civilization. Sturzo sees that this civilization, on the basis of a kind of cultural imperialism, tends

> in its development towards complete conquest of the entire world in a system of normalized relationships we call international law, in a possible organized structure whose beginning, weak but important, is the League of Nations, in a prevailing civilization which, despite all negations, is a Christian civilization.[21]

The structure of this international organization, according to Sturzo, created an axis around which new international structures could arise, a phenomenon which, as noted in the introduction to the Italian edition of his book (1954), intensified after the Second World War, even in the context of the relative weakness of the UN (which was a continuation of the situation under the League of Nations). Institutions proceeding from the birth of the League of Nations, such as international arbitration, the World Court, and the International Labor Organization, were representative of this new development. Consequently—and this is a very important element of Sturzo's thought—the power of individual nations was greatly reduced by the concrete operation of international organizations, partly because national independence became linked to international interdependence defined by structures established by the international community, but also because the complexity created by the international community undermined the effort of states to reshape international law to accord with their interests alone.

The totalitarian State and the question of democracy

It is difficult to separate these topics, which Sturzo referred to in various works during his exile. The heritage of the Leonian assertion that democracy must be Christian or not exist at all appears to have inspired Sturzo to create an approach whereby democracy is measured by religious freedom and the relationship between the Church and the State, implying that both parties accept democracy, but more generally that any guarantee against a totalitarian state ultimately comes from the presence of a Christian civilization.

Sturzo maintained that the twentieth century saw the creation of "three great totalitarian states of different natures, but each national and founded on administrative and political centralization, on militarism, on a monopoly on education, and on a closed economy."[22] He condemned the universalist aspirations of the Soviet Union, the theory of racial superiority of Germany, and the national and imperial mythos of fascism as having become revolutionary, racial, and statist cults. These states posed a serious challenge to freedom, suppressing political liberty and encroaching upon personal freedom, demonstrating that "the diametrical opposition between the liberal and the totalitarian states will vanish as soon as the guarantee of freedom ceases to function."[23] Clearly influenced by the French philosopher Jacques Maritain, Sturzo supplements this assertion with a theory about the forceful suppression of the primacy of spiritual questions in totalitarian states. Sturzo saw this to be the total eclipse of religion that was foreshadowed by the tendency towards a pantheistic ethics among the nineteenth-century liberal states.[24]

The relationship between Church and State[25]

On the eve of the outbreak of the Second World War, Sturzo published a book on the relationship between the Church and the State.[26] This work retraces this relationship from its beginnings, highlighting the scope of its author's interests, but the methodology he chose—revealed in the subtitles of the French and Italian editions ("étude de sociologie juridique" (a study of legal sociology) and "studio sociologico-giuridico" (a sociological-legal study), respectively)—generates its most interesting conclusions in the final part, which focuses on the two centuries prior to the book.

For Sturzo, the fundamental sociological characteristics of Christianity produce, through the consciences of believers, an impact on how societies manifest themselves in history. Therefore, the relationship between Church and State cannot be contextualized solely as a relationship between two institutions with resulting political and legal implications, but rather as a relationship that, in essence, expresses a conflict of conscience between citizen and believer, at times latent, at times palpable. According to Sturzo, this conflict "can take a legal or political form, depending on circumstances; but its source is always a conflict of conscience."[27] This synthesis in the section on the secular state and the Church in the years after the French Revolution gives the author the ability to range from law to politics and history to international relations, viewing everything from the unifying perspective of its relevance to this conflict of conscience.

Sturzo identifies the Church's rejection of the liberal state as a mistake. In his view, despite certain principles that contradict particular elements of Christianity, "The secular state developed a remarkable ethical aspect informed by Christian values. . . . [T]he inability of many to recognize this and instead to unreservedly defend the historical position of the Church was a mistake."[28] From this point of view, he holds that the liberal revolutions of 1848 opened the door to a new chapter by allowing new popular movements with a vision of and success in integrating Catholics (as well as socialists) into the national states as protagonists of history (though some of these states would transform from secular to totalitarian in the coming century). This negative evaluation of the Catholic Church's position leads to his assessment of the first of what he deems the emblematic characteristics of the confessional state; he calls the Restoration's attempt to preserve or reconstruct a confessional state embarrassing, formalist, equivocal,[29] and responsible for producing detachment in the people from both Church and State.[30]

Given the new state of affairs in the twentieth century, Sturzo believed that the Church

> cannot do other than deal with secular states, as they currently exist, on the basis of the religious morals and respect for the human person foundational to Christianity. Meanwhile, the church must grant all that is not antithetical to Christianity to the state, or better yet, to worldly society; since that society is essentially secular, the church must keep its own personality and autonomy all the more visible and strong.[31]

This acknowledgment, according to Sturzo, is necessitated by the inevitable conflict between Christianity and the totalitarian state conceived as a Weltanschauung, especially when, as in the twentieth century, the totalitarian state attempts to restrict freedom. A concordat therefore serves two functions: in some cases it is merely regulatory, while in others, such as the concordat with the Third Reich, it is implicitly cooperative.

The final chapter of this crisis between Church and State, in his opinion, was the debate over the system of international organization that came into being with the creation of the League of Nations. This crisis transcended the boundaries of other international crises to become "a moral crisis . . . of relationships between countries, peoples, and races, a crisis of permanent negotiation, of the values of Christian civilization that still survive in modern secular states and in the League of Nations."[32]

The Lateran Pacts

After the signing of the Lateran Pacts, Sturzo published a series of articles on the solution of the Roman Question.[33] In fact, he had already noted in 1926 that the "political conflict" was almost entirely extinguished, and all that remained was a "religious dispute about the independence and legal freedom of the Holy See."[34] He believed that the Porta Pia breach of 1870, through which Italian soldiers entered Rome to complete the unification of Italy, did not mark the end of the papacy, but rather the end of "a particular means of guaranteeing papal independence that was no longer adapted to the *temporum conditioni et necessitati*."[35]

As for the Lateran Treaty of 1929, between the Kingdom of Italy and the Holy See, he held that the most suitable situation for the Holy See was to be without territory, similar to the status of the League of Nations. Possession of territory "would create a list of civil, economic, and police needs and duties that would increase the papal administration's dependence on the Italian state."[36] Therefore, Sturzo concluded that the Vatican's ongoing depoliticization would continue and that the impact of its religious actions would increase. He later clarified his views in two articles in *Il Pungolo* in March 1929: he saw that the end of a "political Vatican would come about when its legal situation was definitive and unchangeable, and that then the "church in Italy would exist with complete freedom, as in the United States. This solution is too radical for antifascism and also for the Vatican."[37]

While his immediate reaction focused particularly on the solution to the Roman Question, Sturzo subsequently took up the subject of concordats at great length. He believed that the primary aim of the Holy See was to resolve the Roman Question, and that the signing of the concordat was meant to "ensure Catholic influence in the Kingdom of Italy,"[38] while the Fascist government intended to use the concordat to integrate the Church into the totalitarian ethical framework of the State while maintaining the State's secular character. The result was a "duel of grudging compromises, of insinuations left unsaid but clear to the initiated, of general and convoluted statements that were enough to have an impact, sordid arguments, truces of ostensible friendship, reciprocal praise, generous gifts, and significant losses on both sides."[39] Sturzo saw within the ambiguous desire to reestablish a Catholic state, including the concordat Pius XI used to try to change Italy into a confessional state,[40] echoes of the "unhappy experience in Austria of Dolfüss and Schuschnigg," "the all-too personal experience of Salazar in Portugal," and Franco's "national and Catholic Spain." The topic of the Catholic state had come up again: Sturzo thought it could not be revived even in the form of a church allied with dictatorial states under the banner of social conservatism.[41]

His thought is best summarized in his view that the years before the war, which involved an irreconcilable diarchy between the two forms of society embodied by the Church and the state, represented for the Church the age of "the persuasive power of conscience . . . the ability of the Christian citizen to bend state power, or to oppose it in the name of Christian morals, in the name of an ethical principle pervading collective life and of the necessity inherent to and formative of a state or a civilization."[42]

Conclusion

Sturzo's political and institutional thought was initially expressed by the synthesis between political program and a party intended to bring about that program. Its charge was to "meld the party's innovation with the country's historical Christian tradition,"[43] and it aimed to supplant nineteenth-century liberalism. The civil society's pluralistic perspective, which was safeguarded by its various organizations, including the party, was brought into crisis following its confrontation with fascism after the fascists seized power in Italy

The resultant political and theoretical crisis caused Sturzo, in the years of his exile, to adopt a different framework of social pluralism. His familiarity with the Anglo-Saxon world and culture, combined with the knowledge of French culture he acquired during his education, led him to see totalitarianism, the negation of social pluralism, and the decline of the democratic state created by fascism,[44] as the institutional and ideological result of Europe's interwar political crisis.

This view is responsible for his assertion, further emphasized after World War II, that

> the difference between dictatorial and democratic systems lies neither in their theoretical underpinnings nor in their practical administration of the government. . . . Rather it is the democratic respect for political liberty that allows for a dialogue, however ineffective, between the holders of power and free citizens, singly or in association.[45]

This theory is echoed in another paper dating from the same period.[46]

The theme of a possible decline in democracy reappears in a hypothesis, devised around the same time, on the consequences of a hypothetical alliance between capitalism and communism. In Sturzo's view, the effect would be that "their totalitarianism would comprise every human activity" and "our modern society would have to deal with the consequences of surviving under this political and social 'monism', . . . which would weaken one by one all the institutions Judeo-Christian civilization has constructed to defend the human being."[47] From this perspective, even the Anglo-American and Scandinavian democracies, where "Christian ideas and sentiments throughout the periods of reform, counter-reform and subsequent modernization" were best preserved, "are no longer capable of finding authentic moral principles." Faced with the forms of individuality leading to the "centralizing state" which creates "the conditions for totalitarianism," these democracies were in danger of collapse.

Along with this assessment that reemphasizes the importance of "Christian ideas and sentiments," Sturzo explored society and international organizations. Although he emphasized the need for states to conserve the fruit of the Judeo-Christian conception of ideology and morals upon which modern civilization was founded, he argued that international organizations need to find "an original principle to form an international conscience for all peoples." While this principle is absent, international organizations cannot be expected to do more than "provide a *forum* for discussion and a *market* for transactions."[48] These assessments, which consider "an idea of the *state* as existing outside of its own citizens"[49] and the denial of a "moral basis for the judicial construction of current international law,"[50] encapsulate Sturzo's entire arc: taking stock of the lack of a "theory of the state which is substantially and truly Christian," and proposing the need for a philosophical and theological vision of society founded on democracy.

Notes

1 Chabod, 43.
2 Traniello, "Luigi Sturzo nuovo intellettuale."
3 Traniello, "Don Sturzo."
4 Ibid.
5 De Rosa, *Luigi Sturzo*, 51.
6 See Fantappiè, 198–261.

7 Royal Decree, February 10, 1889, n. 5921, approving the unified code of municipal and provincial law, art. 127.
8 De Rosa, *Luigi Sturzo*, 472.
9 Canavero.
10 De Rosa, *Luigi Sturzo*, 82.
11 Sturzo, "I problemi della vita nazionale dei cattolici," in *La croce di Costantino*, 240.
12 Ibid., 238.
13 Ibid., 245.
14 Sturzo, "I problemi del dopoguerra," in *Opera omnia*, second series, vol. 3, 32–58.
15 "Today, a rush of freedom is coming from America, which if it is not a complete acknowledgement of the church's position in society . . . is simply a freedom that admits all legitimate consequences of a moral and religious principle as foundational, essential to the composition of the state." Ibid., 42–3.
16 "Popular and Christian-social parties in the postwar period differ from their their predecessors mainly in that their orientation was marked . . . by the attempt to form their own political visions on the problem of the state." Sturzo, *Opera Omnia*, first series, vols. 5–6, 167.
17 Sturzo, *Opera Omnia*, first series, vol. 2.
18 Cfr. supra note 14.
19 Sturzo, "I problemi del dopoguerra," 36.
20 Sturzo, *La comunità internazionale*, 3.
21 Ibid., 29.
22 Sturzo, *Opera Omnia*, first series, vol. 4, 29. *Politica e morale* was published simultaneously in French and English: Sturzo, *Politics and Morality*, trans. Barbara Barkley Carter (London: Burns Oates & Washbourne, 1938); Sturzo, *Politique et moral* (Paris: Libraire Bloud et Gay, 1938).
23 Sturzo, *Chiesa e Stato*, 2: 168.
24 "Often . . . examining the character of the modern state and its logical progression towards a secular state, we have foreseen that its natural end-state is a totalitarian state." Sturzo, *Chiesa e Stato*, 2: 167. Cf. Craveri.
25 I have intentionally maintained the order of these two words used by Sturzo in the title of his work.
26 Sturzo, *Église et État*; Sturzo, *Church and State*. In Italian: Sturzo, *Opera Omnia*, first series, vols. 5–6.
27 Sturzo, introduction to *Chiesa e Stato*, 1: xxvi (referencing the introduction to the French edition).
28 Sturzo, *Chiesa e Stato*, 2: 218.
29 Ibid., 92.
30 This embarrassing union between church and state was missing a connective element to link people to temporal and religious power. The church didn't mediate between the people and temporal power, and neither did the state mediate between the people and the state: both instead increased their detachment from the people.

Ibid., 93.
31 Ibid., 234.
32 Ibid., 214.
33 Sturzo, "Discussioni sulla soluzione della questione romana," in *The Review of Reviews*, London, February 15, 1929, in *Opera Omnia*, second series vol. 6/1, *Miscellanea londinese 1925–30*, 172–6; Sturzo, "Sulla questione romana," in *Miscellanea londinese 1925–1930*, 177–8; Sturzo, "Atteggiamenti pratici verso il Trattato del Laterano," in *Miscellanea londinese 1925–1930*, 178–80; Sturzo,

"September 20, 1870–September 20, 1929," in *Miscellanea londinese 1925–1930*, 210–14.
34 Sturzo, "La Questione Romana," in *Miscellanea londinese 1925–1930*, 118–28.
35 Sturzo, *Chiesa e Stato*, 2: 129.
36 Sturzo, "Discussioni," 174.
37 Sturzo, "Atteggiamenti," 180.
38 Sturzo, *Chiesa e Stato*, 2: 178.
39 Ibid., 175.
40 "The terms of the concordat are predominantly confessional, and the spirit of the Fascist state remained unaltered."
Ibid., 178.
41 Ibid., 244.
42 Ibid., 241.
43 Ardigò, 70.
44 "Fascism . . . after crushing all resistance and opposition over the course of four years (1922–1926) proclaimed the state totalitarian (the word 'totalitarian' comes from Mussolini and did not previously exist in the Italian lexicon)."
45 Sturzo, *Politica e morale*, 384.
46 "The modern state has become totalitarian and could remain so even while maintaining (often just as a veneer) democratic forms, which will remain guarantees of the principles of freedom inasmuch as they resist" Luigi Sturzo, "*Teorie politiche dei cattolici*," *Opera omnia*. Third series, *Scritti vari vol. 5* Scritti storico-politici (1926–1949) a cura di Lucio Brunelli, Rome 1984, 238.
47 Sturzo, "*Nazionalismo*," 77.
48 Ibid., 228.
49 Sturzo, "*Politica e morale*," 368.
50 Ibid., 308.

Bibliography

Works by Sturzo

Sturzo, Luigi. *Church and State*. London/New York: Geoffrey Bles Longmans Green, 1939.

Sturzo, Luigi. *Église et État. Étude de sociologie historique*. Paris: Les éditions internationales, 1938.

Sturzo, Luigi. "I problemi della vita nazionale dei cattolici." Caltagirone, December 24, 1905. In *La croce di Costantino. Primi scritti politici e pagine inedite sull'Azione Cattolica e sulle autonomie comunali*. Edited by Gabriele De Rosa. Rome: Edizioni di Storia e Letteratura, 1957.

Sturzo, Luigi. *La croce di Costantino. Primi scritti politici e pagine inedite sull'Azione Cattolica e sulle autonomie comunali*. Edited by Gabriele De Rosa. Rome: Edizioni di Storia e Litteratura, 1957.

Sturzo, Luigi. *Opera omnia*. Edited by Istituto Luigi Sturzo. First series, *Opere*. 12 vols. Bologna: Zanichelli, 1960–78. Some volumes republished 2001–03.

Sturzo, Luigi. *Opera omnia*. Edited by Istituto Luigi Sturzo. Second series, *Saggi—Discorsi—Articoli*. 12 vols. Bologna/Rome: Istituto Luigi Sturzo, 1956–98.

Sturzo, Luigi. *Opera omnia*. Edited by Istituto Luigi Sturzo. Third series, *Scritti vari*. 7 vols. Bologna/Milan/Rome/Soveria Mannelli: Zanichelli, Istituto Luigi Sturzo, Cinque Lune, Gangemi, Rubbettino, 1962–2009.

Sturzo, Luigi. *Opera omnia*. Edited by Istituto Luigi Sturzo. *Scritti aggiunti*. 5 vols. Rome: Istituto Luigi Sturzo, Cinque Lune, Edizioni di Storia e Letteratura, 1974–85.
Sturzo, Luigi. *Politics and Morality*. Translated by Barbara Barkley Carter. London: Burns Oates & Washbourne, 1938.
Sturzo, Luigi. *Politique et moral*. Paris: Libraire Bloud et Gay, 1938.

A complete bibliography of the writings and works of Sturzo can be found in: Cassiani, Gennaro, Vittorio De Marco, and Giampaolo Malgieri, eds. *Bibliografia degli scritti di e su Luigi Sturzo*. Rome/Soveria Mannelli: 2004. This is the seventh volume of the third series of *Opera Omnia*.

Works Cited in the Text

Antonetti, Nicola. *Luigi Sturzo e la costituzione repubblicana*. Soveria Mannelli: Rubbettino, 2017.
Ardigò, Achille. "L'innovazione sturziana e la destoricizzazione di oggi." In *Luigi Sturzo e la democrazia europea*, edited by Gabriele De Rosa, 67–74. Rome: Laterza, 1990.
Barbieri, Luigi. *Influenze sturziane su un documento post conciliare. Introduzione allo studio dell'Enciclica Caritas in veritate di Benedetto XVI*. Naples: Edizioni Scientifiche Italiane, 2012.
Barbieri, Luigi. "Laicità e diritto nel pensiero di Luigi Sturzo. Osservazione critiche." In *Universalità e cultura nel pensiero di Luigi Sturzo*, edited by Gabriele De Rosa, 261–75. Soveria Mannelli: Rubbettino, 2001.
Barbieri, Luigi. "Tra storia e diritto: problematiche giuridiche nella produzione scientifica di Luigi Sturzo." In *Studi in onore di Piero Bellini*, edited by Mario Tedeschi. Vol. 1, 17–40. Soveria Mannelli: Rubbettino, 1999.
Bellia, Santo. *Chiesa e Stato nel pensiero di Luigi Sturzo*. Turin: Sei, 1956.
Borgo, Gianni. *Lo Sturzo americano (1940–1946). Strategie politiche e culturali*. Naples: Guida, 2017.
Canavero, Alfredo. "Filippo Meda." *Annali di Storia moderna e contemporanea* 3 (2015): 107–28.
Chabod, Federico. *L'Italia contemporanea 1919–1948*. Turin: Einaudi, 1961.
Condorelli, Mario. "Chiesa e Stato in Luigi Sturzo." In Mario Condorelli, *Scritti di storia e diritto*, 290–327. Milan: Giuffrè, 1996. First published in *Luigi Sturzo nella storia d'Italia. Atti del Convegno Internazionale di Studi promosso dall'Assemblea Regionale Siciliana (Palermo-Caltagirone 26–28 novembre 1971)*. Vol. 1, 311–27. Rome: Edizioni di Storia e Letteratura, 1973.
Craveri, Piero. "Luigi Sturzo, il mondo cattolico, lo Stato liberale: evoluzione e attualità delle sue considerazioni." In *Universalità e cultura nel pensiero di Luigi Sturzo, Atti del convegno promosso dall'Istituto Luigi Sturzo, Roma 28–29–30 ottobre 1999*, edited by Gabriele De Rosa, 245–60. Soveria Mannelli: Rubbettino, 2001.
D'Angelo, Augusto. *De Gasperi, le destre e l'operazione Sturzo. Voto amministrativo del 1952 e progetti di riforma elettorale*. Rome: Studium, 2002.
De Rosa, Gabriele. *Luigi Sturzo*. Turin: UTET, 1977.
De Rosa, Gabriele, ed. *Luigi Sturzo e la democrazia europea*. Bari: Laterza, 1990.
De Rosa, Gabriele, ed. *Universalità e cultura nel pensiero di Luigi Sturzo. Atti del convegno promosso dall'Istituto Luigi Sturzo, Roma 28–29–30 ottobre 1999*. Soveria Mannelli: Rubbettino, 2001.

Fantappiè, Carlo. *Chiesa romana e modernità giuridica*. 2 vols. Milan: Giuffrè, 2008.
Felice, Flavio. *Il contributo di Luigi Sturzo alle scienze sociali*. Cantalupa: Effatà, 2006.
Felice, Flavio. "Le libéralisme radical des premières années du XXe siècle en Italie. Maffeo Pantaleoni—Antonio De Viti de Marco." In *Histoire du libéralisme en Europe*, edited by Philippe Nemo, 619–50. Paris: Presses Universitaires de France, 2006.
Fruci, Alessandro. *Diritto e stato nel pensiero di Luigi Sturzo*. Rome: Nuova Cultura, 2012.
Fruci, Alessandro. *La comunità internazionale nel pensiero politico di Luigi Sturzo*. Rome: Aracne, 2009.
Fruci, Alessandro. *La dimensione giuridica in Luigi Sturzo*. Modena: Editrice Mucchi, 2013.
Guasco, Maurilio. *Romolo Murri. Tra la "Cultura sociale" e "Il domani d'Italia" (1898–1906)*. Rome: Studium, 1988.
Malgeri, Francesco, ed. *Luigi Sturzo nella storia d'Italia. Atti del Convegno Internazionale di Studi promosso dall'Assemblea Regionale Siciliana (Palermo-Caltagirone 26–28 novembre 1971)*. 2 vols. Rome: Edizioni di Storia e Letteratura, 1973.
Mosca Manuela, ed. *Antonio de Viti de Marco. Una storia degna di memoria*. Milan: Bruno Mondadori, 2011.
Piva, Francesco, and Francesco Malgeri. *Vita di Luigi Sturzo*. Rome: Cinque lune, 1972.
Tortarolo, Edoardo. "Salvemini: An Italian Historian as Political Refugee." *Storia della storiografia* 69/1 (2016): 83–100.
Traniello, Francesco. "Don Sturzo. Modello nuovo di intellettuale cattolico." In *Luigi Sturzo e la democrazia europea*, edited by Gabriele De Rosa, 443–8. Bari: Laterza, 1990.
Traniello, Francesco. "Luigi Sturzo nuovo intellettuale." In *Dai Quaderni a Gandhi. Studi di storia religiosa in onore di Ettore Passerin d'Entrèves*, edited by Francesco Traniello, 243–75. Bologna: Il Mulino, 1988.

23 Francesco Carnelutti (1879–1965)

Giovanni Chiodi

Biographical introduction

Francesco Carnelutti was born in Udine on May 15, 1879.[1] After completing his classical studies, he attended the Faculty of Law at the University of Padua, graduating on November 21, 1900. His pandectist thesis, *Universitates iuris et facti*, was supervised by Vittorio Polacco, an elegant, pure civil lawyer whom the disciple would always recognize as his master and as the best of his Paduan professors. In his third year he trained as a practitioner, and he was called to the bar in 1901. He recounts the experience in his autobiography, in which he describes with great affection the Venetian forensic world of the turn of the century, which he enjoyed more than the plain Paduan academic environment.[2]

Carnelutti's scholarly activity began almost by chance, driven by the desire to answer the call for collaboration put out by the *Rivista di Diritto Commerciale*, founded by Cesare Vivante and Angelo Sraffa, for which Carnelutti expressed endless—if somewhat hyperbolic—admiration, describing it as "the most beautiful legal journal in the world."[3] Determined to exploit this opportunity, he sent an *articoluccio* to Sraffa, who agreed to publish it in the first issue. This was the beginning of a partnership that turned out to form the basis of a real training ground for developing the mind of the young Carnelutti.

In 1905, spurred on by Sraffa, he applied for a position as a lecturer in commercial law at the University of Padua after meeting Federico Cammeo, a distinguished master of administrative law, who became Carnelutti's second mentor. Carnelutti gave his first courses at Padua in 1909–10 and at the Bocconi University in Milan in 1909–12, where he was in charge of labor and industrial law. The path he was on led him to hold the chair at Catania after winning the competition decided by a commission chaired by Cesare Vivante. Carnelutti took up a position as an extraordinary professor of commercial law on October 6, 1912, and for two academic years (1912–14) he was in charge of civil law as well, having to replace the prominent scholar Nicola Coviello.

The Catania environment was very dear to Carnelutti, who had an exceptional appeal to students and created a network of true friends with many of his colleagues. This was true to such an extent that, when he won the chair of commercial, maritime, and industrial law at the Venice School of Commerce and was about to be appointed (scheduled for March 15, 1914), he revoked his acceptance. The fact remains, however, that he aimed to move to another university. In July 1914 (on the eve of the First World War), to unblock the situation, Cammeo intervened by advising Carnelutti to apply for the position of professor of civil procedure in Padua, and he also suggested the subject of Carnelutti's first monograph. Carnelutti seized the opportunity: he felt the need to broaden his horizons and decided to direct his studies towards civil procedure. In one busy summer in 1914, he finished his book, *La prova civile*, which was dedicated to Vittorio Polacco and published in 1915. This single essay on the doctrinal panorama of the time, together with his numerous other publications, ensured that he took first place (in second position was Piero Calamandrei) in the Paduan competition of April 1915, judged by a commission chaired by Carlo Lessona and comprising Giuseppe Chiovenda, Giuseppe Messina, Alfredo Rocco, and Federico Cammeo. Called to Padua as an extraordinary professor of civil procedure and judiciary on October 16, 1915, Carnelutti was promoted to full professor in July 1916 by another prestigious commission (again including Chiovenda and Lessona, along with Antonio Castellari, Enrico Redenti, and Vincenzo Simoncelli). The writings he produced during this first scholarly phase already reflected a superb Carnelutti in fine form, as they showed a proud man endowed with extraordinary speculative power and marked interpretative freedom.

In 1935 Carnelutti moved from Padua to the University of Milan, where he held the position of professor of civil procedural law. This marked the beginning of some very productive years, in which Carnelutti extended his interests to other areas of legal knowledge. In the last years of the Milanese magisterium, his interest in his "secret love"—[4]criminal law—grew. Following a further academic opportunity offered to him, Carnelutti agreed to take up the chair of criminal law, beginning on October 29, 1943. The *Lezioni di diritto penale* (1943), a further stage in his development of a general theory of law, dates from this period.

After the armistice and the fall of fascism, Carnelutti, who considered himself a "political reprobate,"[5] took refuge in Switzerland as a guest of the federal judge Plinio Bolla, in Bellinzona. He made use of his time in forced exile by reading, teaching, and writing. He was in fact one of the professors of Geneva's university campus, where he delivered special courses in criminal law throughout 1944. In winter 1944, he wrote a book dedicated to the Swiss Confederation, *La guerre et la paix*, which quotes the 1943 manifesto of the Ventotene European federalist movement. In this period, he also wrote *La storia e la fiaba* (1945) and one of his most inspired books, *Dialoghi con Francesco*, printed in 1947.

Back in Italy, Carnelutti transferred to the Sapienza University of Rome, which was to be the last port of his academic career. Carnelutti, who in 1936 had failed to be named chair of civil procedural law that had been left vacant by Chiovenda, was appointed chair of criminal procedure by the Faculty of Law headed by Filippo Vassalli on February 20, 1946. He commenced his post on February 28 with the prolusion *La lotta del diritto contro il male*, dedicated to the problem of punishment. His three-year period at La Sapienza (1946–49) bore witness to his becoming the protagonist of a new mission: to give a more complete scientific form to criminal procedural law, the "Cinderella" of the juridical disciplines. This is the rather ironic and provocative title he gave to the essay opening the *Rivista processuale* of 1946,[6] which was "a kind of manifesto"[7] that urged continuing on the path of the scientificization of a discipline that was now autonomous from substantive criminal law. This latest adventure, which naturally benefitted from Carnelutti's consummate experience as one of the most prestigious togas in Italy, took on the features of a true apostolate to which Carnelutti devoted his usual energy, and which, on the scientific side, led to the production of two complementary works: *Lezioni sul processo penale* (1946–47) and *Questioni sul processo penale* (1950). Retiring from his teaching in 1949, Carnelutti published a critical essay, with which he launched new reasoning on the activity of judging.[8]

Major themes and contributions

Private, commercial, and labor law: an overview

The writings of the young Carnelutti are stimulating for their freshness, the variety of their topics, and the originality of their perspective. In the articles he wrote for the *Commerciale*, he was determined to "break the closed circle of books."[9] He was attracted by the law in action, by the cases experienced by men in the flesh instead of by "sleeping puppets."[10] He considered himself an observer of real problems: if he had been an artist, he would have been an expert in realism; if he had been a doctor, he would have been a "clinician of the law."[11] This would seem to be a departure from the systematic tendencies of the science of its time, but it is not so, because the young scholar aimed at the scientificization of case law. It was not enough for him to analyze a particular case; rather, he wanted to return to the fundamental principles and build an orderly and coherent system of concepts. He considered himself an enfant terrible and avant-garde because he was also interested in new problems in the emerging disciplines of labor and industrial law, of which he was one of the founding fathers.

We can grasp the novelty of his perspective by examining the articles he wrote that were later collected in volumes. A common feature they share is that of closely following the development of case law. But the concrete case is only the starting point for Carnelutti's conceptual engineering, which always featured original constructions, even if they were sometimes singular. This quality emerges from the *Studi di diritto civile* (1905–15), the epicenter of which is the law of obligations and contracts, with profiles pertaining to general theory, the labor contract, the promise of sale and agrarian contracts. But the work also presents important and more general developments on the concepts of domicile, residence and dwelling, on the distinction between legal personality and patrimonial autonomy, and on energies as the object of juridical relations. His vision of the rules for the interpretation of the contracts contained in the civil code was very modern: in a 1922 article, going against the dominant doctrine in Italy, he claimed that these rules had the nature of authentic legal norms, whose violation allowed for seeking recourse at the Court of Cassation.[12]

The core of commercial law production, at this stage of activity, is summarized in two collections. *Studi di diritto industriale* (1916), including articles from 1907 to 1914, shows that Carnelutti was intent on tracing the main lines of areas that were then largely unexplored, such as industrial property, copyright, and competition law. The *Studi di diritto commerciale* (1917), including articles from 1904 to 1915, offers an impressive snapshot of the complex of problems that the young Carnelutti was able to deal with: silence as acceptance in contracts, company communion, shares and actions, rights of members in the liquidation of commercial companies, commercial contracts—mediation, mandate, shipment, transport, insurance, and current account—stock exchanges, bankruptcy, and bills of exchange.

An emphasis should be placed on his contributions to labor law. Carnelutti was the first Italian jurist to believe in the value of social laws and to try to integrate them into the civil law system.[13] He was convinced of the expansive capacity of the special laws on the employer's liability: rather than minimize them as exceptions to the general rules of civil law, such as external and transient ones, he argued for their extensive interpretation. The two volumes *Infortuni sul lavoro (Studi)* (1913–14), which collected what he called "battle writings"[14] around controversial issues dealt with in courts, are impressive particularly on the methodological level. Here, a discussion is already outlined on the complexity of the law—not reduced to the legislative sources alone. Carnelutti also saw in this unplowed field (almost snubbed by the most orthodox civilians) an opportunity to exercise his brilliant qualities as an inventor of concepts and a system builder. He claimed that the employer's liability for accidents was contractual and had to be coordinated with the labor contract regime.

Alongside these studies, Carnelutti made considerable contributions in the field of labor law concerning important problems of industrial society, such as the nature of the labor contract, the discipline of dismissal, the effects of the strike, and the management of collective labor conflicts. These writings, however, also reveal a conservative profile that was typical of other exponents of liberal legal doctrine, as shown by his views on the collective regulation of the employment relationship—the unresolved node of liberal society and symptomatic of its understanding of state interventionism.[15] In this field, there is a gap with respect to Carnelutti's promotion of the welfare state that extends beyond the constraints of current legislation. When considering the powers of trade unionism, on the other hand, Carnelutti was reluctant to abandon the individualistic vision of labor contracts and favored state intervention that ended up privileging authority over freedom. As early as 1909, in fact, he felt the inadequacy of privatistic tools to overcome the disparity of workers' contractual strength, but he expressed his opposition to the use of strikes and lockouts to resolve collective conflicts. Instead, he called for a prohibition in the public-services sectors and essential-goods industries, although he pointed out that his position differed from the reactionary policies of the past.[16]

Collective bargaining was perceived as a better instrument than the law to regulate collective relations because it was more flexible and gave groups the freedom of self-determination. But for Carnelutti, strikes and lockouts—as violent acts of war—could not be used as a means of exerting pressure. In their place, Carnelutti in 1911 imagined an intervention by the state that aimed at offering a coercive and authoritarian solution to such conflicts if open negotiation was not successful: conciliation and mandatory binding arbitration were the lesser evils when compared to the uncontrolled development of social conflict.[17]

In the 1920s and 1930s, labor and trade-union law, which were key to the economic policies of the fascist regime, were the subject of important reflections in the dimension of corporatism as well. In 1927, in addition to his most celebrated essay on the general theory of law of obligations,[18] Carnelutti published the *Teoria del regolamento collettivo dei rapporti di lavoro*, which he understated as "a first scientific mottling" of the novelties provided by the 1926 labor law—a link between the liberal-conservative Carnelutti of the Giolitti age and the Carnelutti who was a supporter of corporatism without wearing the political uniform of fascism. In 1933, he published the *Teoria giuridica della circolazione*, a work which arranged negotiable instruments within the general theory of contracts as revisited from an economic point of view. It was a volume written with the usual speed for didactic needs, which Tullio Ascarelli considered to be Carnelutti's most inventive book in the field of commercial law.[19]

Once the labor law of April 3, 1926, was enacted, recognizing unions and collective agreements according to the strict directives of Minister of Justice Alfredo Rocco, Carnelutti praised it and saw within it a key to continuity.[20] In doing so, he weakened the authoritarian scope of the law and did not seem to perceive the totalitarian and statualist aspect of Rocco's project, which emptied the trade unions of any effective autonomy to incorporate them into the state. Favorable to a purified nonconflictual syndicalism,[21] Carnelutti approved of the legislative prohibition of strikes and lockouts (which returned to being criminally sanctioned) and looked with confidence at the forms of resolution of the collective conflict envisaged as substitutes for the collective agreement. Furthermore, the collective agreement was not considered an expression of collective autonomy. Its features could not be explained by the categories of private law alone, which remained those of the individual order. Carnelutti proposed an original thesis, arguing that the collective agreement represented a hybrid: it had the body of a contract but the soul of the law; it was a contract in form but a command in substance.[22] The *erga omnes* effectiveness and the binding nature of the collective agreement could be explained only by the belief that the unions—public bodies—exercised a quasi-legislative power over workers and entrepreneurs. The collective agreement was similar to a law: it was an abstract command, even if less abstract than the law; it was the manifestation of a normative power that was not an expression of true autonomy but of heteronomy, because autonomy was conceivable only from an individualistic perspective. The collective agreement was therefore halfway between public and private. Labor litigation itself, regulated by the law of 1926, was narrowly interpreted as a "pseudo-collective" process, which did not allow unions to promote all possible types of individual litigation sentences.[23]

Carnelutti's attitude towards trade-union freedom and collective bargaining was therefore ambiguous and characterized by conservative pressure. On one hand, the collective agreement remained the best means of resolving collective conflicts, but on the other, the state had an obligation to prevent the conflict from degenerating into social damage and upsetting the status quo. The same ideas were also expressed at the dawn of the new republican constitutional state after the fall of fascism. Carnelutti's opposition to the recognition of the right to strike, now provided for in Article 39 of the Constitution, remained intransigent. This was a right that Carnelutti did not hesitate to define as being "of war." The only alternative to striking, besides the contractual solution, even after the failure of the fascist corporative experience, was to appeal to a judge. Corporatism, in this version, was saved and removed from its historical connection to the fascist regime, which had indeed reduced and eventually destroyed its beneficial potential.[24]

The construction of civil procedural law

The refoundation of civil procedural law was the most important chapter of Carnelutti's impressive scientific career, which can be summarized by recalling some salient episodes. In the youthful phase of this career, the book *La prova civile* (1915) emerged as the first attempt to create a general theory of proof in Italian legal culture. Carnelutti submitted the commonplaces on the proof to a conceptual and linguistic purification operation that had long been paradigmatic. To do this, he drew inspiration mainly from German scholars, even if the final synthesis was entirely personal.

To begin with, the scope of the litigation, according to Carnelutti, was not so much to ascertain the truth as it was to resolve a conflict or a dispute. In the lexicon of the author, it aimed at a "formal fixation of facts."[25] The point of reasoning is the conviction that truth is singularly absolute or material: "truth is like water: it is pure, or it is not truth."[26] If the truth could only be absolute, it followed that the formal truth, which was obtained through the trial, was classified as a "nontruth,"[27] even though it might by chance coincide with the material truth. Carnelutti, at this stage, did not believe that the truth sought through the trial, precisely because it was relative, could be qualified as such. From this point of view, the qualification of "disappointed absolutist" is relevant.[28] For proof, therefore, he understood the "process of fixing the controversial fact by the judge":[29] a definition that clearly defined the object (or theme) of the proof as consisting of disputed facts. Carnelutti's other important ideas concern the structure of the proof. Carnelutti stated that there is a distinction between direct and indirect proof (in which he included testimony, documents, confessions, and circumstantial evidence) and affirmed the superiority of direct proof over indirect. Moreover, Carnelutti offered innovative insights into testimony, distinguishing it from expertise and proposing a broader concept than the traditional one. Nevertheless, in subsequent studies, Carnelutti expressed his mistrust of this kind of evidence, which he considered to be in too many cases fallacious, to the extent that he considered it a "necessary evil" only in the absence of documentary evidence.[30] For this reason, he stressed the importance of accurately criticizing testimony based on a knowledge of psychology.[31] Finally, while supporting the judge's free conviction, Carnelutti considered it useful that the legal system provided for rules of legal evidence.

During the twenty-year period that he spent in Padua (1915–35), Carnelutti, while continuing to provide important contributions in other subjects, was deeply involved in civil procedural law. From *homo novus* of the discipline, he became one of its undisputed masters thanks to a prodigious capacity to work and a strong theoretical foundation that led him to write works of broad conceptual and systematic commitment. In doing so, he expanded on the teachings of Giuseppe Chiovenda, who was the promoter of the autonomy of civil procedural law. The main products of these exceptional scientific activities are the *Lezioni di diritto processuale civile* (1920–31). In these volumes, the design of a general theory began to take shape and was eventually fulfilled in the *Sistema di diritto processuale civile* (1936–39).[32]

A milestone that marked the renewal of procedural studies in Italy was the 1924 foundation of the *Rivista di diritto processuale civile*, which became not only the best outlet for Carnelutti's thoughts but also the main intellectual workshop of the discipline. Based on the model of the much-admired *Rivista di diritto commerciale*, with a double direction entrusted respectively to a master and to a younger director who oversaw the organizational aspects, Carnelutti reserved for himself the second role and turned to Chiovenda for the first. The editor-in-chief was Piero Calamandrei.[33]

Two years later, Carnelutti was called by Minister of Justice Alfredo Rocco to join the subcommittee chaired by Lodovico Mortara charged with drawing up the new code of civil procedure. The 1926 draft was a key piece of Carnelutti's work as a legislator, which he considered one of the jurist's missions.[34] Carnelutti took on an arduous task in a controversial field after the projects of Chiovenda and Mortara had not obtained the necessary consent. The structure and contents of the draft were very personal. For this reason, in addition to the unconventional lexicon used, the work was not unanimously welcomed by the subcommittee, which preferred to rework it, although this distorted its original spirit.

In Carnelutti's approach, civil litigation is basically grounded on the initiative of the parties, which prevails over the powers of the judge. Although these judicial powers have increased in accordance with a public vision of the trial, they have not increased so much as to lose their liberal connotation.

In the law of evidence, the principle according to which "the judge cannot use a proof when it has not been proposed by the parties" (Art. 105) is solemnly proclaimed, but not without limits: the party has indeed "the burden of offering all the evidence at its disposal," otherwise, the judge may decide as if the evidence were against it (Art. 106); the parties must show their cards from the beginning, and for this purpose the project does not hesitate to establish several preclusions (Art. 219, 239), even if it confirms the *ius novorum* in appeal.

Realism also led Carnelutti to mitigate and constrain many innovations supported by Chiovenda. First was the principle of orality, of which he approved, but which he allowed to be waived if the parties agree or if the judge deems the waiver appropriate. On this point, his reasoning was tinged with skepticism. He did not believe that civil litigation could improve by establishing orality with a simple legislative stroke of the pen.[35] Orality requires judges and lawyers to be culturally prepared, which was not the case in practice and therefore could not be introduced without risk. Here the practical experience of Carnelutti, as opposed to abstract reforms written only on paper, was very important. It is a warning repeated on various occasions and in different historical phases: "the whole problem of litigation is above all a problem of men."[36] The consequence of this attitude is a careful balance between orality (rule) and writing (exception) according to a principle that Carnelutti called "of elasticity." Writing applies in principle to pleadings and offers of evidence, and orality to conclusions in the trial, but written discussion can also be allowed (Art. 240, 255).

Second, immediacy—that is, immediate contact with the evidence—was considered a cornerstone of civil litigation, just as Chiovenda had taught. Nevertheless, Carnelutti was not so intransigent as not to admit derogations, such as the admissibility of the division of labor between the judge delegate and the court in the taking of evidence (Art. 229). The judge delegated by the court seems to Carnelutti, at this stage of his thought, a necessary expedient for the court to be more agile. He was also convinced from direct experience that the "infamous mediateness" was many times more useful than immediacy.[37]

Third, the principle of concentration of the proceeding in one or a few hearings was set out and was another important element of the orality system enunciated by Chiovenda. To this end, he considered it appropriate to limit the appeals to the court during the pretrial phase, which in practice caused unnecessary slowness.

With his draft, Carnelutti proposed a more elastic procedure, which remained within the parameters of liberal civil litigation. The rejection of his text does not mean that it was not taken into account in further stages of reform. It is undeniable, however, that the new 1940 code aimed to establish a different system. Most notable was its influence on the Vatican and the Brazilian codes of civil procedure, and on the Italian laws of individual labor disputes (1928–34).

After this experience, Carnelutti was no longer part of the technicians in charge of laying the foundations of the new code. The resumption of his activity as a scientific consultant coincided with the appointment of Dino Grandi to the Ministry of Justice. Official contact resumed in 1939, and after that date, Carnelutti, who was not a member of the Fascist Party and did not profess the political ideas of the regime, became part of a restricted committee that comprised the magistrate Leopoldo Conforti and the other two most distinguished proceduralists of the time, Calamandrei and Redenti. When the code was promulgated on October 28, 1940, Carnelutti devoted a broad analysis to it in the *Istituzioni del nuovo processo civile italiano* (1941), which was to support its choices,[38] even though he soon recognized its failure. Nonetheless, he imputed this failure to the ill will of the legal profession, which he claimed was unwilling to change its inveterate habits.[39] In later essays, Carnelutti claimed the paternity of many solutions offered by the code, such as the controversial new figure of the investigating judge,[40] who replaced the delegated judge of the court. He also criticized every step backwards and every yielding with respect to the principle of orality that was carried out by the legislators of the Italian Republic, who were accused of leaving the jurists on the bench and not consulting them.[41]

Moreover, his commitment to the direction of the *Rivista di diritto processuale*, as the journal was now significantly renamed after the year of his *Rinascita* (1946), did not diminish. He continued to write items and to review everything and everyone (even himself) in his caustic, hypercritical, and cutting style, offering both fiercely scathing and also generously positive opinions.

Encounters with the theory of law, philosophy, and religion

Carnelutti's first attempt at reflection in this field is represented by the *Metodologia del diritto* (1939), which attracted the appreciation of the philosopher Giuseppe Capograssi.[42] More complex was the *Teoria generale del diritto*, whose first edition dates to 1940. It marked a turning point in the career of Carnelutti, who liked to compare himself to a traveler eager to visit new places and new spaces. This book was the first experiment of its kind in Italian legal literature. It was an ambitious formal theory of law that was written by a jurist and not by a philosopher of law. Consequently, it attracted dissent and misunderstanding but also motivated criticism and generated some sincere praise. No wonder the author considered it "his highest quality and most dangerous book."[43] Questionable, controversial, and subjected to continuous readjustments, it was undoubtedly fascinating.

This shift towards the grounds of general theory, the philosophy of law, and metaphysics deeply marked Carnelutti's scientific activity and was also a reaction to painful personal events that contributed to bringing the man closer to the Christian faith. In the early 1940s, in fact, Carnelutti launched other stimulating intellectual adventures. He published two autobiographical novels, *Mio fratello Daniele* (1940) and *La strada* (1941), the *Meditazioni* (I–II, 1942–43), the *Interpretazione del Pater Noster* (1941), the *Meditazione sull'Ave Maria* (1943), and *Il problema della pena* (1943). These writings are all connected: Carnelutti tells his readers about himself, his aspirations, and his readings, and together he used them to broaden his horizons beyond the boundaries of positive law. He was so dissatisfied with disciplinary gatekeeping that he devoted himself to biblical and evangelical exegesis. Carnelutti was aware of these transversal incursions into territories that were "forbidden" to the jurist,[44] so he turned into a *maître à penser*, ironizing about his alleged incompetence to reason about philosophy and metaphysics ("I am not a philosopher nor a critic nor an artist"[45]). He admitted the need to write books that "escape from the law" and were "clandestine books" and "metajuridical."[46]

In the 1940s, Carnelutti revised his general theory of law, which was his life's goal, and he was willing to critically review many of the positions he had held in the past in his constant search for perfection. In the midst of the crisis of positivism, he reflected on the problem of justice, vigorously emphasized "the cost of legal certainty,"[47] and claimed the primacy of natural law. Most relevant are, among others, the pages he wrote about the book *La certezza del diritto* (1943) by the philosopher Flavio Lopez de Oñate, which were opposite to the legalism of Calamandrei.[48] The major fruit of his incessant work of rethinking his general theory of law is represented by the second edition of the *Teoria generale del diritto* (1946).[49] Not coincidentally, in the reprint of *La prova civile* (1947), he defined himself as "a tireless constructor of concepts."[50]

To supplement this magnum opus, whose third and final edition was published in 1951, in the following years he dedicated himself to many minor writings that nevertheless responded to a logical thread of thought that gave them continuity. For this reason, Carnelutti gathered them in the second and third volumes of his *Discorsi intorno al diritto*, published in 1953 and 1961, as a sort of spiritual testament. To complete the picture, we must add *Arte del diritto* (1949), the Italian version of the *Seis Meditaciones sobre el Derecho* (1948), which refers to the period of Carnelutti's conferences in Latin America. Carnelutti's interpretation of American society can be found in the "booklet" *America* (1950), which counteracts the novel of the same title by Kafka.

Our jurist, after having done all the jobs in the field of law,[51] and after having been the consultant for a film and written a cinematographic script (*Un uomo in prigione*, 1953), even wore the clothes of the popularizer, writing books and joining radio broadcasts in the 1950s. These conversations are collected in small volumes, which compensate for the loss of the soundtrack.[52] A splendid diary of his readings, which serves "to not forget the best of the books," meaning the "fragments, hints, sketches, ideas put together in bulk," comprised the collections titled *Tempo perso* (1952, 1953, 1955).

His talks at the Cini Foundation in Venice also led to publications that interwove the themes of law, ethics, and religion. The figure of Carnelutti as a Christian jurist can be found almost everywhere in the writings of his later years, particularly in his works dedicated to criminal justice. More specifically, this image of him is found in the items that propose a reading of the Christian message contained in the Bible, in the parables of the Gospel, in the Hail Mary, and in the Our Father.[53] In these meditations, the elderly master challenged himself with examining the toughest philosophical—religious problems and confessed that he was more interested in man and his otherworldly destiny, in the "mystery of the process" and in what was "beyond the law."

For this reason, too, the trial remained a privileged observatory whose problems absorbed him, both in the synthesis *Diritto e processo* (1958) and in the *Principi del processo penale* (1960), "a book that only an old man, full of experience and sadness, can write."[54] Moreover, Carnelutti collected seven of his criminal defenses in the volume *Controvento* (1961), which he recommended to read as a complement to the previous ones, although it included only "scores" without the "music" of his eloquence. They were all trials by media from the 1940s to the early 1960 in which he had to fight against the current of adverse popular judgment.

At a later age, Carnelutti was tempted by a new legislative experience: he became one of the actors in the laboriously epic reform of the 1930 code of criminal procedure. According to Carnelutti, the code should have been completely redone and not simply "restored."[55] Therefore, he took over the chair of a commission appointed by Minister of Justice Guido Gonella in 1962. He prepared two "project schemes" in which, among other innovations, he proposed the abolition of the investigation and of the investigating judge, replaced by a preliminary inquiry conducted by the public prosecutor, the purpose of which was to ascertain the probability and not the certainty of the crime; the validation of the measures limiting freedom; the cross-examination; and the abolition of acquittals based on lack of evidence. His proposals gave rise to a heated debate.[56]

Carnelutti died in Milan in 1965, leaving behind an immense bibliography that is still not fully recorded today.[57] His last article, dedicated to the essence of judging, which he believed was founded not only on science but also on faith, appeared in the *Rivista di diritto processuale* of 1965, immediately after a nostalgic and bitter farewell to his friends, in which he reaffirmed his love for the law, despite the conviction that one must go beyond its borders to truly understand it.[58]

Conclusions

Carnelutti's reputation as the major proceduralist of his time (together with Piero Calamandrei) remains enshrined in the Draft Code of Civil Procedure of 1926, and his two complementary enterprises: the *Lezioni* and the *Sistema*. The *Sistema*, inter alia, is part of his works that were translated into Spanish. This undertaking contributed to spreading his teachings across national borders, especially in Latin American countries, where he was repeatedly invited to give lectures.[59] The importance of these pages is enhanced by the fact that Carnelutti's huge interpretative construction overlapped with a code of civil procedure conceived on the French model and completely detached from the categories of which he made use. It is therefore one of the greatest monuments of Italian legal science of the twentieth century.

Alongside these contributions, Carnelutti offered reflections of a methodological, philosophical, and metaphysical nature. While the clothes of the jurist were getting tighter, he aimed to think higher—although he was aware that his incursions often moved on sandy ground. We can measure Carnelutti's intellectual contribution not only by his profound and prolific work on a general theory of the process, but also by his method, which was based on the observation of reality. If, as a systematic jurist, he concluded a historical cycle, in the analysis of case law and in the legal clinic—as an essential stage in legal education—Carnelutti, one of Italy's top lawyers, was a forerunner, pointing the way. Another of Carnelutti's legacies was the foundation of the first legal journal of the discipline, *Rivista di diritto processuale*, which remains a lively laboratory of ideas. In the individual disciplines he practiced, he experimented with new constructions in commercial, industrial, and labor law, in civil procedural law, and finally in criminal and criminal procedural law (much less in constitutional law, unlike others like Calamandrei). He was also a forerunner in developing the general theory of law and was the only jurist of his time who had the courage to enter a field that after him was increasingly cultivated. Carnelutti also made headway as a Christian jurist. Not only did he measure himself directly against the meaning of the sacred texts by offering original interpretations, but his work as a jurist was also inspired by Christian teachings that deeply affected his general theory of law and his conception of punishment. In this vein, much of Carnelutti's legacy remains to be discovered.

Notes

1 The biographical account draws on Carnelutti's works, mainly *Mio fratello Daniele* and *La strada*, and on the records deposited in Roma, Archivio Centrale dello Stato, *Ministero della Pubblica Istruzione*, *Direzione generale Istruzione Universitaria*, *Divisione prima (1940–1970)*, *Fascicoli personali dei professori ordinari*, 3° versamento 1940–70, b. 101.
2 Carnelutti, *Mio fratello Daniele*, 97–110.
3 Carnelutti, "Scuola italiana del diritto," 125.
4 Carnelutti, *Lezioni di diritto penale*, i.
5 Carnelutti, "Addio, Chiovenda," 121.
6 Carnelutti, "Cenerentola." See Miletti.
7 Carnelutti, "La malattia del processo penale italiano," 1.
8 Carnelutti, "Torniamo al giudizio." See Picardi, "L'esame di coscienza del vecchio maestro."
9 Carnelutti, "Lettera ai miei discepoli," in *Questioni sul processo penale*, v–x, at vi.
10 Carnelutti, *La strada*, 89.
11 Carnelutti, "Clinica del diritto" (1935), in *Discorsi*, 183–97.
12 Carnelutti, "L'interpretazione dei contratti e il ricorso in Cassazione," in *Studi di diritto processuale*, 391–420.
13 See Grossi, 97–8, 101–2, 125–8; Cazzetta, *Scienza giuridica, leggi sociali*, 155–69.
14 Carnelutti, *Infortuni sul lavoro (Studi)*, vii.
15 See, among others, Cazzetta, "L'autonomia del diritto del lavoro," 531–43; also Romagnoli.
16 Carnelutti, "Sul contratto di lavoro relativo ai pubblici servizi assunti da imprese private" (1909), in *Studi di diritto industriale*, 121–51.
17 Carnelutti, "Le nuove forme di intervento dello Stato nei conflitti collettivi del lavoro" (1911), in *Studi di diritto industriale*, 245–58. See Costa, 380–8; Cazzetta, 69–169.
18 Carnelutti, *Diritto e processo nella teoria delle obbligazioni*.
19 Ascarelli, 997.
20 See Stolzi, 48–62, 81–96, 237–68.
21 Carnelutti, "Sindacalismo."
22 See, e.g., Carnelutti, *Teoria del regolamento collettivo dei rapporti di lavoro*, 108; "Sindacalismo"; "Contratto collettivo," *Il diritto del lavoro* 2 (1928): 181–5; id., "Nuove riflessioni sul comando collettivo."
23 Carnelutti, "Funzione del processo del lavoro," *Rivista di diritto processuale civile* 7/1 (1930): 109–12.
24 Carnelutti, "Stato Democratico: Stato Corporativo," in *Verso il corporativismo democratico*, 247–55.
25 Carnelutti, *La prova civile*, 29, 31.
26 Ibid., 32.
27 Ibid., 54.

28 See Taruffo, "Carnelutti e la teoria della prova," 402.
29 Carnelutti, *La prova civile*, 59.
30 Carnelutti, "Lineamenti della riforma del processo civile di cognizione" (1929), in id., *Studi di diritto processuale*, IV, 372.
31 Carnelutti, "La critica della testimonianza," *Rivista di diritto processuale civile* 6/1 (1929): 171–7; id., "Il testimonio, questo sconosciuto!", ibid. 12 (1957): 177–85.
32 See Denti, "Sistematica e post-sistematica nell'evoluzione delle dottrine del processo."
33 Further details in Cipriani, *Storie di processualisti e di oligarchi*, 252–8; id., "Quel lieto evento di tanti anni fa."
34 *Progetto del codice di procedura civile presentato alla Sottocommissione Reale per la riforma del Codice di Procedura Civile* (Padua: CEDAM, 1926). For a discussion, see Tarello; Picardi, "Riflessioni critiche"; Cipriani, *Storie*, 259–94; Denti, "Francesco Carnelutti."
35 Carnelutti, "Lineamenti," 381.
36 See, e.g., Carnelutti, *Lezioni di diritto processuale civile*, III, 192.
37 Carnelutti, "La critica della testimonianza," 176–7.
38 See also Carnelutti, "Nuovo processo civile italiano," *Foro italiano*, 66/4 (1941), 25–30; id., "Carattere del nuovo processo civile italiano," *Rivista di diritto processuale civile* 18 (1941): 35–52.
39 Francesco Carnelutti, "Polemica sulla riforma del processo civile," ibid., 1 (1946): 148–9. See Cipriani, *Il codice di procedura civile tra gerarchi e processualisti*, 53–78.
40 Carnelutti, "Storia e natura del giudice istruttore." See Cipriani, *Ideologie e modelli del processo civile*, 165–73 and 121–55.
41 Carnelutti, "Addio, Chiovenda."
42 See Irti.
43 Carnelutti, *Mio fratello Daniele*, 27.
44 Carnelutti, *Meditazioni*, 7.
45 Ibid., 5.
46 Carnelutti, *Mio fratello Daniele*, 2, 65.
47 Carnelutti, "La certezza del diritto" (1943), in *Discorsi*, II, 15–29, 22.
48 Carnelutti, "Nuove riflessioni intorno alla certezza del diritto" (1950), and "Bilancio del positivismo giuridico" (1951), in *Discorsi*, II, 151–61 and 241–60. See Grossi, 278–9, 283–4; Stolzi, 261–3.
49 See Bobbio.
50 Carnelutti, *La prova civile*, 4.
51 Carnelutti, *La strada*, 211.
52 *Colloqui della sera (a tempo perso)* (1954); *Il canto del grillo* (1955); *Il sole si leva al tramonto* (1956); *Le miserie del processo penale* (1957); *Il segreto della vita* (1959); *Vita da avvocato* (1961). See also *Come nasce il diritto* (1954); *Come si fa un processo* (1954).
53 *Chiose al Vangelo di Matteo* (1949); *Interpretazione del Pater noster* (1950, 1961); *Meditazione sull'Ave Maria* (1955); *I dialoghi del Vangelo e la civiltà* (1956); *Figure del Vangelo* (1958); *Il granello di senapa (Parabole del Vangelo)* 1959; *Il discorso della libertà (sul Vangelo di Giovanni)* 1960; *Il poema di Gesù* (1961); *Maria e le altre donne* (1962). See also Francesco Carnelutti, "Ordinamento giuridico e morale cristiana" (1944), and id., "I valori giuridici del messaggio cristiano" (1950), in id., *Discorsi*, II, 1–14, 185–202.
54 Prefazione, 1.
55 Carnelutti, *Verso la riforma del processo penale*, 11.
56 See Pisani.

57 See Tarello, 525–98; Tracuzzi, "Mio 'padre' Francesco," xxix–xxxiii.
58 Carnelutti, "Lettera agli amici"; "Verità, dubbio, certezza."
59 See Couture.

Bibliography

Ascarelli, Tullio. "La dottrina commercialistica italiana e Francesco Carnelutti" (1960). In id., *Problemi giuridici*. Vol. 2, 983–99. Milan: Casa Editrice Dott. A Giuffrè, 1959.

Bobbio, Norberto. "Francesco Carnelutti, teorico generale del diritto" (1949). In id., *Studi sulla teoria generale del diritto*, 1–52. Turin: Giappichelli Editore, 1955.

Cappellini, Paolo. "Qualcosa oltre le leggi. Plaidoyer per (l'ultimo?) Carnelutti." In *Ordo iuris. Storia e forme dell'esperienza giuridica*, 259–83. Milan: Giuffrè, 2003.

Caprioli, Severino. "L'incognita Carnelutti, ovvero il professor X e le sue albe." *Rivista trimestrale di diritto e procedura civile* 70/2 (2016): 373–97.

Carnelutti, Francesco. "Addio, Chiovenda." *Rivista di diritto processuale* 3/1 (1948): 121–31.

Carnelutti, Francesco. "Cenerentola." *Rivista di diritto processuale* 1/1 (1946): 73–8.

Carnelutti, Francesco. *Diritto e processo nella teoria delle obbligazioni*, Milan: Giuffrè, 1927; Reprinted 2006.

Carnelutti, Francesco. *Discorsi intorno al diritto.* Padua: CEDAM, 1953.

Carnelutti, Francesco. *Infortuni sul lavoro (Studi)*. Vol. 1. Rome: Athenaeum, 1913.

Carnelutti, Francesco. "La malattia del processo penale italiano." *Rivista di diritto processuale* 17 (1962): 1–8.

Carnelutti, Francesco. *La prova civile. Parte generale. Il concetto giuridico della prova.* Milan: Giuffè Editore, 1947; Reprinted 1992.

Carnelutti, Francesco. *La strada.* Rome/Milan: Tumminelli & C. Editori, 1941.

Carnelutti, Francesco. "Lettera agli amici." *Rivista di diritto processuale* 20 (1965): 1–3.

Carnelutti, Francesco. *Lezioni di diritto penale. Il reato.* Milano: Giuffrè, 1943.

Carnelutti, Francesco. *Lezioni di diritto processuale civile.* Vol. 3. Padua, 1923; Reprinted Padua: CEDAM, 1986.

Carnelutti, Francesco. *Meditazioni.* Vol. 1. Rome/Milan: Tumminelli, 1943.

Carnelutti, Francesco. *Mio fratello Daniele.* Reprinted Milan: Giuffrè, 2006.

Carnelutti, Francesco. "Nuove riflessioni sul comando collettivo." *Archivio di studi corporativi* 3 (1932): 145–57.

Carnelutti, Francesco. *Questioni sul processo penale.* 2nd ed. Bologna: Cesare Zuffi, 1950.

Carnelutti, Francesco. "Scuola italiana del diritto." In id., *Discorsi intorno al diritto.* Padua: CEDAM, 1937.

Carnelutti, Francesco. "Sindacalismo." *Il diritto del lavoro* 1 (1927): 4–9.

Carnelutti, Francesco. "Stato Democratico: Stato Corporativo." In *Verso il corporativismo democratico*, 247–55.

Carnelutti, Francesco. "Storia e natura del giudice istruttore." *Rivista di diritto processuale* 10/1 (1955): 157–63.

Carnelutti, Francesco. *Studi di diritto industriale.* Rome: Athaeneum, 1916.

Carnelutti, Francesco. *Studi di diritto processuale.* Padua: CEDAM, 1925.

Carnelutti, Francesco. *Teoria del regolamento collettivo dei rapporti di lavoro. Lezioni di diritto industriale.* Padua: CEDAM, 1927.

Carnelutti, Francesco. "Torniamo al giudizio." *Rivista di diritto processuale* 4/1 (1949): 165–74.

Carnelutti, Francesco. "Verità, dubbio, certezza." *Rivista di diritto processuale* 20 (1965): 4–9.

Carnelutti, Francesco. *Verso la riforma del processo penale*. Naples: Morano, 1963.

Cazzetta, Giovanni. *Scienza giuridica e trasformazioni sociali. Diritto e lavoro in Italia tra Otto e Novecento*. Milan: Giuffrè, 2007.

Cipriani, Franco. "Francesco Carnelutti a quarant'anni dalla scomparsa." In Francesco Carnelutti, *Vita di avvocato. Mio fratello Daniele. In difesa di uno sconosciuto*, xi–xl. Milan: Giuffrè, 2006.

Cipriani, Franco. "Francesco Carnelutti e la procedura civile." *Il giusto processo civile* 2 (2010): 319–45.

Cipriani, Franco. *Ideologie e modelli del processo civile. Saggi*. Naples: Edizioni Scientifiche Italiane, 1997.

Cipriani, Franco. *Il codice di procedura civile tra gerarchi e processualisti. Riflessioni e documenti nel cinquantenario dell'entrata in vigore*. Naples: Edizioni Scientifiche Italiane, 1992.

Cipriani, Franco. "Quel lieto evento di tanti anni fa." *Rivista di diritto processuale* 46 (1991): 225–38.

Cipriani, Franco. *Storie di processualisti e di oligarchi. La procedura civile nel regno d'Italia (1866–1936)*. Milan: Giuffrè, 1991.

Coccopalmerio, Domenico. *Francesco Carnelutti. Il "realismo giuridico italiano"*. Naples: Edizioni scientifice Italiane, 1989.

Consolo, Claudio. "Le opere e i giorni nel percorso vocazionale di Carnelutti: dalla 'Commerciale' alla 'Processuale'." *Giustizia civile* 4 (2016): 665–98.

Costa, Pietro. *Lo Stato immaginario. Metafore e paradigmi nella cultura giuridica italiana fra Ottocento e Novecento*. Milan: Giuffrè, 1986.

Couture, Eduardo I. "Carnelutti y nosotros. Un capítulo de sociología de la cultura." In *Scritti giuridici in onore di Francesco Carnelutti*. Vol. 1, 315–34. Padua: CEDAM, 1950.

Denti, Vittorio. "Francesco Carnelutti e le riforme del processo civile." *Rivista trimestrale di diritto e procedura civile* 50/2 (1996): 407–17.

Denti, Vittorio. "Sistematica e post-sistematica nell'evoluzione delle dottrine del processo" (1986). In id., *Sistemi e riforme. Studi sulla giustizia civile*, 13–39. Bologna: Il Mulino, 1999.

Denti, Vittorio, and Michele Taruffo. "La Rivista di diritto processuale civile." *Quaderni fiorentini* 16 (1987): 631–64.

Grossi, Paolo. *Scienza giuridica italiana. Un profilo storico 1860–1950*. Milan: Giuffrè: 2000.

Irti, Natalino. "La 'Metodologia del diritto' di Francesco Carnelutti." *Rivista di diritto civile* 34/1 (1988): 775–86.

Miletti, Marco. "Un vestito per Cenerentola. L'identità del diritto processuale penale all'alba della Repubblica." In *Diritti individuali e processo penale nell'Italia repubblicana*, edited by Daniele Negri and Michele Pifferi, 363–93. Milan: Giuffrè, 2011.

Picardi, Nicola. "L'esame di coscienza del vecchio maestro." *Rivista di diretto processuale* 41 (1986): 536–43.

Picardi, Nicola. "Riflessioni critiche in tema di oralità e scrittura." In *Studi in memoria di Carlo Furno*, 703–37. Milan: Giuffrè, 1973.

Pisani, Mario. "Variazioni in tema di 'Bozza' Carnelutti per un nuovo c.p.p." *Rivista di diritto processuale* (2010): 83–91.

Romagnoli, Umberto. "Francesco Carnelutti e il diritto del lavoro." *Rivista trimestrale di diritto e procedura civile* 50/2 (1996): 419–44.

Romagnoli, Umberto. "Francesco Carnelutti, giurista del lavoro." *Lavoro e diritto* 23/3 (2009): 373–401.

Stolzi, Irene. *L'ordine corporativo. Poteri organizzati e organizzazione del potere nella riflessione giuridica dell'Italia fascista*. Milan: Giuffrè, 2007.

Tarello, Giovanni. "Carnelutti, Francesco." *Dizionario biografico degli italiani* 20 (1977): 452–56.

Tarello, Giovanni. "Francesco Carnelutti ed il progetto del 1926." *Materiali per una storia della cultura giuridica* 4 (1974): 499–598.

Taruffo, Michele. "Carnelutti e la teoria della prova." *Rivista trimestrale di diritto e procedura civile* 70/2 (2016): 399–408.

Taruffo, Michele. *La giustizia civile in Italia dal '700 a oggi*. Bologna: Il Mulino, 1980.

Tracuzzi, Gianluca. "Mio 'padre' Francesco. Approccio introduttivo." In Francesco Carnelutti, *Il canto del grillo*, edited by Gian Pietro Calabrò, xi–xxxiii. Padua: CEDA, 2014.

Tracuzzi, Gianluca. "Teoria generale del diritto, filosofia e fede nel pensiero di Francesco Carnelutti." *Rivista di diritto processuale* 4–5 (2018): 1154–76.

24 Alcide De Gasperi (1881–1954)

Olivier Descamps

Leader of democratic Italy after the Second World War, Alcide De Gasperi reintroduced his country into the community of European peoples. He lived all his political commitments as a convinced Catholic[1] and played a crucial role in the formation of European unity. De Gasperi is one the fathers of Europe along with two other Christians: Robert Schuman and Konrad Adenauer. His Catholicism was inspired by his universalist and fraternal vision of a united Europe. He gave nobility to the political movement of Christian democracy and dreamed of the restoration of *Res Publica Christiana*.

A pious youth in the Austro-Hungarian Empire

Son of Amadeo De Gasperi and Maria Morandini, Alcide was born on April 3, 1881, in Pieve Tesino, in the province of Trento, which was under Austrian control.[2] His father was a civil servant of the Austro-Hungarian Empire. The first-born child, Alcide was followed by a sister, Maria, and two brothers, Mario and Augusto; Mario became a priest very close to Alcide.

Alcide lived his first years in the mountains and developed a passion for alpinism, a sport that gave him the habits of patience and consistency. But his environment was especially turned to Catholicism. His parents were practicing Catholics and instilled in him a pious education as they regularly attended mass and recited the rosary in the family. De Gasperi was thus inspired by the values of the Gospel taught by his parents, who strove to observe all of God's commandments and sought to practice charity in every moment.

De Gasperi attended a Catholic college and was an excellent pupil in Italian and philosophy. He was interested in social issues and studied the encyclical *Rerum novarum*, issued in 1893 by Pope Leo XIII. This text was the basis of De Gasperi's first commitment to social action. In Trent, De Gasperi came into contact with Don Celestino Endrici, a priest with a background in the best Roman Catholic universities who had earned two doctoral degrees (in philosophy and theology). This cleric had a very important role in spreading the influence of the encyclical as he sought to implement its main ideas. De Gasperi shared his political analysis of socialism. Indeed, the social teachings of Catholicism had similar aims, though a different way of achieving justice on earth.[3] De Gasperi worked for the diocesan paper, *La Voce cattolica*, and the Catholic workers' publication, *Fede e lavoro.*

After graduating with a bachelor's degree, he went to Vienna to study philology and philosophy[4] with the aim of seeking a career in teaching. The choice of studying in Vienna was his only option because his family did not have enough money to pay the expensive fees of an Italian university. He attended all the lessons of Ernst Commer, a professor of theology with a neo-scholastic point of view. Commer developed a conception of the Catholic Church as a hierarchically ordered society, a perfect one without need for reform and conceived as the unity of the faithful behind their pastors.

At that time, the capital of the Austro-Hungarian Empire was the crossroads of many different cultures, and De Gasperi developed a real respect for minorities. Unfortunately, the first months were very difficult; he suffered from hunger and the cold. During this difficult time, he and a friend, Felix, received assistance in the form of a daily bowl of soup from the famous Friars Minor Conventual Church (*Minoritenkirche*). These hardships made his faith deeper, and he found solace in liturgy and the rosary.

His faith seemed to be innate and was surely the consequence of his mother's influence. It was a living faith, rooted in real life without desire for intellectual speculation, and nurtured especially through social activities. In order to improve his situation, De Gasperi gave lessons to young children and managed to rent an apartment. In Vienna, he was interested in Italian migrants. The president of the Catholic Labor Federation entrusted him with the mission of distributing leaflets to promote Leo XIII's encyclical in Voralberg—work that was very difficult because he had to face strong criticism.

A new experience began for De Gasperi when Don Commer brought him in 1902 to Rome, where De Gasperi was impressed by the cradle of Catholicism. They attended an audience with Pope Leo XIII and were received by a number of prelates in the Roman Curia. Moreover, De Gasperi met Romolo Murri, a prominent member of the Christian democracy movement, whose ideas and social reformism he appreciated without sharing Murri's condemnation of modernism after the encyclical *Pascendi* (1907). As member of the University Association of Catholics in Trentino (UACT), Murri was elected the organization's secretary in September 1901. On this occasion, he gave a speech in which he invited the audience to promote the rebirth of Christianity.

When De Gasperi became president of UACT in 1902, he asserted the main aspects of the organization's program: advocacy of Catholics, Italians, and democrats, but Catholics first, and then Italians. De Gasperi believed that Catholicism gave voice to popular interests and social renewal in opposition to atheist socialism. His point of view drew criticism because he advocated the superiority of being Catholic over being Italian. For this, he was accused of supporting the Austro-Hungarian Empire. During this period, Catholics took part in the politico-institutional events of their party. Founded in 1904, the Popular Political

Union of Trentino made a clear distinction between social action and political movement.[5]

After the First World War, this criticism continued to be directed at De Gasperi, who was viewed as a supporter of Austria. But as leader of the UACT, he proposed the creation of an Italian university in Trieste, triggering strong opposition from German students. The Austro-Hungarian government feared the development of irredentism, which sought the unification of all Italian territories. In 1906, however, the central government agreed to founding only an Italian school of law in Innsbrück. But a demonstration by the German students led police to apprehend one hundred thirty-six Italian students, including De Gasperi, and to put them in jail for twenty days.[6]

When he left prison, thanks to the intervention of Enrico Conci, a member of Parliament, De Gasperi graduated in philology before returning to Trent. After going home, he took over the newspaper *La voce cattolica*, a powerful vehicle for the dissemination of ideas. In 1906 the newspaper from the diocese of Trento was renamed *Il Trentino*, whose mission De Gasperi outlined: to promote the introduction of the principles of Christianity into the state and public life; to defend the Italian fatherland; and to support the Catholic social movement and the advent of Christian democracy. Then De Gasperi initiated his political career, joining the Popular Political Union of Trentino, the Austrian Christian Democracy Party, of which he became one of the main leaders.

In 1907 and 1908, the party achieved its first electoral successes by meeting the need to secularize the Catholic movement for the sake of greater political consensus. Elected in 1909 town councilor of Trento, located in the Tyrol, De Gasperi became representative of Trentino, a province in northern Italy,[7] in the Austrian Parliament in 1911. His political action[8] was focused on the improvement of the living standards of the people of Trentino, and the conservation of Italian nationality and Catholic religion for this part of the empire. It seems odd, but there was a real policy of Germanization with the aim of eradicating the Latin and Catholic roots of Trentino. An interesting anecdote tells of the modification of De Gasperi's name from Degasperi by a parliamentary civil servant.

Beyond this anecdote, his political thoughts were based on the project of economic improvement. He believed that the role of economic associations and cooperatives was determinative. When the First World War broke out, he was in favor of neutrality because he thought that a war against the empire would have negative consequences for Trentino. He decided to go to Rome to meet different important actors, such as Pope Benedict XV, the foreign minister Sidney Sonnino, and the Austrian ambassador to discuss the situation of Trento and the defense of its rights in exchange for neutrality.

The war between Italy and Austria-Hungary began on May 1915, and the imperial government decided to deport inhabitants of Trentino. The newspaper *Il Trentino* had to stop publication. De Gasperi, as a member of the Parliament, exerted continuous efforts to make the situation of deportees less difficult. He was not authorized to go to his province for three years, but meanwhile, he denounced the bad behavior of the local staff against the people of Trentino. In 1917, the new emperor recalled the Parliament, and De Gasperi—presenting to his colleagues a picture of the desperate conditions of refugees—developed a humanitarian approach to the issue.

A christian democrat elected representative amid fascist turmoil

At the end of the First World War, De Gasperi sought refuge in Switzerland after the proclamation of the will of the Italian population in Austrian-occupied territories to become part of Italy. He went to Milan and Rome, where he received a warm welcome as a symbol of the reintegrated lands. The Italian government gave him the responsibility of repatriating the refugees.

Returning to Trent, De Gasperi changed the name of the newspaper to *Il nuovo Trentino*. The paper maintained the same editorial line with the reference to the Catholic social principles. De Gasperi joined the Italian Popular Party (IPP), founded by Don Luigi Sturzo in 1918, and presided over the first congress of this new political organization, which had been inspired by the social doctrines of the Catholic Church. De Gasperi was elected a member of Parliament for Trent in 1921 before becoming chairman of the parliamentary group of IPP. At the same time, his private life experienced a great change. He met Francesca Romani, the daughter of his friend Pietro, and in his epistolary relationship with her we can read their deep common spirituality. In 1922 they married and they had four children (Maria Romana, Lucia, Cecilia, and Paola).

His political action was based on the IPP's program with the support for decentralization and regionalization. De Gasperi accompanied Don Sturzo to Germany with the aim of gathering a union of parties inspired by Christianity to struggle against nationalism and communism. Unfortunately, Italy was undergoing a political crisis, and all the means used to avoid the worsening of the situation failed. In fact, socialists and Christian democrats could not reach agreement. The progression of the fascists and their march on Rome led the king, Victor Emmanuel III, to ask Mussolini to take office and to form a government on October 22, 1922.

Mussolini offered the IPP two government departments. Don Sturzo refused, but the parliamentary commission gave its agreement. De Gasperi agreed with this decision in the name of protecting freedom and national institutions. He thought that it could be possible to maintain fascism within the law. During the fourth congress of the IPP, the party decided to continue participating in the government under certain conditions but condemned violence. The head of the government, however, did not agree with this position and requested the resignation of both IPP ministers.

The IPP divided between those with a fascist inclination and those opposed to fascism. New violence against Catholic associations and trade unions led De Gasperi to firmly condemn the violence. Some clerics supported the regime and asked for the resignation of Don Sturzo. The papacy did not really support the

Italian People's Party (IPP) because Pope Pius XI believed that the Catholic Church's issues could be resolved by negotiations with Mussolini. The pope's position brought about the resignation of Don Sturzo and the end of the IPP.

In 1924, the general elections triggered a polemic by the socialist Giacomo Matteotti, who denounced the results. His subsequent abduction and assassination propelled a contest that led to the famous Aventine Secession, in which all opposition parties withdrew from the Parliament. De Gasperi wanted to consolidate the opposition against the dictatorship and sought to reinforce links with the socialists. Criticism from clergy, who spoke highly of the regime, brought about a hardening of the conditions. In the face of a real threat against the Christian democrats, Don Sturzo decided to leave Italy. Mussolini assumed total power and criticized De Gasperi.

In June 1925, De Gasperi organized the last congress of the IPP. Before the audience, he made his point of view clear: he defended the natural rights of human beings, the family, and society against those of the State. But because of many threats and the lack of papal support, he had to flee. Through Milan, he and his wife tried to reach Rome, but they were arrested on the road to Trieste and taken to Rome, where they were imprisoned at Regina Coeli. While his wife was released, he remained in jail for three years, writing many letters and reading the Bible and religious and historical books.

In a parody of a trial in May 1927, De Gasperi was sentenced to three years in prison. After appeal, the sentence was reduced to two years. During this hard time, his faith gave him a particular faculty of resistance. When he experienced stomach problems, he was transferred to a hospital under police supervision, and there his humanity led him to develop friendly relationships with his guards, giving them lessons or writing letters for them. He was even able to write two books—one about the encyclical *Rerum novarum* and the other about Christian corporatism with a focus on the figure of François-René de la Tour du Pin. De Gasperi lived this experience of incarceration as an atonement. When Mussolini visited Bishop Endrici's diocese, the bishop advocated for the release of De Gasperi, who was effectively set free in July 1928. However, he remained under house arrest in Rome to prevent any contact with the people of Trentino, where he enjoyed great popularity. His situation was difficult, and Bishop Endrici helped him by proposing a translation of a German book. Once again, De Gasperi's deep faith was a solid support.

Exile in the Vatican and opposition to fascism

In 1929, negotiations between the Vatican and the fascist government were in process. De Gasperi obtained a position at the Vatican Library thanks to Bishop Celestino Endrici and Giovanni Mercati, the prefect of the Vatican library.[9] In February 1929, a paradox came true with the Lateran Pacts, which were at one and the same time a success for the fascist regime and the birth of Vatican City as a state. This treaty gave a real legal existence to the papacy and allowed the organization of diplomatic services. De Gasperi was concerned that the consequences of the collaboration between State and Church could create confusion between fascism and Catholicism.

In his position at the library, De Gasperi took advantage of this opportunity to reinforce his international understanding.[10] He read the main authors of social Catholicism and corporatism and began to write many articles under a pseudonym (Spectator), especially analyses of the international situation in the newspaper *L'illustrazione Vaticana*. In 1934 he began to comment on the works of Jacques Maritain. He completely agreed with the philosophy of the French author, with whom he shared the same conception of human dignity, the spiritual vocation of human beings, and the idea that the common good of the city is necessarily based on the search for justice and love.

De Gasperi worked in a simple, modest, and dignified way, a real lesson in humility. In this period, the situation in Germany worsened, and he denounced all theories, especially those associating racism and Catholicism. De Gasperi was an opponent of totalitarianism, racism, and heightened nationalism. For him, communism and fascism were in contradiction to all Catholic principles. In this period, too, he was a loving and protecting father of his children, a concrete sign of Providence. In 1935, before undergoing surgery for an inguinal hernia, he wrote his testament, in which he entrusted God to look after his daughters. In this text he asked his wife to tell his children all the ideals of human goodness and Christian democracy he had fought and suffered for. He asserted that they could learn the sense of justice, of Christian fraternity, and of liberty by reading all his old letters. At the same time, Mussolini decided to develop a colonial policy with the invasion of Ethiopia and the beginning of an Italian empire. In 1938, De Gasperi commented on the letter written by German bishops defending the freedom of the Church and denouncing the enslavement of the German people to Hitler's regime.

During the Second World War, De Gasperi attended meetings of the anti-fascist parties and wrote the principles for a new political formation: Christian democracy based on Christianism. In 1943 he drew up an important manifesto for a new party with Guido Gonella: the reconstructive ideas of Christian democracy.[11] In this document, De Gasperi, who wrote once again under a pseudonym, and Gonella asserted the main characteristics and aims of this new party. They considered the major aspects of the Catholic movement to be the promotion of freedom (freedom of education), the respect due to human beings, and social justice. They proposed that the new movement should be far from Marxism and capitalism and should defend social solidarity, representative democracy, separation of powers, and administrative decentralization. His ideas were influenced by Pius XII, who advocated the creation of federal institutions functioning on the basis of the subsidiarity principle.[12] De Gasperi also considered a new League of Peoples with real equal rights and conceived a new international order.

In September 1943 De Gasperi joined the Lateran territory because of the German occupation of Italy. There, he found all the leaders of the national liberation committee, in particular its president, Ivanoe Bonomi. De Gasperi took part in the committee, where his moderation and his rejection of ideological points of view gave him charisma. After the end of the war, the main question was the choice for a new regime: democracy or monarchy? De Gasperi was in favor of monarchy, but the House of Savoy had compromised with fascism, and the only possible regime was a republican one. He thus advocated freedom and the choice by the people. Christian democrats preferred the republic and bicameralism.

At the same moment, Italy faced an important problem of hunger. This was the reason why De Gasperi talked to the United Nations Relief and Rehabilitation Administration, an organization created by the Allies to help populations suffering from misery because of war. As a result of his intervention, a lot of humanitarian aid was directed to Italy, and every month until 1947 several ships of food arrived to help alleviate the hardship.

In July 1944 De Gasperi became secretary of the Christian Democracy Party. As secretary of the party, De Gasperi was appointed minister without portofolio in Bonomi's cabinet, and one year later, he became minister of foreign affairs in the second Bonomi cabinet and then in the cabinet of Feruccio Parri. In November 1944, Bonomi's government faced a crisis because of epuration in the administration—the criminal trial of officials who had collaborated with the fascists. De Gasperi supported Bonomi and refused the constitution of a government with socialists and communists. A new government was formed, and he kept the position of minister of foreign affairs. He understood the importance of this ministry because it made for easier contact with the Allies, who decided the fate of Italy.

Prime minister of Italy

On December 19, 1945, King Humbert II asked De Gasperi to form a government. Until 1953, he would form eight successive cabinets. On June 1946, two key moments of postwar Italian history intervened: general elections and a referendum about the choice between monarchy and democracy. Christian Democracy won the elections, and the voters chose a republic for their regime. The first president of the republic, Enrico De Nicola, asked De Gasperi to form a government.

At that moment, the main problem was the uncertain fate of the country in the postwar peace treaties. In August 1946, De Gasperi defended his country by differentiating between the Italian people and the fascist regime. He did not hesitate to recall Italy's collaboration with the Allies after 1943 as well as all that the West owed to Italy. De Gasperi explained the new aspect of the Italian regime, which combined the humanitarian aspirations of Mazzini, the universalist conceptions of Christianity, and the international hopes of workers.[13] In his conclusion, we can read his Christianity and the principle of fraternity, the sources of many moral and material enrichments of the West. After this speech, the French delegation decided to moderate its requirements against Italy.

In September 1946, De Gasperi decided to leave his position as political secretary of the Christian Democracy Party. He believed that the reconstruction of Italy should be led concomitantly with the construction of a new European and world order. One of the most important actions was to restore Italy's place in the world. That was the reason why, in January 1947, he went to the United States at the invitation of the US Congress. He appeared as the new face of democratic Italy. In a speech in Cleveland, Ohio, De Gasperi asserted his faith in democracy, the regime that he considered to be the only one that could make possible freedom of expression, freedom of the press, and freedom of initiative.[14] His views immediately won for Italy a trade treaty and huge American financial support. In different speeches, De Gasperi presented the United States as a model of democracy and evoked the "united states of Europe." He asserted that a true democracy requires that the world be organized in a common system for the promotion of justice, equality, and progress. His Christian faith made it easier for the American people to favor him, even more so after a mass in New York city.

When he returned to Italy, a political crisis occurred because of all the subsidies provided by the Americans. Socialists and communists contested this financial support, which they viewed as collaboration with capitalism. In May 1947 a new government was formed, one of whose ministers was Carlo Sforza, who had had considerable experience in diplomacy since the end of the nineteenth century. Sforza, as minister of foreign affairs, had to represent Italy when the Marshall Plan was discussed in Paris. Beyond the criticisms, the new government coincided with the ratification of the peace treaty, and the Marshall Plan prompted many violent contestations and a new constitution in December 1947. General elections took place in the context of the Cold War. Christian democrats won a large number of seats in the democratic parliament in the spring of 1948. The situation was difficult after the aggression of Palmiro Togliatti, general secretary of the Italian Communist Party. De Gasperi had to decide whether to involve the army, but the violence stopped because of the intervention of communist leaders.

One of the christian fathers of united Europe

During the Second World War, several drafts of a proposal for a united Europe were prepared. The desire for unity and peace led to the creation of many Europist movements. De Gasperi agreed with these conceptions of a new Europe that would foster fraternal relationship among all the nations. Besides, he had shared this point of view with Don Sturzo since 1919. On the basis of such Christian principles as humanism and fraternity, a common market could become a means to avoid new conflicts among nations. In Italy, a famous manifesto for a united Europe was written in 1941 by Altiero Spinelli and Ernesto Rossi in Ventotene. Spinelli agreed with De Gasperi about the need for unification of Europe. He was involved in the important movement in favor of European unification. After the war, many different groups supported this goal of unifying Europe.

In 1948 De Gasperi accepted the honorary presidency of the European movement in which Winston Churchill and the Belgian socialist Paul-Henri Spaak were prominent. During the first years after the war, different treaties were signed dealing with the crucial issue of the fate of Germany. De Gasperi pleaded in favor of reintegrating Germany among nations. He defended mutual assistance and friendly relationships in culture and economics. Moreover, he considered the creation of a united Europe to be a means of perpetual peace, a way to freedom and justice.[15]

Fundamentally, De Gasperi made all of these efforts in order to reintroduce Italy among the nations. In November 1948 he developed his ideas about European federalism during the Grandes Conférences Catholiques in Brussels.[16] This Brussels speech[17] presented his conceptions of democracy. For its moral basis, he took the example of Belgium, which had a free government and offered a model of society for the future. He shared values that he recognized in the Belgian democracy: freedom of conscience and freedom for different institutions against state centralization. And he continued with the American Revolution and its limitation of powers. He asserted a "realistic and philosophical pessimism"[18] as an appropriate political attitude to protect political liberty. Three main elements were connected in his conception: liberty, peace, and justice. He asserted that the will for peace should lead to European unification with the reintegration of Germany.

In January 1949 Italy was admitted to participation in the Council of Europe. Before the Chamber of Deputies, De Gasperi asserted that Italy was on the cusp of joining the European family. The council was created on May 5, and Italy recovered a new dignity. The political divisions over participation in the Altantic Pact, or NATO, triggered much criticism against him. At the same time, he was received by the pope, who applauded his doctrine and his Christian way of life. As in the past, De Gasperi's policy was inspired by the social doctrine of the Catholic Church, and he believed that the morality of the Gospel had an impact on social life.

In the 1950s, the European project entered a new phase as countries developed a real will for change. As the international situation and the Cold War threatened the peace, opposition between the United States and the Soviet Union spurred a European reaction. De Gasperi was aware of the impact of bipolarism, and he backed the integration of the Atlantic Pact. In April 1950 De Gasperi asserted before a convention of the Nouvelles Équipes Internationales that economic integration did not mean automatically a way to political integration.[19] He developed many efforts to make a political European community possible. De Gasperi advocated for a supranational structure, a federal state, with respect for nationalities but an avoidance of extreme nationalism. He was convinced of the chance for Italy to become involved in the formation of a European union.

The European "big bang" occurred with the Schuman Declaration on May 9, 1950, proposed by the French Catholic minister of foreign affairs, Robert Schuman.[20] Italy was the first country to endorse the declaration. De Gasperi agreed with the content of the declaration, which aimed to build a federative Europe beyond trade unions and economic forces. The desire to build a united Europe was above all based on the aspiration to maintain peace and security in a free and democratic West. On the basis of the Schuman Declaration, negotiations were conducted, and the Italian government presented some demands, including protection of the free movement of labor.[21] The treaty of Paris (April 1951) established the first European community: the European Coal and Steel Community (ECSC).

Among the institutions of the new economic community, an assembly was created, whose first president was De Gasperi. The institutional framework of the ECSC constituted the framework for later drafts. In June 1951, De Gasperi met with Konrad Adenauer, chancellor of West Germany, a Christian, who thanked De Gasperi for his intercession in behalf of Adenauer's country. Both shared the same approach to introducing Christian influences into politics. At the same time, the Italian situation was difficult, and De Gasperi's seventh government decided to back the development of industry and agriculture.[22]

The success of the ECSC aroused an enthusiastic movement of new communities, such as the European Defense Community, established in March 1952 by the Treaty of Paris. De Gasperi considered this new step as a means for struggling against nationalism by the constitution of a European army. In the Treaty of Paris, De Gasperi succeeding in convincing delegates to insert into the draft Article 38,[23] which entrusted to the provisional assembly of the EDC the task of elaborating statutes for a new community: the European Political Community.[24] In fact, he believed that a unified European army could lead to another step for the construction of Europe.

Opposition arose against De Gasperi's point of view, but he backed all solutions in favor of federalism before the Council of Ministers. In December 1951 he gave a speech in Strasbourg before the consultative assembly of the Council of Europe, in which he insisted on the need for federalism. He recommended establishing a central body "in which the national wills of all the countries meet, become specific, and nurture each other in a higher fusion."[25] In September 1952 the Pleven plan for the EDC was approved by all six ministers of foreign affairs of the ECSC in Luxembourg. The main idea was to find the best way to protect the fragile peace in the difficult time of cold war. Six months later, the EPC statutes were adopted by the provisional assembly.

At that time, De Gasperi was the first to receive the famous Charlemagne Prize. During the award ceremony, he evoked the spiritual origins of Europe in a speech. For him, the future would be built not with the use of force or the spirit of conquest but rather with the patience of democratic method and a spirit of agreement in respect of freedom.[26]

In 1953, despite his successes, De Gasperi lost the general elections and had to step down from the presidency. Yet he continued to pursue his commitment in favor of European construction. In April 1954 he proposed to an audience of the European Parliamentary Conference the basis of the European idea with its Christian roots and the need for peace. Two months later, he presented his political testament before the congress of Italian Christian Democracy. He died on August 19, 1954, in Borgo Valsugana. Had he lived longer, he would have known the failure of his project for the EDC because of the negative vote by the French National Assembly.

In sum, the personal life and political commitment of De Gasperi were placed under the light of his deep faith. Despite his intensive political life, he kept a daily time for meditation, prayers, and reading of the Bible or the Church Fathers. In his political life, he sought to apply all the main Christian principles: fraternity, benevolence, peace, justice, and respect. His political views were inspired by the social doctrines of the Catholic Church, especially the encyclical *Rerum novarum*, issued in 1893 by Pope Leo XIII.

Notes

1 Canavero, vii.
2 Audisio and Chiara, 152.
3 De Gasperi, *Scritti e discorsi politici*, vol. 1, 27.
4 Pombeni, *Il primo De Gasperi*, 51.
5 Preda, *De Gasperi: European Founding Father*, 21.
6 Ibid., 20.
7 Before its annexation to Italy in 1919, the present Trentino-Alto-Adige was a part of the Austro-Hungarian Empire in the province of Südtirol.
8 Arnoulx de Pirey, 57.
9 See Melloni.
10 See Formigoni.
11 De Gasperi, *Discorsi politici*, Vol. 2, 19–20.
12 Preda, *De Gasperi: European Founding Father*, 54.
13 De Gasperi, *L'Europa. Scritti e discorsi*, 31.
14 Ibid., 50.
15 Ibid., 7.
16 Preda, *De Gasperi: European Founding Father*, 155.
17 De Gasperi, *L'Europa: scritti e discorsi*, 55.
18 Ibid., 63.
19 De Gasperi, *L'idea europea nel solidarismo cristiano.*
20 Gerbet, 360.
21 Preda, *De Gasperi: European Founding Father*, 205.
22 Craveri, *De Gasperi*, 573–93.
23 Article 38:

1. Within the period provided for in Section 2 of this Article, the Assembly shall study:

   (a) the creation of an Assembly of the European Defense Community elected on a democratic basis;
   (b) the powers which might be granted to such an Assembly;
   (c) the modifications which should be made in the provisions of the present Treaty relating to the other institutions of the Community, particularly with a view to safeguarding an appropriate representation of the States.

In its work, the Assembly will particularly bear in mind the following principles:

> The definitive organization which will take the place of the present transitional organization should be conceived so as to be capable of constituting one of the elements of an ultimate Federal or confederal structure, based upon the principle of the separation of powers and including, particularly, a bicameral representative system.

The Assembly shall also study problems to which the coexistence of different organizations for European cooperation, now in being or to be created in the future, give rise, in order to ensure that these organizations ure coordinated within the framework of the federal or confederal structure.

2. The proposals of the Assembly shall be submitted to the Council within six months from the date on which the Assembly shall have assumed its functions. These proposals will then be forwarded, together with the opinion of the Council, by the President of the Assembly to the Governments of the member States, which, within three months from the date of the receipt of these proposals, shall call a conference for the purpose of examining them. See on the website http://aei.pitt.edu/5201/1/5201.pdf (last connection: 06/30/2019).

24 Kaiser, 282–3.
25 Address given by Alcide De Gasperi (Strasbourg, December 10, 1951) www.cvce.eu/obj/address_given_by_alcide_de_gasperi_strasbourg_10_december_1951-en-a8597705-5863-43d9-9a50-4f0133a17a02.html (Accessed: March 26, 2020).
26 De Gasperi, *L'Europa. Scritti e discorsi*, 170.

Bibliography

Arnoulx de Pirey, Elisabeth. *De Gasperi, le père italien de l'Europe.* Paris: Pierre Téqui, 1991.

Audisio, Giuseppe, and Alberto Chiara. *Les fondateurs de l'Europe unie selon le plan de Jean Monnet.* Paris: Salvator, 2004.

Ballini, Pier Luigi. *Alcide De Gasperi.* Vol. 3: *Dalla costruzione della democrazia alla nostra patria Europa, 1948–1954.* Rome: Soveria Mannelli, Rubbettino, 2009.

Bigaran, Mariapia. "Alcide De Gasperi: The Apprenticeship of a Political Leader." *Modern Italy, Journal of the Association for the Study of Modern Italy* 14/4 (2009): 425–30.

Canavero, Alfredo. *Alcide de Gasperi. Cristiano, democratico, europeo.* Rome: Soveria Manelli, Rubettino, 2003.

Canavero, Alfredo. "La formation européenne de Alcide de Gasperi." In Sylvain Schirman, *Robert Schuman et les Pères de l'Europe*, 285–91.

Canavero, Alfredo, et al. *Alcide De Gasperi.* Vol. 1: *Dal Trentino all'esilio in patria, 1881–1943.* Rome: Soveria Mannelli, Rubbettino, 2009.

Cau, Maurizio. "Alcide de Gasperi: A Political Thinker or a Thinking Politician?" *Modern Italy, Journal of the Association for the Study of Modern Italy* 14/4 (2009): 445–57.

Cau, Maurizio. *De Gasperi e la Prima guerra mondiale.* Trento: Fondazione Bruno Kessler Press, 2015.

Conze, Eckart, Gustavo Corni, and Paolo Pombeni, eds. *Alcide De Gasperi: un percorso europeo.* Bologna: Il Mulino, 2005.

Craveri, Piero. *De Gasperi.* Bologna: Il Mulino, 2006.

Craveri, Piero. "La contribution des représentants des partis laïcs à la politique européiste de De Gasperi." In Sylvain Schirman, *Robert Schuman et les Pères de l'Europe*, 293–305.

De Gasperi, Alcide. *Alcide De Gasperi nel Trentino asburgico, a cura di Elena Tonezzer, Mariapia Bigaran e Maddalena Guiotto.* Bologna: Il Mulino, 2006.

De Gasperi, Alcide. *Diario 1930–1943.* Critical edition with commentary by Marialuisa Lucia Sergio. Bologna: il Mulino, 2018.

De Gasperi, Alcide. *Discorsi parlamentari.* Rome: Carlo Colombo, 1973.

De Gasperi, Alcide. *L'Europa: scritti e discorsi*, edited by Maria Romana De Gasperi. Brescia: Morcelliana, 2004.

De Gasperi, Alcide. *L'idea europea nel solidarismo cristiano.* Sorrento, 1950. Available at www.pro-europa.eu/europe/it/alcide-de-gasperi-lidea-europea-nel-solidarismo-cristiano/ (Accessed 06/20/2019).

De Gasperi, Alcide. *Scritti di politica internazionale 1933–1938.* Vatican City: Libreria editrice vaticana, 1981.

De Gasperi, Alcide. *Scritti e discorsi politici: edizione critica, Coordinamento scientifico di Paolo Pombeni, coordinamento editoriale di Giuliana Nobili Shiera.* Bologna: Il Mulino, 2006.

De Gasperi, Alcide. *Scritti e discorsi politici.* Vol. 1: *Coordinamento scientifico di Paolo Pombeni; coordinamento editoriale di Giuliana Nobili Shiera.* Bologna: Il mulino, 2006.

De Gasperi, Alcide. *Scritti e discorsi politici: edizione critica.* Vol. 2: *Alcide De Gasperi dal Partito popolare italiano all'esilio interno, 1919–1942, a cura di Mariapia Bigaran e Maurizio Cau.* Bologna: Il Mulino, 2007.

De Gasperi, Maria. *La mia patria Europa.* Preface by Alcide De Gasperi. Milan: Mondadori, 1969.

Formigoni, Guido. "L'Europa vista dal Vaticano: De Gasperi commentatore della politica internazionale." In Conze, Corni, and Pombeni, *Alcide De Gasperi: un percorso europeo*, 169–93.

Gerbet, Pierre. "De Gasperi, Alcide." In *Dictionnaire historique de l'Europe unie*, edited by Pierre Gerbet, Gerard Bossuat, and Thierry Grosbois. Paris: André Versailles, 2009.

Kaiser, Wolfram. *Christian Democracy and the Origins of European Union.* Cambridge: Cambridge University Press, 2007.

Melloni, Alberto. "Alcide De Gasperi alla biblioteca Vaticana (1929–1933)." In Conze, Corni, and Pombeni, *Alcide De Gasperi: un percorso europeo*, 141–68.

Pombeni, Paolo. *Il primo De Gasperi. La formazione di un leader politico.* Bologna: Il Mulino, 2007.

Preda, Daniela. *De Gasperi: European Founding Father.* Brussels: Peter Lang, 2017.

Preda, Daniela. *De Gasperi federalista europeo.* Bologna: Il Mulino, 2004.

Preda, Daniela. "L'action européenne de De Gasperi et la contribution du réseau catholique européen autour de lui." In Sylvain Schirman, *Robert Schuman et les Pères de l'Europe*, 307–23.

Schirman, Sylvain, ed. *Robert Schuman et les Pères de l'Europe. Cultures politiques et années de formation. Acte du colloque de Metz du 10 au 12 octobre 2007 organisé par la Maison de Robert Schuman et le Réseau des Maisons des Pères de l'Europe.* Brussels: Peter Lang, 2008.

Taverni, Barbara. "For Italy in a Changing World: The Political Apogee of Alcide De Gasperi, 1948–1954." *Modern Italy, Journal of the Association for the Study of Modern Italy* 14/4 (2009): 459–71.

Valori, Gino. *Degasperi al Parlamento austriaco.* Florence: Parenti, 1953.

25 Arturo Carlo Jemolo (1891–1981)

Carlo Fantappiè

Introduction

Arturo Carlo Jemolo (born in Rome on January 17, 1891, and dying there on May 12, 1981) was a rich and original personality, complex and multifaceted, of considerable depth and importance in the academic, cultural, and social landscape of twentieth-century Italy.

Jemolo is considered one of the most distinguished Italian jurists for the vastness of the themes he dealt with in every field of law, even though he devoted himself mainly to ecclesiastical law, that is, the study of state legislation on religious confessions. He taught this discipline in the universities of Sassari (1920–22), Bologna (1923–25), Milan's Cattolica del Sacro Cuore (1925–27), and Rome (1933–61). Owing to the importance of his work, Jemolo can be considered the refounder of ecclesiastical law in the twentieth century: he helped to make this typical discipline of the Italian tradition appreciated abroad, giving it an innovative character in methodology and doctrine. Moreover, his activity was not limited to legal sciences, to which he devoted himself as a scholar and a legal professional.[1] Jemolo cultivated with great mastery the history of theological and canonical doctrines, especially in the modern age, and the history of the relations between State and Church in contemporary Italy.[2]

In any case, his personality and commitment go beyond the strictly academic sphere to occupy the cultural and social sphere. As an *engagé* intellectual, Jemolo worked for the daily newspaper *La Stampa* from 1955 to 1981 and wrote many essays for prestigious secular cultural magazines, such as Mario Pannunzio's *Il Mondo*, Piero Calamandrei's *Il Ponte*, Ferruccio Parri's *Astrolabio*, and Giovanni Spadolini's *Nuova Antologia*. He also participated in radio broadcasts of RAI. Finally, he carried out functions of scientific advice for various government institutions; in particular, in 1976 he participated in the work of the Commission for the Revision of the Lateran Concordat, chaired by Guido Gonella.

Cultural education

Due to the premature loss of his father, Luigi, Jemolo remained very close to his mother, Anna Adele Sacerdoti, a Piedmontese of Jewish origin. She was related to the Momigliano family, which gave birth to two other well-known scholars, Arnaldo and Attilio.

Jemolo's intellectual training—which took place before the First World War at the University of Turin and later in the cultural environment of Rome—was marked by great masters: the Kantian philosopher Pietro Martinetti, the economist and statesman Luigi Einaudi, the legal historian Federico Patetta, the political doctrines theorist Gaetano Mosca, and the ecclesiastical law and history scholar Francesco Ruffini, his graduation supervisor in 1911.[3]

In addition to his Jewish cultural background and Turin's academic environment, the formation of Jemolo was influenced especially by two significant figures, very different from each other. The first was a Catholic priest of modernist orientation, excommunicated by the Catholic Church: Ernesto Buonaiuti. Jemolo met him in Rome in 1919, became part of his community, and, despite differences of opinion on modernism, remained in contact with Buonaiuti until his death, receiving religious stimuli that were crucial to Jemolo's vision of the relations between religious society and political society.

The second figure who represented a sort of spiritual beacon for Jemolo was the idealist philosopher Benedetto Croce, with whom he was to put himself for many years in a position of *concordia discors*. Jemolo appreciated Croce's anti-Enlightenment orientation, his emphasis on the ethical and social values of Christianity, and, above all, his secular conception of state and culture.

It is significant that Jemolo's most widely read and best-known volume in Italy and abroad—[4] *Church and State in Italy, 1850–1950*—reflects Croce's view that the State and the Church represent "the antithesis and synthesis of the two eternal moments of strength (or utility) and of moral life." A dialectic tension always remains between these two historical magnitudes, with the purpose of keeping the "moral conscience" of humanity awake. But it is not possible to foresee either the alternation of their functions or the internal laws of their relations.[5]

Main themes and contributions

As mentioned earlier, Jemolo's work focused mainly on ecclesiastical law. This discipline did not yet have a well-defined approach, despite the great importance that the conflicts between Church and State had had in the history of the Italian unitary state. The discipline swung between legal dogmatics and the history of State-Church relations, between state law and the law of religious confessions, between public law and private law.

The vision of the relationship between State and Church

Jemolo's early legal works move in the orbit of the discipline of administrative law. Both his monograph *L'amministrazione ecclesiastica* (Ecclesiastical administration) of 1916 and his first textbook, *Elementi di diritto ecclesiastico* (Elements of ecclesiastical law), of 1927 were influenced by the formalist doctrine and liberal principles of Vittorio Emanuele Orlando. Indeed, Jemolo analogically applied the schemes of the State's public organization to Church bodies and conceived of the religious freedom of other confessions in terms of mere protection of religious beliefs.

Towards the end of the 1930s, we witness a definite *antiformalist turn* in Jemolo's thought. This change was not abrupt; rather, it was prepared by more than twenty years of study and developed in line with the tradition of his influences. He had become particularly aware of the historicity of law, of the importance of political doctrines and psychological phenomena in the life of religions.[6]

On the basis of these premises, one understands the controversy of 1938 with his colleague Aldo Checchini on method in ecclesiastical law and on the study of the relationship between State and Church.[7] On one hand, Jemolo opposed the tendency to make ecclesiastical law a branch of private international law or to transform it into a new entity such as "concordatory law" (that is, the law of concordat), because the individuals concerned and the territory of their actions are always included in the state legal system. On the other hand, he relativized the value of the theoretical classifications of the State-Church relations (confessionalism, jurisdictionalism, separatism, etc.), which "have never had a clear legal meaning," and whose only purpose is to provide "the historian and the politician" with some orientation.[8]

Law should not be considered as an entity isolated or isolable from social reality; rather, its emergence and evolution are influenced by a mixture of external factors of a metalegal, mostly political, nature. In the relations between religious confessions and states, the dynamics of political forces weigh more than any legal formula; moreover, state or religious legal norms cannot be isolated from the reality or social environment in which they are formulated and must be applied.[9]

The value of this critique is not limited to ecclesiastical law but concerns legal theory. Jemolo theorized the *inadequacy of the dogmatic conception* in a very fine contribution to the debate about the value and use of legal concepts in which the most important Italian jurists took part between 1935 and 1942. The aim of Jemolo's contribution was to make jurists aware of the unbridgeable gap that will always exist between concepts and the reality of things.[10]

In Jemolo's thought, the reply to Checchini of 1938 became a fundamental step towards establishing the *autonomous, original, and unitary character* of ecclesiastical law within the framework of legal disciplines and plural legal sources. Indeed, for Jemolo, there is a clear distinction between interstate relations at the level of private international law and the forms of connection between the State legal system and the Church legal system. That is, he refuses to admit in general a *renvoi* of state norms to canon law norms, and this implies a specific approach to the problems that are the subject of ecclesiastical law.

An exemplary case is represented by the relations between *canonical marriage and civil marriage* after the 1929 Concordat.[11] The concurrence of Church jurisdiction and State jurisdiction requires an analysis under different normative aspects (canonical, civil, administrative, etc.), the use of principles, methods, and techniques of different disciplines, and the weighing of different reasons or arguments, so as to propose a solution consistent with the normative requirements of the different legal systems (the Church and the State). This effort to bring back conceptual unity to a body of law to which different legal systems contribute simultaneously under different profiles, shows that the purpose of ecclesiastical law is ultimately to rebuild the *unity of legal experience*.[12]

Civil society and religious society

After the antiformalist turn of 1938, another great turning point in the development of Jemolo's methodology is to be found in *Premesse ai rapporti tra Stato e Chiesa* (Introduction to the relationship between Church and State) of 1965. This change can be summarized with the shift from the formula "state and Church" to that of "civil society and religious society." The starting point is no longer the dialectical opposition between the two most representative institutions in the modern history of Europe but, on one hand, the new theory of social groups acting within the State and, on the other, the principle of common interests. The historical-legal and institutional vision is replaced by a historical-sociological vision centered on the idea of social groups, which institutionalize primary or original belongings and reflect the common needs of people. The legal notion of "interest" is the way in which these aspirations are represented and legitimized.[13] The "religious interests" of a group of citizens come together in an organized structure called "religious confession," which tends to form a complete society, with its own laws, legal bodies, established authorities, and social rites. The two most important and organic types of groups are "state groups" and "religious groups."[14]

The peculiarity of the relations between the two societies, religious and state, is that the two groups, in their contacts or contrasts, are made up of the same people. The European history of the second millennium attests to a long series of antithetical positions that arise either from the Church's tendency to consider the State as a subordinate organization meant to collaborate in its higher aims, or from the State's tendency to subjugate the Church, or at least to delimit its powers and functions. After the rise of democracies and constitutional states, this contrast mainly concerns the problem of citizens' religious freedom and the different "tables of values"—civil and religious—of which the two societies become bearers. Although this contrast should not be exaggerated (because civil society has been shaped by Christian ideas and values), it can never be annulled or delimited within defined spheres. Underlying it are, in fact, *different orientations and perspectives*, which often lead to unequal or conflicting assessments, options, and behavior in the face of unforeseeable situations.

Ethical State, freedom principle, and secular conscience

Both the State and the Church are bearers of a historical mission and a set of values that are different but equally necessary. Neither institution can waive its duties. The presence of the State is a condition for guaranteeing both a plural associated life and a plural religious life of citizens. In Jemolo's thought, the dynamic contrast between the Church and the State, between religious and political values, represents an essential bridge to arrive at the concept of *secularism* (a concept expressed in Italian through the adjective *laico* and the noun *laicità*).[15] Each community has to face this problem in relation to the principles of its own legal system, its own religious and cultural traditions, and its specific forms of social organization. There is a big difference between the American model, which allows religious confessions a great deal of freedom, and the European model, which assigns to the state tasks relating to every aspect of life.

Faith in the ethical state, the bearer of an autonomous morality, requires a will to live in a climate of freedom, the rejection of violence, and the acceptance of the pluralistic idea of the state "as a great association of people with a common morality and common interests but not the same ideas on everything, especially on things concerning religion."[16] Jemolo was very aware that believers and non-believers have different conceptions of freedom. While the latter also understand it as a freedom not to believe, for the majority of the former it is connected to the concept of truth and the path to goodness, whereby "the ideal will always be a world where unbelief has no place, where only one truth is taught without any risk of constantly calling it into question."[17]

His thought, inspired by a clearly liberal conception, differs considerably from the Catholic conception of the state. Only a *regime of separation* between the two societies allows us to welcome those who are not part of the religious society into the state society, without discrimination of any kind.[18]

On one hand, Jemolo denied that *natural law* provides a basis for common ground between the two societies, since natural law principles are neither neutral nor universally accepted. On the other hand, he wanted to avoid a mutual indifference between "Catholic conscience" and "secular conscience," for such indifference would lead to a loss of values.[19] To overcome this serious aporia, Jemolo proposed the radical option of "*believer's secularism*," by which he meant a series of mandatory concessions of the believer to the needs of the state, but also the believer's will to respond actively to their consequences. A *secular conscience* of believers should (1) accept the "diversity of conceptions" found in society; (2) recognize that the state must inspire its laws and its activities to a concept of common good to all citizens; (3) allow, though reluctantly, the state to admit in its legislation

> what for him as a believer is sin, and the propaganda of that which for him is such, leaving to free competition, between religious and nonreligious people, the task of dispelling sin, of ensuring that sin, although permitted by the legal norm, is never committed.[20]

The inevitable and necessary gap between *law and sin*, between *sin and crime*, which implies for the believer the "legal tolerance *of evil*," reflects the dialectic between civil society and religious society as well as between the two "tables of values" in perennial and productive conflict.

The *Lezioni di diritto ecclesiastico* (Lessons in ecclesiastical law) (1933–79)

Jemolo's contribution to ecclesiastical law was not limited to the methodological aspect; it also took the form of a constant work of critical reflection on Italian ecclesiastical legislation throughout his long teaching. His *Corsi* and *Lezioni di diritto ecclesiastico* have become an essential reference for scholars in this field. We can distinguish three major phases of the evolution of his doctrine in relation to as many historical events: the Concordat of 1929, the Republican Constitution of 1948, and the Second Vatican Council of 1962–65.

During the phase from the stipulation of the Lateran Pact to the collapse of the fascist regime, Jemolo's doctrine focused on three essential problems. First, the limitation of the *confessional character of the modern state.* In it "one cannot think of a religion of the state as a complete acceptance of dogmas, beliefs, the discipline of a given religion, and, above all, as a concern to attain eternal salvation."[21] Second, the distinction between *modern state and Catholic state*, which implies that the former is not obliged to "recognize limitations to its own legal system, to its own right of government, deriving from a superior system (natural law or divine law or church law)."[22] Finally, the defense of the legitimacy of *civil marriage* after the concordat of 1929. Jemolo also elaborated a comprehensive doctrine on the distribution of state competences in matters of *concordatory marriage* (the regime of matrimonial cohabitation, the effects of marriage, the civil law enforceability of judgments of nullity, etc.).

With the Second World War and the collapse of the fascist regime, Jemolo's doctrinal attitude deeply changed. In the booklet *Per la pace religiosa d'Italia*, (Towards religious peace in Italy), published in 1944, he expressed his new positions on ecclesiastical policy: rejection of the concordat, return to liberal separatism (freedom for all religious confessions without discrimination), elimination of privileges, and application of the common law to the institutions of the Catholic Church.

The second phase of Jemolo's doctrinal work, running from 1948 to 1965, focused on three points. First of all, the problem of the limits of the Church's activity in the life of the State. Article 7 of the Italian Constitution—a constitution which he considered abstract, idealistic, and vague—does not imply that the Church, in the free exercise of its spiritual power and jurisdiction, can derogate from the general norms of the Constitution and treat citizens unequally, despite the transposition of the 1929 concordat. The State has the duty to protect citizens' legal rights, even when the Church, for its own reasons, imposes a sanction on citizens.[23]

A second point concerned the *protection of the organizational freedom* of religious confessions other than Catholic, which, despite Article 8 of the Italian

Constitution, continued to be discriminated against or persecuted in the early years of the republic and, for several other decades, were not regulated on the basis of "agreements" between the State and the representatives of those confessions.[24]

A third aspect was the commitment to revise the crime of ***contempt for the Catholic religion***, a rule considered discriminatory against non-Catholics and, in any case, limiting any form of criticism of the institutional religion of the Catholic Church. Instead, Jemolo proposed to retain the prohibition but broadening it to include insulting of any ideal entity or doctrine of a religious or political movement shared by citizens.[25]

With the consolidation of the democratic conception of the state and the Second Vatican Council, there began a new and irreversible phase in the history of relations between the Church, societies, and states. Jemolo especially appreciated the declaration *Dignitatis Humanae* of Vatican II, which proclaims religious freedom as a natural right of every individual and affirms the "full respect that the person deserves who acts upon convictions, who seeks the truth, even if he or she reaches conclusions contrary to those of the church."[26] After the Council, Jemolo advocated a vision of the state that definitively surpasses the confessional qualification, which has now become a label, and a vision of the Church "*freed from the privileges of concordat.*" Concordats are justified only in cases in which the Church has to regulate its relations with authoritarian regimes.[27]

The problems of religious freedom

In the last phase of Jemolo's doctrinal development, the centrality of constitutional law in matters of individual and collective rights and freedoms emerges. The volume *Problemi pratici della libertà* (Practical problems of freedom)—a small masterpiece of practical philosophy—is meant to be an introduction to the problem of religious freedom. Its aim is to break the dogmatic and conventional schemes widespread in Italian society, and to introduce a new method of analysis to start solving this particular type of controversy.

Jemolo chose to apply to freedom issues a method based on the weighting of principles and to use argumentative techniques instead of logically deductive ones. To solve these problems, we need to resort to "despised casuistry," because there is no single solution, not even for the same individual. Nor can one delegate to others—not even to the confessor—a solution which ultimately refers to ***each individual's conscience.*** Therefore, there cannot be a "juridical dogmatics" of religious freedom; on the contrary, a unitary and concrete reflection can and must be made that seeks to unify, under the categories of law, the different perspectives in which freedom is expressed and revealed in different forms.

Religious freedom is not only the first freedom that has historically emerged, but also the fundamental one. For the religious person, indeed, "nothing matters more than this aspect of life, the possibility of communicating with God in the ways one feels best."[28] Religious freedom cannot be identified with freedom of conscience, nor can it be restricted to the individual sphere, but it must project itself into the life of groups and religious confessions recognized by the law.

One of the most controversial practical problems is the relationship between *freedom and parity* in the religious field. The traditional doctrine of ecclesiastical law presented two conflicting positions. Whereas Francesco Scaduto affirmed the need for equal treatment of all religious confessions, Francesco Ruffini believed that each one should be given not the same treatment but rather what is due to it. The former gave priority to the principle of abstract and ideal equality; the latter took into account the special legal status of the Catholic Church in Italy because of its preeminence.

Although the two goods of equality and freedom are inseparable, the tendency is now to emphasize the primacy of equality over freedom. To the collective conscience, there can be no justification for different treatment in the freedom of association of religious confessions, political parties, trade unions, etc., nor for discriminatory treatment in terms of facilities, aid, favors, honors, etc. A state which subsidizes only one confession does not respect the principle of parity; a state which subsidizes all confessions with sums "fixed in proportion to the number of their members" does not violate the principle of equality.[29] Likewise, it is not acceptable for the State officially and consistently to promote a confession in public religious ceremonies. The same guarantees and facilities should then be extended to associations of atheists or agnostics, or associations operating in fields parallel to religions. The basic criterion of state action must be its usefulness for all citizens.

A second edition of the work appeared in 1972 with a new introduction aimed at clarifying the different historical perspective of the problems of freedom. Jemolo had to note bitterly that, in that decade, faith in freedom and progress had disappeared; that institutions were threatened by political terrorism; that the principle of *Realpolitik* had established itself in international relations; that a flattening of social values had taken place; that freedom and equality were no longer complementary; and, lastly, that "the great opposition lay in the economic and noneconomic" and no longer, as for Einaudi and Croce, in the affirmation or denial of "political liberties." It was the sad conclusion of an old liberal who saw the sunset of the ideal for which he had fought.

Conclusions

We can summarize the contribution of Jemolo's thought on two levels: as a scholar of the relations between State and Church, and as a jurist and political thinker. I begin with the fixed points in the relations between State and Church:

1 the ideal of the *secular State* as a bearer of values equally essential for social coexistence as those proclaimed by the Church;
2 the acceptance of the *principle of separation* of State and Church. Hence the criticism of the ecclesiastical concordat, considered an invalid instrument for guaranteeing a just balance in the relations between State and Church and not even advantageous for both;

3 the principle of *equality of citizens* before the law of the State, whether or not they belong to a religious confession;
4 the claim that *religious law is divorced from the laws of the State*. Once the idea of two distinct areas, the Church and the State, is accepted, and the guarantees of religious freedom for all citizens and religious confessions are defined, it is necessary to draw the corollary of the diversity of values and criteria of evaluation. Not everything that is condemned by the Church must be condemned by state law;
5 the proposal of a "believer's secularism," that is, the principle of a *secular conscience* of the faithful citizen as well as of the atheist or agnostic citizen;
6 the perpetuity of the *contrasts between State and Church*, and therefore the impossibility of drawing up rigid and stable borders. Such conflicts are rooted in diverse inner attitudes and assessments of reality rather than in criteria of objective and rigorous rationality;
7 a *historical-political vision* of State/Church relations that connects, without confusing, the legal factor with history and politics, and that values the decisive weight of citizens' *religious sentiment* rather than the legal structure of religious institutions. This aspect led Jemolo, around 1960, to take an interest in the religious sociology of Gabriel Le Bras in order to grasp the phenomena of secularization and to stress the distance between the *prescribed* and *practiced religiousness.*

The figure of Jemolo as a jurist covers the entire span of Italian legal theory: from the early decades of the twentieth century to the methodological turn of the sixties. Despite some involvement with the fascist regime, due not so much to political opportunism as to fidelity to the principle of legality,[30] his teaching is to be considered "the common heritage of the legal culture—and not only legal—of this century" from the point of view of method in the study of relations between states and churches, of the approach to the problem of religious freedom, and of historical-legal research in the field of canon law and ecclesiastical law.[31]

His fundamental maxim was the duty never to stray from the paths of freedom, even when the stakes involved what he considered "the supreme good, to have people believe in God, and follow Christian law."[32] For Jemolo, religious freedom is never a final achievement; it must always be defended, respected, and extended through education to reason and aversion to violence.[33] Hence the need to overcome all prejudice and the need for clarity and impartiality: a sort of *ethical skepticism* applied to law as to ideologies. We need to combat the elements of confusion hidden in conventional language and thought, which mostly result from conformist attitudes. Precisely because of his antidogmatic and nonconformist character, he called himself a man of doubt, or even a "mal-pensant."

The jurist's task too can be summed up in his duty of "clarification" towards citizens. It is a matter of distinguishing the lust for power from the power of the law, of eliminating the confusion between the law of today and that of tomorrow, of persuading citizens that justice and legality are intrinsically different. The jurist must also clarify the articulation of demands for justice in different social spheres:

the "religious society" that embodies the culmination of justice for the believer; the "political group" that, in view of carrying out a common program, requires greater solidarity from its members; the *civitas*, where the law "establishes only the minimum ethic necessary for an orderly coexistence," leaving to morality the stimulus for citizens to achieve "much more than that minimum."[34]

Jemolo was often described as a "liberal Catholic"; in fact he would have rejected this label too, although he preferred to be called a "liberal and Catholic." He was a deeply liberal man, who defended the value of the state and freedom unflinchingly, even against the degeneration of political terrorism, and at the same time a deeply Catholic man, who remained always faithful to the Church of Rome and always criticized reform movements that did not come from within it.[35] In any case, Jemolo lived and accepted first of all in himself the challenge of contrasting liberal and Catholic values, maturing a rare awareness of the conflict between the external and the internal forum.

Notes

1 During his long career as a lawyer, Jemolo collected notes and comments in *Gli occhiali del giurista.*
2 His bibliography exceeds 950 titles. See Cassandro, Leoni, and Vecchi, 53–190.
3 Francesco Ruffini (1863–1934), renowned scholar of ecclesiastical law and author of the classic *Religious Liberty.*
4 This work, published in Turin in 1948, received five editions and five reprints until 1990. See bibliography for French and English translations.
5 Croce, "Stato e Chiesa," (1931].
6 For the historical-legal method: Jemolo, *La questione della proprietà ecclesiastica.* For the sentimental and not only doctrinal conception of religious life: Jemolo, *Il giansenismo.*
7 Jemolo, "La classifica dei rapporti."
8 Jemolo, "Posizione particolare."
9 Jemolo, *Premesse*, 9; Jemolo, *Lezioni*, 5th ed., 31.
10 See Cesarini Sforza, Jemolo, and Pugliatti, *La polemica.*
11 Jemolo, *Il matrimonio nel diritto canonico*; Jemolo, *Il matrimonio.* In his writing "La famiglia e il diritto," (1949), Jemolo stated that "the family always appears as an island that the sea of law can touch, but only touch."
12 Jemolo, *Il matrimonio*, 19.
13 Jemolo, "Sul concetto di interesse religioso," in Jemolo, *Tra diritto e storia*, 115–33.
14 Jemolo, *Premesse ai rapporti*, 1–4.
15 See Alessandro Ferrari, "State and Churches in Italy."
16 Jemolo, *Premesse ai rapporti*, 89.
17 Ibid., 85.
18 Jemolo, *Coscienza laica*, 35–44.
19 Ibid., 42. See also Jemolo, *La crisi dello Stato moderno*, 150–1.
20 Jemolo, *Coscienza laica*, 44.
21 Jemolo, *Lezioni*, 2nd ed., 26–7.
22 Ibid., 27–30.
23 Jemolo, *Lezioni*, 5th ed., 68–78. Jemolo's position was prompted by a well-known legal case in 1958. The bishop of Prato had indicated as "public concubines" a couple married in civil ceremony and had excluded them from any participation in religious activities as "public sinners."

24 Ibid., 85–119.
25 Jemolo, "Vilipendio."
26 Jemolo, *Costume e diritto*, 470.
27 Jemolo, "Posizione particolare," 208.
28 Jemolo, *Problemi pratici della libertà*, 130.
29 Ibid., 68.
30 See Fantappiè, "Il conflitto delle fedeltà."
31 Gismondi; De Luca, "Jemolo 'canonista'"; Spinelli; Berlingò.
32 Jemolo, "Posizione particolare," 207.
33 Jemolo, *Lezioni*, 5th ed., 25.
34 Jemolo, "Attività intellettuale e vita morale."
35 See Fantappiè, *Arturo Carlo Jemolo*, 91–147.

Bibliography

Accademia Nazionale dei Lincei. "Arturo Carlo Jemolo tra diritto e cultura." In *Giornata lincea nel centenario della nascita di Arturo Carlo Jemolo. Atti dei Convegni Lincei, Roma 18 dicembre 1991*. Roma: Accademia Nazionale dei Lincei, 1993.

Bellini, Piero. "Il contributo metodologico di Aldo Checchini e Arturo Carlo Jemolo alla scienza del diritto ecclesiastico e il significato del loro magistero." In *La tradizione dottrinale nel diritto ecclesiastico*, edited by Mario Tedeschi, 54–84. Napoli: Jovene, 1994.

Berlingò, Salvatore. "Jemolo e il diritto canonico." In *La lezione di un maestro. Atti del Convegno in memoria di Arturo Carlo Jemolo (Torino, 8 giugno 2001)*, edited by Rinaldo Bertolino and Ilaria Zuanazzi, 115–37. Turin: Giappichelli, 2005.

Cassandro, Giorgia, Alessia Leoni, and Fabio Vecchi, eds. *Arturo Carlo Jemolo. Vita ed opere di un italiano illustre: un professore dell'Università di Roma*. Naples: Jovene, 2007.

Cesarini Sforza, Widar, Arturo Carlo Jemolo, and Salvatore Pugliatti. *La polemica sui concetti giuridici*, edited by Natalino Irti. Milan: Giuffrè, 2004.

Croce, Benedetto. "Stato e Chiesa in senso ideale e loro perpetua lotta nella storia." In id., *Etica e politica*, 394–400. Milan: Adelphi, 1994.

Dalla Torre, Giuseppe. *Un altro Jemolo*. Rome: Edizioni Studium, 2013.

De Luca, Luigi. *Diritto ecclesiastico ed esperienza giuridica*. Milan: Giuffrè, 1976.

De Luca, Luigi. "Jemolo 'canonista'." *Il diritto ecclesiastico* 83 (1982): 25–32.

Fantappiè, Carlo. *Arturo Carlo Jemolo. Riforma religiosa e laicità dello Stato*. Brescia: Morcelliana, 2011.

Fantappiè, Carlo. "Il conflitto delle fedeltà: Arturo Carlo Jemolo e il fascismo." In *I giuristi e il fascino del regime (1918–1925)*, edited by Italo Birocchi and Luca Loschiavo, 159–90. Rome: Roma Tre-Press, 2015.

Ferrari, Alessandro. "State and Churches in Italy: From Liberal Separation to Democratic Laicità." *Jahrbuch für Europäische Verwaltungsgeschichte* 14 (2002): 1–42.

Ferrari, Silvio. *Ideologia e dogmatica nel diritto ecclesiastico italiano. Manuali e riviste 1929–1979*. Milan: Giuffrè, 1979.

Galante Garrone, Alessandro. *I miei maggiori*, 225–50. Milan: Garzanti, 1984.

Gismondi, Pietro. "Jemolo, lo studioso di diritto ecclesiastico." *Il diritto ecclesiastico* 83 (1982): 24.

Jemolo, Arturo Carlo. "Attività intellettuale e vita morale." *Archivio di filosofia* 14 (1945): 122–3.

Jemolo, Arturo Carlo. *Chiesa e stato in Italia dal Risorgimento ad oggi*. Turin: Einaudi, 1948. French translation: *L'Eglise et L'Etat en Italie, du Risorgimento à nos jours*. Paris: Editions du Seuil, 1960; English translation: *Church and State in Italy, 1850–1950*. Oxford: Blackwell, 1960.

Jemolo, Arturo Carlo. *Coscienza laica*. Edited by Carlo Fantappiè. Brescia: Morcelliana, 2008.

Jemolo, Arturo Carlo. *Costume e diritto*. Vicenza: Neri Pozza, 1968.

Jemolo, Arturo Carlo. *Gli occhiali del giurista*. 2 vols. Padua: Cedam, 1970 and 1985.

Jemolo, Arturo Carlo. *Il giansenismo in Italia prima della rivoluzione*. Bari: Laterza, 1928.

Jemolo, Arturo Carlo. *Il matrimonio*. Turin: Utet, 1961.

Jemolo, Arturo Carlo. *Il matrimonio nel diritto canonico*. Milan: Vallardi, 1941; new edition Bologna: Il Mulino, 1993.

Jemolo, Arturo Carlo. "La classifica dei rapporti tra Stato e Chiesa." *Archivio giuridico "Filippo Serafini"* 99 (1938): 3–31.

Jemolo, Arturo Carlo. *La crisi dello Stato moderno*. Bari: Laterza, 1954; new edition Rome/Bari: Laterza, 1991.

Jemolo, Arturo Carlo. *La questione della proprietà ecclesiastica nel Regno di Sardegna e nel Regno d'Italia durante il quarantennio 1848–1888*. Turin: Bocca, 1911; new edition Bologna: Il Mulino, 1974.

Jemolo, Arturo Carlo. *Lezioni di diritto ecclesiastico. Il diritto ecclesiastico dello Stato italiano*. 2nd ed. Città di Castello: Tipografia Leonardo da Vinci, 1934; 5th ed. Milan: Giuffrè, 1979.

Jemolo, Arturo Carlo. "Posizione particolare della Chiesa Cattolica." *Il diritto ecclesiastico* 80 (1969): 206.

Jemolo, Arturo Carlo. *Premesse ai rapporti tra Chiesa e Stato*. Milan: Giuffrè, 1965.

Jemolo, Arturo Carlo. *Problemi pratici della libertà*. 2nd ed. Milan: Giuffrè, 1972.

Jemolo, Arturo Carlo. *Stato e Chiesa negli scrittori politici italiani del Seicento e del Settecento*. Turin: Bocca, 1914; new edition Naples: Morano, 1972.

Jemolo, Arturo Carlo. *Tra diritto e storia (1960–1980)*. Milan: Giuffrè, 1982.

Jemolo, Arturo Carlo. "Vilipendio: delitto o contravvenzione?" *La cultura* (1964): 337ff.

Lariccia, Sergio. *Arturo Carlo Jemolo. Un giurista nell'Italia del Novecento*. Rome: Carocci, 2015.

Margiotta Broglio, Francesco. "Jemolo, Arturo Carlo." In *Dizionario Biografico degli Italiani*. Vol. 62, 196–201. Rome: Istituto per la Enciclopedia Italiana, 2004.

Pertici, Roberto. *Chiesa e Stato in Italia. Dalla Grande Guerra al nuovo Concordato (1914–1984)*. Bologna: Il Mulino, 2009.

Ruffini, Francesco. *Religious Liberty*. Translated by J. Parker Heyes, with a preface by J.B. Bury. London: Williams/Norgate/New York: G.P. Putnam's Sons, 1912.

Spinelli, Lorenzo. "I rapporti tra Stato e Chiesa nella dottrina di Jemolo." *Il diritto ecclesiastico* 83 (1982): 33–9.

Valbusa, Paolo. *I pensieri di un malpensante. Jemolo e trentacinque anni di vita repubblicana*. Venice: Marsilio, 2008.

26 Giovanni Battista Montini (Pope Paul VI) (1897–1978)

Jean-Pierre Schouppe

Biographical note

Giovanni Battista Montini, born on September 26, 1897, in Concesio, in the Italian province of Brescia, was the second child of Giorgio Montini and Giuditta Alghisi. His father was a legal expert, representing the Catholic movement in his province and directing the review *Il Cittadino di Brescia*. After studying in a Jesuit primary school and graduating for A levels in the public school of Arnaldo da Brescia, Giovanni Battista entered the local seminary as a day student. Nurtured in a Catholic environment that was both patriotic and open to progress, he was well aware of the dangers of modernity. His oratory school teachers constantly reminded him of them. Searching for an innovation-friendly apologetics, he founded the periodical *La Fionda* in 1918 (with Andrea Trebeschi). On May 29, 1920, he was ordained priest in the Brescia Cathedral. A few months, later he became a boarding student in the Lombard College of Rome before entering the Academy of Ecclesiastical Nobles in November 1921. This is the diplomatic academy of the Holy See and was his first direct connection to the legal field.

As attaché to the nunciature of Warsaw for a few months, in 1923 he was appointed ecclesiastical assistant of the Roman Circle of the FUCI, the Italian Catholic Universities Federation, while pursuing his legal academic training. He received his *laurea* in canon law at the Law Faculty of Milan (in December 1922), supplemented by a civil law degree at the *Utriusque iuris* Institute of the Palazzo dell'Apollinare (July 3, 1924). At the start of the academic year, beginning October 1, and at the behest of Cardinal Giuseppe Pizzardo, Montini began serving as attaché to the secretary of state. He seems to have enjoyed the tasks entrusted to him by the Roman Dicastery less than he did the training activities taken up at the FUCI, for which he became a national ecclesiastical assistant in October 1925.[1] In 1930–37, he was in charge of teaching pontifical diplomatic history at the *Utriusque Iuris* Institute of the Apollinare. On March 9, 1933, he resigned from his national ecclesiastical assistantship at the FUCI. On December 13, 1937, he was appointed deputy secretary of state. In 1939 he founded the information office for prisoners of war, including Jews, before creating the *Ecclesia* review three years later. On November 29, 1952, he was promoted to the post of vice secretary of state for general affairs, thereby reaching the height of his influence on Pope Pius XII. Yet on November 1, 1954, Pius appointed him archbishop of Milan. This decision was subject to a number of diverging interpretations: was it an alienation from the Roman Curia? A preliminary stage for the papacy? Both reasons at once?[2] In any event, his nomination to the archdiocese of Milan should not be interpreted as a form of punishment but as an ideal pastoral preparation. He would indeed be consecrated cardinal in the Basilica of St. Peter, but not until December 15, 1958—and on the basis of a decision made by the successor to Pius XII.[3]

His pontificate began in June 1963. The two main challenges he met were the continuation of the Second Vatican Council, launched by John XXIII, as well as its correct implementation. This council enabled the Catholic Church to proceed with a cautious *aggiornamento*, a reform of the Church in its continuity, as Pope Benedict XVI later emphasized in his famous speech to the Roman Curia. As much as the council deserves credit for its promulgated acts, it would be inappropriate to diminish the relative importance of the part played by Paul VI in them. In his station of "pope within the council,"[4] he intervened actively, sometimes even energetically, during certain sessions, reserving to his own authority some particularly touchy issues: clerical celibacy, responsible fatherhood, and the invocation of Mary as Mother of the Church.

The implementation of Vatican II clearly concerned itself with canon law, and in particular a reform of the 1917 Code of Canon Law that John XXIII had announced in convening the council. The Code's reviewing *coetus*, or study group, set up on March 25, 1963, was supported by Pope Paul throughout his entire pontificate. The promulgation of a double codification—the Latin and the Eastern codes—later materialized under John Paul II's pontificate: the Code of Canon Law (*Codex iuris canonici*, or CIC, 1983) and the Code of Canons of the Eastern Churches (*Codex canonum ecclesiarum orientalium*, or CCEO, 1990). Paul VI, to his credit, promoted many other projects and the promulgation of several canon standards: the Roman Curia's reform, the promotion of the Synod of Bishops, the amendment of procedures for papal elections, the modernization of Vatican diplomacy, the recasting of the nuncio's function, and so on.

Paul VI died on August 6, 1978, in his Castel Gandolfo residence. He was declared blessed on October 19, 2014, and canonized on October 14, 2018.

His main contributions to law

As a student, Montini probably would have preferred to research ecclesiastical history, yet he dedicated himself to a diplomatic career and taught pontifical diplomacy at the Apollinare. Moreover, he invested himself passionately in the formation of young Italian academics from the FUCI, whom he endeavored to steer clear of fascist brain washing. The political career of Alcide De Gasperi is a telling illustration of Montini's own activities. While having a classical intellectual foundation, Paul VI was an admirer of the philosopher Jacques Maritain. He therefore believed in dialoguing with modern culture and preferred to distance himself from other less open-minded Catholics with respect to contemporary issues. This was one of the reasons why he decided to resign from the FUCI.[5]

His work as secretary of state seemed increasingly a humdrum, if not embarrassing, burden: treaties concluded by the Holy See implied a certain level of connivance with fascist or Nazi regimes; thus one could hardly marvel at the signing of the concordat with Germany or the Lateran Pact, despite their undeniable importance for the independence and recognition of the legal entity of the Holy See. The *addetto* nonetheless applied his know-how and expertise to it so successfully as to attain the position of deputy representative of the secretary of state.

The main legal contributions of Paul VI being the red thread of this chapter, it seems befitting to identify them clearly. In the absence of substantial or outstanding legal publications, his main contributions probably came from his diplomatic and canonical activity at the service of the Catholic Church. First, in his role as a player on the Vatican II stage, he (sometimes energetically) steered bills towards certain essential directions. Second, his activity as a legislator and canon law reformer holds a prominent place. To this we should add an international chapter, seeing his career in the light of battles he fought for human rights and religious freedom while serving pontifical diplomacy and concordats as a pope. Last, we should note his work of promoting ecumenism as well as some of his ad hoc interventions in major ethical issues.

Paul VI as a player in Vatican II

As the archbishop of Milan, Montini had done his best to prepare the clergy and the organized laity for the great event of the Second Vatican Council with an appropriate pastoral. Two documents he drafted in person, the *Votum* and the pastoral letter *Pensiamo al Concilio*, should be noted. In the beginning, however, he experienced some disappointment because of a number of factors: the often-mediocre quality of the antiquated patterns developed by the Roman Curia, the absence of a comprehensive plan, and a lack of true leadership. After the death of John XXIII, on May 31, 1963, Paul VI received the council in inheritance—and gradually attempted to remedy its shortfalls. New patterns were conceived of in broader circles that included academic ecclesiastics worldwide. In parallel to this, moderating bishops from various nationalities were appointed to better inspire the council's work.

In the ecclesiastical field, Paul VI remained careful to denounce conciliary theses which tended to emerge in the course of collegial discussions. The *Nota Riservata* written by Bishop Larraona on the *De Ecclesia* blueprint especially concerned him. Its disclosure on the night before the third session of the council preempted the stated pattern of amendments just before the convening of the actual session. Regarding the substance of the *Nota*, the pope wondered whether it might not turn out to be contradictory to admit two supreme sources of authority in the Church. Would such a formula risk favoring a drift from monarchy to diarchy and therefore strike a blow to a dimension of divine law? So he sent a firm call for order in a handwritten manuscript dated October 18, 1964.

A synthesis suggested by Father Wilhelm Bertrams, a canon lawyer from the Gregorian University, inspired in him the notion of collegiality. Starting from the Tridentine debates, this Jesuit exploited the distinction between divine and human law:

> The episcopal function is of divine law inasmuch as in the episcopal consecration are entrusted the gift of the Holy Spirit and the power to rule the Church. . . . [T]he episcopal function [also] belongs to human law, as the canonical mandate clearly establishes the scope and power extensions conferred onto the consecrated one."[6]

A number of theologians deemed inconceivable that the existence of the College of Bishops should depend at all on a canonical decision by the pope and considered such legal distinctions as perfect examples of "legalism." However, in the specific case of Paul VI, such legal distinctions represented the royal path he needed to conciliate the primacy of the pontifical prerogatives with the college's rights. By May/June 1964, he submitted to the doctrinal commission a series of amendments to the *De Ecclesia* text.

The end of the third session of the council was marked by several personal interventions into points of engagement by Paul VI in accordance with his convictions. One of these communications made on his initiative to the assembly concerned the *Nota explicativa prævia*, which he wished to add to the Church's constitution *Lumen gentium*, so as to restrict the scope of this text on episcopal collegiality. He emphasized the fact that the

> Collegium is not to be understood in a strictly legal understanding of the word, that is as a group of peers, who would delegate their power to the president, but rather as a stable group, whose structure and authority must be deduced from revelation.

This second aspect would point to a couple of conditions required in order to become a member of the College of Bishops: "episcopal consecration and hierarchical communion with the head of the college and other members." This communication made a clear distinction between the sacramental—and divine—basis of the College of Bishops, on one hand, and, on the other hand, the concrete exercise of that collegial power which, according to Paul VI, depended on canonical decisions made according to standards approved by the supreme authority. Bertrams's idea manifested itself in filigree here: if the episcopal function (*munus*) of divine law is conferred by sacrament, power (*potestas*) requires the pope through his canonical mission to intervene by means of hierarchical communion. The other points of the *Nota* aimed at preventing the risk of both a diarchical government and a conciliatory drift, bearing in mind that the essential aim was to avoid making a cleavage between "the Roman prelate and the bishops" but rather to extol one "between the Roman prelate alone and the Roman prelate taken as a solidary whole with his bishops."

Among other suitable interventions by Paul VI, here in relation to the Eucharist, was the encyclical *Mysterium fidei*, which states quite clearly the sacrificial nature of the mass, the real presence, and the matter of transubstantiation. Within the conciliary assembly, he took a stance regarding divine revelation which, after Archbishop Bea's intervention, turned out to trigger a nearly unanimous approval of the *Dei Verbum* constitution.

Paul VI, canon law reformer

Time magazine's headline referring to the pope in September 1965 was titled a "Reluctant Revolutionary," because the reforms then started at Vatican II were only at their very beginning. The reforming will of Paul VI focused essentially on reforming the Church with respect to liturgy and the three main areas of the Roman Curia, the bishops' synod, and the holy college.

At a liturgical level, the *Sacrosanctum Concilium* constitution was intended not to initiate any new rite; it simply established a framework of law for the general restoration of liturgy. Its purpose was to promote a better turnout of the faithful by resorting to national languages and adapting liturgies to the various local traditions. A few weeks after the promulgation of the constitution, on January 25, 1964, the *Consilium ad exsequendam Constitutionem de Sacra Liturgia* was founded, attended by forty-two bishops and presided over by Archbishop Lercaro. His main task consisted in implementing and revising the liturgical reform and texts, so as to facilitate the involvement of the faithful, but also to introduce the use of vernacular languages during concelebrations and communions. The Latin language originally was to be replaced only partially (outside the canon); the concept then spread under the influence of episcopal conferences, which enjoyed vast competences in this field. Paul VI was under a lot of pressure, so much so that after the consultation process with the ad hoc commission, he agreed to have all of the canon of the mass translated. Letting go of the obligation to use Latin to celebrate the Eucharist, although derogations were foreseen, was perceived by many as an irredeemable loss of the universal language of the Church, compounded by inaccurate liturgical translations or transpositions. The Roman Missal of St. Pius V (1570) was replaced by a *Novus Ordo* after April 3, 1969. Following numerous criticisms, a revised new edition of "Paul VI's missal" was published, in which the sacrificial nature of mass as well as the substantial presence of Christ throughout the Eucharist were more clearly spelled out. Although this major liturgical reform, not always easily managed or controlled by the *Consilium*, was not faultlessly exempt from some regrettable negative side effects still perceivable to this day, the positive benefits reaped by the faithful from this reformed liturgy are to be credited to Paul VI.

The motu proprio *Ecclesiae Sanctae* (August 6, 1966) established new norms for implementing the Vatican Council, namely, the adoption of new structures, such as the episcopal conferences, the personal prelatures, the presbyterial council, the college of consultors, the pastoral council, and others.

Another crucial stake of this reform was the Roman Curia's reform. Some people favored internationalization of the Curia, while others wanted its replacement by a holy college of the universal Church, like that of the Melkite patriarch of Antioch. The conciliary decree on the pastoral task of bishops, *Christus Dominus*, called for a "new organization" of the Curia. The experience acquired by Paul VI in his former role of deputy to the State Secretariat made him an ideal candidate for becoming the kingpin of such a reform. In his first speech to the Curia, he had asked it to back up his project in order to set the aggiornamento example, wished for by John XXIII. A phenomenon then took place, described by Cardinal Ratzinger, as a decoupling of the ancient "Curia-papacy" loyalty to form a new one: "papacy-council."[7]

The reform took place gradually by a step-by-step approach, congregation after congregation. Thus, the replacement of the Holy Office by the Congregation for the Doctrine of the Faith made the former lose its inquisitorial character as well as its prominence. The Apostolic Constitution *Regimini Ecclesiae Universae* (August 15, 1967) instituted a global reform of the Curia in the wake of those adopted by Sixtus V (1588) and Pius X (1908).[8] The State Secretariat was strengthened, assuming a prime role in coordination and control at the expense of the Congregations. "Public Affairs" (formerly the "first section of Extraordinary Affairs") were taken away from the State Secretariat's portfolio. A new body, the Prefecture for Economic Affairs of the Holy See, henceforth would coordinate the Holy See's administration of assets. The limitation of curial offices to a renewable maximum of five years and age limits were among the novelties. The reform was overall quite welcome, even though some wished that it had been bolder.

Structural reforms extended to the pontifical court and the Vatican's finances. On March 28, 1968, several decisions were taken concerning them.[9] The suppression of the pontifical state had rendered a pontifical court not only superfluous but wholly inappropriate. It was therefore to be replaced by a pontifical household, and a series of tasks and functions of a purely honorific and hereditary nature were suppressed by the same token (motu proprio *Pontificalis Domus*, March 28, 1968). The pope renounced his tiara, ecclesiastical titles were simplified (only apostolic prothonotaries, prelates of honor, and chaplains remained); guard corps were reduced to three (the Swiss Guard, the Palatine Guard, and the papal police); and the same day, a consulting body for the Vatican City State was established (motu proprio *Una struttura particolare*).

Fiscal consolidation of the Holy See and the Vatican was yet another kettle of fish. The president of the Bank of Rome, Vittorio Veronese, addressed to Paul VI a report (1963) (conserved in the Istituto Sturzo of Rome) which indicated several sensitive points in matters of transparency and monitoring of activities of the Institute of Religious Works (IOR). He made repeated attempts to address the issue, writing a letter to the private secretary of the pope, Don Pasquale Macchi. In 1967, following a decision by the Italian government, tax exemptions in the

Vatican were limited and shares of the IOR were sold among Italian companies, without questioning the autonomy of the institute as such.

The synod of bishops represented another major objective. It was commonly admitted that an ecclesiological readjustment in favor of the bishops' college was needed after Vatican I had put the emphasis on the Roman pontiff's infallibility without having had time to inquire in depth about the specific role of diocesan bishops. The synod as a consultative body of the episcopate filled the need for a readjustment in favor of the implementation of the collegiality principle, but the modalities of its implementation required a period of running in. Moreover, it was necessary to decentralize the Church's government by granting more competences to the bishops' conferences, which involved a certain amount of risk. The Italian Episcopal Conference (CEI), under the stewardship of Cardinal Siri, seemed at times to serve as a bastion of resistance for what was later called the Vatican II "minority" work. The call for loyally contributing to the success of the council launched by the pope was not immediately followed, so he had to appoint a new chair to the college—Cardinal Giovanni Colombo. Gifted with new statutes, the CEI turned into a true plenary body of the Italian episcopate.

The first bishops' synod kicked off in Rome on September 29, 1967 and lasted a month. Paul VI had determined its objectives: to thicken the link between the pope and bishops while supporting the former in the exercise of his ministry. If the synod did reflect the "image" of the council as well as its "spirit and method,"[10] it nonetheless distinguished itself from the council by its composition, authority, and objectives. The lack of concrete results from the synod demonstrated the fact that its modus operandi still lacked efficiency, while a number of leaks and infringements on the confidentiality principle were to be deplored at the coordination center for communications of the synod, which resulted in an increased divergence from the pope's vision for the nature and functions of that synod.

The next episode opened during the extraordinary synod on October 11, 1969, with a speech by the pope in the Sistine Chapel. To certain declarations made by Cardinal Suenens on the subject of "co-responsibility" within the Church, Paul VI countered that the Church was no democracy, and that the supreme responsibility entrusted to Peter and his successors could not be conditioned by the authority, as high as it might be, of the episcopal college, whose authority (said he) we are first in wanting to honor, but which would not exist if the pope did not accept their vote.[11] In the synod's conclusions, he quelled the bishops' claims regarding the conference reports of the bishops and the Holy See, and he tempered the reinforcement of the expertise of the synod's secretariat.

Promoting episcopal collegiality could lead one to think that "cardinalcy" and the pope's election within a conclave made of cardinals no longer were topical to the agenda. During the 1969 synod, the desire was expressed for the synod to play a more active part in the pope's election. The synod therefore started summoning ordinary public consistories, the third of which specified the mutual complementarity between the bishops' and the cardinals' collegia, while stressing their consultative nature, subordinate to the supreme office of the Vicar of Christ. In his effort to remain faithful to tradition, Paul VI also saw the need for incorporating some adjustments to the conclave. He excluded cardinals over eighty years old (motu proprio *Ingravescentem Aetatem*, November 21, 1970). He gave up on the idea of associating to the College of Cardinals some of the synod's representatives elected at the general council of this very synod's secretariat. And finally, by limiting to 120 the maximum number of electors (Ap. Const. *Romano Pontefice eligendo*, October 1, 1975), he instilled a new life into the conclave.

To close down the chapter concerning institutional reforms, we should further highlight the support granted by Paul VI to the *Codex* reform, initiated shortly before the start of his pontificate, as well as to the *Lex Fundamentalis Ecclesiae* project. If the latter certainly contributed to improving the *imago Ecclesiae* and to giving a fundamental normative base to the Latin and Oriental Catholic Churches, it is also true that the spirit of the times was imbued with so much anti-legalism that many simply were not ready for such a goal. Nevertheless, these realizations made it possible to start a salutary questioning, and several canons—among others, those touching on the fundamental rights and obligations of the faithful of the Church—found their place in the two codes then in progress.

Paul VI and international law

Paul VI expanded his presence at the Holy See on the international front in several ways. This section focuses on four of those ways: pontifical diplomacy, the promotion of human rights, the defense of religious freedom, and the ICO.

Among the reforms affecting international law, one should take a close look at pontifical representatives. Indeed, as the former professor of the history of nunciatures at the Apollinare Academy, Paul VI was fully aware of the complementarities between papal diplomacy and the ecclesial mission,[12] and he knew very well that the surrender of diplomatic representation that some seemed to call upon—as if it were a simple remnant of the pre-conciliary "perfect legal society"—was unfounded. The *Sollicitudo omnium Ecclesiarum* motu proprio of June 24, 1969, had to meet the requirements formulated by the conciliary decree on bishops: by defining more clearly the role of nuncios in contrast with that of diocesan bishops, and by further internationalizing the nuncios' office. If this document states indeed that the pontifical representative (nuncio) should not hamper the pastoral activity of bishops, thereby meeting the expectations of a majority of the episcopate, it also reiterates the supreme pontiff's prerogatives over local churches. A dual momentum is therefore imparted: an inward pull towards the heart of the Church and another pull towards the pope that moves back (via the nuncios) towards the periphery. The nuncio should be a bishop embodying papal presence to and for each particular church. This mainly concerns the *ad intra* diplomacy, which, contrary to the 1917 Code, benefits from a priority status without the *ad extra* diplomacy being neglected. The exclusive right to represent the Church to other states or international bodies and organizations is strongly recalled, making sure to make no concessions to the affirmations of *Gaudium et spes* number 76c or to the future canon 362 of the CIC 1983, regarding the papal right to appoint and send out legates *ad intra et ad extra* (canon originating directly in the CIC 1917). As for the concordat policy, it fared even better than simply overriding qualified criticism, by winning over "antipublicist" prejudices while adjusting the concordat instrument to the needs of the present.[13]

Since the *Pacem in terris* encyclical of John XXIII, the social mandate of the Catholic Church appealed not only to classical natural law but also to human rights. If Pius XII had not deemed it wise to approve the Universal Declaration of Human Rights in 1948, John XXIII did so in *Pacem in terris*, while maintaining certain reservations. These concern mainly the lack of clarity with respect to the foundation of human rights, given the ambiguity of the concept of human dignity, especially when interpreted in an immanentist way, lending itself to political and ideological manipulation. If the Catholic magisterium often adopted a negative tone in its declarations à propos public liberties and human rights, it was largely owing to a specific liberal and modern nineteenth-century context that clearly displayed aggressive antipathy towards the Church. Since those days, human rights have entered the "signs of the time" to which the Church intended to pay tribute. Paul VI followed in the steps of John XXIII in promoting human rights. Among other statements, he delivered a well-received speech in front of the United Nations General Assembly, in which he morally ratified the institution and presented the Holy See as "expert in humanity."[14]

The Catholic magisterium currently backs human rights in their universal, inalienable dimension, which fosters among others the respect for any person's religious freedom, whether believer or not, and also for any religious or philosophical grouping. The pope's visit to the UN took place the day after the approval of the declaration on religious freedom (adopted with a large majority of votes); it could thus be tagged a papal "UN passport."[15]

In total attunement with *Dignitatis humanae*, which Paul VI bravely defended—from its provisory format to the end of the third conciliary session—in the light of the American theologian John Courtney's quite decisive contribution and that of his Italian colleague Pietro Pavan, the courageous bet was to treat religious freedom as a fundamental "civil right," thus breaking off from the traditional attitude of analyzing issues primarily or even exclusively in terms of "truth rights." Without denying the existence of a moral obligation for each and every person to search for the truth and try to conform his or her behavior to it (a duty that the text often reminds readers of, at the explicit request of Paul VI), a legal space had been created to host the fundamental right of religious truth: namely a fundamental right possessed by any member of civil society by dint of his or her human dignity, whether in the right or wrong with respect to the revelation's truths. The following sentence of the declaration expresses in a particularly satisfying way the notion lying at the core of religious freedom as a fundamental right: it is paramount that "in religious matter, none be ever constrained to act against his conscience nor impeded to act within fair limits, according to his conscience, whether in private in public, alone or in association with others" (Decl. *Dignitatis humanae*, number 2). Despite this "negative" formulation of religious (individual) freedom, the declaration recognizes in its number 4 a community base or institutional dimension as well as a description of its main contents.

Conciliary documents should be read in a consistent manner, each in the light of the others. In terms of religious freedom, the declaration should thus be completed by the broader—and more "positive"—picture given by *Libertas Ecclesiae*, as *Gaudium et spes* explains. Its number 76c exposes the major "publicists'" principles meant to govern relations between the Catholic Church and political community: independence of the Church and State, each in its respective sphere, as well as the promotion as much as possible of various forms of cooperation between the two. All agreements, even informal ones, are welcome. The concordat as a legal tool is not explicitly mentioned, but it is fair to ask whether it was meant to be, in a concilium of such highly pastoral nature. Since then, the multiplication of bilateral international treaties amply attests to the implicit presence of this legal instrument throughout conciliary thought. With *Dignitatis humanæ*, the Catholic Church does have a cornerstone text to serve as the basis of article 18 of the Universal Declaration of Human Rights (1948) and of article 9 of the European Convention for Human Rights (1950); but let us not forget that it anticipates by a few years article 18 of the UN's international Pact Relating to Civic and Political Rights (1966), and it would therefore be acclaimed as a source of inspiration by many religious academic, legal, and political circles.

Paul VI supported the *Ostpolitik* consistently carried out by Cardinal Casaroli under the last months of John XXIII's pontificate. The aim was to bet on negotiation and peaceful coexistence in order to obtain at least a minimal degree of liberty for local churches and peace in relationship to the Soviet Union. These basic principles worked well together with Montini's old-time determination not to take a position between both superpowers and to stay *super partes*. He also encouraged the Helsinki conference and, in general, any work carried out in the framework of the Conference (later Organization) for Security and Cooperation in Europe, which led to significant results in the field of religious freedom.

Finally, resorting to the legal form of the International Catholic Organizations (ICO)—now abandoned—enabled a proactive and diversified Church presence on the international stage, with the support of the Information Center of the ICOs of Geneva.[16]

Paul VI's magisterium is extremely dense. It encompasses everything from the programmatic encyclical *Ecclesiam suam*, which established the tone of dialogue for the pontificate, all the way through to its spiritual will, as his exhortation Ap. Const. *Evangelii nuntiandi* (December 8, 1975) is often considered to be, even though it was not literally his last writ. In those different writings, he addresses several times the issue of human rights as well as various aspects of the Church's social doctrine. How could we not mention the *Populorum Progressio* encyclical (March 26, 1967), the prophetic content of which can be summed up in just one sentence—still as topical as ever nowadays: "Development is peace's new name."[17] Four years later, with *Octogesima adveniens* on the occasion of the eightieth anniversary of the *Rerum Novarum* encyclical, he drew Christians' attention to upcoming issues such as urbanization, immigration, and ecology.

Ecumenism and ethics

Pope John XXIII made a point of promoting ecumenism among the main objectives of Vatican II: it was the first ecumenical concilium to which non-Catholic observers were invited. Paul VI shared this open-mindedness. Suffice it to note the contacts he selected among the reformist churches as deputy representatives, then even as archbishops.[18] Whereas initially the issue of religious freedom had been intertwined with ecumenism, the coordination commission decided in April 1964 to turn the chapter on religious freedom and ecumenism into a separate declaration, which would eventually develop into *Dignitatis humanae*, and to dedicate a specific text to that subject. This document on ecumenism was subjected to heated debates and numerous amendments. When it was about to be put to the ballot, Paul VI announced the introduction of about twenty changes by authority. This was the third decision he made "in conscience" by the end of the third session, in order to safeguard the truth and doctrine of the Church, while resting assured of the support of a majority of its conciliary fathers. This attitude, perceived as quite "directive," created some serious tensions but did not prevent the text from being quasi unanimously adopted, on November 21, 1964. The decree on ecumenism (*Unitatis redintegratio*) thus was born. It was later accompanied by supporting documents: the decree on Eastern Catholic churches (*Orientalium Ecclesiarum*) and the declaration *Nostra Ætate* on non-Christian religions. The lifting of the anathemas between the Roman and Byzantine churches (1965) and the suspension *a divinis* of Monsignor Lefebvre (1976) count among his strong actions.

Next to "Paul VI's creed," certain moral debates need further signaling under the aegis of his pontificate: the publication of a number of articles in the *Concilium* review and the promulgation of a Dutch catechism inflamed passions. From 1965, Cardinal Ottaviani had drawn the pope's attention to some possible moral hazards. Paul VI finally was drawn into the anxiety generated by the turn of events. A crisis in the priesthood already was in full swing. Paul VI firmly defended priests' celibacy in the *Sacerdotalis Cælibatus* encyclical (June 24, 1967). The *Humanae Vitae* encyclical's publication (July 29, 1968) was undoubtedly both the most courageous and the most polemical of his gestures. In view of the central principle to the magisterium in this regard, that is the inseparability of the affective and procreative aspects of the sexual act, he pronounced himself against contraceptive means used by spouses, authorizing the so-called natural ones only under certain conditions. This item number 10 of the encyclical raised a lot of protest, including among several bishops' conferences. The creation of the international theological commission on April 30, 1969, reporting to the Congregation for the Doctrine of Faith, reflects an appeasement attempt. Towards the end of his pontificate, in his *Persona humana* declaration (December 29, 1975), Paul VI even braced himself to clarify the Church's position on major aspects of sexual ethics. The prophetic dimension of this successor of Peter thus reinforced itself over the last years of his pontificate.

Conclusion

This chapter has especially focused on the personal qualities as well as the contributions of Pope Paul VI in the legal field. However, a biography differently oriented could have highlighted other facets, including his great human sensitivity, which was reflected particularly at the end of his pontificate, then also the sequestration and assassination of the Italian politician Aldo Moro: Paul VI greatly suffered for this event and intervened personally by making an autographed appeal to the "men of the Red Brigades." If Paul VI can be considered a "great jurist," it is probably not because of the exceptional level of his legal diplomas, the importance of his university teaching, or his theoretical publications in this area. If he may be said to have contributed to law in a remarkable way, his contribution is chiefly confined to the domain of canon law as well as to the practice and teaching of diplomacy. His basic motivation was above all that of a pastor, but a pastor according to God's heart, with broad horizons, without excluding anyone. His commitment to ecumenical progress is a reflection of this. His legal work consisted mainly of his activity as a canonical and liturgical legislator—particularly in his capacity as the pope who inherited Vatican II—both during the council and its aftermath. He truly marked an entire era of the Catholic Church, and his beneficial influence continues today. But in the legal part of his work, we should not forget his zeal for human rights, including his historic speech at the UN, and his efforts to find just solutions to ethical issues. In sum, all his intense life as pastor and jurist, filled with overcoming trials and pitfalls, can be explained only by the faith of one who holds firmly the helm of Peter's boat and by the holiness confirmed in his recent canonization.

Notes

1 His notes dedicated to FUCI students are essentially of a philosophical order: Paul VI, *Coscienza universitaria*.
2 The appointment of Montini as archbishop of Milan in 1954 unfolded between November 1952 and November 1954. Three main hypotheses about the reason for his appointment were formulated concerning, alternatively, his personal relation to politics, Russian Communism, or his opinion on the Catholic Action movement. Reference could be made among others to Chenaux, 119–25.
3 This time he appeared at the top of the appointed cardinals' list and received John XXIII's encouragements during the first hearing, at which the pope quoted this extract from the Holy Scriptures about him: *Amicus fidelis, protector fortis.* Also see the future Pope Paul VI's autobiographical note published in Macchi, 88.
4 A. Melloni, in Alberigo et al., 34.
5 Regarding the causes for his resignation, see among others Chenaux, 64–6.
6 Cfr. Bertrams.
7 Ratzinger, 86.
8 Cfr. Uginet.
9 Regarding the Church's central between 1968 and 1878, see d'Onorio.

10 Paul VI, Speech of September 30, 1967, at the beginning of the Synod's work, in *Documents pontificaux de Paul VI*, Vol. 6 (1967), 715–16.
11 Cfr. Paul VI, Speech of October 11, 1969, in *Documents pontificaux de Paul VI*, Vol. 8 (1969), 693.
12 Cfr.Dupuy.
13 This emerges from the documentation collected by Broglio.
14 Paul VI, *Address of the Holy Father Paul VI to the United Nations Organization*, October 4, 1965, w2.vatican.va.
15 Prignon, 61.
16 On this account see Joblin, 529–46.
17 Cfr. Cardia and Benigni.
18 Cfr. Congar, "L'œcuménisme de Paul VI."

Bibliography

Alberigo, Giuseppe, et al. *Storia del concilio Vaticano II.* 5 vols. Bologna: Il Mulino, 1995–2001.

Bertrams, Wilhelm. "La collegialità episcopale." *Civiltà Cattolica* 115 (1964): 436–55.

Cardia, Carlo, and Rita Benigni, eds. *A 50 anni dalla "Populorum Progressio". Paolo VI il Papa della modernità, giustizia tra popoli e l'amore per l'Italia.* Roma: Roma Tre-Press, 2018.

Chenaux, Philippe. *Paul VI. Le souverain éclairé.* Paris: Éd. du Cerf, 2015.

Chiron, Yves. *Paul VI, Le pape écartelé.* Paris: Perrin, 1993.

Congar, Yves. *Mon Journal du Concile.* 2 vols. Paris: Éd. du Cerf, 2002.

Congar, Yves. "L'œcuménisme de Paul VI." In École Française de Rome, *Paul VI et la modernité*, 807–20.

De Giorgi, Fulvio. *Paolo VI, il papa del Moderno.* Brescia: Morcelliana, 2015.

D'Onorio, Joël Benoît, "Paul VI et le gouvernement central de l'Église." In École Française de Rome, *Paul VI et la modernité*, 614–45.

Dupuy, André. "Paul VI et la diplomatie pontificale." In École Française de Rome, *Paul VI et la modernité*, 455–77.

École Française de Rome. *Paul VI et la modernité d l'Église.* Rome: Studium, 1984.

Hebblethwaite, Peter. *Paul VI: The First Modern Pope.* Glasgow: Harper Collins, 1993.

Paul VI, Pope. *Insegnamenti di Paolo VI.* Città del Vaticano: Libreria Editrice Vaticana, 1963–1978.

Istituto Paolo VI. *Notiziario.* Brescia, 1979–2017.

Joblin, Joseph."Paul VI et les institutions internationales." In École Française de Rome, *Paul VI et la modernité*, 529–46.

Macchi, Pasquale. *Paolo VI nella sua parola.* Brescia: Morcelliana, 2001.

Margiotta Broglio, Francesco. "I Concordati di Paolo VI." In École Française de Rome, *Paul VI et la modernité*, 479–528.

Paul, VI, Pope. *Coscienza universitaria. Note per gli student.* Rome: Studium, 1930.

Paul VI, Pope. *Documents pontificaux de Paul VI.* Saint-Maurice: Ed. Saint-Augustin, 1967—.

Prignon, Albert. *Journal conciliaire de la 4e session.* Edited by L. Declerck and A. Haquin. Louvain-la-Neuve: Peeters, 2003.

Ratzinger, Joseph. *Mon Concile Vatican II. Enjeux et perspectives.* Perpignan: Artège, 2011.

Riccardi, Andrea. *Il potere del papa. Da Pio XII a Paolo VI*. Roma-Bari: Laterza, 1988.

Schouppe, Jean-Pierre. *Diritto dei rapporti tra Chiesa e comunità politica. Profili dottrinali e giuridici*. Roma: EDUSC, 2018.

Tornielli, Andrea. *Paolo VI, L'audacia di un papa*. Milano: Mondadori, 2009.

Toscani, Xenio, ed. *Paolo VI. Una biografia*. Brescia: Istituto Paolo VI/Studium, 2014.

Uginet, François-Charles. "La constitution 'Regimini Ecclesiae Universae'." In École Française de Rome, *Paul VI et la modernité de l'Église*, 603–13.

Index

For Product Safety Concerns and Information please contact our EU representative GPSR@taylorandfrancis.com
Taylor & Francis Verlag GmbH, Kaufingerstraße 24, 80331 München, Germany

www.ingramcontent.com/pod-product-compliance
Lightning Source LLC
LaVergne TN
LVHW052216200926
848481LV00001B/122
9780367508715